Quantitative Development Policy Analysis

Quantitative Development Policy Analysis

Elisabeth Sadoulet
Alain de Janvry

THE JOHNS HOPKINS UNIVERSITY PRESS
BALTIMORE AND LONDON

The Johns Hopkins University Press
2715 North Charles Street
Baltimore, Maryland 21218-4319
The Johns Hopkins Press Ltd., London

Library of Congress Cataloging-in-Publication Data

Sadoulet, Elisabeth, 1945–
Quantitative development policy analysis / by Elisabeth
Sadoulet and Alain de Janvry.
        p.   cm.
Includes index.
ISBN 0-8018-4782-6
1. Economic   policy—Mathematical   models.   I.   De
Janvry, Alain.   II. Title.
HD75.5.S23   1995
338.9'001—dc20   94-21401

A catalog record for this book is available from the British Library.

Contents

List of Figures xi

List of Tables xii

Preface xiv

Chapter 1. The Quantitative Analysis of Development Policy 1
    1.1. Approaches to Development Theory: The Role of the State and Policy 1
    1.2. Rationales for Government Intervention 3
        1.2.1. Efficiency Oriented Interventions 3
        1.2.2. Nonefficiency Oriented Interventions 4
    1.3. Conceptual Framework 5
    1.4. The Role of Quantitative Policy Analysis 7
    1.5. Criteria for Policy Evaluation 10
        1.5.1. Welfare 11
        1.5.2. Political Feasibility 23
    Exercise 1. Production Function: Technological Change and Factor Substitutability 25
    References 29

Chapter 2. Demand Analysis 32
    2.1. Objectives of Demand Analysis and Role of Theory 32
        2.1.1. Demand Analysis for Policy Making 32
        2.1.2. Alternative Approaches to the Analysis of Demand 33
    2.2. Theory of Consumer Behavior and Demand Analysis 34
        2.2.1. Basic Model 34
        2.2.2. Separability and Stepwise Budgeting 36
    2.3. Estimation of Engel Functions 37
    2.4. Estimation of Price Elasticities from Cross-Sectional Data* 38
    2.5. Estimation of Complete Demand Systems 41
        2.5.1. The Linear Expenditure System 42
        2.5.2. The Almost Ideal Demand System 43
        2.5.3. The Generalized Almost Ideal Demand System 44
        2.5.4. Estimation Problems* 44
        2.5.5. Effects of Household Characteristics* 46
    2.6. Examples 47
        2.6.1. LES and AIDS Estimations 47
        2.6.2. Numerical Values 48
        2.6.3. Quantity and Quality Elasticities 49
    2.7. Policy Implications 49
        2.7.1. Setting Commodity Priorities in Agricultural Research for Nutritional
              Improvement 49
        2.7.2. The Relationship between Calorie Intake and Income 51
    Exercise 2. Food Subsidies in Morocco 52
    References 59

Chapter 3. The Profit Function Approach to Supply and Factor Demand 61
    3.1. The Basic Theory of Production 62
        3.1.1. The Pro_.t Function 62
        3.1.2. The System of Output Supply and Factor Demand 63
    3.2. Examples of Profit Functions and Derived Systems of Output Supply and Factor
          Demand 64
        3.2.1. Normalized Cobb-Douglas 64
        3.2.2. Generalized Leontief 65
        3.2.3. Normalized Quadratic 65
        3.2.4. Translog 66
    3.3. Cost Function and Associated Systems of Factor Demands 66
    3.4. Estimation of the System 67
    3.5. Examples 68
        3.5.1. The Role of Public Goods in the Punjab 68
        3.5.2. Agricultural Price Policy in Argentina 70
    3.6. Short-Run versus Long-Run Supply Response 72
    3.7. Aggregate Supply Response 73
        3.7.1. Linking the Aggregate Elasticity to the Factor Supply 75
        3.7.2. Econometric Estimates 76
    Exercise 3. Price Incentives and Public Goods for Indian Agriculture 78
    References 82

Chapter 4. Supply Response: Expectations Formation and Partial Adjustment 84
    4.1. Alternative Approaches to the Measurement of Supply Response 84
        4.1.1. Structural Form Approaches: Estimation of the Structure and Derivation of
                the Supply Response 84
        4.1.2. Reduced Form Approaches: Direct Estimation of the Supply Response 85
    4.2. Nerlovian Models of Supply Response 86
        4.2.1. The General Nerlovian Supply Response Model 86
        4.2.2. Restricted Nerlovian Supply Response Model 88
        4.2.3. Simplified Models with either No Partial Adjustment or No Expectations
                Formation 88
    4.3. Results Using Nerlovian Models of Supply Response 90
    4.4. Examples of Nerlovian Models 92
        4.4.1. Supply Response of Maize in Thailand under Risk 92
        4.4.2. Supply Response under Controlled Prices in Egypt 92
        4.4.3. Other Supply Response Studies 95
    4.5. Producer Response to Lagged Prices and the Dynamics of Markets 96
    4.6. Alternative Expectations Models 98
    4.7. The Rational Expectations Approach* 99
        4.7.1. General Model 99
        4.7.2. Estimating Supply Response 100
        4.7.3. Criticisms of the Rational Expectations Approach 102
    Exercise 4. Supply Response for Groundnuts in Sub-Saharan Africa 102
    References 110

Chapter 5. Behavior and Welfare under Risk 112
    5.1. Price Determination and Sources of Fluctuations 112
    5.2. Impact of Price Risk on the Level and Variability of Agricultural Income 113
    5.3. Measuring the Cost of Risk 116
        5.3.1. Certainty Equivalent Income and Risk Premium 116
        5.3.2. Risk Aversion 118
        5.3.3. Utility Functions with Constant Absolute or Relative Risk Aversion 119
        5.3.4. The Magnitude of Income Risk 120
    5.4. Welfare and Supply of Risk-Neutral Farmers 120
    5.5. Welfare and Supply of Risk-Averse Farmers 122
    5.6. The Household's Response to Price Risk* 124
    5.7. Instruments of Price Stabilization 126
    5.8. Market Integration and Price Stabilization 127
    5.9. Measures of Food Security at the National Level 129
    5.10. Example: Evaluation of the Brazilian Price Band Proposal 132
    Exercise 5. Food Security in India 134
    References 138

Chapter 6. Household Models 140
    6.1. Household Behavior and Policy Analysis 140
    6.2. Integrating Producer, Consumer, and Worker Decisions into a Household
          Problem 141
        6.2.1. Producer Problem 141
        6.2.2. Consumer Problem 142
        6.2.3. Worker Problem 142
        6.2.4. Consumer-Worker Problem 142
        6.2.5. Household Problem 143
    6.3. Specification of a Household Model 143
        6.3.1. Home Time 143
        6.3.2. Definition of the Household Unit 144
        6.3.3. Who Decides? 144
        6.3.4. Net Buyers versus Net Sellers of Food and/or Labor 144
    6.4. Separable Household Model with Perfect Markets 145
        6.4.1. The Model and Its Solution 145
        6.4.2. Comparative Statics Results 146
        6.4.3. Empirical Results with Separable Models 148
    6.5. Household Model with Market Failures 149
        6.5.1. Why Markets Fail 149
        6.5.2. A Household Model with Market Failures and Credit Constraint 151
        6.5.3. Empirical Results with Nonseparable Models 154
    6.6. When and How to Use a Household Model 159
        6.6.1. When to Use Which Approach? 159
        6.6.2. Econometric Estimation of Household Models and Tests of Separability* . 160
        6.6.3. Econometric Estimation of Supply or Marketed Surplus When There
                Are Price Bands 162
        6.6.4. Calibration and Simulation with a Household Model 163
    6.7. Intertemporal Household Models 164

6.7.1. Basic Intertemporal Consumption Model under Certainty: Life-Cycle
          Model 164
6.7.2. Permanent Income Model under Income Uncertainty 165
6.7.3. Liquidity Constraint and Household Strategies to Mitigate Risk 166
6.7.4. Empirical Evidence on Risk Coping and Risk Management 167
Exercise 6. Household Responses to Price Incentives 168
References 173

Chapter 7. Price Distortions: Indicators and Partial Equilibrium Analysis 176
7.1. Reference Prices 176
7.2. Indicators of Protection and Incentives 178
     7.2.1. Nominal and Real Protection 178
     7.2.2. Effective and Real Effective Protection 179
     7.2.3. Effective Subsidy Coefficient (ESC) 182
     7.2.4. Producer and Consumer Subsidy Equivalents (PSE and CSE).................... 183
     7.2.5. Direct, Indirect, and Total Nominal Protection Rates 184
7.3. Indicators of Comparative Advantage 185
7.4. Partial Equilibrium Analysis of Price Distortions 189
     7.4.1. The Concepts of Consumer and Producer Surplus 189
     7.4.2. Measurement of the Partial Equilibrium Effects of an Export Tax on
              Agriculture 191
     7.4.3. Partial Equilibrium Analysis of Other Price Interventions 193
7.5. Effective Protection When Domestic and Foreign Commodities Are Imperfect
     Substitutes* 204
7.6. Political Economy of Price Distortions 206
Exercise 7. Effects of Price Distortions and Investment in Research on Efficiency
              and Welfare 208
References 212

Chapter 8. The Real Exchange Rate 214
8.1. Market and Effective Exchange Rates 214
8.2. The Market for Foreign Currency and the Real Exchange Rate 215
8.3. The Equilibrium Exchange Rate 218
     8.3.1. The Purchasing Power Parity Equilibrium Exchange Rate 218
     8.3.2. The Elasticity Approach 219
8.4. Forces Affecting the Real Exchange Rate 221
     8.4.1. Shift in Export Earnings from Productivity Change or Commodity Boom . 223
     8.4.2. Shift in Import Demand from Price Shock or Expansionary Domestic
              Policies 225
     8.4.3. Capital Outflow or Debt Accumulation 225
     8.4.4. Trade Policies 226
8.5. Impact of Trade Distortions on the Real Exchange Rate 228
     8.5.1. The Elasticity Approach 228
     8.5.2. The Three-Sector Model and the ω Factor* 229
     8.5.3. Estimating the Equilibrium Exchange Rate with the ω Approach* 232
Exercise 8. Exchange Rate and Trade Policies in Pakistan 233
References 239

Chapter 9. Transactions Costs and Agrarian Institutions 241
    9.1. Efficiency: Technical, Allocative, and Economic 242
        9.1.1. Definitions 242
        9.1.2. Measurements 244
    9.2. Technical Change and Productivity Growth* 248
        9.2.1. Disembodied Technical Change 248
        9.2.2. Total Factor Productivity 250
        9.2.3. Discrete Measures of Technical Change and TFP 251
        9.2.4. Biased Technical Change 252
    9.3. Efficiency and Productivity under Transactions Costs 254
        9.3.1. The Concepts of Transactions Costs and Effective Prices 254
        9.3.2. Measurement of Efficiency under Transactions Costs 255
        9.3.3. Measurement of Total Factor Productivity under Transactions Costs 256
    9.4. Household Behavior under Transactions Costs and Productivity Differentials 258
        9.4.1. A Model of Household Behavior 258
        9.4.2. Determinants of the Relation between TFP and Farm Size 261
    9.5. Transactions Costs and Institutional Solutions: Sharecropping 262
    Exercise 9. Relationship between Farm Size and Productivity: The Economics of
               Land Reform 266
    References 270

Chapter 10. Input-Output Tables, Social Accounting Matrices, and Multipliers 273
    10.1. Social Accounting Matrices 274
    10.2. Example: A Social Accounting Matrix for Ecuador, 1980 276
    10.3. Construction of a SAM: Data Requirements 280
    10.4. The Measure of Agricultural Surplus 281
    10.5. The Input-Output Model 285
        10.5.1 Equations 285
        10.5.2 Interpretation and Extension 287
    10.6. SAM Multipliers 288
    10.7. Applications and Extensions of the SAM Multiplier Analysis 291
    Exercise 10. Input-Output and Social Accounting Matrix Multipliers in Morocco 295
    References 301

Chapter 11. Multimarket Models 302
    11.1. The Multimarket Approach 302
        11.1.1. Consistency Frameworks 303
        11.1.2. Mathematical Programming Approaches 303
        11.1.3. Industry and Sectoral Econometric Models 306
    11.2. Structural Logic of the Model 307
    11.3. Equations of a Multimarket Model 309
    11.4. Writing and Solving a Multimarket 311
    11.5. Examples of Multimarket Analyses of Agricultural Policy 312
        11.5.1. Incidence of the Green Revolution and Public Investments in India 312
        11.5.2. Stabilization Policies and Agriculture in Senegal 320
    11.6. Conclusion 323
    Exercise 11.1. A Multimarket for the Grain-Livestock Sector in North Africa 323

Exercise 11.2. Policy Simulation with a Multimarket for Brazil 332
References 339

Chapter 12. Computable General Equilibrium Models 341
   12.1. The Structure of CGE Models 342
      12.1.1. Agents and Their Behavior 342
      12.1.2. Market Equilibrium 342
      12.1.3. Macroconstraints 343
      12.1.4. Homogeneity and Numéraire 343
   12.2. The Macroeconomics of CGE Models 344
      12.2.1. Foreign Trade and the Real Exchange Rate 344
      12.2.2. The Labor Market Closure 348
   12.3. Construction of CGE Models 349
      12.3.1. Flow Chart and Functional Specifications 349
      12.3.2. Data Requirements 353
      12.3.3. Alternative Closure Rules: Structuralist Models 354
      12.3.4. Exogenous Variables: Definition of Shocks and Policies 355
   12.4. Examples of CGE Analysis of Policy Scenarios 356
      12.4.1. GATT and Increase in Food Import Price for Low-Income Countries 356
      12.4.2. Stabilization Policies in Response to External Shocks: Efficiency,
             Welfare, and Political Feasibility 358
   12.5. Extensions and Recent Developments 361
   12.6. When to Use a CGE 362
   Exercise 12. The Economics of Food Subsidies in a Computable General Equilibrium
          Model 363
   References 371

Appendix. Some Mathematical Tools 373
   A.1. Elasticity 373
   A.2. Taylor Expansion and Log-Linearization of a Function 375
   A.3. Optimization Problems 377
   A.4. Functional Forms of Production Functions 383
   A.5. Functional Forms of Demand Systems: Derivation of Elasticities 386

Author Index 388

Subject Index 392

* Sections marked with an asterisk contain more difficult material.

List of Figures

1.1.   Base run and simulation of stabilization policies in Ecuador 8
1.2.   Consumer surplus 12
1.3.   Equivalent variation, compensatory variation, and consumer surplus 14
1.4.   Income profile of rural Mexico, 1984 19
1.5.   Lorenz curve for rural Mexico, 1984 20
1E.1.   Impact on production of a neutral technological change 28
2.1.   Alternative forms of Engel functions 39
5.1.   Production fluctuation in a closed economy 114
5.2.   World price fluctuation in an open economy 114
5.3.   Welfare effect of production risk on a risk-neutral producer 115
5.4.   Measuring risk aversion 117
5.5.   Supply of risk-averse producers under risk 122
5.6.   Availability of maize, Kenya 131
6.1.   Causal ordering in the separable household model 146
6.2.   Price bands and credit constraint 153
7.1.   Producer and consumer surplus 190
7.2.   Effects of an export tax on efficiency and welfare 192
7.3.   Price distortions on tradables 195
7.4.   Price distortion on nontradables 198
7.5.   Exchange rate overvaluation 199
7.6.   Technological change 200
7.7.   Multiple interventions 202
7.8.   Trade distortions and environmental protection 203
7E.1.   Impact of technological change and an export tax on the production and consumption of
        wheat 208
8.1.   Real exchange rates, Ecuador, 1960–1985 218
8.2.   The elasticity approach to the equilibrium exchange rate 219
8.3.   Alternative measure of the equilibrium exchange rate, Colombia, 1960–1983 221
8.4.   Real exchange rate analysis 224
8.5.   Real exchange rate and trade balance 227
9.1.   Technical and allocative efficiency in the product space 242
9.2.   Technical and allocative efficiency in the factor space 243
9.3.   Bias of technological change 253
9.4.   Frontier and average stochastic profit functions 256
9.5.   Choice of optimum contract 265
11.1.   Generic structure of a multimarket model 308
11.2.   Partial equilibrium analysis of price distortions in the Senegal multimarket 321
11E.1. Partial equilibrium analysis of price distortions in the Brazilian multimarket 335
11E.2. Multimarket for Brazil: Soybeans 336
12.1.   Foreign trade in a CGE 344
12.2.   Macroeconomic balance in a CGE 346
12.3.   Increase in foreign capital inflow 347
12.4.   Change in world price 348
12.5.   CGE flow chart 352
A.1.   Engel functions 374
A.2.   Price elasticity of demand 375

List of Tables

1.1.   Parameters of the linear expenditure demand system, United States, 1948–78 16
1.2.   Income distribution of rural population, Mexico, 1984 18
1.E.1. Production function: Technological change and factor substitutability 27
2.1.   A comparison of elasticities for LES and AIDS 47
2.2.   Estimates of price and income elasticities of food, crops, or individual commodities 48
2.3.   Demand elasticities for Java, 1981 49
2.4.   Impact of a 10% increase in supply on per capita calorie intake 50
2.E.1. Food subsidies in Morocco 54
2.E.2. Food subsidies in Morocco: Policy analysis 54
3.1.   Semiarid India: Price elasticities and shares of income by crop 69
3.2.   Estimated agricultural supply system in Argentina 71
3.3.   Output supply and input demand elasticities, North Indian district, 1959–1975 74
3.4.   Effects of infrastructure on agriculture 77
3.E.1. Price incentives and public goods in Indian agriculture 79
4.1.   Alternative specifications of Nerlovian models of supply response 89
4.2.   Price elasticity of supply of agricultural products in less developed countries 91
4.3.   Estimated area response for maize, Thailand, 1937–63 93
4.4.   Area response elasticities for maize, Thailand, 1937–63 94
4.5.   Estimated area response for crops, Egypt, 1950–1975 95
4.6.   Area response elasticities, Egypt crops 96
4.E.1. Supply response for groundnuts in Sub-Saharan Africa: Base data 104
4.E.2. Supply response for groundnuts in Sub-Saharan Africa: Data preparation and
        simulation results 105
4.E.3. Supply response for groundnuts in Sub-Saharan Africa: Regression results 106
5.1.   Evaluation of a price band for Brazil, 1977–1986 133
5.E.1. Food security in India 136
6.1.   Empirical results with separable household models (price elasticities) 148
6.2.   Household model with market failures, Africa: Impact of 10% increase in price
        of cash crops 155
6.3.   Structural characteristics of small and medium farms, Haute Chaouia, Morocco 157
6.4.   Simulation of household behavior: ASAP responses, Morocco 158
6.E.1. Household responses to price incentives 170
7.1.   Index of nominal and real protection coefficients for cereals and export crops in selected
        African countries, 1972–1983 180
7.2.   Price distortions and comparative advantages, Côte d'Ivoire, 1985 182
7.3.   Protection of agriculture compared with manufacturing in selected developing countries,
        1960 and 1970–1980 183
7.4.   Direct, indirect, and total nominal protection rates for agricultural products 186
7.5.   Nominal and effective protection and domestic resource costs for major commodities,
        Morocco, 1970-1982 188
7.6.   Regressions for nominal protection coefficients, 1960–1984 207
7.E.1. Effects of price distortions and investment in research on efficiency and welfare 209
8.1.   Index of real exchange rates in selected African countries 217
8.2.   Colombia, equilibrium exchange rates 222
8.E.1. Exchange rate and trade policies in Pakistan: Data 234
8.E.2. Exchange rate and trade policies in Pakistan: Equilibrium exchange rate 236
8.E.3. Exchange rate and trade policies in Pakistan: Omega approach 238

9.1.   Frequency distribution of profit loss in Basmati rice production in Pakistan, 1982 256
9.2.   Determinant of profit inefficiency among Basmati rice producers in Pakistan, 1982 257
9.E.1. Relationship between farm size and productivity 267
10.1.   Structure of a social accounting matrix 275
10.2.   Social accounting matrix, Ecuador, 1980 277
10.3.   Social accounting matrix distinguishing between agriculture and nonagriculture 282
10.4.   Social accounting matrix distinguishing between agriculture and nonagriculture,
        Ecuador, 1980 283
10.5.   The input-output model 285
10.6.   Input-output and social accounting matrix multipliers, Ecuador, 1980 290
10.7.   Policy simulations with SAM multipliers, Ecuador, 1980 292
10.8.   Transmission of influence in a village: SAM approach with supply-constrained agriculture . 294
10.E.1. Input-output and social accounting matrix multipliers in Morocco, 1980: Data 296
10.E.2. Input-output and social accounting matrix multipliers in Morocco: Policy simulations 298
11.1.   Simulated effects of technical change and increased exports, India 314
11.2.   Simulated effects of increased agricultural investment and input subsidies 316
11.3.   Untargeted food subsidies and urban ration shops 318
11.4.   Structure of the multimarket for Senegal 320
11.5.   Results of agriculture pricing analysis, Senegal 322
11.E.1. A multimarket for the grain-livestock sector in North Africa 324
11.E.2. A multimarket for the grain-livestock sector in North Africa: Income distribution 331
11.E.3. Policy simulation with a multimarket for Brazil: Structure of the model 332
12.1.   Equations of the computable general equilibrium model 350
12.2.   Impact of a 20% increase in price of cereals on poor African and Asian countries 357
12.3.   Simulations of stabilization policies in response to terms of trade and debt shock in Ecuador 360
12.E.1. The economics of food subsidies in a computable general equilibrium model: Data and
        parameters 364
12.E.2. The economics of food subsidies in a computable general equilibrium model: Simulation 365
12.E.3. Food subsidy policy with alternative financing: Simulation with a CGE 366

Preface

Policy reforms are an integral and continuing feature of economic development. In recent years, many countries have accelerated the pace of reforms due to a variety of causes that include adjustment to the debt crisis and recurrent external price shocks, exhaustion of central planning as an approach to accelerated economic growth, lessons derived from the successes achieved by other countries, transitions to democracy that make poverty, equity, and sustainability issues more important, significant advances in economic theory, and ideological shifts. These reforms address a staggering range of issues, from the microeconomic to the sectoral and macroeconomic levels. At the microeconomic level, policy reforms include changes in access to assets for households and in property rights, diffusion of information on new technological options, measures to reduce transactions costs through new institutions and contracts, incentives and direct assistance to resource reallocation and new investments through price and nonprice instruments, and promotion of grassroots organizations. At the sectoral level, policy reforms include changes in public investment priorities toward infrastructure, irrigation, research, extension, and education; trade policies affecting tariffs, taxes, and quantity restrictions; land reform, rural development, and food-for-work programs; changes in regional institutions mobilizing savings and delivering credit and insurance; and regulations to internalize externalities as well as to enhance sustainability. At the macroeconomic level, policy reforms include stabilization policies to reduce inflation, balance of current accounts deficits, and government budget deficits; liberalization of trade, exchange rates, financial transactions, and foreign investment; privatization, deregulation, and redefinition of the role of the state in the economy; tax reforms; and food subsidies and other welfare programs in health, education, and housing to reduce absolute poverty and improve the satisfaction of basic needs.

While analysis of many of these policy issues takes us into uncharted territory, economic theory has much to offer in providing guidelines to help conceptualize and design policy reforms. The ability to simulate the implications of alternative proposals is fundamental to assist objective policy debates. For this purpose, models must be built and quantitative values given to their parameters. If behavioral relations and parameter values are uncertain, counterfactual experiments with alternative specifications of behavior and plausible ranges of parameter values are a better basis for policy making than subjective debates that leave the door wide open to ideological discourse and obfuscation. While extensive description and comparative history are fundamental entry points into any policy debate, understanding the causal determinants of predicted consequences and obtaining an order of magnitude of expected impacts requires going one step beyond these approaches into quantitative modeling and policy simulation. In the latter, while economic analysis inevitably gives particular attention to the role of prices, we place a strong emphasis on the role of public goods and of structural, technological, and institutional instruments in policy.

Policy analysts have typically had at least some, and often extensive, formal training in economics. However, translation of scholarly economic principles into useful and reliable policy reasoning does not follow directly from knowledge of economic theory and is rarely done adequately. As a result, much economic training remains academic and is not utilized in policy analysis; much policy making continues to be done under the veil of ignorance and, at best, loose understanding of causal relations. Bridging the gap between theory and policy analysis requires acquiring the practice of applying the concepts, theories, and methods of economics to the very purpose of policy analysis.

In an era where microcomputers are widely available, and at least the simple technology of spreadsheets is accessible to all policy analysts, the tremendous analytical capabilities these offer should be used to inform policy analysis. Doing so stimulates the development of useful databases, helps provide quick answers to policy questions, and transforms the informational content of policy debates. For students doing thesis research on policy questions, this technology has the potential of revolutionizing their approach to research and the rigor of their work. Finally, as we have repeatedly witnessed when using this book for teaching in university environments, a quantitative approach to economic reasoning and a policy orientation in economic analysis can deeply transform the teaching of economics and quantitative methods as it gives it a concrete purpose that helps screen the essential from the superfluous and guide teaching toward problem solving.

It is the objective of this book to assist policy analysts and development economists in using the techniques of quantitative policy analysis. It integrates the theoretical exposition of the most useful economic concepts and models for quantitative policy analysis with computer exercises which show what data are required, how the models should be constructed and solved, and what types of policy questions they can be used to address. To integrate theory with policy analysis, the book is structured as a set of 12 subjects and 12 computer exercises. It can be used to teach either a full-time, two-week course (with some topics deleted according to time and interests) or a 12-week course with a lecture and a laboratory each week. Several of the more difficult chapters deserve more than one week of work, and the course can easily extend over a full 15-week semester. Topics covered include micro issues of consumer demand, production and supply, response to risk, household behavior, and transactions costs and agrarian institutions, as well as sectoral and macro problems of trade distortions and real exchange rate, partial equilibrium analysis of policy interventions, food security strategies, multimarket modeling, input-output tables and social accounting matrices, and computable general equilibrium models.

The book is designed for the present and future technicians of policy analysis organizations and for their teachers. This includes master's students in economics or agricultural economics, policy analysts with the equivalent of a master's or a solid bachelor's degree in economics or agricultural economics, officers in international organizations with teaching or research functions, and faculty members in graduate programs. The course taught with this book can, however, be adapted to a wide range of levels by using subsets of the materials presented: we have given it to students with only a few courses in economics and minimal knowledge of quantitative methods, as well as to Ph.D.'s needing retooling and more specific expertise in policy analysis. To help adapt materials to different levels of audience preparedness, the more difficult subjects are marked with an asterisk (*). An appendix with the mathematical tools most commonly used through the book is included, and students should read this material first.

For the sake of simplicity, but also to show that extraordinarily useful policy exercises can be conducted with only a modest microcomputer and a spreadsheet, the exercises are constructed on Lotus (and Excel). Evidently, further work in the policy areas covered in the exercises will lead most analysts to use more sophisticated software packages and more complete policy models. While some preliminary knowledge of Lotus is desirable, the exercises lead the students gradually to the more demanding operations. The exercises are constructed to take the students through the paces of modeling, data entry, estimation, policy simulation, and analysis of policy implications. Students are usually encouraged to work as teams of two on one microcomputer to allow cooperation and debates.

Each chapter presents the theoretical materials to be developed in class, followed by an exercise corresponding to the lecture. For students, the exercises provide a text and a spreadsheet (on diskette). The exercise texts have been written from the perspective of Lotus users, but most of the operations are identical on Excel and Lotus. The only differences students will have to deal with are for matrix manipulations, regressions, and graphs as Excel offers functions that can be used directly to perform these operations while Lotus does not. For the instructor, the exercises are accompanied by a spreadsheet with the solutions and a brief discussion of the answers. Some of the exercises are based on materials adapted from the research monographs of the International Food Policy Research Institute (IFPRI) in Washington, D.C., and we use a multimarket for Brazil developed by the Agricultural and Rural Development Department of the World Bank.

This book started with the encouragement of Antonio Perez from the FAO in Rome, who asked us to prepare a manual for policy analysis in support of the master's programs in agricultural economics in Latin America. We have used succesive drafts to teach in Morocco (master's program in agricultural economics at the Institut Agronomique et Vétérinaire in Rabat), Pakistan (Northwestern Province Agricultural University in Peshawar), Costa Rica (International Institute for Agricultural Cooperation), Italy (master's program in agricultural economics at the Centro di Specializzazione e Ricerche Economico Agrarie per il Mezzogiorno in Portici), France (master's program at the International Mediterranean Institute in Montpellier), Vietnam (State Planning Committee and Economics University in Hanoi), and Egypt (Center for Agricultural Economic Studies at Cairo University). Several generations of our doctoral students at the University of California at Berkeley have also been excellent sources of criticisms and suggestions, and we have freely experimented on them. For the course, an ideal audience is a combination of university students and policy analysts, allowing creative interactions between those closer to theory and methods and those already in the real world of policy making. The book is the accumulation of some eight years of teaching experience, but it will likely never be fully finished, both because of the vastness of the subject and because of the rapid progress of theory and methods on so many fronts. For this reason, we look at the book as an evolving project that will need continuing revisions and extensions. We will consequently be looking forward to receiving comments and suggestions by future users.

We are grateful to the many students who struggled through the exercises; they gave us an opportunity to adjust them so that they, we hope, ended up being both challenging and feasible within the time and computational constraints of the course. We are also grateful to many faculty members and officers of development agencies who helped by inviting us to offer the course and by organizing the many details required. Hadi Esfahani cooperated on earlier versions of the book and gave us many ideas for the design of the exercises. Finally, we are indebted to several critical readers of the text, including Erik Thorbecke, Tracy Hart, and Bradford Mills. We dedicate this book to the next generation of economists in our two families, Loïc Sadoulet and Laurent de Janvry, in compensation for our biased influence in their choice of career.

Quantitative Development Policy Analysis

CHAPTER ONE

The Quantitative Analysis of Development Policy

1.1. Approaches to Development Theory: The Role of the State and Policy

The objective of development economics is to identify, analyze, and recommend development strategies that the less developed countries (LDCs) could follow in order to catch up economically with the more advanced nations. Such strategies must also satisfy a set of idiosyncratic goals that are part of what constitutes "development," for example, reduction in absolute poverty, greater equality and equity, participatory governance and social stability, and sustainability in resource use. Over the centuries, starting with the European countries in "relative economic backwardness" compared with England, which used extensive state intervention to achieve "great spurts in industrial development" (Gerschenkron, 1962), development strategies have assumed many definitions. Each of these strategies proposes a differential balance between the roles attributed to the market, the state, and civil organizations. Whereas pre-World War II liberalism and neoclassical development theory (Johnson, 1958) stressed the role of the market, influential schools of thought that stressed the role of the state emerged during the 1960s and 1970s: dependency theory (Cardoso and Faletto, 1969), development economics (Hirschman, 1981), growth-with-equity (Adelman, 1975), and basic needs (Streeten, 1979). Exhaustion of import substitution industrialization (ISI) and the debt crisis in the 1980s induced a neoliberal critique of these strategies, calling for a descaling of the role of the state and attributing greater influence to market forces (Krueger, 1974). In the 1990s, as many countries slowly emerge from the debt crisis through successful stabilization and adjustment policies, a "new development economics" is also emerging. Here the key role of market liberalization is well recognized. A scaled-down but essential strategic role is assigned to the state, and much greater importance is attributed to the developmental role of civil organizations, from the household to the community and to different forms of grassroots organizations and contractual arrangements (Stiglitz, 1985; Bardhan, 1988). It is from the perspective of this new development economics that this book is written.

In development economics, much attention has been devoted to agriculture and the rural sector. This is because agriculture plays a fundamental role in the economy of the LDCs, both in terms of size of an economic sector and an element of a development strategy. In the low-income countries, agriculture accounts for 32% of gross domestic product (World Bank, 1992). From a social welfare standpoint, it accounts for 61% of labor force employment in all the developing countries and 73% in the least developed (UNDP, 1992). The rural areas are also where absolute poverty is concentrated. The incidence of poverty is estimated to be 49% in the rural sector of developing countries as opposed to 32% in the urban areas (data exclude China; United Nations, 1989). In Latin America, the incidence of poverty is 60% in the rural areas and 36% in the urban sector (ECLAC, 1990).

Except for the few countries that have a strong export base in another sector of the economy (e.g., petroleum) or are already well established in the international market for manufacturing goods, agriculture has a key role to play in a development strategy. This role has been amply described by economic historians (e.g., Ohkawa and Rosovsky, 1960, for Japan), conceptualized in the classical development literature (Kuznets, 1964), and introduced in dual economy models (Ranis and Fei, 1961). It includes functions as a provider of capital (through land and other taxes, forced deliveries, invisible transfers through terms of trade adverse to agriculture, agricultural savings invested in other activities, and the payment of land rents to absentee or diversified landlords), foreign exchange, and labor to the other sectors of the economy. In recent years, the role of agricultural incomes as a source of effective demand for domestic manufacturing has also been stressed through the analysis of linkage effects (Mellor, 1986; Hazell and Ramasamy, 1991; Adelman, 1984). As a consequence, whereas the role of agriculture and rural development for growth and social welfare had been neglected in the development strategies that stressed industrialization by import substitution (Hirschman, 1958; Sen, 1960), it has increasingly been restored as a key element of a development strategy; for instance, in Mellor's "agriculture on the road to industrialization" and in Adelman's "agricultural development-led industrialization." In this book, the development policies analyzed will consequently focus importantly on agriculture, while maintaining a perspective on intersectoral interactions and micro-macro relations.

While government intervention in managing development strategies has been pervasive, from the catching-up strategies of Litz and Bismark in the eighteenth century to the post-World War II ISI strategy of the Economic Commission for Latin America, there is no sector of the economy where intervention has been more pervasive than agriculture, and this in both the less and the more developed countries (MDCs). Interventions include farm subsidies in the MDCs, usually through price support programs; taxation of agriculture in the LDCs through overvalued exchange rates, industrial protectionism, and export taxes; price stabilization interventions through food stocks and variable levies; food self-sufficiency and food security objectives; minimum acreage (cotton in Egypt) and maximum acreage planted (land set-asides in the United States and Europe); consumer food subsidies through cheap food policies, fair price shops, and food stamps; input subsidies, particularly to credit and fertilizers; monopolistic control of markets through parastatal agencies; regulation of competition on agricultural markets; direct income (decoupling) and assets (land reform) transfers; and public investment in agriculture such as infrastructure, irrigation, research, and extension. In general, the dilemma of these interventions—and the challenge for policy analysts—is that government controls only a few instruments (e.g., price through trade instruments) while each intervention has a multiplicity of consequences, both intended and unintended. These consequences include short- and long-run allocative efficiency, income distribution and welfare, fiscal and foreign exchange balances, sustainability of resource use, and political response. As we will argue, it is because of the complexity of these consequences that quantitative analysis of policy is so necessary and at the same time so difficult to perform satisfactorily.

Why have governments intervened so extensively in agriculture? As Gardner said, "agricultural policy is both ubiquitous and contentious" (Gardner, 1987). Because interventions induce a multiplicity of consequences, they are also motivated by a multiplicity of desired effects. Some of these interventions contribute to enhancing the efficiency of resource use and, hence, the aggregate level of income. Others clearly pursue nonefficiency objectives, which often will have an efficiency cost. By creating net social gains (increasing the size of the pie), policies that enhance efficiency can achieve political feasibility either if there are no losers or if compensation of losers by gainers can be managed. Policies which have nonefficiency objectives can achieve political feasibility directly or through political management if they create efficiency gains. If they do not, the political feasibility of nonefficiency goals depends on the relative political power of gainers and losers. Identifying the incidence and magnitude of these gains and losses is thus fundamental to managing the political feasibility of policy reforms.

1.2. Rationales for Government Intervention

Following theory, there are a number of arguments that have been advanced to legitimize government intervention (Stiglitz, 1987).

1.2.1. Efficiency Oriented Interventions

The efficiency rationale for government intervention is based on policy makers' perceptions that markets are failing to perform adequately in conveying price signals, in allowing low-cost transactions, or in prompting entry in a sector of economic activity, resulting in suboptimal use of resources for achieving maximum aggregate income. This includes both long recognized forms of market failure, such as public goods, externalities, economies of scale, and imperfect competition, as well as more recently recognized forms such as transactions costs and imperfect information.

1.2.1.1. Public Goods
Pure public goods are in principle nonrival (use by one does not preclude use by another) and nonexclusive (use cannot be rationed). It is consequently impossible for a private entrepreneur to supply these goods, and the state is called into being the supplier. In many situations, the state has the ability to recover costs through taxation of commodities, regional taxation, or the levying of user fees. Public goods include infrastructure development, such as roads and large-scale water projects, and the provision of new technologies that cannot be patented.

1.2.1.2. Externalities
In this case, the full costs and benefits of an activity are not fully reflected in the costs paid by private entrepreneurs or the returns they can capture. The result is either under- or overprovision of the good. Underprovision typically affects the delivery of public health and educational services, where individuals would only capture part of the benefit of their expenditures in acquiring these services. Overprovision includes production activities that generate pollution, soil erosion upstream that reduces the hydroelectrical and irrigation capacity of reservoirs downstream, and use of common property resources, where lack of cooperation imposes a cost on all others. In this case, state intervention may be required to manage a scheme of taxes and subsidies, to enforce regulatory controls, or to create a market for emission permits.

1.2.1.3 Economies of Scale
If there are already established firms that have achieved economies of scale and learning-by-doing, new entrants are barred. This justifies strategic interventions of the state, seeking to protect or subsidize new firms until they have reached the critical size and experience that allows them to compete. This reasoning has provided the rationale for the strategies of catching-up and import substitution industrialization: the state protects infant industries until they are able to compete in an open economy. It also underlies the new theories of strategic trade where

export subsidies and temporary tariffs are used to take advantage of increasing returns (Krugman, 1990).

1.2.1.4 Market Power

If economies of scale lead to natural monopoly, government regulation of market power will be necessary to keep prices as close as possible to marginal costs, as opposed to allowing monopoly pricing. This applies to utility companies and the need to rule on price setting. Even without economies of scale, the unchecked functioning of markets does not reproduce competition, and it is the role of government to be the regulator of competitive behavior.

1.2.1.5 Transactions Costs and Imperfect Information

Many markets fail because the costs of using the market for a transaction are too high relative to the benefits the transaction yields. Transactions costs include not only transportation costs but also the consequences of imperfect and asymmetrical information that lead to adverse selection and moral hazards as a consequence of the opportunistic behavior it allows. Adverse selection results, for instance, from the fact that those who buy insurance tend to be those most at risk or that those who are willing to pay high interest rates may, on average, be worst risks (Stiglitz and Weiss, 1981). Moral hazards are created by incentives to take greater risks when insured or to shrink on the job when paid a fixed wage. This results in the need to incur costs in recruitment, negotiation, monitoring, enforcement, and giving incentives to self-monitor. Rural markets thus typically fail to deliver insurance, credit, management, and supervision, inducing the emergence of agrarian institutions that will fulfill, through face-to-face relations, the functions markets do not provide. In other situations, private response is insufficient and government intervention is justified; for instance, in changing property rights, in redistributing assets, in fomenting the emergence of institutions for the local management of savings and loans, and in delivering information.

1.2.2. Nonefficiency Oriented Interventions

Government intervention is also motivated by objectives other than efficiency. It can be in response to self-interested government officials' concerns with the income consequences of the outcome of market forces and efficiency oriented policies, or in response to the demands of organized interest groups; generally it is a combination of both (Zusman, 1976).

1.2.2.1. Welfare: Poverty Reduction and Income Distribution

If markets work, efficiency is not affected by the distribution of asset ownership, but the distribution of income is determined by the distribution of assets. If not all markets work, transactions costs establish a relation between asset ownership and efficiency. This distribution may not be what the government would like, motivating policy interventions. Income redistribution can be achieved either ex ante relative to production through assets redistribution, or ex post through systems of taxes and subsidies. If markets work, questioning the distribution of assets is neutral on efficiency. This is not the case if some markets fail, then asset distribution may improve welfare at the cost of efficiency, or efficiency at the cost of welfare, or improve both simultaneously. Land reform that redistributes land toward family farms with lower production costs because they have lower transactions costs on labor may belong to the last category, reconciling efficiency and welfare objectives. In addition, government interventions such as rural development, support to microenterprises, and human capital formation can be targeted to selectively increase the productivity of asset use by the poor.

1.2.2.2. Sustainability and Intergenerational Equity

Sustainability requires that the level of per capita utility achieved by this generation should not imply such depletion of natural assets that the following generation could not reach at least an equal level of per capita utility. Utility is derived not only from income but also from the existence and option values offered by natural assets. Because the long-run level of substitution between natural and man-made assets is lower than was commonly thought some years ago, when greater technological optimism prevailed, achieving sustainability requires caution in the use of natural assets and disruption of the resilience of natural systems. Since future generations are not present to lobby for the cause of sustainability, it is typically the role of government to assume implementation of a sustainability constraint on current development programs.

1.2.2.3. Security: Food and Other Aspects

Security is an important dimension of welfare. This requires that the poor be able to successfully engage in consumption smoothing. The policy instrument to use for this purpose depends on the sources of income the poor have and the institutional mechanisms they use to gain access to food. For net buyers, this will require interventions to stabilize price, which can be achieved through international trade controls (variable levies and quotas), buffer stocks, price fixing and rationing, and use of futures markets. For net sellers, it is stabilizing income, not the prices of what they produce, which is important. This requires calling on irrigation, diversification, and crop insurance schemes. Access to credit for consumption smoothing is an effective mechanism for allowing the poor to assume greater risks in income generation and, thus, to achieve both efficiency and welfare gains. Policies and programs, such as food subsidies and social funds, are also introduced to compensate for the welfare effects of unexpected external shocks.

The purpose of this book is to provide a framework and quantitative analytical techniques for the assessment of these policies.

1.3. Conceptual Framework

In this book, the analysis of the economy and of policy options is progressively built from the microeconomic analysis of consumers, producers, and households to the partial equilibrium analysis of single markets, sectoral policy analysis, macroeconomic policies, and the links between these different levels of policy analysis. The theoretical basis is fundamentally microeconomic in spirit. The paradigm of microeconomic theory is the study of the behavior of individual economic agents in a given technological, institutional, and resource environment which defines the options they have (Kreps, 1990). Our approach to market, sectoral, and macroeconomic analyses then derives from the aggregation of their actions in a global institutional framework that coordinates and aggregates the behavior of individual agents.

In the standard microeconomic approach, economic agents are the individual consumers and producers, and the government. To the two types of private agents, consumers and producers, we add households. The household entity is meaningful whenever the same decision-making unit makes both production and consumption decisions. We will see that the household's decisions differ from the juxtaposition of producer and consumer decisions when markets are incomplete. Since this seems to be a pervasive situation, particularly in the developing countries, the household is important as an institution that internalizes many transactions instead of selling all it produces, hiring all factors it uses, and buying all goods it consumes.

All private agents are considered to be optimizing agents. They control private resources in an environment which is defined by technology, institutions, domestic and international markets, availability of public goods, and policies. These resources are traditionally time, human capital, land, and capital for producers, income for consumers, and the sum of all of these for households. Given the environment, they allocate their resources to maximize an objective function, typically utility for consumers and households and profit for producers.

Government actions are defined over the policy instruments which it controls, principally tax rates, subsidies, public investment, fiscal deficit, and foreign debt. Policies are considered exogenous; that is, we neither define a welfare function for the state that assigns weights to different objectives nor specify any actual decision rules for the making of policy. Consequently, we are not engaging in normative policy analysis whereby the optimum policy is derived from maximization of the government's objective function under the constraints of the operation of the economy. Instead, we engage in policy simulation and trace the implications of each policy alternative according to a multiplicity of criteria we will specify later: efficiency, welfare and equity, and political feasibility. Our purpose is not to treat government as an endogenous policy-making institution (Persson and Tabellini, 1990) and focus on explaining the policy-making processes. Instead, we take policies as exogenous and trace out, by simulation, their multiple implications.

The organization and operation of the economy are described by the distribution of resource endowment (distribution of fixed factors of production and household characteristics), the institutional framework that rules the interaction among agents, and the prevailing constraints (external constraints on debt accumulation, for example). In traditional economic analysis, the market, and in particular the impersonal competitive market, constitutes the institutional framework; prices are the only link among agents. However, when for various reasons (imperfect information and transactions costs, for example) markets do not perform well, alternative institutions may emerge to perform the transactions more efficiently. This gives an economic rationale for the formation of these institutions, where the most efficient among alternative institutions would, in principle, be the ones that prevail. This is the approach taken by recent developments in the theory of institutions, as opposed to the more traditional literature, which confined itself to tracing the effects of specific institutions on economic activity.

In modeling there is often a dilemma between realism and theory. We focus here on an intermediate level between these two, working with models that are sufficiently flexible and detailed to capture the relevant aspects of reality while remaining as close as possible to economic theory. This approach to modeling tries to replicate (while greatly simplifying) the actual mechanisms of the real economy, where many agents independently maximize their own welfare functions and jointly but inadvertently determine the aggregate outcome. In such a context, policy makers can only indirectly affect the outcome by modifying, with the policy instruments they control, the incentives and constraints that apply to individuals. This contrasts with central planning models, in the traditions of input-output and linear programming analyses, where the process of resource allocation is performed by a central agent, just as in a command economy (Tinbergen, 1952). It also contrasts with analyses at shadow prices, considered in the policy analysis matrix (PAM) (e.g., Monke and Pearson, 1989), which evaluate policies in an environment where there would be no distortions and all markets would clear. Here we consider the actual environment, with the distortions and market imperfections that characterize it, and simulate policy alternatives within this context or within a context modified by specific policy interventions, without engaging in global first-best policy exercises.

1.4. The Role of Quantitative Policy Analysis

In policy analysis, there is a gap between the realm of pure theory and the real world that policy makers face (Dervis, de Melo, and Robinson, 1982). Assisting the policy debate requires more than the qualitative insights given by pure theory; it requires quantification of the various mechanisms analyzed by theory. As it is easy to miss many of the complex indirect effects of a policy, empirical modeling can help reveal these effects. In addition, quantitative analysis allows running sensitivity tests to clarify the role of key behavioral assumptions and important parameter values. Quantitative modeling thus allows tracing back disagreements and differences on policy choices to specific behavioral assumptions and causal relations, empirical values given to parameters, and choices of normative objectives. With multiple objectives, including efficiency and nonefficiency objectives as listed above, that cannot be aggregated in any uniquely acceptable welfare function, quantitative policy analysis enables quantification of tradeoffs and better-informed policy debates leading to the choice of which policies to implement.

There are two steps in quantitative policy analysis. The first step consists of constructing a model, $y = f(x, z)$, where x are uncontrollable exogenous variables, z are policy instruments, and y are endogenous variables, some of which enter into the definition of criteria for policy evaluation that we will detail later (see Fox, Sengupta, and Thorbecke, 1966). Solving the model for the observed levels x_{obs} of x and the policy package z_{obs} that was actually implemented yields the solution $\hat{y}$, which is usually called the base run of the model. This solution is either one value for each endogenous variable if the model is static or a sequence of values if intertemporal.

Calculating the base run has four purposes. First, close replication of the observed impact of the policy package in place is essential to *validate* the model. If one follows an econometric approach, where the parameters of f have been estimated as $\hat{f}$ to replicate the data as closely as possible, the base run is the predicted values $\hat{y} = \hat{f}(x_{obs}, z_{obs})$, and statistical criteria of goodness of fit are used to assess the accuracy of the model. If quantification of the model is done with a "calibration" procedure because we do not have enough observations to estimate econometrically the parameters of f (a procedure to be described in more detail later), validation criteria are looser, as they rely on nonunique choices of parameters to replicate the observed data as well as possible. In all cases, model validation is based on seeking to minimize the difference $y_{obs} - \hat{y}$. If this difference remains unsatisfactorily large, new rounds of estimation and calibration are called for.

For illustrative purposes we show, in Figure 1.1, the base run for GDP between 1985 and 1991 obtained with a computable general equilibrium (CGE) model for Ecuador that will be used in Chapter 12. The base run does not exactly replicate the observed levels of GDP because the model omits a number of uncontrollable exogenous factors, for instance, the 1987 earthquake which disrupted the export of oil and many other aspects of the economy. In general, however, the base run has been calibrated to replicate the general tendency of the economy. The values of the policy variables and of the exogenous variables used for the base run were those which were effectively observed in Ecuador during these years (i.e., x_{obs}, z_{obs}). In this case, the policy package consisted in a mix of restrictive fiscal (F) and monetary (M) policies and trade liberalization (TL) that were introduced as part of a stabilization package to counteract the disequilibria created by the debt crisis and the fall in petroleum prices in the early 1980s.

Figure 1.1. Base run and simulation of stabilization policies in Ecuador

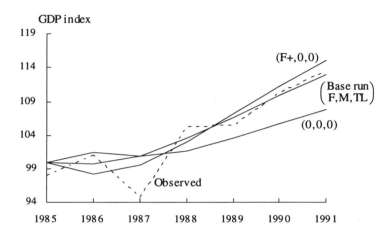

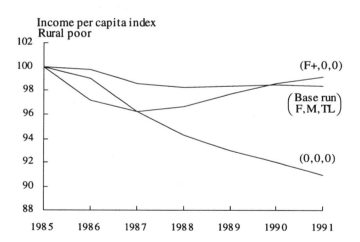

Policies are referred to as F for fiscal, M for monetary, and TL for trade liberalization.

Second, the base run yields predicted values for some endogenous variables which are *not directly observable*. This typically applies to income data, for instance, the per capita income of the rural poor as shown in Figure 1.1. The base run thus allows one to infer what was the effect of the observed historical sequence (x_{obs}, z_{obs}) on these unobservable endogenous variables. In

Ecuador we see that, owing to population growth and the particular distribution of the benefits from growth, the per capita real income of the rural poor fell slightly while the policy package implemented was successful in restoring economic growth.

Third, simulation on the base run can be used to *decompose* the effects on y of specific noncontrollable factors x_i, such as an external price shock, or of specific policy instruments z_i, such as fiscal policy, which, jointly with the other x_{-i} and the other z_{-i}, determine the values predicted by the base run (the notation z_{-i} means all z excluding z_i). In this case, the question asked is typically of the type: what is the effect $\Delta\hat{y}$ of an exogenous marginal change $\Delta\bar{z}_i$ in policy instrument z_i, given the observed levels of the other exogenous variables x and policy instruments z_{-i}, that is,

$$\Delta\hat{y} = \hat{f}\left(x_{obs}, \ z_{i\,obs} + \Delta\bar{z}_i, \ z_{-i\,obs}\right) - \hat{y} \quad ?$$

In the simpler linear models, the individual contributions of the different elements of the policy package and uncontrollable exogenous variables during the period of analysis may be readily read from the parameters. In the more complicated models, this is done by simulation: the components of the policy package actually implemented and of the set of intervening factors can be changed one at a time by a marginal amount to trace out their separate effects through the solution of the model, thus revealing their relative contributions to the observed outcome. This helps the policy analyst develop an understanding of the specific consequences of each policy component and a feel for the sensitivity of the solution to the parameters attached to each policy instrument.

Fourth, the base run is used as the *benchmark* against which to measure the impact of counterfactual policy scenarios. If, for instance, we want to know what would have happened had a particularly policy package (e.g., stabilization policies) not been introduced, or what would have been the impact of an alternative policy (e.g., confining stabilization policies to stronger fiscal austerity, without monetary contraction and trade liberalization), the impact of these counterfactual policies should be assessed not against the status quo ante (i.e., the preshock state of the economy), but against the predicted state of the economy as it would have evolved as a consequence of the shock without implementation of the alternative policies, that is, against the base run. Choosing the base run as the benchmark for policy evaluation as opposed to the status quo ante can make a major difference: if the shock introduces a recession and the policy results in partial compensation for the shock, assessing the policy against the status quo ante would blame the residual recession on the policy. This is an error that has all too often been made in assessing the effectiveness of stabilization policies, resulting in strong indictments against implementation of these policies that were not always justified. This is, for instance, the methodology Cornia (1987) followed for UNICEF in looking at the time evolution of countries with IMF-assisted stabilization programs over the period 1980–85 and judging the effectiveness of the stabilization program by comparing the terminal with the initial year.

In Figure 1.1, the counterfactual experiment of not responding to the debt and price shocks by introducing the observed stabilization package (F, M, TL) is represented by (0, 0, 0). In this case we see that, compared with the base run, a short-run stagnation would have been avoided, but that growth starting in year 2 would have been sharply inferior. Clearly, it took some political determination to sacrifice short-term for long-term growth. Without stabilization policy, the welfare of the rural poor would have fallen dramatically and continued to deteriorate through the years.

The fallacy of assessing a policy against the status quo ante as opposed to the base run is readily visible by looking at the per capita income of the rural poor in Figure 1.1. In this case, the IMF-style stabilization package that was introduced was unable to redress the decline in per capita income, and is thus easily exposed to criticism by confusing shock and policy response. When compared with the counterfactual (0, 0, 0) of not introducing a stabilization program, we see that the decline in per capita income would have been far worse than actually occurred. Alternatively, without model building, the counterfactual used could have been the status of the rural poor in countries that were exposed to the same external shocks but did not introduce a stabilization package. This is difficult to do without modeling, however: shocks and policy responses differed widely across countries, making cross-country comparisons difficult, and there is in general insufficient direct information available on the income of the poor which, consequently, needs to be predicted.

Once the base run has been secured, the second step in quantitative policy analysis consists in using the models to simulate alternative policies that might be considered by policy makers. For instance, policy could have focused the stabilization package on the use of stronger fiscal austerity, without monetary and trade interventions, represented by (F+, 0, 0) in Figure 1.1. Compared with the base run, this would have induced a short-run recession and slower growth in the first four years, since the multiplier effects of fiscal expenditures would have been lost without much gain in crowding-in private investment and controlling inflation, both of which have payoffs only over the medium run. By the fifth year, however, fiscal austerity has a payoff in terms of stronger GDP growth relative to the base run. Undoubtedly for political reasons, the policy package that Ecuador chose to implement, and that is represented by the base run, was milder in the short run, but at the cost of a more mediocre long-run performance.

In quantifying models, several approaches can be followed, some more academic and demanding and some more pragmatic and timely. The more academic approach consists in estimating econometrically all the relations involved in the model. While desirable, this approach often entails large efforts at data collection and econometric estimation and may delay the initiation of policy dialogue beyond convenience. The other approach consists in gathering empirical information from previous studies and, on that basis, making a best guess about the likely value of model parameters. These parameters are scaled to satisfy all the constraints imposed by theory. Model calibration can also be performed to assess how well the model reproduces observed changes. Sensitivity analysis on the parameters retained allows identification of the critical parameters on which precise information should be obtained. This helps define priorities for additional econometric analysis without delaying the initiation of a policy dialogue on the basis of first guesses. In general, it is this pragmatic approach which we prefer.

1.5. Criteria for Policy Evaluation

Policy evaluation has to be conducted in relation to the rationales given to government intervention. In this book, we do not ask whether a particular policy has been successful in achieving the government's intended goal. This is because we do not know what the government's intended goals were: we do not know what its welfare function is, nor how it is being influenced by the demands of special interests. The government's stated goal cannot be taken at face value, since strategic behavior often requires the government to make statements which are at odds with its true objectives. Instead, we use a number of criteria and measure the policy impact on each, leaving it to the policy maker to subsequently use this information to make policy choices. The evaluation criteria used are efficiency, welfare, sustainability, and political feasibility, all of which rely on measures of income or welfare effects on household groups.

Efficiency measures are the most straightforward. They usually consist of measures of aggregate product or income at the level of the unit analyzed. This will be measured by real GDP at the national level and by real sectoral product at the sectoral level. It is more difficult to specify measures of welfare and political feasibility. Here we will not use the criterion of sustainability, since the quantitative techniques we analyze are not intertemporal. Consequently, we turn to the specification of indicators for the quantification of the welfare and political feasibility criteria.

1.5.1. Welfare

1.5.1.1. Change in Utility
Theoretically, the welfare of an agent should be measured by the value of its own objective function. Hence, it should be measured as the level of profit for a producer and of utility for a consumer or a household.

Consider the case of a consumer, who is assumed to behave as if maximizing a well-behaved utility function $u(q, z)$ defined over the quantities of commodities consumed q and environmental and personal characteristics z, subject to a budget constraint y. Substituting into u the demand function $q(p, y, z)$ derived from this constrained maximization gives the indirect utility function, $v(p, y, z)$, which is the maximum utility that the consumer can reach for given prices p and income y. Using this function, the welfare impact on the consumer of a change in income and price from (p^0, y^0) to (p^1, y^1) could be evaluated as:

$$\Delta u = v\left(p^1, y^1, z\right) - v\left(p^0, y^0, z\right).$$

However, the utility functions u and v are not fully defined. This is because consumer theory is based only on the preference ordering of commodity bundles q and any other monotonic transformation of u would represent exactly the same preference ordering. Hence, the utility functions are used only to rank preferences, and the actual values of the levels or the changes in utility are not really meaningful. Such functions are said to be ordinal, as opposed to cardinal, and they cannot give a measurable indicator of welfare. Alternative measures of welfare consequently need to be sought. For this purpose, a number of monetary measures of change in welfare have been proposed, based on the concepts of consumer surplus, compensated and equivalent variation, and real income.

1.5.1.2. Consumer Surplus
A monetary measure S of the welfare change between states (p^0, y^0) and (p^1, y^1) can be defined as the sum of the change in income and a monetary value ΔCS of the change in utility due to the price change:

$$S = y^1 - y^0 + \Delta CS,$$

where ΔCS is the change in consumer surplus in the markets where prices change (Johansson, 1987, p. 24).

The concept of consumer surplus is commonly used in measuring the welfare effect of a single price change. Figure 1.2 shows the standard demand curve (also called the Marshallian demand), which refers to the demand for a commodity as a function of its own price, for a given income and all other prices fixed. If the consumer consumes q^0 at price p^0, the consumer surplus is measured by the area CS^0 below the demand curve and above the price line. To obtain an intuitive interpretation, note that the demand curve represents the marginal utility of consumption. Consumption of one extra unit of good at R, for example, brings RP utility, and for that reason the consumer would be willing to pay RP for that unit. As one goes down the demand curve, each additional unit of consumption brings a lower level of utility, and consumption will be set at q^0 when the purchase price is p^0. With the price of all units equal to p^0, however, PQ measures a surplus in utility above the cost incurred for consumption of the unit at R. This surplus decreases as one moves down along the demand curve, and at q^0 the marginal utility of consumption is equal to its price p^0 and there is no surplus. Thus, the sum of all these surpluses in utility is measured by the area CS^0. When the consumer increases consumption to q^1 in response to a reduction in price to p^1, the increase in consumer surplus ΔCS is measured by the area p^0ABp^1.

The consumer surplus is an appealing measure of consumer benefits from price change because of its interpretation in terms of excess of willingness to pay over what is actually paid.

Figure 1.2. Consumer surplus

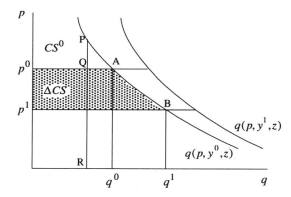

It is also easy to compute, since it is based on the elasticity of demand, which is easy to estimate. Furthermore, the corresponding money measure S can be shown to be equal to the change in indirect utility, Δv, divided by the marginal utility of money. Hence, under the restrictive hypothesis of constant marginal utility of money, S is a good measure of change in utility.

However, the consumer surplus is not well defined when there are multiple price changes or a simultaneous income-price change. The second case also is illustrated in Figure 1.2. Suppose that the consumer enjoys both an increase in income from y^0 to y^1 and a decrease in price from p^0 to p^1. One could evaluate the price adjustment first along $q(p, y^0, z)$ and then the income adjustment; or income could be adjusted first, and then the consumer surplus evaluated along the curve $q(p, y^1, z)$. The two welfare measures are quite different. A similar reasoning applies when several prices change. Hence, the change in consumer surplus due to multiple price and income changes depends on the order in which these changes are considered or, more generally, on the adjustment path. In other words, in this case there is no unique monetary measure of welfare change between two discrete points based on the consumer surplus concept.

1.5.1.3. *Compensating and Equivalent Variations*

Compensating and equivalent variations are welfare measures similar to the consumer surplus, but they do not suffer from the path dependency deficiency evoked above. The compensating variation (*CV*) is the amount of money which, when taken away from the consumer after the price and income change, leaves him with the same level of utility as before the change. It is defined as:

$$v\left(p^1, y^1 - CV, z\right) = v\left(p^0, y^0, z\right).$$

If the economic change brings about an increase in welfare, as in the previous example of income increase and price decrease, *CV* represents the maximum amount that the person will be willing to pay to accept the change. If the economic change brings a welfare loss, *CV* is the negative of the minimum amount that the person would require as a compensation for the change.

The equivalent variation (*EV*) is the amount of money which, when paid to the consumer, achieves the same level of utility before the change that would be enjoyed with the economic change. It is defined by:

$$v\left(p^1, y^1, z\right) = v\left(p^0, y^0 + EV, z\right).$$

If the economic change would bring about an increase in welfare, *EV* represents the minimum amount that the person requires to accept foregoing the change. For an economic project with a welfare loss, this is the maximum amount the person will be willing to pay to avoid the change.

These two concepts of compensating and equivalent variations can be related to what is called the compensated or Hicksian demand curve, which gives the demand for a commodity as a function of its own price for a constant level of utility, and not for a constant level of income as on the Marshallian demand curve. These curves are represented in Figure 1.3, in relation to the Marshallian demand curve. The *CV* is the area to the left of the compensated demand at u^0, while *EV* is the area to the left of the compensated demand at u^1. Although this relationship of *CV* and *EV* with a demand curve is very similar to what was used to compute the consumer surplus, this is not an operational concept, since the Hicksian demand curve cannot be directly observed or estimated. However, it does show that, when there is a single price change, $CV < \Delta CS < EV$, and the consumer surplus ΔCS can be a good approximation for *CV* or *EV*, if income effects are not too large.

Useful analytical expressions for *CV* and *EV* are based on the concept of the expenditure function. The expenditure function $e(p, u, z)$ is the minimum income which is necessary to reach the level of utility u at given price p. This expenditure function is directly related to the indirect utility function $v(p, y, z)$. It is found by solving $v(p, y, z) = u$ for $y = e$. Using the expenditure function, *CV* and *EV* can be written as:

$$CV = y^1 - y^0 - \left[e\left(p^1, u^0, z\right) - e\left(p^0, u^0, z\right)\right]$$

$$EV = y^1 - y^0 - \left[e\left(p^1, u^1, z\right) - e\left(p^0, u^1, z\right)\right].$$

The appealing characteristic of these two measures is that they are path independent and, hence, lead to a unique measure of impact of any combined price and income change. Their limitation is that each relies on one specific level of utility: CV is defined in reference to u^0, while EV is defined in reference to u^1. Hence, they cannot really reflect welfare changes when there is a change in utility brought about by an income-price change.

Figure 1.3. Equivalent variation, compensatory variation, and consumer surplus

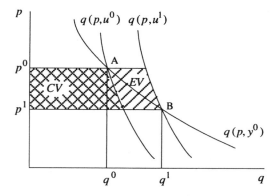

The interpretations of CV and EV as willingness to pay to accept and forego a change is also an interesting feature when applied to policy-induced changes in income and prices. First, willingness to pay can be meaningfully added across households. If the total sum of willingness to pay and compensation requirements as computed with CV is positive, it suggests that a proper compensating scheme could make the policy acceptable to everyone. In that respect, CV gives an interesting base for the design of compensating schemes that makes everybody at least as well off after the policy as before, which is the definition of a Pareto optimal policy (Just, Hueth, and Schmitz, 1982). Similarly, if the sum of all EV is positive, it indicates that a compensating scheme exists that could make it acceptable to everyone to forego the policy change. Limited compensation schemes targeted at special population groups can also be designed with these CV and EV measures.

1.5.1.4. *Real Income and the Choice of Price Index*

The simplest of all commonly used indicators of welfare is real income, defined as nominal income divided by a price index, real $y = y/P$. The impact of a combined price-income change is measured by:

$$\frac{\Delta \text{real } y}{\text{real } y} = \frac{\Delta y}{y} - \frac{\Delta P}{P}.$$

Use of this indicator raises the question of the definition of a true price index P which should be the ratio of the minimum expenditure required in current period 1 and in base period 0 to achieve a constant level of utility for a particular consumer group. Typical candidates are the Laspeyres price index P_L with weights equal to the quantities in the base period,

$$P_L = \sum_i q_i^0 p_i^1 / \sum_i q_i^0 p_i^0 ,$$

and the Paasche price index P_P with weights equal to the quantities in the current period,

$$P_P = \sum_i q_i^1 p_i^1 / \sum_i q_i^1 p_i^0 .$$

In the Laspeyres index, the price change is measured on the basis of the consumption structure prior to the change in income and price. Hence, the index does not take into account the expenditure reallocation to adjust for changes in prices and income. In most cases, one would expect a shift away from the commodities whose prices increase most and toward commodities which become relatively cheaper. Hence, if all prices do not change proportionally, the consumer price index computed with fixed consumption shares most likely overestimates the increase in the true price index and underestimates the decrease, in both cases biasing the welfare change unfavorably. The degree of bias introduced in the measure of welfare change depends on the flexibility that the consumer has in adapting consumption patterns. This, in turn, depends on the substitutability in consumption among the commodity groups which are considered and on the extent of the differences in individual price changes. The Paasche index does the opposite, namely it understates the increase and overstates the decrease in the true price index. Thus the true price index lies somewhere in between the Laspeyres and Paasche indexes. This has led Fisher (1922) to suggest using the geometric mean of the Laspeyres and Paasche indexes as an approximation to the true index, an index which has become known as Fisher's Ideal Price Index,

$$P_F = \sqrt{\frac{\sum_i q_i^0 p_i^1 \sum_i q_i^1 p_i^1}{\sum_i q_i^0 p_i^0 \sum_i q_i^1 p_i^0}}.$$

The main reason for using real income as an indicator of welfare is its simplicity. When changes are not too large, or when substitutabilities among commodities are not very high (e.g., because we are working at a high level of aggregation on large commodity groups that substitute poorly for each others), real income can be a good proxy for welfare change.

1.5.1.5. *Example of Computation of Welfare Indicators*
For this example, we use an aggregated version of the demand system reported in Table 2.1. Total consumption is aggregated in four items: food, housing, other nondurables, and durables.

The direct utility u, indirect utility v, expenditure function e, and corresponding demand system q, to which we will return in more detail in Chapter 2, are defined by:

$$u = \prod_{i=1}^{n}(q_i - c_i)^{b_i}$$

$$q_i = c_i + \frac{b_i}{p_i}(y - \sum_k p_k c_k)$$

$$v = (y - \sum_k p_k c_k)\lambda \ , \text{ with } \ \lambda = b_0 / \prod_k p_k^{b_k}$$

$$e = \sum_k p_k c_k + v \prod_k p_k^{b_k} / b_0,$$

where b_i and c_i are parameters and $b_0 = \prod b_i^{b_i}$. The parameters are given in Table 1.1. All prices are initially normalized to one. With this information, we can compute utility, $u^0 = v^0 = \$225$, income and expenditure, $y^0 = e\ (p^0, u^0) = \$2874.1$, and the marginal utility of money $\partial v / \partial y = \lambda = 0.297$.

Table 1.1. Parameters of the linear expenditure demand system, United States, 1948-78

	b_i	c_i (1972\$)	Base consumption (1972\$)	Consumption with food price increase	
				Quantities (1972\$)	Percent change
Food	0.088	494	561	551	−1.8
Housing	0.250	291	481	468	−2.6
Other nondurables	0.488	1,122	1,492	1,468	−1.6
Durables	0.174	209	341	333	−2.5

Source: Blanciforti, Green, and King, 1986.

Consider now a 10% increase in the price of food. Because of the income effect, consumption of all items declines. The new values for utility and expenditures are: $u^1 = v^1 = \$208.6$, $e\ (p^1, u^0) = \$2929.9$, $e\ (p^0, u^1) = \$2818.8$, $P = 1.0195$, and real income $= \$2819.1$.

Compensating and equivalent variation are calculated as: $CV = \$55.8$ and $EV = \$55.3$. The change in real income is $\$55.0$. The change in utility is 16.42. This, divided by the marginal utility of money, gives $\$55.3$. As will be seen in detail in Chapter 7, the change in consumer surplus can be calculated as:

$$\Delta CS = q^1 (p^1 - p^0) + 0.5(q^1 - q^0)(p^1 - p^0) = \$55.6.$$

These results show that all these measures are close to each other. They indicate that the 10% increase in the price of food induced a loss in welfare between $\$55.0$ and $\$55.8$ monetary units, or 1.91% to 1.94% of the initial income of $\$2874$.

1.5.1.6. Aggregate Welfare*

The aggregate concept of welfare corresponding to *EV* and *CV* at the national level is based on the trade expenditure function (Lloyd and Schweinberger, 1988). The trade expenditure function is defined as:

$$B(p,u,z) = \sum_h e(p,u_h,z_h) + e(p,u_g) + e(p,u_I) - g(p,z),$$

where $e(p, u_h, z_h)$, $e(p, u_g)$, and $e(p, u_I)$ are the expenditure functions corresponding to the utility achieved by household *h*, by the government *g*, and by investment expenditures *I*, respectively, and $g(p, z)$ is the domestic revenue, equal to GDP plus tariff revenues. *B* represents the necessary transfer to the country to achieve the levels of utility $u = (u_h, u_g, u_I)$ at given price *p* and characteristic/endowment *z*. Welfare changes due to either a shock or a policy that would alter income and prices can be measured by:

$$CV = -B(p^1,u^0,z) + B(p^0,u^0,z), \quad \text{and}$$

$$EV = -B(p^1,u^1,z) + B(p^0,u^1,z).$$

Aggregate welfare is also measured by either real GDP or by real absorption, which is the sum of private consumption, government consumption, and investment in real terms. Since a country can run a deficit, real GDP and real absorption may be significantly different. Real absorption is a better indicator of the actual welfare of the population, while real GDP measures its productive capacity.

1.5.1.7. Poverty

While there is a broad consensus that poverty alleviation should be a main concern in policy design, the measurement of poverty is itself the subject of intense debate. The basic requirement for the measurement of poverty is the definition of a poverty line which delineates the poor from the nonpoor. Disputes around the choice of a poverty line arise because the standard of living is a multidimensional concept, and there is no objective standard for what constitutes basic requirements. For that reason, some policy analysts prefer to use physical measures related to a specific requirement on which there may be greater consensus, such as nutrition or health, as the basis to define poverty. Capitalizing on this, the definition of a poverty line in terms of income is often done by first calculating the expenditure required to achieve a minimum nutritional intake and then inflating this expenditure by an appropriate ratio to take into account nonfood requirements.

Assuming that one has defined such a poverty line y^*, several measures of the extent of poverty exist. The most commonly used index is the headcount ratio, $H = n/N$, the share of households which are below the poverty line (*n*) in total population (*N*). This index, however, does not give a measure of the extent of poverty for the poor. Other indicators overcome this shortcoming. One is the income gap *I*, defined as:

$$I = \frac{1}{ny^*} \sum_{i \in P} (y^* - y_i),$$

where $(y^* - y_i)$ measures, for individual *i* in poverty, the gap between income and the poverty line, *P* is the set of all poor, and *n* is the total number of poor. This income gap is represented in

Figure 1.4 with data from rural Mexico. To build the income profile curve, income recipients are ranked by increasing income. This information is commonly reported by population groups, as in Table 1.2. The income gap is measured by the area between the poverty line and the income profile of the population, with proper normalization.

As the income gap I does not take into account the number of poor, it is often suggested that the product $P_1 = H\,I$ would be more satisfactory:

$$P_1 = \frac{1}{Ny^*} \sum_{i \in P} (y^* - y_i).$$

Table 1.2. Income distribution of rural population, Mexico, 1984

	Population N (percent)	Quarterly income y (pesos)	Cumulative population (percent)	Cumulative income (percent)	Poverty indices $(y-y^*)$	$(y-y^*)^2$	Income distribution Area under Lorenz curve	Theil index
Poor	11.3	147	11.3	4.7	188	35,526	448	
	9.3	195	20.6	10.0	140	19,479	441	
	8.8	219	29.4	15.5	116	13,482	416	
	8.1	233	37.5	21.0	102	10,432	362	
	7.3	278	44.9	26.8	57	3,266	345	
	6.2	284	51.1	31.9	51	2,646	263	
	5.6	304	56.7	36.8	31	934	227	
Nonpoor	14.1	363	70.8	51.6			534	
	4.2	389	75.0	56.2			127	
	4.3	428	79.3	61.5			120	
	3.6	440	82.9	66.1			86	
	3.0	492	85.9	70.3			67	
	3.0	499	88.9	74.6			54	
	2.7	547	91.6	78.8			42	
	2.2	657	93.7	82.9			30	
	2.5	759	96.2	88.3			27	
	2.0	829	98.2	93.0			14	
	1.8	1,324	100.0	100.0			6	
Poor	$H = 56.7$	226			685	85,766	3,608	0.028
Nonpoor	43.3	508						0.073
All	100	348					Gini = 0.28	$T = 0.136$
					$I = 3.6$			$T_b = 0.080$
					$P_1 = 2.0$	$P_2 = 0.8$		$T_w = 0.056$

Source: Levy, 1990.
Note: Poverty line defined at 335 pesos.

P_1 measures the level of income transfer needed to bring all poor to the poverty line, normalized to Ny^*. The shortcoming of this index is that it does not capture inequality among the poor, since a dollar of income gap for the extreme poor has the same weight as a dollar of income gap for those who are just under the poverty line.

Figure 1.4. Income profile of rural Mexico, 1984

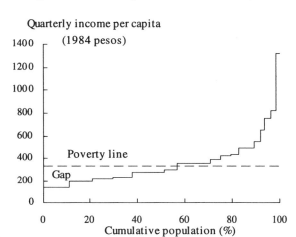

The Sen poverty index, which combines the standard poverty measures, H and I, with a measure of the inequality within the poverty group, is defined as:

$$S = H [I + (1 - I) G_p],$$

where H and I are the headcount and income gap defined above, and G_p is the Gini coefficient of inequality among the poor, defined in the next section.

Alternatively, and to better capture the importance of extreme poverty, Foster, Greer, and Thorbecke (1984) have suggested the following index:

$$P_2 = \frac{1}{Ny^{*2}} \sum_{i \in P} (y^* - y_i)^2.$$

One property of this index, which proves to be convenient in policy analysis, is that it is decomposable across subgroups. Hence, the aggregate poverty index P_2 of a population is a weighted average of the indices P_{2k} calculated for groups k of size N_k:

$$P_2 = \sum_k \frac{N_k}{N} P_{2k}.$$

1.5.1.8. Inequality

Defining adequate measures of inequality has also given rise to a large body of literature. A simple statistical indicator of income inequality is the coefficient of variation of income, $cv(y) = \sigma(y) / \bar{y}$, ratio of the standard deviation of income $\sigma(y)$ to mean income $\bar{y}$. This coefficient has the advantage of being unit-free. A more complete way to analyze income distribution is to construct the Lorenz curve. This is illustrated in Figure 1.5, which shows the distribution of income in rural Mexico in 1984. On the *x*-axis, the cumulative percentage of population is reported, and the *y*-axis represents the cumulative percentage of the income they control. The curve in Figure 1.5 indicates that the poorest 21% of the population receive 10% of total income (point A), and the poorest 71% receive 52% (point C). With a perfectly equal income distribution, the Lorenz curve would be the first diagonal, since any percentage of the population would

Figure 1.5. Lorenz curve for rural Mexico, 1984

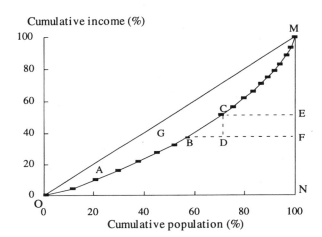

receive the same percentage of total income. The greater the level of inequality, the farther away the Lorenz curve lies from the 45 degree line OM.

A convenient shorthand summary of the relative degree of inequality can be obtained by calculating the ratio of the area between the diagonal and the Lorenz curve, divided by the total area of the triangle under the diagonal. This is the Gini coefficient:

$$\text{Gini} = \frac{\text{area G}}{\text{area OMN}}.$$

The Gini coefficient varies from 0 (perfect equality) to 1 (perfect inequality). Gini coefficients for countries with high inequality typically lie between 0.5 (e.g., Mexico) and 0.7 (e.g., Jamaica), while more egalitarian countries have Gini coefficients in the range of 0.4 (India) to 0.3 (Indonesia) (UNDP, 1992).

The analytical expression of the Gini coefficient is based on the measure of the area OBMN under the Lorenz curve, computed as the sum of triangles like BCD and rectangles like CDFE.

If the Lorenz curve were constructed with individual income data, the lengths BD and EF would be equal to $100/N$ and $100\,y_i/Y$, which are the percentage shares of individual i in total population N and in total income Y. This gives:

$$\text{Area OBMN} = \left[\sum_i \frac{1}{2} \frac{1}{N} \frac{y_i}{Y} + \sum_i \frac{y_i}{Y} \left(\frac{N - r_i}{N} \right) \right] \times 10000 , \text{ and}$$

$$G = \frac{2}{N\bar{y}} \left(-\frac{Y(N+1)}{2} + \sum_i y_i r_i \right) = \frac{2}{N\bar{y}} \text{cov}(y, r),$$

where r_i is the rank of individual i when the population is ordered by increasing income and cov(.) is the covariance between the income and rank series (Pyatt, Chen, and Fei, 1980).

Another inequality measure is Theil's (1987) entropy index, defined as:

$$T = \sum_{i=1}^{N} (y_i/Y) \ln \frac{y_i/Y}{1/N}.$$

This measure varies from 0 (complete equality) to $\ln N$ (complete inequality). Some authors prefer a transformed Theil index $T^* = 1 - e^{-T}$ which varies from 0 to $1 - 1/N$, and hence from 0 to 1 when $N \to \infty$. A convenient property of the Theil index is that it can be decomposed into between-group and within-group components. Assume that there are several groups k with population N_k, group income y_k, and Theil index T_k. The inequality index T can be written as the sum $T = T_w + T_b$ of the total within-group inequality index,

$$T_w = \sum_k (y_k/Y) T_k ,$$

and the between-group inequality index,

$$T_b = \sum_k (y_k/Y) \ln \frac{y_k/Y}{N_k/N} .$$

T_w is a weighted average of the within group inequality indices T_k, T_b characterizes inequality between the groups, and y_k/Y and N_k/N are the income and population shares of each group.

1.5.1.9. Decomposition of Income Inequality by Source of Income.

An interesting element of the analysis of income inequality is to measure the contribution of the different sources of income (agricultural income, nonagricultural income, remittances, etc.) to overall income inequality and to determine whether any particular source contributes to increase or decrease income inequality.

Let total income y of an individual consists of income y^s from S sources. The decomposition of the variance of income y is written:

$$\text{var}(y) = \sum_s \text{var}(y^s) + \sum_{s' \neq s} \text{cov}(y^s, y^{s'}) = \sum_s \text{cov}(y^s, y).$$

In this expression, the covariance between income y^s and total income y measures the contribution of income y^s to the variance of income y.

The corresponding decomposition of the coefficient of variation is expressed as:

$$cv(y) = \frac{\operatorname{var} y}{\sigma(y)\,\bar{y}} = \sum_s \frac{\bar{y}^s}{\bar{y}} \frac{\operatorname{cov}(y^s, y)}{\sigma(y)\sigma(y^s)} \frac{\sigma(y^s)}{\bar{y}^s} = \sum_s \frac{\bar{y}^s}{\bar{y}} \rho(y^s, y)\,cv(y^s),$$

where $\rho(y^s, y)$ is the coefficient of correlation between y^s and y.

Hence, a source of income y^s will increase income inequality $cv(y)$ if it is positively correlated to overall income y. The importance of its contribution increases with its own inequality $cv(y^s)$, its correlation with total income $\rho(y^s, y)$, and its share in income $\bar{y}^s / \bar{y}$.

An income source s is sometimes defined as inequality increasing (decreasing) if enlarging its share in total income increases (decreases) total inequality. Based on the decomposition of the coefficient of variation, the sth income source is inequality increasing if $\rho(y^s, y)\,cv(y^s)/cv(y)$ is larger than unity.

A similar decomposition can be performed on the Gini coefficient:

$$G = \frac{2}{N\bar{y}} \operatorname{cov}(y, r) = \frac{2}{N\bar{y}} \sum_s \operatorname{cov}\left(y^s, r\right) = \sum_s \frac{\bar{y}^s}{\bar{y}} R_s G_s,$$

where G_s is the Gini coefficient of the sth source of income and R_s is the correlation ratio expressed as:

$$R_s = \frac{\operatorname{cov}\left(y^s, r\right)}{\operatorname{cov}\left(y^s, r^s\right)}.$$

The decomposition of the Gini coefficient can also be written:

$$\sum_s w_s g_s = 1, \text{ where } w_s = \bar{y}^s / \bar{y} \text{ and } g_s = R_s G_s / G.$$

Contribution of the sth source of income to total inequality is hence measured by the factor inequality weight, $w_s g_s$. From the Gini coefficient decomposition, the sth source of income is inequality increasing (decreasing) if its concentration coefficient g_s is greater (less) than unity.

Using these different methods, Adams (1991) analyzed the respective contributions of agricultural income, nonagricultural income, and international remittances to rural income inequality in Egypt in 1986-87. He found that, while international remittances have a large Gini coefficient (0.93), their contribution to overall inequality is only 22% because they have a small share of total income (9.6%). In contrast agricultural income makes the largest contribution to overall inequality (66%) despite a moderate Gini coefficient (0.51) because it represents a large share of total income (57.7%).

1.5.1.10. *Example of Calculation of Poverty and Inequality Indices*

We use the income data for rural Mexico reported in Table 1.2. The original household data have been ranked by increasing income levels before being grouped into classes. The classes usually either are classes of same size (like deciles) or are defined by regular income intervals (e.g., 0–150, 150–200, etc.).

Using a poverty line of 335 pesos (of 1984), which had been defined on the basis of an expanded food budget, the exact limit between poor and nonpoor falls within the seventh or eighth group. With the necessary approximation due to grouped data, we consider the seventh group to be in poverty and the eighth group to be above poverty. This gives $H = 56.7\%$ of the rural population as poor. The poverty gap is 685.5 or $I = 3.6\%$ of the "minimum" income for the poor (number of poor × poverty line). It also represents $P_1 = 2\%$ of the "minimum" income of the total population (total population × poverty line). An appealing normalization for the income gap is to compare it with total income. The poverty gap of 685.5 represents 2% of total rural income (34,780). The index P_2, equal to 0.8, does not have a similar intuitive interpretation.

Computation of the Gini coefficient is given in Table 1.2. The area under (or to the right of) the Lorenz curve is approximated by the sum of a rectangle CDEF and a triangle BCD for each income group. In Table 1.2, the total area under the Lorenz curve is calculated to be equal to 3608. As area OMN is equal to 5000, the Gini coefficient is equal to 0.28. This Gini coefficient indicates a relatively low level of inequality within the rural population of Mexico, an accomplishment of the extended land reform program launched after the revolution of 1910.

The Theil index is also computed on the basis of these data. Total inequality is equal to 0.136, which can be decomposed into 0.056 for the average inequality within the two groups, poor and nonpoor, and 0.080 for inequality between the two groups. Inequality among the nonpoor is, as expected, much greater than inequality among the poor.

The distribution of income is often done under a different format, with income classes representing socioeconomic groups (small farmers, traders, civil servants, etc.) rather than income brackets. Socioeconomic groups are assumed to be well defined and stable and to represent homogenous groups in term of sources of income as opposed to deciles, which have a composition that is redefined whenever the incomes of different households rise and fall. Hence, socioeconomic groups are better used to analyze the differential impact of shocks and policy changes than groups defined on income levels. However, socioeconomic groups are not convenient for the computation of poverty and inequality indices, as households of similar income levels may pertain to different groups. Therefore, one needs to know the income distribution within each group. This is usually done by estimating a standard distribution (Pareto or lognormal) and assuming that it stays invariant in the policy simulation. The change in overall levels of poverty and inequality is then calculated from the changes in average income of each class. An example will be given in Chapter 12.

1.5.2. Political Feasibility

A policy that does not pass the test of political feasibility is a utopian proposition. Even if introduced, it will be challenged and will not be sustainable. For this reason, an important criterion for the evaluation of policy scenarios is assessment of the political feasibility of a policy based on the real income effects it has on the groups that have political weight. In that sense, political feasibility is quite distinct from efficiency and welfare. In general, one may think that it should act as a constraint on policy making: any policy considered should first satisfy the constraint of political feasibility. Once we have verified that it does, the efficiency and welfare implications of the policy can be assessed meaningfully. Political feasibility can, of course, be achieved through political management (i.e., through the packaging of policies to achieve political feasibility), even if it has efficiency and welfare costs.

If a policy is Pareto optimum in the sense that nobody is made worse off while some are made better off, the policy can be thought to be politically feasible. If a policy creates net social gains, then political management is feasible in that the gainers could compensate ex post the politically relevant losers. The question is to identify who the latter are and how much income transfer would be necessary to acquire their political support. If ex post income redistribution is not possible, in particular because the institutions necessary to make it credible that compensation will effectively take place are missing, then the policy has to be politically feasible through its own income effects. Political management is still feasible, but it has to be done through the packaging of policies, as opposed to straight tax-subsidy income transfers. To define the policy packaging that will achieve political feasibility at the minimum efficiency and welfare cost, it is necessary to construct an index of political feasibility.

An index of political feasibility (F) can be constructed on the basis of the government's criterion function established in the theory of public choice (Becker, 1983). It is a weighted sum of the rates of change in real income $\dot{y}_k$ that a particular policy creates for group k,

$$F = \sum_k I_k \dot{y}_k, \quad \sum_k I_k = 1,$$

where the weights I_k represent the relative levels of influence that each group exercises on government. These weights should be specified to capture the institutional process of policy making. Several options are available (see Dervis, de Melo, and Robinson, 1982):

a. One person, one vote: $I_k = n_k / n$, where n_k is the size of group k and n is total population size. This weighting scheme captures the role of numbers in policy making.

b. One dollar, one vote: $I_k = y_k / \sum y_k$, where y_k is average per capita income in group k. This weighting scheme captures the role of economic power in influencing policy making.

c. Combined roles of numbers and economic power: $I_k = n_k y_k / n\bar{y}$. In this case, the government's criterion function becomes:

$$F = \sum_k I_k \dot{y}_k = \frac{\sum n_k dy_k}{n\bar{y}},$$

which is the rate of change in total income induced by the policy (with $\dot{y} = dy / y$).

d. If only the political opinion of the urban rich or the rural rich matters in policy making, then $I_k = 1$ for that class.

e. More complex indices can be built to try to capture the role of coalitions among groups, the inducement to free ride when groups become large, the formation of expectations regarding the gains from policy when there is imperfect information, and perceived relative deprivation inducing a greater lobbying response (see de Janvry, Fargeix, and Sadoulet, 1992).

In the following chapters, the implications of policy simulations will be characterized by the effects they have on these different indices: efficiency, poverty, equity, and political feasibility.

Exercise 1
Production Function: Technological Change and Factor Substitutability

In this exercise (file 1PRODUCT), we look at the effect of the technological constraints, as characterized by the production function, on the optimal behavior of the producer. We show the importance of technological progress, not only in directly increasing the output from a given bundle of input, but also in increasing the productivity of labor and, thus, in promoting employment creation. We study the determinant role of the substitutability between the factors of production in conditioning the elasticity of producer supply in response to price incentives. We also show how this substitutability can critically affect the change in distribution of income induced by a change in factor prices.

We use a constant elasticity of substitution (CES) production function, in which production q is obtained from two factors of production, capital $\bar{k}$ and labor l, according to the following relationship:

$$(1) \quad q = a\theta_0 \left[\alpha(\theta_k \bar{k})^{-\rho} + (1-\alpha)(\theta_l l)^{-\rho} \right]^{-1/\rho},$$

where a is the scale parameter ($a > 0$); α is the share parameter ($0 < \alpha < 1$); θ_0, θ_k, and θ_l are efficiency measures that are used to characterize neutral, capital-saving, and labor-saving technological change, respectively; and ρ is a direct transformation of the elasticity of substitution σ between $\bar{k}$ and l:

$$\rho = \frac{1-\sigma}{\sigma} \quad \text{or} \quad \sigma = \frac{1}{\rho+1}, \text{ which shows that } \quad -1 < \rho < 0 \quad \text{ for } \sigma > 1$$

$$0 < \rho \quad \text{ for } \sigma < 1.$$

For a given value of capital, the physical marginal productivity of labor is given by:

$$(2) \quad \frac{\partial q}{\partial l} = (a\theta_0 \theta_l)^{-\rho}(1-\alpha)\left[\frac{q}{l}\right]^{1+\rho}.$$

Capital is considered a fixed factor, whose availability cannot be altered in the short time span considered here, while labor is a variable factor that can be purchased in any desired amount, at a given wage w. Profit-maximizing behavior from the producer then determines the optimum labor use and the supply curve as functions of technology, availability of the fixed factor $\bar{k}$, and prices (price of output p and price of labor w):

$$(3) \quad l = \frac{\theta_k \bar{k}}{\theta_l}\left[\frac{1}{\alpha}\left(\frac{p}{w}(1-\alpha)a\theta_0\theta_l\right)^{\sigma\rho} - \frac{(1-\alpha)}{\alpha}\right]^{1/\rho}, \text{ and}$$

$$(4) \quad q = l\left[\frac{w}{p}(a\theta_0\theta_l)^{\rho}\frac{1}{1-\alpha}\right]^{\sigma}.$$

There are no intermediate inputs, so that total sales pq are equal to total revenue, which is decomposed into labor cost wl and the residual return to the fixed factor. The return per unit of fixed capital is computed as $(pq - wl)/\bar{k}$.

The spreadsheet in Table 1E.1 is organized in three parts. The first block (rows 3 to 14) gives the parameters of the production function. The second block (rows 15 to 28) is used to study the technological constraint by computing production [equation (1)] and marginal productivity of labor [equation (2)] as functions of labor input l. The third block is used to perform the simulation of the optimal choice of the producer, with its labor demand [equation (3)] and output supply [equation (4)], and to compute some derived measures of technological choice (k/l and q/l), and of income distribution (return to capital and labor shares in total revenue).

Vertically, the first three columns are used to set different values of the exogenous variables (labor l in the production function, and price p and wage w in the model of optimal behavior). Different simulations can then be performed with these values, with each simulation using three columns.

First, examine the cells containing the parameters E5–E13. Note that in E13, ρ is calculated according to the formula given above. All the other cells contain numbers which can be changed to perform different simulations. Check now that the formulae in E19 and F19 correspond to equations (1) and (2) above, and see how these have been copied in E20–E27 and F20–F27 to compute production and marginal labor productivity at different levels of employment (values of labor in cells A19–A27). In the following block, the exogenous variables are entered in A33–A42 and B33–B42, and an intermediate variable p/w which often appears in the formulae is computed in column C. Check the formulae for labor demand (E33), output supply (F33), the computation of the supply elasticity (G34), the capital-labor ratio (E46), average labor productivity (F46), the return per unit of fixed capital (E59), and labor share in total income (F59).

1. Technological Change

Simulate the impact of a neutral technological change. To do this, first copy the complete set of calculations done for simulation 1 (area E5–H68) into the space reserved for the second simulation (I5). Then, in cell I9 change the value of θ_0 from 1 to 1.1. The new production function is given in I19–I27. To compare it with the former production function (in E19–E27), report these two series on a graph.

To make a graph in lotus, call up the sequence /Graph to reach the graph menu. Then, define the type of graph and fill in the data. Choose a scatter diagram by calling up Type, highlighting XY, and pressing Return. To enter the values of labor for the x-axis, choose X, press Return, highlight the range A19–A27, and press Return again. Similarly, to enter the series of production: choose A, press Return, highlight the range in which you have computed the first production function (E19–E27), and press Return. Choose B, press Return, highlight the range in which you have computed the second production function (I19–I27), and press Return. You can view the graph by pressing View. Add titles to your graph by calling up Options Title First, enter the title, press Return, and Quit. Add a legend, too, by calling up Options Legend, and entering titles for the two series (use titles that are informative, like theta0 = 1 and theta0 = 1.1 for these two curves, respectively). Go back into the graph menu; you can view the graph again and save it. Graphs cannot be printed directly from Lotus. Therefore, you need to save your graph twice. First, call up Name Create, and save the graph as a Lotus file that

	A	B	C	D	E	F	G	H	I	J	K	L	M	N
1	Table 1E.1. Production function: Technological change and factor substitutability													
2														
3	Parameters					Simulation 1				Simulation 2				
4						theta0 = 1				theta0 = 1.1				
5	sigma				.80									
6	a				25.00									
7	alpha				.30									
8	k				3.00									
9	theta 0				1.00									
10	theta k				1.00									
11	theta L				1.00									
13	-rho				-.25									
15	Variation of production with labor input													
16						Marginal								
17	Labor					productivity								
18	L				Production	of L								
19	2.00				56.2	20.3								
20	3.00				75.0	17.5								
21	4.00				91.5	15.7								
22	5.00				106.5	14.3								
23	6.00				120.3	13.3								
24	7.00				133.1	12.4								
25	8.00				145.2	11.7								
26	9.00				156.6	11.1								
27	10.00				167.5	10.6								
29	Optimal behavior													
30	Factor demand and supply function													
31					Labor	Output	Supply							
32	Price	Wage	p/w		demand	supply	elasticity							
33	.037	1.00	.037		.82	28.9								
34	.042	1.00	.042		1.23	39.5	2.7							
35	.047	1.00	.047		1.74	50.8	2.4							
36	.052	1.00	.052		2.32	62.5	2.2							
37	.057	1.00	.057		2.98	74.7	2.0							
38	.062	1.00	.062		3.71	87.0	1.9							
39	.067	1.00	.067		4.52	99.5	1.8							
40	.072	1.00	.072		5.39	112.0	1.7							
41	.077	1.00	.077		6.32	124.5	1.6							
42	.082	1.00	.082		7.32	137.0	1.5							
44	Technology													
45					Capital/L	Output/L								
46					3.7	35.4								
47					2.4	32.0								
48					1.7	29.2								
49					1.3	27.0								
50					1.0	25.1								
51					.8	23.4								
52					.7	22.0								
53					.6	20.8								
54					.5	19.7								
55					.4	18.7								
57	Return to fixed factor and income distribution													
58					Rent to k	wL/pq								
59					.084	76.4								
60					.141	74.4								
61					.216	72.8								
62					.311	71.3								
63					.425	70.0								
64					.560	68.9								
65					.715	67.8								
66					.891	66.8								
67					1.088	65.9								
68					1.306	65.1								

you can recall with the sequence Name Use whenever you are in this spreadsheet. Name it "$Q(L)$," for example. Then, by calling up Save, you save the graphs as a .pic file that you will not be able to access and modify later; you will use this file only to print from another program. Save this graph under the same name $Q(L)$.pic (see Figure 1E.1).

These graphs show production to be an increasing function of labor. Looking at the slope of the functions, what can you say about the evolution of marginal productivity of labor as labor use increases? How does technological change affect the marginal productivity of labor?

Now, consider the optimal behavior of the producer, represented in the labor demand and output supply functions. For a given price and wage, $p = 0.057$ and $w = 1$ for example, what are the optimal labor demand l_1 and output supply q_1 corresponding to $\theta_0 = 1$, and l_2 and q_2 corresponding to $\theta_0 = 1.1$? By how much does output increase when the 10% technological change takes place? This output increase can be decomposed in two components: the first is the direct effect of technological change when labor is kept at the same level. This is the move upward

Figure 1E.1. Impact on production of a neutral technological change

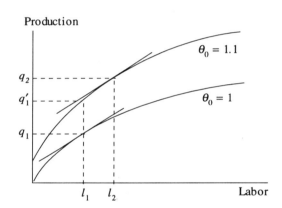

from one production function to the other at l_1, represented by the move from q_1 to q_1' in Figure 1E.1. To find the value of q_1', give the value of 2.98 to labor in cell A20, and read the corresponding value of production in E20. The second is due to the increase in labor use from l_1 to l_2 in response to the increase in labor productivity, which produces a move from q_1' to q_2. What is the relative importance of these two components in this case?

2. Substitutability among Factors of Production and Supply Elasticity

Set θ_0 back to 1 in the simulation 2, and now perform three simulations with σ equal to 0.5, 0.8, and 1.2, respectively. Compare the production functions. When labor input increases from 3 to 6, for example, how does the production level change in the three cases? How does labor productivity change? Derive from this the meaning of substitutability among the factors of production.

Now, look at the supply function. Starting from the same price, $p = 0.057$, for which all three supply functions take approximately the same values, suppose that the output price increases to 0.062. By how much do output and labor demand increase in the three cases? Symmetrically, when the price decreases, how do output and labor demand change with different values of σ? What can you conclude about the relationship between substitutability among factors and supply elasticity? Explain. Draw the supply functions for the three values of σ on the same graph.

Observe the variations in profit (return to the fixed factor) with these price variations. Compare the increases in profit when the output price increases. Compare the declines in profit when output price declines. Can you see how flexibility in production allows the producer to adjust labor use in response to a price change and, thus, to protect the profitability of the fixed factor?

3. Substitutability Among Factors of Production and Factor Shares in Income

In this question, you will analyze how the labor income changes when the wage changes. Set the output price at 0.057 in A33–A42, and give values to the wage rate running from 0.75 to 1.20 in B33-B42. Observe how the labor share changes in the value of production when the wage rate increases from 1 to 1.20 or decreases from 1 to 0.75. Contrast the cases when σ is smaller and greater than one. Explain this by looking at the changes in labor use in response to wage movement.

References

Adams, Richard. 1991. *The Effects of International Remittances on Poverty, Inequality and Development in Rural Egypt.* Washington, D.C.: International Food Policy Research Institute, Research Report 86.

Adelman, Irma. 1975. "Growth, Income Distribution, and Equity-Oriented Development Strategies." *World Development* 3:67–76.

Adelman, Irma. 1984. "Beyond Export-Led Growth." *World Development* 12:937–49.

Bardhan, Pranab. 1988. "Alternative Approaches to Development Economics." In *Handbook of Development Economics*, edited by H. Chenery and T. N. Srinavasan. Amsterdam: North-Holland.

Becker, Gary. 1983. "The Theory of Competition Among Pressure Groups for Political Influence." *Quarterly Journal of Economics* 93:372–400.

Blanciforti, Laura, Richard Green, and Gordon King. 1986. *U.S. Consumer Behavior Over the Postwar Period: An Almost Ideal Demand System Analysis.* Giannini Foundation Monograph No. 40. Davis: University of California.

Cardoso, Fernando, and Enzo Faletto. 1969. *Dependencia y desarrollo en America Latina.* Mexico City: Siglo XXI.

Cornia, Andrea. 1987. "Adjustment Policies, 1980–1985: Effects on Child Welfare." In *Adjustment with a Human Face.* Volume I, *Protecting the Vulnerable and Promoting Growth*, edited by A. Cornia, R. Jolly, and F. Stewart. Oxford: Clarendon Press.

de Janvry, Alain, André Fargeix, and Elisabeth Sadoulet. 1992. "The Political Feasibility of Rural Poverty Reduction." *Journal of Development Economics* 37:351–367.

Dervis, Kemal, Jaime de Melo, and Sherman Robinson. 1982. *General Equilibrium Models for Development Policy.* Cambridge: Cambridge University Press.

ECLAC (Economic Commission for Latin America and the Caribbean). 1990. *Magnitud de la pobreza en America Latina en los años ochenta.* LC/L.533. Santiago: ECLAC.

Fisher, Irving. 1922. *The Making of Index Numbers.* Boston: Houghton Mifflin.

Foster, James, Joel Greer, and Erik Thorbecke. 1984. "A Class of Decomposable Poverty Measures." *Econometrica* 52:761–66.

Fox, Karl, Jati Sengupta, and Erik Thorbecke. 1966. *The Theory of Quantitative Economic Policy with Applications to Economic Growth and Stabilization.* Amsterdam: North-Holland.

Gardner, Bruce. 1987. *The Economics of Agricultural Policies.* New York: Macmillan.

Gerschenkron, Alexander. 1962. *Economic Backwardness in Historical Perspective.* Cambridge: Harvard University Press.

Hazell, Peter, and C. Ramasamy. 1991. *The Green Revolution Reconsidered: The Impact of High-Yielding Rice Varieties in South India.* Baltimore: Johns Hopkins University Press.

Hirschman, Albert. 1958. *The Strategy of Economic Development.* New Haven: Yale University Press.

Hirschman, Albert. 1981. "The Rise and Decline of Development Economics." In *Essays in Trespassing: Economics to Politics and Beyond*, edited by A. Hirschman. Cambridge: Cambridge University Press.

Johansson, Per-Olov. 1987. *The Economic Theory and Measurement of Environmental Benefits.* Cambridge: Cambridge University Press.

Johnson, Harry. 1958. *International Trade and Economic Growth.* Cambridge: Harvard University Press.

Just, Richard, Darrell Hueth, and Andrew Schmitz. 1982. *Applied Welfare Economics and Public Policy.* Englewood Cliffs, N.J.: Prentice-Hall.

Kreps, David. 1990. *A Course in Microeconomic Theory.* Princeton: Princeton University Press.

Krueger, Anne. 1974. "The Political Economy of the Rent Society." *American Economic Review* 64:291–303.

Krugman, Paul. 1990. *Rethinking International Trade.* Cambridge: The MIT Press.

Kuznets, Simon. 1964. "Economic Growth and the Contribution of Agriculture: Notes on Measurement." In *Agriculture in Economic Development*, edited by C. Eicher and L. Witt. New York: McGraw-Hill.

Levy, Santiago. 1990. *Poverty in Mexico: Issues and Policies.* Washington, D.C.: World Bank, Latin American and Caribbean Operations Division.

Lloyd, Peter, and A. G. Schweinberger. 1988. "Trade Expenditure Functions and the Gains from Trade." *Journal of International Economics* 24:275–97.

Mellor, John. 1986. "Agriculture on the Road to Industrialization." In *Development Strategies Reconsidered*, edited by J. Lewis and V. Kallab. New Brunswick, N.J.: Transaction Books.

Monke, Eric, and Scott Pearson. 1989. *The Policy Analysis Matrix for Agricultural Development.* Ithaca: Cornell University Press.

Ohkawa, Kazushi, and Henry Rosovsky. 1960. "The Role of Agriculture in Modern Japanese Economic Development." *Economic Development and Cultural Change* 9:43–68.

Pyatt, Graham, Chau-Nan Chen, and John Fei. 1980. "The Distribution of Income by Factor Components." *Quarterly Journal of Economics* 95:451-73.

Persson, Torsten, and Guido Tabellini. 1990. *Macroeconomic Policy, Credibility, and Politics.* New York: Harwood Academic Publishers.

Ranis, Gustav, and J. C. Fei. 1961. "A Theory of Economic Development." *American Economic Review* 51:533–65.

Sen, A. K. 1960. *Choice of Techniques.* Oxford: Basil Blackwell.

Stiglitz, Joseph. 1985. *Economics of Information and the Theory of Economic Development.* Working Paper 1566. New York: National Bureau of Economic Research.

Stiglitz, Joseph. 1987. "Some Theoretical Aspects of Agricultural Policies." *The World Bank Research Observer* 2:43–60.

Stiglitz, Joseph, and Andrew Weiss. 1981. "Credit Rationing in Markets with Imperfect Information." *American Economic Review* 71:393-410.

Streeten, Paul. 1979. "A Basic Needs Approach to Economic Development." In *Directions in Economic Development*, edited by K. Jameson and C. Wilber. Notre Dame, Ind.: University of Notre Dame Press.

Theil, Henri. 1987. *Economics and Information Theory.* Chicago: Rand McNally.

Tinbergen, Jan. 1952. *On the Theory of Economic Policy.* Amsterdam: North-Holland.

UNDP (United Nations Development Program). 1992. *Human Development Report.* New York: Oxford University Press.

United Nations. 1989. *Report on the World Social Situation.* New York: United Nations.

World Bank. 1992. *World Bank Development Report, 1992.* Washington D.C.: Oxford University Press
for the World Bank.

Zusman, Pinhas. 1976. "The Incorporation and Measurement of Social Power in Economic Models."
International Economic Review 17:447–62.

CHAPTER TWO

Demand Analysis

2.1. Objectives of Demand Analysis and Role of Theory

The objective of analyzing individual consumer behavior is to explain the level of demand for the commodities an individual consumes given the structure of relative prices faced, real income, and a set of individual characteristics such as age, education, professional status, type of household to which he belongs, and geographical environment (for example, rural versus urban). If demand is analyzed directly at the regional or the national level, it is affected by both the average level of these variables in the unit of analysis and by their distribution across the population. A policy analyst will typically ask the question, "What is the income or price elasticity of good x for consumers in a particular subgroup (social class, income strata) or for all consumers in a region or country?"

2.1.1. Demand Analysis for Policy Making

There is a wide range of development policy questions for which knowledge of consumer behavior is important. One is the definition of policy interventions to improve the nutritional status of particular individuals, households, or individuals within households such as infants and pregnant women. On this subject, there has been an active controversy about the magnitude of the income elasticity of calorie intake compared with the income elasticity of food expenditures. As the income of poor people rises, it is likely that they will trade quality for quantity of food and thus substitute away from calories toward nonnutrient characteristics of foods such as taste and variety. If this is the case, the income elasticity of calorie intake could be significantly lower than the income elasticity of food expenditure. Schemes of income transfers to the poor would thus have a much smaller nutritional impact and would require much larger transfers to achieve a quantum of nutritional improvement. In this debate, Behrman and Deolalikar (1990) have argued that increases in income will not result in any significant improvements in nutrient intakes, while Strauss and Thomas (1990) and Subramanian and Deaton (1992) have shown that calorie elasticity is indeed lower than expenditure elasticity, but nevertheless significantly positive.

Another area of policy analysis is a country's strategy of food subsidies. The key issue here is to determine which commodities to subsidize in order to minimize the budgetary cost of nutritional improvement of the malnourished. To achieve this, an ideal commodity for distribution is one consumed in large quantities by the poor and little by those with adequate diets, thus minimizing leakages toward the latter (Timmer, Falcon, and Pearson, 1983). Subsidizing one commodity will create not only direct nutritional gains through that commodity, but indirect gains as well, as the consumption of nonsubsidized goods increases due to the purchasing power released by acquisition of the subsidized commodity. Assessing the total nutritional effect of the subsidy thus requires capturing the complex reallocation of consumer expenditures across commodities in response to the price change. Food prices may be reduced through direct price interventions or through the allocation of public budgets to agricultural research on specific foods. In this case, a country may tailor its agricultural research strategy to its nutritional improvement objectives (Pinstrup-Andersen, de Londoño, and Hoover, 1976).

Finally, knowledge of the demand structure is essential for sectoral and macroeconomic policy analysis. In the very short run, with production relatively inflexible, changes in the structure of demand are the main determinants of observed changes in market prices for nontradable goods and of imports and exports for tradable goods. In the medium and long runs, the structure of final demand is an important element of more complete models (such as multimarket and CGE models that we analyze in subsequent chapters) that seek to explain the levels of production and consumption, price formation, trade flows, income levels, and government fiscal revenues. For these models, complete systems of demand equations need to be estimated that satisfy the consumers' budget constraints as well as consistency in choices. Several systems adequate for this purpose will be analyzed here.

2.1.2. Alternative Approaches to the Analysis of Demand

Methodologically, there are two approaches that can be followed to estimate the parameters of demand equations. One consists of specifying estimable single-equation demand functions in a pragmatic fashion without recourse to economic theory. A typical situation, for instance, is to estimate from time series data the income and price elasticities for a commodity i in a constant elasticity demand equation such as:

$$\ln q_i = a_i + \sum_j E_{ij} \ln \frac{p_j}{P} + \eta_i \ln \frac{y}{P} + \sum_k b_{ik} \ln z_k,$$

where:

q_i = quantity purchased of good i per capita,

p_i, p_j = prices of good i and of selected other commodities j which are close substitutes or complements,

y = total expenditure per capita,

P = consumer price index,

E_{ij} = direct and cross-price elasticities,

η_i = expenditure elasticity,

z_k = household characteristics, time (to account for steady changes in tastes, in the distribution of income, and in the quality of products), and other exogenous variables, and

b_{ik} = elasticities of demand with respect to z_k.

The use of relative prices (p_i/P) and real income (y/P) as exogenous variables makes the demand equations homogenous of degree zero in prices and income. This ensures that there is no "money illusion" in demand in the sense that it is not affected by a proportional increase in all prices and income.

This pragmatic approach is attractive in its simplicity, yet it has serious drawbacks. First, the choice of functional forms for the demand equations and of the variables to be included is arbitrary. The guidelines used are usually a combination of common sense, interest in specific elasticities, computational convenience, and goodness of fit criteria. This leaves doubt whether the estimated equation is actually derived from consumer behavior and, if it is, what type of behavior is implied.

Second, the functional form used above postulates constancy of the elasticities over all values of the exogenous variables. Although this is convenient for policy analysis, it is evident that this can be true only over a short range of prices and income. Typically, commodities that are luxuries (high income elasticities) become necessities (low income elasticities) when per capita income increases. A third drawback is that the set of demand equations estimated in this fashion leads to predictions which do not satisfy the budget constraint that limits total expenditure. This is because the estimated parameters in general do not satisfy the restrictions imposed on them by demand theory.

An alternative approach to the estimation of demand equation parameters uses the theory of demand as a guideline for the choice of functional forms and variables to be included. In particular, the theory allows (1) the derivation of estimable functional forms of demand equations from mathematically specified models of consumer choice and (2) the imposition of constraints on demand parameters to reduce the number of independent parameters to be estimated to manageable numbers relative to the data available. In the following section, we will briefly outline the basic theory of consumer behavior and critically present some of the recent advances which have been extensively used for empirical analysis and policy making.

2.2. Theory of Consumer Behavior and Demand Analysis

2.2.1. Basic Model

The basic objective of the theory of consumer behavior is to explain how a rational consumer chooses what to consume when confronted with various prices and a limited income. At this level of generality, the main usefulness of the theory for empirical purposes is that it establishes a set of constraints which demand parameters must satisfy, thus limiting the number of independent parameters to be estimated and ensuring consistency in the results obtained.

Consider an individual consumer whose utility function is $u(q, z)$, where q is the vector of quantities of n commodities on which a consumption decision must be made and z are individual characteristics. The amount of income which can be spent is y, imposing a budget constraint $p'q = y$, where p' is an n-dimensional row vector of prices. The consumer's objective function is to maximize utility with respect to q, subject to the budget constraint $p'q = y$. This can be rewritten as:

$$\underset{q,\lambda}{Max}\ u(q,z) + \lambda(y - p'q),$$

where λ is a Lagrange multiplier (see the Appendix).

The solution to this maximization problem is a set of n demand equations:

$$q_i = q_i(p, y, z), \quad i = 1, \ldots, n.$$

These n equations contain:

n income slopes $\dfrac{\partial q_i}{\partial y}$ or income elasticities $\eta_i = \dfrac{\partial q_i}{\partial y}\dfrac{y}{q_i}$, and

n^2 price slopes $\dfrac{\partial q_i}{\partial p_j}$ or price elasticities $E_{ij} = \dfrac{\partial q_i}{\partial p_j}\dfrac{p_j}{q_i}$.

Goods can be categorized according to the signs and magnitudes of these elasticities as follows:

Categorization with respect to the income elasticity:

   Normal good: $\eta_i > 0$ ($\eta_i > 1$ luxury; $0 < \eta_i < 1$ necessity)
   Neutral good: $\eta_i = 0$
   Inferior good: $\eta_i < 0$.

Categorization with respect to the own-price elasticity:

   Non-Giffen good: $E_{ii} < 0$ ($E_{ii} < -1$ elastic; $E_{ii} > -1$ inelastic)
   Giffen good: $E_{ii} > 0$.

Categorization with respect to the cross-price elasticity:

   Gross substitutes: $E_{ij} > 0$
   Gross complements: $E_{ij} < 0$.

There are a number of constraints that these parameters must satisfy. They are:

a.   The *Engel equation* that derives from the budget constraint:

(1) $\displaystyle\sum_i p_i \frac{\partial q_i}{\partial y} = 1$ or $\displaystyle\sum_i w_i \eta_i = 1$,   where $w_i = \dfrac{p_i q_i}{y}$ are the budget shares.

b.   The *n Cournot equations* that also derive from the budget constraint:

(2) $\displaystyle\sum_i p_i \frac{\partial q_i}{\partial p_j} = -q_j$ or $\displaystyle\sum_i w_i E_{ij} = -w_j$,   for $j = 1, \ldots, n$.

c.   These two sets of equations together give the *n Euler equations* (that are consequently not additional restrictions) that state there is no money illusion; that is, that if all prices and income increase in the same proportion, demand remains unchanged:

(2′) $\displaystyle\sum_j E_{ij} + \eta_i = 0$, $i = 1, \ldots, n$.

d.   The $n(n-1)/2$ *Slutsky equations* that express symmetry in substitution effects:

(3) $E_{ij} = \dfrac{w_j}{w_i} E_{ji} + w_j(\eta_j - \eta_i)$,   for $i \neq j = 1, \ldots, n$.

Using equations (1), (2) or (2′), and (3), the $n + n^2$ parameters of the system of demand equations are thus reduced to a smaller number of independent parameters, namely,

$$(n + n^2) - 1 - n - \frac{n(n-1)}{2} = \frac{1}{2}(n^2 + n - 2).$$

Theory thus allows substantial reduction in the number of parameters to be estimated and, hence, in the amount of data needed for that purpose. If, for example, n is 10, the demand equations contain 110 parameters. The 56 constraints on these, however, imply that only 54 of them are independent.

For empirical work, time series data are usually needed to observe price changes and estimate price elasticities. However, these time series are generally short; and the number of independent parameters left by theory, even after imposing all constraints, remains excessive. Additional constraints, consequently, need to be added by making the general model of consumer choice more restrictive. This can be accomplished with use of the concept of separability.

2.2.2. *Separability and Stepwise Budgeting*

The basic idea of separability is intuitively appealing. It postulates that commodities which interact closely in yielding utility can be grouped together while goods which interact only in a general way through the budget constraint are kept in separate groups. Items used for food, clothing, housing, transportation, and entertainment could thus constitute separable groups. While carrots and tomatoes compete closely in satisfying food utility, and movies and plays entertainment utility, carrots and movies compete for overall utility in a way similar to tomatoes and plays. Another way of understanding the idea of separability is through the concept of stepwise budgeting in the making of consumer choices. Due to the complexity for consumers in making choices among a very large number of alternatives, income is first allocated to budget categories, also called wants, such as food, clothing, and housing. In a second stage, the food budget is allocated to specific items such as carrots and tomatoes. It can be shown that, if separability in wants exists, the exact same final choices are made in two stages as in one single decision. Empirically, existence of separability reduces further the number of independent parameters to be estimated.

Several types of separability have been postulated, some more restrictive than others (see Brown and Deaton, 1972). The most restrictive, and also the most empirically useful, is one introduced by Frisch (1959), where each commodity belongs to a separate group (pointwise separability). The utility function is thus written as:

$$u = u_1(q_1) + \ldots + u_n(q_n).$$

This implies "want independence" in the sense that the marginal utility (*MU*) of a good i is independent of the quantity consumed of any other good j:

$$MU_i = \frac{\partial u}{\partial q_i} = \frac{du_i}{dq_i}, \quad \frac{\partial MU_i}{\partial q_j} = 0.$$

Because goods are not likely to be inferior, it implies that all goods are gross complements to each other. It is, consequently, an approach that works fairly well when dealing with commodities that are themselves broad aggregates, such as food, clothing, and housing. In this case, the cross- and own-price elasticities take the following forms, respectively:

$$E_{ij} = -\frac{w_j}{\omega} \eta_i \eta_j - w_j \eta_i, \quad i \neq j,$$

$$E_{ii} = \frac{1}{\omega} \eta_i (1 - w_i \eta_i) - w_i \eta_i,$$

where:

$\omega = \dfrac{\partial \lambda}{\partial y} \dfrac{y}{\lambda}$ is the "flexibility of money,"

$\lambda = \partial u^* / \partial y$ is the marginal utility of income, and

$u^*(p, y) = u(q(p, y))$ is the indirect utility.

Note that price elasticities are obtained as a function of the budget shares, the income elasticities, and the parameter ω. If ω is known, the price elasticities can be derived from cross-sectional household survey data which give measures of the budget shares and estimations of the income elasticities. In a sense, this is an extreme case where restrictive theoretical specifications allow for an estimation of behavior in response to price changes without even requiring observation of prices.

The flexibility of money can be measured from knowledge of the own-price elasticity, the income elasticity, and the budget share for one separable group i:

$$\omega = \frac{\eta_i (1 - w_i \eta_i)}{E_{ii} + w_i \eta_i}.$$

This is commonly done using the food group since it is the one for which prior knowledge of these elasticities tends to be most reliable.

The flexibility of money has been estimated for a large number of countries and time periods. Estimates range from -3 at low levels of per capita income (e.g., in Argentina and Chile) to -1.1 in the United States. In order to predict likely levels of ω, an empirical relation can be estimated between the measured ω and the corresponding level of real income. One such relation is:

$$\ln(-\omega) = 1.87 - 0.60 \ln(y/P), \quad R^2 = 0.46,$$
$$\underset{(6.6)}{} \quad \underset{(-4.9)}{}$$

where y/P is real per capita income in 1957–59 dollars, with $P = 100$ in the base year, and the numbers in parentheses are t-statistics (see Bieri and de Janvry, 1972).

2.3. Estimation of Engel Functions

In those situations where all we have are cross-sectional data from household budget surveys which do not contain observations in price variations, we are limited to the estimation of Engel curves:

$$q_i = q_i(y, z), \quad i = 1, \ldots, n.$$

where z denotes characteristics that vary across households, including family size, education, and geographical location. A question of interest here is how consumption patterns vary between households at different income levels. The parameter to express this is the income elasticity.

The Engel curves specified for estimation should have several desirable properties: (1) they should satisfy the budget constraint (predicted expenditure for each commodity should add up to total expenditure); (2) they should be able to represent luxuries, necessities, and inferior goods; (3) they should have variable income elasticities due to the empirical fact that income elasticities tend to decline as income increases; and (4) the consumption of many commodities should reach a saturation point as income increases.

Four forms of Engel functions which have been commonly used are the following:

Engel curve	Mathematical formula	Income elasticity
Linear	$q = a + by$	$\eta = \dfrac{q-a}{q} = \dfrac{by}{a+by}$
Double logarithmic	$\ln q = a + b \ln y$	$\eta = b$
Semilogarithmic	$q = a + b \ln y$	$\eta = \dfrac{b}{q} = \dfrac{b}{a + b \ln y}$
Logarithmic reciprocal	$\ln q = a - b \dfrac{1}{y}$	$\eta = \dfrac{b}{y} = a - \ln q$

Figure 2.1, taken from Brown and Deaton (1972), shows the geometric properties of the first three types of Engel curves. All four Engel curves can be estimated by simple regression techniques. Except for the double logarithmic, the other three have variable elasticities. The linear form is the only one which satisfies the Engel aggregation equation, but it gives fits that are usually not as good as the other three, which lack theoretical plausibility. From an empirical standpoint, the semilogarithmic tends to perform best (Prais and Houthakker, 1955).

2.4. Estimation of Price Elasticities from Cross-Sectional Data*

We have seen how cross-sectional expenditure survey data can be used to estimate income elasticities. To estimate price elasticities, short of making the strong assumption of additive separability as in section 2.2.2 above, we need to observe demand patterns under different price conditions. This usually requires time series data. Since consumer characteristics also matter, we would need to have cross-section data, displaying variability in the z's, repeated over time. Such data are rarely available, particularly in the LDCs. This section reports on recently developed techniques for estimating price elasticities using cross-sectional expenditure survey data when there are spatial variations in prices. The data requirements to apply these techniques are household expenditures by commodity, quantity of each commodity consumed, and individual characteristics thought important in explaining consumption behavior. Since the technique relies on spatial variation in prices, it requires that household expenditure data be collected in "clusters," for example, five or more households with access to a same market, which is the way data are usually collected to save on transportation costs for enumerators. The fact that prices vary comes from differential village-specific transactions costs and poorly integrated markets.

Figure 2.1. Alternative forms of Engel functions

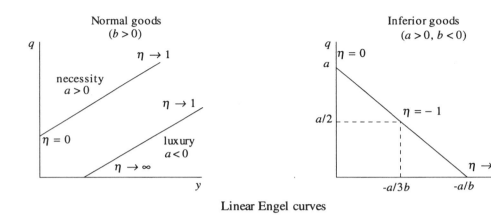

Linear Engel curves

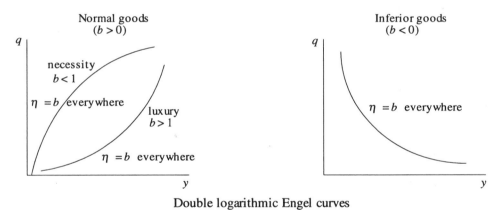

Double logarithmic Engel curves

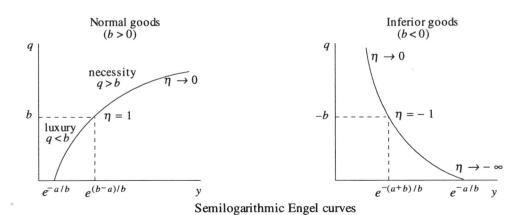

Semilogarithmic Engel curves

Given expenditure and quantity data, the unit values and expenditure shares can be calculated for each household as:

$$\frac{y_i}{q_i} = v_i, \quad \frac{y_i}{y} = w_i,$$

where

y_i = expenditure on good i,
y = total expenditure on all goods,
q_i = quantity of good i,
v_i = unit value of good i, and
w_i = budget share of good i.

It is tempting to estimate price elasticities by regressing the logarithm of quantity on the logarithm of unit value as a proxy for price, and this has indeed frequently been done. However, two problems arise with this approach. First, consumers respond to price movements by changing both the quantity and the quality of a good. For example, one might buy lower-quality cuts of meat as the price of meat rises. Since unit values reflect both price and quality, they will tend to vary less than price. The consequence is that direct estimation of the elasticity of consumption with respect to unit value E_q^v overestimates the true price elasticity E_q^p. Second, since unit value is calculated from quantity, measurement errors result in a spurious negative correlation between quantity and unit value. For example, if a household underreports quantity for a correct statement of expenditures, the derived v is overestimated.

Deaton (1988, 1990) has developed a method which adjusts for these effects and yields a consistent estimate of price elasticity. The method assumes that there are no price variations within clusters, and hence that unit value variations across households in a same cluster are only due to quality differentials and measurement errors. This allows one to use within-cluster variations in demand to estimate the impact of income and consumer characteristics on demand, including the quality effect. This relation can then be used to remove the predicted effects of income and household characteristics on demand and to explain the residual cross-cluster variations in demand by price only.

Considering for simplicity the case of only one good (see Deaton, 1988, for the case of several goods) the two basic equations for estimation are:

(4) $w_{hc} = \alpha_1 + \beta_1 \ln y_{hc} + \gamma_1 z_{hc} + \theta_1 \ln p_c + f_c + u_{1hc}$,

demand equation (which corresponds to an AIDS functional form, as we will see in section 2.5.2 below),

(5) $\ln v_{hc} = \alpha_2 + \beta_2 \ln y_{hc} + \gamma_2 z_{hc} + \theta_2 \ln p_c + u_{2hc}$,

unit value equation that captures the quality effect of income and consumer characteristics, where:

w_{hc} = share of budget devoted to the good by household h in cluster c,
y_{hc} = total budget,
z_{hc} = vector of household characteristics,
p_c = unobserved cluster price,
f_c = unobserved fixed cluster effect capturing taste variations across clusters,

v_{hc} = unit value,
u_{1hc}, u_{2hc} = residual error terms.

The estimation technique proceeds in three stages. In the first stage, parameters β_i and γ_i, which measure the influence of income and household characteristics, are estimated with household observations taken in deviation from the cluster mean. In the second stage, the price effect is isolated by averaging equations (4) and (5) over households by cluster. This gives

$$\hat{y}_{1c} = \alpha_1 + \theta_1 \ln p_c + f_c + u_{1c}$$
$$\hat{y}_{2c} = \alpha_2 + \theta_2 \ln p_c + u_{2c},$$

where $\hat{y}_{1c}$ and $\hat{y}_{2c}$ are the following cluster average variables:

$$\hat{y}_{1c} = \frac{1}{n} \sum_h \left(w_{hc} - \hat{\beta}_1 \ln y_{hc} - \hat{\gamma}_1 z_{hc} \right)$$
$$\hat{y}_{2c} = \frac{1}{n} \sum_h \left(\ln v_{hc} - \hat{\beta}_2 \ln y_{hc} - \hat{\gamma}_2 z_{hc} \right).$$

The variables $\hat{y}_{1c}$ and $\hat{y}_{2c}$ measure between-cluster variations attributable to price and a random error component. The parameters θ_1 and θ_2 cannot be estimated by regression in these equations since the prices p_c are not observable. However, the ratio $\phi = \theta_1 / \theta_2$ can be obtained from the covariance of y_1 and y_2. In the third stage, a consistent set of expenditure (η) and price (E) elasticities is then derived from the value ϕ computed above and the relationships that exist between the price and income elasticities of unit value (θ_1 and β_1), expenditure shares (θ_2 and β_2), and quantities (E and η).

2.5. Estimation of Complete Demand Systems

Estimation of single demand functions either from time series data following the pragmatic approach or from price variations across clusters in household surveys creates the problem that the quantity projections obtained may not satisfy the requirements of demand theory, particularly the budget constraint. Such predictions are consequently inadequate for use in complete models such as multimarkets (Chapter 11) and CGEs (Chapter 12). For this purpose, complete systems of demand equations which are able to take into account consistently the mutual interdependence of large numbers of commodities in the choices made by consumers need to be specified and estimated.

Three demand systems have received considerable attention because of their relative empirical expediency. They are the Linear Expenditure System (LES) developed by Stone (1954), the Almost Ideal Demand System (AIDS) developed by Deaton and Muellbauer (1980), and the combination of these two systems into a Generalized Almost Ideal Demand System (GAIDS) proposed by Bollino (1990). Other complete demand systems found in the literature but not as widely used are the Rotterdam model of Theil (1976) and Barten (1969) and the translog model of Christensen, Jorgenson, and Lau (1975).

2.5.1. The Linear Expenditure System

The Linear Expenditure System (LES) is the most frequently used system in empirical analyses of demand. It derives from the Stone-Geary utility function, which is pointwise separable:

$$u = \prod_{i=1}^{n}(q_i - c_i)^{b_i} \quad \text{or} \quad u = \sum_{i=1}^{n} b_i \ln(q_i - c_i) \quad \text{with} \begin{cases} 0 < b_i < 1 \\ \sum_i b_i = 1 \\ q_i - c_i > 0 \end{cases}.$$

The c's are usually interpreted as minimum subsistence or "committed" quantities below which consumption cannot fall. The demand functions derived from maximization of this utility function under a budget constraint constitute the LES:

$$p_i q_i = c_i p_i + b_i \left(y - \sum_j c_j p_j \right), \quad i = 1, \ldots, n.$$

This shows that the b's are the marginal budget shares, $\partial pq/\partial y$, which tell how expenditure on each commodity changes as income changes. Since $b_i > 0$, this system does not allow for inferior goods. $\sum c_j p_j$ is the subsistence expenditure and the term $(y - \sum c_j p_j)$ is generally interpreted as "uncommitted" or "supernumerary" income which is spent in fixed proportions b_i between the commodities.

An important drawback of this system is that it implies linear Engel functions, a specification not supported by empiricism and that can at best be true only over a short range of variation of y. If the equations are to be used for predictions, only short-term predictions can consequently be made. The price and income elasticities in these equations are (see derivation in the Appendix):

$$E_{ii} = -1 + (1 - b_i)\frac{c_i}{q_i}, \quad E_{ij} = -\frac{b_i c_j p_j}{p_i q_i}, \quad \eta_i = \frac{b_i}{w_i},$$

where w_i is, as before, the budget share of commodity i. The flexibility of money can also be measured as

$$\omega = -\frac{y}{y - \sum_j c_j p_j}.$$

Like all pointwise-separable models, the LES model is better applied to large categories of expenditure than to individual commodities, since it does not allow for inferior goods and implies that all goods are gross complements ($E_{ij} < 0$). Estimation of the LES is difficult due to nonlinearity in the coefficients b and c, which enter in multiplicative form. Two iterative approaches have been followed to overcome this difficulty.

The most common and relatively less sophisticated technique is a two-stage iterative procedure. It exploits the fact that, for given b, the LES is linear in c:

(6) $\quad p_i q_i - b_i y = c_i(p_i - b_i p_i) - \sum_{j \neq i} c_j(b_i p_j).$

Similarly, for given c, the LES is linear in b:

(7) $\quad p_i q_i - c_i p_i = b_i \left(y - \sum_j c_j p_j \right).$

The iterative estimation sequence is as follows. Start with an initial value of b and estimate the c in (6) using ordinary least squares (OLS) regression without intercept. Then, given this estimate of the c, estimate b in (7), again by OLS regression without intercept. The iteration continues until the sequence converges to stable estimates of b and c. An improved estimation method that treats (6) and (7) as a system of equations has been proposed by Parks (1969).

The other approach which has been used to estimate the LES is based on the technique of full information–maximum likelihood. It requires a computer algorithm that solves for a non-linear system of equations.

2.5.2. *The Almost Ideal Demand System*

The Almost Ideal Demand System (AIDS) derives from a utility function specified as a second-order approximation to any utility function. The demand functions are derived in budget share form as:

$$\frac{p_i q_i}{y} \equiv w_i = a_i + \sum_j b_{ij} \ln p_j + c_i \ln \frac{y}{P},$$

where w_i is the budget share, P is a price index defined as:

$$\ln P = a_o + \sum_k a_k \ln p_k + \frac{1}{2} \sum_j \sum_k b_{jk} \ln p_k \ln p_j,$$

and the parameters are subject to the following restrictions:

$$\sum_i a_i = 1, \quad \sum_i b_{ij} = 0, \quad \sum_i c_i = 0, \quad \sum_j b_{ij} = 0, \quad b_{ij} = b_{ji}.$$

Deaton and Muellbauer (1980) suggest approximating the price index P by the Stone geometric price index:

$$\ln P^* = \sum_i w_i \ln p_i.$$

This linear approximation is all the better if there is collinearity in prices over time. The equation to be estimated is thus:

$$w_i = a_i^* + \sum_j b_{ij} \ln p_j + c_i \ln \frac{y}{P^*},$$

where $a_i^* = a_i - c_i \ln \phi$ and $P = \phi P^*$ is the approximation to P. The linear-approximate AIDS should be estimated as a system of equations with the above-mentioned restrictions on the parameter estimates. The price and income elasticities can be derived from the parameter estimates as (see derivation in the Appendix):

$$E_{ii} = -1 + \frac{b_{ii}}{w_i} - c_i, \quad E_{ij} = \frac{b_{ij}}{w_i} - \frac{c_i}{w_i}w_j, \quad \eta_i = 1 + \frac{c_i}{w_i}.$$

The AIDS implies a money flexibility value of minus one (Blanciforti, Green, and King, 1986).

2.5.3. *The Generalized Almost Ideal Demand System*

The Generalized Almost Ideal Demand System (GAIDS) combines the LES and AIDS models, preserving some of the interesting features of the LES (the concept of committed and supernumerary expenditures) while adding flexibility to the estimated elasticities (Bollino, 1990). The basic idea is to replace in the LES the fixed proportions (b_i) in the allocation of supernumerary expenditures (y^S) by an AIDS specification that makes this allocation a function of income and prices. The equation to be estimated is:

$$q_i = c_i + \frac{1}{p_i}\left[\alpha_i + \sum_j \gamma_{ij} \ln p_j + \beta_i \ln \frac{y^S}{P}\right]\left(y - \sum_j c_j p_j\right), \quad i = 1, \ldots, n,$$

where $y^S = y - \sum_j c_j p_j$, under the constraints

$$\sum_i \alpha_i = 1, \quad \sum_i \gamma_{ij} = 0, \quad \sum_i \beta_i = 0, \quad \sum_j \gamma_{ij} = 0, \quad \gamma_{ij} = \gamma_{ji}.$$

Calling $AIDS_i$ the square bracket in the GAIDS equation and $w^S = y^S/y$ the supernumerary share, the price and income elasticities are:

$$E_{ii} = -1 + \left(1 - AIDS_i - \beta_i\right)\frac{c_i}{q_i} + \frac{w^S}{w_i}\left(\gamma_{ii} - \beta_i w_i\right),$$

$$E_{ij} = -\frac{c_j p_j}{p_i q_i}\left(AIDS_i + \beta_i\right) + \frac{w^S}{w_i}\left(\gamma_{ij} - \beta_i w_j\right), \quad \text{and}$$

$$\eta_i = \frac{AIDS_i + \beta_i}{w_i}.$$

These expressions simplify to the LES elasticities for $AIDS_i = b_i$ and $\gamma_{ij} = \beta_i = 0$.

2.5.4. *Estimation Problems**

There are three econometric problems which deserve caution in estimating the AIDS or GAIDS systems.

2.5.4.1. Probit Analysis of Decision to Consume

During the survey period, some of the goods may not have been consumed by some of the households, implying zero values for the corresponding observations of the endogenous variable in the regression equations. The dependent variable is thus truncated, creating a bias in the OLS estimates, since the assumption of zero correlation between independent variables and error term is violated. This problem is solved by using a two-stage estimation procedure proposed by Tobin (1958) that combines a probit analysis with a standard OLS (see Hein and Wessells, 1990). In the first stage, the decision by an individual (k) to consume the particular item (i) or not is modeled as a probit as:

$$\text{Prob}\left(q_{ik}^{*}=1\right) = \text{Prob}\left(f_{ik}\left(p_{k}, y_{k}, z_{k}\right) + u_{ik} > 0\right)$$

where q_{ik}^{*} is equal to one if the kth household consumes the ith commodity and zero otherwise; p_{k}, y_{k}, and z_{k} are the prices, income, and characteristics that apply to that household; and u_{ik} an error term. The probit estimation gives the inverse Mill's ratio:

$$\lambda_{ik} = \phi\left(f_{ik}\right) / \Phi\left(f_{ik}\right),$$

where ϕ is the probability density function and Φ the cumulative density function of the standard normal distribution. In the second stage, this ratio is used as an additional exogenous variable in the OLS estimation of the demand equation in order to correct for the bias created by use of a limited dependent variable. (See also Maddala, 1983, Chapter 8. These regression options are programmed in most econometric packages.)

2.5.4.2. Seemingly Unrelated Regressions

Demand equations appear to be unrelated, since none of the endogenous quantities or budget shares appear on the right-hand side of the equations. This is not the case, however, since error terms across equations are correlated by the fact that the dependent variables need satisfy the budget constraint (e.g., the budget shares in AIDS and GAIDS sum to one). While an OLS estimate of these equations would be consistent and unbiased, the estimation method developed by Zellner (1962) for Seemingly Unrelated Regressions (SUR) provides estimates that are more efficient. In a first stage, OLS is used to estimate the variance-covariance matrix among residuals; in a second stage this estimated matrix is used in a generalized least squares estimation. Since the covariance matrix among residuals is singular because the residuals satisfy the budget constraint, the typical procedure consists in deleting one of the equations of the demand system. The parameters from the deleted equation can be calculated from the parameters of the other equations through the restrictions on parameters. Barten (1969) has suggested an Iterated Seemingly Unrelated Regression (ITSUR) routine which produces results that are invariant to the equation deleted.

2.5.4.3. Imposition of Inequality Restrictions

Demand parameters need to satisfy a number of exact restrictions, and these must be imposed on the estimators. Equality constraints are imposed by using a restricted least squares approach. Imposition of inequality restrictions is more demanding. Bayesian estimation methods have been developed for this purpose by Geweke (1986). In the Bayesian approach, prior beliefs are combined with sample information into a posterior distribution from which point estimates of the parameters and confidence intervals are then derived. Here, the demand system is first estimated without the inequality constraints, yielding a vector of unconstrained parameter estimates and their distribution. Prior information is then introduced by truncating this distribution. The expected value of this truncated distribution then becomes the parameter vector to be used in the calculation of the elasticity estimates. This method was applied to an AIDS for meat in Canada by Chalfant, Gray, and White (1991) and by Rose (1992) to a GAIDS with a Mexican household consumption panel.

2.5.5. Effects of Household Characteristics*

Households differ by a set of characteristics $(z_k, k = 1, ..., s)$ such as age and sex composition, race and religion, and urbanization status that affect the pattern of demand. From a policy standpoint, it is important to estimate the impact of these characteristics on demand to establish the determinants of observed household-specific consumption levels, help target government programs such as food aid on particular classes of households, and determine the amount of assistance needed to bring the malnourished to acceptable consumption standards. Since the budget constraint needs to be satisfied, any increase in expenditure on some commodities due to a change in z_k must be compensated by a corresponding decline in the consumption of the other commodities. Hence, the z_k parameters are constrained to satisfy the s constraints:

$$\sum_{i=1}^{n} p_i \frac{\partial q_i}{\partial z_k} = 0 \quad \text{for all } k.$$

Several approaches have been followed to incorporate household characteristics in the estimation of complete demand systems. The idea is to introduce additional parameters into the original system and postulate that household characteristics affect demand only through these parameters (Goungetas and Johnson, 1992).

2.5.5.1 Translating Approach

Using the same idea as in the LES, we postulate that characteristics affect demand only through "translation" parameters (c_i) that represent subsistence or "necessary" levels of demand. Hence, quantities are decomposed into:

$$q_i = c_i + \overline{q}_i(p, \ y - \sum_j c_j p_j), \ \text{where} \ c_i = \sum_k a_{ik} z_k,$$

which contains ns parameters to be estimated (Pollak and Wales, 1978).

2.5.5.2. Scaling Approach

The idea here is to use scaling parameters (m_i) to reflect the number of "equivalent persons" in the household measured in a scale specific to each commodity i. This corresponds to replacing, in the standard demand model, quantities q_i by scaled quantities q_i/m_i and prices p_i by scaled prices $p_i m_i$. The demand equations to be estimated are then:

$$q_i = m_i q_i(p_1 m_1, ..., p_n m_n, y), \ \text{where} \ m_i = 1 + \sum_k b_{ik} z_k,$$

adding again ns parameters to be estimated (Barten, 1964).

These two methods can also be combined as done by Gorman (1976). Results obtained under the different approaches were compared by Pollak and Wales (1981).

2.6. Examples

2.6.1. LES and AIDS Estimations

Blanciforti, Green, and King (1986) estimated a LES and a linear-approximate AIDS using U.S. expenditure data over the period 1948–78 for 11 aggregate commodity groups: food, alcohol plus tobacco, clothing, housing, utilities, transportation, medical care, durable goods, other nondurable goods, other services, and other miscellaneous goods. Partial comparative results are given in Table 2.1. With the LES, by definition all goods are gross complements ($E_{ij} < 0$)

Table 2.1. A comparison of elasticities for LES and AIDS

Commodity group	LES elasticities		AIDS elasticities	
	Expenditure	Own–price	Expenditure	Own–price
Food	0.43	−0.21	0.35	−0.51
Alcohol plus tobacco	0.22	−0.08	0.22	−0.25
Clothing	0.58	−0.24	0.92	−0.38
Housing	1.57	−0.57	0.28	−0.39
Utilities	1.17	−0.38	0.64	−0.67
Transportation	1.09	−0.38	0.47	−0.47
Medical care	1.99	−0.61	0.79	−0.70
Durable goods	1.39	−0.52	3.93	−0.04
Other nondurable goods	1.39	−0.45	1.46	−1.21
Other services	0.96	−0.36	0.83	−0.28
Other miscellaneous goods	0.64	−0.22	0.42	0.03

Source: Blanciforti, Green, and King, 1986.

and all expenditure elasticities are positive. All estimated own-price elasticities are estimated to be negative and inelastic ($E_{ii} > -1$). Finally, the average flexibility of money is equal to −3.0.

With the AIDS, only durable goods and other nondurable goods are estimated in the model to be luxuries ($\eta_i > 1$). Of the 11 direct price effects, 10 are negative, with the 11th not significantly different from zero. Of the 110 cross-price elasticities (not reported in Table 2.1), 60 are negative, indicating complementary goods, and the other 50 are positive, indicating substitute goods. However, most of the cross-price coefficients are not statistically significantly different from zero. Finally, tests of the homogeneity condition lead to rejection for 5 of the 11 commodities, suggesting that homogeneity conditions do not necessarily hold in the aggregate.

Comparing results from the two models, expenditure elasticities tend to be lower for the AIDS model than the LES model, and own-price elasticities tend to be higher. While all goods are by definition gross complements in the LES, the AIDS estimates complementary and substitute goods in roughly equal numbers. The estimate of the flexibility of money also differs between the two models. The AIDS implies a value of –1.0, which is closer to estimates for the United States than the LES of –3.0.

The overall results suggest that the less restrictive functional form of the AIDS model allows more realistic estimates of expenditure elasticities, cross-price elasticities, and flexibility of money parameters. Estimation is also significantly easier for the AIDS model, since linear estimation techniques can be employed.

2.6.2. Numerical Values

The literature offers a vast number of estimates of direct and cross-price elasticities of demand that serve as guidelines for what is expected to be found in further econometric studies and for the construction of "guesstimated" policy analysis models such as partial equilibrium (Chapter 7), multimarkets (Chapter 11), and CGEs (Chapter 12). Useful compilations of elasticities include those by Scandizzo and Bruce (1980) (selectively reproduced in Table 2.2) and by Sullivan, Wainio, and Roningen (1988).

Table 2.2. Estimates of price and income elasticities of food, crops, or individual commodities

Product	Country	Period	Own-price	Income or expenditure	Cross-price	R^2
Food	Chile	1964	–0.45*	0.45*	—	—
	Greece	1958-65	–0.49*	0.67*	—	0.99
	Peru	1950-58	–1.01*	0.99*	—	0.99
	South Korea	1955-68	–0.47	0.72[a]	—	0.99
	Philippines	1953-65	–0.35	0.52[a]	—	0.99
	Taiwan	1955-68	–0.41	0.57[a]	—	0.99
	Thailand	1960-69	–0.68	0.84[a]	—	0.98
Foodgrains	Bangladesh	1963-79	–0.17*	0.30*	—	—
	India	1951-66	–0.34*	0.49*	—	—
	Jamaica	1959-68	–0.47	0.58[a]	—	0.93
Total cereals	India	1951-68	–0.50*	0.79	—	0.57
	Ghana	1953-70	–2.32	0.71	–2.22 (yams)	—
Rice	India	1951-68	–0.75*	0.94*	—	0.57
	Ghana	1953-70	–1.25*	0.71*	–0.58 (cereal)	—
Wheat	India	1951-68	–0.22	1.06	—	0.87
	West Pakistan	1963-64	–0.10	0.21[a]	—	—
	Argentina	1963	–0.03	0.16	0.60 (rice)	—
Cassava	Ghana	1953-70	–0.64	0.82	0.85* (rice)	—
Potatoes	Argentina	1963	–0.13*	0.04	—	—
Pulses	West Pakistan	1963-64	–0.05 to –0.08	0.16[a]	—	—
Edible oils	West Pakistan	1963-64	–0.05 to –0.8	0.5[a]	—	—
Milk	West Pakistan	1963-64	–0.29 to –0.38	1.02[a]	—	—
	Argentina	1963	–0.29	0.17*	—	—

Source: Scandizzo and Bruce, 1980.
[a]Reported without the statistical information.
*Significant at 10% level.

2.6.3. Quantity and Quality Elasticities

Deaton (1989) estimated price and income elasticities from household survey data in Java. With this approach, the elasticity of demand of any food item is decomposed into a quality component and a quantity component. Table 2.3 reports the results obtained. The total expenditure elasticity of demand for fresh fish is equal to 1.3, which decomposes into a quantity component of 1.08 and a quality component of 0.22. In general, however, the quality components of expenditure elasticities are very small, suggesting that these food groups are fairly homogenous in quality. In this case, unit values are good proxies for prices. The quantity elasticities show that maize and cassava hardly respond to income, while meat, wheat, fruit, and fresh fish are luxury goods ($\eta_i > 1$). Direct price elasticities tend to be low (in absolute value) for the goods which are also necessities.

Table 2.3. Demand elasticities for Java, 1981

Commodity	Share of total budget (percent)	Elasticity of quality with respect to total expenditure	Elasticity of quantity with respect to total expenditure	Elasticity of quantity with respect to price
Rice	24.5	0.03	0.49	−0.42
Wheat	0.5	0.10	1.57	−0.69
Maize	5.8	−0.00	0.09	−0.82
Cassava	1.3	0.02	0.14	−0.33
Roots	0.6	0.17	0.71	−0.95
Vegetables	5.6	−0.04	0.67	−1.11
Legumes	3.7	0.04	0.85	−0.95
Fruit	1.9	0.07	1.39	−0.95
Meat	2.1	0.09	2.30	−1.09
Fresh fish	2.9	0.22	1.08	−0.76
Dried fish	2.8	0.06	0.57	−0.24

Source: Deaton, 1989.

2.7. Policy Implications

2.7.1. Setting Commodity Priorities in Agricultural Research for Nutritional Improvement

A given agricultural research budget can be allocated to generate exogenous changes in the supply of a large number of alternative commodities. The question addressed here is how best to improve the nutritional status of the urban poor in Colombia (Pinstrup-Andersen, de Londoño, and Hoover, 1976). A complete matrix of direct and cross-price elasticities of demand for 18 food items was estimated from cross-sectional data and the flexibility of money under the want independence assumption (although, as correctly argued by Brandt and Goodwin, 1980, this assumption may not be warranted at such a fine level of disaggregation). Starting from an exogenous rate of change in the supply of each of the 18 commodities, the new market equilibria (given by the rates of change in equilibrium prices and quantities) are then calculated, using the matrix of price elasticities of demand and setting the short-run elasticity of supply equal to zero. The predicted changes in total demand are then allocated across income groups on the basis of demand elasticities specific to each group. Using transformation coefficients to convert food into calories, the direct impact of the supply shift in commodity *i* on calorie consumption is the increase in consumption of *i* while the indirect impact is the sum of the adjustments in the consumption of all other foods. The net effect is the sum of these two effects, and it gives the change in calorie consumption brought about by an increase in the supply of commodity *i*.

Before supply increases, the households in income stratum 1, which represent 18.3% of all households in the city of Cali, are deficient in calorie consumption, with only 89% of their calorie intake requirements satisfied. The results in Table 2.4 show that the net impact of a 10% increase in supply on per capita calorie intakes among the deficient stratum is highest for basic staples such as rice, maize, and cassava. By contrast, increasing the supply of beef and milk is largely wasted in increasing the calorie consumption of the nondeficient strata. It is notable that some commodities have large negative indirect effects that can eventually fully cancel the positive direct effects on calorie consumption. This is the result of the high direct- and cross-price elasticities (absolute value in excess of one) of these foods, their large shares in total expendi-

Table 2.4. Impact of a 10% increase in supply on per capita calorie intake

Food for which supply has increased	Deficient stratum				Nondeficient stratum		
	Direct effect	Indirect effect	Net effect	% reduction in deficiency	Direct effect	Indirect effect	Net effect
Beef	14.6	−6.5	8.1	3.4	23.7	1.0	24.6
Milk	6.2	−3.0	3.1	1.3	10.1	0.4	10.5
Rice	36.1	6.9	43.0	18.2	31.8	−1.0	30.8
Maize	38.2	0.1	38.3	16.2	22.2	−2.2	20.0
Beans	7.8	0.3	8.1	3.4	5.3	0.0	5.3
Peas	0.2	−0.7	−0.4	−0.2	0.6	0.2	0.8
Potatoes	10.9	4.2	15.1	6.4	6.4	−2.6	3.8
Cassava	17.3	5.8	23.1	9.8	10.1	−11.2	−1.1
Vegetables	2.6	−1.6	1.0	0.4	2.4	0.3	2.6

Source: Pinstrup-Andersen, de Londoño, and Hoover, 1976.

tures, and their relatively high nutrient content. When the supply of one of these foods increases, total consumer outlay for the food increases. Due to the budget constraint, outlays on other foods tend to decrease as reflected by the cross-price elasticities, causing the net result of a smaller nutritional impact than that of the direct effect alone. With some items, such as peas and tomatoes, the net effect can be negative, with the paradoxical result that increasing the supply of these foods may end up reducing the calorie intake of a deficient group.

Finally, it is notable that the reduction in calorie deficiency that results from an increase in supply is small, with most of the nutritional benefits captured by the nondeficient groups. With a zero supply elasticity, a 10% increase in the production of rice and maize would reduce calorie deficiency by 18% and 16%, respectively. The greater the elasticity of supply response, the less the fall in price induced by a same percentage increase in supply and the less the increase in consumption. Hence, if the elasticity of supply response is one, the same calorie increases are reduced to 6% and 5%, respectively. Thus, we draw two important conclusions: (1) The choice of budgetary allocation across commodities in agricultural research does have an impact on who will benefit nutritionally. While not the sole goal in agricultural research, nutritional implications for the poor should be taken into account when establishing commodity priorities in agricultural research, particularly if considering no other policy intervention. (2) Because malnutrition is the outcome of absolute poverty, however, significant declines in malnutrition require a more direct approach that raises the incomes of the poor or transfers food to them in the form of food subsidies. Although new technology resulting in shifts in supply and reduced prices is important to improving human nutrition, the full nutritional potential of such technology is reached only if accompanied by rapid increases in incomes and food availability among low-income groups.

2.7.2. The Relationship between Calorie Intake and Income

The calorie (c) elasticity with respect to price and income derives directly from the price and demand elasticities of demand for food items and technical coefficients (a_{ci}) measuring the calorie content of each food i. The calorie elasticities with respect to the price of a food i (E_{ci}) and to income (η_{ci}) are:

$$E_{ci} = \frac{dc/c}{dp_i/p_i} = \frac{\sum_j a_{cj}q_j E_{ji}}{\sum_j a_{cj}q_j}, \quad \text{and } \eta_{cy} = \frac{dc/c}{dy/y} = \frac{\sum_j a_{cj}q_j \eta_j}{\sum_j a_{cj}q_j}.$$

There are substitutions between quantity of calories and quality of food as income increases, leading to a shift to higher nutrient cost foods. As a result, it is no surprise that the income elasticity of calorie intake is smaller than the income elasticity of food expenditures. There has been an intense debate on the magnitude of the calorie elasticity. Earlier estimates by Knudsen and Scandizzo (1982) for five LDCs had found income elasticities of calories in the range of 0.53 to 0.74 for the lowest income quartile. Using much more detailed data, with estimations of nutrient-expenditure elasticities for 120 foods in South India, Behrman and Deolalikar (1987) found that these elasticities are not significantly different from zero: as incomes rise, consumers shift to higher food quality and higher nutrient cost foods. This was, however, challenged by Strauss and Thomas (1990) with data from Brazil and by Subramanian and Deaton (1992) with data from Maharastra in India. Using flexible functional forms, these researchers showed that the calorie-expenditure relation is positively sloped for the lowest three quartiles of per capita expenditures. While this elasticity is less than that for food expenditure, it is significantly different from zero, in the 0.25 to 0.3 range in the lowest expenditure decile in Brazil and 0.3 to 0.5 in rural Maharastra.

The analysis of calorie consumption has been extended to the intrahousehold allocation of food, particularly after initial studies revealed a strong gender bias against female children (Sen and Sengupta, 1983). A controversy has also arisen here between those who look at the household as a single decision-making unit and those who use a bargaining approach between household members. Following the first approach, Rosenzweig and Schultz (1982) hypothesized that parents make allocations of food to children based on the present value of the future contributions which the child is expected to make to family income. This is confirmed by their finding that, in areas of rural India with greater female employment, households invest more in female children, resulting in improved nutrition and lower mortality rates for these children. Following the second approach (Folbre, 1984; McElroy, 1990), women have greater bargaining power within the household in areas where they have higher fallback options outside the household determined in particular by greater access to the labor market. A key issue for the bargaining approach is that income may not be pooled within the household, and that income controlled by women may have a greater impact on child nutrition and health than income controlled by men, an effect empirically confirmed by Thomas (1990) for Brazil. The impact of the opportunity cost of time for husbands and wives on the intrahousehold allocation of food can derive from both a joint household utility function and a bargaining model. Senauer, Garcia, and Jacinto (1988) estimate the relative allocation of calories within households for husbands, wives, and children in the rural Philippines. They find that the mother's wage rate has a positive impact on the calorie allocation for children, while that of the husband has a negative impact, suggesting the importance of improving the employment conditions of women in order to improve intrahousehold resource allocation toward children.

Finally, studies of intrahousehold calorie-price responsiveness are important to design schemes of food subsidies in relation to individual types within households. Empirical analyses show that price elasticities differ across members and foods, and these differences tend to be large. For southern India, Behrman and Deolalikar (1990) find that price elasticities tend to be more negative for female members, implying that food price increases during the lean season or drought years fall disproportionately on this group. As a consequence, they are the group most at risk as prices fluctuate. Regarding different foods, an increase in the price of sorghum, the main staple in the diet, has a negative effect on nutrient intake, but increases in the prices of rice and milk have strong positive impacts. A positive relation suggests that households value nonnutritional attributes of food in their choices. This also suggests that price subsidies on foods other than inferior ones such as sorghum may actually reduce the nutrient intake of household members. Garcia and Pinstrup-Andersen (1987) similarly find that the calorie intake of children in the Philippines is positively related to the price of rice, while that of the whole household is negatively related, suggesting caution in the choice of foods to be subsidized in terms of the differential nutritional welfare of household members: a subsidy to the price of rice may improve household nutrition but worsen that of children.

Exercise 2
Food Subsidies in Morocco

Morocco has maintained for many years an expensive system of untargeted food subsidies that absorbed, in the early 1980s, as much as 10% of the government budget. Attempts at scaling down these subsidies as part of the stabilization program that followed the end of the phosphate boom and reduced capacity to borrow on the international financial market have been highly conflictive. Subsidies on meat, butter, and other dairy products have been removed since the early 1970s, but attempts at raising the prices of soft wheat, edible oils, and sugar have been strongly opposed, leading to deadly street riots.

This food subsidy policy exercise (file 2DEMAND) is based on the study by Laraki (1989). The objective is to explore alternative ways of reducing the government's food subsidy budget while preserving the real income or the nutritional status of the poor. Although we limit ourselves to the rural sector, a similar analysis can be conducted for the urban sector. After having estimated a complete system of demand for the rural sector, we simulate the impact that alternative redefinitions of the food subsidy program would have on three policy criteria:

The real income of the rural poor (y),

Their calorie intake (q_c),

The government's food subsidy budget (B).

Data on rural household expenditures on 6 food categories and on nonfood for 10 income deciles are reported in cells A7–J19 of Table 2E.1. Since we have only cross-sectional expenditure data, we can estimate price elasticities either using the separability hypothesis with a chosen flexibility of money as explained in section 2.2.2 or the Deaton approach presented in section 2.4. We start with the first and will proceed with estimates obtained by Laraki using the second.

1. Budget Shares and Engel Functions

An interesting contrast in the patterns of consumer expenditures across income deciles is given by calculating the budget shares (w) in cells A33–J44 and plotting them in a graph against total expenditures. Contrast in particular the changes in budget shares for soft and hard wheat across deciles. Which of these grains is a necessity and which is a luxury? On another graph, you can also contrast the budget shares for all the basic foods (soft wheat, hard wheat, barley, edible oils, and sugar) to the budget shares for other foods (which include milk, eggs, meats, and fruits and vegetables) and for nonfood items. Note that there are no inferior goods and the level of expenditure on all seven categories increases with income.

Using the household expenditure data across households, estimate double logarithmic Engel functions. You should first transform the data into logarithms in cells A20–J31. Then use the regression option in Lotus. Transcribe the income elasticities η_i obtained (denoted e in the spreadsheet) in a row of results in your spreadsheet (Estimated e on row 50).

Recall that the income elasticities must satisfy the Engel aggregation,

$$\sum_i w_i \eta_i = 1.$$

You should therefore calibrate the estimated elasticities so they satisfy this constraint expost. To do this, enter the budget shares w for decile 1 in row 49 and calculate the Engel aggregation (weighted sum) for the estimated elasticities. Divide all the estimated elasticities by this sum to calculate the calibrated elasticities in row 51.

2. Calculation of the Price Elasticities

The study by Laraki (with results that are modified here) uses the Deaton technique to estimate the direct and cross-price elasticities from cross-sectional data. That study does not give us elasticity estimates for other foods and for nonfoods. We will consequently rely on the separability hypothesis to calculate the direct elasticities for these two categories and their cross-price elasticities with all other goods. We will calculate this for the poorest rural decile with a flexibility of money $\omega = -4$.

A	B	C	D	E	F	G	H	I	J
1	**Table 2E.1. Food subsidies in Morocco**								
2									
3									
4		Soft	Hard						Total
5		wheat	wheat	Barley	Edible oils	Sugar	Other foods	Nonfoods	expenditure
6									
7	**Household expenditures (1984 dirhams)**								
8	Income deciles								
9	1 poorest	230	68	95	135	162	662	1105	2456
10	2	232	145	203	290	319	1711	1703	4603
11	3	163	203	285	447	447	2521	2190	6256
12	4	203	203	355	507	507	3293	2728	7795
13	5	243	304	426	669	608	3831	3274	9355
14	6	210	420	490	700	700	4482	4113	11115
15	7	249	499	499	748	665	5653	5095	13409
16	8	399	698	598	897	797	6579	6373	16342
17	9	362	966	604	1087	966	8090	8744	20818
18	10 richest	754	1885	754	1319	1319	12817	20419	39267
19									
20	**Logarithm of expenditures**								
21	Income deciles								
22	1 poorest								
23	2								
24	3								
25	4								
26	5								
27	6								
28	7								
29	8								
30	9								
31	10 richest								
32									
33	**Budget shares (w)**								
34	Income deciles								
35	1 poorest								
36	2								
37	3								
38	4								
39	5								
40	6								
41	7								
42	8								
43	9								
44	10 richest								
45									
46	**Estimated elasticities for rural decile 1**								
47									
48	Income elasticities (e)								Weighted sum
49	w decile 1								
50	Estimated e								
51	Calibrated e decile 1								
52									
53	Price elasticities (E)								
54	Flexibility of money	-4							
55	Soft wheat						0.00	0.00	
56	Hard wheat						0.00	0.00	
57	Barley						0.00	0.00	
58	Edible oils						0.00	0.00	
59	Sugar						0.00	0.00	
60	Other foods	0.00	0.00	0.00	0.00	0.00		0.00	
61	Nonfoods	0.00	0.00	0.00	0.00	0.00	0.00		
62									

	A	B	C	D	E	F	G	H	I	J
63		Table 2E.2. Food subsidies in Morocco: Policy analysis								
64		Decrease the food subsidies budget while protecting nutritional status of the poor (poorest decile rural households)								
65										
66			Soft	Hard						
67			wheat	wheat	Barley	Edible oils	Sugar	Other foods	Nonfoods	Total
68										
69		**Initial structure of consumption and subsidies**								
70		Budget shares (w)								
71		Calorie shares (c)	0.27	0.09	0.31	0.14	0.12	0.07	0.00	1.00
72		Subsidy shares (b)	0.54	0.00	0.00	0.32	0.10	0.04	0.00	1.00
73		c/w								
74		Income elasticities (e)								
75		Subsidies budget (B)	115			68				212
76										
77										
78		**Calibrated price elasticities**								
79										
80		Soft wheat	-0.75	0.09	0.17	-0.02	0.02	0.03	0.01	
81		Hard wheat	0.23	-0.35	0.06	0.24	-0.48	-0.42	-0.57	
82		Barley	0.38	0.06	-0.36	-0.05	0.08	-0.38	-0.50	
83		Edible oils	-0.07	0.13	-0.04	-0.61	0.18	-0.18	-0.28	
84		Sugar	0.00	-0.19	0.05	0.16	-0.55	-0.07	-0.15	
85		Other foods	-0.05	-0.04	-0.07	-0.05	-0.04	-0.48	-0.38	
86		Nonfoods	-0.06	-0.03	-0.06	-0.05	-0.05	-0.23	-0.64	
87										
88		**Worksheet for policy experiment**								
89										
90		**Policy instruments**								
91		dp/p exogenous	0.50	0.00	0.00	0.00	0.00	0.00	0.00	
92		**Endogenous changes**								
93		dq/q								
94		ds/s								
95		dS/S								
96										
97		**Results of policy experiment: Indicators of real income, calorie, and budget cost**								
98										
99		100*dy/y			y is the real income of rural decile 1					
100		100*dqc/qc			qc is the calorie intake of rural decile 1					
101		100*dB/B			B is the government budget on food subsidies to rural decile 1					
102										
103		**Record of results: Alternative subsidy schemes**								
104										
105		Experiments	1	2	3	4				
106		**Exogenous price changes**								
107		dp/p wheat	0.50							
108		dp/p barley								
109		dp/p oils								
110		**Endogenous policy criteria**								
111		100*dy/y	-4.68							
112		100*dqc/qc	-3.91							
113		100*dB/B	-55.17							

To do this, recall that the formulas for the direct and cross-price elasticities under the separability hypothesis are:

$$E_{ii} = \frac{1}{\omega} \eta_i (1 - w_i \eta_i) - w_i \eta_i,$$

$$E_{ij} = -\frac{w_j}{\omega} \eta_i \eta_j - w_j \eta_i, \quad i \neq j.$$

In cells A53–I61, the cross-price elasticities with other foods and nonfoods have already been calculated with the separability formula. Calculate the direct price elasticities for other foods and nonfoods in cells H60 and I61, respectively.

3. Relative Calorie Contribution of Different Foods

For each commodity consumed by rural decile 1, we know the budget share w, the calorie share c, the subsidy share b, and the income elasticity η. Calculate the ratio c/w. Note that the calorie contributions per kilogram of soft wheat, hard wheat, and barley are about equal but that the price of barley is half that of the wheats. What does the ratio c/w suggest for the redesign of the food subsidy scheme if we want to protect the calorie intake of the rural poor while reducing the cost to government? Contrast this to the current structure of subsidy shares.

Cells A77–I86 give a complete matrix of price elasticities where the diagonal elements are the same as those you calculated in H60 and I61 but where the cross-price elasticities have been calibrated to satisfy all the constraints on price elasticities imposed by the Cournot and Slutsky equations given in section 2.2.1.

4. Policy Criteria for the Evaluation of Food Subsidy Programs and Policy Alternatives

The government would like to reduce its food subsidy budget while preserving the real income and/or the calorie intake of the poor. There are, consequently, three indicators which we should use to assess the effects of a change in the food subsidy program:

Real Income Effects

If $P = \sum q_i^0 p_i$ is the Laspeyres consumer price index for rural decile 1, the rate of change in this indicator induced by given rates of change in prices is:

$$\frac{dP}{P} = \sum_i \frac{q_i^0 p_i}{P} \frac{dp_i}{p_i} = \sum_i w_i \frac{dp_i}{p_i}.$$

Using as an indicator of welfare the real income $y = \bar{y} / P$, where $\bar{y}$ is a constant nominal income, the rate of change in real income is:

$$\frac{dy}{y} = -\frac{dP}{P} = -\sum_i w_i \frac{dp_i}{p_i}, \quad \text{where the } w_i\text{'s are the budget shares.}$$

Calorie Intake Effects

Taking into account the direct and all the cross-price effects, the rate of change in quantity consumed of food i in response to given rates of change in prices is:

$$\frac{dq_i}{q_i} = \sum_j E_{ij} \frac{dp_j}{p_j}.$$

If a_i is the calorie content of a unit of food i, then total calorie intake is:

$$q_c = \sum_i a_i q_i.$$

The rate of change in calorie consumption induced by given price changes is:

$$\frac{dq_c}{q_c} = \sum_i \frac{a_i q_i}{q_c} \frac{dq_i}{q_i} = \sum_i c_i \frac{dq_i}{q_i},$$

where the c_i's are the calorie shares in total calorie consumption.

Budgetary Effects

Food subsidies create a price wedge between the equilibrium market price p^m and the subsidized consumer price p^s. The unit subsidy s_i on food i is:

$$s_i = p_i^m - p_i^s.$$

The total subsidy budget on the rural poor is:

$$B = \sum_i s_i q_i.$$

The share of each food in the subsidy budget is:

$$b_i = \frac{s_i q_i}{B}.$$

The rate of change in the government's subsidy budget can consequently be measured as:

$$\frac{dB}{B} = \sum_i b_i \left(\frac{ds_i}{s_i} + \frac{dq_i}{q_i} + \frac{ds_i}{s_i} \frac{dq_i}{q_i} \right) \equiv \sum_i b_i \frac{dS_i}{S_i},$$

where the b_i's are the initial subsidy shares and where we have defined

$$\frac{ds_i}{s_i} + \frac{dq_i}{q_i} + \frac{ds_i}{s_i} \frac{dq_i}{q_i} = \frac{dS_i}{S_i}.$$

If we introduce a subsidy to a food j that was not subsidized before, its cost $s_j q_j$ has to be added to the subsidy budget. The change in the government's subsidy budget thus becomes:

$$\frac{dB}{B} = \sum_i b_i \frac{dS_i}{S_i} + \frac{s_j q_j}{B} = \sum_i b_i \frac{dS_i}{S_i} - \frac{(dp_j / p_j) w_j y}{B},$$

where y is total expenditure.

In the case of Morocco, the subsidized prices of soft wheat and edible oils are 66% of the corresponding equilibrium market price. A 50% increase in the prices of soft wheat and edible oils, two subsidized foods, hence eliminates the food subsidy on these items. Thus,

$$s_i = p_i^m - p_i^s = \frac{1}{2} p_i^s, \quad i = \text{soft wheat, edible oils.}$$

The rate of change in these subsidies (row 94) is:

$$\frac{ds_i}{s_i} = -\frac{dp_i^s}{s_i} = -2\frac{dp_i^s}{p_i^s}.$$

We can calculate the initial subsidy budget B on the rural poor as follows. From row 72, we see that the subsidy shares of soft wheat and edible oils are 0.54 and 0.32, respectively, thus representing 86% of the total B. The cost of these subsidies is:

$$0.86 \; B = s_1 q_1 + s_4 q_4 = \frac{1}{2} p_1^s q_1 + \frac{1}{2} p_4^s q_4,$$

which can be solved for B on row 75.

5. Policy Experiments

Conduct the following experiments:

Experiment 1. Eliminate the food subsidy on soft wheat, which currently absorbs 54% of the food subsidy budget. What are the effects on real income, calorie intake, and the government's subsidy budget? Paste your results in the "Record of Results" area of the spreadsheet, keeping track of the exogenous price changes that you have made (in this case $dp/p = 0.50$ for soft wheat).

Experiment 2. Eliminate the subsidy on edible oils instead of that on soft wheat. How do the implications differ from the impact of eliminating the food subsidy on soft wheat and why?

Experiment 3. While eliminating the food subsidy on edible oils, introduce a subsidy to barley which is much cheaper nutritionally. By how much would you have to lower the price of barley in order to keep constant the nutritional status of the rural poor? (Proceed to change the price of barley until the calorie impact is zero.) Does it create significant savings for government?

Experiment 4. Now eliminate the food subsidy on soft wheat instead of that on edible oils, and protect the nutritional status of the poor by subsidizing barley. By how much do you now need to lower the price of barley? Which of these alternative subsidy schemes would you recommend to the Moroccan government?

References

Barten, A. P. 1964. "Family Composition, Prices, and Expenditure Patterns." In *Econometric Analysis for National Economic Planning*, edited by P. Hart, G. Mills, and J. Whitaker. London: Butterworth.

Barten, A. P. 1969. "Maximum Likelihood Estimation of a Complete System of Demand Equations." *European Economic Review* 1:7–73.

Behrman, Jere, and Anil Deolalikar. 1987. "Will Developing Country Nutrition Improve with Income? A Case Study for Rural South India." *Journal of Political Economy* 95:492–507.

Behrman, Jere, and Anil Deolalikar. 1990. "The Intrahousehold Demand for Nutrients in Rural South India: Individual Estimates, Fixed Effects, and Permanent Income." *Journal of Human Resources* 25:665–96.

Bieri, Jurg, and Alain de Janvry. 1972. *Empirical Analysis of Demand under Consumer Budgeting*. Giannini Foundation Monograph no. 30. Berkeley: University of California, Department of Agricultural and Resource Economics.

Blanciforti, Laura, Richard Green, and Gordon King. 1986. *U.S. Consumer Behavior over the Postwar Period: An Almost Ideal Demand System Analysis*. Giannini Foundation Monograph no. 40. Davis: University of California, Department of Agricultural Economics.

Bollino, Carlo. 1990. "A Generalized Version of the Almost Ideal and Translog Demand Systems." *Economics Letters* 34:127–29.

Brandt, John, and Joseph Goodwin. 1980. "The Impact of Increasing Food Supply on Human Nutrition: Implications for Commodity Priorities in Agricultural Research and Policy: Comment." *American Journal of Agricultural Economics* 62:588–91.

Brown, Alan, and Angus Deaton. 1972. "Survey of Applied Economics: Models of Consumer Behavior." *Economic Journal* 82:1145–1236.

Chalfant, James, Richard Gray, and Kenneth White. 1991. "Evaluating Prior Beliefs in a Demand System: The Case of Meat Demand in Canada." *American Journal of Agricultural Economics* 73:476–90.

Christensen, Laurits, Dale Jorgenson, and Lawrence Lau. 1975. "Transcendental Logarithmic Utility Functions." *American Economic Review* 65:367–83.

Deaton, Angus. 1988. "Quality, Quantity, and Spatial Variations of Price." *American Economic Review* 78:418–30.

Deaton, Angus. 1989. "Household Survey Data and Pricing Policies in Developing Countries." *World Bank Economic Review* 3:183–210.

Deaton, Angus. 1990. "Price Elasticities from Survey Data: Extensions and Indonesian Results." *Journal of Econometrics* 44:281–309.

Deaton, Angus, and John Muellbauer. 1980. "An Almost Ideal Demand System." *American Economic Review* 70:312–26.

Folbre, Nancy. 1984. "Market Opportunities, Genetic Endowments, and Intrafamily Resource Distribution: Comment." *American Economic Review* 74:518–20.

Frisch, Ragnar. 1959. "A Complete Scheme for Computing All Direct and Cross Demand Elasticities in a Model with Many Sectors." *Econometrica* 27:177–96.

Garcia, Marito, and Per Pinstrup-Andersen. 1987. *The Pilot Food Price Subsidy Scheme in the Philippines: Its Impact on Income, Food Consumption, and Nutritional Status*. Monograph no. 61. Washington, D.C.: International Food Policy Research Institute.

Geweke, John. 1986. "Exact Inference in the Inequality Constrained Normal Linear Regression Model." *Journal of Applied Econometrics* 1:127–41.

Gorman, W. 1976. "Tricks with Utility Functions." In *Essays in Economic Analysis: Proceedings of the 1975 AUTE Conference*, edited by M. Artis and A. Nobay. Cambridge: Cambridge University Press.

Goungetas, Basile, and Stanley Johnson. 1992. *The Impact of Household Size and Composition on Food Consumption: An Analysis of the Food Stamp Program Parameters Using the Nationwide Food Consumption Survey, 1977–78*. Monograph 92-M5. Ames: Iowa State University Center for Agricultural and Rural Development.

Hein, Dale, and Cathy Wessells. 1990. "Demand Systems Estimation with Microdata: A Censored Regression Approach." *Journal of Business and Economic Statistics* 8:365–71.

Knudsen, Odin, and Pasquale Scandizzo. 1982. "The Demand for Calories in Developing Countries." *American Journal of Agricultural Economics* 64:80–6.

Laraki, Karim. 1989. "Ending Food Subsidies: Nutritional, Welfare, and Budgetary Effects." *World Bank Economic Review* 3:395–408.

Maddala, G. S. 1983. *Limited-Dependent and Qualitative Variables in Econometrics*. Cambridge: Cambridge University Press.

McElroy, Marjorie. 1990. "The Empirical Content of Nash-Bargained Household Behavior." *Journal of Human Resources* 25:559–83.

Parks, Robert. 1969. "Systems of Demand Equations: An Empirical Comparison of Alternative Functional Forms." *Econometrica* 37:629–50.

Pinstrup-Andersen, Per, Norha Ruiz de Londoño, and Edward Hoover. 1976. "The Impact of Increasing Food Supply on Human Nutrition: Implications for Commodity Priorities in Agricultural Research and Policy." *American Journal of Agricultural Economics* 58:131–42.

Pollak, Robert, and Terence Wales. 1978. "Estimation of Complete Demand Systems from Household Budget Data: The Linear and Quadratic Demand Systems." *American Economic Review* 68:348–59.

Pollak, Robert, and Terence Wales. 1981. "Demographic Variables in Demand Analysis." *Econometrica* 49:1533–51.

Prais, Sigbert, and Hendrik Houthakker. 1955. *The Analysis of Family Budgets*. Cambridge: Cambridge University Press.

Rose, Donald. 1992. "Planning for Nutrition in Rural Mexico: A Case Study in Household Food Consumption Behavior." Ph.D. dissertation, University of California at Berkeley, Department of Agricultural and Resource Economics.

Rosenzweig, Mark, and T. Paul Schultz. 1982. "Market Opportunities, Genetic Endowments, and Intrafamily Resource Distribution: Child Survival in Rural India." *American Economic Review* 72:803–15.

Scandizzo, Pasquale, and Colin Bruce. 1980. *Methodologies for Measuring Price Intervention Effects*. Staff Working Paper no. 394. Washington, D.C.: The World Bank.

Sen, A. K., and S. Sengupta. 1983. "Malnutrition of Rural Children and the Sex Bias." *Economic and Political Weekly* 18:855–64.

Senauer, Benjamin, Marito Garcia, and Elizabeth Jacinto. 1988. "Determinants of the Intrahousehold Allocation of Food in the Rural Philippines." *American Journal of Agricultural Economics* 70:170–80.

Stone, Robert. 1954. "Linear Expenditure Systems and Demand Analysis: An Application to the Pattern of British Demand." *Economic Journal* 64:511–27.

Strauss, John, and Duncan Thomas. 1990. "The Shape of the Calorie-Expenditure Curve." Economic Growth Center Discussion Paper no. 595. New Haven: Yale University.

Subramanian, Shankar, and Angus Deaton. 1992. "The Demand for Food and Calories: Further Evidence from India." Unpublished paper: Princeton University Research Program in Development Studies.

Sullivan, John, John Wainio, and Vernon Roningen. 1988. *A Data Base for Trade Liberalization Studies*. Washington, D.C.: USDA, Economic Research Service, Agriculture and Trade Division.

Theil, Henri. 1976. *Theory and Measurement of Consumer Demand*. Amsterdam: North-Holland.

Thomas, Duncan. 1990. "Intra-household Resource Allocation: An Inferential Approach." *Journal of Human Resources* 25:633–64.

Timmer, Peter, Walter Falcon, and Scott Pearson. 1983. *Food Policy Analysis*. Baltimore: Johns Hopkins University Press.

Tobin, James. 1958. "Estimation of Relationships for Limited Dependent Variables." *Econometrica* 26:263–85.

Zellner, Arnold. 1962. "An Efficient Method of Estimating Seemingly Unrelated Regressions and Tests for Aggregation Bias." *Journal of the American Statistical Association* 57:348–68.

CHAPTER THREE

The Profit Function Approach to Supply and Factor Demand

The objective of Chapters 3 and 4 is to analyze the supply side of the economy and determine how producers will respond to changes in product and factor prices, in technology, and in access to certain constraining factors of production. This analysis is central to policy decisions in that it helps us understand the impact that alternative policy packages or external shocks may have on the producers themselves. Through the changes it induces in commodity supply and factor demand, the analysis of production response, like that of demand in the previous chapter, is an essential component of models that seek to explain market prices, wages and employment, external trade, and government fiscal revenues. Whether the systematic taxation of agriculture can be held largely responsible for the poor performance of the sector in many developing countries is an important debate in this period of policy reform. The impact on growth of reforms aimed at reducing this taxation depends on the elasticity of supply response of agriculture, a central issue of the following analysis. In this chapter, we will also treat the symmetrical issue, all too often neglected, of the role of nonprice factors in production, where some of these factors are delivered by government while others can be privately obtained.

There are two elements in determining a producer's response. One is the technological relation that exists between any particular combination of inputs and the resulting levels of outputs; this is represented by the production function. The other is the producer's behavior in choice of inputs, given the level of market prices for a commodity and factors that can be traded, and the availability of fixed factors whose quantity cannot be altered in the period of analysis. Integration of these two elements leads to the definition of the profit or the cost function, which gives the maximum profit or the minimum cost that a farmer can obtain given the environment, and to a direct method to determine the optimal decision on output supply and factor demand. This is the approach described in this chapter. It is fundamentally a systems approach, with prices and nonprice factors treated very symmetrically. However, neither uncertainty nor rigidity in implementation of the optimum decisions is considered here. In Chapter 4, we present models of supply response which, by contrast, explicitly specify the formation of expectations for unknown future prices and the adjustment lags in production, but usually treat lightly the roles of competitive crops, inputs, and fixed factors, concentrating on the direct response of one particular crop to its own price. The role of risk in production decisions is developed in Chapter 5.

In studying supply response, it is important to distinguish between specific crops and broad agricultural aggregates, and between short-run and long-run responses. These two points are discussed in the last two sections.

3.1. The Basic Theory of Production

3.1.1. The Profit Function

Let the production function of a farm be given by:

(1) $h(q, x, z) = 0,$

where q is the vector of output quantities, x is the vector of variable input quantities, and z is a vector of fixed factor quantities. Variable inputs are usually labor, fertilizer, water, pesticides, seeds, hours of rented tractor use, and such, which can be purchased in the desired quantities. Fixed factors are either private factors that cannot be acquired in the time span analyzed (land, equipment), public factors (infrastructure and extension services), or exogenous features (such as weather and distance to market).

If w and p are the prices of inputs and outputs, respectively, the producer's restricted profit is $p'q - w'x$ (the symbol $'$ indicates transposition of a vector, and "restricted" profits means that only variable costs are subtracted from gross revenues). The producer is assumed to choose the combination of variable inputs and outputs that will maximize profit subject to the technology constraint:

(2) $\displaystyle \max_{x,q} \; p'q - w'x, \quad \text{s.t.} \; h(q, x, z) = 0.$

The solution to this maximization problem is a set of input demand and output supply functions that can be written as:

(3) $x = x(p, w, z)$ and $q = q(p, w, z).$

Substituting these expressions into the definition of profit gives the *profit function*, π, which is the maximum profit that the farmer could obtain given the prices, w and p, the availability of fixed factors, z, and the production technology, $h(\cdot)$:

(4) $\pi = p'q(p, w, z) - w'x(p, w, z) = \pi(p, w, z).$

It can be proved that, under mild regularity conditions, there is a one-to-one correspondence between the production function and the profit function. If, for example, the production function is a Cobb-Douglas, the profit function also takes that form. This is established as follows. Consider the Cobb-Douglas production function, $q = ax^{\alpha}z^{\beta}$. Maximization of profit, $pax^{\alpha}z^{\beta} - wx$, is given by the first-order condition:

(5) $pa\alpha x^{\alpha-1}z^{\beta} - w = 0.$

The optimum level of input is:

$$x = \left(a\alpha z^{\beta} \frac{p}{w} \right)^{\frac{1}{1-\alpha}}.$$

The corresponding optimum level of output and maximum profit are:

$$q = a^{\frac{1}{1-\alpha}} \left(\alpha \frac{p}{w} \right)^{\frac{\alpha}{1-\alpha}} z^{\frac{\beta}{1-\alpha}} \quad \text{, and}$$

(6) $\quad \pi = a^{\frac{1}{1-\alpha}} \alpha^{\frac{\alpha}{1-\alpha}} (1-\alpha) z^{\frac{\beta}{1-\alpha}} p^{\frac{1}{1-\alpha}} w^{\frac{-\alpha}{1-\alpha}} .$

However, this correspondence cannot always be established analytically, and in what follows we will take the functional form of the profit function as directly given. For a function to be admissible as a profit function, it must be nonnegative, monotonically increasing (decreasing) in prices of outputs (inputs), convex, homogenous of degree zero in all prices, and, if the production function displays constant return to scale, homogenous of degree one in all fixed factors. Examples of profit functions are the Cobb-Douglas, the generalized Leontief, the quadratic, and the translog.

If there is a single output, the *normalized profit function*, π^*, is defined as the ratio of the profit function to the price of the output. It is a function of the relative prices of the inputs, $w^* = w/p$, and of the fixed factors, that is, $\pi^* = \pi^*(w^*, z)$.

3.1.2. The System of Output Supply and Factor Demand

The profit function has two interesting properties: its derivative with respect to the price of a product is equal to the supply function of that product; and its derivative with respect to the price of an input is equal to the negative of the demand function of that input. That is:

(7) $\quad \dfrac{\partial \pi}{\partial p_i}(p, w, z) = q_i \quad$ and $\quad \dfrac{\partial \pi}{\partial w_k}(p, w, z) = -x_k .$

These relations, called the Shephard duality lemma, are proved by differentiating the profit function (4) and taking advantage of the first-order conditions of the maximization problem (2).

This symmetry in outputs and inputs can be further exploited by treating inputs as negative outputs. Let us define the vector q as representing both inputs and outputs as follows:

$$q = \begin{pmatrix} q \\ -x \end{pmatrix} \quad \text{with price} \quad p = \begin{pmatrix} p \\ w \end{pmatrix}.$$

Under this symmetrical notation, p can now be either a product or a factor price. When positive, q is the quantity of a product and, when negative, the quantity of a factor. The relations (7) above can now be written:

(8) $\quad q_i = \dfrac{\partial \pi}{\partial p_i}(p, z).$

These supply and demand functions satisfy the following properties:

a. *Homogeneity.* Output supply and factor demand functions are homogenous of degree zero in all prices and, if production displays constant returns to scale, homogenous of degree one in all fixed factors.

b. *Symmetry.* Symmetry of the second-order derivatives of the profit function implies that:

$$\frac{\partial q_i}{\partial p_j} = \frac{\partial q_j}{\partial p_i}.$$

The same properties can be written in terms of elasticities:

a. *Homogeneity.* The sum of the elasticities of any output or input with respect to all prices is equal to zero, and, if production displays constant return to scale, the sum of its elasticities with respect to the fixed factors is equal to one:

$$\sum_j E(q_i / p_j) = 0 \quad \text{and} \quad \sum_m E(q_i / z_m) = 1.$$

b. *Symmetry.* The cross-price elasticities are inversely proportional to the corresponding profit shares:

$$\frac{E(q_i / p_j)}{E(q_j / p_i)} = \frac{s_j}{s_i} \quad \text{with} \quad s_i = p_i q_i / \pi.$$

3.2. Examples of Profit Functions and Derived Systems of Output Supply and Factor Demand

3.2.1. Normalized Cobb-Douglas

This is the model used by Yotopoulos and Lau (1979) in their earlier studies when they pioneered the approach. They consider a single output with a Cobb-Douglas production function. The derived normalized profit function also has a log-linear form:

$$\ln \pi^* = a + \sum_i \alpha_i \ln w_i^* + \sum_m \beta_m \ln z_m.$$

This function is homogenous of degree zero in all prices. Homogeneity of degree one in the fixed factors prevails if and only if

$$\sum_m \beta_m = 1.$$

The equations for the factor demands and output supplies are:

$$x_i = -\frac{\partial \pi^*}{\partial w_i^*} = -\alpha_i \pi^* / w_i^*$$

or $$\ln x_i = [a + \ln(-\alpha_i)] + \sum_j (\alpha_j - \delta_{ij}) \ln w_j^* + \sum_m \beta_m \ln z_m$$

and $$q = \pi^* + \sum_i w_i^* x_i = \left(1 - \sum_i \alpha_i\right) \pi^*$$

or $\quad \ln q = \ln\left(1 - \sum_i \alpha_i\right) + a + \sum_i \alpha_i \ln w_i^* + \sum_m \beta_m \ln z_m$,

where δ_{ij} is the Kronecker index (= 1 if $i = j$ and 0 if $i \neq j$).

These expressions reveal how restrictive the Cobb-Douglas system is. The cross-price elasticities of the different input demands (x_i) with respect to the price of one of them (w_j) are constant and all equal (to α_j), while the direct price elasticity of demand of that input (x_j) is $\alpha_j - 1$. The elasticities with respect to given fixed factors are constant and all equal to β_m.

3.2.2. Generalized Leontief

The profit function is written as:

$$\pi = \sum_{i,j} b_{ij} \sqrt{p_i p_j} + \sum_{i,m} b_{im} \, p_i z_m \quad \text{with} \quad b_{ij} = b_{ji}.$$

This function is homogenous of degree one in all prices but not with respect to the fixed factors. The equations for the factor demands and output supplies are:

$$q_i = b_{ii} + \sum_{j \neq i} b_{ij} \sqrt{p_j / p_i} + \sum_m b_{im} \, z_m.$$

In this system, the price elasticities are not constant, but they can be computed at any given value of prices and quantities with the following expressions:

$$E_{ij} = b_{ij} \sqrt{p_j / p_i} \, / 2q_i, \quad i \neq j, \quad \text{and} \quad E_{ii} = -\sum_{j \neq i} E_{ij}.$$

3.2.3. Normalized Quadratic

Profit and prices are normalized by the price of the nth commodity:

$$\pi^* = \pi / p_n = a_0 + \sum_i a_i p_i^* + \frac{1}{2} \sum_{i,j} b_{ij} p_i^* p_j^* + \sum_{i,m} b_{im} p_i^* z_m, \quad i,j = 1, \dots, n-1, \text{ with } b_{ij} = b_{ji},$$

where $p_i^* = p_i / p_n$ is the vector of normalized output and input prices. The profit function is homogenous in prices but not with respect to the fixed factors. The derived system of output supply and factor demand is:

$$q_i = a_i + \sum_j b_{ij} p_j^* + \sum_m b_{im} z_m.$$

Supply for the nth commodity, whose price served as a numéraire, is:

$$q_n = \pi^* - \sum_i p_i^* q_i = a_0 - \frac{1}{2} \sum_{i,j} b_{ij} p_i^* p_j^*.$$

The elasticities can be computed at any particular value of prices and quantities as:

$$E_{ij} = b_{ij} p_j^* / q_i, \quad i, j \neq n,$$

$$E_{nj} = \frac{1}{s_n} \sum_i s_i E_{ij} \quad \text{and} \quad E_{nn} = -\sum_i E_{ni},$$

where the s_i are the profit shares.

3.2.4. Translog

The translog profit function is very commonly used. It is a second-degree function in prices and fixed factors. As such, it can be considered as a second-order approximation of any function, just as a Cobb-Douglas function gives the first-order linear approximation. It is a flexible model with variable elasticities, and as such it does not suffer from the very restrictive characteristics of the Cobb-Douglas. The profit function is written as:

$$
\ln \pi = a_0 + \sum_i a_i \ln p_i + \sum_m b_m \ln z_m + \frac{1}{2} \sum_{i,j} b_{ij} \ln p_i \ln p_j
$$
$$
+ \frac{1}{2} \sum_{m,n} c_{mn} \ln z_m \ln z_n + \sum_{i,m} d_{im} \ln p_i \ln z_m.
$$

(9)

Restrictions on the parameters that ensure homogeneity with respect to both prices and fixed factors are:

$$b_{ij} = b_{ji}, \quad c_{mn} = c_{nm}, \quad \sum_i a_i = 1, \quad \sum_m b_m = 1, \quad \text{and} \quad \sum_i b_{ij} = \sum_m c_{mn} = \sum_i d_{im} = \sum_m d_{im} = 0.$$

The derived factor demand and output supply functions are:

$$(10) \quad q_i = \frac{\pi}{p_i} \left[a_i + \sum_j b_{ij} \ln p_j + \sum_m d_{im} \ln z_m \right]$$

with the corresponding elasticities:

$$(11) \quad E_{ij} = s_j + b_{ij} / s_i \quad \text{and} \quad E_{ii} = -1 + s_i + b_{ii} / s_i.$$

3.3. Cost Function and Associated Systems of Factor Demands

The cost function approach is similar to the profit function approach. Starting again from the production function (1), the producer is assumed to minimize costs to produce a given level of output:

$$\text{Min}_x \, w'x \quad \text{s.t.} \quad h(q, x, z) = 0.$$

The solution to this minimization problem is a set of input demands:

$x = x(w, z, q),$

and the cost function is the corresponding minimum variable cost of producing the given output, $c(w, z, q)$. Like a profit function, the cost function completely characterizes the producer's behavior, as it includes both the technological constraint from the production function and the behavior of the producer. The cost function is positive; it is nondecreasing, concave, continuous, and homogenous of degree one in input prices. It is also nondecreasing in the level of output q and does not include the fixed costs, that is, $c(w, z, 0) = 0$. By the Shephard duality theorem, one shows that the input functions are the derivative of the cost function with respect to the input prices:

$x_i = \partial c / \partial w_i.$

The impact of output on cost is measured by the elasticity of cost with respect to output, $\partial \ln c / \partial \ln q$, or by its inverse $(\partial \ln c / \partial \ln q)^{-1}$ called the elasticity of size. For cost-minimizing firms, the elasticity of size is equal to the elasticity of scale.

The most commonly used cost functions are:

a. *The linear cost function.* $c(w, q) = q \sum \alpha_i w_i$, which is associated with a Leontief production function.

b. *The Cobb-Douglas cost function.* $c(w, q) = A(q) \prod w_i^{\alpha_i}$, which is associated with a Cobb-Douglas production function.

c. *The CES cost function.* $c(w, q) = A(q) (\sum \beta_i w_i^{-\rho})^{-1/\rho}$ which corresponds to a CES production function (with an elasticity of substitution equal to the inverse of the elasticity of substitution in the cost function).

d. *The translog cost function.* $\ln c(w, z, q) = \alpha + \sum \beta_i \ln x_i + \sum \beta_{ij} \ln x_i \ln x_j$, where x represents either an input price w_i, the output level q, or a fixed input z_m.

From each of these functional forms, a system of input demand can be derived. Empirical analyses with costs functions proceed in exactly the same way as analyses based on profit functions. Binswanger (1974) gives an example of this approach for the estimation of a system of factor demand for India.

3.4. Estimation of the System

What are the data requirements for the estimation of the profit function or of the system of output supply and factor demand equations described above? The data need to contain sufficient variability in all the exogenous variables, that is, in the fixed factors and prices. Variability in fixed factors is usually greater in cross-sectional farm-level data than in time series data. Price variability, however, is usually fairly small across households (although a proper account of the transactions costs incurred by different households would usually reveal greater variability in effective prices paid by the different households than the casual recording of market prices) and is greater in time series data. Thus, a combined cross-sectional and time series data set is ideal (e.g., as used by Bapna, Binswanger, and Quizon, 1984, for India; Esfahani, 1987, for Egypt). However, estimations have also been made with farm-level data covering several regions (Sidhu and Baanante, 1981, for India) and with long time series (e.g., data for 1940 to 1980 used by Fulginiti and Perrin, 1990, for Argentina).

From the theoretical section above, we see that two procedures can be followed to estimate supply response from a profit function approach. The first is to estimate the profit function itself, based on observations of farmers' profits and of the exogenous variables, prices and fixed factors. However, farmers' profits are usually computed on the basis of observations of outputs and inputs rather than directly observed. Availability of this complete information allows direct estimation of the derived system of output supply and factor demand. This is the most commonly used approach. This estimation is also less demanding in information: even if some data on inputs or outputs are missing (in which case profit cannot be calculated), estimation can be performed by dropping the corresponding equations. All the equations are jointly estimated, with the exception of the profit function, which is not linearly independent but rather a linear combination of the individual equations. Only when one of the factor demand or output supply equations is eliminated, as in the translog function, can both the profit equation and the derived system be used simultaneously.

At this point, note that systems of output supply and factor demand equations can exist independent of profit maximization behavior, as long as the behavior of individual agents is sufficiently stable over time and can be aggregated over farmers. This implies that estimated systems are useful for economic analysis regardless of whether they are derived from the theory of profit maximization. For a system to be compatible with a profit function, however, it needs to satisfy the four types of constraints introduced above: homogeneity in prices, symmetry, monotonicity, and convexity of the underlying profit function. Two different approaches have been taken in the estimation of the systems with respect to these constraints. The first is to estimate the total system without any constraint and to test for the constraints (either globally or separately), thereby providing a test of profit maximization (Lopez, 1980). The tests of symmetry and homogeneity are standard tests on linear transformations of parameters. The monotonicity and convexity of the profit function are usually checked at certain points only, the average point or selected data points, by verifying that its first derivatives have the correct sign and that the characteristic roots of the matrix of second-order derivatives are all nonnegative. The second approach requires performing an estimation under constraints, imposing, in particular, the homogeneity and symmetry conditions on the parameters. Monotonicity and convexity, if they are not automatically satisfied, are not always tested for (see Ball, 1988, for a test and imposition of convexity constraints). Econometrically, none of these estimations is difficult, as all the models are linear in their parameters.

3.5. Examples

3.5.1. The Role of Public Goods in the Punjab

Bapna, Binswanger, and Quizon (1984) estimated a cropping system for the semiarid tropical areas of India, with data from a 19-year time series of 93 districts. The production system includes five crops (wheat, sorghum, other coarse cereals, chickpeas, and other crops); three variable factors of production (fertilizer, labor, and bullocks); and five fixed factors not under the farmer's control (rainfall, extent of use of high-yielding varieties, extent of irrigation, road density, and regulated market density). However, the estimated system is incomplete because of the lack of reliable data on labor and bullock use and on bullock prices. Thus, two input equations are missing, and bullock price is not included in the equations. Both the generalized

Leontief and the normalized quadratic models were used, and they were found to give very similar results.

As output prices are not known at the time of planting, expected prices were used with the following lag structure (Chapter 4 will introduce different specifications for the formation of price expectations):

$$p_{it}^e = 0.71\, p_{i,\,t-1} + 0.29\, p_{i,\,t-2}.$$

The system was estimated imposing the symmetry constraint. Table 3.1 reports the elasticities computed at sample means for the normalized quadratic model. It should be noted that these elasticities are not constant but depend on sample values of prices and quantities. In economic

Table 3.1. Semiarid India: Price elasticities and shares of income by crop

	Wheat	Sorghum	Other coarse cereals	Chickpeas	Other crops	Fertilizer
Crop prices						
Wheat	0.33	−0.39*	−0.14	0.08	−0.07	1.48*
Sorghum	−0.35*	0.77*	0.16	0.00	−0.13	−1.46*
Other coarse	−0.05	0.06	0.23	−0.41	0.08	−0.30
Chickpeas	0.03	0.00	−0.48*	0.46	−0.03	−0.46
Other crops	−0.12	−0.26	0.41	−0.14	0.25	0.64
Factor prices						
Fertilizer	−0.12*	0.14*	0.07	0.09	−0.03	0.03
Wages	0.29*	−0.32	−0.26	−0.08	−0.08	0.08
Fixed variables						
Rain	0.51*	−0.06	−0.31*	0.30*	0.00	0.36
HYV	−0.05	−0.05	−0.11*	−0.04	−0.11*	−0.06
Irrigation	0.31*	0.27	0.51*	0.27*	0.57*	1.53*
Road density	−0.24	0.34*	1.42*	−0.22	1.04*	4.44*
Market density	0.10	−0.11	0.01	−0.05	−0.17	0.17
Share of crop in aggregate crop revenue						
	0.19	0.23	0.09	0.08	0.41	--[a]

Source: Bapna, Binswanger, and Quizon, 1984.
*Significant at the 5% level.
[a]Not applicable.

applications, the parameters themselves and the functional forms of the output and demand functions should, therefore, be used to compute simulated values. How do these results fare with respect to theory?

a. Five of the six direct price elasticities have the expected sign (positive for outputs and negative for inputs); the direct price elasticity of fertilizer has the wrong sign but is not significantly different from zero. Surprisingly, sorghum is found the most responsive with an elasticity of 0.77. This is not consistent with the usual view that the supply of a subsistence crop with a small market surplus is not responsive to price change. Wheat and chickpeas are also fairly responsive with elasticity of 0.33 and 0.46. This confirms (although mildly) that farmers are price responsive despite the very harsh environment under which they operate.

b. Cross-price elasticities in such a system do not have a definite expected sign. Among crops, complementarity may arise from particular rotation features or from particular patterns of use of the different fixed factors. Price elasticities of crops with respect to inputs are not necessarily negative in a systemwide approach; the increase in the price of one single factor induces restructuring of the pattern of production, including increases in certain crops and decreases in others.

c. The most interesting finding in this analysis is that the role of the nonprice factors, particularly public goods such as road density and market regulation, is very significant. This is demonstrated by the very high elasticity of fertilizer use with respect to road density. The results show that price incentives, public investment in roads and irrigation, and institutional change in access to high-yielding varieties and market regulation are all important determinants of high output levels.

As can be judged by the small number of parameters that are significantly different from zero, the econometric performance of this model is not very good. This is a relatively general outcome for econometric estimations based on duality with microlevel data, which have been less satisfactory than with aggregate data. One should not be too surprised, however, as these models represent an extreme simplification of the complex microlevel decision framework, which ignores such important features as risk aversion, imperfect markets, incomplete information, dynamic adjustments, and sequential decision making.

3.5.2. Agricultural Price Policy in Argentina

Fulginiti and Perrin (1990) estimated a translog model of the agricultural sector in Argentina using time series data over the long period 1940 to 1980. They consider seven crops; three variable inputs (capital, labor, and an aggregate of fertilizer, seeds, and chemicals); and three fixed factors (land, rainfall, and time in years as a proxy for technological change).

Estimation of the translog system is done on the share equations:

$$(12) \quad s_i = a_i + \sum_j b_{ij} \ln p_j + \sum_m d_{im} \ln z_m,$$

where $s_i = p_i q_i / \pi$ is the share of output sale (a positive number) or input purchase (a negative number) in profit. As the sum of the shares is equal to one, the system is not linearly independent, and one equation has to be eliminated. The coefficients of the eliminated equation are identifiable from the restrictions. The system was estimated with imposition of the symmetry and homogeneity constraints.

Table 3.2 gives the parameters and the corresponding elasticities calculated at mean value of shares. Except for linseed, all the own-price supply elasticities are high, between 0.7 and 1.5. Of the 21 cross-price elasticities, 15 are positive, indicating complementarity relationships among the commodities. In other words, as the price of a commodity rises, new inputs are drawn into general production (note the input elasticities in response to product prices), causing an increase in the production of other products as well. The elasticity of beef supply in response to a general

Table 3.2. Estimated agricultural supply system in Argentina

A. Parameter estimates restricted for symmetry and homogeneity

Quantities	Intercept	Prices Beef	Wheat	Corn	Sunflower	Linseed	Soybean	Sorghum	Capital	Labor	Others	Land	Rain	Time
Beef	6.43	1.17	-0.84	-0.41	-0.14	-0.10	-0.01	-0.13	0.10	0.27	0.01	0.07	-0.01	-0.06
Wheat	0.47		1.31	-0.48	-0.03	-0.12	0.03	-0.18	0.17	-0.03	0.17	0.21	-0.20	0.01
Corn	-1.45			0.88	-0.11	-0.04	0.00	0.01	0.09	0.00	0.04	-0.02	0.30	-0.28
Sunflower	-0.98				0.28	0.04	-0.01	0.01	-0.09	0.04	0.02	0.03	-0.05	0.01
Linseed	-0.34					0.09	0.01	0.01	0.05	0.06	0.00	0.02	0.07	-0.09
Soybean	-0.36						0.05	0.01	-0.06	-0.01	-0.02	0.02	-0.05	0.02
Sorghum	-0.15							0.24	-0.01	0.00	0.04	-0.05	0.03	0.02
Capital	-1.05								-0.10	0.00	-0.16	-0.16	-0.11	0.27
Labor	0.38									-0.22	-0.11	-0.01	-0.03	0.13
Others	-1.95										-0.09	-0.02	0.05	-0.02

B. Estimated own- and cross-price elasticities

Quantities	Beef	Wheat	Corn	Sunflower	Linseed	Soybean	Sorghum	Capital	Labor	Others
Beef	1.17	0.10	0.08	0.03	0.02	0.02	-0.02	-0.95	-0.26	-0.20
Wheat	0.15	1.42	-0.15	0.10	-0.04	0.07	-0.12	-0.82	-0.53	-0.07
Corn	0.22	-0.29	1.48	-0.11	0.02	0.04	0.12	-0.82	-0.48	-0.19
Sunflower	0.22	0.58	-0.33	1.10	0.38	-0.03	0.14	-1.67	-0.23	-0.17
Linseed	0.27	-0.26	0.08	0.49	-0.08	0.15	0.16	-0.62	0.08	-0.27
Soybean	0.78	1.75	0.57	-0.14	0.54	0.66	0.42	-2.96	-0.78	-0.85
Sorghum	-0.19	-1.03	0.55	0.21	0.18	0.13	1.56	-1.11	-0.44	0.14
Capital	1.08	0.65	0.34	0.23	0.07	0.09	0.10	-1.94	-0.49	-0.13
Labor	0.63	0.89	0.43	0.07	-0.02	0.05	0.09	-1.03	-1.03	-0.07
Others	0.83	0.21	0.29	0.08	0.10	0.09	-0.05	-0.48	-0.12	-0.97

Source: Fulginiti and Perrin, 1990.
Note: Weighted mean square error for system = 1.598 with 297 degrees of freedom.

increase in all output prices is 1.4 (calculated as the sum of the elasticities of beef supply with respect to all commodity prices). As the elasticities for the other commodities are similarly high, it shows that a general rise in product prices, if not offset by higher input prices, would induce a relatively elastic response of aggregate output. Elasticities with respect to input prices are, in general, negative. The sizes of these elasticities suggest that policies affecting credit and wages will have noticeable effects on output levels as well as input use.

This model has been used to assess the impact of Argentine policies that have raised input prices and lowered the producer prices of most products. First, policies have to be characterized in terms of a percentage price wedge. Summarizing information on these 40 years of policy, the authors estimate that ad valorem export taxes resulted in average wedges of 10% for beef, 15% for soybeans, and 25% for the other crops. Similarly, the exchange rate policy is assumed to have induced an 18% overvaluation of the currency; import restrictions, a 26% increase in the price of capital; and minimum wage regulations, a 10% increase in wages. Using the model above, prediction of percentage changes in quantities can then be made at a given value of profit shares. The authors conclude that elimination of export taxes alone would have increased production from 15% for beef to almost 96% for soybeans, which gives an average of 27% for aggregate production. Elimination of import restrictions would have about the same overall effect (29%). The output effect of an exchange rate devaluation would be 14%, while eliminating the minimum wage regulation would increase average output by only 4%.

Possible problems with the analysis are the use of partial equilibrium for such large changes and consideration of an average situation over as long a time period as 40 years.

3.6. Short-Run versus Long-Run Supply Response

In the definition of the production function (1) above, an important distinction was made between variable inputs, which can be acquired in any desired quantity at a given price, and fixed factors, whose quantities are given for the decision period analyzed. The price elasticity, which depends on the impact of the price on the use of variable factors only, is thus a short-run concept. If most factors used in agriculture are fixed in the short run, as it is often claimed, then supply elasticity is close to zero. However, price incentives and increased profitability in agriculture will induce adjustment of some of the fixed factors over a longer period of time. Among those fixed factors some, such as weather or distance to markets, are truly exogenous and cannot be altered. Others, such as irrigation from tube wells, herds of livestock, or equipment, are private inputs that can be acquired through investment involving a certain time lag. Others still, like large-scale irrigation, roads, and electrification, are public investments. Although public policy cannot be considered totally driven by profitability, the theory of induced innovation asserts that the provision of public goods is partially responsive to profitability. Taking proper account of these long-run effects of price incentives, the long-run production response of agriculture is clearly greater than what is captured by considering only adjustments in the variable inputs.

Let us decompose the vector z in three categories: k for private fixed factors, k^* for public goods, and t for the truly exogenous factors. The long-run response is defined by allowing k and k^* to adjust to prices, to the exogenous factor t, and to a variable representing government policy G. The derived system of supply and demand becomes:

$$q = q(p, k, k^*, t),$$
$$k = k(p, k^*, t),$$
$$k^* = k^*(p, G),$$

and the long-run elasticities E_{ij}^L are defined by:

$$E_{ij}^L = \frac{\partial \ln q_i}{\partial \ln p_j} + \sum_l \frac{\partial \ln q_i}{\partial \ln k_l} \left(\frac{\partial \ln k_l}{\partial \ln p_j} + \sum_m \frac{\partial \ln k_l}{\partial \ln k_m^*} \frac{\partial \ln k_m^*}{\partial \ln p_j} \right) + \sum_m \frac{\partial \ln q_i}{\partial \ln k_m^*} \frac{\partial \ln k_m^*}{\partial \ln p_j}$$

$$(13) \qquad = E_{ij}^S + \sum_l E(q_i / k_l) \, E(k_l / p_j) + \sum_m E(q_i / k_m^*) \, E(k_m^* / p_j)$$

$$+ \sum_{l,m} E(q_i / k_l) \, E(k_l / k_m^*) \, E(k_m^* / p_j).$$

Similarly, the long-run supply responses with respect to the t variables are:

$$E^L(q_i / t_n) = E_{in}^S + \sum_l E(q_i / k_l) \, E(k_l / t_n) + \sum_m E(q_i / k_m^*) \, E(k_m^* / t_n).$$

Using this approach on data very similar to those used in the Bapna, Binswanger, and Quizon study described above, Evenson (1983) estimated these two sets of elasticities. In his analysis, the t variables include population density, research expenditures, high-yielding varieties, and rainfall. Private investments, k, include irrigation intensity, cropped area, and farm size. Public investments, k^*, which respond to price changes, are electrification and roads. To avoid simultaneity problems, Evenson introduces a time lag on prices in the equation defining the k and k^* variables, implying a delay in the implementation of investment. The results are reported in Table 3.3.

Using equation (13), long-run direct price elasticities have been calculated when only the private variables are allowed to respond to price changes and when both private and public variables change. In most cases, the long-run elasticity is, as expected, substantially higher than the short-run elasticity. In the case of rice, for example, the increase from 0.39 to 0.96 stems from the fact that rice production responds positively to irrigation, net cropped area, and farm size, while private investment in these three factors also responds positively to an increase in the price of rice. This example illustrates the mechanism of supply response by farmers who must invest in order to substantially increase the production of a profitable crop. The unexpected result on wheat, which has a large negative long-run price elasticity, comes from the seemingly contradictory result that wheat production responds positively to irrigation intensity while irrigation itself responds negatively to an increase in the wheat price. These results also illustrate the dual role of a public good. The availability of high-yielding varieties, for example, influences the production of rice, wheat, and the use of fertilizers both directly in the short run and indirectly in the long run through an induced investment in irrigation.

3.7. Aggregate Supply Response

In studying the elasticity of supply response in agriculture, a critical distinction must be made between the response of an individual crop and that of broad agricultural aggregates.

Table 3.3. Output supply and input demand elasticities, North Indian districts, 1959–1975

A. Elasticities of output supply and input demand

Elasticity with respect to	Wheat	Rice	Coarse cereals	Other crops	Fertilizer	Bullock labor	Tractors	Labor
Price								
Wheat	0.37*	−0.21*	0.22*	−0.03	−0.01	0.02	0.01	0.00
Rice	−0.13*	0.39*	−0.08	−0.03	−0.20*	0.01	−0.05	−0.06*
Coarse cereal	0.07*	−0.04	0.04	−0.04*	−0.16	−0.01	0.11	0.09*
Other crops	−0.06	−0.09	−0.23*	0.18*	0.35*	0.01	−0.02	0.01
Fertilizer	0.00	0.04*	0.06	−0.02*	0.20*	−0.04*	0.16	0.12*
Bullock	−0.03	−0.02	0.03	0.01	−0.44*	−0.01	−0.01	0.05*
Tractor	0.00	0.00	−0.01	0.00	0.04	0.00	−0.08	−0.16*
Labor	0.23*	−0.08	−0.04	−0.05	0.22*	0.02*	−0.10	−0.06*
Fixed factor and exogenous variables								
Electrification	−0.03	0.01	0.06*	0.08*	0.25*	0.01*	0.03	−0.03*
Roads	−0.11	−0.47*	0.37*	−0.36*	−0.33*	−0.09*	0.29*	0.03
Irrigation intensity	1.12*	0.27*	0.92*	0.28*	1.20*	0.06*	1.85*	0.12*
Net cropped area	−0.14	1.49*	1.05*	0.61*	0.29	−0.02	−1.27*	0.04
Farm size	0.22*	0.38*	−0.03	−0.21*	−0.74*	0.06*	0.69*	−0.29*
Indian research	0.02	−0.09*	−0.10*	0.18*	0.25*	0.00	0.54*	−0.08*
High–yielding varieties	0.28*	0.11*	−0.07*	−0.13*	0.26*	0.01*	−0.12*	0.03*
Rainfall	0.16*	0.41*	−0.17*	0.02	0.46	0.01*	0.21*	0.06*

B. Long–run direct price elasticities

	Wheat	Rice	Coarse cereals	Other crops	Fertilizer	Bullock labor	Tractors	Labor
Private fixed factors	−0.88	0.96	0.71	0.28	0.10	0.04	−1.31	−0.05
All fixed factors	−0.76	0.50	0.76	−0.03	0.00	−0.07	−1.41	−0.07

C. Elasticities of fixed factors

	Electricity	Roads	Irrigation	Net crop area	Farm size	Literacy	Research intensity	Laborers/ cultivators
Wheat price	−1.74*	−0.64*	−1.12*	−1.08*	−0.64*	−0.38*	0.32*	−0.80*
Rice price	1.91*	1.03*	0.91*	0.17*	0.16*	0.10*	0.33*	0.01
Coarse cereal prices	2.88*	−0.31*	0.56*	0.16	0.15	−0.38*	−0.51*	0.36*
Other crops price	−3.05*	0.15	−1.30*	0.87*	0.31*	0.45*	0.20*	0.24
Fertilizer price	−1.44*	−0.78*	−0.22	0.01	−0.22	−0.07	1.61*	−0.36
Bullock price	0.05	1.25*	0.29*	−0.78*	0.24*	0.28*	0.28*	0.04
Tractor price	2.35*	−0.64	−0.53	−0.19	−0.70*	−0.80*	−2.74*	−0.89*
Labor price	0.61*	−0.15	1.19*	0.10	0.45*	0.38*	−0.15*	0.65*
Population density	0.14	0.61	0.45	0.56	−0.69	0.50	1.02	0.67
Research expenditures	0.13	0.07	−0.12	0.09	0.09	−0.02	0.69	0.01
High–yielding varieties	0.05	−0.02	0.15	0.07	−0.03	0.05	0.13	0.21
Rainfall	−0.43*	−0.41*	−1.14*	0.03	0.02	−0.30*	0.00	0.22

Source: Evenson, 1983.
*Asymptotic $t > 1.5$

While individual crops do respond strongly to price factors, even in the short run, the growth in any crop usually takes resources away from other crops. So the price elasticity of all agriculture is very low in the short run. The problem is that the main factors of agricultural production— total land, labor, and capital—are fixed in the short run. Aggregate agricultural production can grow only if additional resources are devoted to agriculture or if technology changes. The long-run response to increased profitability thus occurs through slowing emigration from rural areas and increasing investment in agriculture and rural areas.

3.7.1. Linking the Aggregate Elasticity to the Factor Supply

There is an interesting quick calculation that can give an order of magnitude for the price elasticity of aggregate production Q. For simplicity, let the production function be approximated by a Cobb-Douglas in the variable factors x_i (at price w_i) and one fixed factor z:

$$Q = \prod_i x_i^{\mu_i} z^v.$$

The associated supply function derived from profit maximization is:

(14) $\quad Q = p^{\frac{\mu}{1-\mu}} \prod_i (\mu_i / w_i)^{\frac{\mu_i}{1-\mu}} z^{\frac{v}{1-\mu}}, \quad$ where $\quad \mu = \sum_i \mu_i.$

This shows that the supply elasticity, $\mu /(1 - \mu)$, is directly linked to the degree of homogeneity of production with respect to the variable inputs. The parameter μ_i can be approximated by the share of the input i in the value of production and μ by the share of all variable inputs. If, for example, the different factor shares are 0.14 for land, 0.16 for livestock, 0.09 for fertilizer, 0.06 for tractors, 0.01 for irrigation, 0.38 for labor, and 0.16 for the residual fixed factors, public and private capital, then assuming that only fertilizer, tractors, and irrigation can adjust in the short term gives a supply elasticity of $0.16/0.84 = 0.19$.

All the theory discussed until now, including the last result on the aggregate supply elasticity, is based on the distinction between variable and fixed factors. Such a dichotomy suggests a zero supply elasticity for the fixed factors and an infinite supply elasticity for the variable inputs. While this may be true for an individual farmer, it cannot hold for the whole sector. For instance, a very large increase in fertilizer demand cannot be matched by unlimited supplies at the current price. In addition, supply of some "fixed" inputs can be changed somewhat if prices justify it and if time is allowed. Taking these considerations into account, the analysis can be generalized by introducing explicitly the factor supply functions. In doing so, we extend the partial analysis of the supply model to integrate the factor markets, an approach that will be further developed in Chapter 11 with multimarket models. In this general case, the supply elasticity is written (Mundlak, 1985):

$$E(Q/p) = \frac{1}{\dfrac{1-\mu}{\mu} + \sum_i E_{iQ} s_i / \varepsilon_i},$$

where $E_{iQ} = \partial \ln x_i / \partial \ln Q$ is the elasticity of x_i along the expansion path (i.e., for the optimum factor combination) obtained under constant prices, s_i is the share of input i in the variable cost (equal to μ_i/μ for the Cobb-Douglas case), and ε_i ($\varepsilon_i \neq 0$) is the supply elasticity of the variable input x_i.

In order to obtain a quick order of magnitude, consider again the Cobb-Douglas with all the factors variable, which gives $E_{iQ} = 1$, and consider the unrealistic assumption where $\varepsilon_i = \varepsilon$. In this case, the elasticity of supply is simply equal to ε, the elasticity of factor supply.

Alternatively, consider the case where some inputs are fixed. To simplify, group all inputs into two classes, a variable aggregate with elasticity of supply ε_x and a fixed aggregate with shares μ and $1 - \mu$, respectively. In this case, E_{iQ} is $1/\mu$ for the variable factor and zero for the fixed factor, and the elasticity of aggregate output becomes:

$$E(Q/p) = \frac{\mu}{1 - \mu + 1/\varepsilon_x}.$$

This expression clearly shows how the supply elasticity of the product is modified by the supply elasticity of the variable factor. Thus, for $\mu = 0.16$ and $\varepsilon_x = 1$, the product supply elasticity is 0.09 instead of 0.19 obtained above under the assumption of $\varepsilon_x = \infty$.

3.7.2. Econometric Estimates

An estimate of the aggregate supply response can be derived from estimation of a disaggregated system of individual crops of the type described above. Consider, for example, the estimated system in Table 3.1. The implied aggregate supply elasticity with respect to an overall price increase is a weighted average of the individual crop elasticities:

$$E(Q/p) = \sum_i E(Q/p_i) = \sum_{i,j} s_j E(q_j/p_i),$$

where s_j is the share of crop j in aggregate crop revenue. While the results of direct individual crop price elasticities range from 0.25 to 0.77, the aggregate elasticity is only 0.05. Bapna and his associates also directly estimated an aggregate supply elasticity for a larger region which includes the subregion for which the elasticity matrix is shown. They found an aggregate elasticity of only 0.09, which is consistent with the implied elasticity from crop responses.

Most aggregate supply models follow the Nerlovian approach (presented in the next chapter), where fixed factors are generally omitted. There are few direct estimations of the aggregate supply response which explicitly specify the contribution of nonprice factors as is done for individual crops in the system approach described in this chapter. The results of the few studies where this has been done are described in Binswanger (1989) and Binswanger, Yang, Bowers, and Mundlak (1987) and can be summarized as follows:

a. The short-run aggregate response of agriculture to price changes is low. Note, however, that this does not imply that price policy reforms are not important. Given the very high levels of direct and indirect taxation that have prevailed in agriculture (see Chapter 7), structural adjustment may bring price changes on the order of 100%. Assuming an overall elasticity of even 0.1 or 0.2, such price reforms will result in a significant aggregate response.

b. Public investments and services have a strong effect on agriculture. Table 3.4 shows that infrastructure, services, and human capital strongly affect aggregate output and the demand for fertilizers and tractors. Roads are a clear example of infrastructure with a strong impact. From India's study, regulated markets (featuring a formal auction mechanism to sell individual farmers' output) can be seen as a low-cost government investment with a powerful output effect and, in the cross-country study, broader literacy is shown to boost output as well as the demand for fertilizer.

c. While research and extension have been shown in other studies to have a strong effect on the production of individual crops, their impact on aggregate supply is much lower, in much the same way that aggregate price elasticity is lower than individual elasticities.

Table 3.4. Effects of infrastructure on agriculture

	Aggregate crop output	
	Cross–country	India
Prices		
Output price	−0.05*	_ [a]
International output price[b]		0.13*
Fertilizer price	0.0	−0.12*
Urban wage	−0.05*	0.05
Interest rate		−0.001
Infrastructure		
Total irrigation[c]	1.62*	
Government canal irrigation		0.03
Rural road density	0.12*	0.20*
Paved roads[c]	0.26*	
Electrification		0.03*
Services		
Regulated markets		0.08*
Commercial banks		0.02*
Extension	0.02	
Human capital		
Rural population density	0.12*	
Adult literacy rate[c]	0.54*	
Primary school		0.33*
Life expectancy	1.76*	
Technical		
Research	0.00	
Rainfall		0.07*
GDP per capita	0.21*	
Number of observations	580	1,785

Source: Binswanger, 1989.
[a]Blanks indicate data not available.
[b]To circumvent simultaneity problems, an index of international prices is used as an instrumental variable for domestic prices.
[c]Coefficients are not in elasticity form: irrigation, paved roads, and adult literacy are ratios expressed as a percentage. The coefficients in the table give the increase in the dependent variable for a one point increase in the independent percentage.
*Statistical significance at 10% or more.

d. Because output is so dependent on private investment, one would expect credit to be a critical factor in aggregate response. A study of the role of credit in India found that the main effect of institutional credit growth and higher lending volumes has not been a substantial increase in aggregate crop output but rather a substitution of capital for labor. Thus, the credit-supply approach to agricultural growth pursued over the last three decades in India has failed to generate employment or to reach its agricultural output objectives.

e. Because fixed factors have strong effects on output, an explanation of long-run supply requires an analysis of the determinants of change in these factors themselves. Result show that farmers, government, and providers of services all respond to agroclimatic potential. As public infrastructure and services are targeted to the better agroclimatic regions, more workers migrate to these regions. Private investment is then attracted by this abundance of natural resources, labor, and infrastructure. And private suppliers of services respond to the better opportunities associated with good agroclimate, improved infrastructure, and high private investment.

Exercise 3
Price Incentives and Public Goods for Indian Agriculture

This exercise consists of an analysis of output supply and factor demand with a system of equations derived from the profit function. The subjects addressed are: (1) the interdependencies between tradable and nontradable products and the consequences that price policies have on each; (2) the contrasts between the price elasticity of a single product and the elasticity of aggregate supply; (3) the respective roles of price and structural variables in the determination of output levels. On this last point, the exercise will analyze the importance of public goods in conditioning the response of producers to price incentives, and the contrast between short-run and long-run price elasticities calculated by taking into account the changes in the structural variables induced by price variations. Prepare a report in which the results to the following questions are discussed with reference to these subjects.

The problem presented here (file 3PROFIT) is largely inspired by Evenson's 1983 study, "Economics of Agricultural Growth: The Case of Northern India." We consider a system of production with three crops (wheat, rice, and coarse cereals), produced with three variable factors (labor, bullock traction, and tractors), and two fixed factors (irrigation, and research and extension). The impact of other fixed factors we do not wish to investigate (such as land, rainfall, etc.) has been incorporated in the model's constant term. The model is derived from a normalized quadratic profit function. The system of product supply and factor demand is written as:

$$q_i = a_o + \sum_j b_{ij}(p_j / w) + \sum_k b_{ik} z_k, \quad i = 1, \dots, 6, \quad j = 1, \dots, 5, \quad k = 1, 2,$$

where q_i represent the three products and three variable factors (positive values for the products and negative values for the factors), p_i / w their prices relative to wage (w), and z_k the structural variables.

The first part of Table 3E.1 gives the parameter estimates for the a's and the b's. The supplementary row, "Research × own price," will be used for the analysis of cross effects and is ignored for the moment. On the right, column J reports the average values of the exogenous variables in the sample. Irrigation is measured by the percentage of crop land irrigated, research

Table 3E.1. Price incentives and public goods in Indian agriculture

Parameters of the derived output supply and factor demand equations

Exogenous variables	Wheat	Rice	Coarse cereals	Bullock power	Tractor	Labor	Irrigation	Average base values exogenous variables	Elasticities (Wheat)	
Intercept	-18185	-3970	-520	-34677	568	1990			Wheat price	.36
Wheat price/wage	5441	-2133	450	-507	-200	-35		1.09	Rice price	-.12
Rice price/wage	-2133	4569	-800	-277	-37	-3858		0.96	Coarse cereals price	.04
Coarse cereals price/wage	450	-800	2607	-147	-60	-1888		1.48	Bullock price	-.02
Bullock price/wage	-507	-277	-147	430	-9	-1853		0.78	Tractor price	-.01
Tractor price/wage	-200	-37	-60	-9	250	-6102		0.76	Irrigation	1.14
Irrigation (% land)	531	90	175	-54	-20	-740		35.00	Research-extension	.73
Research and extension	56	55	60	18	-2	30		214.00		
Research*wheat price/wage								232.19	Wage	-.24
Estimated base values	16360	11586	21857	-33418	-718	-30111				

(endogenous variables, values in constant prices)

Simulations

	Quest.#2 Wheat p 10%	Quest.#2 Rice p 10%	Quest.#3 Tradables 15%	Quest.#4 Irrigation 10%	Quest.#4 Res&Ext 10%	Quest.#5 Wheat p 10%LR
Exogenous variables						
Wheat price/wage	1.09	1.19				
Rice price/wage	.96	.96				
Coarse cereals price/wage	1.48	1.48				
Bullock price/wage	.78	.78				
Tractor price/wage	.76	.76				
Irrigation	35.00	35.00				
Research and extension	214	214				
Research*wheat price/wage	232	255				
Endogenous variables						
Wheat	16360	16950				
Rice	11586	11355				
Coarse cereals	21857	21906				
Total crops	61133	61624				
Bullock	-33418	-33473				
Tractor	-718	-740				
Labor	-30111	-30115				
Total factors	-56791	-56854				
Profit/wage	4342	6608				
Percent change over base value						
Wheat	.00	3.61				
Rice	.00	-2.00				
Coarse cereals	.00	.22				
Total crops	.00	.80				
Bullock	.00	.16				
Tractor	.00	3.02				
Labor	.00	.01				
Total factors	.00	.11				
Profit/wage	.00	52.21				
Estimated irrigation						

and extension by cumulated expenditures in constant price over the past 5 years, and quantities of product and input in values in constant prices.

1. The price and fixed factor elasticities in this model are variable. Therefore, their values can be calculated only for a given value of the exogenous variables. Using the average value observed in the sample, the price elasticities of supply of wheat are calculated in column L:

$$E(q_i / p_j) = (b_{ij} \ p_j / w)(1 / q_i),$$

$$E(q_i / w) = -\left(\sum_j b_{ij} \ p_j / w \right)(1 / q_i) = -\sum_j E(q_i / p_j), \quad \text{and}$$

$$E(q_i / z_k) = b_{ik} z_k / q_i .$$

Complete the table of price and fixed factor elasticities of supply for the other products and of demand for the factors. Note, in cell L23, that the formula used to calculate the elasticity with respect to wage is different from the others. Discuss the results in terms of complementarity/substitutability between products and between factors. Verify the signs of the other price elasticities, that is to say, for the products in relation to the prices of factors and for the factors in relation to the prices of products. Analyze, in particular, why the signs for the elasticities of factor demand have been reversed. Contrast the values of the elasticities of supply and factor use with respect to the two structural variables.

2. Simulations of the impact of changes in the exogenous variables are given in the lower part of Table 3E.1. The first entries of that part of the table include the values of the exogenous variables; the second give the predicted levels of production and factor use; and last, beneath, the third block reports the percentage changes in the endogenous variables relative to their base values. The first column reproduces the base values. In the second column, the price of wheat is increased by 10%. The new values are 16,950 for wheat production, 11,355 for rice production, and so on. This corresponds to an increase of 3.6% for wheat, a decrease of 2% for rice, and so on. (Dividing these results by 10 also gives you the different direct- and cross-price elasticities with respect to the wheat price.) Notice that even if an increase in the price of wheat can induce a slight increase in the production of that product, this occurs at the cost of a decrease in the production of rice, and therefore the impact on aggregate agricultural output will be low. Repeat this exercise for an increase in the price of rice. Comment on your results.

3. Considering wheat and rice as tradable products, considering that the price of tractor services is linked to the international price of imported tractors, and considering that the services of draught animals and labor are not tradable, what will be the impact of an exchange rate devaluation of 15% on agricultural production? Simulate for that purpose the impact of a simultaneous increase of 15% in the prices of wheat, rice, and tractor services. You should observe a drop in the production of the nontradable product. It is precisely this reallocation effect which a policy of exchange rate devaluation attempts to achieve. Going beyond the framework of this production model, what can be expected for the evolution of the demand for nontradable products and, therefore, for their equilibrium prices? In our case, there is complementarity between nontradables and wheat, and substitutability with rice is not very strong. The fall in production of nontradables is consequently not large. Analyze the perverse effect of a devaluation on the utilization of tractors, even though these are imported.

4. We will consider that the structural variables represent respectively a private investment (tube well irrigation) and a public investment (research and extension). Simulate in columns G and H the effects of a 10% increase in each of these structural variables. Analyze the impact on the production structure. Compare the total increase in outputs with the total increase in factors. What can be induced about the total factor productivity of the variable factors?

5. The structural variables, considered fixed in the short run, change in the long run. Private investment is often considered to respond to global profitability and, therefore, to product and factor prices. Based on the study cited above, add in column I, under the heading "irrigation," the coefficients of an equation that determines the level of the private structural factor, here irrigation. This equation is written:

$$irrigation = 10.09 + 20 \, p_{wheat} \, / \, w + 0.015 \, research \, .$$

You see, in this equation, the effects of price incentives and of complementarity between public goods (research) and private investment (irrigation). Introduce the parameters of this new equation in column I (that is, 10.09 in cell I10, and so on) and an additional row (row 70) in the block of endogenous variables in which you calculate the estimated value of the irrigation variable. The expression that you must enter is analogous to those used in the calculation of supply of different products or of factor demand. To calculate the long-run price elasticity which includes these investments, proceed in two stages:

a. Use your simulation of a 10% increase in the price of wheat in column D. Read the new values for irrigation in cell D70.

b. Report the value in cell I39 as the new irrigation level and combine it with the effect of a 10% increase in the price of wheat.

Compare this long-run price elasticity of wheat production with the short-run elasticity of question 2. Print and/or save your results, as the model will be changed in the following questions.

6. The impact of a public good is often considered as a factor increasing the elasticity of supply response. In order to reflect this, we can add a cross term, product of the research variable by the price of the product, corresponding to the following model:

$$q_{wheat} = a_o + (5441 + 33 \, research) \, p_{wheat} \, / \, w + \sum_{j \neq wheat} b_{ij} \, p_j \, / \, w + \sum_k b_{ik} \, z_k \, .$$

This is done in row 22, in the column of the wheat equation, by addition of the variable $research \times p_{wheat} \, / \, w$. In this cell, C22, introduce the value 33 for the corresponding parameter. Reduce the value of the intercept sufficiently (by subtracting the product 33×232.19, which is the average value of the new variable) in order to reproduce the base values with this new equation. Check that this is indeed the case in the first column of simulations. With this new model, calculate the direct price elasticity for wheat by simulating the impact of an increase in the price of wheat. Compare this with the simple elasticity obtained earlier in question 2.

7. The following equations represent the total impact of public investment (in research and extension) on wheat production:

$$q_{wheat} = a_o + (5441 + 33 \ research) \ p_{wheat} / w + \sum_{j \neq wheat} b_{ij} \ p_j / w + 56 \ research + 531 \ irrigation,$$

where $irrigation = 10.09 + 20 p_{wheat} / w + 0.015 \ research$.

These equations show that the total impact of public investment on wheat production can be decomposed into three related effects.

First, in the short run, a change in research investment affects wheat production directly. This was simulated in question 4 by increasing research and extension by 10%.

Second, a change in public investment will also indirectly affect wheat production by changing the way production responds to a change in price (i.e., a change in research investment changes the own price elasticity of wheat production). To simulate these two effects together, create a column labeled 7(a) in the spreadsheet that you have just modified for question 6. In this column increase the research and extension variable by 10% as was done in question 4. The variable *research × wheat price* in row 42 correspondingly increases. Now simulate the impact of this new set of exogenous variables on the endogenous variables.

Third, in the long run, a change in public investment will also have an indirect effect through the impact of public investment on investment in irrigation. To simulate the three effects together, extend the row labeled "estimated irrigation" across the bottom of all simulations. This row now shows the long-run impact of each simulated change in exogenous variables on investment in irrigation. The "estimated irrigation" in column 7(a) shows the long-run impact of a 10% increase in public investment in research on private investment in irrigation. Report this "estimated irrigation" to row 39 of a new column labeled 7(b). In this same column increase the research and extension variable by 10% as was done in 7(a). All other exogenous variables remain at base levels. Simulate the impact of this new set of exogenous variables on the endogenous variables.

Analyze these results.

References

Ball, Eldon. 1988. "Modeling Supply Response in a Multiproduct Framework." *American Journal of Agricultural Economics* 70:813–25.

Bapna, Shanti, Hans Binswanger, and Jaime Quizon. 1984. "Systems of Output Supply and Factor Demand Equations for Semiarid Tropical India." *Indian Journal of Agricultural Economics* 39:179–202.

Binswanger, Hans. 1974. "A Cost Function Approach to the Measurement of Factor Demand and Elasticities of Substitution." *American Journal of Agricultural Economics* 56:377–86.

Binswanger, Hans. 1989. "The Policy Response of Agriculture." *World Bank Economic Review*, Proceedings of the Annual Conference of Development Economics, 231–58.

Binswanger, Hans, M. C. Yang, Alan Bowers, and Yair Mundlak. 1987. "On the Determinants of Cross Country Aggregate Agricultural Supply." *Journal of Econometrics* 36:111–31.

Esfahani, Hadi Salehi. 1987. "Technical Change, Employment, and Supply Response of Agriculture in the Nile Delta: A System-wide Approach." *Journal of Development Economics* 25:167–96.

Evenson, Robert. 1983. "Economics of Agricultural Growth: The Case of Northern India." Unpublished paper, Yale University, Economic Growth Center.

Fulginiti, Lilyan, and Richard Perrin. 1990. "Argentine Agricultural Policy in a Multiple-Input, Multiple-Output Framework." *American Journal of Agricultural Economics* 72:279–88.

Lopez, Ramon. 1980. "The Structure of Production and the Derived Demand for Inputs in Canadian Agriculture." *American Journal of Agricultural Economics* 62:38–45.

Mundlak, Yair. 1985. *The Aggregate Agricultural Supply Response.* Working Paper no. 8511. Rehovot, Israel: Center for Agricultural Economics Research.

Sidhu, Surjit, and Carlos Baanante. 1981. "Estimating Farm-Level Input Demand and Wheat Supply in the Indian Punjab Using a Translog Profit Function." *American Journal of Agricultural Economics* 63:237–46.

Yotopoulos, Pan, and Lawrence Lau. 1979. "Resource Use in Agriculture: Applications of the Profit Function to Selected Countries." *Food Research Institute Studies* 17:11–22.

CHAPTER FOUR

Supply Response: Expectations Formation and Partial Adjustment

4.1. Alternative Approaches to the Measurement of Supply Response

We have seen in Chapter 3 that there are two types of elasticities of supply response for which policy makers need information: those of individual activities and that of the sector aggregate. In general, the elasticity of supply response will be much higher for crops than for the sector, particularly in the short run. This is because response by crops can be obtained by reallocating variable factors across crops, whereas aggregate response requires expansion of area or of other fixed factors, technological change, or shifting from more fixed-factor extensive to more fixed-factor intensive activities (such as from wheat to vegetables), all of which are slower and more difficult to achieve than variable factor reallocation. For crops, supply response can be studied for yield, area, or output. Here again, we can predict a ranking of elasticities, with the elasticity of yield smaller and more unstable than the elasticity of area and, a fortiori, than that of output, which is the sum of the former two. Finally, the elasticity of supply response increases with time as desired factor reallocation becomes more complete and as factors which are fixed in the short run, of both private and public origins, can become variable. The long-run elasticity of supply response can thus eventually be very high depending on the elasticity of supply response of these fixed factors (Mundlak, 1987).

These observations give us a ranking of elasticities (E) of supply response as follows:

$$E_{aggregate} < E_{crop},$$
$$E_{yield} < E_{area} < E_{output},$$
$$E_{short\ run} < E_{long\ run}.$$

The theory of production developed in Chapter 2 suggests that there are a number of alternative approaches to estimation of the elasticities of supply response, both at the structural and at the reduced form levels.

4.1.1. Structural Form Approaches: Estimation of the Structure and Derivation of the Supply Response

4.1.1.1. Production Function Estimation from Cross-Sectional Data

Farm surveys give data on output, variable inputs, and fixed-factor levels from which a production function can be estimated. Using the first-order conditions for profit maximization, the supply responses can then be derived. The production function needs to be given a functional form such as Cobb-Douglas, constant elasticity of substitution (CES), translog, or generalized power (Debertin, 1986; Heathfield and Wibe, 1987). The derived supply functions for the Cobb-Douglas, CES, and translog production functions are given in the Appendix. This approach, while undemanding in data, has problems. A simultaneity bias between inputs and output will occur unless experimental data are used or we are in an economy with set prices. Derived elasticities are long run in nature as we observe full factor reallocations and correct price expectations across farms. Thus, partial adjustment or adaptive expectations are not taken into account, which, as we will see in Nerlovian models, results in overestimating the short-run elasticity of supply response. And a great deal of sensitivity of the derived supply elasticities hinges on the choice of functional form for the production function, which is largely arbitrary.

4.1.1.2. Linear Programming

This is basically the same approach as above except that the production function is specified as a set of fixed coefficients and the profit maximization problem includes a set of effective constraints. Again, only cross-sectional data are needed. The advantage is the possibility of a very detailed specification of the complexity of production systems, including the nature of the production technology (e.g., interrelationships among crops due to rotations) and the specificity of the constraints (e.g., seasonal labor constraints). Supply response is derived by parametric programming, solving for optimal quantities as prices vary.

4.1.1.3. Production Function with Observed Price Variations

In this case, the production function and the first-order conditions can be estimated simultaneously. Observing price variations requires either time series data (which show little variability in fixed factors unless the series is very long, as in the Fulginiti and Perrin study reviewed in Chapter 3), or cross-sectional data over time (which is highly demanding), or a single cross section with observed differences in farm-level effective prices (with problems of quality differentials as in the Deaton methodology for the estimation of demand parameters from unit values reviewed in Chapter 2). This last approach is promising, but not frequently used, as farm surveys rarely record both quantities and values in the transactions observed and do not obtain a full characterization of transactions costs.

4.1.1.4. Profit Function Approach

As seen in Chapter 3, the profit function can be estimated from a combination of cross-sectional and time series data, or from cross-sectional data that show interfarm variations in effective prices or from a long run time series that shows variations in fixed factors. The supply and factor demands are then derived analytically.

4.1.1.5. Complete Structural Models

Complete models of the farm sector or of the whole economy can also be estimated and the supply function derived by simulation. Such models include multimarket and general equilibrium models that are developed in Chapters 11 and 12.

4.1.2. Reduced Form Approaches: Direct Estimation of the Supply Response

4.1.2.1. Ad Hoc Specifications of Supply Response Including Partial Adjustment and Expectations Formation

This is the nature of the Nerlovian models studied in this chapter. Time series data are used for only the commodity under study and the prices of a few directly related commodities. With only minimal theoretical and data demands, however, it is not surprising that the results have more often than not been unreliable.

4.1.2.2. Estimation of Complete Systems of Supply Deriving from a Profit Function

In this case, the restrictions on parameters across equations are imposed so that the resulting system derives rigorously from a profit function. Estimation procedures were discussed in Chapter 3.

4.1.2.3. Estimation of Structural Models of Supply and Demand Equilibrium

This includes cobweb models and rational expectations models where both prices and quantities are endogenous. It also includes multimarket models that are developed in Chapter 11.

4.2. Nerlovian Models of Supply Response

A central problem in the estimation of the supply response equation derived in Chapter 3,

$$q = q(p, z),$$

is that producers respond to expected as opposed to actual prices. Usually, the *observed prices* are market or effective farm-gate prices after production has occurred, while production (planting) decisions have to be based on the prices farmers *expect* to prevail several months later at harvest time. Because of the time lag involved in agricultural production, modeling the formation of expectations is thus an important issue in the analysis of agricultural supply response.

Another problem is that the *observed quantities* may differ from the *desired* ones because of adjustment lags in the reallocation of variable factors. When the price of a crop changes, it may take several years before farmers can reach their desired production patterns at the new price. Therefore, before applying the model to the actual data, one has to specify these adjustment lags explicitly. In the following sections, we discuss Nerlovian models which are built to handle these two dynamic processes (Nerlove, 1956, 1958).

4.2.1. The General Nerlovian Supply Response Model

Models of supply response can be formulated in terms of yield, area, or output response of individual crops, for instance, the desired area to be allocated to a crop in period t is a function of expected relative prices and a number of shifters:

(1) $\quad q_t^d = \alpha_1 + \alpha_2 p_t^e + \alpha_3 z_t + u_t.$

In this equation, q_t^d is the desired cultivated area in period t; p_t^e is the expected price (or, more generally, a vector of relative prices including the price of the crop itself, prices of competing crops, and factor prices, with one of these prices chosen as numéraire); z_t is a set of other exogenous shifters, principally private and public fixed factors and truly exogenous variables such as weather; u_t accounts for unobserved random factors affecting the area under cultivation and has an expected value of zero; and the α_i's are parameters (or elasticities if the variables are expressed logarithmically) with α_2 the long-run coefficient (elasticity) of supply response.

Because full adjustment to the desired allocation of land may not be possible in the short run, the actual adjustment in area will be only a fraction δ of the desired adjustment:

(2) $\quad q_t - q_{t-1} = \delta(q_t^d - q_{t-1}) + v_t, \qquad 0 \le \delta \le 1,$

where q_t is the actual area planted of the crop, δ the *partial-adjustment coefficient*, and v_t a random term with zero expected value.

The price the decision maker expects to prevail at harvest time cannot be observed. Therefore, one has to specify a model that explains how the agent forms expectations based on actual and past prices and other observable variables. For example, in a formulation that represents a learning process, farmers adjust their expectations as a fraction γ of the magnitude of the mistake they made in the previous period, that is, of the difference between the actual price and expected price in $t - 1$:

$$p_t^e - p_{t-1}^e = \gamma(p_{t-1} - p_{t-1}^e) + w_t, \qquad 0 \le \gamma \le 1, \quad \text{or}$$

(3) $\quad p_t^e = \gamma p_{t-1} + (1-\gamma)p_{t-1}^e + w_t,$

where p_{t-1} is the price that prevails when decision-making for production in period t occurs, γ is the *adaptive-expectations coefficient*, and w_t is a random term with zero expected value. An alternative interpretation of this learning process is that the expected price is a weighted sum of all past prices with a geometrically declining set of weights:

$$p_t^e = \gamma \sum_{i=1}^{\infty} (1-\gamma)^{i-1} p_{t-i},$$

where the right-hand side geometric series is the solution to equation (3), which gives the certainty equivalent to p_t^e.

Since p_t^e and q_t^d are not observable, we eliminate them from equations (1), (2), and (3). Substitution from equations (1) and (3) into equation (2) and rearrangement give the reduced form:

(4) $\quad q_t = \pi_1 + \pi_2 p_{t-1} + \pi_3 q_{t-1} + \pi_4 q_{t-2} + \pi_5 z_t + \pi_6 z_{t-1} + e_t,$

where:

$\pi_1 = \alpha_1 \delta\gamma,$

$\pi_2 = \alpha_2 \delta\gamma,$ the short-run coefficient (elasticity) of supply response,

$\pi_3 = (1-\delta) + (1-\gamma),$

$\pi_4 = -(1-\delta)(1-\gamma),$

$\pi_5 = \alpha_3 \delta,$

$\pi_6 = -\alpha_3 \delta(1-\gamma),$

$e_t = v_t - (1-\gamma)v_{t-1} + \delta u_t - \delta(1-\gamma)u_{t-1} + \alpha_2 \delta w_t.$

Equation (4) is the estimable form of the supply response model defined by equations (1), (2), and (3). This reduced form is overidentified, since there are six reduced-form coefficients π but only five structural parameters (α_1, α_2, α_3, γ, and δ). To obtain a unique solution for the latter, a nonlinear constraint must be imposed on the parameters of the reduced form:

$$\pi_6^2 - \pi_4\pi_5^2 + \pi_3\pi_5\pi_6 = 0.$$

The model should be estimated using nonlinear, maximum-likelihood techniques, and correction needs to be made for serial correlation in the error terms (see Table 4.1 for the structure of the residuals displaying serial correlation). The structural coefficients can be solved with the following equations:

$$\delta^2 + (\pi_3 - 2)\delta + 1 - \pi_3 - \pi_4 = 0,$$

$$\gamma = 1 + \pi_4 /(1 - \delta),$$

$$\alpha_1 = \pi_1 / \delta\gamma,$$

$$\alpha_2 = \pi_2 / \delta\gamma, \text{ the long-run coefficient (elasticity) of supply response,}$$

$$\alpha_5 = \pi_5 / \delta.$$

The short-run price response is estimated by π_2, and the long-run price response is calculated as α_2, where $\alpha_2 = \pi_2/\delta\gamma \geq \pi_2$ since both δ and $\gamma \leq 1$. As expected, the long-run supply response exceeds the short-run supply response.

4.2.2. Restricted Nerlovian Supply Response Model

If exogenous shifters (z) are not included in the model, then $\alpha_3 = 0$ in the structural form and $\pi_5 = \pi_6 = 0$ in the reduced form. The reduced-form equation then becomes:

$$q_t = \pi_1 + \pi_2 p_{t-1} + \pi_3 q_{t-1} + \pi_4 q_{t-2} + e_t.$$

Because δ and γ enter the remaining reduced-form coefficients symmetrically, the model is underidentified, and no solution can be found for δ and γ. However, the short-run and long-run price responses can be calculated as π_2 and $\alpha_2 = -\pi_2/(\pi_3 + \pi_4 - 1)$, respectively. The error term is the same as with the general model and indicates the presence of serial correlation (see Table 4.1). This model can be estimated with OLS or generalized least squares to correct for serial correlation.

4.2.3. Simplified Models with either No Partial Adjustment or No Expectations Formation

We give in Table 4.1 a number of additional estimable versions of the Nerlovian model where there is either no partial adjustment $(\delta = 1)$ or no expectations formation $(\gamma = 1)$. The former would apply to crops where there are no specialized fixed factors of any significance and adaptation can be complete in one period, implying $q_t = q_t^d$. The latter applies to situations where administered prices are announced at planting time, such as in the case of Egypt, which we analyze later in this chapter. In this case, $p_t^e = p_{t-1}$. This latter model is exactly identified and has frequently been used when forward guaranteed prices are announced. Note that in all models with either $\delta = 1$ or $\gamma = 1$, the long-run elasticity of supply response is $\alpha_2 = \pi_2 /(1 - \pi_3)$. All these models have p_{t-1} and q_{t-1} as exogenous variables and must consequently be carefully distinguished on the basis of the z variables included. Note that, when no z variables are present, the restricted models with either $\delta = 1$ or $\gamma = 1$ cannot be distinguished from one another at the level of the reduced form.

Table 4.1. Alternative specifications of Nerlovian models of supply response

Supply response models	A priori information	Reduced form	Structural parameters	Restrictions	Estimators	Residuals
Partial adjustment and adaptive expectation	None	p_{t-1}, q_{t-1}, q_{t-2}, z_t, z_{t-1}	$\alpha_1, \alpha_2, \alpha_3$, δ, γ	$\pi_6^2 - \pi_4\pi_5^2 + \pi_3\pi_5\pi_6 = 0$	$\delta^2 + (\pi_3 - 2)\delta + 1 - \pi_3 - \pi_4 = 0$, $\gamma = 1 + \pi_4/(1-\delta)$, $\alpha_1 = \pi_1/\delta\gamma$, $\alpha_2 = \pi_2/\delta\gamma, \alpha_3 = \pi_5/\delta$	$\alpha_2\,\delta\,w_t$ $+\delta[u_t - (1-\gamma)\,u_{t-1}]$ $+[v_t - (1-\gamma)\,v_{t-1}]$
Adjustment and expectations, restricted	$\alpha_3 = 0$	p_{t-1}, q_{t-1}, q_{t-2}	α_1, α_2, δ, γ	None	$\alpha_1 = \alpha_2\pi_1/\pi_2$, $\alpha_2 = -\pi_2/(\pi_3+\pi_4-1)$, δ and γ not estimatable	Same
Expectations only	$\delta = 1$	p_{t-1}, q_{t-1}, z_t, z_{t-1}	$\alpha_1, \alpha_2, \alpha_3$, γ	$\pi_6 = -\pi_3\pi_5$	$\gamma = 1 - \pi_3$, $\alpha_1 = \pi_1/\gamma, \alpha_2 = \pi_2/\gamma, \alpha_3 = \pi_5$	$u_t - (1-\gamma)u_{t-1}$ $+ \alpha_2 w_t$
Expectations restricted	$\delta = 1$, $\alpha_3 = 0$	p_{t-1}, q_{t-1}	α_1, α_2, γ	None	$\gamma = 1 - \pi_3$, $\alpha_1 = \pi_1/\gamma, \alpha_2 = \pi_2/\gamma$	Same
Adjustment only	$\gamma = 1$	p_{t-1}, q_{t-1}, z_t	$\alpha_1, \alpha_2, \alpha_3$, δ	None	$\delta = 1 - \pi_3$, $\alpha_1 = \pi_1/\delta, \alpha_2 = \pi_2/\delta, \alpha_3 = \pi_5/\delta$	$\delta u_t + v_t$
Adjustment restricted	$\gamma = 1$, $\alpha_3 = 0$	p_{t-1}, q_{t-1}	α_1, α_2, δ	None	$\delta = 1 - \pi_3$, $\alpha_1 = \pi_1/\delta, \alpha_2 = \pi_2/\delta$	Same
Extrapolative naive	$\gamma = 1$, $\delta = 1$	p_{t-1}, z_t	$\alpha_1, \alpha_2, \alpha_3$	None	$\alpha_1 = \pi_1, \alpha_2 = \pi_2, \alpha_3 = \pi_5$	u_t
Extrapolative naive and restricted	$\gamma = 1, \delta = 1$, $\alpha_3 = 0$	p_{t-1}	α_1, α_2	None	$\alpha_1 = \pi_1, \alpha_2 = \pi_2$	u_t

4.3. Results Using Nerlovian Models of Supply Response

Nerlovian models are quite practical, and their numerous variants have been applied to many crops in many countries. However, it is fair to say that, compared with a correct theoretical specification of supply response as derived from the theory of producer behavior in Chapter 3, many formulations have not been careful about specification of the estimated equations. Specifically, the estimated supply functions should be homogenous of degree zero in prices, include the prices of both competing crops and important factors, and make explicit the role of fixed factors. In contrast, the profit function approach is both more theoretically rigorous and more demanding in terms of data. But, users of the profit function approach have, in general, not paid attention to the mechanisms of expectations formation for prices and of partial adjustment in production. Clearly, the best of what the two approaches offer needs to be integrated. How this is done depends, in each particular case, on the objectives of the analysis and the data availability, seeking to strike a balance between rigor and convenience. For the moment, theory is on the side of the profit-function approach, but empirical results have been sketchy and poor. While theory is badly mistreated in most Nerlovian specifications, they offer a very large body of empirical results on which policy makers may rely, if taken with a grain of salt.

A compilation of elasticity estimates using the Nerlovian approach is given in Table 4.2. In general, the short-run price elasticity of acreage response ranges between 0 and 0.8 while the long-run acreage response is between 0.3 and 1.2 (Rao, 1989). Askari and Cummings (1976) and a number of others have attempted to identify reasons why price elasticities (E) vary across countries and commodities. Their findings and other studies suggest that the following matter:

a. Higher price and yield risks decrease E (Behrman, 1968; Just, 1977).

b. Multiple cropping and irrigation afford more flexibility in land use and thus increase E.

c. Minor crops have a higher E because they are easier to shift around.

d. Higher household income, larger farm size, and greater asset ownership increase E as they facilitate access to credit and reduce risk aversion.

e. Sharecropping reduces E due to the disincentive which output sharing implies.

f. Education and access to extension services increase E.

g. Market failures for other products (e.g., for food crops in estimating E for cash crops) and for factors (e.g., labor, credit, and insurance) decrease E for the crops with markets (see Chapter 6 on household models).

h. Availability of low-priced consumer goods that can be purchased with cash earnings increases E for cash crops.

i. Greater market integration, implying a lower share of households producing exclusively for home consumption, increases the regional E (see Chapter 6).

The aggregate supply response shows short-run elasticities between 0.1 and 0.3 and long-run elasticities between 0.4 and 0.5. As we saw in Chapter 3, the Nerlovian approach tends to underestimate the long-run response as it either completely fails to specify the role of fixed factors or fails to take into account the elasticity of supply response of the fixed factors themselves to price (Mundlak, 1985).

While we do not develop this here, the same methodology used for supply response can be used to estimate the elasticities of factor demand and of marketed surplus response.

Table 4.2. Price elasticity of supply of agricultural products in less developed countries

Product	Country	Period	Price elasticities		R^2
			Short–run	Long–run	
Agricultural production	Argentina	1950–74	0.21 to 0.35	0.42 to 0.78	—
Foodgrains	India	1951–64	–0.06 to 0.42	—	—
Rice	Thailand	1951–65	0.39	0.31	0.48
	India	1960–69	0.19 to 0.24	0.64 to 0.68	—
	Pakistan	1949–68	0.12	0.17	—
	Bangladesh	1949–68	0.13	0.19	—
	Philippines	1972–74	0.4 to 0.7	0.7 to 1.0	—
	Indonesia	1951–62	0.20	—	0.69
	Malaysia	1951–62	0.23	1.35	0.61
	Taiwan	1962–72	0.22	0.97	—
	South Korea	1960–71	0.24	2.00	—
	Sri Lanka	1953–74	0.21	0.99	—
	Egypt	1953–72	0.08	0.08	0.43
	Iraq	1960–71	0.66	1.57	0.59
Wheat	India	1950–67	0.10	0.13	—
	Pakistan	1950–68	0.07	0.21	—
	Egypt	1953–72	0.91	0.44	0.83
	Syria	1961–72	0.64	3.23	0.57
	Iraq	1962–71	1.59	1.96	0.70
	Jordan	1955–67	0.20	0.23	0.66
	Lebanon	1951–72	0.56	0.58	0.29
	Kenya	1950–69	0.31	0.65	—
Barley	India	1951–64	0.53	0.60	0.88
	Pakistan	1951–68	0.03	0.02	—
	Brazil	1970–71	0.22 to 0.62	2.5 to 1.1	—
	Syria	1961–72	0.27	0.40	0.50
	Iraq	1951–60	0.51	0.35	0.74
	Jordan	1955–67	2.85	4.04	0.52
	Lebanon	1951–72	0.17	0.22	0.67
	India	1960–69	0.11 to 0.13	0.14 to 0.16	—
Maize	Kenya	1950–69	0.95	2.43	—
	Egypt	1953–72	0.04	0.09	0.89
	Syria	1947–60	0.51	0.69	0.84
	Jordan	1955–66	6.13	6.40	0.60
	Lebanon	1953–72	0.13	0.29	0.93
	Sudan	1951–65	0.23	0.56	—
Cassava	Thailand	1955–63	1.09	1.09	0.14
Millet	Syria	1961–72	1.21	1.60	—
	Sudan	1951–65	0.09	0.36	—
	Iraq	1961–70	0.88	1.85	0.82
	India	1951–65	0.83 to 0.90	—	0.49
Sorghum	India	1947–65	0.02 to 0.20	0.03 to 0.28	0.70
	Sudan	1951–65	0.31	0.59	—
Potatoes	Syria	1950–60	0.65	1.30	0.87
	Lebanon	1957–72	0.54	0.58	0.73

Source: Scandizzo and Bruce, 1980.

4.4. Examples of Nerlovian Models

4.4.1. Supply Response of Maize in Thailand under Risk

An interesting extension of the Nerlovian supply model is Behrman's (1968) study of the area response of maize in eight provinces of Thailand using time series data from 1937 to 1963. He stated a four-equation structural model as follows:

$$A_t^d = a_0 + a_1 p_t^e + a_2 y_t^e + a_3 \sigma_{pt} + a_4 \sigma_{yt} + a_5 M_t + u_{1t},$$

$$A_t = b_0 + A_{t-1} + \delta(A_t^d - A_{t-1}) + u_{2t},$$

$$p_t^e = c_0 + p_{t-1}^e + \gamma(p_{t-1} - p_{t-1}^e) + u_{3t},$$

$$y_t^e = \hat{y}_t, \; y_t = d_0 + d_1(R_t - \overline{R}) + d_2 t + d_3 t^2 + u_{4t},$$

where:

A^d, p^e, y^e = desired area, expected price (deflated by a price index of competing crops), and expected yield,

A_t, y_t = area and yield, respectively,

$\hat{y}$ = predicted yield for $R_t = \overline{R}$,

σ_{pt} and σ_{yt} = standard deviations of price and yield in last three periods,

M_t = malaria death rate,

$R_t, \overline{R}$ = rainfall in t and average rainfall,

t = time trend.

Substituting the latter three equations in the first to eliminate all unobservable variables, the reduced form equation for area planted is of the type $A = Xb + w$, where the variables X are $p_{t-1}, A_{t-1}, A_{t-2}, \hat{y}_{t-1}, \hat{y}_{t-2}, \sigma_{pt}, \sigma_{p,t-1}, \sigma_{yt}, \sigma_{y,t-1}, M_t$, and M_{t-1}. Behrman used a maximum-likelihood procedure to estimate this reduced form equation directly with respect to the structural form parameters a_0 to a_6, b_0, δ, c_0, and γ. His results for maize plantation are reported in Table 4.3. Table 4.4 gives the short-run and long-run elasticities at the sample mean. As shown by the R^2s, this model explains a considerable portion of the variation in planted area in all eight provinces, but this is not due to price response coefficients which are in all cases statistically insignificant. By contrast, the expected yield is a strong determinant of area planted. So is price risk which has a negative effect on area planted as greater risk in the gross return of a crop leads farmers to plant more of other crops. Area adjustment and price expectation coefficients play minor roles and were set equal to one in most provinces.

4.4.2. Supply Response under Controlled Prices in Egypt

Cuddihy (1980) estimated a model of area response for the five major crops of Egyptian agriculture: long-season berseem (Egyptian clover), cotton, wheat, maize, and rice. For price, he used revenue per feddan (1 feddan = 1.035 acres) of each crop deflated by a real wage index. Using revenue per feddan is an interesting way of combining price and yield expectations when both are assumed to be exogenous. The choice of deflator, the real wage index, is based on the fact that labor cost is a large share of the variable costs of agricultural production in Egypt. Expectations are formed with a one-year lag, as in section 4.2.4. The expected yields y_i^e of the five crops are all included in the model, and no shifter is used.

The structural form of the model is thus:

Table 4.3. Estimated area response for maize, Thailand, 1937-63

Province	Constant	Expected price (a_1)	Expected yield (a_2)	Price risk (a_3)	Yield risk (a_4)	Malaria death rate (a_5)	Area adjustment (δ)	Price expectation (γ)	R^2
Nakhornsawan	−3.64 (2.6)	a	3.04 (6.2)	−0.26 (2.9)					0.81
	5.50 (4.2)			−0.43 (2.8)		−0.22 (2.4)			0.45
	0.37 (1.2)	1.70 (1.5)		−0.95 (2.0)					0.20
Sara–buri	−1.57 (2.2)		1.35 (2.6)	−0.07 (2.1)					0.92
Lopburi	−8.71 (6.6)	0.54 (0.3)	4.05 (10.4)	−0.12 (2.8)			0.69 (3.8)	1.27 (6.7)	0.96
Nakhornratsima	−5.02 (1.6)	0.97 (1.0)	3.51 (2.1)	−0.71 (2.1)			0.54 (2.3)		0.85
Phitsnulok	4.76 (3.7)		4.36 (7.6)	−0.15 (1.3)					0.82
Phicit	0.60 (0.4)		1.89 (4.8)	−0.40 (1.6)	−0.46 (1.1)				0.75
	7.42 (5.7)			−0.22 (0.7)	−0.46 (1.0)	−0.40 (4.2)			0.70
Phetchabun	9.99 (1.9)	6.70 (1.5)	3.94 (2.8)				0.32 (1.2)		0.73
Sukhothai	11.0 (6.1)		5.58 (8.1)	−0.28 (2.0)	−0.12 (1.8)				0.89
	3.8 (5.2)			−0.55 (2.6)	−0.20 (1.3)	−0.17 (2.1)			0.39

Source: Behrman, 1968, pp. 322–23.

t-statistics in parentheses.

[a]Corresponding variable was not used.

Table 4.4. Area response elasticities for maize, Thailand, 1937-63

Province	Short-run elasticities of area planted with respect to					Long-run elasticities of area planted with respect to				
	Price	Yield	Price risk	Yield risk	Malaria death rate	Price	Yield	Price risk	Yield risk	Malaria death rate
Nakhornsawan	1.92	4.88	−1.19 to −2.09	a	−0.85	1.92	4.88	−1.19 to 2.09		−0.85
Sara-buri		2.24	−0.34				3.96	0.62		
Lopburi	1.58	4.71	−0.30			1.81	6.83	−0.44		
Nakhornratsima	0.27	1.36	−0.21			0.41	2.52	−0.40		
Phitsnulok		2.44	−0.22				2.44	−0.22		
Phichit		1.41	−0.16 to −0.28	−0.35	−12.27		1.41	−0.16 to −0.28	−0.35	−12.27
Phetchabun	4.47	3.68				14.17	11.68			
Sukhothai		7.73	−0.36 to −0.70	−0.15 to −0.26	−0.22		7.73	−0.36 to −0.70	−0.15 to −0.26	−0.22

Source: Behrman, 1968, p. 325.
[a]Corresponding variable was not used.

$$A_t^d = \alpha_1 + \sum_i^5 \alpha_{2i} p_{it}^e + \sum_i^5 \alpha_{3i} y_{it}^e + u_t,$$

$$A_t - A_{t-1} = \delta\left(A_t^d - A_t\right) + v_t,$$

$$p_{it}^e = p_{i,t-1}, \quad \text{i.e., } \gamma = 1 \quad \text{(administered prices)},$$

$$y_{it}^e = y_{i,t-1}, \quad \text{(naive expectations)}.$$

The reduced form of the model is written as:

$$A_t = \pi_1 + \sum_{i=1}^5 \pi_{2i} p_{i,t-1} + \pi_3 A_{t-1} + \sum_{i=1}^5 \pi_{5i} y_{i,t-1} + (\delta u_t + v_t),$$

where:

$$\pi_1 = \alpha_1 \delta,$$

$$\pi_2 = \alpha_2 \delta, \text{ short-run elasticity of supply response,}$$

$$\pi_3 = 1 - \delta,$$

$$\pi_5 = \alpha_3 \delta,$$

$\alpha_2 = \pi_2 /(1 - \pi_3)$, long-run elasticity of supply response.

The data set has 26 annual observations, from 1950 to 1975.

The estimation results are shown in Table 4.5. Table 4.6 presents the supply elasticities. About one-third of the estimated coefficients are significantly different from zero at the 5% level, and the R^2s indicate that a large part of observed variation in the cultivated areas is explained by the model. An interesting aspect of Cuddihy's model is that unlike most other studies, where crops are considered in isolation, area responses of the main crops are estimated together so that the interactions among them can be examined. However, his results have several problems, probably reflecting the fact that resource allocation in Egyptian agriculture has

Table 4.5. Estimated area response for crops, Egypt, 1950–1975

Crop (feddan)	Form of equation	Constant	Estimation of coefficients of area planted with respect to revenues (in LE/feddan)					Area adjustment coefficient	R^2
			Wheat	Rice	Maize	Cotton	Long berseem		
Wheat	Linear	1172 (3.3)	25.8 (3.4)	−7.2 (−1.3)	−9.6 (−1.1)	1.1 (0.4)	−6.3 (−2.0)	0.89 (0.5)	0.72
Rice	Linear	11.7 (0.3)	−11.7 (−0.9)	7.5 (1.0)	6.2 (0.5)	0.7 (0.2)	5.0 (0.9)	0.30 (2.9)	0.78
Maize	Linear	1549 (6.5)	29.1 (4.9)	a	−18.0 (−3.6)	4.8 (2.3)		1.24 (1.4)	0.82
Cotton	Linear	1409 (2.8)		3.6 (0.7)		−2.7 (−0.7)	−9.5 (−1.9)	0.69 (1.5)	0.34
Long berseem	Loglinear	1.92 (2.5)	0.05 (0.5)		−0.11 (−1.0)	−0.25 (−2.3)	−0.02 (−0.3)	0.10 (7.6)	0.96

Source: Cuddihy, 1980.
t-statistics in parentheses.
aCorresponding variable was not used.

been highly intervened by government, leaving to revenues a relatively secondary role. The presence of some negative own-revenue effects does not make economic sense. Also, some revenue terms have been arbitrarily omitted in the equations for maize, cotton, and berseem. Finally, the cross-revenue effects are not always consistent. For example, in the estimate of the equation for wheat, one finds that maize is its competitor, while the maize equation indicates that wheat is a complement.

4.4.3. Other Supply Response Studies

The adaptive expectations model has been applied to a number of specialized supply response models such as beef and tree crops. For beef, because animals are both a capital good and a product, structural models predict that the short-run supply response to an increase in the price of cattle should be negative, while the long-run should be positive (Jarvis, 1974). This is, however, not a strong conclusion and slight changes in specification of the model can lead to positive short-run supply response (Paarsch, 1985). Empirically, both negative and positive short-run supply responses have been obtained, and most frequently nonsignificant coefficients (Nelson and Spreen, 1978; Antonovitz and Green, 1990).

Structural models for perennial crops have stressed the determinants of new investment in tree plantations. In a model for Brazilian coffee, Wickens and Greenfield (1973) developed a three-equation structural model with: (1) a vintage production function where potential produc-

Table 4.6. Area response elasticities, Egypt crops

| | Elasticities of area planted with respect to revenues | | | | | | | | | |
| Crop | Short–run | | | | | Long–run | | | | |
	Wheat	Rice	Maize	Cotton	Berseem	Wheat	Rice	Maize	Cotton	Berseem
Wheat	0.41	−0.16	−0.16	0.04	−0.12	0.46	−0.18	−0.16	0.04	−0.13
Rice	−0.32	0.28	0.15	0.04	0.14	1.05	0.91	0.52	0.15	0.47
Maize	0.41	[a]	−0.29	0.13		0.33		−0.19	0.13	
Cotton		0.06		−0.09	−0.13	0.95	0.09		−0.12	−0.19
Berseem	0.05		−0.10	−0.24	−0.02	0.05		−0.11	−0.25	−0.02

Source: Cuddihy, 1980.
[a]Corresponding variable was not used.

tion is a function of the number of trees surviving and technological change, (2) an investment function where the number of trees planted is a function of lagged planting and current price, and (3) a supply response equation where the proportion of potential production that is harvested is explained by lagged prices. The reduced form supply function derived from this structural model is estimated and shows the importance of longer lags in the supply of tree crops compared to field crops. For the analysis of rubber supply in Sri Lanka, Hartley, Nerlove, and Peters (1987) focused on the uprooting and replanting of trees as opposed to new plantings as in the previous study. They specify a three-equation model with replanting, production, and new plantings. Their results show a strong positive long-run response of replantings to variations in the expected price and generally insignificant response to current price.

4.5. Producer Response to Lagged Prices and the Dynamics of Markets

The empirical analysis of supply using partial adjustment and adaptive expectations has had fundamental implications for the making of agricultural policy. It has shown that, together with fixed factors and other shifters of supply, prices do indeed matter. LDC government interventions that suppress prices through marketing boards and cheap food policies will tend to induce stagnation; MDC government interventions that support farm incomes through price support will tend to create costly farm surpluses.

The key implication of these models is that existence of a lag between decisions on inputs and the output level achieved requires that predictions be made about product prices in order to make input decisions. Product price predictions will consequently affect the level of output and future prices. If producers' price foresight is imperfect, price expectations can induce market dynamics such as price oscillations and instability in prices and production.

In a simple model where $\gamma = 1$ (static expectations where the expected price only depends on current prices) and there is no partial adjustment $(\delta = 1)$, the market equilibrium will be determined as follows:

Supply response: $\quad S_t = Ap_{t-1} + B \quad$ (sellers respond to past prices)

Consumer demand: $\quad D_t = ap_t + b \quad$ (there is zero excess demand at the price offered by suppliers)

Market equilibrium: $\quad S_t = D_t \quad$ (nontradable commodity).

This is the famous cobweb model developed by Ezekiel (1938) and Waugh (1964), which they used to explain the unstable performance of many agricultural commodity markets. The solution to this model, assuming that $p = p_0$ at $t = 0$, is (Henderson and Quandt, 1971):

$$p_t = \left(p_0 - \frac{B-b}{a-A} \right) \left(\frac{A}{a} \right)^t + \frac{B-b}{a-A},$$

which gives the time path of p_t as a function of t. A dynamic market equilibrium is achieved if prices stabilize, i.e., if $p_t = p_{t-1}$ as $t \to \infty$. This requires that $p_t = (B-b)/(a-A)$. For this to occur, the first right-hand term in the p_t equation must tend to zero as $t \to \infty$, which will be the case if $A/a =$ slope S / slope $D < 1$, assuming normal slopes for supply and demand, i.e., $A > 0$ and $a < 0$. Thus:

if $A/a < 1$, the market oscillates toward a stable equilibrium price and quantity;

if $A/a > 1$, the market oscillates toward unstable and explosive equilibrium.

With foresight based on lagged prices, the cobweb model derives from the adaptive expectations hypothesis. It thus implies rational behavior from the standpoint of individual producers if this is the type of information which they have about the future. However, the cobweb model implies collective producer irrationality: all together, farmers always produce more or less than the social optimum given by equilibrium between supply and demand (Wright, 1994). If competitive producers knew the underlying supply and demand model and had rational expectations, actual output would be independent of previous prices as opposed to specification in the Nerlove and cobweb models. If government were better informed than producers and knew the underlying supply and demand which producers do not, this would justify government intervention which could stabilize the market by setting forward prices at the market clearing level, thereby helping producers to remedy their own imperfect knowledge. Indeed, this is the policy implication which Waugh had derived from his analysis of the cobweb model. But farmers themselves could acquire this information and develop rational expectations behavior. This is the formulation which we analyze in the following section.

In recent years, the adaptive expectations model has declined in popularity in favor of rational expectations formulations. This is because the latter are far more intellectually appealing, even though they have, to this date, not proved econometrically superior.

The fact remains that the cobweb model explains commonly observed market behavior. Williams and Wright (1991) show that this is not necessarily incompatible with rational expectations behavior by producers. In a model where there is rational expectations by producers and there are competitive storage activities, the result would be a cobweb-like market behavior if the market is subject to exogenous independent shocks. In this case, the forward price is a function of current price: a large current harvest will lead to expectations of lower future prices through the accumulation of stocks. This will decrease planned output. The result is negative serial correlation among realized production levels in successive years, as predicted by the cobweb model when there are positive stocks. Storage induces a partial linkage between current prices and expected prices, thus rationalizing the logic of the adaptive expectations model and the possibility of cobweb-like behavior of farm commodity markets.

4.6. Alternative Expectations Models

Given the generally unsatisfactory performance of Nerlovian models, other specifications of the formation of product price expectations have been sought. Alternative approaches basically fall into three categories: those that rely on econometric techniques to identify a lag structure from past prices; those that make use of additional information available to producers about future prices; and the rational expectations approach that relies on economic theory to specify the mechanism of future price formation.

Econometric techniques specify a forecasting equation for p_t^e as an autoregressive moving-average (ARMA) process of order (p, q) in past prices as follows:

$$(5) \quad p_t^e = \sum_{i=1}^{p} \alpha_i p_{t-i} + \sum_{j=1}^{q} \gamma_j \varepsilon_{t-j},$$

where ε is white noise. Substituting in (1), the parameters of the ARMA model (5) are estimated jointly with the other structural parameters using time series estimation techniques (see Judge et al., 1988; for an application, see Antonovitz and Green, 1990).

Additional information on prices typically combines futures prices (p^f), government price support programs (p^s), and cash prices (p) in a weighted average. In (1), expected price becomes:

$$p_t^e = \beta_1 p_t^f + \beta_2 p_t^s + \beta_3 p_{t-1} \text{ with } \sum \beta_i = 1.$$

Estimation of these weights allows to determine the relative importance of futures, support, and cash prices in the formation of farmers' expectations. Chavas, Pope, and Kao (1983) find that price support programs explain much of the supply response for corn in the United States, while Gardner (1976) shows that futures prices are a good substitute for cash price lagged one year. However, futures prices do not fully capture government decisions, indicating that support price needs to be added separately.

Anderson, Dillon, and Hardaker (1977) suggest using a conditional price expectations model where the expected price is derived from a joint distribution of market and support prices. The mean support price, $E(p^s)$, the standard deviations of market and support prices, σ_p and σ_{p^s}, and the correlation between market and support price, corr(p, p^s), are calculated each year on the basis of observed data for the previous five years. If p and p^s are jointly normally distributed, the mean of the conditional distribution of market prices for a given announced support price p_t^{s*} is:

$$p_t^e = E\left(p \mid p^s = p^{s*}\right) = E(p) + \text{corr}(p, p^s)\frac{\sigma_p}{\sigma_{p^s}}\left(p_t^{s*} - E(p^s)\right).$$

The expected market price $E(p)$ is approximated by either the lagged cash price p_{t-1} or the futures price p_t^f (see Shideed and White, 1989).

Empirical tests of the relative predictive power of these alternative specifications of price expectation show that not one model dominates the rest. To the contrary, since different market participants seem to use different ways of forming expectations, expectations are heterogenous and the best approach consists of combining these different approaches (Shonkwiler and Hinckley, 1985; Antonovitz and Roe, 1986).

The rational expectations formulation, originally developed by Muth (1961), is the third option.

4.7. The Rational Expectations Approach*

4.7.1. General Model

As seen above, the Nerlovian specification of adaptive expectations is based on the history of past prices with weights declining geometrically over time. The expectation formation model is thus:

$$p_t^e = f(\text{past prices}) = \gamma \sum_{i=1}^{\infty} (1-\gamma)^{i-1} p_{t-i}.$$

This approach has been criticized on the following grounds:

a. Price weights are ad hoc as opposed to being the explicit outcome of an optimization process.

b. Price predictions underuse the information available to the decision maker: (1) on the structural process of price formation, for which one should use knowledge of both supply and demand or whatever more complete structural model is the best available predictor; (2) on available forecasts about the exogenous variables that affect this process; and (3) on anticipated policy changes that affect price formation, a process that corresponds to the "Lucas critique" (Lucas, 1976).

Rational expectations, by contrast, use the model's prediction of the endogenous variables, including price, to form expectations. Instead of being based on past prices, forecasts are thus based on knowledge of a structural model of price determination, exogenous forecasts of the independent variables in this model, and expectations about the policy instruments in the model (Fisher, 1982; Eckstein, 1984). The expectations formation model is thus:

$$p_t^e = f(\text{model predictions} \mid \text{exogenous variable forecasts and expected policy changes}).$$

The general model we want to estimate is:

(6) $By_t + Ay_t^e + \Gamma_1 x_{1t} + \Gamma_2 x_{2t} = u_t,$

where y_t is a vector of observable endogenous variables, y_t^e is a vector of unobservable expected variables, x_{1t} is a vector of uncertain exogenous variables (including policy variables), and x_{2t} is a vector of certain exogenous variables. In this model, structural parameters will be identified if the number of exogenous variables is greater than the number of expected variables (Wallis, 1980). The rational expectations hypothesis consists in postulating that expectations y_t^e are given by the model predictions y_t^e at the time when the predictions are formed, given information x_{1t}^* on the exogenous and policy variables x_{1t} at that time:

$$y_t^e = E(y_t \mid \text{information on } x_{1t}^* \text{ and } x_{2t}).$$

The model can be rewritten as:

$$By_t + Ay_t^e = -\Gamma_1 x_{1t} - \Gamma_2 x_{2t} + u_t,$$

or, taking expected values at the time when the prediction is made,

$$E(By_t + Ay_t^e) = (B + A) y_t^e = -\Gamma_1 x_{1t}^* - \Gamma_2 x_{2t}.$$

Solving for y_t^e gives:

$$y_t^e = -(B + A)^{-1}(\Gamma_1 x_{1t}^* + \Gamma_2 x_{2t}).$$

Substituting in (6),

$$By_t = -A(B + A)^{-1}\Gamma_1 x_{1t}^* - \Gamma_1 x_{1t} - A(B + A)^{-1}\Gamma_2 x_{2t} - \Gamma_2 x_{2t} + u_t,$$

where all variables are either directly observed (x_{1t}, x_{2t}) or predicted (x_{1t}^*) by, for example, an ARMA of the type $x_{1t}^* = \phi x_{1,t-1} + \varepsilon_t$, $E(\varepsilon_t) = 0$, where ϕ is known.

4.7.2. Estimating Supply Response

Like in the cobweb model, the supply and demand equations for an agricultural commodity are (omitting the subscript t, which is common to all variables):

Supply : $q = \gamma_{13} + \alpha_{12} p^e + \gamma_{11} x + u_1,$

Demand : $p = \gamma_{23} - \beta_{21} q + \gamma_{22} y + u_2,$

where x includes either input prices (with a negative sign) or policy variables such as a fertilizer quota (with a positive sign), and y is income.

Under the rational expectations hypothesis, the expected price is the model equilibrium price at the time for which the prediction is made:

$$q^e = \gamma_{13} + \alpha_{12}p^e + \gamma_{11}x^*,$$
$$\beta_{21}q^e = \gamma_{23} - p^e + \gamma_{22}y^*,$$

where x^* and y^* are predicted exogenous variables as seen at the time for which the price expectation is made.

We solve this system by multiplying the supply function by $-\beta_{21}$ and adding the two equations:

$$0 = (\gamma_{23} - \beta_{21}\gamma_{13}) - (1 + \beta_{21}\alpha_{12})p^e - \beta_{21}\gamma_{11}x^* + \gamma_{22}y^*,$$

or $$p^e = \frac{1}{1 + \beta_{21}\alpha_{12}}\left[(\gamma_{23} - \beta_{21}\gamma_{13}) - \beta_{21}\gamma_{11}x^* + \gamma_{22}y^*\right].$$

Thus, if the input price x^* is expected to fall (or the fertilizer quota to rise), the expected commodity price p^e falls as supply is expected to rise. Replacing in the supply function, we obtain:

$$q = \left[\gamma_{13} + \frac{\alpha_{12}(\gamma_{23} - \beta_{21}\gamma_{13})}{1 + \beta_{21}\alpha_{12}}\right] - \frac{\alpha_{12}\beta_{21}\gamma_{11}}{1 + \beta_{21}\alpha_{12}}x^* + \frac{\alpha_{12}\gamma_{22}}{1 + \beta_{21}\alpha_{12}}y^* + \gamma_{11}x + u_1,$$

or $$q = \pi_0 + \pi_1 x^* + \pi_2 y^* + \gamma_{11}x + u_1,$$

where all variables are either observed or predicted exogenously.

The policy variable x thus has both a direct effect γ_{11} and an indirect effect, $-(\alpha_{12}\beta_{21}\gamma_{11})/(1 + \beta_{21}\alpha_{12}) < \gamma_{11}$, which is of opposite sign but smaller than the direct effect.

The exogenous variables are predicted as:

$$x^* = \phi_1 x_{t-1} + \phi_2 x_{t-2},$$
$$y^* = \phi_3 y_{t-1},$$

where the ϕ's have been estimated separately. The system of equations to be estimated is:

Supply : $q = \pi_0 + \pi_1\phi_1 x_{t-1} + \pi_1\phi_2 x_{t-2} + \pi_2\phi_3 y_{t-1} + \gamma_{11}x + u_1,$

Demand: $p = \gamma_{23} - \beta_{21}q + \gamma_{22}y + u_2.$

The supply equation contains lagged values of the exogenous variables in the demand equation. Note, however, that, in contrast to the Nerlovian adaptive expectations model, it does not contain lagged values of the endogenous variable. Nonlinear cross-equation restrictions on the supply equation parameters should be imposed in order to allow identification of the structural parameters of the supply function, particularly identification of the price response coefficient α_{12}.

4.7.3. Criticisms of the Rational Expectations Approach

While rational expectations offers a more logical approach to the formation of expectations than adaptive expectations, it suffers from both conceptual and empirical drawbacks. Theoretically, the approach tends to exaggerate the rationality of the decision-making process through which expectations are formed. Specifically:

a. Agents may not use all the information that could be available to them because acquiring it is costly. They also may appear not to use all the information available to them because change is costly and may exceed the resulting gains.

b. Agents may not use this information as "intelligently" as the model; that is, they do not know the model, or they have an incomplete understanding of the mechanisms of price determination. They may, however, be buying these predictions from economists like us or from specialized forecasting services that presumably have complete information and are using the model for predictive purposes.

c. Agents may not know how to forecast the exogenous variables and policy changes.

Empirically, rational expectations has, to this date, not proved its superiority to more ad hoc specifications of expectations formation such as the Nerlovian adaptive adaptations (Lovell, 1986). However, the approach suggests a rich research agenda to transcend the informality of adaptive expectations. To make progress in specifying the mechanism of expectations formation, what is needed is a more accurate understanding of how agents actually form their opinions about expected prices based on who they are, how they think about the future, their cost of accessing information, the quality of that information, and their expected benefits from using it.

Exercise 4
Supply Response for Groundnuts in Sub-Saharan Africa

In this exercise (file 4SUPPLY) you will estimate groundnut acreage responses to groundnut and millet producer prices using a data set based on the agricultural situation in Senegal from 1960 to 1988. Groundnuts are extremely important to the Senegalese economy, representing the major source of cash income for farmers and the principal source of export earnings for the country as a whole. A government-controlled marketing board determines the producer price for the crop and extracts the difference between the world price and the producer price as government revenue. Traditionally, because world prices have been higher than producer prices, the export surplus has been a major source of government revenue. However, the dramatic decline in world groundnut prices in the late 1980s forced the government to become a net subsidizer of the sector. The impact on farmers from the removal of this subsidy became a central issue in the policy debate over whether to continue government control of the sector or to let the private market determine producer prices.

Braverman and Hammer, in a study examined later, construct a multimarket model which predicts the effects of groundnut pricing policies on groundnut production and other crop prices and quantities, as well as on consumer and producer welfare. The price elasticities estimated in this exercise form the basis for such a model. The exercise will estimate long- and short-run elasticities.

Model specifications are based on the price determination mechanisms observed in Senegal. Groundnut prices are set by the marketing board and known before production. Cereal prices de facto fluctuate with supply and demand and are not known to the farmer at the time of planting. Therefore, the effect of cereal prices on groundnut acreage is modeled as a lagged expectation of previous years' prices. Rainfall is also not known before planting and is modeled as an expectation based on rainfall in the previous years. Two alternative lagged-expectation functions are compared for this variable in the exercise. We will also look at the effect on production of the structural adjustment policies implemented since 1979.

To improve the significance of the results, some marginal modifications have been made on the original data.

1. Data Preparation

The first step in data preparation is to properly deflate prices and create lagged expectation variables for cereal prices and rainfall. The basic data for the exercise are contained in Table 4E.1. Column A contains the year, column B the area planted in that year, columns C and D the prices, in current CFA (Communauté Financière Africaine) francs, of groundnuts and millet per metric ton, column E rainfall in millimeters, and column F the consumer price index. The groundnut and millet prices in columns G and H are deflated by the consumer price index (CPI) to 1961 CFA.

Table 4E.2 is reserved for data preparation. As all the models tested in this model use logarithm of variables, column B contains the logarithm of area. Column C contains a one-year lag of the acreage variable in column B. As shown in Chapter 4, a one-year lag area variable is used in the specification of most Nerlovian supply response models and will be included in all the model specifications tested in this exercise. Because the price of groundnuts is known to farmers at planting, no expectation operator is needed. Thus, column D contains the current year real price of groundnuts, expressed in logarithm. However, because the price of millet after harvest is not known at planting, expectations must be formulated. As seen in the theoretical model studied in the chapter, this leads to the use of the one-year lagged variable in the reduced-form model, as reported in column E. Similarly, future rainfall levels are not known at planting time. Two alternative specifications of expectations are formulated and tested in this exercise: a one-year lag expectations operator, $R_t^e = R_{t-1}$ and a previous three-year mean lag expectations operator, $R_t^e = (R_{t-1} + R_{t-2} + R_{t-2})/3 \equiv R_{t-(1-3)}$. These variables are shown in logarithmic value in columns F and G, respectively. The final variable to be used in the models is a dummy variable for the structural adjustment. Senegal initiated an agricultural sector adjustment program in 1979. This variable will be used to test the hypothesis that the program had a significant impact on the response of acreage to price.

2. Graph of Observations

Before doing any statistical analysis, you should make a graph of the evolution of groundnut acreage and of some of the potential explanatory variables, like price, over time. This gives a good support from the description of the phenomenon to analyze, and often suggests variables to consider. Make sure that you label the variables and title the graphs. Save your acreage graphs as "Area."

	A	B	C	D	E	F	G	H
1	Table 4E.1. Supply response for groundnuts in Sub-Saharan Africa: Base data							
2								
3								
4								
5								
6		Area in	Current prices			Consumer	Real prices	
7		groundnuts	Groundnuts	Millet	Rainfall	price	Groundnuts	Millet
8	Year	(1,000 ha)	(CFA/mt)		(mm)	index	(1961 CFA/mt)	
9								
10	1960	1323	20500	22000	817	0.95	21652	23236
11	1961	1230	22000	22500	685	1.00	22000	22500
12	1962	1233	21500	23000	609	1.07	20101	21503
13	1963	1185	21500	25000	699	1.14	18873	21945
14	1964	1055	20600	25000	830	1.21	17039	20678
15	1965	1016	20600	25800	660	1.26	16401	20541
16	1966	1017	21000	22000	897	1.28	16355	17134
17	1967	1064	18000	23000	886	1.32	13678	17477
18	1968	1091	18000	23000	457	1.31	13730	17544
19	1969	1097	21200	24000	841	1.37	15520	17570
20	1970	1051	23100	23000	496	1.42	16256	16186
21	1971	1060	23100	29000	745	1.51	15288	19193
22	1972	1087	25500	22000	428	1.60	15977	13784
23	1973	1280	41500	37000	461	1.69	24513	21855
24	1974	1020	41500	35000	556	1.95	21282	17949
25	1975	1201	41500	42000	801	2.37	17533	17744
26	1976	1175	41500	55000	573	2.51	16508	21877
27	1977	1079	41500	65000	437	2.67	15520	24308
28	1978	970	41500	45000	637	2.87	14445	15663
29	1979	995	41500	45000	666	3.11	13344	14469
30	1980	1097	50000	45000	418	3.52	14209	12788
31	1981	1216	60000	55000	573	3.73	16100	14759
32	1982	1148	60000	75000	553	4.37	13730	17162
33	1983	925	60000	85000	337	4.88	12303	17429
34	1984	873	75000	95000	492	5.46	13741	17406
35	1985	750	75000	100000	546	6.16	12175	16234
36	1986	789	90000	100000	735	6.54	13761	15291
37	1987	823	90000	110000	809	6.82	13191	16122
38	1988	787	70000	115000	500	6.54	10700	17579
39								
40								

Table 4E.2. Supply response for groundnuts in Sub-Saharan Africa: Data preparation and simulation results

	A	B	C	D	E	F	G	H	I	J	K	L	M	N	O	P
				Prices (1961 CFA)					Estimated area in groundnuts		High price of	Estimated area in groundnuts under alternative policy				
												High price		High price	High price	High price
43		Area in				Rainfall	Previous three year mean rainfall	Agricultural structural adjustment			groundnuts	High price with	No structural	without	with	without
44		groundnuts	Lag area in	Groundnuts	Last year millet	last year			Model 1	Best model ?	new Pgt	struct. adj.	adjustment	struct. adj.	struct. adj.	struct. adj.
45	Year	(1,000 ha)	groundnuts					1979 - 88	(1,000 ha)	(1,000 ha)	(CFA/mt)	(1,000 ha)	(1,000 ha)	(1,000 ha)	(1,000 ha)	(percent change)
46		$\ln A_t$	$\ln A_{t-1}$	$\ln P_{gt}$	$\ln P_{m,t-1}$	$\ln R_{t-1}$	$\ln R_{t-(1-3)}$	DUM								
47	t															
48	1960	7.19		9.98					1323							
49	1961															
50	1962															
51	1963															
52	1964															
53	1965															
54	1966															
55	1967															
56	1968															
57	1969															
58	1970															
59	1971															
60	1972															
61	1973															
62	1974															
63	1975															
64	1976															
65	1977															
66	1978															
67	1979															
68	1980															
69	1981															
70	1982															
71	1983															
72	1984															
73	1985															
74	1986															
75	1987															
76	1988															

Working space for regression

	A	B	C	D	E	F
82	Year	Dependent variable		Independent variables		
83		variable				
84	t	$\ln A_t$	$\ln A_{t-1}$	$\ln P_{gt}$	$\ln P_{m,t-1}$	$\ln R_{t-1}$
85	1960	7.19		9.98		

Table 4E.3. Supply response for groundnuts in Sub-Saharan Africa: Regression results

Dependent variable	Constant	Lag area $\ln A_{t-1}$	Prices (1961 CFA) Current groundnut $\ln P_{gt}$	Prices (1961 CFA) Millet $\ln P_{m,t-1}$	Rainfall last year $\ln R_{t-1}$	Rainfall Three-year average $\ln R_{t-(1-3)}$	Structural adjustment 1979-88 Additive DUM	Structural adjustment 1979-88 On price DUM*$\ln P_{gt}$	R^2 [adjusted]	Elasticities (at mean values) w.r.t. Groundnut price Short	Groundnut price Long	Millet price Short	Millet price Long
1. lnAt	1.62 (1.8)	0.676 (5.4)	.349 (3.9)	-.341 (-3.9)	.09 (1.8)				0.82 [.79]				
2. lnAt													
3. lnAt													
4. lnAt													
5. lnAt													

Note: t-statistics in parentheses; elasticities with structural adjustment in curly brackets; adjusted R2 = 1-[T/(T-K)](1-R2), where T is the number of observations and K the number of exogenous variables.

Describe the evolution of acreage and price. What does it suggest in terms of the role of price incentive? In which periods does it seem that the acreage decision may have been affected by something other than the groundnut price?

3. Testing Supply Response Models

This portion of the exercise tests several alternative specifications of the Nerlovian supply response model using ordinary least squares regression techniques. The first specification is:

$$(1) \quad \ln A_t = b_0 + b_1 \ln A_{t-1} + b_2 \ln p_{gt} + b_3 \ln p_{m,t-1} + b_4 \ln R_{t-1},$$

where:

A_t = area of groundnuts planted in time t,
p_{gt} = price of groundnuts, in 1961 CFA, at time t,
$p_{m,t-1}$ = price of millet, in 1961 CFA, at time $t-1$,
R_{t-1} = rainfall at time $t-1$.

To perform the regression with Lotus, all exogenous variables need to be placed next to each other. It is thus necessary to create a special working space in which the appropriate data will be placed for each regression. This is done in row 80 and below. The data needed to estimate this model are arranged with the dependent variable ($\ln A_t$) in column B and the independent variables in columns C–F. To copy the data from Table 4E.2 to this space, use the option /Range Value, then select the range that you want to copy, A47–F76, and the position this should be copied to, A84. This option /RV copies the values themselves, as opposed to /C, which would copy the formulae. To use the Lotus regression options, press /Data Regression. A number of options are presented in the box on the right. The Y-range option asks for the range of the dependent variable to be included in the regression. (Note that data from 1960 cannot be included since the lagged variables do not have observations for that year.) The range should be set to B86–B113. The X-range option asks for the range of the independent variables to be included in the regression and should be set to C86–F113.

Output range tells Lotus that the output of the regression should be placed to the right and below A117, which is an empty space and does not interfere with the calculations in the rest of the worksheet.

The option Intercept allows regressions to be run without an intercept if necessary. Since we want an intercept (b_0) in the model, set the option to compute.

You are now ready to execute the regression. To do so choose Go. The estimated coefficients, their standard deviations, and important measures of regression performance immediately appear in the range A117–F125. Scroll down to see these results. To see which coefficients correspond to which variables, simply copy the range C84–F84 onto the range C123–F123.

Interpreting the Results

The goodness of fit of a regression is assessed by its coefficient of determination, R^2. The estimated coefficient of a particular variable is significantly different from zero if it is more than 1.7 times the standard deviation away from zero. To evaluate the significance levels of estimated coefficients, go to cell C126 and enter +C124/C125. This gives the *t*-statistic. Copy the formula onto the range D126–F126. Note that for the first specification of the model, R_{t-1}, p_{gt}, and $p_{m,t-1}$ are significant. Examine the results: aside form statistical significance, do the own- and cross-price responses conform with results expected from economic theory?

Table 4E.3 in Q41-AD62 is used to record the regression results. The coefficient estimates and *t*-statistics obtained above are reported in the first two rows. Compare your results with those in the table and make sure there are no mistakes. In the rest of the exercise, your task is to estimate alternative specifications of the Nerlovian supply response model and record them in Table 4E.3.

You can also visualize the goodness of your estimation by plotting on the same graph both the observed and estimated areas. For this, prepare in Table 4E.2 a column of estimated values. In cell I48, for the year 1960, you enter the observed value (+B10). Then you recursively compute the estimated value with the equation just estimated. In cell I49 you enter the formula:

$$+@\exp(1.62+0.68*@\ln(I48)+0.349*D49-0.341*E49+0.091*F49)$$

[the exponential function is @exp()] and copy down the formula for all the years.

Select your graph "Area" by choosing /Graph Name Use, then add the series of the estimated values (I49–I76) for acreage in the B option. Change the title of the graph to "Observed and Estimated Areas for Groundnuts." Add a legend and save this new graph.

You are now ready to view the graph. Take a minute to admire your work. How well is the model replicating the observation? Which years are not predicted correctly? Why?

Alternative Specifications of the Nerlovian Supply Response Model

Estimating alternative specifications of the model entails changing the dependent variables included in the model. Try alternative specifications. Use, for example, $\ln R_{t-(1-3)}$ the logarithm of the average rainfall in times $t-1$, $t-2$, and $t-3$, instead of $\ln R_{t-1}$:

(2) $\ln A_t = b_0 + b_1 \ln A_{t-1} + b_2 \ln p_{gt} + b_3 \ln p_{m,t-1} + b_4 \ln R_{t-(1-3)}$.

You should try also using the dummy variable for the adjustment period, either as an additive variable,

(3) $\ln A_t = b_0 + b_1 \ln A_{t-1} + b_2 \ln p_{gt} + b_3 \ln p_{m,t-1} + b_4 \ln R_{t-1} + b_5 DUM_t$,

or as a multiplicative variable that modifies the price responsiveness :

$$\ln A_t = b_0 + b_1 \ln A_{t-1} + (b_2 + b_5 DUM_t) \ln p_{gt} + b_3 \ln p_{m,t-1} + b_4 \ln R_{t-1}.$$

To estimate this last case, create a new variable $S_t = DUM_t \times \ln p_{gt}$, and use the equation:

(4) $\ln A_t = b_0 + b_1 \ln A_{t-1} + b_2 \ln p_{gt} + b_3 \ln p_{m,t-1} + b_4 \ln R_{t-1} + b_5 S_t$.

You can also try using both dummies simultaneously:

(5) $\ln A_t = b_0 + b_1 \ln A_{t-1} + b_2 \ln p_{gt} + b_3 \ln p_{m,t-1} + b_4 \ln R_{t-1} + b_5 DUM_t + b_6 S_t$.

To estimate model specification (2), simply copy the variable $\ln R_{t-(1-3)}$ from (G47–G76) into the working space now occupied by $\ln R_{t-1}$. The first year that data are available for these variables is 1963, so 1960–62 should not be included in the dependent or independent variable ranges for this regression. The independent variable range should now be set to C88–F113. Place the regression output below the output for the first regression and record your results in Table 4E.3. Follow a similar procedure for the remaining specifications. Experiment with different combinations of the variables, in search of the best model.

Compare the economic results (the parameter values) and the statistical qualities of the alternative specifications. Choose the best model. Discuss the sign of the parameters, that of the structural adjustment variable in particular. What are the elements of a structural adjustment policy that should act negatively on groundnut production, and what are those that should act positively? Which ones seem to dominate in this case?

4. Policy Uses of Estimates

The estimated parameters are of value only in their usefulness for policy analysis. In this final section of the exercise, you will use the results recorded in Table 4E.3 to calculate short- and long-run elasticities as well as impacts from 15% increases in groundnuts and millet prices.

Calculating Elasticity Estimates

The convenient feature of the log-linear specification is that the elasticity estimates do not vary with the point at which they are evaluated, and the short-run elasticities are simply equal to the parameter estimates of the price variables: $E^{sr}_{groundnuts} = b_2$ and $E^{sr}_{millet} = b_3$. The long-run elasticities are calculated as follows:

$$E_i^{lr} = \frac{E_i^{sr}}{1 - b_1}.$$

Calculate the short- and long-run elasticities for your models.

Calculating Impacts from Price Changes

Consider now only the model that best explains the groundnut acreage decision. Estimation of the impact of price changes on groundnuts production can be done by using the estimated model to predict acreage response under alternative scenarios of price changes. Consider, for example, the following model (model (5) above):

$$\ln A_t = b_0 + b_1 \ln A_{t-1} + b_2 \ln p_{gt} + b_3 \ln p_{m,t-1} + b_4 \ln R_{t-1} + b_5 DUM_t + b_6 S_t .$$

First, create a column of estimated area in J44–J76 as follows:

$$\hat{A}_t = \exp(b_0 + b_1 \ln \hat{A}_{t-1} + b_2 \ln p_{gt} + b_3 \ln p_{m,t-1} + b_4 \ln R_{t-1} + b_5 DUM_t + b_6 S_t),$$

which would serve as reference. In column K, create a new vector of real prices p^1_{gt} for groundnuts that incorporates a 15% increase in prices from 1961 to 1988. This represents a policy in which the price increase occurs in 1961 and from then on the change is maintained. Create the corresponding variable $\ln p^1_{gt}$ and then estimate a new vector of areas:

$$\hat{A}_t^1 = \exp(b_0 + b_1 \ln \hat{A}_{t-1} + b_2 \ln p_{gt}^1 + b_3 \ln p_{m,t-1} + b_4 \ln R_{t-1} + b_5 DUM_t + b_6 S_t).$$

The comparison of $\hat{A}_t^1$ and $\hat{A}_t$ gives you the impact of the price policy. You can compute the percentage changes (in column O), or view these on a graph. Comment.

Repeat the same procedure without the variables *DUM* and *S* in columns M and N, with percentage change in column P. This tells you what would have been the impact of the price policy in the absence of a structural adjustment program. Compare these two results. What can you infer from them? Does structural adjustment make supportive price policies more or less necessary than in normal times? Explain why.

References

Anderson, Jock, John Dillon, and Brian Hardaker. 1977. *Agricultural Decision Analysis.* Ames: The Iowa State University Press.

Antonovitz, Frances, and Richard Green. 1990. "Alternative Estimates of Fed Beef Supply Response to Risk." *American Journal of Agricultural Economics* 72:475-88.

Antonovitz, Frances, and Terry Roe. 1986. "A Theoretical and Empirical Approach to the Value of the Information in Risky Markets." *Review of Economics and Statistics* 68:105-14.

Askari, Hossein, and John Cummings. 1976. *Agricultural Supply Response: A Survey of the Econometric Evidence.* New York: Praeger.

Behrman, Jere. 1968. *Supply Response in Underdeveloped Agriculture: A Case Study of Four Major Annual Crops in Thailand. 1937–1963.* Amsterdam: North–Holland.

Chavas, Jean-Paul, Rulon Pope, and Robert Kao. 1983. "An Analysis of the Role of Futures Prices, Cash Prices, and Government Programs in Acreage Response." *Western Journal of Agricultural Economics* 8:27-33.

Cuddihy, William. 1980. *Agricultural Price Management in Egypt.* Staff Working Paper no. 388. Washington, D.C.: World Bank.

Debertin, David. 1986. *Agricultural Production Economics.* New York: Macmillan.

Eckstein, Zvi. 1984. "A Rational Expectations Model of Agricultural Supply." *Journal of Political Economy* 92:1–19.

Ezekiel, Mordecai. 1938. "The Cobweb Theorem." *Quarterly Journal of Economics* 52:431–443.

Fisher, Brian. 1982. "Rational Expectations in Agricultural Economics Research and Policy Analysis." *American Journal of Agricultural Economics* 64:260–65.

Gardner, Bruce. 1976. "Futures Prices in Supply Analysis." *American Journal of Agricultural Economics* 58:81-84.

Hartley, Michael, Marc Nerlove, and Kyle Peters. 1987. "An Analysis of Rubber Supply in Sri Lanka." *American Journal of Agricultural Economics* 69:755-61.

Heathfield, David, and Soren Wibe. 1987. *An Introduction to Cost and Production Functions.* Atlantic Highlands, N.J.: Humanities Press International.

Henderson, James, and Richard Quandt. 1971. *Microeconomic Theory: A Mathematical Approach.* New York: McGraw-Hill.

Jarvis, Lovell. 1974. "Cattle as Capital Goods and Ranchers as Portfolio Managers: An Application to the Argentine Cattle Sector." *Journal of Political Economy* 82:489-520.

Judge, George, Carter Hill, William Griffiths, Helmut Lütkepohl, and Tsoung-Chao Lee. 1988. *Introduction to the Theory and Practice of Econometrics.* New York: John Wiley & Sons.

Just, Richard. 1977. "Estimation of an Adaptive Expectations Model." *International Economic Review* 18:629-44.

Lovell, Michael. 1986. "Tests of the Rational Expectations Hypothesis." *American Economic Review* 76:110–24.

Lucas, Robert. 1976. "Economic Policy Evaluation: A Critique," In *The Phillips Curve and Labor Markets*, edited by K. Brunner and A. Meltzer. Amsterdam: North–Holland.

Mundlak, Yair. 1985. *The Aggregate Agricultural Supply Response.* Working Paper no. 8511. Rehovot, Israel: Center for Agricultural Economics Research.

Muth, John. 1961. "Rational Expectations and the Theory of Price Movements." *Econometrica* 29:315-35.

Nelson, Glenn, and Thomas Spreen. 1978. "Monthly Steer and Heifer Supply." *American Journal of Agricultural Economics* 60:117-25.

Nerlove, Marc. 1956. "Estimates of Supply of Selected Agricultural Commodities." *Journal of Farm Economics* 38:496-509.

Nerlove, Marc. 1958. *The Dynamics of Supply: Estimation of Farmers' Response to Price.* Baltimore: Johns Hopkins University Press.

Paarsch, Harry. 1985. "Microeconomic Models of Beef Supply." *Canadian Journal of Economics* 18:636-51.

Rao, Mohan. 1989. "Agricultural Supply Response: A Survey." *Agricultural Economics* 3:1–22.

Scandizzo, Pasquale, and Colin Bruce. 1980. *Methodologies for Measuring Agricultural Price Intervention Effects.* Staff Working Paper no. 394. Washington, D.C.: World Bank.

Shideed, Kamil, and Fred White. 1989. "Alternative Forms of Price Expectations in Supply Analysis for U.S. Corn and Soybean Acreages." *Western Journal of Agricultural Economics* 14:281-92.

Shonkwiler, Scott, and Suzanne Hinckley. 1985. "A Generalized Supply Response/Factor Demand Model and Its Application to the Feeder Cattle Market." *Western Journal of Agricultural Economics* 10:245-53.

Wallis, Kenneth. 1980. "Econometric Implications of the Rational Expectations Hypothesis." *Econometrica* 48:49–73.

Waugh, Frederik. 1964. "Cobweb Models." *Journal of Farm Economics* (now *American Journal of Agricultural Economics*) 46: 602–614.

Wickens, M.R., and J.N. Greenfield. 1973. "The Econometrics of Agricultural Supply: An Application to the World Coffee Market." *The Review of Economics and Statistics* 55:433-440.

Williams, Jeffrey, and Brian Wright. 1991. *Storage and Commodity Markets.* Cambridge, England: Cambridge University Press.

Wright, Brian. 1994. "Dynamic Perspectives on Agricultural Policy Issues." *American Journal of Agricultural Economics* 75:1113-25.

CHAPTER FIVE

Behavior and Welfare under Risk

This chapter explores how risk affects the optimal behavior and the welfare of rural house-holds as well as the food security of a nation. Yield and output price risks are introduced in section 5.1, and we consider the situation when they are correlated. Sections 5.2 to 5.5 explain the basic theory of supply when there is only one crop, no credit or insurance markets, and no storage, so that risk in production is directly transmitted as an income and consumption risk. For this presentation, we draw heavily on the work of Newbery and Stiglitz (1981). The basic measures of cost of risk and risk aversion are presented in sections 5.2 and 5.3. The behavior of risk-neutral farmers is considered in section 5.4. We show that, even if a farmer is indifferent between a risky return and a safe return, risk has an important effect on behavior. The theory of supply for risk-averse farmers is discussed in section 5.5. Risk generally shifts the supply curve inward, except for very risk-averse farmers who work harder in order to avoid disastrous out-comes. Section 5.6 considers households who both produce and consume. In the context of relatively segmented markets, the welfare cost of price fluctuations is higher for these house-holds than for pure producers, but they can partly insure themselves against price extremes by increasing food production. This has important policy implications for the role of market inte-gration. Section 5.7 shifts the analysis of risk to the national level and discusses alternative schemes commonly used for domestic price stabilization. Section 5.8 looks at different tests of the degree of market integration since well-integrated markets across space and commodities would allow targeting price stabilization efforts on only a few locations and commodities. Sec-tion 5.9 gives a brief introduction to the measurement of national food security. Section 5.10 concludes the chapter by examining a price stabilization scheme for an open economy, using Brazil as an example.

5.1. Price Determination and Sources of Fluctuations

Producers face two types of risks, production and price risks. Production (or yield) risks are those which arise because of natural causes such as variation in rainfall, weather, pests, or dis-eases. Yield fluctuations are largest for an individual plot of land. Therefore, a particular pro-ducer may reduce exposure to yield risk by farming geographically dispersed plots of land and diversifying crops. At the country level, fluctuations are also reduced by the diversity of cli-matic conditions. This is confirmed by Valdés and Konandreas (1981), who report on fluctua-tions of staple food production from 1961 to 1976. They find food production to be relatively stable in most large low-income countries (with coefficients of variation between 6% and 9% for India, Bangladesh, Indonesia, the Philippines, Sri Lanka, Ghana, Nigeria, Brazil, and Mexico), while variability is very high in most of the smaller countries, particularly North African and Middle Eastern countries (with coefficients of variation close to 30% in Algeria, Libya, and Morocco; 40% in Syria; and 65% in Jordan).

Price risks affect the prices of the commodities farmers produce and the inputs they buy. Because output price risk seems to be the most important element of farmers' decision-making processes, we concentrate our analysis on the impact of output price risk and ignore input price fluctuations. Newbery and Stiglitz (1981) report coefficients of variation of detrended real international market prices from 1951 to 1975 which range from 20% to 58%, with the following commodity figures: jute 20%, coffee 26%, cotton 30%, cocoa 31%, rubber 40%, and sugar 58%.

At the market level, price and production risks are intimately related. Hence, at a country level, a critical difference is whether the commodity is a nontradable or a tradable. For a nontradable, assuming fluctuations in demand to be negligible, the original source of risk lies in the fluctuation of domestic production. Price fluctuations are then directly linked to production fluctuations as low (high) equilibrium prices clear the market when production is high (low), implying a negative correlation between production and prices. For a tradable commodity, the fluctuations of price and domestic production will usually not be correlated. Because prices are given by world market equilibrium, they vary with the world supply and demand, which is not affected by domestic production unless the country is a large producer or buyer in the world market. At the farmers' level, prices are exogenous. However, local rural markets in developing countries are often isolated from national and international markets by high transportation and marketing costs. As yield fluctuations are highly correlated within a small area, local prices, determined by local production and demand, are both highly volatile and, for individual farmers, strongly negatively correlated with their own production. Hence, such farmers face both yield and price risks, with a level of correlation between these risks that depends on the level of regional market integration.

Given the long duration of the agricultural production process, an important distinction must be made between the ex ante supply schedule and the ex post supply curve. The ex ante supply schedule used for decisions made at the start of the season depends on expected future returns and is based on an average variability of yield and price. A theme of this chapter will be to characterize how this schedule is affected by risk as well as by alternative policies that reduce risk. At harvest time, the ex post supply curve depends on the weather and on ex ante decisions on input use. It does not, however, depend on the realization of price, since at harvest time producers can no longer respond to price incentives. This is illustrated in Figures 5.1 and 5.2, where the ex ante supply curve S is upward sloping and the ex post curve is represented by vertical lines. A low and a high realization around the ex ante optimal choice of J are shown in Figure 5.1.

5.2. Impact of Price Risk on the Level and Variability of Agricultural Income

Although many policy interventions are aimed at reducing the variability of prices, the more fundamental concern of farmers is not price but income variability. As we will see below, stabilization of price need not contribute to the stabilization of income. In certain cases, in fact, it will increase the variability of income.

Assuming that the ex ante supply function is invariant with risk, consider the closed economy case where the only source of price variability is that induced by production variability (Figure 5.1). Let q be the realization of production. The income of the farmers is $y = pq$. Assuming that the demand has a constant price elasticity $(-\varepsilon)$, the market clearing price will be:

$$p = q^{-1/\varepsilon},$$

which fluctuates with q.

Figure 5.1. Production fluctuation in a closed economy

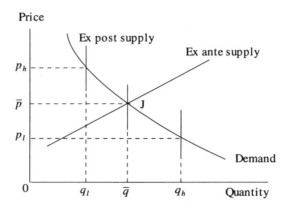

Figure 5.2. World price fluctuation in an open economy

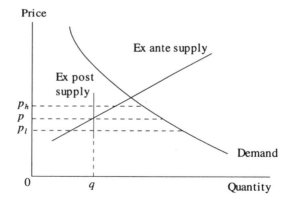

Note first that if prices are to be stabilized, they must be fixed at the level $\bar{p}$ for which consumption is equal to average production $\bar{q}$ (i.e., at $\bar{p} = \bar{q}^{-1/\varepsilon}$, which is not the average of the fluctuating price). At a higher price, stocks will surely accumulate over time, and at a lower price the country will run out of supply, since demand is above average supply. In both cases, the economy could not remain closed to international trade.

With stabilization of prices, the income of farmers is $y = \bar{p}q$, with the mean value $Ey = \bar{p}\bar{q} = \bar{q}^{1-1/\varepsilon}$. Without intervention, the income is $y = pq = q^{1-1/\varepsilon}$, with mean value $Ey = E(q^{1-1/\varepsilon})$. The comparison of these two averages depends on the value of ε (Figure 5.3). If the elasticity of demand is greater than one, the income curve is concave in q and the average value of the variable income, $E(q^{1-1/\varepsilon})$, is lower than the income obtained with a stabilized

Figure 5.3. Welfare effect of production risk on a risk-neutral producer

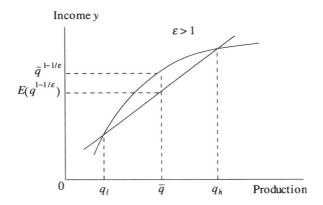

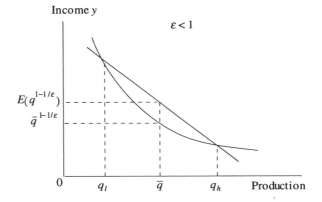

price. If the elasticity is less than one, which would typically be the case for food products, the converse is true, and price stabilization decreases the average income received by the farmer.

If we measure income instability by the variance of the logarithm of income, then:

$$\text{var}(\ln y) = \begin{cases} \text{var}(\ln q) & \text{with price stabilization,} \\ (1-1/\varepsilon)^2 \, \text{var}(\ln q) & \text{without price stabilization.} \end{cases}$$

Whether stabilization reduces or increases the variability of income depends on whether ε is smaller or greater than 1/2.

In summary, if $\varepsilon < 1/2$, price stabilization decreases both the average and the variability of y; if $1/2 < \varepsilon < 1$, it decreases the average and increases the variability of income; and if $\varepsilon > 1$, price stabilization increases the average and the variability of income. Hence, there is no doubt that price stabilization is unfavorable to producers when demand elasticity is in the (1/2, 1) interval. For $\varepsilon < 1/2$ or $\varepsilon > 1$, producers face a trade-off between average level and variability of income. Whether they benefit from price stabilization depends on how they value the cost of risk.

5.3. Measuring the Cost of Risk

The first question here is to define the welfare of a farmer whose income is uncertain. This welfare function will serve to measure the welfare cost of risk. It will also give the basis of the theory of behavior under risk, if one assumes, as it is most logical, that farmers maximize their welfare. In the standard model of producer behavior where farmers operate under certainty, the welfare function is profit. This also applies to risk-neutral farmers who are indifferent between a safe income and a risky income of the same expected value. For risk-averse farmers, two broad approaches have been used. In the first, risk is defined as the probability that income will fall below a predetermined disaster level. Following this definition, various *safety-first* models have been developed (Pyle and Turnovsky, 1970). In Roy's model, producers choose the production plan which minimizes the probability that income will fall below the disaster level. In Telser's model, producers maximize their expected profit subject to the condition that the probability of falling below the disaster level is lower than a specified value. The second approach is an extension of the standard theory of consumer behavior. In this theory, consumers behave as if they had a utility function, defined over the consequences of their choice (in the case of the consumer, it is defined over the quantities consumed), and make their choices to maximize this utility. For choices involving risk, one can similarly show that, under certain assumptions, agents behave as if they were maximizing the expected value of the utility that they can derive from the outcome of their actions. This gives the *expected utility* model. It is usually thought that the expected utility model is a relatively general approach, while the safety-first model applies more specifically to situations where there is a clear discontinuity at the disaster level entailed, for example, by starvation or bankruptcy, which results in a drastic change of status for the agent (Buschena and Zilberman, 1992). In the rest of this chapter, we stay with the expected utility model.

5.3.1. Certainty Equivalent Income and Risk Premium

Assuming that the producer's welfare is measured by the expected utility of income, we can now measure the risk cost of a risky income. Consider the utility function u defined over the income y. Risk aversion corresponds to a concave utility function as shown in Figure 5.4. To see this, assume that the random income y takes either one of two values, a low and a high value, with equal probability:

$$y = \begin{cases} \bar{y} - \delta & \text{with probability } 1/2 \\ \bar{y} + \delta & \text{with probability } 1/2. \end{cases}$$

The expected utility of this random outcome is the average value of the two utility levels, $Eu(y)$, which is less than the utility $u(\bar{y})$ associated with the sure income $\bar{y}$. The producer would prefer the sure income $\bar{y}$ to the uncertain income of the same average value and is therefore said to be risk-averse. Conversely, if one had considered a convex utility function, the expected utility derived from the uncertain income would be higher than the utility corresponding to the sure income. The producer would prefer uncertainty to security at the same average income and therefore would be a risk taker.

Figure 5.4. Measuring risk aversion

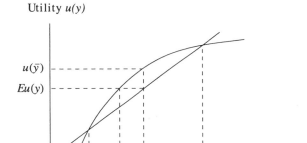

The difference between $u(\bar{y})$ and $Eu(y)$ is a measure of the cost of risk in terms of the welfare of the producer. One can also measure this cost in monetary terms by asking what would be the sure income that would give the producer the same utility as this random income. This is the certainty equivalent income, $\hat{y}$, defined by:

$$u(\hat{y}) = Eu(y),$$

and represented in Figure 5.4. The difference between $\hat{y}$ and $\bar{y}$ gives the amount of average income that the producer is ready to give up to exchange random income for sure income. It is referred to as the *risk premium*:

$$\rho = \bar{y} - \hat{y}.$$

The magnitude of the risk premium depends on both the shape of the utility function and the probability distribution of y. The more curved the utility function, the larger the risk premium for a given range of fluctuation of y. Hence, the agent's level of risk aversion is reflected by the curvature of the utility function. And, for a given utility curve, the larger the fluctuation in income and hence δ, the larger the risk premium. This represents the riskiness of income. In the definition of the risk premium given above, these two elements cannot, however, be easily separated. We now give a more precise measure of risk aversion as well as an approximate but explicit formula for the risk premium as a function of risk aversion and riskiness of income.

5.3.2. Risk Aversion

Consider a second-order Taylor expansion of the utility of the random income y around the average income $\bar{y}$:

$$u(y = \bar{y} + h) \approx u(\bar{y}) + hu'(\bar{y}) + \frac{1}{2}h^2 u''(\bar{y}),$$

where h is a random variable assuming values $\pm\delta$ with equal probability. Taking the expected value of this expression, and given that $Eh = 0$ and $Eh^2 = \delta^2$, we find:

$$Eu(y) \approx u(\bar{y}) + \frac{1}{2}\delta^2 u''(\bar{y}).$$

Similarly, we can use a Taylor expansion of the utility of the certainty equivalent income $\hat{y}$ around $\bar{y}$:

$$u(\hat{y} = \bar{y} - \rho) \approx u(\bar{y}) - \rho u'(\bar{y}).$$

Recall that $\hat{y}$ is defined by $Eu(y) = u(\hat{y})$. Setting equal these two expressions gives an approximation for the risk premium ρ:

$$\rho \approx -\frac{1}{2}\delta^2 \frac{u''(\bar{y})}{u'(\bar{y})}.$$

In this expression, the risk premium contains two multiplicative elements, the riskiness of income, expressed by the variance δ^2 of income, and the ratio u''/u', which is independent of the variability of y and measures the curvature of the utility curve. This last term captures the concept of risk aversion. More specifically, one defines:

$$\text{Absolute risk aversion: } A = -\frac{u''(\bar{y})}{u'(\bar{y})}$$

$$\text{Relative risk aversion: } R = -\bar{y}\frac{u''(\bar{y})}{u'(\bar{y})}.$$

The risk premium, that is, the cost of risk, can then be written as:

$$\rho \approx \frac{1}{2}A \, \text{var}(y) \quad \text{or} \quad \frac{\rho}{\bar{y}} \approx \frac{1}{2}R\,\sigma_y^2,$$

where σ_y is the coefficient of variation of income which is equal to standard deviation of $y/\bar{y}$.

These last relationships give some insights into the meaning of relative and absolute risk aversion. Take, for example, two farmers with respective average incomes of 100 and 1000. Assume that risk is multiplicative, with a coefficient of variation σ_y of 20%. This gives respective standard deviations of 20 and 200. With an assumption of constant relative risk aversion, R, the cost of risk is proportional to the average level of income, that is, the two farmers are prepared to give up $R\%$ of their income to avoid fluctuations. The richer farmer, with an average income and standard deviation 10 times higher than the poorer farmer, is ready to pay a premium 10 times higher than the poor counterpart. In contrast, assuming constant absolute risk aversion gives costs of risk equal to $200A$ and $20,000A$, respectively, or a cost of risk 100 times higher for the richer farmer. This example suggests that the assumption of constant absolute risk aversion is implausible over a wide range of income. This, however, does not prevent use of a constant A to analyze the decisions of a given individual. Conventional wisdom is that A declines with income or wealth, and R is relatively constant in the middle range of income. However, neither of these assumptions adequately reflects the high cost of risk at a very low level of income. In such an income range, we would expect R to increase as income falls.

A few remarks are in order in reference to these calculations:

a. The risky income may not be total income. Farmers may have secure labor income or remittances. Because they are concerned with fluctuations of total income rather than solely of agricultural income, the calculation of cost of risk has to be done with respect to total income, y. This means that the lower the share of the risky income in y, the lower the coefficient of variation σ_y, and the lower the cost of a given agricultural risk. Furthermore, because utility is really produced by consumption and not income, one can argue that if individuals have sufficient wealth, their consumption should not be very sensitive to fluctuations in their income, and risk should be defined on wealth and not on income. However, the quantification of wealth is difficult. Alternatively, one can base the evaluation of risk on income and consider that wealth influences the coefficient of risk aversion. In any case, one of the few empirical studies on this measure shows farmers to be responsive to income and not to wealth (Binswanger, 1980).

b. The cost of risk, ρ, increases with the risk aversion of the bearer and with the square of risk. This has important implications for risk sharing. Transferring risk to a less risk-averse individual will decrease the cost of risk. Landlords, middlemen, or individuals with higher incomes and assets would usually be less risk averse than small farmers, and shifting risk to them is efficient. Also, if one assumes constant absolute risk aversion, by dividing the risky income among several persons, the cost of risk borne by each individual is lower, and the total cost of risk is thus reduced. This can be seen as follows. The absolute size of the risk premium is $\rho = 1/2\, A \operatorname{var}(y)$. Hence, if we divide the risky income among n individuals, the variance of income will be divided by n^2, and the total cost of risk by n. This, however, does not hold under the assumption of constant relative risk aversion.

5.3.3. *Utility Functions with Constant Absolute or Relative Risk Aversion*

For any particular utility function, risk aversion, whether relative or absolute, will vary with the level of income. Two utility functions are particularly useful in solving problems under uncertainty.

The utility function with constant relative risk aversion:

$$u(y) = \frac{y^{1-R}}{1-R} \quad \text{for } R \neq 1, \quad \text{and} \quad u(y) = \ln y \quad \text{for } R = 1.$$

The utility function with constant absolute risk aversion:

$$u(y) = -k\, e^{-Ay}.$$

5.3.4. The Magnitude of Income Risk

How large is the coefficient of variation of agricultural income? In a widely referenced study, Roumasset (1976) estimated the income risk of rice production in the Philippines. He found that rain-fed rice produced using traditional techniques had a coefficient of variation σ of 20%, while the use of modern techniques, which increased mean income, raised σ to 50%. For irrigated rice, traditional techniques yielded a σ of 25%, while modern techniques almost doubled average income but yielded a σ of 33% to 42%. Another study by Schluter and Mount (1976) of 33 unirrigated farms in the Surat District of India over six years showed σ ranging from 5% to 32%, with an average value of 17%.

Empirical measures of risk aversion followed two approaches. In the first approach, experiments are designed in which farmers are asked to choose among alternative hypothetical lotteries, which differ by their average return and risk. In an experiment conducted in India, Binswanger (1980) found that farmers' choices are consistent with the expected utility model, as opposed to safety-first types of behavior; individuals are sensitive to fluctuations in income rather than to the impact that these have on their wealth; and attitude toward risk is quite well approximated by a constant relative risk aversion over income with a coefficient R between 0.3 for small fluctuations and 1.7 for larger fluctuations. This coefficient of constant relative risk aversion over income rather than wealth is often called the coefficient of partial risk aversion. Critics of this approach argue that farmers may not react to these hypothetical gambling situations as they would to their actual production decisions.

The second approach attempts to infer the parameters of risk attitude from the observed behavior of farmers. It consists in a comparison of the marginal product of a factor at the profit-maximizing optimum with the marginal product at the observed decision, based on an econometrically estimated production function. The difference between profit maximizing and observed levels of factor use is attributed to attitude toward risk. Moscardi and de Janvry (1977) conducted such a study of farmers in Puebla, Mexico, postulating a safety-first approach, in which the cost of risk is equal to $K\bar{y}\sigma_y$. They found a mean value of the risk aversion coefficient K equal to 1.12, which would correspond to a coefficient of relative risk aversion of about 2 if σ was 0.5, a correspondence suggested by Newbery and Stiglitz (1981). The difficulty with this approach is that, because risk is measured as a residual term, it will tend to capture many other factors not accounted for by the model, from a misspecification of the model itself to existence of household-specific credit constraints and transactions costs.

Combining these two types of measures gives orders of magnitude for the cost of income risk. If fluctuations in income are measured with a σ of 20% and relative risk aversion is 2, the welfare loss due to risk is 4% of mean income. With a σ of 40%, the welfare loss rises to 16% of income.

5.4. Welfare and Supply of Risk-Neutral Farmers

Consider an individual farmer, with production q as a function of a single input x and a random factor θ:

$$q = \theta f(x), \quad \text{with} \quad E\theta = 1, \quad \text{var } \theta = \sigma_\theta^2.$$

The output price p is also random, but the input price w is not, and profit $y = pq - wx$ is correspondingly random. A risk-neutral farmer maximizes expected profit:

$$Ey = E(pq) - wx = \overline{p}\overline{q} + \text{cov}(p,q) - wx.$$

Thus, given a negative correlation between the individual's own production and the market price, expected profit will be lower under uncertainty than under certainty. This would happen in a relatively isolated market, for example, where a good year for this individual would usually correspond to a good year for most of the other producers and, hence, to a fall in local market price. The intuitive reasoning behind this result is that, as the producer receives a low price whenever output is high, and a high price whenever output is low, for average production the farmer receives a price lower than the average price (Figure 5.1). This shows that risk affects the welfare of even risk-neutral producers.

Furthermore, because $\text{cov}(p,q)$ is also a function of x, the optimal choice of x, that which maximizes Ey, is affected by the presence of risk. For instance, specify the stochastic nature of p as:

$$p = \overline{p} - b(\theta - 1) + v, \quad \text{with} \quad Ev = 0, \quad \text{and} \quad E\theta v = 0.$$

Price variability has two components: an element perfectly correlated with output risk, and another uncorrelated to output risk. With this specification, $-b$ is the coefficient of correlation between θ, the risk element in production, and p. Therefore,

$$\text{cov}(p,q) = -b\sigma_\theta^2 f(x).$$

The producer's maximization problem,

$$\underset{x}{\text{Max }} Ey = E(pq) - wx = E\{[\overline{p} - b(\theta - 1) + v]\theta f(x)\} - wx,$$

yields:

$$(\overline{p} - b\sigma_\theta^2)f'(x) = w.$$

This shows that the producer behaves as if the price were $\hat{p} = \overline{p} - b\sigma_\theta^2$. This discounted price, called the "action certainty equivalent price," is the nonrandom price which leads to the same behavior as the random price.

A common graphic representation is shown in Figure 5.5, where risk is seen as shifting the supply curve inward. The difference between the marginal cost curve and the pseudo–supply curve is the markup $-b\sigma_\theta^2$. The farmer chooses the level of input such that marginal cost of production is equal to the certainty equivalent price $\hat{p}$ of the expected price $\overline{p}$. Note that while this pseudo–supply curve conveniently represents the producer's decision, it cannot be used to compute profit and surplus. The short-run supply will be a vertical line fluctuating around $\overline{q}$, taking at any time t the value q_t, for example. Corresponding prices and revenues are also fluctuating, taking, for example, the values p_t and $p_t q_t$ at time t, respectively. Profit is random and is measured as the difference between the variable revenue and the nonrandom cost under the marginal cost curve.

Note also that the relationship between $\hat{p}$ and $\bar{p}$ depends on the specification of risk. With additive risk on supply or a different model of price formation, the markup will take different forms and may not be constant.

In the case that we have developed here, the welfare of the risk-neutral producer Ey can also be written as a function of $\hat{p}$:

$$Ey = (\bar{p} - b\sigma_\theta^2)\bar{q} - wx = \hat{p}\bar{q} - wx.$$

This expression does not always hold, as it depends on the specification of risk. In general, the "welfare certainty equivalent price" $\hat{p}'$, defined by $Ey = \hat{p}'\bar{q} - wx$, is different from $\hat{p}$.

In conclusion, we have shown that:

a. Even risk-neutral producers are affected by risk if there is any correlation between their own production and the price level. This will more likely occur in relatively segmented markets and with more homogenous conditions of production across producers.

b. For a producer, a negative correlation between production and the market price induces a lower expected profit than under certainty.

c. Some cases, for example, under multiplicative risk, can induce a lower marginal return to input use and an inward shift of the supply curve.

d. Consequently, price stabilization will usually induce an outward shift of the supply curve. This comes as a correction to our assumption in section 5.2, where we assumed that price

Figure 5.5. Supply of risk-averse producers under risk

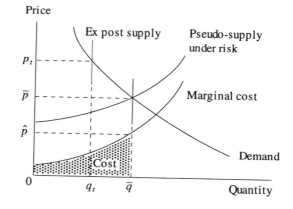

stabilization did not affect the supply curve. This supply effect enhances the argument of section 5.2 by providing another justification for a stabilized price lower than the average of the random price.

5.5. Welfare and Supply of Risk-Averse Farmers

The risk-averse farmer maximizes not expected income, but rather expected utility:

$$\text{Max } Eu(y) = Eu\big[p\theta f(x) - wx\big].$$

To simplify the analysis, assume that the farmer uses only personal labor, with marginal utility w, and that the utility function is separable in revenue and leisure. Equivalently the utility is assumed additive in revenue and cost, that is, $Eu\big[p\theta f(x) - wx\big] = Eu\big[p\theta f(x)\big] - wx$. Assume also that the farmer has a constant relative risk aversion R on fluctuating income. The farmer's problem is rewritten as:

$$\text{Max}_{x}\left\{E\left[\frac{(p\theta f(x))^{1-R}}{1-R}\right] - wx\right\}.$$

The two random terms p and θ can be combined in one random variable, $r = p\theta$, which gives the random return associated with one unit of expected quantity $f(x)$. The first-order condition of this problem gives:

$$E(r^{1-R})f(x)^{-R}f'(x) - w = 0.$$

Under certainty, r is always equal to its average value $\bar{r}$ and the first-order condition is:

$$\bar{r}^{1-R}f(x)^{-R}f'(x) - w = 0.$$

If $R < 1$, $E(r^{1-R}) < \bar{r}^{1-R}$, and $f(x)^{-R}f'(x)$ under risk is higher than under certainty. As $f(x)^{-R}f'(x)$ is a decreasing function of x, input use x under risk is lower than under certainty. Conversely, if $R > 1$, input use and supply under risk are higher than under certainty.

To grasp the intuition behind this result, note that the marginal utility of effort x is:

$$u'(x) = r^{1-R}f(x)^{-R}f'(x) - w.$$

This can be decomposed into the marginal income produced by increasing effort, $dy / dx = rf'(x)$, the utility of each marginal unit of income, $du / dy = [rf(x)]^{-R}$, and the constant marginal cost of effort w. With risk aversion, the marginal utility of income, du/dy, declines with income. Values of R greater than one represent a very concave utility function and thus a steep decline of the marginal utility of income as income rises. This decline overwhelms the increase in income, $rf'(x)$, implying that the marginal utility of effort, du/dx, declines when r increases. Hence, high risk aversion places a high value on increased output at lower realizations of the random price. The utility of marginal effort is not only decreasing but also concave in r. Therefore, when risk increases, the expected value of a marginal unit of effort increases and producers work harder to avoid the extreme situations. With milder risk aversion, $R < 1$, an increase in r induces a decline in the marginal utility of income but an increase in the marginal utility of effort, although at a decreasing rate. Risk induces a decline in expected marginal return to effort and, hence, a decline in effort.

Although the effect of risk on effort and production is ambiguous, the effect on welfare is always negative. To see this, denote by $d\sigma$ a change in risk. The marginal effect on welfare is:

$$\frac{dW}{d\sigma} = \frac{d(Eu(y) - wx)}{d\sigma} = \frac{\partial(Eu(y) - wx)}{\partial x}\frac{dx}{d\sigma} + \frac{\partial Eu(y)}{\partial \sigma}.$$

The first term is zero because producers are assumed to adjust their effort x to maximize their welfare, and the second term is negative since the utility is concave in the random term r.

In conclusion:

a. When risk increases, risk-averse producers will decrease their effort if they are mildly risk averse but increase their effort if they are very risk averse.

b. Whether a program that attempts to reduce income risk will induce an overall increase or decrease in output depends on the distribution of risk aversion across producers. However, if it does produce an increase in total supply, this may induce a lowering of the average price. This will in part curtail the anticipated benefit from price stabilization.

c. In all cases, risk decreases the producers' welfare.

5.6. The Household's Response to Price Risk*

To this point, we have concentrated on the effect of uncertainty on producers' welfare and behavior. We have not addressed the issue of the impact of price fluctuations on consumers. Without going into details, one can imagine that consumers will usually be risk averse with respect to fluctuations of the prices of what they consume. However, whereas producers fear low prices, consumers fear high prices. The question then is whether these two effects compensate for each other for rural households which both consume and produce the same commodities; the answer is yes. Comparing a net selling household with a pure producer, we will see that the household which consumes part of its production holds a type of insurance against low prices. In the case of a net buying household, home production of a part of its consumption needs serves as an insurance against high prices. Hence, because net selling households are partly protected against risk, they tend to produce more than pure producers with the same level of risk aversion. Net buying households also tend to produce more than pure producers because this provides them with a consumption insurance. Very risk-averse food-deficit households produce more under uncertainty than under certainty in order to reduce exposure to extreme prices.

Consider a household which produces only one agricultural good that it also consumes. Consider the case of price fluctuations only. Abstracting from the prices of all the other commodities that the household purchases, its indirect utility function is:

$$u(y, p), \quad \text{where } y = pf(x) - wx + T,$$

where T represents other sources of income. The input level x that maximizes the expected utility of the household is given by:

$$Eu'_y\big[pf'(x) - w\big] = Eu'_y\, pf'(x) - Eu'_y\, w = Eu'_y\,\bar{p}\Big[1 + \sigma_{u'_y}\sigma_p\, \mathrm{cor}(u'_y, p)\Big]f'(x) - Eu'_y\, w = 0.$$

As seen before, the impact of risk on production behavior relies on the sign of the correlation between u'_y and p. If p and y were not correlated, input use would be determined by $\bar{p}\,f'(x) = w$, independent of risk. If p and y are correlated, which is the case here, then input use and supply response are affected by risk. There are two elements in the influence of p on u'_y: one is a production effect, where an increase in price p induces an increase in income y and, hence, a decrease in marginal utility of income. The consumption effect counters this: an increase in price reduces the real income, thus inducing an increase in the marginal utility of income. The net of the two can be shown in the following approximation obtained by a Taylor expansion:

$$(1) \quad \text{cor}(u'_y, p) \approx \sigma_p^2 \left(R(s_p - s_c) + \eta s_c \right)$$

$$(2) \qquad\qquad = \sigma_p^2 \left(R s_p - s_c (R - \eta) \right),$$

where R is the coefficient of relative risk aversion, η the income elasticity of consumption c of the food item, $s_c = pc/y$ the share of food consumption in total expenditure, and $s_p = pf(x)/y$ the share of the risky income in total income. Pure producers are defined as not consuming their own production, that is, $s_c = 0$.

These expressions reveal the determination of the degree of self-sufficiency of the household as critical in the impact of uncertainty on production:

a. For net selling households [defined by $f(x) > c$, or $s_p > s_c$], expression (1) is always negative. Hence, the marginal utility of income is negatively correlated with price, and input use and production under risk are lower than under certainty. As for pure producers, the negative effect of risk increases with risk aversion R.

b. For food-deficit households, expression (1) is negative for low values of R and positive for large values of R. Hence, net buying households with mild risk aversion behave as producers in reducing their production. Very risk-averse households increase their production in response to increases in risk.

c. The negative effect of risk on production is lower for households than for pure producers. This is seen in expression (2), as the income elasticity η is usually lower than R. A positive $R - \eta$ indicates that a household produces more than a pure producer with the same risk aversion. This is because consumption of its own production in years of very low prices ensures a certain level of utility to some of its product which is not marketed at the low price.

Econometric studies of attitude toward risk like those of Antle (1989) and Moscardi and de Janvry (1977) are usually based on the observed gap between expected revenue and marginal cost. What we now know is that, if the agent is a household, this gap depends not only on risk aversion R, but also on the income elasticity and the level of self-sufficiency.

In terms of welfare effect, Finkelshtain and Chalfant (1991) show that the risk premium is equal to:

$$\rho \approx \delta^2 \left(-\frac{1}{2} \frac{u''_{yy}}{u'_y} + \frac{u''_{yp}}{u'_y} \right).$$

This risk premium is higher for households than for pure producers whenever u''_{yp} is positive, that is, when price and marginal utility of income are negatively correlated. Hence, despite the compensating role that consumption and production have on each other, and the adjustment made in production, the negative welfare effect of risk is higher on households than it is on producers. Households thus suffer a higher cost from risk in food price and, at the same time, produce more food than pure producers.

In the context of a combined cash crop–food crop production system and presence of both production and price risks, Fafchamps (1992) has used a similar argument to show that small farm households will tend to allocate relatively more of their resources to food crops and will be less responsive to price and technical opportunities in cash crop production than commercial farmers. This bias toward food production is due to the volatility of food prices and their correlation with individual production, inducing households to self-insure through higher food production.

This suggests an important entry point for policy aiming both at increasing the supply response of cash crops and relieving smallholders from the high welfare cost of risk. Food market integration would reduce the volatility of local prices and their correlation with individual production. The rationale for food self-sufficiency would decrease, and peasants would allocate their resources following a standard portfolio approach with an optimum diversification based on relative profitability and riskiness of the different crops. Market integration can be promoted by infrastructure investments, by removing regulatory impediments to domestic trade, and by direct support to trade through government shops or credit to the private sector.

5.7. Instruments of Price Stabilization

Preoccupation with the high welfare costs of price volatility has led many countries to establish schemes for domestic price stabilization. Although the explicit objective of these schemes is only to stabilize prices, they often result in support or taxation on the average price. A common example is that of export taxation by marketing boards. Another is the fixation of a price floor for staples without a symmetric price ceiling, which raises the average price while stabilizing it. While there may be a case for such changes in the average price, it must be seen as a separate issue, at least analytically if not politically. This is not to say that the stabilized price must be equal to the average of the fluctuating price. In a closed economy, the stabilized price must balance supply and demand, as modified by stabilization. Storage and administrative costs involved in price stabilization programs must also be imputed to the program. Taxation and price supports, however, must be viewed as a separate issue, as their objective is to transfer income from one group to another.

To measure the instability of a time series, it is necessary to extract the time trend of the series. This is done as follows:

a. Perform a regression using the logarithm of real price p as the dependent variable and time t as the independent variable:

$$\ln p_t = a + bt + \varepsilon,$$

where b is the annual growth rate of real price p, and ε a random error.

b. Compute the estimated values $\hat{p}_t = e^{a+bt}$ and the relative residuals

$$\hat{u}_t = (p_t - \hat{p}_t)/\hat{p}_t.$$

c. An index $I(p)$ of the variability of the series p is given by the standard deviation of $\hat{u}$:

$$I(p) = \sqrt{\frac{1}{n}\sum_t \hat{u}_t^2}.$$

In a cross-country analysis of price stabilization schemes, Knudsen and Nash (1990) compare instability indices of domestic prices with instability indices of international prices. Their study includes 15 crops across 37 developing countries and covers the period 1967–1981. In general, they find these programs to be successful. Domestic prices of grains were more stable than international prices on average by 15 percentage points, beverages by 7 percentage points, and fiber by 4 percentage points. However, in a number of cases, despite "stabilization" schemes, domestic prices were actually more unstable than the border price equivalent. This happened in 9% of the cases for grains, 31% for beverages, and 35% for fiber.

There are different types of institutions for price stabilization. An important differentiating characteristic among these institutions is whether or not they physically handle commodities. The first group includes marketing boards and buffer stock schemes. Marketing boards, which are common in Africa, have been denounced as major budget burdens. Without denying the possibility of administrative inefficiency, the deficits of these agencies in general derive from the fact that they manage pricing policies with goals that combine stabilization and redistribution. In the case of staple goods, high procurement prices are set to support producers, and, at the same time, low delivery prices are set to favor consumers. Such pricing policies make it impossible for private traders to operate profitably. Hence, even if this was not the original intention, marketing boards end up forced to carry out the total trading. In such cases, even a small discrepancy between unit cost and selling price may cause enormous losses. Alternatively, government agencies may tax producers of export crops as a revenue base. As parallel markets develop, the size of operation of the marketing board, its income base, and the foreign earning controlled by the government all shrink.

Variable tariffs and subsidies on imports and exports form the second group of price stabilizing institutions. In many countries, export taxes are not explicitly and systematically set with an eye toward price stabilization. However, some stabilization is generally achieved as export taxes are decided on a year-to-year basis, with ad hoc adjustments to variations in international prices. A major drawback of these variable tax schemes is that they transfer all the instability onto the government budget, making planning difficult. There is in addition a tendency to expand expenditures when revenues are high, with asymmetric difficulties in the necessary cuts in bad years. This instability tends to boost expenditures and generate deficits. A solution to this problem is to create a buffer fund for export commodities as in Papua New Guinea. When the world price is high, a tariff is levied and the proceeds are put in a fund which is used for subsidies when the world price is low. The rules for fixing the tax level are well established, with a tax rate equal to half the difference between world price and the previous 10-year average. This self-financing scheme has been successful in reducing instability in prices by 46% (Knudsen and Nash, 1990).

Analyses of price stabilization have led to the following general recommendations: it is better to avoid handling the commodity itself; partial stabilization gives a better benefit-cost ratio than total stabilization; and the average price should approximate the average market price to avoid an ever-increasing disequilibrium of reserves (Knudsen and Nash, 1990).

5.8. Market Integration and Price Stabilization

We have seen that price stabilization can be achieved through either buffer stocks or trade. Whichever approach is followed, the cost of stabilization is reduced if internal markets are well integrated in the sense that price movements are transmitted across spatially dispersed markets and across commodities: in this case, it will be sufficient to stabilize prices in one central market to which others are related and the price of one fundamental commodity to which the prices of other commodities are related. Since markets in LDCs are suspected of fragmentation and spatial oligopoly pricing (Basu and Bell, 1991), a number of recent studies have addressed the issue of testing empirically the degree of market integration.

Different approaches have been followed to test spatial market integration. The simplest approach is to see if there exist high correlations between prices in different markets (Blyn, 1973). Alternatively, we can see whether differences in market prices exceed transfer costs across markets (Hays and McCoy, 1977) or exceed normal seasonal fluctuations (Delgado, 1988). A more powerful approach consists in taking into account the structure of price determination across markets. The basic model was formulated by Ravallion (1986) who considered a radial distribution of markets where one central market with price p_r is related to n feeder markets not directly related to each others with prices p_i. The model of spatial price determination is thus:

$p_r = p_r(p_1,...,p_n,x_r)$ central market price,

$p_i = p_i(p_r,x_i)$, $i = 1,...,n$ feeder markets prices,

where the x are market-specific seasonal and exogenous variables which affect price formation. For estimation purposes, the dynamic structure of the feeder market price equations is specified as a function of past prices with a general structure of l lags as follows:

$$(3) \quad p_{it} = \sum_{j=1}^{l} \alpha_{ij} p_{i,t-j} + \sum_{j=0}^{l} \beta_{ij} p_{r,t-j} + \gamma_i x_{it} + e_{it}, \ i = 1,...,n.$$

Estimation of this equation, typically with monthly price quotations, can be used to test the following hypotheses about market integration:

Segmentation of market i: present and past central market prices do not influence the ith local market. In this case: $\beta_{ij} = 0, j = 1,...,l$.

Short-run market integration: a price increase in the central market is fully and immediately passed on the ith market without lagged effects. This corresponds to the criterion of equal spatial prices over time, net of transfer costs, established by Takayama and Judge (1971). In this case, $\beta_{i0} = 1$, $\beta_{ij} = \alpha_{ij} = 0, j = 1,...,l$.

Long-run market integration: under long-run equilibrium, a permanent price change in the central market is fully passed over time to the feeder markets, but potentially through lagged effects. Solving (3) for the long-run equilibrium change dp_i due to a change dp_r in the central market price gives:

$$dp_i = \sum_{j=1}^{l} \alpha_{ij} dp_i + \sum_{j=0}^{l} \beta_{ij} dp_r, \quad \text{or} \quad dp_i = \frac{\sum_{j=0}^{l} \beta_{ij}}{1 - \sum_{j=1}^{l} \alpha_{ij}} dp_r.$$

The corresponding test of long-run market integration is thus: $\sum \alpha_{ij} + \sum \beta_{ij} = 1$.

If the market structure is not one of radial central-feeder markets, but more generally of pairwise interlinked rural markets, the test of integration is done by evaluating all pairwise price relationships (i, j) in the spatial relations considered as opposed to the pairwise relationships (i, r) (Faminow and Benson, 1990).

If there is only one lag, the feeder market price equations simplify to:

$$(4) \quad p_{it} = \alpha_i p_{i,t-1} + \beta_{i0} p_{rt} + \beta_{i1} p_{r,t-1} + \gamma_i x_{it} + e_{it},$$

which can be written in first differences as:

$$(5) \quad \Delta p_{it} = (\alpha_i - 1)(p_{i,t-1} - p_{r,t-1}) + \beta_{i0}\Delta p_{rt} + (\alpha_i + \beta_{i0} + \beta_{i1} - 1)p_{r,t-1} + \gamma_i x_{it} + e_{it}.$$

This relates the change in local price to past spatial price differentials, the current change in central market price, past central price, and market-specific exogenous variables. Since there is less multicollinearity in this difference equation (5) than in the price equation (4), it is this equation that is estimated. The tests of market integration are then:

Market segmentation: $\beta_{i0} = \beta_{i1} = 0$.
Short-run market integration: $\beta_{i0} = 1, \beta_{i1} = \alpha_i = 0$.
Long-run market integration: $\alpha_i + \beta_{i0} + \beta_{i1} - 1 = 0$.

With one lag and no x variables, Timmer (1987) suggests an index of market connectedness (*IMC*) defines as:

$$IMC = \frac{\alpha_i}{\beta_{i0} + \beta_{i1}}$$

which takes a value of zero for short-run integration and ∞ for full segmentation.

There is, however, a simultaneity problem in the estimation of the Δp_{it} equation (5) since Δp_{rt} is by definition endogenous as it is related to price formation in the local markets. Ravallion thus uses an instrumental variable approach to predict Δp_{rt} in a two-stage least squares estimation. Alderman (1993) has extended this framework to test for intercommodity price transmission in food markets in Ghana.

Results, in general, show that market integration is far from perfect. In his study of rice markets in Bangladesh, Ravallion finds that market efficiency varies both over seasons and during periods of famine. As to price transmission across commodities, Alderman finds that it is far from perfect in Ghana, attributing this to the fact that traders tend to specialize in one commodity, thus segmenting the process of acquiring information across commodities. In this case, stabilizing the price of one commodity would only partially carry to the price of other commodities.

Recent econometric advances in the theory of cointegration of time series have also been used to test the long-run integration of markets (Alderman, 1993; Alexander and Wyeth, 1994).

5.9. Measures of Food Security at the National Level

Food security is of utmost importance to all countries. Even though food security commands high priority in many policy debates, it is too often confused with or reduced to concepts of price stabilization or food self-sufficiency, which are only some of the many potential components of a food security strategy. It is beyond the scope of this chapter to fully address strategies for food security. However, to the extent that production and price risks are elements of the problem, we will briefly describe an aggregate measure of food security related to them.

In simple terms, food security is defined as access by all people at all times to food sufficient for a healthy life (Reutlinger, 1986). A controversial but unavoidable concept underlying this definition is that of "sufficient" food. Two types of food insecurity are commonly distinguished: chronic and transitory. Chronic food insecurity refers to situations where access to food is, on average, below the required level and is rooted in poverty. Temporary food insecurity refers to a short-run food decline due to fluctuations in income (e.g., because of illness or unemployment), production, or prices. These two types of food insecurity are closely related, since a household or a country that is in normal times close to the minimum level of food is more apt to fall into transitory food insecurity. Specific causes of food insecurity vary across countries, regions, and households. Hence, food security must be tackled with an array of policy instruments geared to these specific sources of risk.

While food security involves access to food by all individuals, it is defined and measured at different levels: country, region, household, or individual. The monitoring of food security at the household or individual level requires intensive household surveys, with appropriate measures of food intake. These surveys are usually taken at one point in time. Hence, they measure existing situations but neither the trends nor the fluctuations in consumption and thus cannot be used to rigorously measure food security. They may, however, be used in cross-sectional analyses to establish the relationship between nutritional status and socioeconomic and demographic variables such as income, wage, price ratios, assets, migration, gender, and education. These socioeconomic variables can then be used as proxies to analyze the level of food security, to predict the effect of external events, and to monitor the impact of different policies.

At the country or regional level, food security can, to some extent, be monitored in terms of indicators of production, availability, trade, stocks, and prices (Valdés and Konandreas, 1981). Availability is defined as:

Availability (C) = production − intermediate use and waste + net imports − increase in stocks.

Availability is an aggregate concept of final consumption, sometimes called "apparent consumption" or "disappearance," as opposed to a measure taken directly from the observation of consumption itself. Data on intermediate use and waste are not always available, in which case they are estimated as a given percentage of production.

Food security is analyzed in terms of the mean $\overline{C}$, trend $\hat{C}_t$, and variability $I(C)$ of availability and its components. From these, several indicators of food security have been used:

a. If the growth rate of availability is approximately zero, a mean-variance measure can be used:

$$\overline{C} - \frac{1}{2} A \operatorname{var}(C),$$

where A is the coefficient of absolute risk aversion.

b. By assuming that the relative residual $\hat{u}$ of availability follows a normal distribution, $N(0, \sigma_u)$, one can compute the probability that availability will fall below a minimum level C_m:

$$\operatorname{Prob}(C < C_m).$$

c. When there is a definite trend in the series, the probability that availability falls below a certain percentage α of the trend value is calculated as:

$$\text{Prob}(C < \alpha\hat{C}).$$

More specifically, these indicators are calculated as follows:

$$\text{Prob}(C < C_m) = \text{Prob}\left(\frac{C - \overline{C}}{\sigma(C)} < -\frac{\overline{C} - C_m}{\sigma(C)}\right) = 1 - F_{(\overline{C} - C_m)/\sigma(C)},$$

$$\text{Prob}(C < \alpha\hat{C}) = \text{Prob}\left(\hat{u} = \frac{C - \hat{C}}{\hat{C}} < -(1 - \alpha)\right) = \text{Prob}\left(\frac{\hat{u}}{I(C)} < -\frac{1 - \alpha}{I(C)}\right) = 1 - F_{(1-\alpha)/I(C)},$$

where $\alpha(C)$ is the standard deviation of C, $I(C) = \sigma_u$ the index of variability of C, and F the cumulative normal distribution.

In comparative studies of staple food consumption for the period from 1961 to 1976, Valdés and Konandreas (1981) found coefficients of variability of 6% to 8% for Asian countries and 15% to 25% in African countries. Correspondingly, the probability of falling below 95% of the

Figure 5.6. Availability of maize, Kenya (in thousand tons)

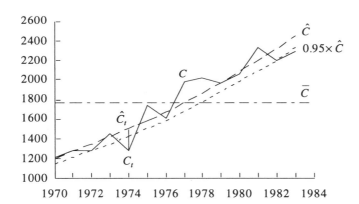

trend value is 20% to 27% in Asian countries and 37% to 42% in African countries. In the latter case, this implies that one should expect consumption to fall below 95% of the trend in about two years out of five. In the case of Kenya, represented in Figure 5.6, the index of variability of consumption is 10%, which gives:

$$\text{for } \alpha = 0.95, ((1 - \alpha)/I(C))\ F_{0.5} = 0.69,$$

or a probability of 31% of falling below 95% of the trend line. In fact this has occurred three times (1974, 1982, and 1983) over the 15-year period examined (data from Pinckney, 1988).

5.10. Example: Evaluation of the Brazilian Price Band Proposal

In trying to avoid large price shocks in the 1980s, Brazil used erratic and short-term policy interventions rather than any explicit policy of price stabilization. In 1987, however, a price band rule was proposed for the major crops. The principle of a price band rule is that the government announces a reference price and a band around this reference price. When the market price fluctuates within the price band, the government does not intervene. When the price hits one of the borders of the band, the government intervenes with imports, exports, or changes in stocks to maintain the price at the limit. The setting of the reference price depends on whether the commodity is a tradable or a nontradable. For a nontradable, the reference price is built on a long-term trend of the equilibrium domestic price. For a tradable, the reference price is set on a long-term trend of international price. Braverman, Kanbur, Salazar Brandão, Hammer, Rezende Lopes, and Tan (1990) analyzed the potential impact of the rules proposed in 1987. We summarize their results for a nontradable (beans) and a tradable (rice).

As noted in section 5.3.2, the cost of fluctuation of income is measured by $(1/2)R\sigma_y^2\bar{y}$. When government intervention modifies the average income of the producers by Δy and its fluctuations by $\Delta\sigma_y^2$, the total benefits of the intervention are measured by:

$$B_p = \Delta y - \frac{1}{2} R \, \Delta\sigma_y^2 \, \bar{y}.$$

The first term, called the "transfer benefit," indicates the gain or loss to all producers due to the change in average income, irrespective of their attitudes toward risk. The second term is the "pure benefit" from stabilization, which depends on each producer's risk aversion.

Braverman et al. (1990) used this approach to evaluate the risk costs of alternative pricing policies. They compared the historical observations under free trade and under a price band rule. For the beans sector, the free-trade price is the price which clears the market. Thus, its calculation requires both a supply and a demand function. Braverman et al. (1990) chose linear functions and solve for q and p over time:

$$q_t^s = a + bp_t$$
$$q_t^d = c + dp_t$$
$$q_t^s = q_t^d,$$

with the parameters b and d corresponding to average supply and demand elasticities of 0.36 and –0.50, respectively. Application of a price band rule on these computed equilibrium prices requires stocking or destocking whenever the price hits the lower or upper limit of the band. These limits are set at 17% below and above the long-run price. The long-run price, in turn, is defined as a 60-month moving average of past prices. For each of these simulated price series, the corresponding supply and demand are computed. Note, however (and this is an inconsistency in the analysis), that production is a function of price rather than of the expected price and the variability of prices, as the analysis in this chapter would suggest.

Historically, the average real price received by farmers for beans was Cr$10 per kilogram in 1986 cruzeiros, as noted in Table 5.1. These prices were very unstable, with a coefficient of variation around the trend of 30%. Producers' revenue was also characterized by a high degree

Table 5.1. Evaluation of a price band for Brazil, 1977–1986 (in 1986 cruzeiros)

	Price		Production		Producer income		Risk premium[b]		Efficiency cost
	Average (Cr$/kg)	σ^a (%)	Average (1000 tons)	σ^a (%)	Average (million Cr$)	σ^a (%)	Average (million Cr$)	% of revenue (%)	(million Cr$)
Beans									
Historical data	10.0	30	2,120	16	16,115	19	387	2.4	420
Free trade	10.2	35	2,132	17	16,573	33	1200	7.2	0
Band rule	8.3	12	1,976	24	13,264	26	596	4.5	
Wheat									
Historical data	3.1	14	2,240	27	7,091	39	717	10.1	
Free trade	2.5	11	2,026	30	5,265	37	479	9.1	0
Band rule	2.7	7	2,083	29	5,645	31	361	6.4	125

Source: Braverman et al., 1990.

[a]σ = Coefficient of variation around trend.

[b]Assuming constant relative risk aversion of 1.33

of variability, although less than that of prices. The risk premium that risk-averse producers would be willing to pay to have this instability eliminated, assuming a relative risk aversion of 1.33, is equal to 2.4% of their income. Under free trade, prices are slightly higher on average but more volatile. Thus, the existing policies have embodied producer price tax and stabilization components. Producers' revenue is also higher and more variable than under the implemented policy. The band rule is effective in reducing the variability in prices to a coefficient of variation of 12%. However, the average price is 18.6% lower. This happens despite a symmetric definition of the band around the trend price because the price fluctuations are not symmetric around the trend. Because the upper limit of the band is hit eight times while the lower limit is hit twice, a better definition of the band should leave a wider band above the average than below. Despite stabilizing prices, this policy does no better job at stabilizing producer income than the absence of a price band.

Government intervention in the wheat market is strong, with set producer and consumer prices and government-controlled marketing. With producer prices above and consumer prices below the world market, imports are larger than under free trade, and the government operation generates a large fiscal deficit. For wheat, the free-market price is the world market price. The price band is defined with a 12% margin above and below a reference price (calculated as a 60-month average of past world market prices corrected for transportation costs). Table 5.1 summarizes the results of the evaluation of the free-trade and the price band proposal. On average, the producer price was kept 23% above the world price. However, the domestic price has been more volatile than the free-trade price. The increase in risk cost associated with domestic intervention is equal to Cr$238 million, or 3.3% of producers' income. The price band policy would reduce the fluctuations in income compared with the historical data and with free trade. The risk benefit to producers is Cr$241 million, which has to be compared with the policy efficiency cost of Cr$125 million, defined as the sum of changes in consumer surplus, producer surplus, and government revenues (see Chapter 7).

Exercise 5
Food Security in India

This food security exercise (file 5FOODSEC) is based on the study by de Janvry and Sadoulet (1991). The objective is to analyze the achievement of India in terms of food security at the national level, during the period from 1950 to 1987, and characterize the evolution of the country's policy in combining strategies of production, imports, and stocks. We look at the two concepts of chronic and transitory food security by decomposing the analysis of a time series into its trend and its fluctuations.

Basic data on food grains supply are reported in Table 5E.1.

1. Self-Sufficiency

We first look at the issue of food self-sufficiency, a concept which is different from but often confused with food security. For this purpose, compute the indicator of import dependency, defined by the ratio of imports over total domestic supply, itself equal to the sum of imports and net production. Report this series on a graph. Save this graph under the name MDEPEND.pic.

Comment on the evolution of self-sufficiency. Recall that 1965 is the year when the Green Revolution started in India.

2. Components of Food Availability

The concept of food availability will be used to characterize food security. It is defined as follows:

Net availability = net production + imports – increase in stock.

Complete the table by computing net availability as defined above (note that you are given levels of stocks, not changes of stocks). Report both net food production and net food availability on the same graph. Similarly, report total imports and stocks on a third graph. A breaking point of 1966 appears on these figures, suggesting two distinct periods in India's food security policy.

3. Trend and Fluctuations of Production

The production performance is analyzed in terms of trend and fluctuations. The trend of a series x is measured by the estimated average growth rate during the period, which is given by the slope m of the regression of $\ln x$ on time t:

$\ln x = a + mt.$

The fluctuation of a series is measured by the coefficient of variation around the trend. This is the standard deviation std of the relative deviations around the trend:

$$I(x) = \text{std } [(x_t - \hat{x}_t) / \hat{x}_t],$$

where $\hat{x}_t = \exp(a + mt)$ is the estimated value for x_t.

To complete this analysis on production, prepare a table with columns containing t and $\ln q$. Perform two regressions of $\ln q$ using the rows corresponding to 1951–66 first, and then the rows for 1967–87. This gives estimated growth rates of production for the two periods. Add one column of estimated values $\hat{q}$ for q by using the results of the first regression in the cells that correspond to 1951–66, and the results of the second regression for the cells corresponding to the years 1967–87. To visualize your results, you can make a graph with both series q and $\hat{q}$. Add one column containing $(q - \hat{q}) / \hat{q}$, and use the @std function to compute the coefficients of variation separately for the two periods again. Report these values of growth rates and coefficients of variation in Table 5E.1.

Discuss your results by contrasting the two periods. What do they show regarding the growth and the variability of production?

4. Strategy of Food Security

Repeat the same analysis for net food availability. Compare the growth rates of production and availability. You should see that the rate of growth of food availability has decreased in the second period, despite an increasing rate of production. The growth rate of availability is also higher than the growth rate of production in the first period but lower in the second period. Now compare the coefficients of variation. What can you derive from this comparison in terms of food security?

Using the trends in imports and stocks observed in the graphs above, discuss your findings in terms of the choices of strategy for food security followed by India.

5. Per Capita Availability

The achievement in food security may be better judged on a per capita basis. For that purpose, compute the growth rates in per capita availability during the two periods. Discuss.

6. Price Stabilization

Another goal of the Indian food strategy may be the stabilization of prices. To analyze its performance, two domestic prices, one for food grains and an overall price index, as well as an international market price are given. For comparison, compute an index of real price of food grains by dividing the price of food grains by the overall price index and an index of the international price of Thai rice with 1970–71 as a base. Analyze these two series with graph, growth

Table 5E.1 Food security in India

								Prices		Price indices	
							Wholesale price index				Price indices
A	B	C	D	E	F	G	H	I	J	K	L	M
Year	Population (millions)	Net production	Imports	Closing stocks with government (million tons)	Net availability	Import dependency ratio (percent)	Foodgrains (base 1970-71 = 100)	All commodities (base 1970-71 = 100)	International price (Thai rice) (1980 $)	Per capita net availability (kg)	Relative foodgrains price index (base 1970-1971)	International price (Thai rice) (base 1970-1971)
1950	363.4	48.1	4.8	.7			44.5	48.5	604.9			
1951	369.6	48.6	3.9	1.3			49.8	53.3	553.3			
1952	376.1	54.0	2.0	2.0			48.2	45.5	572.5			
1953	382.9	63.2	.8	1.5			48.5	46.3	656.8			
1954	390.2	61.8	.6	1.7			39.3	44.3	607.3			
1955	397.8	60.6	1.4	.9			33.9	40.7	534.0			
1956	405.8	63.3	3.6	.3			43.7	45.7	499.6			
1957	414.3	59.2	3.2	1.2			48.0	48.3	490.0			
1958	423.3	68.9	3.9	.9			50.0	49.3	499.3			
1959	432.7	67.1	5.1	1.4			50.4	51.3	470.5			
1960	442.4	71.8	3.5	2.8			50.1	54.6	434.5			
1961	452.2	72.4	3.6	2.6			48.5	55.9	467.5			
1962	462.0	70.1	4.6	2.3			51.2	56.5	514.5			
1963	472.1	70.6	6.3	2.3			54.0	58.9	490.8			
1964	482.5	78.2	7.5	1.0			66.9	65.9	462.1			
1965	493.2	63.3	10.4	2.1			72.4	71.7	454.3			
1966	504.2	65.0	8.7	2.2			81.5	81.6	524.8			
1967	515.4	83.2	5.7	2.0			106.5	94.1	655.4			
1968	527.0	82.3	3.9	4.0			100.9	93.1	646.2			
1969	538.9	87.1	3.6	4.5			89.5	95.4	569.8			
1970	551.3	94.9	2.0	5.6			96.4	101.3	413.8			
1971	563.9	92.0	.5	8.1			102.1	105.2	351.5			
1972	576.8	84.9	3.6	3.4			114.6	113.0	367.5			
1973	590.0	91.6	5.1	3.1			135.0	131.6	754.3			
1974	603.5	87.4	7.4	2.7			183.6	169.2	959.3			
1975	617.2	105.9	.7	7.9			187.0	175.8	578.2			
1976	631.3	97.3	.6	18.8			150.4	172.4	399.5			
1977	645.7	110.6	.2	17.3			167.2	185.4	388.9			
1978	660.3	115.4	.0	17.1			173.3	185.0	456.5			
1979	675.2	96.0	.0	17.4			179.8	206.5	363.3			
1980	690.1	113.4	.0	11.7			207.3	248.1	433.9			
1981	705.2	116.6	1.2	11.3			236.1	278.4	480.4			
1982	720.4	113.3	2.1	12.8			242.5	285.3	295.6			
1983	735.6	133.3	4.1	15.3			270.4	308.5	286.6			
1984	750.9	127.4	2.3	22.6			275.4	334.0	265.6			
1985	766.1	131.6	.0	24.2			289.5	353.3	225.1			
1986	781.4	124.4	.0	22.6					185.6			
1987			.0	14.0								

136

	A	B	C	D	E	F	G	H	I	J	K	L	M
49	**Table 5E.1 (continued)**												
50	Annual growth rates												
51	1951 - 66		2.4										
52	1967 - 87		2.8										
53	1951 - 87		2.6										
54	Coefficient of variation around trend												
55	1951 - 66		7.3										
56	1967 - 87		7.0										
57	1951 - 87		7.2										
58													

Sources: Government of India, Bulletin on Food Statistics, 1965, 1985, and Economic Survey 1987 - 88; World Bank, Commodity Trade and Price Trends, 1987-88, (Baltimore: Johns Hopkins University Press, 1988).

Working space

Year	Net production			Net availability			Per capita net availability	Relative foodgrains price			Thai rice price	
	Ln	Estimated	(Obs-est)/est	Ln	Estimated	(Obs-est)/est	Ln	Ln	Estimated	(Obs-est)/est	Ln	Estimated
1950												
1951												
1952												
1953												

rates, and coefficient of variations. What can you conclude about the effectiveness of price stabilization in India?

References

Alderman, Harold. 1993. "Intercommodity Price Transmittal: Analysis of Food Markets in Ghana." *Oxford Bulletin of Economics and Statistics* 55:43-64.

Alexander, Carol, and John Wyeth. 1994. "Cointegration and Market Integration: An Application to the Indonesian Rice Market." *Journal of Development Studies* 30:303-28.

Antle, John. 1989. "Nonstructural Risk Attitude Estimation." *American Journal of Agricultural Economics* 71:774–84.

Basu, Kaushik, and Clive Bell. 1991. "Fragmented Duopoly: Theory and Applications to Backward Agriculture." *Journal of Development Economics* 36:145-65.

Binswanger, Hans. 1980. "Attitudes towards Risk: Experimental Measurement Evidence from Rural India." *American Journal of Agricultural Economics* 62:395–407.

Blyn, George. 1973. "Price Series Correlation as a Measure of Market Integration." *Indian Journal of Agricultural Economics* 28:56-59.

Braverman, Avishay, Ravi Kanbur, Antonio Salazar Brandão, Jeffrey Hammer, Mauro de Rezende Lopes, and Alexandra Tan. 1990. *Costs and Benefits of Agricultural Price Stabilization In Brazil.* Policy, Research, and External Affairs Working Paper, WPS 564. Washington, D.C.: World Bank, Agricultural and Rural Development Department.

Buschena, David, and David Zilberman. 1992. "Risk Attitudes over Income under Discrete Status Levels." Unpublished paper. University of California at Berkeley, Department of Agricultural and Resource Economics.

de Janvry, Alain, and Elisabeth Sadoulet. 1991. "Food Self-Sufficiency and Food Security in India: Achievements and Contradictions." In *National and Regional Self-Sufficiency Goals: Implications for International Agriculture,* edited by Ruppel and Kellogg. Boulder, Colo.: Lynne Rienner.

Delgado, Christopher. 1988. "A Variance Components Approach to Food Grain Market Integration in Northern Nigeria." *American Journal of Agricultural Economics* 68:970-79.

Fafchamps, Marcel. 1992. "Cash Crop Production, Food Price Volatility, and Rural Market Integration in the Third World." *American Journal of Agricultural Economics* 74:90–99.

Faminow, Merle, and Bruce Benson. 1990. "Integration of Spatial Markets." *American Journal of Agricultural Economics* 72:49-62.

Finkelshtain, Israel, and James Chalfant. 1991. "Marketed Surplus under Risk: Do Peasants Agree with Sandmo?" *American Journal of Agricultural Economics* 73:557–67.

Hays, H.M., and J.H. McCoy. 1977. "Food Grain Marketing in Northern Nigeria: Spatial and Temporal Performance." *Journal of Development Studies* 14:182-92.

Knudsen, Odin, and John Nash. 1990. "Domestic Price Stabilization Schemes in Developing Countries." *Economic Development and Cultural Change* 38:539–58.

Moscardi, Edgardo, and Alain de Janvry. 1977. "Attitudes toward Risk among Peasants: An Econometric Approach." *American Journal of Agricultural Economics* 59:710–16.

Newbery, David, and Joseph Stiglitz. 1981. *The Theory of Commodity Price Stabilization.* Oxford: Oxford University Press.

Pinckney, Thomas. 1988. *Storage, Trade, and Price Policy under Production Instability: Maize in Kenya.* Research Report 71. Washington, D.C.: International Food Policy Research Institute.

Pyle, David, and Stephen Turnovsky. 1970. "Safety-First and Expected Utility Maximization in Mean-Standard Deviation Portfolio Analysis." *Review of Economics and Statistics* 52:75–81.

Ravallion, Martin. 1986. "Testing Market Integration." *American Journal of Agricultural Economics* 68:102-109.

Reutlinger, Shlomo. 1986. *Poverty and Hunger: Issues and Options for Food Security in Developing Countries.* Washington, D.C.: World Bank.

Roumasset, James 1976. *Rice and Risk: Decision Making among Low-Income Farmers.* Amsterdam: North-Holland.

Schluter, M. G., and Timothy Mount. 1976. "Some Management Objectives of Risk Aversion in the Choice of Cropping Patterns, Surat District, India." *Journal of Development Studies* 12:246–61.

Takayama, Takashi, and George Judge. 1971. *Spatial and Temporal Price and Allocation Models.* Amsterdam: North-Holland Publishing Co.

Timmer, Peter. 1987. *The Corn Economy of Indonesia.* Ithaca, N.Y.: Cornell University Press.

Valdés, Alberto, and P. Konandreas. 1981. "Assessing Food Security Based on National Aggregates in Developing Countries." In *Food Security for Developing Countries*, edited by A. Valdés. Boulder, Colo.: Westview Press.

CHAPTER SIX

Household Models

6.1. Household Behavior and Policy Analysis

Probably no less than a quarter of the world population belongs to farm (peasant) households, and most of this population is in the less developed countries (Ellis, 1988). Agricultural production is often importantly dependent on their performance as farmers, and world poverty is disproportionately found among them, making understanding the determinants of their welfare a prime concern in any strategy of poverty alleviation. The specificity of these households is that they integrate in a single institution decisions regarding production, consumption, and reproduction over time. These households are only semicommercialized in the sense that, even if all markets work, at least some of their production is kept for home consumption and some of their labor resources are used directly for home production. Food produced in excess of household consumption is sold on the product market, and family labor supplied in excess of use on the home plot is sold on the labor market. If production is less than consumption and/or labor supplied less than needs for the plot, the household is a net buyer of food and/or a net employer of labor. In this case, cash expenditures to buy food have to come from other sources of income such as the sale of cash crops or of labor. When not all markets work, some households may be completely autonomous in food and/or labor, even when they participate to markets for other goods such as cash crops and other factors such as fertilizers or credit. Other specificities of peasant households are the importance of behavior toward risk, existence of household members with different opportunity costs and eventually captive within the household, a life cycle that differentially redefines the opportunity costs of family members over time, and a great multiplicity of activities both in agriculture and off-farm, including wage labor and microenterprises (von Braun and Pandya-Lorch, 1991; Reardon, Delgado, and Matlon, 1992). As we will see in Chapter 9, peasants usually belong to agrarian communities which offer them contractual opportunities to access factors, insurance, and credit when markets fail.

The analysis of peasant households is important for policy analysis. When all markets work, the only linkage between production and consumption decisions is through the level of farm income achieved in production. When not all markets work, there are direct interrelations between production and consumption decisions. In both cases, policies that affect the price of goods (factors) both produced (used) and consumed (sold) thus have complex implications for production and welfare. Important policy questions this raises are whether peasant households will over time tend to differentiate in landless workers and commercial farmers, and thus disappear as a social category, or whether they can be competitive and, if so, which category of peasants will tend to dominate, starting from a heterogenous set of households. As we shall see, the answers to these questions very much depend on the nature of transactions costs that characterize different households and the quantity of productive assets they control. Politically, disappearance or permanence of a peasantry has often had serious implications on policy making, as exemplified by the Mexican reforms of the land tenure system, Japanese and French agricultural trade policy, and transitions to socialism in many African and Asian countries.

The construction of household models started with the work of Chayanov in the 1920s as part of the debate between populists and Bolsheviks in Russia, where households faced no labor market and had flexible access to land, yielding the concept of demographic differentiation as the optimum work effort changed through the life cycle (Harrison, 1975). More recently Becker (1965) formalized in the "new home economics" the process of time allocation within the household when labor has an opportunity cost and utility is derived not directly from goods purchased, but from Z-goods produced in the household with purchased goods and family time. The full version of the neo-classical farm household model was developed by Barnum and Squire (1979) and further elaborated by a series of authors in a book edited by Singh, Squire, and Strauss (1986).

6.2. Integrating Producer, Consumer, and Worker Decisions into a Household Problem

In economic theory, the problems of production decisions, consumption decisions, and labor supply decisions are usually analyzed separately through the behavior of three classes of agents:

a. Producers, who maximize net revenues with respect to levels of products and factors, subject to constraints determined by market prices, fixed factors (private assets and public goods), and technology. This was examined in Chapter 2.

b. Consumers, who maximize utility with respect to the quantities of goods consumed, subject to constraints determined by market prices, disposable income, household characteristics, and tastes. This was analyzed in Chapter 3.

c. Workers, who maximize utility with respect to income and home time (often referred to as leisure), subject to the constraints determined by the market wage, total time available, and worker characteristics.

Formally, this has been modeled as three separate agents who solve the following three problems:

6.2.1. Producer Problem

Definitions:

One product: q_a with price p_a

Two variable factors: x with price p_x

l (labor) with price w

Fixed factors and firm characteristics: z^q (fixed capital, farm size).

Structural form of the model:

$$\underset{q_a, x, l}{\text{Max}} \ \pi = p_a q_a - p_x x - wl, \ \text{profit}$$

$$\text{s.t.:} \ g(q_a, x, l; z^q) = 0, \ \text{production function.}$$

Reduced form of the model:

Supply function: $q_a = q_a(p_a, p_x, w; z^q)$

Factor demands: $x = x(p_a, p_x, w; z^q)$

$l = l(p_a, p_x, w; z^q)$

Maximum profit: $\pi^* = \pi^*(p_a, p_x, w; z^q)$.

6.2.2. Consumer Problem

Definitions:

Two products: c_a with price p_a (agricultural good)

c_m with price p_m (manufactured good)

Disposable income: y

Household characteristics: z^c.

Structural form of the model:

$$\underset{c_a, c_m}{\text{Max}}\; u(c_a, c_m; z^c), \quad \text{utility function}$$

s.t.: $p_a c_a + p_m c_m = y$, budget constraint.

Reduced form of the model:

Demand functions: $c_i = c_i(p_a, p_m, y; z^c), \quad i = a, m.$

6.2.3. Worker Problem

Definitions:

Home time: c_l

Time worked: l^s

Total time endowment available: E

Worker characteristics: z^w.

Structural form of the model:

$$\underset{c_l, y}{\text{Max}}\; u(c_l, y; z^w), \quad \text{utility function}$$

s.t.: $y = w l^s$, income equation,

$c_l + l^s = E$, time constraint.

These two constraints can be collapsed into one equation:

$w\, c_l + y = w\, E$, full income constraint.

Reduced form of the model:

Demand function for home time: $c_l = c_l(w, E; z^w).$

Because the worker is also a consumer, these last two problems can be integrated into one single decision taken by the consumer-worker.

6.2.4. Consumer-Worker Problem

Definitions:

Characteristics of the consumer-worker: z^{cw}.

Structural form of the model:

$$\underset{c_a, c_m, c_l}{\text{Max}} \quad u(c_a, c_m, c_l; z^{cw}), \quad \text{utility function}$$

$$\text{s.t.:} \quad p_a c_a + p_m c_m = wl^s = y, \quad \text{budget constraint,}$$

$$c_l + l^s = E, \quad \text{time constraint.}$$

These two constraints can be collapsed into one equation:

$$p_a c_a + p_m c_m + w c_l = w E, \quad \text{full income constraint.}$$

Reduced form of the model:
  Demand functions: $\quad c_i = c_i(p_a, p_m, w, E; z^{cw}), \quad i = a, m, l.$

6.2.5. Household Problem

In the case of a household, the decision maker is engaged simultaneously in production, consumption, and work decisions. The three problems must be integrated into one single household problem.

Definition:
  Characteristics of the household: z^h.

Structural form of the model:

$$\underset{q_a, x, l, c_a, c_m, c_l}{\text{Max}} \quad u(c_a, c_m, c_l; z^h), \quad \text{utility function}$$

$$\text{s.t.:} \quad g(q_a, x, l; z^q) = 0, \quad \text{production function,}$$

$$p_x x + p_m c_m = p_a(q_a - c_a) + w(l^s - l), \quad \text{cash constraint,}$$

$$c_l + l^s = E, \quad \text{time constraint.}$$

The last two constraints can be collapsed into one equation:

$$p_a c_a + p_m c_m + w c_l = \pi + wE = y^*, \quad \text{full income constraint,}$$

where $\pi = p_a q_a - p_x x - wl$, farm restricted profit.

6.3. Specification of a Household Model

Before analyzing the solution of the household model, it is important to clarify the nature of the assumptions which are made in the construction of the structural form of the model.

6.3.1. Home Time

A household model integrates production, consumption, and work decisions. Consumption decisions include the choice of home time in trade-off with the consumption of goods that would need more income and hence more work. Home time is time which is not spent in directly productive and labor market activities. It includes family maintenance (cooking, fetching wood and water, tending the house); family reproduction (pregnancies, rearing the children, attending the elders); socialization (relationships within the family and with neighbors and the community, festivals, religious practices); and leisure (relaxation, pleasure, and sleep). Only a small fraction of home time is thus "time off," particularly for women, and it is evidently quite different from the concept of leisure often identified with this allocation of time (Ellis, 1988).

6.3.2. Definition of the Household Unit

The concept of household varies widely across cultures. It ranges from the Western nuclear household to the African extended family system. Definition of the unit of analysis thus requires careful prior description of the subject analyzed. The key element in defining the household is identifying the decision-making unit which sets the strategy concerning the generation of income and the use of this income for consumption and reproduction. It is thus in general associated with the group that shares the same abode or hearth. There are no simple rules, however, and careful understanding of the decision-making process being analyzed must be obtained in each case, calling for an interdisciplinary approach to the specification of the unit of analysis.

6.3.3. Who Decides?

We consider here only models where there is a single decision-making process. This excludes highly relevant bargaining models where the household has several decision makers with unequal bargaining strengths who interact in a cooperative repeated game (Bourguignon and Chiappori, 1992; McElroy, 1990). As we have seen in Chapter 2, income may not be pooled under bargaining and consumption choices may be quite different for income controlled by women and men. In this chapter, the single decision-making process we consider characterizes either a situation where a single household member decides on behalf of the others (a patriarch or matriarch) or one where there is enough consensus among members to treat internal dissensions as a minor consideration. In this consensual household, resources are pooled into a unique strategy and consumption is shared, although by no means necessarily equally between household members, as we shall see.

6.3.4. Net Buyers versus Net Sellers of Food and/or Labor

Because production and work decisions affect the level of income achieved, whether a household is a net seller or a net buyer of a commodity (food or labor) whose price has changed has vastly different consequences for its welfare. A higher price for a food item thus lowers the welfare of a net buyer of food while raising the welfare of a net seller, usually a large farmer with a marketable surplus. For net sellers of labor, typically smallholders with little land and large families, a higher wage raises welfare while lowering it for net buyers for whom it is a production cost. In situations where perfect markets exist for all products and factors, most of the action in household models thus comes from whether households are net buyers or net sellers of products and factors. This differential position is principally determined by inequalities in access to productive assets and differential transactions costs in relating to markets.

6.4. Separable Household Model with Perfect Markets

6.4.1. The Model and Its Solution

If perfect markets exist for all products and factors, including the different categories of family labor, all prices are exogenous to the household and all products and factors are tradables with no transactions costs. In this case, production and consumption/work decisions can be taken in terms of these prices, which determine the opportunity costs of all products and factors owned by the household. As is typical when all markets work and there are no transactions costs, it is immaterial whether the household consumes its own products or sells them to buy what it needs to consume. Similarly, it is immaterial whether the household uses its own labor or sells it to hire what it needs to produce. Under these conditions, the household behaves as if production and consumption/work decisions were made sequentially. Perfect markets are sufficient, but not necessary for separability. As we shall see later, there is separability whenever prices are exogenous and markets are used, even if sale and purchase prices are not identical. When a household model is separable, it can be solved recursively in two steps:

a. First, the *production problem* is solved:

$$\max_{q_a, x, l} \pi = p_a q_a - p_x x - wl$$

$$\text{s.t.:} \quad g(q_a, x, l; z^q) = 0, \quad \text{production function.}$$

Reduced form of the model:

Supply function: $q_a = q_a(p_a, p_x, w; z^q)$
Factor demands: $x = x(p_a, p_x, w; z^q)$
$$l = l(p_a, p_x, w; z^q)$$
Maximum profit: $\pi^* = \pi^*(p_a, p_x, w; z^q)$.

b. Second, the *consumption/work problem* is solved, given the level of profit π^* achieved in production:

$$\max_{c_a, c_m, c_l} u(c_a, c_m, c_l; z^h), \quad \text{utility function}$$

$$\text{s.t.:} \quad p_x x + p_m c_m + w c_l = \pi^* + wE, \quad \text{full income constraint,}$$

$$c_l + l^s = E, \quad \text{time constraint.}$$

Reduced form of the model:
Demand functions: $c_i = c_i(p_a, p_m, w, y^*; z^h), \quad i = a, m, l,$
where $y^* = p_a q_a - p_x x - w l + w E$.

This recursive solution can be visualized in Figure 6.1, which gives the causal ordering through which variables are determined. Note that the only hinge between production and consumption decisions is π^*. Because p_a and w enter into both production and consumption decisions, the key issue for policy analysis is whether these prices represent a benefit or a cost to a particular household. This depends upon whether the household is a net seller of agricultural goods and/or labor, or a net buyer.

Figure 6.1. Causal ordering in the separable household model

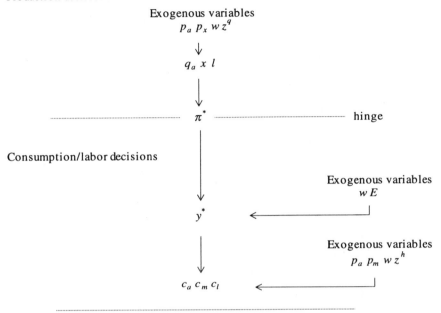

Derived indicators

Marketed surplus	$= q_a - c_a > 0,$	net seller,
	$< 0,$	net buyer
Labor supply	$= l^s = E - c_l$	
Labor balance	$= l - l^s > 0,$	hire in,
	$< 0,$	hire out.

6.4.2. Comparative Statics Results

Though it is not always unambiguous, we can frequently predict analytically what the household's response to price changes will be.

6.4.2.1. Elasticity of Consumption for Food with Respect to the Price of Food
Differentiating the demand function for food with respect to the price of food yields:

$$\frac{\partial c_a}{\partial p_a} = \frac{\partial c_a}{\partial p_a}\bigg|_{y^*=const} + \frac{\partial c_a}{\partial y^*}\frac{\partial y^*}{\partial p_a} = \frac{\partial c_a}{\partial p_a}\bigg|_{y^*=const} + q_a\frac{\partial c_a}{\partial y^*}.$$

The first term on the right-hand side can be decomposed into substitution and income effects using the Slutsky equation (see Appendix):

$$\frac{\partial c_a}{\partial p_a} = \frac{\partial c_a}{\partial p_a}\bigg|_{u=const} - c_a \frac{\partial c_a}{\partial y^*} + q_a \frac{\partial c_a}{\partial y^*} = \frac{\partial c_a}{\partial p_a}\bigg|_{u=const} + (q_a - c_a)\frac{\partial c_a}{\partial y^*}.$$

The first term on the right is the substitution effect and is negative. Because food is a normal good, $\partial c_a/\partial y^*$ is positive. Consequently, the sign of the second term is determined by the household status as a net seller, $(q_a - c_a) > 0$, or a net buyer, $(q_a - c_a) < 0$, of food. The net of the two terms on the right thus gives the following result: for net buyers, such as landless workers and small farmers, the result $\partial c_a/\partial p_a < 0$ is unambiguous. However, if the marketed surplus of net sellers is large enough, the second term may overwhelm the first, and $\partial c_a/\partial p_a$ can be > 0.

6.4.2.2. Elasticity of Demand for Home Time with Respect to Wage

Differentiating the demand function for home time with respect to wage, and decomposing as before, yields:

$$\frac{\partial c_l}{\partial w} = \frac{\partial c_l}{\partial w}\bigg|_{u=const} + (E - c_l - l)\frac{\partial c_l}{\partial y^*} = \frac{\partial c_l}{\partial w}\bigg|_{u=const} - (l - l^s)\frac{\partial c_l}{\partial y^*}.$$

Again, the first term on the right-hand side is negative. The second term $(l - l^s)$, the household's labor balance, may be positive for large farmers who hire in labor and negative for small farmers who hire out labor. While this elasticity may have either sign, we can conclude the following:

For households who hire in, the elasticity is unambiguously negative. Thus, wage is a cost. A rising wage leads to a fall in income and to less consumption of home time.

For landless workers and small farmers who hire out, the elasticity can be of either sign. Wage is a revenue. At low levels of income, it is likely that the income elasticity of leisure will be high, since so little of it is consumed. In this case, the consumption of leisure may well increase as wage rises and the household becomes more accommodated.

6.4.2.3. Elasticity of Marketed Surplus with Respect to the Price of Food

When very poor farmers produce a marketed surplus of food, it may happen that this surplus falls when the price of food rises, creating a perverse response for policy makers. For this reason, forced deliveries of cereals have frequently been imposed on peasants in Egypt and in India. This can be seen as follows:

Define the marketed surplus of food (ms_a) as: $ms_a = q_a - c_a > 0$. The response of marketed surplus to price is:

$$\frac{\partial ms_a}{\partial p_a} = \frac{\partial q_a}{\partial p_a} - \frac{\partial c_a}{\partial p_a}\bigg|_{u=const} - ms_a \frac{\partial c_a}{\partial y^*}.$$

The first term on the right-hand side is the supply response in production and is positive. The second term is unambiguously positive. The third term, for a normal good, is negative. While the net will generally be positive, very poor households may have such a high income elasticity of food consumption that the entire expression is negative. This effect will be reinforced by a low elasticity of supply response and a low substitution effect between food and other goods. A negative marketed surplus response for foodgrains has been observed by Bardhan (1970) for a sample of villages in Punjab and Uttar Pradesh and for small farmers in the Delhi Territories by de Janvry and Kumar (1981).

6.4.3. Empirical Results with Separable Models

Table 6.1 gives a compilation of household responses to changes in the price of food and in the wage in seven low-income countries (Singh, Squire, and Strauss, 1986). Two households are contrasted, a pure consumer/worker household (landless) and a farm household with a mar-

Table 6.1. Empirical results with separable household models (price elasticities)

Countries	Demand for food		Demand for nonagricultural commodity		Labor supply	
	Landless	Landed	Landless	Landed	Landless	Landed
With respect to the price of food (p_a)						
Taiwan	−0.72	0.22	0.13	1.18	0.21	−1.59
Malaysia	−0.04	0.38	−0.27	1.94	0.08	−0.57
Korea	−0.18	0.01	−0.19	0.81	0.03	−0.13
Japan	−0.87	−0.35	0.08	0.61	0.16	−1.00
Thailand	−0.82	−0.37	0.06	0.51	0.18	−0.62
Sierra Leone	−0.74	−0.06	−0.03	0.14	0.01	−0.09
Northern Nigeria	−0.05	0.19	−0.14	0.57	0.03	−0.06
With respect to the wage rate (w)						
Taiwan	0.14	−0.03	0.05	−0.12	−0.12	0.17
Malaysia	0.06	−0.08	0.29	−0.35	−0.07	0.11
Korea	0.16	0.01	0.77	0.05	0.00	0.11
Japan	0.29	0.15	0.39	0.25	0.15	0.45
Thailand	0.57	0.47	0.62	0.52	0.08	0.26
Sierra Leone	0.47	0.37	0.78	0.57	0.14	0.26
Northern Nigeria	0.06	0.02	0.04	0.01	0.01	0.01

Source: Singh, Squire, and Strauss, 1986.

keted surplus of food (landed). The results show that consumption of food by the landless always falls when the price rises, but that consumption by the landed rises in Taiwan, Malaysia, Korea, and Nigeria, where marketed surpluses are sufficiently large to create positive income effects that overwhelm the direct negative price effect. Consumption of the nonagricultural commodity always rises among the landed, who have a positive marketed surplus and hence rising incomes. Consumption of the nonagricultural commodity rises among the landless when it is a substitute for food, as in the case of Taiwan, Japan, and Thailand, but falls when it is a complement. Finally, labor supply, which is the complement to home time, always rises among the landless when the price of food rises as their real incomes fall. By contrast, it always falls among the landed as incomes rise, indicating an increased consumption of home time.

When it is the wage that rises, the landless increase food and nonagricultural consumption as their incomes improve. While the effect is small, labor supply falls with wage in Taiwan and Malaysia, suggesting that the income elasticity of leisure is very high. However, it increases in all other countries. Among the landed, only in Taiwan and Malaysia does wage appear to be a cost, indicating that the landed are net buyers of labor. This leads to a fall in the consumption of food and the nonagricultural commodity. The landed of all other countries represented behave as net sellers of labor, so consumption rises when the wage increases. Household labor supply always increases with wage: in Taiwan and Malaysia, family labor substitutes for hired labor; in the other countries, hiring out increases.

These examples show that, in separable household models, contrasted responses across households come from differential status regarding the net sale of products and labor. While this is interesting, it is clear that there is much more to household behavior than the transmission of income effects in production to consumer response. We now turn to this richer specification of household models.

6.5. Household Model with Market Failures

6.5.1. Why Markets Fail

Up to this point, the household model has been developed under conditions where perfect markets exist; that is, where all products and factors are tradables and where the opportunity cost of any product or factor held by the household is its market price. Under this condition, separability holds, and the producer side of the model can be solved prior to the consumer/worker side, with farm profits serving as the hinge between the two problems. Ownership of the variable factors is irrelevant for production decisions and affects consumption decisions only through income level, which is itself determined by ownership.

The farm household is, however, typically located in an environment characterized by a number of market failures for some of its products (e.g., some foods, particularly the most perishable or bulky, or those with high price risk) and for some of its factors (e.g., child labor or family labor with low access to the labor market or facing discrimination). An extreme case of market failure is simply nonexistence of a market, for example, due to a fully enforced legal prohibition on certain transactions. Typically, however, some type of market exists for any good or factor, be it only abroad or in the underground economy. In spite of this, a market may fail for a particular household when it faces wide price margins between the low price at which it could sell a commodity or factor and the high price at which it could buy that product or factor. Faced with this wide price band, the household may be better off choosing self-sufficiency in that good or factor if its subjective price (defined as the price which equates its supply and demand) falls inside the band. The magnitude of the price band may be increased by one or more of the following factors:

a. *Transactions costs*, which include distance from the market and poor infrastructure that increase transportation costs, high marketing margins due to merchants with local monopoly power, high search and recruitment costs due to imperfect information, and supervision and incentive costs on hired labor.

b. *Shallow local markets*, which imply a high negative covariation between household supply and effective prices. In this case, when the harvest is good and the household could have a marketed surplus, the price falls because all other households also have plentiful harvests and the subjective equilibrium price remains within the price band. Conversely, when there is a drought and household supply falls, so does the supply of all other households. The ensuing sharp rise in price may force the household to remain self-sufficient.

c. *Price risks and risk aversion* influence the effective price used for decision making. As we saw in Chapter 5, the certainty equivalent price used for decision making is the expected price discounted by a markup that reflects the level of risk and the degree of risk aversion. Sales prices are discounted negatively to hedge against risk. Purchase prices are discounted positively for the same reason. The greater the level of price risk and the greater the aversion to risk, the wider the effective price band becomes and the higher the likelihood of market failure.

A frequent cause of market failure is limited access to working capital credit. The seasonality of agricultural expenditures and revenues implies that the household not only has to satisfy an annual cash income constraint, with total expenditure less or equal to total revenue, but also to balance its budget during the lean season when there are high expenditures for consumption and input purchase and few revenues. With limited access to credit, the budget balance becomes a constraint, where expenditures have to remain less or equal to the sum of revenues during the period, accumulated savings, and credit availability. Hence, a credit constraint limits the optimum production or consumption choices. The price of any good that enters the credit constraint, either to relax the constraint as it creates liquidity or to tighten it as it uses liquidity, is marked up by the shadow value of credit. The decision prices of goods that relax the credit constraint—the daily sale of milk or family labor, for example—are marked up positively, increasing their production and/or sale. Conversely, the decision prices of goods that require credit—such as chemical fertilizers and hired labor—are also marked up positively, reducing their purchase and inducing import substitution. Exogenous market prices are consequently no longer the full opportunity cost of the goods that enter the credit constraint. If the household is facing a price band for any of these goods, the price band is now shifted upward for the goods and factors that enter into the credit constraint, and greater credit scarcity increases the magnitude of the shift.

With market failure, the corresponding good or factor becomes a nontradable. Its "price" is no longer determined by the market but internally to the household as a shadow price. When a household needs to decide what to produce and how to earn income in different activities in a situation where some markets fail, then there is no longer "separability" between production and consumption decisions. The household's production/income problem must be determined simultaneously with its consumption decisions. This is when the household approach to policy analysis becomes essential. In this case, we can no longer study separately the farm/firm side of the household without looking at its consumption decisions at the same time.

In Figure 6.1, nonseparability appears in the fact that the determination of shadow prices is based on endogenous variables that are on both sides of the income hinge. If there is market failure for food, the shadow price of food p_a^* is obtained by equilibrium between production q_a and consumption c_a of food. If there is a market failure for labor, the shadow wage w^* is determined by equality between farm production labor needs l and household labor supply l^s.

The contrast between separability and nonseparability can thus be summarized as follows:

a. If the market is used for a transaction, the household behaves *as if* it were deciding sequentially: production first and consumption/work after. Production decisions are identical to those of a pure producer. Consumption decisions are affected by the level of income reached in production. For both decisions, *market prices* serve as decision prices. The relevant price is the sale price if the household is a net seller and the purchase price if it is a net buyer.

b. If the market is not used for a transaction, that is, when the subjective equilibrium price falls within the price band, the household behaves *as if* a market existed within the household for the nontradable. Equilibrium of supply and demand on this fictitious market determines a *shadow price* that serves as the decision price for the household.

6.5.2. A Household Model with Market Failures and Credit Constraint

6.5.2.1. Definitions
Goods produced, including both food and cash crops: $q > 0$
Factors used, including both family labor and purchased factors: $q < 0$
Goods consumed, including food, purchased goods, and home time: $c > 0$
Household initial endowment, including time available to each household member: E
Net transfers received, including remittances: S
Access to credit: K
Exogenous effective market prices: $\bar{p}$
Endogenous decision prices: p^*
Number of goods: n products and factors, m consumption goods, t tradables, and nt nontradables.

6.5.2.2. Classification of Goods and Factors
Goods, and equivalently factors, are decomposed into three categories, each with a different rule for price formation which will be established in section 6.5.2.3:

Tradables which are not subject to a credit constraint, *TNC*. For these goods, the decision price is the farm-gate price, also referred to as the effective market price.

Tradables subject to a credit constraint, *TC*. For these goods, we will see that the decision price is the effective market price marked up by the shadow value of credit as determined by the credit constraint.

Nontradables, *NT*. For these goods, the decision price is the endogenous shadow price as determined by equilibrium between supply ($q_i + E_i$) and demand (c_i) within the household.

The two tradable categories (*TNC* and *TC*) together constitute the tradable category T.

To which of these three categories a particular good pertains is an endogenous choice. In what follows, we nevertheless specify the household model as if this classification had already been achieved. At the end of the chapter, we address the issue of testing for the tradability or nontradability of each good and factor.

6.5.2.3. The Model and Its Solution
The household's problem is to:

(1a) $\text{Max}_{c,q} \ u(c, z^h)$

subject to the following constraints:

(1b) $\sum_{i \in T} p_i(q_i + E_i - c_i) + S \geq 0,$ cash constraint,

(1c) $\sum_{i \in TC} p_i(q_i + E_i - c_i) + K \geq 0,$ credit constraint,

(1d) $g(q, z^q) = 0,$ production technology,

(1e) $p_i = \bar{p}_i, \quad i \in T,$ exogenous effective market prices for tradables,

(1f) $q_i + E_i = c_i, \quad i \in NT,$ equilibrium conditions for nontradables.

The Lagrangian associated with the constrained maximization problem is written as:

$$L = u(c, z^h) + \lambda \left[\sum_{i \in T} \bar{p}_i(q_i + E_i - c_i) + S \right] + \eta \left[\sum_{i \in TC} \bar{p}_i(q_i + E_i - c_i) + K \right] + \phi\, g(q, z^q)$$

$$+ \sum_{i \in NT} \mu_i(q_i + E_i - c_i).$$

The three types of goods can be treated symmetrically in the solution of the model by defining endogenous decision prices p^* as follows:

(2a) $p_i^* = \bar{p}_i, \quad i \in TNC,$

(2b) $p_i^* = \bar{p}_i(1 + \lambda_c), \quad \lambda_c = \eta / \lambda, \quad i \in TC,$

(2c) $p_i^* = \mu_i / \lambda, \quad i \in NT.$

After manipulation of the first-order conditions, the reduced form of the model can be written as follows. Production decisions regarding all tradables and nontradables are represented by a system of supply and factor demand functions in the decision prices p^*:

(3a) $q = q(p^*, z^q).$

On the production side, the household thus behaves as if it were maximizing profit using the p^* prices. Optimum levels of products and factors yield maximum profit:

(3b) $\pi^* = \sum p_i^* q_i.$

On the demand side, decisions are also made in terms of the p^* prices. Using (1b), (1c), (1d), (1e), (1f), and (2), the full-income constraint in p^* prices is written:

(3c) $\sum_i p_i^* c_i \leq \pi^* + \sum_i p_i^* E_i + S + \lambda_c K = y^*,$

and the demand system is:

(3d) $c = c(p^*, y^*, z^h).$

On the consumption side, the household thus behaves as if it were maximizing utility using the p^* prices and y^*.

For tradables, the decision prices are the effective market prices, or farm-gate prices, $\bar{p}_i$ given in equation (1e). For the nontradables, the decision prices are the shadow prices μ_i / λ, where λ is the marginal utility of cash given by constraint (1b) and μ_i the marginal utility of endowment in nontradable i given by equilibrium condition (1f). For the credit-constrained tradables, the decision prices are given by the market prices and the marginal utility of credit λ_c (or η) introduced by the credit constraint (1c).

The roles of these prices in decision making are illustrated in Figure 6.2. The endogenous markup λ_c on the price of the credit-constrained tradables serves to raise the decision price of

Figure 6.2. Price bands and credit constraint

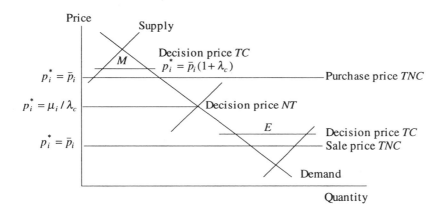

E = exports (sales)
M = imports (purchases)
NT = nontradable
TC = tradable credit-constrained
TNC = tradable not credit-constrained
p^* = decision prices
p = effective farm-gate prices
λ_c = price markup on credit-constrained transactions

both credit-constrained tradable products and factors with a positive marketed surplus. Even though these goods are transacted at the market price $\bar{p}$, their supply increases and their home use falls, since $p^* > \bar{p}$, reflecting the fact that higher sale of these goods and factors helps ease the credit constraint. Similarly, the endogenous markup λ_c raises the decision price of the credit-constrained tradables of which the household is a net buyer, inducing it to produce more of them for import substitution and to use less of them in production and consumption. Even though the transaction occurs at the market price $\bar{p} < p^*$, purchases of these goods and factors are reduced to accommodate the credit constraint.

The model to be solved is thus composed of the following five blocks of equations:

Production decisions: n equations (3a) for n products and factors, and one equation (3b) for profits.

Consumption decisions: one equation (3c) for full income and m equations (3d) for m consumption goods.

Cash constraint: equation (1b).

Credit constraint: equation (1c).

Equilibrium conditions for price formation: t equations (1e) for the tradables and nt equations (1f) for the nontradables.

The model thus has $n + m + t + nt + 4$ equations to solve for n product and factor levels, m consumption levels, t decision prices of tradables, nt nontradable decision prices, profits, full income, and the shadow prices of cash and credit.

Because the decision prices of nontradables and of credit-constrained tradables are endogenous, production and consumption decisions are not separable. This system of equations consequently needs to be solved simultaneously. Since this is analytically intractable, as is often the case in models with policy relevance, a computable version of this model needs to be specified, which we will discuss in section 6.6.4.

6.5.3. Empirical Results with Nonseparable Models

6.5.3.1. Market Failures in Food and Labor in Africa

We present first in Table 6.2 results from a nonseparable model that captures the structure of an African household with the following features (de Janvry, Fafchamps, and Sadoulet, 1991):

Products: a cash crop and a food crop,

Factors: labor and fertilizer,

Consumption: food, manufactured goods, and home time.

The study is motivated by the observation that peasants appear to governments as unresponsive to price incentives in the production of cash crops, while peasants perceive themselves as constantly trying to adjust to labor shortages or food scarcities, leading a life of great instability. These contradictory visions of the peasantry are reconciled by analyzing the role of market failures that occur as a consequence of eventually wide price bands in food and labor. For that purpose, four alternative structural conditions are considered (there is no credit constraint in this model):

Market failures for both food and labor,

Market failure for labor only,

Market failure for food only,

Absence of market failure.

The model questions how households respond to a 10% increase in the price of cash crops under these different structural conditions. The results in the last column of Table 6.2 show that, when there are no market failures, the household increases factor use and shifts its resources from food, with a 5.4% decline in production, to cash crops, which increase by 9.9%. As real income increases, more food, manufactured goods, and leisure are consumed. Since both home time and labor used in production rise, the hiring of outside labor increases by 6.1% to fill the deficit. And since less food is produced while more is consumed, demand for food on the market increases by 7.9%. These results are analogous to those observed in Table 6.1, with no market failures and transmission of income effects from production to consumption. Here, at the initial equilibrium point, the household is exactly self-sufficient in labor and food.

When both markets fail, by contrast, the elasticity of supply response of cash crops drops from 0.99 to 0.18, showing very little response. This is due both to an inability to reduce food production by any significant amount, since the family needs to feed itself while income rises, with only some substitution in consumption between food and the manufactured good, and to an inability to use more labor in production since the consumption of leisure rises slightly as income improves. Output response mainly comes from increased use of fertilizers. On the consumption side, the only reward to peasants is increased consumption of manufactured goods.

Table 6.2. Household model with market failures, Africa: Impact of 10% increase in price of cash crops (percentage change over base)

	Market failures			
	Food and labor	Labor	Food	None
Consumption				
Food	−0.5	3.0	−0.8	2.1
Leisure	0.4	0.6	4.0	2.7
Manufactured goods	15.8	7.7	9.5	5.6
Production				
Food crop	−0.5	−6.4	−0.8	−5.4
Cash crop	1.8	9.3	5.5	9.9
Fertilizer	4.7	2.8	3.1	2.2
Labor	−0.6	−1.0	3.9	1.7
Prices				
Food crop	8.8	—[a]	5.8	—
Cash crop	10.0	10.0	10.0	10.0
Fertilizer	—	—	—	—
Labor	9.3	4.5	—	—
Manufactured goods	—	—	—	—
Residual balances				
Net labor supply[b]	—	—	−10.6	−6.1
Marketed surplus of food[b]	—	−10.1	—	−7.9

Source: de Janvry, Fafchamps, and Sadoulet, 1991.
[a]No change relative to base value.
[b]Net labor supply in percent of household labor effort and marketed surplus in percent of food production.

No wonder, thus, that peasants appear to government as unresponsive to price incentives. Internally, by contrast, the perception of food and labor scarcities is represented by the sharp rises in shadow prices, by 8.8% and 9.3%, respectively. It is thus not at all surprising that peasants consider themselves stressed to respond to external incentives, however imperceptible this response may be to outsiders.

When the labor market fails but the food market is used, the shock can be exported on the food market. The household responds by shifting out of food production and buying food instead, as demonstrated by an elasticity of cash crops production of 0.93%. This allows an increase in food consumption, but without a corresponding increase in leisure, since the family needs to produce the labor effort.

Finally, when it is only the food market that fails, response in cash crops is enhanced, as revealed by an elasticity of 0.55%, by hiring labor from the outside. This allows an increase of the consumption of leisure, but not that of food, which declines slightly as resources are shifted to cash crops.

Other questions that can be asked with this type of model are: How does the household adjust to a fall in the price of manufactured goods? Can, in particular, cheaper manufactured goods serve as an incentive for peasants to increase production of cash crops (see Berthélemy and Morrisson, 1987; Azam and Besley, 1991) or is the desired increased production of cash crops better induced through imposition of a monetary head tax? How does technological change in the production of food affect the use of family labor in food production and hence the supply of cash crops? These questions are analyzed in de Janvry, Fafchamps, and Sadoulet (1991).

6.5.3.2. *Market Failure for Child Labor and Credit Constraint in Morocco*

The response of Moroccan households to a sharp rise in the price of cereals brought about by an agricultural structural adjustment program (ASAP) is analyzed in a model with the following features (de Janvry, Fafchamps, Raki, and Sadoulet, 1992):

Products: hard wheat, soft wheat, coarse grains, fruits and vegetables, animal forage, milk, meat, and handicrafts.

Factors: coarse grains used as animal feed, animal forage, machinery, and fertilizers; male, female, and child labor; and fixed factors to which correspond depreciation costs.

Consumption: hard wheat, soft wheat, coarse grains, fruits and vegetables, milk, meat; male, female, and child home time; other consumption goods; and savings.

Table 6.3 shows how the base information for two types of households—small and medium farmers—is organized. This information is derived from household surveys in the Haute Chaouia. An important feature of these farms is that animal production is partly done by using child labor for herding small flocks in common grazing lands. Nontradable child labor can thus be used as a substitute for tradable coarse grains and animal forage in meat and milk production. Goods are partitioned into three groups:

Nontradables: milk and child labor.

Tradables, credit-constrained: animal forage, machinery, fertilizer, and male and female hired labor.

Tradables, not credit-constrained: all other products and factors.

The model is completed with a system of supply and factor demand deriving from a generalized Leontief profit function and a demand system that derives from a translog indirect utility function.

When cereals prices rise, other prices rise as well, in particular that of animal forage, due to competition in production. Hence, the ASAP policy is specified as a vector of exogenous price changes (given in footnote to Table 6.4) for most tradable goods and factors. The results in Table 6.4 show that medium farmers, whose economy is largely cereals oriented, gain much more than small farmers, whose economy is largely livestock oriented. The credit constraint is highly binding on the medium farmers: all credit-constrained factors are marked up by 16.6%,

Table 6.3. Structural characteristics of small and medium farms, Haute Chaouia, Morocco (in 1000 dirham unless otherwise indicated)

Farm types	Total resources Small	Medium	Resources per hectare Small	Medium	Production or availability Small	Medium	On-farm use Small	Medium	Consumption and home time Small	Medium	Net sale Small	Medium	Family labor used on farm Small	Medium
Structural characteristics														
Average farm size (ha)	5.1	22.8												
Capital	3.0	12.0	0.59	0.53										
Animals (livestock units)	4.9	7.1	0.96	0.31										
Product and factor use														
Hard wheat					2.00	8.56			0.85	2.38	1.15	6.17		
Soft wheat					0.44	6.73			1.43	1.72	-0.99	5.01		
Coarse grains					2.95	12.07	2.78	5.40	1.61	1.55	-1.44	5.13		
Fruits and vegetables					1.64	4.40			2.18	4.48	-0.54	-0.08		
Forage (TC)					0.41	0.92	1.39	2.74			-0.99	-1.83		
Milk (NT)					0.74	1.54			0.74	1.54				
Meat					8.54	14.09			1.71	4.04	6.83	10.05		
Handicrafts & services					1.20	2.92					1.20	2.92		
Machinery (TC)							0.04	3.42			-0.04	-3.42		
Fertilizers (TC)							0.85	5.02			-0.85	-5.02		
Male labor (TC)					8.86	12.84	3.56	6.60	2.94	7.90	2.36	-1.66	3.56	4.94
Female labor (TC)[a]					4.43	6.42	2.54	2.55	1.60	5.61	0.30	-1.74	2.54	0.81
Child labor (NT)[a]					3.73	5.24	1.82	1.95	1.91	3.28			1.82	1.95
Depreciation of fixed factors							-1.94	-3.53			-1.94	-3.53		
Other consumption goods									3.72	7.72	-3.72	-7.72		
Savings									1.33	4.29	-1.33	-4.29		

Farm types	Total Small	Medium
Total net income	13.55	27.71
Net crops income	5.93	19.74
Net animal income	3.76	5.05
Off-farm income	3.86	2.92

Farm types	Income shares Small	Medium
Net crops income	43.8	71.2
Net animal income	27.8	18.2
Off-farm income	28.5	10.5

Source: de Janvry, Fafchamps, Raki, and Sadoulet, 1992.

Table 6.4. Simulation of household behavior: ASAP responses, Morocco
(percent change over base run unless otherwise indicated)

Farm size	Base run (in 1000 dirham)		ASAP Credit constraint		ASAP No credit constraint	
	Small	Medium	Small	Medium	Small	Medium
Full income	20.01	44.58	1.56[a]	7.2	1.6	7.7
Credit						
Credit deficit (1000 DH)			0.0	0.0	0.4	2.9
Price markup on *TC* (%)			8.4	16.6	0.0	0.0
Consumption						
Home time men	2.94	7.90	1.4	6.1	2.6	8.4
Home time women	1.60	5.61	−5.4	−9.7	10.3	14.4
Home time children	1.91	3.28	−0.9	−1.9	−0.9	−2.8
Consumption goods	12.24	23.43	1.8	9.8	−0.1	5.4
Production						
Hard wheat	2.00	8.56	1.6	1.8	2.0	1.8
Soft wheat	0.44	6.73	2.1	−0.7	8.5	2.3
Coarse grains[b]	0.17	6.67	82.5	8.1	98.6	11.5
Forage[b]	−0.98	−1.82	−2.6	−8.3	−1.5	−3.3
Total crops	3.27	24.54	4.4	1.8	6.5	3.8
Total livestock	9.28	15.63	−1.0	−4.1	−1.0	−1.8
Machinery and fertilizer	−0.89	−8.44	3.1	−2.0	7.1	4.0
Labor men	−3.56	−6.60	−0.5	−5.0	1.0	2.2
Labor women	−2.54	−2.55	0.1	−0.4	0.7	5.5
Labor children	−1.82	−1.95	0.9	3.1	0.9	4.7
Shadow prices (index)						
Labor children	1.05	1.02	12.7	17.1	11.2	13.2
Wage labor						
Men	2.36	−1.66	−1.0	9.1	−4.7	48.7
Women	0.30	−1.74	27.5	−31.8	−59.1	54.4
Marketed surplus						
Hard wheat	1.15	6.17	3.6	−0.5	4.9	1.4
Soft wheat	−0.99	5.01	2.7	−1.2	−2.1	0.5
Meat	6.83	10.05	−1.4	−11.2	−0.6	−4.4

Source: de Janvry, Fafchamps, Raki, and Sadoulet, 1992.
Note: Exogenous price changes: hard wheat 17.8%, soft wheat 14.4%, coarse grains 27.8%, fruits and vegetables 8.7%, animal forage 24%, meats 12.8%, handicrafts 6.1%, machinery and fertilizers 1.5%, other consumption goods 5%, and wages 6.7%.
[a]Equivalent variation in full income to the change in indirect utility at base prices.
[b]Net of intermediate use.

while the markup is 9.4% on small farmers. This reflects the ability of small farmers to relax the credit constraint by selling labor. In contrast, hiring out labor has a high opportunity cost for medium farmers. The credit constraint severely limits the ability of medium farmers to hire labor and to rent machinery and buy fertilizers. The credit constraint thus decreases their supply response on crops from 3.8% to 1.8%. On small farms, the credit constraint induces household members, particularly women, to work more on the labor market. Relaxing this constraint allows women to remain on the farm and allows for the hiring of outside workers.

ASAP induces the redefinition of the farm economy from livestock to crops, resulting in a falling production of milk and meat. Paradoxically, however, rising forage prices induce a substitution in meat production from the use of animal forage to the use of grazing in the commons and hence intensified need for child labor. As a result, the use of children in production increases, their shadow price rises sharply, and their home time falls. Market failure for child labor and access to commons increase the negative effect of ASAP on the livestock economy. In addition, the long-run consequence is increased school absenteeism and increased overgrazing in the commons, thus intensifying two of the traditional aspects of Moroccan underdevelopment.

6.6. When and How to Use a Household Model

6.6.1. When to Use Which Approach?

If there are no market failures and we are interested only in the production side of the farm household, the separability condition eliminates the need for a household approach. Even though production decisions are taken by a household, resources are allocated exactly as proposed in the pure production theory of the firm.

If there are no market failures and we are interested in the consumption side of the household, a household approach may be useful to link the consumption side to the production side ex post through income effects. The gain from use of the household approach as opposed to modeling the consumption side as a pure consumer problem will, however, only be worthwhile if:

a. Farm profit effects due to price changes are large. This will not be the case for minor crops or if there are high substitution effects among products, or among factors if it is the price of a factor that changes, as this allows the household to mitigate the income effect of the price change.

b. Farm profits are a large share of full income. This will not be the case if the household does not farm as its primary economic activity, or if the net income contribution of the farm is small because the farming activity is underpriced.

c. The income elasticity of the commodity that is of interest to the analyst is high. In general, the income elasticity of staples is less than that of luxury foods and nonagricultural commodities. Consequently, transmission of income into quantity effects will be less important for staples than for luxury goods and nonagricultural commodities.

If there are market failures, a household approach is necessary due to breakdown of the separability condition. If, however, the good for which the market fails is secondary in production and consumption, then the loss of studying the household in a nonseparable fashion or of studying producer and consumer/worker decisions separately may not be worth the cost of building a complicated model. Additionally, if the width of the price bands is small, so that neglecting market failures does not significantly misrepresent household behavior, separability may again be acceptable.

When market failures are important, then a nonseparable household approach should be followed.

6.6.2. Econometric Estimation of Household Models and Tests of Separability*

If the household model is separable, its econometric estimation can be divided into two independent parts, the production and the consumption systems. Each of these systems is estimated with the standard consumer and producer approaches seen in Chapters 2 and 3. For the consumption side, this requires measurement of a consistent demand system such as the LES or the AIDS as described in Chapter 2. For the production side, this can be done with a production function, a linear programming specification of the production system (Ahn, Singh, and Squire, 1981), or a profit function approach (Lau, Lin, and Yotopoulos, 1978).

If the model is not separable, the estimation of production and consumption behavior must be done simultaneously. Because the structural model can be written in explicit form only with the use of the nonobservable implicit prices, its estimation is quite complex, and for that reason it is not usually done. Two different approaches to the estimation of the reduced form are found in the literature, and with each of them a corresponding test of separability is associated.

6.6.2.1. Reduced Form Approach

The first approach considers the fully reduced form of the model (Lopez, 1984; Benjamin, 1992). Take the solution of the nonseparable household model given in section 6.5.2.3. Equations (3a) and (3d) give production and consumption decisions as functions of the decision prices p^*, decision income y^*, and the household characteristics z^q and z^h associated with production and consumption decisions. The endogenous p^* and y^* themselves are functions of the exogenous prices $\bar{p}$, the characteristics z^q and z^h, exogenous transfer S, and credit K if the credit constraint is binding. Eliminating p^* and y^* gives the fully reduced forms:

$$q = q(\bar{p}, z^q, z^h, S, K) \text{ for production, and}$$
$$c = c(\bar{p}, z^q, z^h, S, K) \text{ for consumption.}$$

These functions may be estimated as such. With these reduced forms, however, none of the original parameters and hence the constraints that they are supposed to satisfy can be identified. There is no justification for any specific restrictive forms for the system, and any flexible form for the function q and c can be chosen. In particular, one can estimate the demand for a subset of inputs or the supply function without having to deal with a full system. The distinguishing feature of these equations is that the production decisions depend on characteristics z^h of the consumption decisions, as opposed to what would be found in a pure producer model. Hence, one can develop a test of separability of the household model: if the parameters of the z^h variables jointly are significantly different from zero in the production equations, separability is rejected. Following this approach, Lopez (1984), using Canadian data, and Benjamin (1992), with rural Javanese data, have estimated labor demand functions and tested for the significance of demographic variables in these equations. Empirically, Lopez found that production decisions are indeed not separable from consumption decisions, while Benjamin could not reject the separability hypothesis.

In order to measure the importance of the credit constraint on agricultural production, Feder, Lau, Lin, and Luo (1990) contrast the behavior of unconstrained and constrained Chinese households. Since whether households are credit constrained or not is determined by variables which also influence production and consumption decisions, the econometric model is a switching regression with endogenous criterion, which consists of the joint estimation of the probability of being constrained or unconstrained and the production decision:

$$\text{prob(credit constrained)} = f\left(z^q, z^h\right),$$

$$q = q\left(\bar{p}, z^q\right) \quad \text{if the credit constraint is not binding,}$$

$$q = q\left(\bar{p}, z^q, z^h, K\right) \quad \text{if the credit constraint is binding.}$$

Note that K is total liquidity available during the period and not only credit. It includes the cash value of inventories, deposits, and credit. A frequent error of studies that attempt to measure the impact of credit on production decisions is to divide the sample into borrowers and non-borrowers, as opposed to the correct criterion of constrained/unconstrained used here. Indeed, some households may not need credit and hence are not constrained even if they are not borrowing, while other households may have access to credit although they are limited in the amount which they can borrow. The findings of the Feder, Lau, Lin, and Luo study suggest that credit to the constrained households has a small effect on production. This, however, does not mean that credit has a small effect on consumption and welfare.

6.6.2.2. *Predicted Endogenous Prices*

The second approach, followed by Lambert and Magnac (1992), relies on a variation of the explicit form of the solution (3a) and (3d). Consider again the nonseparable model of section 6.5.2.3. Production decisions are taken as if the household was maximizing profit at given characteristics z^q and prices p^*. Equivalently, one can say that the household's production decisions on inputs correspond to a cost minimization:

$$\underset{q}{\text{Min}} \left(\sum_i p_i^* q_i\right)$$

for a given level of output, and subject to the production technology constraint $g(q, z^q) = 0$. Because of its additivity, this global cost minimization can be written as:

$$\underset{q_j}{\text{Min}} \left(\underset{q_i}{\text{Min}} \sum_{i \in T} \bar{p}_i q_i + \sum_{j \in NT} p_j^* q_j\right)$$

where the internal minimization problem $C = \text{Min} \sum \bar{p}_i q_i$ is a cost minimization on the tradable inputs, conditional on the choice of the nontradable inputs. Write this cost function $C = C[\bar{p}, z^q, (q_j)_{j \in NT}, q_{output}]$. A duality theorem very similar to the one we saw for the profit function in Chapter 3 establishes that the optimum q_i are first derivatives of this cost function with respect to their prices. The solution to this minimization problem can be written:

$$q_i = q_i\left[\bar{p}, z^q, (q_j)_{j \in NT}, q_{output}\right], \quad i \in T.$$

In this system, the nontradables q_j play the same role as fixed inputs in a more standard analysis. As they are in fact also variable and endogenous, they are called quasi-fix inputs. Standard functional forms for cost functions and their associated input demand systems are similar to those used for profit functions (Chambers, 1988). The estimation can be done with standard estimation procedures, since all variables are observed. Note, however, that the nontradables q_j of the right-hand side and the output level q_{output} are endogenous. Hence, one needs to correct for potential bias by using instrumental variables. The procedure is then to regress the nontradable q and output level on a number of instruments, substitute their predicted values in the supply system for the tradable inputs, and then estimate the system by OLS.

The solution of the cost minimization for the use of nontradables is:

$$p_j^* + \partial C / \partial q_j = p_j^* + \sum_{i \in T} \bar{p}_i \ \partial q_i / \partial q_j = 0 ,$$

from which one can derive for each household an estimation of the endogenous implicit price p_j^* of the quasi-fix variables.

As discussed in section 6.5.3 above, these implicit prices give an interesting measure of the relative scarcity of the factor for the household. Comparison and test of equality of these implicit prices with effective market prices, if they are observed, also give a test of separability for the household.

6.6.3. *Econometric Estimation of Supply or Marketed Surplus When There Are Price Bands*

An important implication of the existence of price bands and nonseparability is that market participation of the different households is endogenous, and also is the influence of market prices on their supply. This has strong consequences for the estimation of supply response. Each household is responsive to its own decision price, and only when it is participating in the market as buyer or seller is its decision price determined by the market price. Hence, there is a difference between the true underlying supply elasticity of a household, as characterized by its supply function, and the apparent supply response to market price. In fact, the elasticity of the regional supply response will only be a fraction of the underlying true household-level elasticities, as it reflects the impact that market price has only on those households that participate to the market. Standard estimation procedures (as in Chapter 4), which typically ignore this fact, attribute to all households the market price, and directly estimate the regional elasticity of supply response, will underestimate the households' true underlying supply elasticity. With market participation varying across regions, it is not surprising to find in the literature estimations of supply elasticities which are highly inconsistent and generally low (for an elaboration of this subject, see de Janvry and Sadoulet, 1992).

One way to take into account this decision is to jointly estimate the probability of participation in the market (as supplier or as buyer) and the output supply as a function of the market price for those who do participate. Since the two decisions of (1) whether to participate in the market, which results from the joint decision of production and consumption, and (2) how much to produce, are jointly made, estimation of this system has to be performed with proper correction for selection bias (see Maddala, 1983, for a general presentation of estimation with selectivity bias). Using this methodology to estimate marketed surplus of coarse grains in Senegal, Goetz (1992) found that the regional effect of market price on marketed surplus is substantially lower than the underlying true elasticity.

Beyond the important issue of improving the estimation of supply elasticities, this remark stresses the potential for policy entry points alternative to market-level price incentives. It emphasizes in particular the role of policies that increase market participation as an instrument to increase the aggregate response of production to market incentives.

6.6.4. Calibration and Simulation with a Household Model

As usual, the parameters of the household model can either be estimated econometrically (the academic approach) or be guesstimated (the policymaker's approach). If guesstimated, the systems must be calibrated ex post to satisfy all the constraints on parameters.

When the full nonseparable model is not simultaneously estimated, a pragmatic approach consists in calibrating the model as though it were separable, implying that all prices are observed and credit constraints not effective at the base point, and of simulating responses to changes in the exogenous variables and parameters using the nonseparable model. While this is clearly inconsistent, comparing the solutions with and without market failures at least gives us a qualitative idea of the importance of these failures to household behavior.

We proceed as follows. Functional forms are specified for the production system, through specification of a profit function from which supply and factor demand equations are derived, and for the consumption system through specification of an indirect utility function from which a demand system is derived. As we have seen in Chapter 3, a convenient functional form for the profit function is the generalized Leontief:

$$\pi = \sum_{i,j} b_{ij} \sqrt{p_i p_j} + \sum_{i,m} b_{im} p_i z_m^q.$$

Its derived system of output supply and factor demand is:

$$q_i = \sum_j b_{ij} \sqrt{p_j / p_i} + \sum_m b_{im} z_m^q, \quad \text{with } b_{ij} = b_{ji}.$$

To determine the values of the b_{ij} and b_{im} parameters of this system, we typically start from a set of first-guess price and fixed factor elasticities derived from the literature. These elasticities are then calibrated to satisfy the constraints that a generalized Leontief profit function implies. This can be done by using an algorithm that minimizes, with respect to b_{ij} and b_{im}, the sum of the squares of the discrepancies between this initial set of elasticities and a set of new elasticities that derive from the generalized Leontief, keeping constant the diagonal values in which we tend to have the greatest confidence.

First-guess values are also chosen for the price and income elasticities in consumption. They are calibrated using the same algorithm as above to satisfy all the additivity and symmetry constraints implied by a translog indirect utility function:

$$v = \sum_i \alpha_i \ln(p_i / y^*) + \frac{1}{2} \sum_{i,j} \beta_{ij} (p_i / y^*) \ln(p_j / y^*),$$

where $y^* = \pi + \sum_i p_i E_i + S$, full income.

The expenditure system that derives from the translog is:

$$\frac{p_i c_i}{y^*} = \frac{\alpha_i + \sum_j \beta_{ij} \ln p_j / y^*}{\alpha_y + \sum_j \beta_{yj} \ln p_j / y^*},$$

where $\alpha_y = \sum_i \alpha_i = -1$, $\beta_{yj} = \sum_i \beta_{ij}$, and $\beta_{ij} = \beta_{ji}$.

With the nonseparable household model thus quantified, we can proceed to solve the model numerically.

Numerical solution of the separable model is easy, since the reduced-form equations are explicit with a profit function and so are the demand equations. If the production side is a linear program, a simplex-type algorithm must be used. If the model is nonseparable, and some prices thus endogenous, the system of reduced-form equations is nonlinear. It can be solved either with a nonlinear equations package or by log-linearizing the model around the initial base point. In the latter case, only small changes around the base point can be simulated. However, it has the advantage of requiring only inversion of the matrix of endogenous variables coefficients, an operation that can be done on a spreadsheet.

6.7. Intertemporal Household Models

The analyses of household models in previous sections have all concerned choices within one unit of time as function of assets, prices, and household characteristics of the same period. An important other class of household behavior models relates to decisions over time. Consumers have characteristics such as family size and composition that change over time and justify an optimal intertemporal pattern of consumption. Hence, when the life-cycle income flow does not correspond to this desired consumption pattern, or when income fluctuates with external shocks, individuals try to "smooth" their consumption through borrowing and lending and through insurance mechanisms. If, however, this ex post smoothing is difficult to achieve, individuals then adopt income strategies which match as closely as possible their desired consumption path. When ex post consumption smoothing is feasible, there is separability between production and consumption akin to what we found in static models. When imperfect insurance or credit markets prevent perfect smoothing, separability breaks down as production decisions are affected by the desired pattern of consumption (Besley, 1993; Deaton, 1992a).

6.7.1. Basic Intertemporal Consumption Model under Certainty: Life-Cycle Model

The simplest intertemporal model, the life-cycle model, explains how consumption and savings evolve over the life-span of individuals and households. We assume that the individual lives T periods, receives an exogenous flow of income y_t, for $t = 1, ..., T$, and that he has the possibility in any year t to save or borrow at an interest rate r. We assume that he starts with an endowment A_0 and that he is not allowed to be in debt at the end of his life. If we abstract from bequest motives, then assets A_T will be equal to zero at the end of his life. The intertemporal utility of a stream of consumption c_t is assumed to be additively separable in its arguments and take the form:

$$u(c_1,\dots,c_T) = \sum_{t=1}^{T} \frac{1}{(1+\delta)^{t-1}} u(c_t, z_t),$$

where z_t are variables that affect the desired level of consumption, and δ is the discount rate. The discount rate measures the impatience of consumers, in the sense that consumption in the future is given less weight than consumption now, with a decline in weight of $1/(1 + \delta)$ for each additional period.

The consumer problem is to choose the optimal level of consumption, and correspondingly of savings or borrowing s_t, that maximizes his utility:

$$\underset{c_t}{\text{Max}} \sum_{t=1}^{T} \frac{1}{(1+\delta)^{t-1}} u(c_t, z_t),$$

$$\text{s.t.} \quad c_t = y_t - s_t,$$
$$A_t = (A_{t-1} + s_t)(1+r),$$
$$A_T = 0,$$

where A_t represents assets at the end of period t. The second condition represents the evolution of assets, with savings s_t (borrowing, if negative) combining with previous asset holdings and earning an interest rate r.

Substituting $y_t - c_t$ for s_t in the second constraint and replacing $A_{T-1}, \dots, A_1$ by their expression gives the life-time budget constraint:

$$\sum_{t=1}^{T} \frac{c_t}{(1+r)^{t-1}} = A_0 + \sum_{t=1}^{T} \frac{y_t}{(1+r)^{t-1}}.$$

The left-hand side of this expression is the sum of the discounted value of all future consumption, also called the *net present value* of the stream of consumption c_t. The right-hand side is similarly initial assets plus the net present value of the stream of income y_t. What this unique constraint expresses is that, when there is no constraint to saving or borrowing, the only budgetary constraint that applies to consumption is that the total value of consumption over the whole life-time (with yearly value properly discounted) is equal to the total resources available to the consumer. Maximizing utility subject to this life-time budget constraint gives:

$$u'(c_t, z_t) = \left(\frac{1+\delta}{1+r} \right) u'(c_{t+1}, z_{t+1}) = \left(\frac{1+\delta}{1+r} \right)^{t-1} \lambda,$$

where λ is the Lagrange multiplier associated with the life-time budget constraint (Deaton, 1992a). This says that if the discount rate δ is equal to the interest rate r, marginal utility of consumption should be constant over time. Hence, consumption in any period depends on the life-cycle characteristics z_t but not on current income y_t.

6.7.2. Permanent Income Model under Income Uncertainty

When income is uncertain, the standard approach is to replace utility by expected utility, so that the first-order conditions become:

$$u'(c_t, z_t) = \left(\frac{1+\delta}{1+r}\right) Eu'(c_{t+1}, z_{t+1}).$$

This last expression links consumption in year t to expected consumption in year $t + 1$. It shows that expected consumption in year $t + 1$ only depends on the evolution of life-cycle variables z, and not on the income or wealth in period t or earlier, once c_t is known (Deaton 1992a). In the particular case of a quadratic utility function,

$$u(c_t) = -\frac{1}{2}(\bar{c} - c_t)^2,$$

and a discount rate δ equal to the interest rate r, the optimal consumption path is given by:

$$c_t = f(r)\left(A_t + \sum_{k=1}^{T-t} \frac{Ey_{t+k}}{(1+r)^k} \right).$$

This expression shows that consumption at time t only depends on the expected life time wealth at time t, which is composed of wealth at time t and the discounted expected flow of income over the future. Consumption is therefore sensitive to any "permanent" change in income, but not to fluctuations or transitory income variations. By the same token, all "transitory" income should be saved.

6.7.3. *Liquidity Constraint and Household Strategies to Mitigate Risk*

Suppose that borrowing is limited ($s_t \geq -b_0$) and that asset levels must always be non-negative ($A_t \geq 0$). This liquidity constraint implies that the maximum the consumer can spend is his cash in hand, the sum of assets and current income. The liquidity constraint alters fundamentally consumer behavior. First, when the liquidity constraint is binding, consumption is below the optimal level that a nonconstrained consumer would have chosen. This contradicts the permanent income model, and one should observe a relationship between current income and consumption. Second, even if the constraint is not binding on one particular year, the risk that the borrowing constraint might bind in the future induces consumers to save and accumulate assets in provision for such eventualities. Without access to insurance or external credit, consumers must provide for this by accumulating additional assets. It can be shown that increasing variability of future income increases the rate of savings.

Households facing a potential borrowing constraint resort to a wide range of mechanisms beyond savings to mitigate risk. Alderman and Paxson (1992) usefully classify possible strategies into risk management and risk-coping strategies. Risk management strategies are actions undertaken by households to reduce the variability of income. In agriculture, this might include landholdings fragmented in scattered plots, crop diversification, and choice of less risky techniques. Households can also reduce income risk by engaging in diversified activities, participating in the labor market, or through the migration of certain family members. Some contracts such as sharecropping reduce the cost of risk through risk sharing, while others protect households from extreme adversity through limited liability clauses. Risk-coping strategies are ex post actions that smooth consumption given income shocks. Households can spread their income risk intertemporally through savings management as discussed above, or engage in relationships with other households to spread their income shocks across households at any given point in time. Intertemporal smoothing is accomplished through lending and borrowing in formal or informal financial markets, accumulation and sales of assets, and storing of goods for future consumption. Risk sharing across households occurs through formal institutions such as crop insurance, or through informal arrangements of mutual insurance, state-contingent transfers, and gifts among friends and neighbors.

Although it is easier to conceptualize these mechanisms as sequential, the household's decision on how much risk management to do depends on its risk aversion and its ability to smooth consumption through risk-coping mechanisms. Not having access to perfect consumption smoothing techniques forces the household to modify its income generation strategy. Hence, a liquidity constraint breaks the separability between consumption and production decisions over time in intertemporal models as it does in static models.

6.7.4. Empirical Evidence on Risk Coping and Risk Management

Tests of the liquidity constraint and measurements of its impact on production and consumption decisions have recently received considerable attention. A number of studies have tried to directly test for the permanent income model by regressing consumption or savings on a measure of permanent income. The main challenge in this type of analysis is to properly distinguish between the permanent and transitory components of income. Using weather variability as the main determinant of transitory income, Paxson (1992) finds that shocks to the income of Thai farmers are largely saved, although she rejects the strict version of the permanent income hypothesis. Alderman (1992) also finds substantial evidence of consumption smoothing among Pakistani farmers, although to a lesser degree by poorer households.

Alternatively, the ability to smooth consumption can be tested directly from the observation of consumption patterns over time, as derived from the relationship established between marginal utilities above. Using this method on Indian panel data, Morduch (1992) finds contrasts among income groups, with evidence of a borrowing constraint and imperfect consumption smoothing for the landless and small farmers in most villages, but not for the richer farmers.

A perfect risk-sharing mechanism among members of a community would imply that all the households pool and redistribute among each other the fluctuations affecting their income. This does not mean that consumption will be perfectly smooth over time, but that it is protected from households' idiosyncratic shocks and is only affected by the group-level fluctuations in income. In particular, where households in the same community face similar production risks, output price risks, and consumer prices, there is little scope for insurance at the community level. A strong empirical implication of the full risk-sharing model is that controlling for community changes in consumption, the consumption and the income of an individual will not be correlated. Perfect sharing is most likely impossible to achieve because of the intrinsic limit imposed by opportunistic behavior. However, it is still interesting to see whether consumption patterns evidence some degree of sharing. An important issue for these studies is to define the appropriate community: is it the village, a subgroup within the village, the ethnic group, or the family with geographically dispersed members? Empirical analyses include Townsend (forthcoming) and Morduch (1991) for India, Alderman and Garcia (1992) for Pakistan, Deaton (1992b) for Côte d'Ivoire, and Udry (1990) for Nigeria. All these studies reject the full insurance model, but many of the results are consistent with some degree of risk sharing.

A different approach has been taken by Udry (forthcoming), who directly tests for the presence of partial risk sharing attached with one specific transaction: lending-borrowing interpersonal transfers. His findings support the hypothesis that credit contracts have state-contingent repayment obligations, according to which a borrower will repay less if he is facing a negative shock and more if it is the lender who is facing a bad shock.

The hypothesis of risk management behavior by households predicts that income-generating decisions are influenced by risk aversion and consumption decisions if there is a liquidity constraint that prevents ex post optimal consumption smoothing. The main empirical difficulty here is to identify whether the household is constrained or not and the tightness of this constraint. This is similar to what we have seen in the static model where what influences production decisions is the amount of available liquidity if the constraint is binding, or equivalently the shadow price of the liquidity constraint. Furthermore, in the case of an intertemporal model, decisions are affected by the liquidity constraint not only in the years in which the constraint is binding but also in the other years. Hence, it is really the potentiality of being constrained in the future which should be captured. Following his identification of a class of constrained households, Morduch (1992) shows that potentially constrained households display more crop and plot diversification than do other households. Using the data from the same Indian villages, Rosenzweig and Binswanger (1994) show that households with greater wealth opt for a more risky (presumed more profitable) portfolio of activities.

A final remark concerns the direct interaction that may take place between risk-coping actions and income generation when assets used for saving/insurance mechanisms are also productive assets. This is explored by Rosenzweig and Wolpin (1993) in the same Indian villages where savings for the purpose of hedging against future needs and credit constraints is done via the holding of bullocks. The impact of this is twofold. On the one hand, the fact that these productive assets are used for insurance gives them some extra value beyond their marginal productivity in production. This is like a positive externality, and it induces a higher level of accumulation. On the other hand, any sales made in times of negative shocks have negative consequences on future income and, hence, can increase the severity of future occurrence of negative shocks.

Exercise 6
Household Responses to Price Incentives

In this exercise (file 6HHOLD), we use a separable model to simulate the production and consumption behavior of a landed household and compare it with the behavior of a landless household, where income does not derive from agricultural profit. We also look at one case of nonseparability induced by a labor market failure and show how it affects the responsiveness of the household to crop price increases. This exercise is largely based on a model built by Lau, Yotopoulos, Chou and Lin (1981), with producer and consumer behavior estimated with household data from the Province of Taiwan in 1967-68. The first part of Table 6E.1 gives the parameters of a demand system and a profit function for a household. The demand system is a Linear Logarithmic Expenditure System, which is derived from a translog indirect utility function:

$$p_i c_i = y^* (\alpha_{i0} + \sum_k \alpha_{ik} \ln p_k + \alpha_{id} \ln A_d),$$

where y^* is the full income of the household, p_k are the prices of the different goods (agricultural commodity, nonagricultural commodity, and home time), A_d is the number of members in the household, and c is the vector of consumption. Note that the restrictions on these parameters are:

$$\sum_i \alpha_{i0} = 1, \ \sum_k \alpha_{ik} = 0, \ \text{and} \ \sum_i \alpha_{ik} = \sum_i \alpha_{id} = 0.$$

The full income is the sum of profit, the value of the time of all the workers, and exogenous transfers:

$$y^* = \pi + p_l E A_w + S,$$

where p_l is the wage rate, A_w the number of workers, E the total time endowment available per worker, and S net transfers (positive or negative).

The estimated normalized restricted profit function is the Cobb-Douglas:

$$\ln(\pi / p_a) = \beta_0 + \sum_j \beta_j \ln(p_j / p_a) + \sum_k \gamma_k \ln z_k,$$

where the p_j are the prices of the different variable inputs and the z_k are the fixed inputs. In our case variable inputs are labor, animal labor, machine labor, and fertilizer, and fixed inputs are land and capital. The homogeneity constraint is automatically satisfied in this formulation, and the only restriction on the parameters is:

$$\sum_k \gamma_k = 1.$$

Note that the parameter $(-\sum \beta_j)$ has been assigned to the price variable p_a in the corresponding cell of the table.

Output supply q and factor demand x_i are obtained by derivation of the profit function as follows:

$$q = \frac{\partial \pi}{\partial p_a} = \left(1 - \sum_j \beta_j\right) \frac{\pi}{p_a} = (1 + \beta_a) \frac{\pi}{p_a}$$

and

$$x_j = -\frac{\partial \pi}{\partial p_j} = -\beta_j \frac{\pi}{p_j}.$$

Exogenous variables include the structural characteristics of the household (number of dependents and number of workers), its endowment of the fixed inputs of land and capital, transfers S, and all the prices. The household used for the first set of experiments has 7.3 members, among which 3.7 are workers, one hectare of land, and NT$43,045 of capital. It receives a negative net transfer of NT$10,000, which corresponds to other income that do not derive from agricultural production net of fixed rent and household savings (considered exogenous in this simplified model). Its profit income of NT$38,690 represents 52% of its full income. It is this

	B	C	D	E	F	G	H	I	J	K	L
1	Table 6E.1. Household response to price incentives										
2											
3											
4	Parameter values in equations										
5			Exogenous variables								
7		Intercept	Agr.	Nonagric.	Wage	Animal	Mechanical	Fertilizer	Number		
8			price	price		labor price	labor price	price	dependents	Capital	Land
9			(Pa)	(Pna)	(wage)	(Panimal)	(Pmech.)	(Pfert)	(Ad)	(K)	(T)
11	Consumption										
12	Agricultural commodity	0.145	0.025	0.042	-0.067				0.063		
13	Nonag. commodity	0.580	0.042	0.139	-0.181						
14	Home time	0.275	-0.067	-0.181	0.248				-0.063		
15	Production										
16	Profit / Pa	10.550	1.112		-0.826	-0.045	-0.020	-0.221		0.072	0.928
19		Base household		Subfamily farm		Elasticities for the base household				Family farm	
20	Observed exogenous values		Pa +10%		Pa +10%	Pna	Panimal	P fert.	Wage	Base	Pa +10
22	Other income to landed (NT$)	-10000	-10000								
23	Other income to landless (NT$)	28690	28690								
24	Time per worker (days)	365	365								
26	Agric. com. price (NT$/kg)	3.4	3.7								
27	Nonag. com. price (NT$/kg)	26.8	26.8								
28	Home time price, wage (NT$/day)	33.6	33.6								
29	Animal labor price (NT$/day)	46.7	46.7								
30	Mechan. labor price (NT$/hour)	53.2	53.2								
31	Fertilizer price (NT$/kg)	2.3	2.3								
33	Number of workers	3.7	3.7								
34	Number of dependents	7.3	7.3								
35	Quantity of capital (NT$)	43045	43045								
36	Quantity of land (ha)	1.00	1.00								
38	Endogenous variables										
41	Landless household										
42	Total time value (NT$)	45377	45377								
43	Full income (NT$)	74067	74067								
44	Consumption:										
45	Agricultural commodity (kg)	4432	4077								
46	Nonagric. commodity (kg)	1250	1261								
47	Home time (days)	759	745								
48	Labor supply (days)	592	606								
51	Landed household										
52	Producer model										
53	Profit (NT$)	38690	47317								
54	Production (kg)	24033	26720								
55	Labor demand (days)	951	1163								
56	Animal labor (days)	37	46								
57	Mechanical labor (hours)	15	18								
58	Fertilizer (kg)	3718	4547								
60	Full income (NT$)	74067	82694								
61	Consumption:										
62	Agricultural commodity (kg)	4432	4552								
63	Nonag. commodity (kg)	1250	1408								
64	Home time (days)	759	831								
65	Total labor supply (days)	592	519								
67	Marketed surplus (kg)	19601	22169								
68	Net market labor supply (days)	-359	-644								

	B	C	D	E	F	G	H	I	J	K	L
69	Table 6E.1. Household response to price incentives (cont.)										
70		Base household		Subfamily farm		Elasticities for the base household				Family farm	
71			Pa +10%		Pa +10%	Pna	Panimal	P fert.	Wage	Base	Pa +10
72											
73		Comparing columns									
74			D to C	E to C	F to E	G to C	H to C	I to C	J to C	K to C	L to K
75	Growth rates in production										
76	Production		11.2								
77	Labor demand		22.3								
78	Profit		22.3								
80	Growth rates in consumption										
81	Landless household										
82	Agricultural commodity		-8.0								
83	Nonagric. commodity		.9								
84	Home time		-1.9								
85	Labor supply		2.4								
87	Landed household										
88	Agricultural commodity		2.7								
89	Nonagric. commodity		12.6								
90	Home time		9.6								
91	Marketed surplus		13.1								
92	Net labor supply		79.2								

relatively large share of full income which clearly qualifies the household as a peasant household. Remember that the profit income does not include the value of the household labor, even when working on its own land, but rather is a concept of return to the fixed factors only. In each simulation, we will compare two households, a landless household and a landed household. The two households have the same characteristics and, in particular, the same initial income. However, for the landless household all nonlabor income is constant, while the landed household earns part of its income from profits. The transfer S for the landless household is set to NT\$28,690, which is equal to the initial value of profit and transfer of the landed household in order to make them perfectly comparable. This is entered in row 23.

From this set of equations and the exogenous variables, one can simulate the decisions of the household in production and input demand, and in consumption and labor supply. The first block of endogenous variables gives those of the landless household. The next block gives the behavioral variables of the landed household, decomposed into production and consumption. Profit, production, and input demand are first calculated using the formulae above. The full income is then calculated as the sum of the profit, the value of time available to the household, and transfer (other income). Consumption of agricultural and nonagricultural commodities and of home time is then derived. Labor supply is the complement of home time in total time. Marketed surplus of agricultural product is calculated as the difference between output and household consumption, and net labor supply as the difference between total labor supply by the household and demand for labor for production on its own land.

Experiments can be conducted by copying the set of exogenous variables and equations of the first column into adjacent columns and modifying exogenous variables.

1. Agricultural Price Increase

Suppose the price of the agricultural product increases by 10%. What would be the increase in supply? What would be the change in consumption? Compare the results given by the landless household model and by the landed household model. With this landed household, you should see that the income effect may dominate the price effect, resulting in an increase of consumption of agricultural products concurrent with a rise in price. Use rows 73 to 91 to compute percentage changes in production and consumption.

By changing the endowment of the household, one can reduce the importance of its profit income. In the third column repeat a base calculation for a household owning only 0.4 ha of land and NT$17,218 of capital, and in the fourth column simulate the 10% agricultural price increase for this last household. Make sure to compare this subfamily farm to a landless household of the same income. For that purpose, reset the landless household transfer S at its new value. The consumption of agricultural goods by the subfamily farm should decline in response to a price increase, as it would for a landless household, although to a lesser extent. Be careful, in rows 73 to 91, to compute the percentage change between column F and column E.

2. Price Elasticities

For the base household types, calculate and compare the price elasticities of consumption with respect to the price of nonagricultural products, the wage, and the input prices for animal labor and fertilizer.

3. Marketed Surplus

Analyze the elasticity of marketed surplus with respect to the agricultural price. From the first two columns, you can compute the elasticity of marketed surplus for the original household. Explain why it is larger than the production elasticity. Save your file, as you will soon be modifying this model.

Suppose now that the household has a very low supply elasticity, a large share of production used for home consumption, and a low (absolute) consumption price elasticity for the agricultural product. As a result, an increase in price will induce a small increase in production, an increase of income due principally to the value increase of the crop, and a strong increase in consumption. This may result in the "perverse" effect of a decline of the marketed surplus. To simulate this, you must change the parameters of the model. Note that the direct price elasticity of consumption of the Linear Logarithmic Expenditure System is:

$$\frac{p_i}{c_i}\frac{dc_i}{dp_i} = -\left(1 - \alpha_{ii}\frac{y^*}{p_i c_i}\right).$$

To decrease the price elasticity of consumption of the agricultural product with respect to its own price, increase the parameter α_{ii} from 0.025 to 0.260. Adjust the intercept α_{i0} to 0.720 to increase the initial level of consumption. Modify the supply elasticity. As the elasticity with respect to p_a is the sum of the cross-price elasticities, you must change them as well. Try different values that will decrease the agricultural price elasticity to about 0.2. Then, adjust the intercept until the base value of profit is equal to the initial value of NT$38,690. You can compute the base equilibrium for this household in the first column and simulate a price increase of 10% in the second column. Explain the negative change in marketed surplus by analyzing the share of home consumption in production and the changes in these two quantities.

Save this file under a different title than your first, as it has different parameters.

4. Missing Market for Labor

Retrieve the file with the original set of parameters. Define in column K a landed household that is exactly self-sufficient in labor. We suggest starting this from the base household of column C and proportionately decreasing capital and land until labor demand is equal to labor supply. Simulate the impact of a 10% increase in the agricultural price in column L and in the nonagricultural price in column M. When the price of agriculture increases in column L, labor demand increases. The household is thus forced to hire workers from outside. Conversely, when the price of the nonagricultural good increases, home time decreases, labor supply increases, and the household sells some labor on the labor market. Suppose now that the household does not use the labor market. This implies that the household adjusts its behavior to maintain the equilibrium between demand and supply of labor. This constrained behavior can be replicated by using a shadow price for labor which adjusts and acts as a market price to influence the household's behavior. To perform this simulation, first copy columns L and M into new blank columns N and O. Calibrate the shadow wages until supply and demand for labor are in equilibrium. Compare the behavior of this household with a missing labor market and that of the household with perfect markets. Under conditions of missing market, the increase in agricultural price induces a decrease in agricultural production, not an increase. Explain why this occurs. Contrast this behavioral response to that induced by an increase in the nonagricultural price on these two households.

References

Ahn, Choong Yong, Inderjit Singh, and Lyn Squire. 1981. "A Model of an Agricultural Household in a Multi-crop Economy: The Case of Korea." *Review of Economics and Statistics* 63:520–25.

Alderman, Harold. 1992. "Savings, Remittances, and Pensions in Rural Pakistan." World Bank, Agriculture and Rural Development Department, mimeo.

Alderman, Harold, and Marito Garcia. 1992. "Poverty, Household Food Security and Nutritional in Rural Pakistan." Washington, D.C.: International Food Policy Research Institute Research Report.

Alderman, Harold, and Christina Paxson. 1992. "Do the Poor Insure." World Bank, Agriculture and Rural Development Department, WPS 1008.

Azam, Jean-Paul, and Timothy Besley. 1991. "Peasant Supply Response under Rationing: The Role of the Food Market." *European Journal of Political Economy* 7:331–43.

Bardhan, Kalpana. 1970. "Price and Output Response of Marketed Surplus of Foodgrains: A Cross-Sectional Study of Some North Indian Villages." *American Journal of Agricultural Economics* 52:51–61.

Barnum, Howard, and Lyn Squire. 1979. *A Model of an Agricultural Household: Theory and Evidence.* Occasional Paper no. 27. Washington, D.C.: World Bank.

Becker, Gary. 1965. "A Theory of the Allocation of Time." *Economic Journal* 75:493–517.

Benjamin, Dwayne. 1992. "Household Composition, Labor Markets, and Labor Demand: Testing for Separation in Agricultural Household Models." *Econometrica* 60:287–322.

Berthélemy, Jean Claude, and Christian Morrisson. 1987. "Manufactured Goods Supply and Cash Crops in Sub-Saharan Africa." *World Development* 15:1353–67.

Besley, Timothy. 1993. "Savings, Credit, and Insurance." Forthcoming in *Handbook of Development Economics*, Vol. 3, edited by J. Behrman and T. N. Srinivasan.

Bourguignon, François, and Pierre-André Chiappori. 1992. "Collective Models of Household Behavior." *European Economic Review* 36:355-64.

von Braun, Joachim, and Rajul Pandya-Lorch, eds. 1991. *Income Sources of Malnourished People in Rural Areas: Microlevel Information and Policy Implications*. Washington, D.C.: International Food Policy Research Institute, WP on Commercialization of Agriculture and Nutrition no. 5.

Chambers, Robert 1988. *Applied Production Analysis*. Cambridge: Cambridge University Press.

de Janvry, Alain, and Elisabeth Sadoulet. 1992. "Structural Adjustment under Transactions Costs." Paper prepared for the 29th European Association of Agricultural Economists Seminar on Food and Agricultural Policies under Structural Adjustment, Stuttgart, Germany.

de Janvry, Alain, and Praduman Kumar. 1981. "The Transmission of Cost Inflation in Agriculture with Subsistence Production: A Case Study in Northern India." *Indian Journal of Agricultural Economics* 36:1–14.

de Janvry, Alain, Marcel Fafchamps, and Elisabeth Sadoulet. 1991. "Peasant Household Behavior with Missing Markets: Some Paradoxes Explained." *Economic Journal* 101:1400–17.

de Janvry, Alain, Marcel Fafchamps, Mohamed Raki, and Elisabeth Sadoulet. 1992. "Structural Adjustment and the Peasantry in Morocco: A Computable Household Model." *European Review of Agricultural Economics* 19:427–53.

Deaton, Angus. 1992a. *Understanding Consumption*. Oxford University Press.

Deaton, Angus. 1992b. "Saving and Income Smoothing in Côte d'Ivoire." *Journal of African Economics* 1:1-24.

Ellis, Frank. 1988. *Peasant Economics: Farm Households and Agrarian Development*. Cambridge: Cambridge University Press.

Feder, Gershon, Lawrence Lau, Justin Lin, and Xiaopeng Luo. 1990. "The Relationship Between Credit and Productivity in Chinese Agriculture: A Microeconomic Model of Disequilibrium." *American Journal of Agricultural Economics* 72: 1151–57.

Goetz, Stephan. 1992. "A Selectivity Model of Household Food Marketing Behavior in Sub-Saharan Africa." *American Journal of Agricultural Economics* 74:444–52.

Harrison, Mark. 1975. "Chayanov and the Economics of the Russian Peasantry." *Journal of Peasant Studies* 2:389–417.

Lambert, Sylvie, and Thierry Magnac. 1992. "Measurement of Implicit Prices of Family Labour in Agriculture: An Application to Côte d'Ivoire." Unpublished paper, Institut National de la Recherche Agronomique, Paris.

Lau, Lawrence, Pan Yotopoulos, Erwin Chou, and Wuu-Long Lin. 1981. "The Microeconomics of Distribution." *Journal of Policy Modeling* 3:175–206.

Lau, Lawrence, Wuu-Long Lin, and Pan Yotopoulos. 1978. "The Linear Logarithmic Expenditure System: An Application to Consumption-Leisure Choice." *Econometrica* 46:843–68.

Lopez, Ramón. 1984. "Estimating Labour Supply and Production Decisions of Self-Employed Farm Producers." *European Economic Review* 24:61–82.

Maddala, G. S. 1983. *Limited-Dependent and Qualitative Variables in Econometrics*. Cambridge: Cambridge University Press.

McElroy, Marjorie B. 1990. "The Empirical Content of Nash-Bargained Household Behavior." *The Journal of Human Resources* 25:560–84.

Morduch, Jonathan. 1991. "Consumption Smoothing Across Space: Tests for Village-Level Responses to Risk." Mimeo. Department of Economics, Harvard University.

Morduch, Jonathan. 1992. "Risk, Production, and Savings: Theory and Evidence from Indian Households." Mimeo. Department of Economics, Harvard University.

Paxson, Christina. 1992. "Using Weather Variability to Estimate the Response of Savings to Transitory Income in Thailand." *American Economic Review* 82:15–34.

Reardon, Thomas, Christopher Delgado, and Peter Matlon. 1992. "Determinants and Effects of Income Diversification Amongst Farm Households in Burkina Faso." *Journal of Development Studies* 28:264–96.

Rosenzweig, Mark, and Hans Binswanger. 1994. "Wealth, Weather Risk, and the Composition and Profitability of Agricultural Investments." *Economic Journal* 103:56–78.

Rosenzweig, Mark, and Kenneth Wolpin. 1993. "Credit Market Constraints, Consumption Smoothing, and the Accumulation of Durable Production Assets in Low Income Countries: Investment in India." *Journal of Political Economy* 101:223–34.

Singh, Inderjit, Lyn Squire, and John Strauss, eds. 1986. *Agricultural Household Models.* Baltimore: Johns Hopkins University Press.

Townsend, Robert. (forthcoming). "Risk and Insurance in Village India." *Econometrica.*

Udry, Christopher. (forthcoming). "Risk, Insurance in a Rural Credit Market: An Empirical Investigation in Northern Nigeria." *Review of Economic Studies.*

Udry, Christopher. 1990. "Credit Markets in Northern Nigeria: Credit as Insurance in a Rural Economy." *World Bank Economic Review* 4:251–69.

CHAPTER SEVEN

Price Distortions: Indicators and Partial Equilibrium Analysis

Agricultural price policy has been a major instrument of government intervention, with the goal either of increasing the contributions of agriculture to economic development or of enhancing the welfare of farm households. In other instances, price policy has been used to satisfy the rent-seeking demands of special interests. Price distortions against agriculture have been blamed for the stagnation of agriculture in the LDCs (Schultz, 1978) and for the squeeze on agricultural incomes (Sah and Stiglitz, 1984). In the MDCs, price distortions in favor of farmers are blamed for exhausting government budgets and imposing heavy taxes on consumers (Gardner, 1987). In many LDCs, food subsidies also create heavy drains on government budgets. These distortions in agricultural and food prices have become a hotly debated political issue among an array of interest groups representing producers, consumers, governments, international competitors, and environmentalists. The descaling of price interventions in agriculture has been the object of protracted, and only partially successful, negotiations in the Uruguay round of GATT (General Agreement on Tariffs and Trade).

A first level of analysis in assessing agricultural price policy consists of characterizing the magnitude of domestic price distortions through a set of indicators and tracing out the impact of these distortions in a partial equilibrium framework. Even if the analysis is subsequently extended to multimarket and general equilibrium analyses (as in Chapters 11 and 12), a necessary starting point is to first characterize the nature of the distortions in each market. Partial equilibrium analysis of these distortions indeed gives a reliable first-order approximation of their total effects that will rarely be fully overwhelmed by second-round and general equilibrium effects.

In this chapter, we first introduce the concept of reference prices, against which distortions will be measured. We then define a number of widely used indicators of price distortion, such as the nominal and effective rates of protection, and of comparative advantage, such as the domestic resource cost. Next, the tools of partial equilibrium analysis are briefly introduced. They are then used to characterize the efficiency and welfare costs of a vast array of price distortions, such as export taxes and import tariffs, producer and consumer subsidies, taxes and subsidies to factors, overvaluation of the exchange rate, and trade policy interventions to internalize environmental externalities.

7.1. Reference Prices

We start, once more, from the fundamental contrast between tradable and nontradable goods. For *tradables*, the equilibrium price is the border price p^b measured in domestic currency:

$$p^b = e\,p^\$,$$

where e is the exchange rate and $p^{\$}$ the world market price in dollars or other foreign currency.

This price gives the opportunity cost to the country of producing a good and thus helps determine whether the country is an efficient producer of that commodity (Tsakok, 1990). Measuring this price involves several decisions. The first is which international market price to use. Since these prices are notably unstable and distorted, some long-run trend value of the international price should be used, and this requires making a decision as to the relevant time period for analysis. Whether or not this international price is distorted by policy interventions is irrelevant if these distortions are here to stay over the chosen period. Deciding on this is evidently highly complex. What it says, however, is that choice of the international price that will be used requires a solid understanding of the corresponding international commodity markets before a decision can be made.

The second decision is which exchange rate to use. In many countries, the official exchange rate e is vastly overvalued relative to the equilibrium exchange rate e^{*} (see Chapter 8). In this case, the border price p^{b} measured at e underestimates the equilibrium border price p^{b*} measured at e^{*}. Which exchange rate to use depends on the objective of the analysis. If e is used, only *direct* sources of price distortions that originate in commodity-specific trade interventions will be measured; if e^{*} is used, *indirect* distortions due to disequilibrium in the exchange rate will also be captured, and these can be very large, as we shall see.

Third, we need to decide at which geographical point the price distortion will be measured. If we are to compare farm-gate prices to the reference price, the border price must also be calculated at the farm gate. The problem, of course, is that there are as many farm-gate prices as there are farms in the country. Having chosen a particular location, we denote the unit transportation costs as follows:

t_1 between harbor and farm,

t_2 between city and farm, and

t_3 between harbor and city.

The farm-gate "border price" for products sold by the farm is thus:

For an exported product: $p^{b} = e\,p^{\$}(1 - t_1)$,

For an imported product: $p^{b} = e\,p^{\$}(1 + t_3 - t_2)$.

Finally, there are a variety of other costs involved between harbor and farm, including some degree of processing, quality changes, transport losses, storage costs, and seasonality effects. In order to be comparable, the farm-gate price must be correspondingly adjusted by v, the unit marketing and processing costs, thus making the farm-level "border prices" equal to:

$$p^{b} = e\,p^{\$}(1 - t_1 - v) \text{ for exports and } p^{b} = e\,p^{\$}(1 + t_3 - t_2 - v) \text{ for imports.}$$

For *nontradables*, the reference price p_{NT}^{b} is the equilibrium market-clearing price with no government intervention, that is, the price at which supply equals demand for that product. These prices can either be predicted with a model of supply and demand where all price distortions have been removed or estimated as a cost price, the more common method. In this latter case, input-output coefficients a are used. Production factors are decomposed into nontradables (primary factors and nontradable intermediates) for which equilibrium domestic prices p^{d} are used, and tradable intermediates for which border prices are used:

$$p_{NT}^b = \sum_i a_i^{NT} p_i^d + \sum_j a_j^T p_j^b.$$

Since the nontradable intermediates are themselves produced with nontradable and tradable factors, their cost price can also be decomposed and tradable factors priced at the border price. Through successive decompositions of the nontradable component of cost, the only nonborder prices left in the calculation of cost are those of the primary factors that should be measured at their undistorted shadow prices.

Between border and domestic price, a set of *direct* policy interventions can distort prices, including export taxes, import tariffs, trade quotas, and domestic producer and consumer taxes and subsidies. When these interventions create a price wedge between producer and consumer prices, the observed domestic prices are p_p^d at the producer level and p_c^d at the consumer level. A number of indicators can be used to characterize the discrepancy between domestic and border prices and to decompose the origins of this discrepancy.

7.2. Indicators of Protection and Incentives

7.2.1. Nominal and Real Protection

The *nominal protection coefficient* (*NPC*) is the simplest indicator of price distortion and the easiest to measure. It is equal to the ratio of the domestic price of a commodity i to its border price using the official exchange rate:

$$NPC_i = \frac{p_i^d}{p_i^b}.$$

Thus,   if $NPC_i > 1$, producers are protected and consumers taxed,
          if $NPC_i < 1$, producers are taxed and consumers subsidized, and
          if $NPC_i = 1$, the structure of protection is neutral.
Alternatively, this can be written as the *nominal rate of protection* (*NRP*):

$$NRP_i = \left(\frac{p_i^d}{p_i^b} - 1 \right) = t_i.$$

Thus, $p_i^d = p_i^b NPC_i = p_i^b (1 + t_i)$.

If $NRP_i > 0$, producers are protected and consumers taxed; if $NRP_i < 0$, producers are taxed and consumers subsidized. Thus, if $NPC > 1$ or $NRP > 0$, producers receive a price which, after direct interventions, is above the border price, giving them incentives to produce more of the crop than if equilibrium prices prevailed. Whether a commodity is initially taxed ($NRP < 0$) or protected ($NRP > 0$), a rise in the *NRP* between two periods indicates increased protection and a fall indicates increased disprotection.

If the official exchange rate is not at equilibrium, the border price against which the domestic price is compared should be adjusted to remove this additional distortion. Calculating the border price at the equilibrium exchange rate e^*, the *NPC* and *NRP* become the real protection coefficient (*RPC*) and the real rate of protection (*RRP* = *RPC* − 1), which take into account both *direct* price distortions through product-specific price policies as above and *indirect* distortions through the exchange rate.

We measure the degree of exchange rate distortion as *EDist* = e/e^*. This, as we will see in Chapter 8, is proportional to the real exchange rate when e^* is measured by the purchasing power parity (PPP) approach. Then, with $p_i^{b*} = e^* p_i^{\$}$ denoting the border price at the equilibrium exchange rate,

$$RPC_i = \frac{p_i^d}{p_i^{b*}} = \left(\frac{e}{e^*}\right)\left(\frac{p_i^d}{p_i^b}\right) = EDist \cdot NPC_i.$$

In this decomposition of RPC_i, NPC_i measures the *direct* effect, which is product specific, while *EDist* measures the *indirect* effect, which is economywide. If the exchange rate is overvalued, $e < e^*$, $p^b < p^{b*}$, *EDist* < 1, *NPC* > *RPC*, and *NPC* thus overestimates *RPC*.

Table 7.1 gives values for the *NPC* and *RPC* (in index form relative to *NPC* and *RPC* in a base period 1969–71) for a number of African countries in the early 1970s and early 1980s (World Bank, 1986). For cereals, the *NPCs* indicate that there was rising direct protection through trade policies, with domestic prices 22% and 51% above the base period in 1972–73 and 1981–83, respectively. When overvaluation of the exchange rate is taken into account by calculating *RPC*, rising direct protection in 1972–73 turns into a rising total disprotection of 11%. Similarly, the 51% rise in direct protection in 1981–83 is reduced to a total increase in protection of only 9%. There was some direct disprotection of export crops in 1972–83 (7%), which had reversed into slight protection in 1981–83 (2%). However, it is through the official exchange rate that these crops are severely taxed, and this taxation was not significantly weakened over the two periods, as it evolved from 29% in the first to 27% in the second. These results show that indirect disprotection through the exchange rate is very important in African agriculture. The appearance of protection through trade distortions in food crops is eventually fully erased by exchange rate overvaluation. This makes the important point that a significant part of agricultural price policy is via exchange rate policy, not direct price interventions at the commodity level.

7.2.2. Effective and Real Effective Protection

Price distortions affect inputs as well as products. It is often the case, for instance, that disprotection of products is partially compensated by subsidies of some inputs such as fertilizers and fuels and of credit. From the standpoint of farm incentives, it is important to capture the net effect of these distortions. This is done by calculating at the farm level the effective protection coefficient (*EPC*) for a commodity i. For this purpose, inputs are categorized as follows:

Traded intermediate factors (*T*), such as fertilizers, chemicals, and fuels.

Primary factors: land, labor, and fixed capital, such as machinery and buildings.

Nontraded intermediate factors (*NT*): services such as insurance and transportation and other factors for which the international market fails. These intermediate factors are themselves produced with primary factors, traded intermediary factors, and nontraded intermediary factors.

Table 7.1. Index of nominal and real protection coefficients for cereals and export crops in selected African countries, 1972–1983 (1969–1971 = 100)

Country	Cereals				Export crops			
	1972–73		1981–83		1972–73		1981–83	
	Nominal index	Real index	Nominal index	Real index	Nominal index	Real index	Nominal index	Real index
Cameroon	129	90	140	108	83	61	95	75
Côte d'Ivoire	140	98	119	87	92	66	99	71
Ethiopia	73	55	73	49	88	71	101	66
Kenya	115	94	115	98	101	83	98	84
Malawi	85	79	106	100	102	94	106	97
Mali	128	79	177	122	101	83	98	70
Niger	170	119	225	166	82	59	113	84
Nigeria	126	66	160	66	108	60	149	63
Senegal	109	79	104	89	83	60	75	64
Sierra Leone	104	95	184	143	101	93	92	68
Sudan	174	119	229	164	90	63	105	75
Tanzania	127	88	188	95	86	62	103	52
Zambia	107	93	146	125	97	84	93	80
All Sub–Saharan Africa	122	89	151	109	93	71	102	73
Rate of protection relative to 1969–1971 (%)								
Direct effect		22		51		-7		2
Indirect effect		-37		-28		-24		-28
Total effect		-11		9		-29		-27

Source: World Bank, 1986.
Note: The nominal index measures the *NPC* relative to the base period 1969–71 where *NPC* = 100. The real index measures the *RPC* relative to 1969–71 = 100.

180

The nominal *EPC* is: $NEPC_i = \dfrac{Va_i^d}{Va_i^b} = \dfrac{p_i^d - \sum_j a_{ij} p_j^d}{p_i^b - \sum_j a_{ij} p_j^b},$

where Va_i is the value added on primary factors in the production of i measured at domestic prices (d) and at border prices (b) using the official exchange rate, hence the term nominal. The a_{ij} are technical coefficients measuring the number of units of intermediate factor j per unit of production of output i. This indicator can also be expressed in rate form as the nominal effective rate of protection (*NERP*):

$$NERP_i = NEPC_i - 1.$$

If $NEPC_i > 1$ (or $NERP_i > 0$), domestic producers of i are directly protected. The return on their resources is higher than it would be if border prices prevailed, creating incentives to increase the production of this commodity. Protection implies that domestic producers of i can be inefficient relative to foreign producers. By contrast, if $NEPC_i < 1$, domestic producers of i are disprotected, price distortions give them disincentives to the production of i, and they can remain in the production of i only if they are more efficient than foreign producers. If $NEPC_i = 1$, the structure of prices is neutral on incentives. If there were price distortions on the product side, they have been exactly compensated by opposite distortions on the factor side.

Calculation of *NEPCs* is more difficult than calculation of *NPCs*, as it involves making statements about the nature of production technology. While detailed estimation methodologies are given in Balassa (1982) and in Tsakok (1990), we indicate here some of the main issues involved in their calculation:

a. Value added should be calculated as the return to primary factors. This requires extracting the primary factor component from nontraded intermediate factors. Because this is a demanding calculation, alternative calculations of *ERP* vary in their treatment of the role of nontradable intermediates in the calculation of value added:

Simple Corden method. $Va = p -$ unit cost of traded intermediate inputs directly used in production. In this case, value added is the return to primary factors and nontraded intermediates. It consequently overestimates true value added by the cost of the traded component of nontraded intermediates.

Simple Balassa method. $Va = p -$ unit cost of traded intermediate inputs $-$ unit cost of nontraded intermediate inputs. In this case, value added is the return to primary factors *directly* involved in the productive activity. It consequently underestimates true value added by the cost of the primary factors used in the production of intermediate factors.

Sophisticated Corden method. $Va = p -$ unit cost of direct traded inputs $-$ unit cost of traded components of nontraded intermediate inputs. This calculation requires extracting stepwise the traded component of the cost of production of nontraded intermediate inputs. With this decomposition, value added correctly measures the return to: (1) primary factors *directly* involved in the productive activity; and (2) primary factors used in the production of nontraded intermediate factors, that is, the primary factors *indirectly* involved in the productive activity.

b. Production technology is represented by Leontief fixed coefficients. This implies that the price distortions do not affect the nature of the technology used and, in particular, that there is no substitution between traded and nontraded inputs as a result of the price distortions. This is a strong assumption if price distortions have prevailed for some time. If technology is responsive to relative prices, the estimated *EPC*s will be biased.

c. Factor subsidies tend to be highly socially discriminatory, with some producers capturing a significant portion of subsidies to, for example, fertilizers and seeds. This is because these rents are transferred through the forces of the political economy, with relative effectiveness in lobbying affecting how much a particular group of farmers will receive. When this is the case, *EPC*s will vary greatly across producers of the same commodity. Calculations should thus be farm-group specific, as overall statements can be highly misleading of incentives for specific groups of producers.

d. If the official exchange rate differs from the equilibrium exchange rate, the indirect price distortion brought about by the exchange rate should also be taken into account. Measuring the *EPC* and the *ERP* at the equilibrium exchange rate thus gives the real *EPC* (*REPC*) and the real *ERP* (*RERP*).

Table 7.2 gives measurements of *NPC*, *EPC*, and *REPC* for Côte d'Ivoire (Michel, 1987). Cocoa and coffee, the main export crops, are heavily taxed, with *NPC*s equal to 0.56 and 0.39, respectively. Rice, by contrast, is protected by an import tariff, resulting in an *NPC* of 1.12. Imported inputs, particularly small tractors, spare parts, and fuel, are taxed. The *EPC*s of cash crops are for this reason inferior to their *NPC*. Because cocoa and coffee cultivation rarely

Table 7.2. Price distortions and comparative advantages, Côte d'Ivoire, 1985

Product	Nominal protection coefficient *NPC*	Effective protection coefficient *EPC*	Real effective protection coefficient *REPC*	Domestic resource cost *DRC*
Cocoa	0.56	0.48	0.29	0.19
Coffee	0.39	0.34	0.15	0.25
Cotton				
Manual	0.99	0.70	0.51	0.63
Oxen	0.99	0.64	0.45	0.58
Tractor	0.99	0.58	0.39	0.58
Rice, rain fed				
Manual	1.12	1.30	1.11	1.16
Oxen	1.12	1.29	1.10	0.88
Tractor	1.12	1.28	1.09	1.01
Rice, irrigated				
Manual	1.12	1.56	1.37	1.19
Mechanized	1.12	1.50	1.50	0.83
Maize				
Manual	0.61	0.54	0.35	1.15
Oxen	0.61	0.52	0.33	0.85
Tractor	0.61	0.20	0.01	0.97
Groundnuts				
Manual	0.98	0.66	0.47	0.85
Oxen	0.98	0.54	0.31	0.55

Source: Michel, 1987.

employs machinery, the difference between *EPC* and *NPC* is small. In contrast, tractor-intensive cotton production registers a neutral *NPC* of 0.99 and an *EPC* of 0.58, representing high taxation through an import tariffs on factors. However, the *EPC* of rice is higher than its *NPC*, as product-specific fertilizer subsidies further reinforce a 12% protection on the product side. Finally, exchange rate overvaluation implies that the *REPC* is lower than the *EPC*, as the nominal border price is less than the equilibrium border price. The more important the import content on the factor side, that is, for tractorized production as opposed to manual, the more *EPC* tends to overestimate *REPC*. Neutral protection in an *NPC* sense for cotton (0.99) thus becomes 0.58 in terms of *EPC* and 0.39 in terms of *REPC*.

Table 7.3. Protection of agriculture compared with manufacturing in selected developing countries, 1960 and 1970–1980

Country and period	Year	Relative protection ratio[a]
In the 1960s		
Mexico	1960	0.79
Chile	1961	0.40
Malaysia	1965	0.98
Philippines	1965	0.66
Brazil	1966	0.46
Korea	1968	1.18
Argentina	1969	0.46
Colombia	1969	0.40
In the 1970s and 1980s		
Philippines	1974	0.76
Colombia	1978	0.49
Brazil[b]	1980	0.65
Mexico	1980	0.88
Nigeria	1980	0.35
Egypt	1981	0.57
Peru[b]	1981	0.68
Turkey	1981	0.77
Korea[b]	1982	1.36
Ecuador	1983	0.65

Source: World Bank, 1986.
[a]Calculated as EPC_a/EPC_m, where EPC_a and EPC_m are the effective protection coefficients for agriculture and the manufacturing sector, respectively. A ratio greater than 1.00 indicates that protection is in favor of agriculture.
[b]Refers to primary sector.

Table 7.3 compares the *EPC*s between agriculture and manufacturing in the 1960s and in the 1970–80s in a number of countries through calculation of the ratio $EPC_{Agriculture} / EPC_{Manufacturing}$. The results show the extent of discrimination against agriculture in the context of then widespread import substitution industrialization policies, with the exception of Korea, where industrialization was already well advanced and farmers were protected. Discrimination against agriculture has slowly declined over time, with Mexico, Brazil, Colombia, and the Philippines reducing their relative disprotection of agriculture from an average of 0.58 to 0.70.

7.2.3. Effective Subsidy Coefficient (ESC)

Subsidies are also typically given to primary factors used in the production of a particular crop i. Like subsidies to intermediate factors, they tend to be highly unequally distributed across farm groups (h), with the larger farmers or powerful ethnic groups reaping benefits disproportionately. Subsidies may include tax breaks on land or credit subsidies for the financing of working capital. The *ESC* corrects the *EPC* for these differential subsidies compared with the incentives for other unsubsidized, or differently subsidized, groups:

$$ESC_{ih} = \frac{Va_i^d \pm (\text{Differential subsidies on primary factors per unit of output } i)_{ih}}{Va_i^b}.$$

Since value added is measured per unit of output, subsidies also have to be calculated per unit of output. The *ESC* permits one to assess the incentives to the production of i specific to particular classes of farmers.

7.2.4. Producer and Consumer Subsidy Equivalents (PSE and CSE)

These measures are simplifications of the *EPC* and *ESC* calculations because they do not attempt to measure value added, with the difficulties it implies in specifying technology. These indicators correct the *NPC* for input subsidies s and indirect taxes t received by a particular producer or consumer group h per unit of output of a commodity i:

$$PSE_{ih} = \frac{p_{ih}^d + s_{ih} - p_i^b - t_{ih}}{p_i^b}, \qquad CSE_{ih} = \frac{p_i^b + s_{ih} - p_{ih}^d - t_{ih}}{p_i^b}.$$

Channels through which subsidies and taxes occur include direct transfers (income support), input assistance, marketing assistance, and infrastructure support (research and extension). Border prices can also be calculated at the equilibrium exchange rate to account for indirect distortions. These indicators offer simple measures of incentives to produce and consume that have been widely used, for instance, in the GATT negotiations. The Economic Research Service of the USDA periodically publishes calculations of *PSE* and *CSE* for some 40 commodities in 27 countries and the European Community (Webb, Lopez, and Penn, 1990).

7.2.5. Direct, Indirect, and Total Nominal Protection Rates

Instead of using product prices p_i, a better indicator of incentive is given by the terms of trade p_i / p_{NA} for that product, where p_{NA} is a price index of nonagricultural goods (Krueger, Schiff, and Valdés, 1988). We can thus rewrite the real rate of protection $RRP = p^d / p^{b*} - 1$ using terms of trade to yield the real rate of relative protection *RRRP*:

$$RRRP_i = \frac{p_i^d / p_{NA}^d}{p_i^{b*} / p_{NA}^{b*}} - 1,$$

where:

p_i^d / p_{NA}^d is the relative producer price with distortions, and
p_i^{b*} / p_{NA}^{b*} is the relative border price measured at the equilibrium exchange rate e^* and without trade distortions.

This can be rewritten as:

$$RRRP_i = \left(\frac{p_i^d / p_{NA}^d - p_i^b / p_{NA}^d}{p_i^{b*} / p_{NA}^{b*}} \right) + \left(\frac{p_i^b / p_{NA}^d}{p_i^{b*} / p_{NA}^{b*}} - 1 \right).$$

In this decomposition, the first term is a function of trade policies on product i and thus measures the *direct* price interventions. The second term can be written as:

$$\frac{p_i^b}{p_i^{b*}} \frac{p_{NA}^{b*}}{p_{NA}^d} - 1 = \frac{e}{e^*} \frac{p_{NA}^{b*}}{p_{NA}^d} - 1$$

and is a function of exchange rate disequilibrium and of industrial protectionism, that is, of *indirect* price interventions. Exchange rate overvaluation ($e/e^* < 1$) and industrial protectionism $\left(p_{NA}^{b*} / p_{NA}^d < 1 \right)$ both contribute to making this second term negative.

Table 7.4 gives calculations of *RRRP* and of its direct and indirect components for exported and imported food products in a number of LDCs. Indirect sources of distortion swamp direct protection to imported food crops. For exported cash crops, a high level of direct taxation (–11% in both periods) is increased to –36% (1975–79) and –40% (1980–84) by indirect distortions, with extreme exchange rate and industrial distortions in Ghana and Zambia. Food crops are protected by import tariffs in both periods (20% and 21%, respectively), but indirect distortions turn this protection into taxation of 5% and 6% in the two periods. Thus, the main source of anti-agriculture bias during these years was through exchange rate and industrial policies, not through commodity-specific agricultural policies. Among indirect sources of distortion, industrial protection policies taxed agriculture more than did real overvaluation of the exchange rate (Schiff and Valdés, 1992). These results suggest that agricultural price policy has been made at the levels of the Central Bank and the Ministry of Economics in terms of macroeconomic principles more than at the level of the Ministry of Agriculture in terms of sectoral needs and pressures of farm lobbies. While widely publicized, these results must be interpreted with caution as far as disincentives to agriculture are concerned. The period analyzed was characterized by ample compensatory policies on the factor side, through subsidized credit most particularly, which are not taken into account by the indicators of protection used.

7.3. Indicators of Comparative Advantage

While the *EPC* and *NPC* serve to measure levels of incentives, with implications for the efficiency with which the corresponding commodities will be produced, the domestic resource cost (*DRC*) provides a measure of efficiency, with implications for the level of incentives offered to

Table 7.4. Direct, indirect, and total nominal protection rates for agricultural products (%)

Country	Product	1975–79			1980–84		
		Direct	Indirect	Total	Direct	Indirect	Total
Exported products							
Argentina	Wheat	–25	–16	–41	–13	–37	–50
Brazil	Soybeans	–8	–32	–40	–19	–14	–33
Chile	Grapes	1	22	23	0	–7	–7
Colombia	Coffee	–7	–25	–32	–5	–34	–39
Côte d'Ivoire	Cocoa	–31	–33	–64	–21	–26	–47
Dominican Rep.	Coffee	–15	–18	–33	–32	–19	–51
Egypt	Cotton	–36	–18	–54	–22	–14	–36
Ghana	Cocoa	26	–66	–40	34	–89	–55
Malaysia	Rubber	–25	–4	–29	–18	–10	–28
Pakistan	Cotton	–12	–48	–60	–7	–35	–42
Philippines	Copra	–11	–27	–38	–26	–28	–54
Portugal	Tomatoes	17	–5	12	17	–13	4
Sri Lanka	Rubber	–29	–35	–64	–31	–31	–62
Thailand	Rice	–28	–15	–43	–15	–19	–34
Turkey	Tobacco	2	–40	–38	–28	–35	–63
Zambia	Tobacco	1	–42	–41	7	–57	–50
Average		–11	–25	–36	–11	–29	–40
Imported food products							
Brazil	Wheat	35	–32	3	–7	–14	–21
Chile	Wheat	11	22	33	9	–7	2
Colombia	Wheat	5	–25	–20	9	–34	–25
Côte d'Ivoire	Rice	8	–33	–25	16	–26	–10
Dominican Rep.	Rice	20	–18	2	26	–19	7
Egypt	Wheat	–19	–18	–37	–21	–14	–35
Ghana	Rice	79	–66	13	118	–89	29
Korea	Rice	91	–18	73	86	–12	74
Malaysia	Rice	38	–4	34	68	–10	58
Morocco	Wheat	–7	–12	–19	0	–8	–8
Pakistan	Wheat	–13	–48	–61	–21	–35	–56
Philippines	Corn	18	–27	–9	26	–28	–2
Portugal	Wheat	15	–5	10	26	–13	13
Sri Lanka	Rice	18	–35	–17	11	–31	–20
Turkey	Wheat	28	–40	–12	–3	–35	–38
Zambia	Corn	–13	–42	–55	–9	–57	–66
Average		20	–25	–5	21	–27	–6

Source: Krueger, Schiff, and Valdés, 1988.

producers. Whether it is efficient for a country to produce a commodity as opposed to importing it (whether the country has comparative advantage in that commodity, in other words) depends on the opportunity cost of domestic production relative to the value added it creates in foreign currency.

The *DRC* is the ratio of the cost in domestic resources and nontraded inputs (valued at their shadow prices) of producing the commodity domestically to the net foreign exchange earned or saved by producing the good domestically:

$$DRC_i = \frac{\sum_{j=k+1}^{n} a_{ij} p_j^*}{p_i^b - \sum_{j=1}^{k} a_{ij} p_j^b},$$

where:

$j = 1,...,k$ are the traded inputs,

$j = k+1,...,n$ are the domestic resources and the nontraded intermediate inputs,

p_j^* is the shadow price of domestic resources and nontraded intermediate inputs,

p_i^b is the border price of the traded output i measured at the shadow exchange rate,

p_j^b is the border price of the traded input j, also measured at the shadow exchange rate.

The denominator is consequently that of the *EPC*. If *DRC* < 1, the economy saves foreign exchange by producing the good domestically either for export or for import substitution. This is because the opportunity cost of the domestic resources and nontraded factors used in producing the good is less than the foreign exchange earned or saved. In contrast, if *DRC* > 1, domestic costs are in excess of foreign exchange costs or savings, indicating that the good should not be produced domestically and should be imported instead.

An alternative formulation of *DRC* consists in measuring the denominator in dollars. In this case, the *DRC* is in units of domestic currency per dollar, that is, it is a commodity-specific implicit exchange rate. Comparative advantage is assessed by comparing the DRC_i to the shadow exchange rate. If $DRC_i < e$, the commodity should be produced domestically, as the domestic currency cost per dollar is less than the opportunity cost measured by e. By contrast, if $DCR_i > e$, the commodity should be imported.

*DRC*s offer useful policy guidelines in deciding which commodities should be produced domestically and which should be imported, and thus in establishing the country's static comparative advantages on an efficiency basis. However, calculation of *DRC*s is highly demanding. Difficulties include:

a. Identifying which are the primary factors and nontraded inputs to be included among domestic resources. As in the calculation of *ERP*, the traded component in the production of nontraded inputs should be factored out stepwise.

b. Establishing the opportunity cost (shadow price) of the domestic resources, that is, the equilibrium prices they would fetch in their next best use.

c. Establishing the technical coefficients of the resources and inputs used, as in the calculation of *ERP*.

d. Finally, estimating the shadow exchange rate to be used in the calculation of p^b or, if the denominator is measured in dollars, against which to compare *DRC*.

Use of the *DRC* in measuring comparative advantage has the additional difficulty of being static while the decision to specialize and trade is dynamic. The infant-industry argument used in import substitution industrialization, for instance, postulates that, by expanding the scale of production and by learning-by-doing, future domestic costs will be reduced. The technical coefficients and the shadow prices used should, consequently, as much as possible, try to reflect these expected changes, not the current conditions of production. This, however, requires a type of information for which more complete models need to be developed.

Calculations of *DRC* in Table 7.2 show that Côte d'Ivoire has strong comparative advantage in cocoa and coffee and good comparative advantages in cotton and peanuts with improved production techniques. Interestingly enough, Côte d'Ivoire is taxing precisely those commodities where it has the strongest comparative advantage. This can be noted through the low *NPC* and *EPC* for these commodities. While a good source of revenues in the short run, these trade taxes compromise reproduction of comparative advantages in the long run.

Table 7.5 gives calculations of *DRC*s for several crops in Morocco over time. The results clearly show that Morocco does not have comparative advantages in sugar beets and sugarcane. On efficiency grounds, it should import sugar instead of producing it domestically at a cost 250% above border price. It has, by contrast, very strong comparative advantages in the production of citrus. Its strong comparative advantages in wheat and barley in 1970 have gradually eroded to the point that Morocco should now be indifferent between producing and importing these cereals, particularly if intensive technologies which are more competitive are not adopted in wheat production. Barley, by contrast, is more competitive when produced under traditional

Table 7.5. Nominal and effective protection and domestic resource costs for major commodities, Morocco, 1970–1982

Product	1970			1982		
	NPC	*EPC*	*DRC*	*NPC*	*EPC*	*DRC*
Hard wheat						
Traditional	0.92	0.95	0.76	1.07	1.31	1.01
Semi-intensive	0.97	1.03	0.48	1.21	1.34	0.90
Soft wheat						
Semi-intensive	0.94	0.98	0.77	1.00	1.21	1.06
Intensive	0.96	1.08	0.53	1.17	1.32	0.98
Barley						
Traditional	0.81	0.82	0.61	1.12	1.23	0.95
Semi-intensive	0.89	0.92	0.85	1.18	1.34	1.01
Maize (semi-intensive)	0.65	0.68	0.65	1.14	1.31	0.78
Pulses (beans)	0.98	1.08	0.96	1.12	1.17	0.80
Sugar beets (irrigated)	1.31	1.83	2.54	1.27	2.25	2.56
Sugarcane	1.30	1.56	2.01	1.24	1.61	2.62
Cotton	0.25	0.91	0.58	0.95	1.43	0.82
Citrus (navels)	0.99	1.04	0.59	0.99	1.18	0.53

Source: Estimates based on a desk study carried out in the World Bank in 1984 and updated in 1985.

technology. This loss of comparative advantage is due to the decline in international wheat and barley prices without a corresponding increase in productivity. Morocco may want to maintain wheat production for food security and farm income purposes. However, on an efficiency basis Morocco should either induce a gradual shift away from wheat into citrus, where this is possible, or boost the international competitiveness of domestic producers through adoption of improved technologies.

7.4. Partial Equilibrium Analysis of Price Distortions

The indicators of price distortion developed above give us a measure of the magnitude of the incentive effects of price policies on producers and consumers. They do not trace out the efficiency, welfare, government budget, and balance-of-trade implications of the distortions they signal. In this section, we turn to a partial equilibrium analysis of the implications of these distortions. The advantage of this approach is its empirical simplicity and the fact that the first-round effects it measures are, in general but not always, an acceptable first-order approximation of the total effects. However, partial equilibrium analysis does not take into account several other important effects, such as income and cost changes that shift the demand and supply functions, interactions across markets with products or factors that are close substitutes or complements in production or consumption, exchange rate effects, and savings-investment and public revenue-public investment effects that may create productivity gains through increases in fixed factors of both private and public origins. As such, partial equilibrium analysis tends to emphasize the static negative effects of distortions while underestimating possible positive dynamic effects of these same distortions. Government revenues from trade taxes may, for instance, be used for the delivery of public goods, the reduction of transactions costs, temporary subsidies to achieve economies of scale, and income redistribution to the poor. To capture some of these indirect effects, this analysis will be extended in later chapters using a multimarket approach in Chapter 11 and a general equilibrium approach in Chapter 12.

7.4.1. The Concepts of Consumer and Producer Surplus

Following Marshall, the concept of consumer surplus provides a measure of consumer welfare as the excess of the price the consumer would be willing to pay for each unit consumed over the price which is actually paid (see Currie, Murphy, and Schmitz, 1971). As we have seen in Chapter 1, this surplus is measured by the area pBA under the demand curve and above the price line (Figure 7.1). The demand curve measures, up to a scalar λ, the marginal utility offered by each unit of the good. The difference between marginal utility, which indicates the maximum price which the consumer would be willing to pay for that unit, and the price actually paid, the market price, is a measure of surplus and, hence, of consumer welfare. The area pBA thus measures the difference between the money value of total utility (area OBAq) and the cost of achieving this utility (area OpAq).

On the producer side, producer surplus is measured by the area CpA, above the supply curve and below the price line. Because the supply curve measures the marginal cost of each unit produced, area OCAq is the total cost of variable factors. Area OpAq is gross revenue. The difference between these two areas, CpA, is revenue above variable cost; that is, it is the "restricted profit" or rent that accrues to the fixed factors. In agriculture, if land is the only fixed factor, if there is imperfect substitutability between land and variable factors, and if variable factors are in infinitely elastic supply, producer surplus is the land rent. Thus, a policy reform that creates a gain in producer surplus results in an increase in land rent. The effects of the policy change are consequently capitalized in land values at the moment when the policy change is known. They create a one-shot gain in wealth for the current landowners that needs to be paid by future entrants in agriculture under the form of higher land prices.

Figure 7.1. Producer and consumer surplus

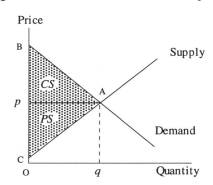

Calculations of producer and consumer surplus depend on specifying a functional form for supply and demand. This proves to be problematic, as functions are econometrically estimated over a small range of prices and quantities. As a result, we know very little of the shape they have toward the origin of the quantity and price axes. Fortunately, we usually only need to measure small changes in producer and consumer surplus around an observed equilibrium point (but, as we will see, this is not enough to measure the welfare gains from technological change). We typically assume that the demand and supply curves are constant elasticity functions around this point, principally because we tend to have better information about the value of supply and demand elasticities than the value of price slopes. In this case, the only data that we need to measure the changes in producer and consumer surpluses created by a given change in price are the initial level of price, the quantities consumed and produced at this price, and the elasticities of supply and demand at the initial production and consumption levels.

Partial equilibrium indicators typically used to assess the impact of a price intervention or of policies that shift the supply and demand curves are:

a. *Welfare effects.* The impact on consumer welfare is measured by the change in consumer surplus (ΔCS) and the impact on producer welfare by the change in producer surplus (ΔPS). This analysis can be disaggregated among consumer and producer groups if they have different initial shares in total consumption and production and/or different price elasticities of demand and supply. For instance, poor consumers typically have a higher elasticity of demand for food with respect to price and a higher share of their total consumption expenditures in food than rich consumers. Small farmers typically have a lower elasticity of supply response and a larger share of their total production in food crops than large farmers.

b. *Government budget effect* (ΔB). Import tariffs and export taxes are sources of government revenues. Producer and consumer subsidies are sources of government outlays. The net of these revenues and expenditures is calculated to give the effect on the government budget.

c. *Rent effects* (ΔR). When quantity restrictions apply on exports or imports, a commodity is transformed from a tradable to a nontradable. The rents the export or import quotas create are appropriated by exporters or importers instead of by government, unless these quotas are auctioned under competitive bidding. If exporters or importers compete among each others to appropriate these rents, they may dissipate in rent-seeking expenditures up to the whole value of the rent (Krueger, 1974).

d. *Efficiency effects*. The net social gain or loss (*NSG, NSL*) to the country is measured as the total of the changes in consumer surplus, producer surplus, government budget effect, and rent effects. As we will see below, an *NSL* can typically be decomposed between an *NSL* in production (*NSLP*) and an *NSL* in consumption (*NSLC*) (Timmer, 1986).

e. *Balance-of-payments effect* (ΔBoP). Changes in exports and imports induced by the policy change are measured. Changes in import costs and export earnings are also measured, and the net gives the change in the balance of trade or payments.

Typically, the sources of price distortion are:

On exportables: export tax, export subsidy, producer subsidy, consumer subsidy, and export quota.

On importables: import tariff, import subsidy, producer subsidy, consumer subsidy, and import quota.

On all tradables: trade prohibition and overvalued exchange rate.

On nontradables: taxes, subsidies, supply control, price support with government storage or dumping of surplus production.

On inputs: taxes or subsidies on inputs used to produce either tradables or nontradables.

Multiple interventions that combine the above.

Monopolistic or oligopolistic pricing.

Other policy instruments that shift supply that are analyzed in partial equilibrium analysis include: technological change in tradables or nontradables; taxes and subsidies and government regulations to reduce environmental externalities.

In the following section, we analyze the partial equilibrium effects of a number of these policy interventions.

7.4.2. Measurement of the Partial Equilibrium Effects of an Export Tax on Agriculture

Consider in Figure 7.2 the case of an ad valorem export tax t that lowers the domestic price p^d below the border price as follows:

$$p^d = p^b (1 + t) = p^b\, NPC,$$

where t is negative since this is a tax, that is,

$$t = NRP = NPC - 1 = (p^d - p^b) / p^b.$$

Denoting areas by numbers as in Figure 7.2, the efficiency and welfare effects are measured as follows:

Change in consumer surplus (ΔCS) = 1
Change in producer surplus (ΔPS) = $-1 - 2 - 3 - 4$

Change in government revenue $(\Delta B) = 3$

Total = net social gain $(NSG) = -2 - 4$, where 2 is the net social loss in consumption $(NSLC)$ and 4 is the net social loss in production $(NSLP)$.

Exports decline from $(q^b - c^b)$ to $(q - c)$. The change in the balance of payments is $\Delta BoP = -p^b(q^b - q + c - c^b)$.

This analysis shows that an export tax on agriculture increases the welfare of consumers, who now face lower domestic prices for that part of domestic production which they absorb. This gain comes from a transfer of revenue equal to area 1 from producers to consumers. Government also gains, as the tax is a source of revenues it did not have before. This gain is equal to

Figure 7.2. Effects of an export tax on efficiency and welfare

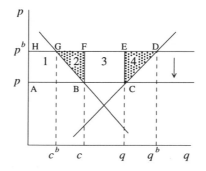

$\Delta CS = 1$; $\Delta PS = -1 - 2 - 3 - 4$;

$\Delta B = 3$; $NSG = -2 - 4$.

area 3, which is transferred from producers to government. Producers, however, lose by more than these two transfers. Their total loss due to lower domestic prices is equal to area $1 + 2 + 3 + 4$. Since areas 2 and 4 are lost by them but not captured by anyone else, they constitute a net social loss that measures the total efficiency loss for the country. This net social loss can be decomposed into two sources of inefficiency: area 2 is the net social loss in consumption. It originates in the fact that consumers now spend more on the commodity that has been cheapened by tax, creating a misallocation of their expenditures which is rational from their standpoint but socially suboptimal. Area 4 is the net social loss in production. It is a loss in efficiency because, while rational from the standpoint of individual producers, resources are being drawn away from the production of this good and used for the production of other goods with lower productivity.

For the purpose of quantitative analysis, it is important to measure the efficiency, welfare, government revenue, and balance-of-trade effects using the following:

p^b = border price that was also the domestic price before tax,

q^b = quantity produced at the border price,

c^b = quantity consumed at the border price,

E_S = elasticity of supply measured at (p^b, q^b),

E_D = elasticity of demand measured at (p^b, c^b), which is negative,

t = export rate of protection.

Two derived measures which we use to simplify notation are:

$W = p^b q^b$ = gross value of production at border price,

$V = p^b c^b$ = value of consumption at border price.

Imposition of an export tax changes the domestic price level and the quantities produced and consumed to:

p^d = domestic price after tax (also denoted p),

q = quantity produced after tax,

c = quantity consumed after tax.

The net social loss in production (*NSLP*), equal to area 4 in Figure 7.2, can be measured as:

$$NSLP = \frac{1}{2}\left(q^b - q\right)\left(p^b - p\right) = -\frac{1}{2}\left(\frac{q - q^b}{p - p^b}\frac{p^b}{q^b}\right)\frac{q^b}{p^b}\left(p - p^b\right)\left(p^b - p\right)$$

$$= \frac{1}{2}E_S\left(\frac{p - p^b}{p^b}\right)^2 p^b q^b = \frac{1}{2}E_S t^2 W,$$

where:

$t = NRP = NPC - 1 = (p / p^b) - 1$, and

$E_S = [(q - q^b)/(p - p^b)](p^b/q^b)$.

Proceeding in similar fashion, we obtain the following measures of efficiency and welfare:

a. *Efficiency effects*

Net social loss in production: $NSLP = 1/2\ E_S\ t^2\ W > 0$,

Net social loss in consumption: $NSLC = -1/2\ E_D\ t^2\ V > 0$,

Total net social loss: $NSL = NSLP + NSLC > 0$.

b. *Welfare effects*

Welfare gain of producers (change in producer surplus):

$\Delta PS = q\ (p - p^b) - NSLP < 0$,

Welfare gain of consumers (change in consumer surplus):

$\Delta CS = -c\ (p - p^b) - NSLC > 0$.

c. *Government budget effects*

Change in government revenue: $\Delta B = (q - c)(p^b - p) > 0$.

d. *Change in the balance of payments*

Change in net exports: $\Delta BoP = -p^b\ (q^b - q + c - c^b) < 0$.

The efficiency loss from a price distortion is smaller the lower these elasticities. Hence, if price response is small, as structuralist economists would argue and which is certainly true in the very short run, a price distortion primarily has income transfer effects with minimal efficiency costs. The higher the elasticities, as monetarist economists would argue is the case and especially in the longer run, the greater the efficiency losses and consequently the smaller the income transfer effects. This can be seen by the fact that, when elasticities are high, areas 2 and 4 absorb a larger share of the total producer loss 1 + 2 + 3 + 4, reducing the relative magnitude of the transfers 1 to consumers and 3 to government. By contrast, efficiency losses are less and income transfer effects greater on poor consumers and small farmers with, respectively, low demand and supply elasticities with respect to price. When one side of the market is more elastic than the other, it is the elastic side that bears the efficiency effect and the inelastic side that bears the income transfer effect. Across commodities, efficient taxation does not require uniformity, but higher tax rates for goods in inelastic demand and lower for goods in elastic demand. This is the important Ramsey rule or inverse elasticity rule in public finance. Implementation of this rule would, however, create a regressive tax system since higher taxes would fall on food while taxes would be low on luxuries, implying a trade-off between efficiency and equity. For administrative purposes and the monitoring of evasion, uniform tax rates are more desirable, explaining why countries have generally preferred neutral taxation.

Even if elasticities are high, the magnitude of the efficiency effects is small, as they vary with the square of the *NRP*. For example, with $E_S = 0.5$ and an export tax with $t = -0.25$, the *NSLP* as a share of the gross value of production before price distortion, $100 NSLP / W$ is equal to 1.6%. This does not mean, however, that these efficiency losses are unimportant. First, an equal amount of resources may be wasted in lobbying and other rent-seeking activities to capture the distributive gains that distortions create. Second, as the elasticity increases in the longer run, so does the magnitude of the efficiency losses, which in time cumulate in large numbers. Finally, in a dynamic sense, the rents and government revenues created along with the efficiency losses may have large social costs if they are not used for investment and productivity-increasing purposes.

7.4.3. Partial Equilibrium Analysis of Other Price Interventions

In Figures 7.3 through 7.8 we present the partial equilibrium analysis of a number of policy interventions.

7.4.3.1. Exportables
a. *Export subsidy (Figure 7.3a): European Community's Common Agricultural Policy (CAP).* CAP is the policy by which the European Community (EC) supports its farmers' incomes. Producer prices are fixed at $p_p = \bar{p}$. Consumers have to pay this price as well; that is, there is no price wedge. This results in an *NSLP* (4) and an *NSLC* (2). Relative to free trade, consumers lose $\Delta CS = -1 - 2$ and producers gain $\Delta PS = 1 + 2 + 3$. As production increases and consumption falls, exports E increase significantly, and the EC must subsidize these exports at a high government budget cost equal to $\Delta B = -2 - 3 - 4$. The net social loss is $2 + 4$. Over the years, the cumulative effect of this policy has transformed the EC into a large exporter, driving down the world market price by Δp^b. The quantities produced and consumed do not change, but the government cost of export subsidies rises by $E \Delta p^b$.

b. *Producer subsidy (Figure 7.3b): United States Farm Policy.* The United States uses a different approach to support its farmers' incomes. It offers them a "deficiency payment" which consists in guaranteeing a fixed producer price, the "target price" set above the border price. Consumers pay the "loan rate," which in principle equals the border price, thus introducing a price wedge. Consumer surplus is not affected ($\Delta CS = 0$), and there is no *NSLC*. Producer surplus increases as in the EC, by $\Delta PS = 1 + 2$, and *NSLP* = 3. The government cost of deficiency payments is $\Delta B = -1 - 2 - 3$. Since the United States is also a large exporter, deficiency payments increase exports and lower the international market price by Δp^b. Consumers gain

Figure 7.3. Price distortions on tradables

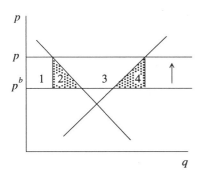

7.3a. Export subsidy

$\Delta CS = -1 - 2; \quad \Delta PS = 1 + 2 + 3;$

$\Delta B = -2 - 3 - 4; \quad NSG = -2 - 4.$

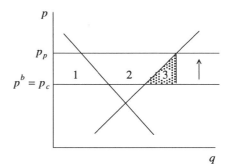

7.3b. Producer subsidy (wedge)

$\Delta CS = 0; \quad \Delta PS = 1 + 2;$

$\Delta B = -1 - 2 - 3; \quad NSG = -3.$

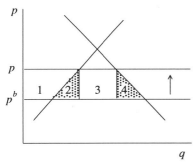

7.3c. Import tariff

$\Delta CS = -1 - 2 - 3 - 4; \quad \Delta PS = 1;$

$\Delta B = 3 > 0; \quad NSG = -2 - 4.$

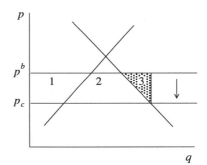

7.3d. Consumer subsidy (wedge)

$\Delta CS = 1 + 2; \quad \Delta PS = 0;$

$\Delta B = -1 - 2 - 3; \quad NSG = -3.$

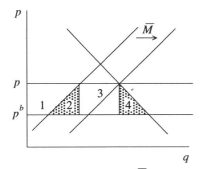

7.3e. Import license ($\overline{M}$)

$\Delta CS = -1 - 2 - 3 - 4; \quad \Delta PS = 1;$

$\Delta B = 0; \quad NSG = -2 - 4; \quad \Delta rent = 3.$

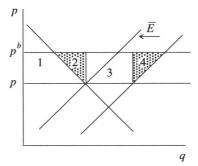

7.3f. Export quota ($\overline{E}$)

$\Delta CS = 1; \quad \Delta PS = -1 - 2 - 3 - 4;$

$\Delta B = 0; \quad NSG = -2 - 4; \quad \Delta rent = 3.$

and increase their consumption, while output level remains the same. The cost to government increases by $q \, \Delta p^b$.

Assuming that the supply and demand curves are the same in Figures 7.3a and 7.3b and that the producer price support is at the same level, we can compare the partial equilibrium effects of U. S. and EC agricultural price policies as follows:

Consumer surplus: $\Delta CS_{US} = 0, \ \Delta CS_{EC} < 0$
Producer surplus: $\Delta PS_{US} = \Delta PS_{EC}$
Exports: $\Delta E_{US} < \Delta E_{EC}$
World market price effect: $-\Delta p^{\$}_{US} < -\Delta p^{\$}_{EC}$
Government budget: $\Delta B_{US} > \Delta B_{EC}$
Efficiency losses: $NSL_{US} < NSL_{EC}$ (as $NSLC_{US} = 0$).

The EC farm policy is less expensive to government, as consumers pay directly part of the farm price support in the form of higher food prices. On the other hand, the efficiency loss in the United States is smaller and the depressive impact of U. S. farm policy on the world market price is also less than the EC's. We thus see that there is a difficult trade-off in farm policy between the level of consumer welfare and budget cost.

European farmers are vociferously resisting a switch to a deficiency payment system, a switch the United States is pressing on Europe in order to reduce the negative impact on the world market price. In principle, the policy reform could be neutral on EC farmers' welfare, as in the move from Figure 7.3a to 7.3b. By shifting part of the cost of farm price support from consumers to government, the policy reform should be endorsed by consumers, in whom farmers would thus find allies. The problem, however, is that it introduces a price wedge which makes existence of the farm subsidies much more visible than before and hence difficult to sustain politically. Under the current system, consumers never see the world market price and hence are not as prone to oppose the subsidies, even though they pay a higher price for them!

7.4.3.2 Importables

a. *Direct protection of imported food products (Figure 7.3c).* Measurements of nominal protection coefficients for cereals in Africa (Table 7.1) and for rice in Côte d'Ivoire (Table 7.2), as well as of direct nominal protection rates for imported food products (Table 7.4), show that these crops have in general been protected through mport tariffs. This has been part of purposeful efforts by governments to achieve a greater degree of food security through increased self-sufficiency, at the cost of efficiency losses and of redistributive effects against consumers introduced by price distortions. In many countries, these policies were introduced in response to the food crisis of the early 1970s which led to skyrocketing world market food prices; in others they were introduced in response to the pressures of farm lobbies. The magnitude of the resulting efficiency and redistributive effects is analyzed in Figure 7.3c. Consumers are taxed ($\Delta CS = -1$ $-2 -3 -4$) while producers gain ($\Delta PS = 1$). The policy is attractive to government which not only satisfies food security and farm incomes objectives, but also captures tariff revenues ($\Delta B = 3$). Redistributive effects from consumers to producers and government are, however, achieved at the cost of an efficiency loss in production (-2) and an efficiency loss in consumption (-4). If the distortion is sustained over time and supply is elastic in the longer run, import substitution will be large, eventually turning imports into exports and what were expected to be budget revenues into costly budget subsidies, as the European Economic Community and Japan learned the hard way.

b. *Cheap Food Policy (Figure 7.3d).* We have seen that a typical aspect of agricultural price policy in the LDCs is to tax exports (Figure 7.2) and to subsidize food imports for consumers (Figure 7.3d). In this latter case, producers are not affected ($\Delta PS = 0$), consumers gain ($\Delta CS = 1 + 2$), and the government incurs the very large cost of the consumer subsidy ($\Delta B = -1 - 2 - 3$), which includes the cost of the efficiency loss in consumption which the price distortion creates ($NSLP = 3$). Combining a consumer subsidy of food with an export tax on cash crops allows the government to eventually balance its budget, but at the cost of a yet higher global distortion.

7.4.3.3. Quantity Restrictions in Trade: Import License (Figure 7.3e) and Export Quota (Figure 7.3f)

Quantity restrictions on trade transform tradables into traded nontradables since the domestic price is now determined by equilibrium between supply after the quota shift and demand. The licenses generate rents for traders. Import quotas (nontariff barriers) are commonly used by countries with balance-of-payments problems to save on foreign exchange. The expectation is that if the import license is given directly to the user of an imported capital good, it does not create a price distortion on this producer. It also gives certainty to the government, as opposed to a tariff, on the exact quantity of foreign exchange expenditure.

With an import quota $\overline{M}$ (Figure 7.3e), imports fall and the domestic price (if there is a domestic market for imports), or the shadow price for the licensee, rises. Consumers lose ($\Delta CS = -1 - 2 - 3 - 4$) while producers gain ($\Delta PS = 1$). There is no gain to government, as the quota rent from selling imports at a domestic price above the import price is captured by importers ($\Delta rent = 3$). The net social loss is $2 + 4$. Alternatively, if the economy was opened to free trade and the nontradable thus transformed into a tradable, the gain from trade would be equal to $2 + 4$. Clearly, the government could capture the importer's rent 3 by auctioning the import quotas. Importers will bid for the right to import until the price equals its shadow value p. Another mechanism whereby the government can appropriate this rent is by setting a tariff equivalent equal to $p - p^b$ with the same impact on trade as the quota. Tarification has the additional advantages of eliminating rent seeking among importers, conveying clear signals to importers, being easy to administer particularly if a uniform tariff is used, and eliminating the possibility of monopoly pricing on the domestic market. For small economies where there may be only one domestic producer of a commodity, trade under tariffs is equivalent to introducing competition at the tariff-adjusted border price.

Export quotas (Figure 7.3f) are often imposed by countries which export wage goods and want to maintain cheap food, at the cost of a loss in foreign exchange earnings. Recurrent export quotas on meat in Argentina are an example of this. In this case, consumers gain ($\Delta CS = 1$), producers lose ($\Delta PS = -1 - 2 - 3 - 4$), and exporters capture a rent ($\Delta rent = 3$). The net social loss $-2 - 4$ is the loss from not practicing free trade. It measures the social opportunity cost of subsidizing consumers through the mechanism of export quotas.

7.4.3.4. Tax and Subsidy on Nontradables

a. *Tax on a nontradable (Figure 7.4a).* An important debate in agricultural price policy is that of the efficiency and welfare effects of a tax on agriculture. When the commodity is a nontradable, we see that, for a given elasticity of demand, the efficiency and welfare implications are vastly different depending on the elasticity of supply. Structuralists argue that elasticity is

low while monetarists maintain that it is high. Using again the Ramsey rule, the implications of
a tax are contrasted as follows:

	Inelastic supply	Elastic supply
Output effect (< 0)	Small	Large
Change in consumer price (> 0)	Small	Large
Change in farm income (< 0)	Large	Small
Tax revenue mainly paid by	Farmers	Consumers
Efficiency loss ($NSG = -2 - 4$)	Small	Large

Based on their presumptions about supply elasticity, it is not surprising that structuralists
argue in favor on a tax on agriculture, if only to generate government revenues that can be used
to shift the supply function through investments in public goods. Monetarists, in contrast, prefer
not to tax agriculture through prices, as this has large efficiency costs. They prefer a neutral tax
on land or income to create revenues for public investment. This tax is, however, usually difficult to administer, and a trade-off then needs to be incurred between inefficient taxation and
efficiency gains from public investment.

   b. *Subsidy on a nontradable (Figure 7.4b).* This occurs when a government supports a
farm price without production control, leaving the market to clear at the quantity produced at the
subsidized price. In this case, both producers and consumers are subsidized ($\Delta CS = 3$, $\Delta PS = 1$).
In principle, it is thus a politically attractive policy for government, typical of the food-price
dilemma: seek to please all constituents by giving high prices to farmers and low prices to

Figure 7.4. Price distortions on nontradables

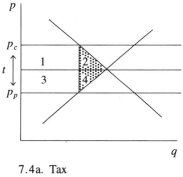

7.4a. Tax

$\Delta CS = -1 - 2$; $\Delta PS = -3 - 4$;

$\Delta B = 1 + 3 > 0$; $NSG = -2 - 4$.

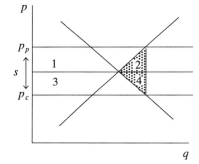

7.4b. Subsidy

$\Delta CS = 3$; $\Delta PS = 1$;

$\Delta B = -1 - 2 - 3 - 4$; $NSG = -2 - 4$.

consumers (Tweeten, 1989). The cost on government is, however, exceedingly high ($\Delta B = -1
- 2 - 3 - 4$), and it is not a zero-sum game since it creates a net social loss ($NSG = -2 - 4$).

7.4.3.5. Exchange Rate Overvaluation
   Particularly in periods of rapid inflation, countries tend to have overvalued exchange rates.
Irrespective of inflation, this is also typically the case in countries that export agricultural prod-

ucts and import manufactured capital and consumption goods, and where there is an urban bias in policy making (Lipton, 1977). Sustaining an overvalued exchange rate requires quantity adjustment on the foreign exchange market, in general through some form of quantity rationing via import licenses.

a. *Exportable (Figure 7.5a).* The welfare effect of overvaluation is a revenue transfer from producers to consumers equal to 1. The net social loss 2 is an income transfer from domestic producers to the country's foreign importers, who have access to the good at a lower price in domestic currency. Exports decline as production of the good falls and its domestic consumption increases.

b. *Importable (Figure 7.5b).* The welfare effect is again a revenue transfer from producers to consumers equal to one. The additional subsidy 2 to consumers is a tax on foreign exporters to the country who, if they are willing to continue to export, receive lower prices for their sales. Imports increase as production falls and demand increases.

Figure 7.5. Exchange rate overvaluation

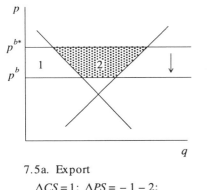
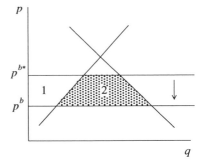

7.5a. Export
$\Delta CS = 1$; $\Delta PS = -1 - 2$;
$NSG = -2$.

7.5b. Imports
$\Delta CS = 1 + 2$; $\Delta PS = -1$;
$NSG = 2$.

In all cases, exchange rate overvaluation benefits consumers of tradables and taxes producers of tradables. It worsens the balance of payments via both lower exports and higher imports. The result is that, even though consumers and importers of capital goods may strongly resist devaluation, overvaluation is sustainable only as long as the foreign exchange crisis can be postponed, for instance, by borrowing from abroad or by quantity rationing on imports.

7.4.3.6. *Technological Change on Nontradables and Tradables*

There is a sharp contrast in the distribution of welfare gains from technological change when the good is a nontradable versus either a tradable or a commodity with government price support. In the case of a nontradable (Figure 7.6a), the price falls and consumers are the main gainers ($\Delta CS = 1 + 2$). This gain to consumers increases if demand is more inelastic. The effect on producers is positive but small. The net social gain ($NSG = 2 + 4$) is fundamentally captured by consumers, and exclusively so if demand is completely inelastic, in which case $NSG = 2 + 4$

$= \Delta CS = 1 + 2$. This explains why consumers should be the ones investing, through government, in agricultural research. In this case, the benefits of technological change are captured by consumers through the "Mill-Marshallian agricultural treadmill" of falling production costs and falling prices as the innovation diffuses through the farm sector (Owen, 1966).

If demand is infinitely elastic (Figure 7.6b), either because the good is a tradable or because the government stands ready to buy and stock all increase in production at the current price (e.g., at the target price in the United States), technological change is neutral to consumers ($\Delta CS = 0$). The gain for producers is the full net social gain ($\Delta PS = NSG = 2$). If the good is a tradable, the country gains through increased exports and foreign earnings, with the whole gain captured by the fixed factor in agriculture, namely land rents. Farmers as a group should thus be highly supportive of technological change in a tradable good. If the good is nontradable, gains can be retained by farmers through government intervention to support the price. In India, a significant part of the gains from the Green Revolution have thus been appropriated by farmers. Even though grains are not traded, farmers were able to use their political clout to change the

Figure 7.6.   Technological change

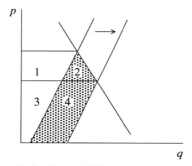   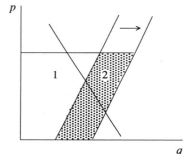

7.6a. Nontradable

$\Delta CS = 1 + 2; \quad \Delta PS = (4 + 3) - (1 + 3);$

$NSG = 2 + 4 \cong \Delta CS.$

7.6b. Tradable or price support

$\Delta CS = 0; \quad \Delta PS = 2;$

$NSG = 2 = \Delta PS.$

government's food security strategy from one based on trade to one based on the carryover of large food stocks, as we saw in Chapter 5. As a result, land values increased sharply in the areas where the Green Revolution had diffused successfully.

Measuring the welfare gains from technological change, as the area between the supply curves before and after the change and the demand curve, has received a great deal of attention, since it allows one to calculate the rate of return from investment in agricultural research. To do this, the measured welfare gain from research is divided by the cost of the innovation. Such calculations were made by Griliches (1958) for hybrid corn in the United States, Peterson (1967) for poultry research, Schmitz and Seckler (1970) for the mechanical tomato harvester in California, Scobie and Posada (1978) for rice in Colombia, Akino and Hayami (1975) for rice in Japan, and Ayer and Schuh (1972) for cotton in Brazil. The difficulty of measuring the welfare gains from technological change is that we need to know the whole area between the supply curves, not just changes in producer and consumer surpluses around an equilibrium point as in the analyses of price distortions. In this case, the functional form given to the supply function (linear or log-linear) has a great impact on the size of the benefits, and we know very little about the shape of the supply function far away from the range of observed prices and quantities. Also important is the nature of the shift in supply induced by technological change (horizontal or pivotal). For a parallel change in linear supply as in Figure 7.6a, the net social gain is measured by:

$$NSG = \dot{q}p_0 q_0 \left(1 + \frac{1}{2}\frac{\dot{q}}{E_S + E_D}\right),$$

where p_0 and q_0 are the equilibrium price and quantity before the supply shift and $\dot{q} = \Delta q / q$ is the proportional shift in supply (see Norton and Davis, 1981, for measurements under alternative specifications of supply and shifts).

Many measurements have been obtained of the rate of return from investment in agricultural research using this methodology, referred to as the index number approach. Results typically range from 20% to 60 %, suggesting that there is underinvestment in agricultural research, since this rate of return is clearly above the social opportunity cost of capital (Ruttan, 1982).

7.4.3.7. Multiple Interventions

Price interventions are frequently combined to achieve simultaneously a variety of policy objectives. Once there is more than one distortion, we are in a second-best world where removal of one distortion may not create an efficiency gain if one distortion was compensating for the efficiency effect of the other. Examples of multiple policy interventions on an imported agricultural commodity are as follows:

a. *Tax on imports to subsidize domestic farm prices.* For example, many countries tax cheap PL 480 wheat imports and use the tax revenue to support the farm price with a wedge (Figure 7.7a). This has been done with wheat in Brazil and milk in Chile (Hall, 1980). It is an effective strategy to generate revenues and use them to promote import substitution if temporary protection is needed to achieve economies of scale and if access to PL 480 is seen as only temporary. This is also the policy followed by Japan to subsidize its wheat producers while taxing its consumers to generate the corresponding revenues.

b. *Producer and consumer subsidy (Figure 7.7b).* This is the same food-price dilemma that we analyzed for a nontradable in Figure 7.4b. It corresponds to the situation where government is yielding to both producer and consumer pressure groups, but at a very high budgetary cost.

c. *Tax on imports and on producers to subsidize consumers (Figure 7.7c).* This corresponds to the Chinese wheat policy, where consumer prices are kept very low and prices paid to producers are also, but to a lesser extent, below world market level (Carter, McCalla, and Schmitz, 1989).

The distributional implications of trade liberalization in two importing countries with contrasted trade distortions like Japan (Figure 7.7a) and China (Figure 7.7c) are markedly different. Evidently, in both cases liberalization creates net social gains. In Japan, it would yield a large gain to consumers, a small loss for producers, and a very small gain or loss for government. In China, the same policy would create a large loss for consumers, a small gain for producers, and a large gain for government. The distributional impacts of trade liberalization, even among importing countries, should thus be carefully assessed in terms of the nature of the preliberalization distortions. These contrasted distributional effects also imply that the political economy of trade liberalization varies widely across countries, with the pressures coming from consumers in Japan and government in China.

Figure 7.7. Multiple interventions

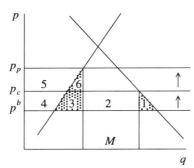

7.7a. Tax on import to subsidize producer price

$\Delta CS = -1 - 2 - 3 - 4; \quad \Delta PS = 4 + 5;$

$\Delta B = 2 - 5 - 6;$

$NSG = -1 - 3 - 6.$

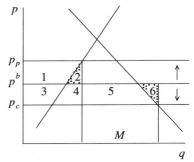

7.7b. Producer and consumer subsidy on importables

$\Delta CS = 3 + 4 + 5; \quad \Delta PS = 1;$

$\Delta B = -(1 + 2) - (3 + 4 + 5 + 6);$

$NSG = -2 - 6.$

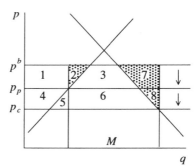

7.7c. Tax on imports and on producers to subsidize consumers

$\Delta CS = 1 + 2 + 3 + 4 + 5 + 6; \quad \Delta PS = -1 - 2;$

$\Delta B = -(4 + 5) - (2 + 3 + 6 + 7 + 8);$

$NSG = -2 - 7 - 8.$

7.4.3.8. *Trade Distortions and Environmental Protection*

In the absence of market failures, laissez-faire maximizes social welfare. This is not the case, however, when there are market failures, in which case price distortions may create efficiency gains. For example, when there is an externality such as pollution, domestic price policy and trade policy can both be used to reduce the externality. We explore here which policy instrument is most effective for this purpose (Vasavada, 1991).

Consider the case of agriculture that uses a polluting input such as insecticides to produce an exported commodity, for example, cotton in El Salvador or vegetables in Guatemala. It is well known that the first best policy is a revenue-neutral factor tax with subsidy, the so-called Pigou-Coase approach to internalizing externalities. This policy induces less use of the polluting input and substitution of nonpolluting inputs. Similarly, a production tax and subsidy could be imposed on a polluting product. However, LDCs are frequently unable to manage schemes of taxes and subsidies for lack of adequate fiscal institutions and enforcement capacity. In this case, trade policy may be used to reduce the externality, but at what efficiency cost?

Figure 7.8 analyzes the case of a polluting export where the private marginal cost curve (private supply) is inferior to the social marginal cost curve (social supply) that includes the

Figure 7.8. Trade distortions and environmental protection

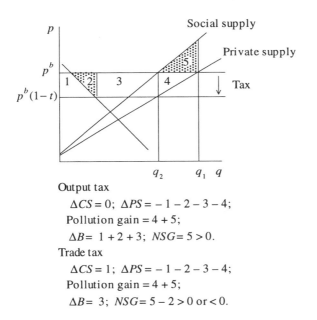

Output tax

$\Delta CS = 0$; $\Delta PS = -1 - 2 - 3 - 4$;

Pollution gain $= 4 + 5$;

$\Delta B = 1 + 2 + 3$; $NSG = 5 > 0$.

Trade tax

$\Delta CS = 1$; $\Delta PS = -1 - 2 - 3 - 4$;

Pollution gain $= 4 + 5$;

$\Delta B = 3$; $NSG = 5 - 2 > 0$ or < 0.

external production cost. At world market price p^b, the country overproduces (q_1) and overexports relative to the social optimum (q_2). The correct level of production and export can be achieved through either an output tax or an export tax, both equal to the rate of taxation t. This gives a positive net social gain in the case of an output tax ($NSG = 5 > 0$) but an undetermined result in the case of a trade tax ($NSG = 5 - 2 > 0$ or < 0).

The trade tax introduces an inefficiency in consumption, since it induces consumers to increase consumption, which reduces the optimum level of exports. Hence, without taking into account costs of implementation, an output tax is a more efficient way than a trade tax to internalize an externality. However, if the differential in implementation costs is greater than the *NSLC* of the trade tax, using the trade instrument is the best way of reducing pollution to the social optimum.

7.5. Effective Protection When Domestic and Foreign Commodities Are Imperfect Substitutes*

All price distortion analyses done so far are based on the dichotomy between tradables and nontradables, with the critical assumption of perfect substitutability between domestic and foreign commodities for the tradables. This is what led to the definition of a reference, or nondistorted, price based on the foreign price for these tradables and to the measure of direct distortions by the trade taxes. This assumption of perfect substitutability may be quite acceptable for specific well-defined commodities of homogenous quality and in fact may apply reasonably well to most agricultural products. However, when one considers any sectoral aggregation of commodities (e.g., light manufacturing, electric home appliances, or canned foods), domestic production and imports are not exactly the same commodities and can only be considered imperfect substitutes. Under these conditions, equality between domestic prices and import prices does not hold in equilibrium, and thus the imposition of a 20% tariff, for example, does not induce the same increase in domestic prices. In this section, we will see a simple single-sector model that illustrates the relationship between foreign/domestic goods substitutability and effective protection.

Consider, for example, an importing sector. Let D be the domestic production, M the imports, and C total consumption, with p_D, p_M, and p their respective prices. Imperfect substitution between domestic production and imports is captured in a demand function that states that the ratio of domestic goods to imports is a function of the relative price of the two commodities:

$$\frac{D}{M} = \frac{1 - s_M}{s_M} \left(\frac{p_D}{p_M} \right)^{-\sigma},$$

where s_M is the share of imports in domestic consumption measured at equal prices.

If ε is the price elasticity of demand for C and μ the price elasticity of supply of D, the market for this sector is written as:

$$C = D + M = p^{-\varepsilon}, \quad \text{where} \quad p = \frac{p_M M + p_D D}{M + D} \quad \text{is the consumer price, and}$$

$$D = p_D^{\mu}.$$

These equations can be solved for the quantities C, D, and M, the producer price p_D, and the consumer price p, as a function of the import price p_M. Differentiation of the system around the initial point where, by proper normalization, all prices are equal to one, gives the following relations for the rates of change in the equilibrium prices:

$$\dot{p}_D = \frac{s_M(\sigma - \varepsilon)}{s_M(\sigma - \varepsilon) + \mu + \varepsilon}\,\dot{p}_M \quad \text{and} \quad \dot{p} = \frac{s_M(\sigma + \mu)}{\sigma + \mu + (1 - s_M)(\varepsilon - \sigma)}\,\dot{p}_M\;.$$

This shows that the elasticities of transmission of the import price on the domestic producer and consumer prices are less than one for all finite values of the elasticity of substitution σ. The change in producer price is negative if σ is lower than the elasticity of demand ε. This comes from the fact that aggregate consumption decreases in response to the aggregate consumer price increase and, with low substitutability between the imported and domestic commodities, consumption of both components decreases. For σ greater than ε, the elasticity of transmission to the producer price increases with the initial share of imports s_M and decreases with the supply elasticity μ. Thus, an increase in the international price will have relatively small effects on the producer price if domestic production is a poor substitute for imports, if the share of imports is small, or if the supply elasticity is large. The consumer price, by contrast, always increases. The rise in consumer price is greater with higher substitutability σ, with lower demand elasticity ε, and with a greater share s_M of imports in total supply. If there is sufficient substitutability (σ greater than ε), then a higher supply elasticity μ reduces the magnitude of the price transmission.

Similarly, on the supply side, selling on the domestic market and selling on the international market are not rigorously equivalent. The commodities may be somewhat different, and the markets certainly are unequally accessible. In that sense also, we can consider commodities for the domestic market and for the foreign market to be imperfect substitutes for the producer, and export taxes may not fully affect the domestic price. A symmetric reasoning can thus be made on the export side. Let X be domestic production, with producer price p_X, and a supply elasticity of μ. Competition for resources between production for the domestic market D and for exports E is also expressed in a supply function which depends on the relative prices of the two commodities. Assume in this case that there are no imports. The domestic market is written:

$$X = D + E = p_X^{\mu}\,, \quad \text{with} \quad p_X = \frac{p_D D + p_E E}{X}\,, \quad \text{and}$$

$$D = p_D^{-\varepsilon}\,.$$

This gives:

$$\dot{p}_D = \frac{s_E(\sigma - \mu)}{s_E(\sigma - \mu) + \mu + \varepsilon}\,\dot{p}_E \quad \text{and} \quad \dot{p}_X = \frac{s_E(\sigma + \varepsilon)}{\sigma + \varepsilon + (1 - s_E)(\mu - \sigma)}\,\dot{p}_E\;.$$

The use of import tariff and export subsidy rates as measurements of protection or distortion may largely overestimate the true direct protection. When protection applies to intermediate inputs, the effective rate of protection similarly overestimates taxation effects. When protection applies to both output and input, and imperfect substitutability lowers the numerator and the denominator of the effective protection, the direction of change is ambiguous. True effective protection may be either greater or lower than simple calculation of the effective rate would entail. This suggests that protection indicators, as calculated in this chapter, should be used with caution and probably used only for commodities that are indeed almost perfect substitutes for foreign products.

7.6. Political Economy of Price Distortions

With price interventions pervasive in both LDCs and MDCs, a large body of literature has emerged seeking to identify the political economic determinants of these interventions (Anderson and Hayami, 1986; Gardner, 1987; Rausser, 1992; Swinnen and van der Zee, 1992). Questions asked are: Why do the LDCs tax their agricultures while the more developed subsidize them extensively? And why are the levels of intervention sharply uneven across commodities? Some of the explanations that have been given are: (1) High indirect taxation on LDC agriculture originated in implementation of import substitution industrialization strategies and in the consequences of Dutch disease episodes (see Chapter 8), while farm lobbies had little power to influence macroeconomic policies. (2) Export taxes on agriculture and import tariffs on food are the main sources of fiscal revenues for LDC governments with weak ability to collect direct taxes. The resistance of governments to abandon agricultural trade taxation subsequently decreases with their rising ability to lower the administrative costs of collecting direct taxes. (3) Product taxation allows governments to selectively compensate farmers through input subsidies and public projects, thus capturing political gains (Bates, 1981). (4) Throughout the agricultural transformation that accompanies economic development, a continued fall in the relative income of farm producers induces strong demands for income support by farmers. (5) The lobbying power of farm lobbies increases through the agricultural transformation because the organizational costs of controlling the free-rider problem in collective action by farmers falls as their number declines and communications improve (Olson, 1965). (6) As farms become more commercialized and more specialized and have a higher share of fixed costs in total costs, the benefits to farmers of engaging in lobbying activity rises. (7) Per capita cost to the rest of society of protecting agricultural incomes is high in the LDCs and falls with the agricultural transformation as population shifts away from agriculture, reducing opposition to the rise in agricultural protectionism. (8) Resistance of industry to agricultural protectionism also falls with economic development as the elasticity of wages with respect to food prices falls (as food budget shares decline) and the elasticity of industrial profits with respect to wage also falls (as capital intensity rises).

In a recent econometric study, Fulginiti and Shogren (1992) used 1960–84 time series data for 18 MDCs and LDCs and a number of commodities (yielding 1,858 data points) to regress *NPC* on a number of indicators of the political-economic determinants of protectionism listed above. Their results, reported in Table 7.6, show the following: (1) The agricultural sector's relative rent-seeking power is represented alternatively by the share of agriculture in GDP, labor force, and consumption. None of these variables is significant, a disappointing result from the standpoint of the theory of public choice. (2) The public revenue potential of agricultural taxation is represented by land per capita and labor productivity. Both are significantly negative, indicating that agriculturally well-endowed countries discriminate more against their agricultural sector and in this fashion extract some of the land rents. (3) The LDCs' preference for commodity over income taxation is represented by the share of agricultural trade in GDP. A significant negative coefficient shows that there is a higher tax on agriculture if a greater share of agricultural commodities is exported. Variables characterizing trade show that exportables are taxed while importables (food) are subsidized. (4) Equity and distributional considerations in policy making are represented by two variables: currency overvaluation, where a significant positive coefficient shows that a low real exchange rate induces pressures for protection, and the indirect nominal protection coefficient (capturing exchange rate distortions and industrial protectionism associated with import substitution industrialization), where a significant negative coefficient indicates less direct taxation of the sector when it is more heavily taxed indirectly. (5) The bias in trade policy toward food, for instance, for food security reasons, is reflected by a

Table 7.6. Regressions for nominal protection coefficients, 1960–1984

Independent variables	Alternative specifications		
	(1)	(2)	(3)
Share of agriculture			
in GDP	−0.01	−0.05	
	(−1.03)	(−1.42)	
in consumption			−0.00
			(−1.13)
Land per capita	−0.25		
	(−4.32)		
Labor productivity		−0.10	−0.11
		(−3.98)	(−4.39)
Share of agriculture trade in GDP		−0.01	−0.01
		(−5.64)	(−4.65)
Exportables	−0.26	0.26	0.24
	(−2.96)	(2.88)	(2.62)
Importables	0.63	0.63	0.62
	(7.28)	(7.22)	(7.10)
Currency overvaluation	0.21	0.22	
	(3.21)	(3.31)	
NRP indirect			−0.30
			(−3.49)
Food	−0.01	−0.02	−0.02
	(−0.52)	(−0.60)	(−0.65)
Income per capita	0.05	0.03	0.05
	(3.92)	(1.67)	(2.34)
Intercept	−0.90	−0.62	−1.13
	(−5.80)	(−2.47)	(−5.22)
R^2	0.62	0.64	0.66

Source: Fulginiti and Shogren, 1992.
Note: *t*-statistics in parentheses.

food dummy. Its nonsignificance suggests that there is no pro-food bias in the *NPC* (but also that this effect may have already been captured by the positive coefficient of the Importable variable). (6) Finally, the level of development, measured by income per capita, captures all the other structural changes accompanying the agricultural transformation not already represented by the included variables. It is significantly positive, as expected.

These results show that self-interests are important in the formation of agricultural policy. Understanding the mechanisms through which these interests influence policy making is fundamental for the design of policy reforms that it may be politically feasible to implement and sustain.

Exercise 7
Effects of Price Distortions and Investment in Research on Efficiency and Welfare

In this exercise (file 7WELF), we use partial equilibrium analysis to calculate the efficiency loss and the welfare effects that are created by an export tax on wheat in Argentina. Part of the export tax is used to fund the National Institute of Agricultural Technology (INTA), which generates new technologies for wheat producers. The export tax thus has an overall negative effect on static efficiency but a positive potential effect through technological change. Here we explore each effect separately and in combination. Figure 7E.1 illustrates the changes in production induced by price distortion and technological change. Let $q(p)$ be the supply function. At world price p^b the supply would be q^b (point C in the figure). At domestic price p, the production q is lower (point F). Technological change moves the production schedule from $q(p)$ to

Figure 7E.1. Impact of technological change and an export tax on the production and
consumption of wheat

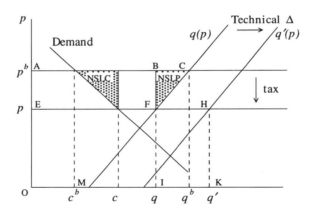

$q'(p)$, inducing a shift in production from F to H at the domestic price. Before technological change occurs, the point which is observed is the actual production, that is, F. Point C has to be derived from knowledge of elasticities and distortions and point H from knowledge of the potential impact of research on productivity.

In the data in Table 7E.1, the distorted price system is characterized by a nominal protection coefficient *NPC* equal to 0.54, that is,

$$NPC = p / p^b = 0.54,$$

	A	B	C	D	E	F	G	H	I
1		Table 7E.1. Effects of price distortions and investment in research on efficiency and welfare							
2									
3									
4									
5			Supply elasticities (ES)			Budget alloc. to research		World market	
6		Structural features	Short run	Medium run	Long run	Medium run	Long run	price + 20%	NPC = 0.75
7									
8		Observed levels (in 1000 MT)							
9		Production q	7033						
10		Consumption c	4746						
11		Exports E	2287						
12									
13		Price elasticities							
14		Supply ES	0.2						
15		Demand ED	-0.3						
16									
17		Trade policy							
18		Nominal protection coefficient NPC	0.54						
19		Border price ($ per MT) pb	122						
20		Domestic price p = NPC*pb	66						
21		Tax rate t* = (pb - p)/p	0.85						
22									
23		Potential levels at border prices							
24		Production qb	8231						
25		Consumption cb	3533						
26		Exports Eb	4698						
27									
28		Welfare effects of	.... taxation ...			....		.. pw increase	.... taxation ....
29									
30		Net social loss in production NSLP	33622						
31		Net social loss in consumption NSLC							
32		Net social loss NSL							
33		Change in consumer surplus ΔCS							
34		Change in producer surplus ΔPS							
35		Change in government revenues ΔB							
36		Net social gain from taxation							
37									
38		Technological change gains from	.... taxation ...			....		.. pw increase	.... taxation ....
39		Share of government tax revenues							
40		allocated to agricultural research k							
41		Elasticity of technology generation a							
42		Output effect of research b*q*(k*B)^a							
43		New level of production							
44									
45		Welfare effects of technological change							
46		Change in producer surplus ΔPS							
47		Change in consumer surplus ΔCS							
48		Change in government revenue ΔB							
49		Net social gain from techn. change							
50									
51		Net effects of technology and	.... taxation ...			....		.. pw increase	.... taxation ....
52									
53		Change in producer surplus							
54		Change in consumer surplus							
55		Change in government revenue							
56		Net social gain							
57									
58									
59		Potential level as % of actual							
60		Production							
61		Consumption							
62		Exports							
63									
64		Welfare change as % of change in producer surplus							
65		Taxation only							
66		Overall							
67									

where p is the domestic price and p^b the world market (that is, border) price. Since the *NPC* is smaller than one, it indicates that wheat is disprotected. We also know the domestic price elasticities of supply and demand for wheat:

Supply: $E_S =$ 0.2 in the short run
                           0.5 in the medium run
                           1.2 in the long run

Demand: $E_D = -0.3$

When measuring relatively large changes in prices and quantities, we use the formula for the average or arc elasticity,

(1) $(q^b - q) / q = E (p^b - p) / p,$

rather than the usual formula for the point elasticity.

Analyze the impact of an export tax on Argentine wheat by answering the following questions:

1. Calculate, with the average elasticity formula above, the levels of production q^b, consumption c^b, and exports E^b that would have prevailed at the international price.

2. Analyze the welfare impact of taxation. This is represented by the move from C to F on Figure 7E.1. The associated loss in producer surplus is the area ACFE, and the net social loss in production the area BCF. Using the formulas in the reminder at the end of the problem set to approximate the welfare triangles, calculate the following measures of welfare changes (you should apply these formulas starting from the observed point F):

The net social loss in production (*NSLP*)
The net social loss in consumption (*NSLC*)
The total net social loss (*NSL = NSLP + NSLC*)
The change in consumer surplus (ΔCS)
The change in producer surplus (ΔPS)
The change in government revenue (ΔB)
The net social gain from taxation ($\Delta CS + \Delta PS + \Delta B$).

According to these results, who gains and who loses from taxation? Is the net social loss (which measures the overall efficiency loss) large or small relative to the income transfers that taxation creates? Is the loss mainly on the consumer side or the producer side? How much does government gain relative to this loss?

3. Since the elasticity of supply response varies with the length of time over which the response is measured, parameterize your results for the short- (0.2), medium- (0.5), and long-run (1.2) elasticities of response.

4. A small share k of the export tax revenues B is assigned to INTA to support research on wheat. Start by saying that it is equal to 2%. Also say that the increase in output created by research is

$$\Delta q / q = b (k B)^a ,$$

where a is the elasticity of production of research which is equal to 0.8 and b is a scalar equal to 0.00014. This is represented on Figure 7E.1 by a shift from F to H. The gross sale revenue (price × quantity) of the producer increases from pq (area EFIO) to pq' (area EHKO). Assuming that the cost of production remains constant (area MFEO), the change in producer surplus is equal to the area FHKI, equal to $p(q' - q)$. To measure the effects of investment in research, calculate for both the medium and the long run:

The output effect of research (Δq)

The new level of output ($q' = q + \Delta q$).

The welfare effects of technological change under price distortions:

    Change in producer surplus

    Change in consumer surplus

    Change in government revenue (do not forget to subtract the cost of research)

    Net social gain from technological change.

Who captures the benefits from technological change in an open economy? Qualitatively, how would this differ in a closed economy?

5. Taxation hurts producers, whereas technological change benefits them. Calculate the net effect of these two interventions by measuring:

    The change in producer surplus from both taxation and technological change

    The change in consumer surplus

    The change in government revenue

    The net social gain. Why is it negative?

Use only medium- and long-run elasticities.

6. Explore parametrically what it would take to make the net social gain positive by changing the share of the tax revenue B that is allocated to research. What is the minimum share that must return to agriculture in the form of research to make the net social effect positive? Look at both medium- and long-run effects.

7. Say that the world market price increases by 20% but that domestic prices remain unchanged. In the original calculation, p^b and t were given, and p was derived. You need to change the corresponding formulas, since now both p^b and p are given, and the new NPC has to be recalculated. Compute now the welfare effect of this world price change (and not the welfare effects of taxation under this new price). Does this rise in world price directly affect producers and/or consumers? Who is the main gainer from this rise in prices? What does it do to agricultural research?

8. Allow now for some trade liberalization by raising the NPC to 0.75 while keeping the world price at its former level of 122\$/MT. Use the potential level q^b and c^b computed in the first column and equation (1) to estimate the new level of q and c. Use the medium-run supply elasticity. Discuss the implications that this trade liberalization has on all sectors including the government budget. Why is the net social gain of taxation cum research now positive? Use this result to weight the relative merits of investment in research financed by trade distortions relative to trade liberalization.

Reminder: Partial Equilibrium Analysis of an Export Tax on Agriculture

The formulas for the calculation of the efficiency and welfare effects of an export tax measured at (p, q) and (p, c), instead of (p^b, q^b) and (p^b, c^b) as in section 7.4.2, are computed as follows. Instead of using the usual definition of the tax rate,

$$t = NRP = NPC - 1 = (p - p^b)/p^b,$$

we use here:

$$t^* = (p^b - p)/p = (1 - NPC)/NPC.$$

Let: $W^* = pq$ the gross value of production at domestic price
$V^* = pc$ the value of consumption at domestic price.

a. *Efficiency effects:*
The net social loss in production (*NSLP*), equal to area FBC, can be measured as:
$NSLP = 1/2 \, (q^b - q)(p^b - p) = 1/2 \, E_S \, t^{*2} \, W^* > 0.$
Similarly, the net social loss in consumption can be measured as:
$NSLC = -1/2 \, E_D \, t^{*2} \, V^* > 0.$
Total net social loss: $NSL = NSLP + NSLC.$

b. *Welfare effects:*
Welfare gain of producers (change in producer surplus):
$\Delta PS = q \, (p - p^b) - NSLP < 0.$
Welfare gain of consumers (change in consumer surplus):
$\Delta CS = -c \, (p - p^b) - NSLC > 0.$

c. *Government budget effect:*
Change in government revenue: $\Delta B = (q - c)(p^b - p).$
Net social gain: $NSG = \Delta CS + \Delta PS + \Delta B.$

d. *Change in the balance of payments:*
Exports decline from $q^b - c^b$ to $q - c$. The loss in foreign exchange earnings is the change in net exports, that is, the change in the balance of payments:
$\Delta BoP = -p^b \, (q^b - q + c - c^b).$

References

Akino, Masakatsu, and Yujiro Hayami. 1975. "Efficiency and Equity in Public Research: Rice Breeding in Japan's Economic Development." *American Journal of Agricultural Economics* 57:1–10.

Anderson, Kim, and Yujiro Hayami. 1986. *The Political Economy of Agricultural Protection.* London: Allen and Unwin, Ltd.

Ayer, Harry, and G. Edward Schuh. 1972. "Social Rates of Return and Other Aspects of Agricultural Research: The Case of Cotton Research in São Paulo, Brazil." *American Journal of Agricultural Economics* 54:557–69.

Balassa, Bela. 1982. *Development Strategies in Semi-industrialized Economies.* Baltimore: Johns Hopkins University Press.

Bates, Robert. 1981. *Markets and States in Tropical Africa.* Berkeley: University of California Press.

Carter, Colin, Alex McCalla, and Andrew Schmitz. 1989. *Canada and International Grain Markets: Trends, Policies, and Prospects.* Ottawa: Economic Council of Canada, Canadian Government Publishing Centre, Ministry of Supply and Services.

Currie, John, John Murphy, and Andrew Schmitz. 1971. "The Concept of Economic Surplus and Its Use in Economic Analysis." *Economic Journal* 18:741–98.

Fulginiti, Lilyan, and Jason Shogren. 1992. "Agricultural Protection in Developing Countries." *American Journal of Agricultural Economics* 74:795–801.

Gardner, Bruce. 1987. *The Economics of Agricultural Policies.* New York: Macmillan Publishing Co.

Griliches, Zvi. 1958. "Research Costs and Social Returns: Hybrid Corn and Related Innovations." *Journal of Political Economy* 66:419–31.

Hall, Lana. 1980. "Evaluating the Effects of PL-480 Wheat Imports on Brazil's Grain Sector." *American Journal of Agricultural Economics* 62:19–28.

Krueger, Anne. 1974. "The Political Economy of the Rent Seeking Society." *American Economic Review* 64:291–303.

Krueger, Anne, Maurice Schiff, and Alberto Valdés. 1988. "Agricultural Incentives in Developing Countries: Measuring the Effect of Sectoral and Economywide Policies." *World Bank Economic Review* 2:255–72.

Lipton, Michael. 1977. *Why Poor People Stay Poor: A Study of Urban Bias in World Development.* Cambridge: Harvard University Press.

Michel, Gilles. 1987. "The Analytical Framework." In *La Côte d'Ivoire en transition*, vol. 3. Washington D.C.: World Bank.

Norton, George, and Jeffrey Davis. 1981. "Evaluating Returns to Agricultural Research: A Review." *American Journal of Agricultural Economics* 63:685–89.

Olson, Mancur. 1965. *The Logic of Collective Action.* Cambridge: Harvard University Press.

Owen, Wyn. 1966. "The Double Developmental Squeeze on Agriculture." *American Economic Review* 56:43–70.

Peterson, Willis. 1967. "Returns to Poultry Research in the United States." *Journal of Farm Economics* 49:656–69.

Rausser, Gordon. 1992. "Predatory Versus Productive Government: The Case of U.S. Agricultural Policies." *Journal of Economic Perspectives* 6:133–157.

Ruttan, Vernon. 1982. *Agricultural Research Policy.* Minneapolis: University of Minnesota Press.

Sah, Raaj, and Joseph Stiglitz. 1984. "The Economics of Price Scissors." *American Economic Review* 74:125–138.

Schiff, Maurice, and Alberto Valdés. 1992. *The Plundering of Agriculture in Developing Countries.* Washington, D.C.: World Bank.

Schmitz, Andrew, and David Seckler. 1970. "Mechanical Agriculture and Social Welfare: The Case of the Tomato Harvester." *American Journal of Agricultural Economics* 52:569–78.

Schultz, Theodore, ed. 1978. *Distortions of Agricultural Incentives.* Bloomington: Indiana University Press.

Scobie, Grant, and Rafael Posada. 1978. "The Impact of Technical Change on Income Distribution: The Case of Rice in Colombia." *American Journal of Agricultural Economics* 60:85–91.

Swinnen, Joe, and F. A. van der Zee. 1992. "The New Political Economy of Agricultural Policies: A Survey with Special Reference to the EC's Common Agricultural Policy." The Wageningen Economic Papers series, Wageningen Agricultural University, The Netherlands.

Timmer, Peter. 1986. *Getting Prices Right: The Scope and Limits of Agricultural Price Policy.* Ithaca: Cornell University Press.

Tsakok, Isabelle. 1990. *Agricultural Price Policy: A Practitioner's Guide to Partial Equilibrium Analysis.* Ithaca: Cornell University Press.

Tweeten, Luther. 1989. "Classical Welfare Analysis." In *Agricultural Policy Analysis Tools for Economic Development,* edited by L. Tweeten. Boulder, Colo.: Westview Press.

Vasavada, Utpal. 1991. "Trade Policy Implications of Sustainable Agriculture." *Canadian Journal of Agricultural Economics* 39:593–606.

Webb, Alan, Michael Lopez, and Renata Penn. 1990. *Estimates of Producer and Consumer Subsidy Equivalents: Government Intervention in Agriculture, 1982–87,* Statistical Bulletin no. 803. Washington D.C.: U.S. Department of Agriculture Economic Research Service.

World Bank. 1986. *World Development Report, 1986.* New York: Oxford University Press.

CHAPTER EIGHT

The Real Exchange Rate

In the previous chapter, we identified two components of price distortions. The first component originated in taxes, tariffs, subsidies, or quantity rationing on a particular product or factor. These direct distortions were characterized by comparing domestic prices with border prices at the official exchange rate, and different indicators were proposed to measure them (*NRP*, *ERP*, and the first term in *RRRP*). The second component originated indirectly in an exchange rate distortion, measured by comparing domestic prices with border prices at the equilibrium exchange rate (*RRP*, *RERP*, and the second term in *RRRP*). The importance of exchange rate distortions for the agricultural sector was revealed by numerous measurements showing that indirect distortions were generally greater than direct distortions.

The analysis of exchange rate distortions is based on the definition and measurement of the equilibrium exchange rate which is the subject of this chapter. As we shall see, movements of the equilibrium exchange rate are the result of several sectoral and macroeconomic policies—trade, official exchange rate, fiscal, and monetary policies—as well as of external shocks. Among causes of change in the equilibrium exchange rate, a distinction needs to be made between normal movement associated with structural or sustainable changes in the economy and movements away from a sustainable equilibrium level induced by policy disequilibria or temporary shocks.

8.1. Market and Effective Exchange Rates

As there is a great deal of confusion in the definition of some of the basic terms used in exchange rate analysis, we first define the concepts that we use throughout this book. The nominal exchange rate e is the price of a foreign currency unit in terms of domestic currency units, the definition adopted in the IMF's *International Financial Statistics*. The measurement unit is therefore LCU/foreign currency (LCU for local currency unit). To simplify the exposition, we will use the dollar sign $ to represent the foreign currency unit. Under a flexible exchange rate regime, the domestic currency, and by extension the exchange rate, are said to *depreciate* when the LCU price of the foreign currency increases, that is, when the exchange rate rises. Conversely, the domestic currency, and thus the exchange rate, *appreciates* when the exchange rate falls. Under a fixed exchange rate regime, the rise and fall of the exchange rate are referred to as exchange rate: *devaluation* and exchange rate *revaluation*.

When there are trade taxes, importers and exporters of different commodities transact the dollar at different effective prices. An import tariff t_{Mi} increases the price of imported good i, while an export tax t_{Ei} decreases the price received by the exporter of the exported good i. The perceived prices of the foreign currency by importers and exporters are $e(1 + t_{Mi})$ and $e(1 - t_{Ei})$, respectively. This is captured in the concept of the *effective exchange rate* for a specific commodity i, which is defined as:

$e_i^{eff} = e(1 + t_{Mi} - t_{Ei})$, where e is the nominal exchange rate in LCU/\$.

The real world contains as many exchange rates as there are foreign currencies. There are also multiple exchange rate regimes in which different exchange rates for the same currency apply to different transactions. The most representative exchange rate, or an average of the main exchange rates for this country, is then chosen for e, and all the discrepancies are aggregated in an equivalent trade tax around this unique exchange rate e.

This joint treatment of trade taxes and exchange rates emphasizes similarities and specificities in their roles. A uniform 10% import tariff and export subsidy would leave all relative prices of tradables equal and thus be equivalent to a 10% devaluation of the exchange rate. Pakistan provides an example of systematic use of trade taxes in lieu of an exchange rate policy, as shown in this chapter's exercise. Pakistan maintained an artificially low nominal exchange rate with import tariffs and export subsidies of 250% and 150%, respectively, during 1960–72 and accommodated a 100% devaluation in 1973 with corresponding decreases in the tariff and subsidy rates. Ecuador used a system of multiple exchange rates from 1982 to 1986, with exchange rates for imports above the official exchange rate, and increased this difference in 1985 with a corresponding decrease in tariffs. A system of specific exchange rates and trade taxes allows for selective protection of certain sectors, but it also tends to create confusion and uncertainty, raise administrative costs, and justify intense political actions by specific interest groups.

8.2. The Market for Foreign Currency and the Real Exchange Rate

Consider now the market for foreign currency. The supply of foreign currency derives from exports and inflows of capital, and the demand for foreign currency from imports and capital outflows. As in any other market, there is a one-to-one relationship between excess demand, which is the balance-of-payment deficit, and the price level, which is the exchange rate. How this market adjusts depends on the exchange rate regime. In a country with a fully flexible exchange rate, a shift in the export supply schedule increases the supply of foreign currency, which induces a decrease in its price. With a stable monetary policy that ensures stability of domestic prices and a fall in the price of the foreign commodities, both sides of the market adjust, with imports increasing and exports decreasing until the balance of trade returns to its original equilibrium. In a fixed exchange rate regime, the equilibrating mechanism is indirect. Increased exports create a surplus in the balance of payments. This generates an additional supply of foreign currency that the Central Bank, under obligation to maintain the exchange rate, must buy. The money supply thus expands and exerts an upward pressure on domestic prices. Imports increase because foreign commodities, whose prices have not risen, become relatively more attractive. Exports decrease because selling on foreign markets is less profitable. The new equilibrium is reached when the deficit returns to its original level.

These examples show that the relevant price on the foreign exchange market is the price of the foreign currency relative to the domestic price level. This is the concept of the *real exchange rate* (*RER*). Many variants of the concept of real exchange rate are used (Dornbusch and Helmers, 1989). In its simplest form, the real exchange rate is defined as a deflated nominal exchange rate e / p^d, where p^d is a price deflator for the domestic currency. This index measures the real price of the dollar but does not adjust for the fact that the dollar itself changes in value over time. A more refined index, which adjusts to changes in the purchasing power of the dollar, is $e p^\$ / p^d$, where $p^\$$ is a general index of dollar prices on the world market. These indices are usually built with the country's own consumer price index (CPI) for p^d and the U.S. wholesale price index (WPI) for $p^\$$. The gross national product (GNP) deflator is sometimes used for the domestic deflator. It has the advantage of a larger coverage than the CPI. However, since it is based on factor prices and hence does not capture the underlying inflation rate except in the case of wage indexation to domestic prices, it is not an appropriate index for countries with high inflation rates. The U.S. CPI would not be a good deflator to use for the dollar deflator because this index includes the price of many domestic services and home goods. The WPI is more representative of internationally traded goods.

This real exchange rate index can be extended to include several trade partners by using a weighted average of specific real exchange rates, with weights equal to the share α_i of each partner in the country's international trade (imports, exports, or both) in a base year:

$$RER = \sum_i \alpha_i \frac{e_i p_i^\$}{p^d} \text{ with } \sum_i \alpha_i = 1.$$

All indices needed for the computation of these exchange rate indicators are readily available on a monthly, quarterly, or yearly basis in *International Financial Statistics*, published monthly by the IMF.

The real exchange rate, which represents foreign prices in local currency units relative to the domestic price, is a good index of the country's competitiveness. A decrease in the real exchange rate means that domestic goods become more expensive and thus less competitive with foreign goods.

Table 8.1 reports the evolution of the real exchange rate for selected African countries from 1973 to 1983. All countries show a substantial decline in their real exchange rates in the 1970s, but dramatic devaluations in the early 1980s reestablished levels of competitiveness comparable to the 1970 levels in most countries.

There is another interpretation of the real exchange rate concept useful for analyzing resource allocation. The underlying adjustment mechanism of the balance of payments, directed by an increase of the exchange rate, for example, is to induce consumers to buy domestic goods instead of imports and, symmetrically, to induce producers to produce tradables, whether import-competing or exportables, rather than nontradables. The relevant exchange rate index for such allocation decisions is therefore p_T / p_{NT}, the relative prices of tradables and nontradables. If the country has sufficiently detailed national accounts, these price indices are built as averages of sectoral prices on the basis of the adequate sectoral partition. Otherwise, import and export price indices, which are regularly published, are used to construct the price of tradables, and the prices of construction and services, the wage level, or even the GDP deflator are used as proxies for the nontradable price. In this approach, traded goods can be subdivided further, and real exchange rates can accordingly be defined for specific commodities or groups of commodities as p_{Ti} / p_{NT}, where p_{Ti} is the price index for a subgroup i of tradables.

Choice of indices of the real exchange rate depends on the purpose of the study. In this chapter, we will alternatively use two indices which, to avoid confusion, we will refer to as *RER1* and *RER2*:

Real exchange rates: $RER1 = ep^\$ / p^d$ and $RER2 = p_T / p_{NT}$.

*RER*1 is sometimes called the purchasing power parity (PPP) real exchange rate. Combining the concepts of real exchange rate and effective exchange rate gives the real effective exchange rate for commodity *i* as:

Real effective exchange rate: $RER_i^{eff} = RER\,(1 + t_{Mi} - t_{Ei})$.

These two real exchange rates for Ecuador are reported in Figure 8.1. Both follow the same overall trends until 1980, with an appreciation in 1960–69, a drastic readjustment in 1970–71, and a regular appreciation again since 1972. They diverge in the 1980s, however. During the

Table 8.1. Index of real exchange rates in selected African countries (1969–1971 = 100)

Country	1973–75	1978–80	1981–83
Cameroon	75	58	80
Côte d'Ivoire	81	56	74
Ethiopia	93	64	67
Ghana	89	23	8
Kenya	88	69	86
Malawi	94	85	94
Mali	68	50	66
Niger	80	56	74
Nigeria	76	43	41
Senegal	71	60	85
Sierra Leone	100	90	73
Sudan	76	58	74
Tanzania	85	69	51
Zambia	90	79	86
All Sub-Saharan Africa	84	62	69
excluding Ghana	83	64	73

Source: World Bank, 1986.
Note: The real exchange rate is defined as the official exchange rate deflated by the ratio of the domestic to the U.S. consumer price deflators. A fall in the index indicates exchange rate appreciation. Data are three-year averages.

1980s, *RER*1 stabilizes, indicating a correspondence between exchange rate movement and inflation, but the price structure changes and *RER*2 falls, following the decline in international prices of major agricultural products in 1981 and of oil in 1982 and 1983. The difference in the sizes of the two real exchange rate adjustments in 1970 and 1971 also reflects a change in external prices. The two-year devaluation returned *RER*1 to its 1961 value, but over these 10 years the relative price of agricultural tradables and *RER*2 had declined. In these two periods, 1961–71 and 1980–85, the stronger decline of *RER*2 thus indicates a loss in the comparative

Figure 8.1. Real exchange rates, Ecuador, 1960–1985

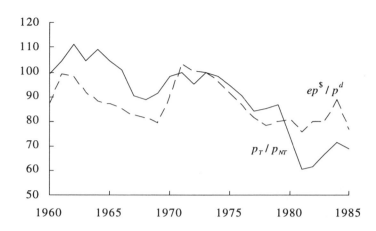

Source: p_T / p_{NT} from Scobie and Jardine, 1988; $ep^{\$} / p^{d}$ computed from data available in *International Financial Statistics*.

advantage of Ecuador due to changes in the international environment, a factor that *RER*1 does not incorporate.

8.3. The Equilibrium Exchange Rate

The concept of equilibrium exchange rate is an exchange rate that would prevail in a nondistorted environment. Determination of the equilibrium exchange rate therefore rests on the understanding of how completely free-floating exchange rates respond to changes in the economic conditions. We will analyze how domestic and foreign inflation, trade disturbances, and capital flows affect the exchange rate and define from these analyses indicators of the equilibrium exchange rate.

8.3.1. The Purchasing Power Parity Equilibrium Exchange Rate

An important determinant of exchange rate movements should be the difference between the domestic rate of inflation and inflation rates in the rest of the world. If domestic inflation exceeds inflation abroad, then, other things being equal, the currency will tend to depreciate. The PPP theory asserts that this effect should be the main explanation for exchange rate movements. Correspondingly, one can define the PPP equilibrium exchange rate in any year in relation to a base year equilibrium exchange rate as:

$$e^{*}(\text{PPP}) = e_0^{*} \frac{p^{d} / p_0^{d}}{p^{\$} / p_0^{\$}},$$

where p_0^d, $p_0^\$$, and e_0^* are the domestic price index, the foreign price index, and the equilibrium exchange rate in the base year. By choosing a base year in which the official nominal exchange rate e_0 was at an equilibrium level, this expression can be used to compute a time series of equilibrium exchange rates. The choice of the base year is, however, the tricky part of this approach. One usually chooses a year in which the balance of payments was roughly in equilibrium or at an acceptable long-term disequilibrium value, and for which this equilibrium was not obtained by exceptional constraints imposed on imports, exports, or capital movements. All necessary data on exchange rate and price indices are readily available in *International Financial Statistics*.

Substituting $p^d/p^\$$ in the definition of the *RER*1 gives:

$$RER1 = \left(e_0^* \frac{p_0^\$}{p_0^d} \right) \frac{e}{e^*(\text{PPP})}.$$

The real exchange rate *RER*1 therefore measures the deviation of the exchange rate from its PPP equilibrium value. In other words, a falling *RER*1 indicates a nominal exchange rate that falls below its equilibrium value. This typically happens when domestic inflation runs high and devaluations are lower than the necessary adjustment. Alternatively the real exchange rate remains constant when the nominal exchange rate mimics the relative inflation rates.

This definition of the equilibrium exchange rate is limited, as it does not consider any shock that would justify a change in the real exchange rate. Typical cases of such shocks are trade disturbances, like the change in the terms of trade that affected Ecuador, and capital flows.

8.3.2. The Elasticity Approach

The elasticity approach estimates the equilibrium real exchange rate that would equilibrate the balance of trade. Let us consider the foreign currency market represented in Figure 8.2. As we have seen above, its price is the real exchange rate. The equilibrium real exchange rate is defined as the rate for which the market is in equilibrium or at an acceptable or sustainable level

Figure 8.2. The elasticity approach to the equilibrium exchange rate

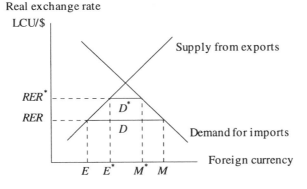

of disequilibrium D^*. If the actual balance-of-trade deficit D is greater than D^*, the observed RER is below its equilibrium value RER^*. The level of exports E^* and imports M^* that would prevail at the equilibrium RER^* can be computed from the observed levels E and M, and the export and import elasticities ε_E and ε_M, as follows:

$$\frac{E - E^*}{E} = \varepsilon_E \frac{RER - RER^*}{RER} \quad \text{and} \quad \frac{M - M^*}{M} = \varepsilon_M \frac{RER - RER^*}{RER}.$$

This shows a relation between the necessary change in the balance-of-trade deficit and the necessary change in the real exchange rate:

$$D - D^* = (M - M^*) - (E - E^*) = (\varepsilon_E E - \varepsilon_M M)(RER^* - RER) / RER.$$

This solves for the equilibrium real exchange rate as a function of the unsustainable part of the deficit $D - D^*$:

$$RER^*(\text{elasticity}) = RER[1 + (D - D^*) / (\varepsilon_E E - \varepsilon_M M)].$$

Note that because ε_M is a negative number, the denominator is always positive and, hence, reduction of the trade balance deficit $(D - D^* > 0)$ requires an increase of the real exchange rate.

This expression can be used to compute a series of nominal equilibrium exchange rates comparable to the PPP equilibrium exchange rate, which is the nominal exchange rate that should prevail at the observed domestic price index:

$$e^*(\text{elasticity}) = e[1 + (D - D^*) / (\varepsilon_E E - \varepsilon_M M)].$$

One difficulty with this approach is the determination of the level of the sustainable deficit, which is somewhat subjective. Debating what deficit is sustainable is, however, unavoidable, as it is a fundamental part of the concept of an equilibrium situation. Another difficulty is the determination of import and export elasticities. Indeed, imports and exports are aggregates of many different products with very different price elasticities, and the meaning and measure of such average elasticities are not clear. In practice, one can estimate import and export functions. Alternatively, one may resort to approximate values derived from the literature. A relatively common use has been to take $\varepsilon_M = -2$ and $\varepsilon_E = 1$. However, Khan and Ostry (1992) report much lower values for the price elasticity of imports, in the range -0.1 to -0.5.

A third approach to the estimation of the equilibrium exchange rate, which derives from the specification of a structural three-sector model, partly resolves this problem of the underlying formation of import and export elasticities. This is discussed in section 8.5.2 below.

Table 8.2 and Figure 8.3 report the calculation of these two equilibrium exchange rates for Colombia. The year 1974 was chosen as the base year for the PPP method because it is the closest to an equilibrium situation, with a balance of trade in equilibrium, moderate capital movements, "normal" terms of trade, a moderate fiscal deficit relative to GDP, and relatively low trade restrictions (García García and Montes Llamas, 1989). The evolution of this indicator shows that the Colombian peso was largely overvalued in the early 1960s but steadily converged to an equilibrium value in 1974 before again becoming overvalued. For the calculation of the equilibrium exchange rate by the elasticity approach, the sustainable deficit was chosen as 2% of GNP. Colombia did not incur a deficit beyond this value until the mid-seventies, with the exception of 1966 and 1971, and even enjoyed a large surplus in the later years of that decade. Accordingly, the equilibrium exchange rate—referred to as elasticity ($D = D^*$) in Table 8.2 and Figure 8.3—varied little from the official exchange rate. It was only in the 1980s that elimination of a balance-of-payment deficit, largely due to debt interest payment, would require a devaluation of the exchange rate of up to 20%. As we will see later, if trade taxes, which serve to restrict imports, were eliminated, a 15% to 20% devaluation of the currency above this level would be needed—elasticity ($D = D^*$ and $t = 0$) in Table 8.2 and Figure 8.3. Comparison of the PPP and elasticity approach equilibrium exchange rates until 1974 indicates that Colombia has been able to maintain a balanced current account despite a PPP-overvalued exchange rate. This is explained by Colombia's ability to sustain, in part through the use of nontariff barriers, an

Figure 8.3. Alternative measures of the equilibrium exchange rate, Colombia, 1960–1983

Ratio of equilibrium to official exchange rate e^*/e

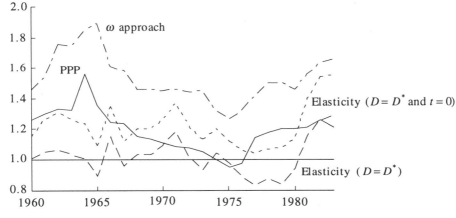

Source: Table 8.2

increasing ratio of exports to GDP, while containing imports to a growth rate lower than that of GDP. The difference between the two curves in the late seventies is, by contrast, foreign in origin, with the large trade surplus due to the coffee boom. If high coffee prices represent a durable structural change, this in turn would denote a change in Colombia's comparative advantage which could sustain a lower equilibrium exchange rate than the PPP calculation would suggest.

8.4. Forces Affecting the Real Exchange Rate

Let us now return to the analysis of the real exchange rate. As in any supply-and-demand analysis, the real exchange rate will change if the underlying supply and demand curves shift. As we have seen above, this will happen regardless of the exchange rate regime chosen. Some

Table 8.2. Equilibrium exchange rates, Colombia

Years	Current balance (million $) 1	Nominal e (pesos/$) 2	CPI (index) 3	U.S. WPI (index) 4	e*(PPP) (pesos/$) 5	Import tariff 6	Export tax 7	Imports (million $) 8	Exports (million $) 9	Surplus due to trade taxes (million $) 10	Sustainable D* (million $) 11	e*(elast) D=D* (pesos/$) 12	e*(elast) t=0 and D=D* (pesos/$) 13	e*(ω) (pesos/$) 14
1960	−87	6.6	1.9	30.7	8.4	.53	.06	496	488	203	81	6.7	7.6	9.7
1961	−145	6.7	2.0	31.0	8.7	.62	−.02	531	465	194	92	7.1	8.5	10.4
1962	−162	6.9	2.1	30.7	9.2	.87	−.02	537	476	241	104	7.3	9.1	12.1
1963	−132	9.0	2.7	30.6	11.9	.87	.02	497	481	241	97	9.3	11.4	15.8
1964	−129	9.0	3.2	30.7	14.1	.99	.03	582	636	309	119	9.1	11.1	16.7
1965	−11	10.5	3.3	31.3	14.2	1.04	.02	430	591	231	124	9.3	11.4	19.9
1966	−288	13.5	4.0	32.3	16.7	.71	.06	639	526	299	114	15.5	18.2	21.7
1967	−73	14.5	4.3	32.4	17.9	.68	.04	464	552	211	118	13.9	16.2	23.0
1968	−164	16.3	4.6	33.2	18.7	.53	.02	615	605	225	120	16.9	19.6	23.8
1969	−175	17.3	5.0	34.5	19.6	.52	.00	648	672	222	129	17.9	20.8	25.2
1970	−293	18.4	5.4	35.7	20.4	.51	.01	802	788	279	145	20.2	23.2	26.7
1971	−454	19.9	5.9	36.9	21.6	.52	−.02	903	754	294	155	23.5	27.4	29.1
1972	−191	21.9	6.7	38.6	23.4	.49	−.09	850	979	199	172	22.1	26.4	31.6
1973	−55	23.6	8.0	43.6	24.8	.50	−.10	983	1,263	213	204	22.1	26.7	34.4
1974	−352	26.1	10.0	51.8	26.1	.36	−.06	1,511	1,495	315	238	27.1	31.3	34.6
1975	−172	30.9	12.3	56.6	29.3	.29	−.08	1,415	1,683	193	260	30.1	34.5	39.2
1976	163	34.7	14.8	59.3	33.7	.35	−.13	1,654	2,202	175	304	30.5	36.6	46.0
1977	375	36.8	19.6	62.9	42.1	.45	−.15	1,970	2,660	264	388	30.7	38.3	52.1
1978	258	39.1	23.1	67.8	46.0	.56	−.06	2,552	3,155	738	463	34.2	41.7	58.7
1979	438	42.6	28.8	76.3	51.0	.55	−.15	2,978	3,441	608	573	35.8	45.8	64.0
1980	−206	47.3	36.5	87.1	56.6	.51	−.06	4,283	3,986	1,221	701	44.4	54.0	68.9
1981	−1,961	54.5	46.5	95.0	66.1	.63	−.05	4,730	3,158	1,678	775	62.7	76.4	85.0
1982	−3,054	64.1	58.0	96.9	80.8	.72	−.04	5,358	3,114	2,123	834	80.9	98.7	104.8
1983	−3,003	78.9	69.4	98.1	95.5	.76	.00	4,464	2,970	1,928	833	101.9	122.3	131.2

Sources: cols. 1–4, 8–9: *International Financial Statistics*; cols. 6–7, 11: García García and Montes Llamas, 1989.

Note: Elasticities for the omega approach (0.9) and trade elasticities (−2 for imports and +1 for exports): García García and Montes Llamas, 1989. D^* is set at 2% of GDP. Surplus (exports−imports) due to trade taxes and equilibrium exchange rates [e^*(PPP), e^*(elasticity), and $e^*(\omega)$]: see text.

of these shifts reflect structural changes, and the corresponding movement of the real exchange rate is to be interpreted as the evolution of an equilibrium rate. Alternatively, some shifts correspond to unsustainable positions or policy-induced distortions, and the corresponding movement of the real exchange rate reflects a disequilibrium situation. Therefore, the diagnostic of a movement of the real exchange rate is not necessarily due to a disequilibrium situation, although this may often be the case. Furthermore, as we will see later, an appreciation in the real exchange rate creates specific difficulties for the country. It is thus crucial to monitor potential disequilibria underlying any such movement of the real exchange rate. We will now see how changes in exports earnings, imports schedules, capital flows, and trade taxes affect the real exchange rate and, in each case, analyze the consequences these may have for the economy. These examples are adapted from Harberger (1986, 1989).

8.4.1. Shift in Export Earnings from Productivity Change or Commodity Boom

A shift in the export schedule (Figure 8.4a) induces a decline in the real exchange rate. One example of such a shift is a general improvement of efficiency in the export sectors, like that enjoyed by Japan since the mid-1950s. In this case, the movement of the real exchange rate can be understood in two ways. First, because Japan's efficiency in producing nontradables did not increase as quickly, the price of nontradables had to increase relative to that of tradables. Consequently, the real exchange rate, $RER2$, had to fall. Alternatively, this can be explained by the foreign exchange market, where export growth produced an increase in income and in the supply of foreign exchange. Since not all newly generated income was spent on imports, the demand for foreign exchange did not increase as quickly. The resulting foreign exchange surplus could only be absorbed through a decline in the real exchange rate, as measured by $RER1$ (see Figure 8.5).

Another example of a sudden increase in foreign exchange supply is that of the oil-exporting countries when the price of oil rose dramatically in 1973–74 and 1979–80. In most cases, decline in real exchange rates followed these oil shocks.

Can these movements be considered adjustments in the equilibrium exchange rate? Yes, in the sense that exchange rate appreciation in all these cases corresponds to an improvement in the country's comparative advantage. However, there are important differences between the case of Japan and that of the oil-exporting countries. As productivity growth in Japan was fairly widespread across tradable sectors, all sectors could withstand the appreciation in the real exchange rate. The decline in the real exchange rate can thus be viewed as a necessary correction, one which compensated for differential improvements in productivity and maintained equilibrium in the relative profitability between nontradable and tradable sectors. In contrast, commodity booms can have dramatic consequences for other sectors. Facing an appreciated exchange rate, and thus a decline in price relative to nontradables and wages, other tradable sectors, such as agriculture and industry, cannot remain profitable. These sectors may even be dismantled as resources flow to the more profitable productive sectors, that is the booming sector and nontradables, and demand shifts to inexpensive imports. This is what is known as the "Dutch disease," in reference to appreciation of the real exchange rate in the Netherlands when it started to export large quantities of North Sea natural gas. In many cases, the sector most affected by this changing price structure has been agriculture. Industrial sectors have often been protected by tariffs and import restrictions in partial compensation for appreciation of the real exchange rate. Again, this equilibrium reflects the new comparative advantage of the country producing

Figure 8.4. Real exchange rate analysis

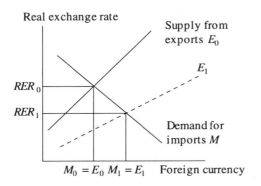

8.4a. Shift in exports earnings

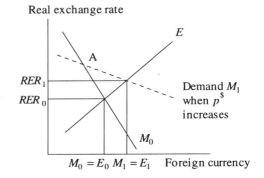

8.4b. Increase in world price of imports

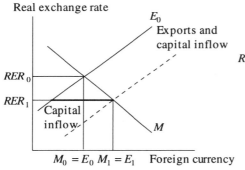

8.4c. Capital inflow spent on nontradables

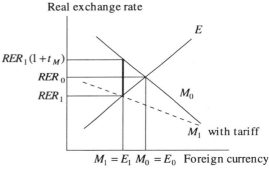

8.4d. Imposition of an import tariff

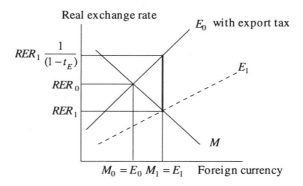

8.4e. Elimination of an export tax

Source: Harberger, 1986.

the booming commodity, yet it implies important restructuring of the whole economy. Furthermore, if, as in the case of oil, the sudden price boom is of short duration, economies find themselves with dismantled tradable sectors at the onset of the downturn of the Dutch disease. Only a few farsighted countries, like Cameroon or Botswana (Hill, 1991), protected themselves against such costly fluctuations by sterilizing foreign earnings abroad and regulating their entry into the country. This avoided an appreciation in the real exchange rate and saved foreign resources for times beyond the short commodity boom. Other mechanisms that can be used to prevent appreciation of the real exchange rate include increased government reserves out of taxation of foreign revenues, repayment of foreign debt, and exports of capital for direct foreign investment in other countries.

8.4.2. Shift in Import Demand from Price Shock or Expansionary Domestic Policies

Symmetrically, a sudden shift in the demand schedule (Figure 8.4b) will induce a readjustment in the real exchange rate. A price increase in imported goods, oil for the importing countries, for example, will induce an increase or decrease in demand for foreign exchange, depending on whether the elasticity of imports is greater or lesser than one. This corresponds to the right and left of A in Figure 8.4b. If demand is inelastic, the balance-of-payment equilibrium is reestablished by a real devaluation. Monetary and fiscal policies also cause important shifts in the demand schedule. Suppose that a government engages in an expansionary monetary and fiscal policy. As a result, aggregate demand increases and output begins to rise. A share of increased demand becomes increased imports. At the same time, exports may decrease if domestic demand exceeds the increase in supply. Thus, an expansionary policy tends to create a deficit in foreign currency and a depreciation of the real exchange rate. In both cases, while depreciation of the exchange rate is an equilibrium response to the shift in the demand schedule, it puts pressure on productive sectors by increasing the price of imported inputs. However, it is also true that a depreciation in the exchange rate increases these sectors' competitiveness on the world market. Whether the net of these two effects generates an expansion or recession depends on the economy's ability to respond to new incentives. However, as we will see in the next section, expansionary policies may also cause harm to the economy through their impact on capital flows.

8.4.3. Capital Outflow or Debt Accumulation

International capital flows constitute the most important element of exchange rate movement and may be linked to fiscal and monetary policies themselves. For example, during a phase of expansionary policy, which is expected to lead to a necessary depreciation of the exchange rate, capital will tend to flow out of the country, in order to protect itself from the loss in foreign exchange value that it would incur through the devaluation. This outflow of capital may, in turn, precipitate a devaluation, as in the case of a successful speculative attack. Conversely, large capital inflows induce real exchange rate appreciation. Indeed, if all the proceeds of the capital movements were spent on imports or on exportables, the real exchange rate should remain unchanged. In the more likely case that a fraction of these revenues is spent on domestic nontradables (Figure 8.4c), the balance of payment exhibits a surplus, thus exerting a downward pressure on the real exchange rate.

This conjugation of capital inflow, debt accumulation, and steady appreciation of the real exchange rate characterized most developing countries in the 1970s. Only if this capital inflow is sustainable can this be considered an equilibrium situation. Whereas foreign remittances from migrant workers can constitute a steady capital inflow, debt accumulation certainly does not. Initial accumulation of debt itself does not pose any particular problem, since it simply implies an adjustment through a decline of the real exchange rate. However, the decline in the real exchange rate decreases the competitiveness of domestic products with respect to foreign products. As the prices of domestic commodities increase, imports become more attractive and exports more difficult. This impedes the development of the tradable sectors. Typically, some of the industrial sectors are protected by import tariffs, yet nonprotected sectors often suffer from a very sluggish growth or actually decline. As in the case of Dutch disease discussed above, debt accumulation causes most of its damage when capital inflows are suddenly interrupted, as was the case in the early 1980s. Economies accustomed to the disequilibrium situation must adjust radically through drastic depreciation of the real exchange rate and reconstruction of competitive tradable sectors. Unfortunately, this reconstruction is more complex than just resetting price incentives and, therefore, may demand a considerable amount of time.

8.4.4. Trade Policies

Trade policies directly affect the real exchange rate. An import tariff (Figure 8.4d), for example, raises the domestic price of the imported commodities and thus reduces their demand. This decreased demand for dollars leads to a decline in the real exchange rate. Similarly, export duties are equivalent to resource costs, as they represent necessary expenditures for exporters. Thus, a decrease in an export tax (Figure 8.4e), or the introduction of an export subsidy, shifts the export supply curve. The resulting increase in supply of dollars leads to a fall in the real exchange rate. Sectoral trade policies thus affect not only the sector to which they are directed but all other sectors through the general equilibrium effect on the real exchange rate. For example, the currency appreciation that follows imposition of an import tariff on industrial commodities partially decreases the real protection enjoyed by the targeted sector. Unfortunately, the other tradable sectors bear the burden of the decreased real exchange rate without the compensating distortion and are thus most negatively affected. As a result, a protection of the industrial sector acts as a tax on the tradable agricultural sectors. The magnitude of the movement of the real exchange rate in response to a trade tax determines the sectoral distribution of the impact of the tariff between real protection of the tariff-protected sector and taxation of the other tradables. In the following section, a model is developed that can be used to predict the order of magnitude of the real exchange rate movement and thus evaluate the real protection given by an import tariff.

In conclusion:

a. Productivity growth in the export sectors, increases in world export prices, domestic restrictive fiscal and monetary policies, foreign capital inflows, debt accumulation, tariff protection, and liberalization of exports all induce an appreciation of the real exchange rate.

b. While this movement in the real exchange rate is always a contingent equilibrium response in the foreign exchange market, it only corresponds to a long-term equilibrium if the original cause of the movement is sustainable, like a productivity increase. Otherwise, it should be viewed as an accommodation to disequilibrium, with adjustment and welfare losses necessary sooner or later.

c. In all cases, the change in the real exchange rate induces restructuring of the economy between tradables and nontradables and, if it originates in sectoral distortions like commercial taxes, implies further restructuring among the different tradables.

The impact of the exchange rate on the economy is illustrated in an analysis of Turkey by Asikoglu and Uctum (1992), in which they argue that the real depreciation of the exchange rate pursued from 1979 to 1988 has induced an important shift in the composition of output toward

Figure 8.5. Real exchange rate and trade balance

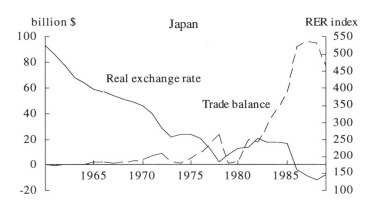

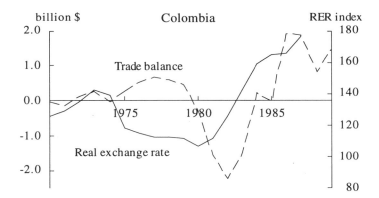

Source: Harberger, 1989.

tradables, an impressive growth of exports, and has been an essential component of the successful overall growth of the economy.

Comparison of the real exchange rates and trade balances of Japan and Colombia (Figure 8.5) illustrates the contrast between a decline in the real exchange rate as a response to a growing balance-of-trade surplus (Japan and Colombia 1974–79) and a depreciation of the real exchange rate made necessary in order to induce recovery of a reasonable trade balance (Colombia 1982–87).

8.5. Impact of Trade Distortions on the Real Exchange Rate

Two approaches can be used to measure the impact of trade distortions on the real exchange rate, one derived from the elasticity approach seen above, and the other from a small three-sector general equilibrium model. Both methods can also be used in a counterfactual manner to compute the equilibrium real exchange rate that would correspond to a free-trade environment.

8.5.1. The Elasticity Approach

The first method is a two-step procedure which evaluates what the change in the balance-of-trade deficit induced by a given trade distortion would be had the real exchange rate remained constant. The elasticity model then calculates the necessary movement in the exchange rate that would prevent this change in the balance of trade. Imposition of an import tariff t_M raises the domestic prices of imports from p_M to $p_M (1 + t_M)$. Using the same elasticity approximation as above, the induced change in imports would be:

$$\Delta M = \varepsilon_M M^* \Delta p \,/\, p = \varepsilon_M M^* t_M,$$

where M^* is the free-trade import volume. Similarly, imposition of an export tax t_E would induce a decrease in the export price to $p_E (1 - t_E)$ and a decrease in exports equal to:

$$\Delta E = -\varepsilon_E E^* t_E.$$

Imposition of both taxes would thus induce a change in the balance-of-trade deficit equal to $\Delta M - \Delta E$. In order for the balance of trade to return to its previous value, a compensating change in the exchange rate is thus necessary. It can be computed by substituting $(\Delta M - \Delta E)$ for $D - D^*$ in the expression that defines the equilibrium real exchange rate above. This gives:

$$RER(\text{with tax}) = RER^*(\text{free trade})\left[1 + \frac{\varepsilon_M M^* t_M + \varepsilon_E E^* t_E}{\varepsilon_E E^* - \varepsilon_M M^*}\right],$$

where M^*, E^*, and RER^* are the imports, exports, and real exchange rate under free trade, respectively. With ε_M negative and ε_E positive, this expression confirms that an import tariff induces a decrease in the real exchange rate, while an export tax induces an increase in the real exchange rate.

This can be used, conversely, to compute the change in the real exchange rate that would be required by the *removal of taxes*. Our departure point is now prices and volumes under the distorted system. The relative change in the import price is $-t_M /(1 + t_M)$, while it is $t_E /(1 + t_E)$ for the export price. The free-trade equilibrium exchange rate is thus:

$$RER^*(\text{free trade}) = RER(\text{with tax})\left[1 + \frac{-\varepsilon_M M t_M /(1 + t_M) - \varepsilon_E E t_E /(1 - t_E)}{\varepsilon_E E - \varepsilon_M M}\right],$$

where E and M are observed exports and imports under the distorted regime.

The corresponding series of nominal equilibrium exchange rates [elasticity $(D = D^*$ and $t = 0)$] are reported for Colombia in Table 8.2 and Figure 8.3. Comparison of the two elasticity approach equilibrium exchange rates indicates that the high level of import tariffs of 40% to 80% induces an overvaluation of the exchange rate by 15% to 20%.

8.5.2. The Three-Sector Model and the ω Factor*

As mentioned above, one weakness of the elasticity approach is that it depends on elasticities of imports demand and exports supply. However, consumers demand commodities (cereals vs. radios) rather than being concerned with the origin of a commodity (imported vs. domestic products), and productive resources are allocated to commodities rather than to markets. Therefore, these elasticities are not well defined, much less easily measured. The purpose of this three-sector model is to explicitly relate the demand for imports and the supply of exports to the production and consumption elasticities of the different commodities in the country. It thus requires formulation of a structural model underlying the reduced form used in the elasticity approach.

Consider the partitioning of the economy into three sectors: importables, exportables, and nontradables. Think of them as roughly representing manufacturing, agricultural, and service sectors, respectively. Let D_i, S_i, and p_i be the demand, the supply, and the price of commodity i. The two tradable commodities are pure tradables, that is, they are perfect substitutes for foreign commodities, with their prices equal to international prices $p_i^\$$ converted into domestic currency and modified by taxes. Equilibrium between supply and demand is obtained through import and export markets for tradables and through determination of an equilibrium price in the nontradables market.

	Sectors		
	Importables	Nontradables	Exportables
Supply	S_M	S_{NT}	S_E
Demand	D_M	D_{NT}	D_E
Price	$p_M = e\, p_M^\$(1 + t_M)$	p_{NT}	$p_E = e\, p_E^\$(1 - t_E)$
Market equilibrium	$M = D_M - S_M$	$S_{NT} = D_{NT}$	$E = S_E - D_E$

As total demand is equal to total revenue in the economy, equilibrium in the nontradables market ensures equilibrium in the balance of trade. This can be seen as follows:

$$e(p_M^\$ M - p_E^\$ E) = p_M(D_M - S_M) + p_E(D_E - S_E) - e p_M^\$ t_M M + e p_E^\$ t_E E$$
$$= -p_{NT}(D_{NT} - S_{NT}).$$

This confirms that the equilibrium variable is the real exchange rate, which can be determined either by solving for the domestic price on the domestic market for a given exchange rate or by solving for the exchange rate on the foreign currency market for a given domestic price. However, since the concepts of elasticities of demand and supply of the nontradable are cleaner, we solve here for equilibrium in the domestic market.

Because we are working with the aggregate domestic demand for nontradables, it is expressed as a function of real income y, different structural variables z that affect the structure of consumption, and relative prices:

$D_{NT} = D_{NT}(p_M / p_{NT}, p_E / p_{NT}, y, z)$, with elasticities μ_M, μ_E, μ_y, and μ_z,

and the supply function is:

$S_{NT} = S_{NT}(p_M / p_{NT}, p_E / p_{NT}, y)$ with elasticities η_M, η_E, and η_y.

Log-linearization of the system gives:

$$\ln D_{NT} = \mu_M (\ln p_M - \ln p_{NT}) + \mu_E(\ln p_E - \ln p_{NT}) + \mu_y \ln y + \mu_z \ln z,$$

$$\ln S_{NT} = \eta_M (\ln p_M - \ln p_{NT}) + \eta_E(\ln p_E - \ln p_{NT}) + \eta_y \ln y,$$

$$\ln p_E = \ln e + \ln p_E^\$(1 - t_E) \text{ and } \ln p_M = \ln e + \ln p_M^\$ (1 + t_M).$$

Equilibrium of the market for nontradables is obtained by equating the first two equations. This solves for the price of nontradables, giving:

$$\ln p_{NT} = \ln e + (1 - \omega)\left(\ln p_E^\$(1 - t_E)\right) + \omega\left(\ln p_M^\$(1 + t_M)\right) + \frac{\gamma_y}{\gamma_M + \gamma_E} \ln y + \frac{\mu_z}{\gamma_M + \gamma_E} \ln z$$

or: $$\ln (e / p_{NT}) = -(1 - \omega)\left(\ln p_E^\$(1 - t_E)\right) - \omega\left(\ln p_M^\$(1 + t_M)\right) - \frac{\gamma_y}{\gamma_M + \gamma_E} \ln y - \frac{\mu_z}{\gamma_M + \gamma_E} \ln z,$$

where:

$$\omega = \frac{\gamma_M}{\gamma_M + \gamma_E}, \ \gamma_M = \mu_M - \eta_M, \text{ and } \gamma_E = \mu_E - \eta_E.$$

Thus, the real exchange rate e/p_{NT} is related to world prices, trade policies, and macroeconomic variables. The parameter ω, called the *incidence* parameter, measures the transmission of an increase in the import price, induced in particular by tariffs, onto the domestic price of the nontradable. Its complement, $(1 - \omega)$, measures the transmission from the export price to the price of the nontradable.

What does this tell us about levels of effective protection provided by trade policies? Suppose that an import tariff of 20% is introduced. If ω is, for example, equal to 0.7, the nontradable price increases by 14%. This means that the price of the importable relative to that of the nontradable, representative of its labor cost, for example, has increased by only 6%. Real protection is not 20% but rather 6%. At the same time, the export sector, whose price has not increased, supports an effective taxation of 14% relative to the nontradable price. The same reasoning applies to an export tax. With an incidence factor of 0.7, an export tax of 20% taxes the export sector by only 6%, while protecting the importable sector by 14%. The incidence factor ω thus indicates how the effect of a trade tax is distributed across the two sectors. With an incidence factor close to one, the price of the nontradable follows closely the price of the importable. Thus, no policy can be effective on the importable sector, neither tax nor subsidies, while the export sector captures the full effect of trade policies, whatever sector was originally targeted. An export tax fully penalizes the export sector, and so does imposition of an import tariff. On the other hand, an incidence factor ω close to zero indicates that the nontradable price will always closely follow the export price and thus that all effects of the trade policy will be borne by importables.

The estimation of the parameter ω is usually performed on a transformation of the expression above. The variable considered on the left-hand side is either the real exchange rate for exports (p_E / p_{NT}), the real exchange rate for imports (p_M / p_{NT}), or the real exchange rate for a weighted average of exports and imports (with weights α and $1 - \alpha$):

$$\ln(p_E / p_{NT}) = \omega \left[\ln(p_E^\$ / p_M^\$) + \ln\left(\frac{1 - t_E}{1 + t_M} \right) \right] - \frac{\gamma_y}{\gamma_M + \gamma_E} \ln y - \frac{\mu_z}{\gamma_M + \gamma_E} \ln z,$$

$$\ln(p_M / p_{NT}) = (1 - \omega) \left[\ln(p_M^\$ / p_E^\$) + \ln\left(\frac{1 + t_M}{1 - t_E} \right) \right] - \frac{\gamma_y}{\gamma_M + \gamma_E} \ln y - \frac{\mu_z}{\gamma_M + \gamma_E} \ln z,$$

or

$$\ln(p_E^\alpha p_M^{1-\alpha} / p_{NT}) = (\omega - 1 + \alpha) \left[\ln(p_E^\$ / p_M^\$) + \ln\left(\frac{1 - t_E}{1 + t_M} \right) \right] - \frac{\gamma_y}{\gamma_M + \gamma_E} \ln y - \frac{\mu_z}{\gamma_M + \gamma_E} \ln z.$$

In certain studies, the empirical difficulty of constructing price indices for exportables and importables has prompted the use of proxies for the real exchange rate. A candidate for proxy is the readily available *RER*1 indicator. A corresponding real effective exchange rate for exportables *RER*1$(1 - t_E)$ can be used instead of p_E / p_{NT}. In this case, the two terms representing trade taxes and external terms of trade are dissociated and appear as independent variables in the regression.

These expressions show that true protection of a tradable, defined as the increase in the relative price of the tradable to that of the nontradable, is in fact determined by the ratio $(1 + t_M)/(1 - t_E)$, and not by individual tax rates. This ratio defines the equivalent tariff of the trade taxes, $T = (1 + t_M)/(1 - t_E) - 1$. True protection for imports and exports is approximated by $(1 - \omega)T$ and $-\omega T$, respectively.

This model specification has an important bearing on the analysis of price distortions. It emphasizes that indicators of price distortions derived from partial equilibrium analysis in the previous chapter may be misleading when large trade taxes apply to a wide range of products.

Valdés (1986a) reported estimations showing a high parameter ω:

Argentina	0.4 to 0.5
Chile	0.5 to 0.6
Colombia	about 0.9
Nigeria	0.6 to 0.9
Peru	about 0.7
Philippines	about 0.8
Zaire	about 0.8.

These results suggest a high degree of substitution between nontradables and importables, and at least one-half of the burden of protection borne by exportables. Since the exports of many LDCs are predominantly agricultural, an import-substitution strategy taxes agriculture substantially more than a comparison of the nominal rates of protection would suggest.

The structural factors that should be incorporated in the z variables of the regressions are those mentioned in section 8.4 which influence the real exchange rate, principally fiscal and monetary policies and foreign capital flows. Empirical studies vary greatly in the coverage of these factors, and many of them do not even introduce any z variables. Reporting on several studies for Latin American countries, Valdés (1986b) found that government expenditures and capital flows have, in most cases, a significant depressive effect on the real exchange rate.

In their study of Argentina over the period 1913–84, Mundlak, Cavallo, and Domenech (1990) argue that the effects of trade policies and macroeconomic variables on the real exchange rate depend on the degree of commercial and financial openness. Using a ratio of the value of trade volume to income to measure trade openness and the ratio of the official to the black market exchange rate to measure financial openness, they treat all the parameters of the equation above as linear functions of the variables of openness. The elasticity of the real exchange rate to the terms of trade, ω, is found to be a function of the trade openness, with an elasticity of 0.29, and the computed value for ω declines from around 0.65 in the 1920s to values in the range 0.20 to 0.30 since 1955.

Edwards (1989) proposes extending the basic model in a different direction. He argues that while the long-run behavior of the real exchange rate is determined by real variables, also known as the *fundamentals* (such as trade regime, terms of trade, real income, and capital inflow), the actual value of the real exchange rate at any point in time is also influenced by nominal variables. Therefore, he includes indices of macroeconomic policies, such as domestic credit or money supply, and the nominal exchange rate in the real exchange rate equation. He also uses the lagged real exchange rate to capture adjustment effects. Estimations done with this extended model support his hypothesis that short-run real exchange rate movements have responded to both nominal and real disturbances. These estimations also give a large coefficient on the lagged real exchange rate, which indicates that the autonomous forces that move the *RER* back to its equilibrium operate fairly slowly. White and Wignaraja's (1992) estimation of the real exchange rate for Sri Lanka is based on a similar model. They find that the real exchange rate reflects 90% of a change in the nominal exchange rate. With an estimated parameter of 0.825 for the lagged real exchange rate, the long-term impact of any exogenous variable is $1/(1 - 0.825) = 5.5$ times higher than the short-term impact. With this model, foreign aid is found to have a relatively small short-run effect but a significant long-run effect on the real exchange rate. Note that the problem of serial correlation would be particularly important in these estimations since, in the presence of a lagged dependent variable, standard OLS estimation would give biased and inconsistent estimates. It is, therefore, important to properly test for autocorrelation. The standard Durbin-Watson statistic is also biased with a lagged dependent variable. An alternative test proposed by Durbin consists of regressing the residuals on their lagged value and the regressors in the model, and testing for the significance of the coefficient of the lagged residual using standard least squares procedure.

8.5.3. *Estimating the Equilibrium Exchange Rate with the ω Approach**

The model developed above can also be used to estimate the equilibrium exchange rate. By setting the balance-of-trade deficit to its equilibrium value D^*, one can estimate the equilibrium exchange rate compatible with this sustainable value:

$$\ln e^*(\omega \text{ approach, } D^*) = \ln e - \frac{\mu_z}{\gamma_M + \gamma_E}(\ln D^* - \ln D).$$

By setting all trade taxes to zero, one can similarly estimate the free-trade equilibrium exchange rate:

$$\ln e^*(\omega \text{ approach, free trade}) = \ln e + (1 - \omega)\ln(1 - t_E) + \omega \ln(1 + t_M).$$

Using an incidence factor ω of 0.9 estimated by García García and Montes Llamas (1989) for Colombia, this free-trade equilibrium exchange rate is compared with the other alternative concepts of equilibrium exchange rates in Table 8.2 and Figure 8.3. Unfortunately, the estimated equation does not contain the balance-of-trade variable, which means that this equilibrium exchange rate cannot include the necessary correction for balance-of-trade disequilibrium. As mentioned above, however, the balance of trade was fundamentally in equilibrium until 1975, and thus comparison remains feasible for this period. The equilibrium exchange rate measured by the ω approach is parallel to but 30% above the equilibrium exchange rate measured by the elasticity approach. This is difficult to justify and may indicate that the high level of 0.9 is an overestimation of the true incidence factor.

Exercise 8
Exchange Rate and Trade Policies in Pakistan

This exercise on exchange rate and trade policies is adapted from the analysis done by Dorosh and Valdés (1990). The direct trade policies implemented in Pakistan are characterized by the equivalent import tariff t_M and export tax t_E rates, reported in Table 8E.1 (file 8EXRATE). The series of macroeconomic data for Pakistan is taken from the IMF's *International Financial Statistics* (*IFS*).

1. Effective Exchange Rates

Table 8E.1 reports the nominal exchange rate e (line af in *IFS*), and the indicators of trade policy distortions $(1 + t_M)$ and $(1 - t_E)$ for the period from 1960 to 1987. Compute the effective exchange rate for exports, $e_E = e(1 - t_E)$, and the effective exchange rate for imports, $e_M = e(1 + t_M)$. Plot e, e_M, and e_E on the same graph. This clearly shows three contrasted periods: 1960–72, 1973–81, and 1981–87. Comment on the respective use of exchange rate and trade policies during these three periods. What are their combined effects on the incentives to imports and exports? How has the trade policy bias between imports and exports evolved over time?

2. The Real Exchange Rate

The above analysis of effective exchange rates ignores changes in the domestic price level and changes in world prices. By contrast, the real exchange rate reflects the changes in the

Table 8E.1. Exchange rate and trade policies in Pakistan: Data

	Trade policies			Prices						Macroeconomic aggregates					
	(1 + tm)	(1 - tx)	e	Pakistan CPI	U.S. WPI	Japan WPI	Japan exch. rate	Unit value of exports	Unit value of imports	Imports	Exports	Remittances	Aid	Governt expenditures	Real GDP (1985
			(Rs/$)	(Index)	(Index)	(Index)	(Yen/$)	(Index)	(Index)	(mn Rs)	(mn Rs)	(mn $)	(mn $)	(mn Rs)	billion Rs)
1960	2.3	1.7	4.8	16.0	30.7	42.8	360.0			2830	1874	0			
1961	2.3	1.7	4.8	16.2	30.6	43.2	360.0			2687	1906	0			
1962	2.4	1.6	4.8	16.1	30.7	42.5	360.0			3195	1891	0			
1963	2.5	1.6	4.8	16.4	30.6	43.3	360.0			3848	1985	0			
1964	2.5	1.6	4.8	17.1	30.7	43.3	360.0			4318	2035	0			
1965	2.9	1.8	4.8	18.0	31.3	43.7	360.0			4534	2516	0			
1966	2.7	1.6	4.8	19.3	32.3	44.7	360.0			3896	2868	0			
1967	2.9	1.6	4.8	20.6	32.4	45.5	360.0			4775	3071	41			
1968	3.0	1.7	4.8	20.7	33.2	45.9	360.0			2913	1913	79			
1969	3.1	1.8	4.8	21.3	34.5	46.9	360.0			2933	1671	107			
1970	3.0	1.7	4.8	22.5	35.7	48.6	360.0			3175	1892	81			
1971	3.2	2.0	4.8	23.5	36.9	48.2	349.3			2946	2225	65			
1972	2.7	1.8	5.6	24.8	38.6	48.6	303.2	20.1	16.7	5473	5776	129	45	8784	217.7
1973	1.5	1.1	10.6	30.5	43.6	56.3	271.7	35.1	23.6	8792	9533	147	43	11128	232.8
1974	1.3	0.9	9.9	38.6	51.8	74.0	292.1	45.4	40.1	15576	10970	177	380	14520	245.7
1975	1.2	1.0	9.9	46.7	56.6	76.2	296.8	40.0	45.5	19508	10416	275	435	19525	257.0
1976	1.4	1.2	9.9	50.0	59.3	80.1	296.6	43.7	43.5	19751	11552	433	500	22390	268.9
1977	1.5	1.2	9.9	55.1	62.9	81.6	268.5	52.3	45.0	22116	11766	884	175	24564	279.1
1978	1.5	1.2	9.9	58.4	67.8	79.5	210.4	59.6	47.5	29513	14605	1420	133	30793	301.4
1979	1.5	1.0	9.9	63.3	76.3	85.3	219.1	69.1	53.7	36707	20355	1578	482	36241	315.9
1980	1.6	1.0	9.9	70.8	87.1	100.5	226.7	73.7	67.0	48373	25923	2218	366	41084	343.4
1981	1.6	1.0	9.9	79.2	95.0	101.9	220.5	76.5	77.0	50912	28538	2195	434	53392	367.2
1982	1.4	1.0	10.6	83.9	96.9	103.7	249.1	83.9	87.0	59098	28275	2793	426	55355	391.2
1983	1.4	1.0	12.7	89.3	98.1	101.4	237.5	90.0	87.4	63795	40320	3116	540	70560	417.7
1984	1.4	1.1	13.5	94.7	100.5	101.1	237.5	100.3	95.9	74921	35994	2942	544	82627	438.8
1985	1.5	1.0	15.2	100.0	100.0	100.0	238.5	100.0	100.0	85656	43645	2710	651	93613	472.2
1986	1.5	1.0	16.1	103.5	97.1	90.9	168.5	121.4	95.2	81550	56336	2676	846	120114	498.1
1987	1.5	1.0	17.2	108.4	99.7	87.5	144.6	133.4	115.5	92521	72583	2440	693	127822	530.3

Source: Cols. 1 & 2: Dorosh and Valdés, 1990; other cols.: International Financial Statistics, Yearbook 1990.

domestic price of traded goods relative to the price of the home or nontradable goods. The real exchange rate is defined by *RER*1:

$$RER = e \, p^w / p^h,$$

where p^w and p^h are the world price of traded goods and the domestic price of home goods, respectively. A weighted average of the wholesale price indices for the United States and Japan, which are the major trading partners of Pakistan, is used to represent the world price:

$$p^w = w_{US} WPI_{US} + w_J WPI_J / (e_J / e_{J,85}),$$

where the weights w are 0.7 for the United States and 0.3 for Japan, WPI_i are the wholesale price indices (line 63 in *IFS*) of the two countries, and $e_J / e_{J,85}$ is an index of the exchange rate of Japan in yen/\$ (we use the current exchange rate divided by the exchange rate in 1985, so that it is equal to one for the base year 1985 used for WPI_i). As for the home goods price, we will use the consumer price index (CPI) of Pakistan.

Construct the series of the real exchange rate *RER*, as well as the effective real exchange rate for exports and imports $RER_E = RER(1 - t_E)$ and $RER_M = RER(1 + t_M)$. Plot these series on a graph and comment on the evolution of real incentives to exports and imports.

3. The Equilibrium Exchange Rate

The PPP approach and the elasticities approach will be used to estimate the equilibrium exchange rate. A comparison of results obtained illustrates the differing concepts of the equilibrium exchange rate underlying these approaches.

3.1. Purchasing Power Parity Approach

A base year is chosen for which the nominal exchange rate is considered to have been at equilibrium. For that purpose, the table of macroeconomic indicators has been completed with the value of imports (line 71v in *IFS*), exports (line 70 in *IFS*), and remittances (measured by the private unrequited transfers, line 77afd in *IFS*). Compute in Table 8E.2 the balance of current account deficit D_0. It is equal to the value of imports less the value of exports and remittances (converted in domestic currency). Examination of this series of deficits indicates that in 1980, the balance of current accounts was approximately in equilibrium. The 1980 exchange rate will thus be retained as an equilibrium exchange rate. The equilibrium exchange rate in year t is then defined by:

$$e_t^*(\text{PPP}) = e_{80} \frac{CPI_t / CPI_{80}}{p_t^w / p_{80}^w},$$

where *CPI* is the domestic consumer price index, p^w is the aggregate foreign price index computed above, and t represents the current year. Compute this series in the reserved space in Table 8E.2.

Make a graph to show its evolution over time.

Table 8E.2. Exchange rate and trade policies in Pakistan: Equilibrium exchange rates

	Effective exchange rates		Real exchange rates				Balance of curr. acc. deficit (mn Rs)	Change BoT def. if T = 0 (mn Rs)	Equilibrium exchange rates			
	ex	em	Aggregate WPI	RER	RERx	RERm			e* (PPP)	e1* (elasticity)	e2*	e3* (omega)
1960			30.00				956	3979		7.3		
1961												
1962												
1963												
1964												
1965												
1966												
1967												
1968												
1969												
1970												
1971												
1972												
1973												
1974												
1975												
1976												
1977												
1978												
1979												
1980												
1981												
1982												
1983												
1984												
1985												
1986												
1987												

236

3.2. Elasticity Approach

We must first evaluate what would be the trade deficit generated by removing the trade taxes. If ε_M is the elasticity of import demand M and ε_E is the elasticity of export supply E, the change in the trade deficit is:

$$\Delta D = \Delta M - \Delta E = \varepsilon_M M \left(\frac{-t_M}{1+t_M} \right) - \varepsilon_E E \left(\frac{t_E}{1-t_E} \right).$$

Since ε_M is negative, ε_E positive, and t_E negative, imports increase and exports decrease, both adding to the deficit increase.

The equilibrium exchange rate is then defined as the exchange rate that would compensate for the elimination of the trade taxes, that is:

$$e1^*(\text{elasticity}) = e \left(1 + \frac{\Delta D}{\varepsilon_E E - \varepsilon_M M} \right).$$

Assuming $\varepsilon_M = -2$ and $\varepsilon_E = 1$, compute this equilibrium exchange rate from 1960 to 1987.

Furthermore, we can compute the equilibrium exchange rate that would be necessary to reach a balanced current account. This is done by eliminating both the induced change in balance-of-trade ΔD and the observed deficit in the balance of current account D_0 computed above:

$$e2^*(\text{elasticity}) = e \left(1 + \frac{\Delta D + D_0}{\varepsilon_E E - \varepsilon_M M} \right).$$

Report the three series of equilibrium exchange rates on the same graph and compare them. Describe the different concepts of equilibrium underlying these measures, and explain why these measures differ so widely over the last seven years.

4. The Omega Approach

4.1. Determination of the Real Exchange Rate

The real exchange rate is affected by external shocks on the foreign prices of imports and exports $\left(p_E^w \text{ and } p_M^w \right)$, trade and exchange rate policies, and changes in the domestic price. Three macroeconomic variables that influence the pattern of consumption, and thus the domestic price, are retained. These are worker remittances, foreign aid, and government expenditures. The equation to be estimated is the following:

$$\ln RER_E = a_1 + \omega \ln \left(\frac{1-t_E}{1+t_M} \right) + a_2 \ln \frac{p_E^w}{p_M^w} + a_3 \ln(RRemit) + a_4 \ln(RAid) + a_5 \ln(RGovt).$$

The ω factor, known as the incidence factor, measures the distribution across sectors of the impact of trade policies.

	A	B	C	D	E	F	G	H	I	J	K	L	M	N	O	P
81	Table 8E.3. Exchange rate and trade policies in Pakistan: Omega approach															
82																
83		RRemit =	RAid =	RGovt =	ln	ln	ln	ln	ln	ln						
84		R/Pw/	Aid/Pw/	G/CPI/	RERx	RRemit	RAid	RGovt	(1-tx)/	Pxw/						
85		GDP	GDP	GDP					(1+tm)	Pmw						
86																
87	1972															
88	1973															
89	1974															
90	1975															
91	1976															
92	1977															
93	1978															
94	1979															
95	1980															
96	1981															
97	1982															
98	1983															
99	1984															
100	1985															
101	1986															
102	1987															
103																
104																
105																
106																
107																

The exogenous variables are defined as follows:

a. The foreign prices are the unit value of exports and imports (lines 74 and 75 in *IFS*).

b. $RRemit = (Remit / p^w) / Real\ GDP$, where *Remit* are the remittances measured by the private unrequited transfers (line 77afd in *IFS*), p^w is the aggregate world price computed above, and *Real GDP* is GDP at constant prices (line 99b.p in *IFS*).

c. $RAid = (Aid / p^w) / Real\ GDP$, where *Aid* is the foreign aid measured by the sum of official unrequited transfers (line 77agd in *IFS*) and exceptional financing (line 79a.d in *IFS*).

d. $RGovt = (Govt / CPI) / Real\ GDP$, where *Govt* is government expenditures (line 82 in *IFS*).

The estimation will be performed for 1972 to 1987 only. The original data for *Aid*, *Govt*, and GDP at constant prices for these years are reported in Table 8E.1. Create a new Table 8E.3 for the transformed data to be used in the regression. Recall that all exogenous variables need to be in columns next to each other to use the regression function in Lotus. Perform the regression and interpret your results.

4.2. *Determination of the Equilibrium Exchange Rate*

Using the omega approach, the equilibrium exchange rate is defined as the nominal exchange rate that would correspond to the elimination of all trade taxes. Using the equation estimated above gives:

$$\ln\left[e\,\frac{p^w}{p^h}\left(1-t_E\right)\right] = a_1 + \omega \ln\left(\frac{1-t_E}{1+t_M}\right) + a_2 \ln\frac{p_E^w}{p_M^w} + a_3 \ln(RRemit) + a_4 \ln(RAid) + a_5 \ln(RGovt),$$

and $\quad \ln\left(e^*\,\frac{p^w}{p^h}\right) = a_1 + a_2 \ln\frac{p_E^w}{p_M^w} + a_3 \ln(RRemit) + a_4 \ln(RAid) + a_5 \ln(RGovt),$

or: $\quad e^*(\omega \text{ approach}) = e(1-t_E)\left[\frac{1-t_E}{1+t_M}\right]^{-\omega}.$

Calculate this time series of equilibrium exchange rates from 1972 to 1987, and report it on the graph. Compare this estimation of the equilibrium exchange rate with the other series. Comment.

References

Asikoglu, Yaman, and Merih Uctum. 1992. "A Critical Evaluation of Exchange Rate Policy in Turkey." *World Development* 20:1501–14.

Dornbusch, Rudiger, and F. Leslie Helmers, eds. 1989. *The Open Economy: Tools for Policymakers in Developing Countries.* New York: Oxford University Press for the World Bank.

Dorosh, Paul, and Alberto Valdés. 1990. *Effects of Exchange Rate and Trade Policies on Agriculture in Pakistan.* Research Report 84. Washington D.C.: International Food Policy Research Institute.

Edwards, Sebastian. 1989. *Real Exchange Rates, Devaluation, and Adjustment.* Cambridge: MIT Press.

García García, Jorge, and Gabriel Montes Llamas. 1989. *Trade, Exchange Rate, and Agricultural Pricing Policies in Colombia.* World Bank Comparative Studies. Washington, D.C.: World Bank.

Harberger, Arnold. 1986. "Economic Adjustment and the Real Exchange Rate." In *Economic Adjustment and Exchange Rates in Developing Countries,* edited by S. Edwards and L. Ahamed. Chicago: University of Chicago Press.

Harberger, Arnold. 1989. "Applications of Real Exchange Rate Analysis." *Contemporary Policy Issues* 7:1–26.

Hill, Catharine. 1991. "Managing Commodity Boom in Botswana." *World Development* 19:1185–96.

Khan, Mohsin, and Jonathan Ostry. 1992. "Response of the Equilibrium Real Exchange Rate to Real Disturbance in Developing Countries." *World Development* 20:1325–34.

Mundlak, Yair, Domingo Cavallo, and Roberto Domenech. 1990. "Effects of Macroeconomic Policies on Sectoral Prices." *World Bank Economic Review* 4:55–79.

Scobie, Grant, and Veronica Jardine. 1988. *Macroeconomic Policy and Agriculture in Ecuador: An Overview*. Research Triangle Park, N.C.: Sigma One Corporation.

Valdés, Alberto. 1986a. "Exchange Rates and Trade Policy: Help or Hindrance to Agricultural Growth?" In *Agriculture in a Turbulent World Economy*. Proceedings of the Nineteenth International Conference of Agricultural Economists, edited by A. Maunder and U. Renborg. Brookfield, VT: Gower.

Valdés, Alberto. 1986b. "Impact of Trade and Macroeconomic Policies on Agricultural Growth: The South American Experience." In *Economic and Social Progress in Latin America*. Washington, D.C.: Inter-American Development Bank.

White, Howard, and Ganeshan Wignaraja. 1992. "Exchange Rates, Trade Liberalization, and Aid: The Sri Lankan Experience." *World Development* 20:1471–80.

World Bank. 1986. *World Development Report, 1986*. New York: Oxford University Press.

CHAPTER NINE

Transactions Costs and Agrarian Institutions

Policymakers have traditionally focused on three important sources of growth for the agricultural sector: (1) factor deepening in response to price incentives, to nonprice factors such as public investment which affect the profitability of private investment, and to the relaxation of constraints on, for instance, access to credit; (2) efficiency gains through greater technical and allocative efficiency by producers in response to better information and education; and (3) productivity gains through technical change as a result of research or the transfer of new technologies. In Chapters 3 (Profit Function), 4 (Supply Response), and 6 (Household Models), we have focused on the analysis of the first source of growth. In this chapter, we turn our attention to the other two sources of growth: efficiency and productivity gains.

In recent years, an additional area of policy intervention has gained increasing attention by observing that many markets are imperfect due to the existence of transactions costs and that, as a consequence, producers face eventually highly different effective farm-gate prices. The existence of transactions costs, in turn, leads farmers to use resources differently from one another, to eventually refrain from market transactions if their subjective equilibria for the production of commodities they also consume or for the use of factors they also own falls within their own price band (Chapter 6), or to use contracts in order to achieve transactions at a lower cost than through the market. As a consequence, important productivity gains can be achieved by reducing transactions costs, allowing greater specialization and exchange, thus suggesting another set of policy interventions to enhance growth. In particular, if transactions costs are related to control over assets or to the effectiveness of producers' organizations, issues such as redistributive land reform and cooperation in grassroots organizations become important policy instruments to achieve not only welfare but also efficiency gains.

Sections 9.1 and 9.2 review the concepts of efficiency and productivity, respectively, and discuss alternative approaches to their measurement. Section 9.3 then introduces the concept of transactions costs and analyzes its implications for the measurement of efficiency and productivity, as well as for the design of the optimum technology from the standpoint of different classes of producers and the state. Section 9.4 applies the concept of transactions costs to a household model. It shows how transactions costs, together with the assets the household controls, explain the differential income strategy which each class of household follows and predict patterns of social differentiation. Household behavior under transactions costs helps explain why there may exist an inverse relationship between total factor productivity and farm size. The implications of this inverse relationship are used to discuss land reform, an important policy arena where efficiency and equity gains are not separable and where there may exist opportunities for policy interventions to achieve both through the same policy instrument. Finally, section 9.5 explores the role of contractual arrangements as a household response to transactions costs. It also briefly introduces the theory of contracts and the reasons why a particular contract may be chosen when there are transactions costs in specific markets.

9.1. Efficiency: Technical, Allocative, and Economic

9.1.1. Definitions

Efficiency of a production unit may be defined as how "effectively" it uses variable resources for the purpose of profit maximization, given the best production technology available, the level of fixed factors z, and product p and factor p_x prices. Maximum efficiency is achieved when the most efficient production function is used and when the marginal value product of

Figure 9.1. Technical and allocative efficiency in the product space

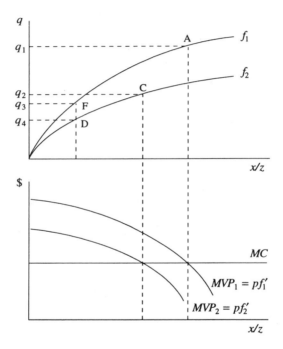

$f=f(x,z)$ production function of variable factor x and fixed factor z

$MVP = pf'$ = marginal value product

MC = marginal cost

each factor on this production function is equal to its price. This maximum efficiency is indicated by point A in both Figure 9.1, when there is only one variable factor x/z, and in Figure 9.2 for a unit isoquant, when there are two variable factors $(x_1/z, x_2/z)$. Assume that the observed producer choice is D in both figures. Relative to maximum efficiency A, inefficiency can be decomposed into two sources:

Technical efficiency (Leibenstein's [1989] X-efficiency). In Figure 9.1, output at D is less than the output level F that could be reached with the same level of input using the best practice production function f_1. In Figure 9.2, the total variable cost TC_4 of producing one unit of output at D is greater than total variable cost TC_3 at F using best practice isoquant I_1 and the same factor ratio than at D. Gaps DF in output (Figure 9.1) and cost (Figure 9.2) are attributed to technical inefficiency.

Allocative efficiency. In Figure 9.1, points C, with technology actually used f_2, and A, with best practice f_1, are allocatively efficient. In Figure 9.2, this corresponds to points C with actual practice I_2 and A with best practice I_1. In the first case, output gaps $q_2 - q_4$ with current technology and $q_1 - q_3$ with best practice are attributed to allocative inefficiencies. In Figure 9.2, this corresponds to cost gaps $TC_4 - TC_2$ with current technology and $TC_3 - TC_1$ with best practice.

Figure 9.2. Technical and allocative efficiency in the factor space

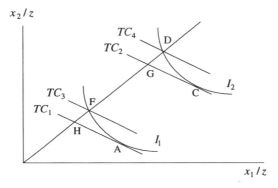

TC = total variable cost; I = unit isoquant

For the sake of measurement, we define the following indices of efficiency:

a. *Efficiency indices in the product space*
Technical efficiency $TE = q_4/q_3$
Allocative efficiency AE
 Along current technology: $AE_c = q_4/q_2$
 Along best practice, once technical efficiency has been achieved: $AE_b = q_3/q_1$.
Economic efficiency $EE = q_4/q_1$. It is equal to the product of technical efficiency and allocative efficiency along best practice: $EE = TE \times AE_b$.

b. *Efficiency indices in the factor space*
Technical efficiency: $TE = TC_3/TC_4 = $ OF/OD
Allocative efficiency
 Along current technology: $AE_c = TC_2/TC_4 = $ OG/OD
 Along best practice, once technical efficiency has been achieved:
 $AE_b = TC_1/TC_3 = $ OH/OF.
Economic efficiency: $EE = TC_1/TC_4 = TE \times AE_b = $ OH/OD. This last measure, and its decomposition in technical and allocative efficiencies, was first proposed by Farrell (1957) and has been widely used.

Clearly, if allocative efficiency is measured along current technology, then the share of allocative efficiency in total efficiency is less than if it is measured along best practice, since $(TC_2 / TC_4)/(TC_1 / TC_4)$ is less than $(TC_1 / TC_3)/(TC_1 / TC_4)$. Because there may be some arbitrariness in the choice of indicators, a clear statement of the definitions used is essential. Measuring allocative efficiency along best practice is consistent with the decomposition of economic efficiency into its technical and allocative components. It also has the advantage that firm-specific, currently used production functions need not be estimated. Instead, all that is needed is estimation of the best practice frontier production function.

9.1.2. Measurements

In addition to choosing appropriate efficiency indices, there are several options to measure the frontier production function. Traditionally, three approaches have been followed.

9.1.2.1. Engineering Approach

Data from experimental plots in farmers' fields can be used to estimate both the best production function available to them and the production function currently in use (Herdt and Mandac, 1981). The design of experimental treatments should allow for variability in factor use, environmental conditions, and quality of technology. The estimated production function could thus include: x, levels of factor used (fertilizers, insecticides, and seeds); z_f, variables that characterize the particular farm's environment (soil quality, water stress, incidence of disease); and z_p, dummies which earmark the use of best practices (quality of fertilizer use, weed control, and insect control). The production function is thus modeled most generally as:

$$q = f(x, z_f, z_p).$$

Assigning the values of a particular farm's environment to z_f yields estimates of the farm-specific f_1 (when z_p is the set to best practice values) and f_2 (when z_p is set to actual practice values) in Figure 9.1. This allows the measurement of technical efficiency (based on the comparison of the two predicted outputs on f_1 and f_2 corresponding to the farmer's observed level of input x) and of either definition of allocative efficiency above.

Once these measures of farmer-specific efficiency have been obtained, they can be regressed econometrically against a set of exogenous variables that characterize the farmers' circumstances. In their study of rice farmers in the Philippines, Herdt and Mandac (1981) thus find that both technical and allocative efficiency are explained by farm size and the number of days when the farm operator was not present on the farm. Smaller farms are, as expected, more efficient, suggesting that larger farms suffer from management difficulties. However, the positive impact that absence of farmer has on efficiency is quite surprising, perhaps suggesting that this time spent off the farm was useful to gather information which enhances the quality of management decisions. Technical efficiency is further explained by the farmers' quality of knowledge of input and output prices as well as by their use of local sources of information. These results suggest that land reform and improved extension services can increase efficiency.

9.1.2.2 Average Production Functions for Subsets of Farms

Another means of capturing differences in technical and allocative efficiencies between prespecified categories of farms (e.g., small versus large farms) is to estimate a production (or profit) function across farms with farm category effects included in both the production function and the first-order conditions in the form of dummy variables. Farm category effects in the production function capture technical efficiency differentials. For example, neutral technological differences imply different levels for the intercept of the production function. Farm category effects in the first-order conditions capture allocative efficiency differentials which indicate the degree to which profits are being maximized.

Yotopoulos and Lau (1973) use this approach to test for differential efficiency between small and large farms, starting from a Cobb-Douglas profit function. As seen in section 3.1.1, in the case of a Cobb-Douglas profit function, the correspondence between production and profit function is analytically feasible; hence, efficiency can be tested from the profit function directly. Consider the corresponding production and profit functions, as established in Chapter 3:

$$q = ax^{\alpha} z^{\beta} \quad \text{and} \quad \pi = a^* z^{\beta^*} p^{1-\alpha^*} w^{\alpha^*},$$

where:

x = labor used in production with corresponding wage w,

z = a fixed factor,

q = output with corresponding price p, and

π = the maximum profit.

The parameters of the profit and production functions are related as follows [equation (6) of Chapter 3]:

$$a^* = a^{\frac{1}{1-\alpha}} \alpha^{\frac{\alpha}{1-\alpha}} (1-\alpha) , \quad \beta^* = \frac{\beta}{1-\alpha} , \quad \text{and} \quad \alpha^* = \frac{-\alpha}{1-\alpha}.$$

The first-order condition [equation (5) of Chapter 3], which establishes allocative efficiency, can also be written:

$$wx / pq = \alpha \quad \text{or} \quad \frac{-wx}{\pi} = \frac{-wx}{pq - wx} = \frac{-\alpha}{1-\alpha} = \alpha^*.$$

The technical efficiency parameter a can be retrieved from the constant term a^* of the profit function. Note, however, that the definition of the profit function has encompassed substituting x for its optimal value, and hence assumes allocative efficiency. In general, the parameter a^* reflects a combination of technical efficiency and allocative efficiency, called profit efficiency. If allocative efficiency holds, however, then profit efficiency implies technical efficiency.

Yotopoulos and Lau (1973) use a time series of farm-level observations to estimate the model:

$$\ln \pi = \ln a^* + \delta_l D_l + \sum_t \delta_t D_t + \alpha^* \ln w + (1-\alpha^*) \ln p + \sum_m \beta_m^* \ln z_m, \quad \text{and}$$

$$\frac{-wx}{\pi} = \gamma_l D_l + \gamma_s D_s,$$

where D_l, D_s, and D_t are dummies for large farm, small farm, and years, respectively. The system of two equations and the accompanying constraints on parameters are estimated using Zellner's seemingly unrelated regression method.

The following tests are then used to analyze efficiency differentials:

i) $\gamma_l = \gamma_s$ for equal levels of allocative efficiency with respect to labor demand by small and large farms,

ii) $\gamma_l = \gamma_s = \alpha^*$ for absolute allocative efficiency with respect to labor demand by small and large farms,

iii) $\delta_l = 0$ for equal level of profit efficiency on small and large farms,

iv) $\gamma_l = \gamma_s$ and $\delta_l = 0$ for equal level of allocative and technical efficiency on small and large farms.

Applying this approach to four years of data (1967–70) for a sample of wheat producers in the Punjab, Sidhu (1974) finds that there are no differences in economic and allocative efficiencies between large and small farms, and thus a fortiori in their technical efficiencies. Results by Yotopoulos and Lau (1973) for India in the earlier period 1955–57 had suggested that small and large farms were equally allocatively efficient, but that small farms were more technically, and hence more economically, efficient than large farms. Sidhu attributes this difference in results to the fact that the superior technical efficiency of small farms before the Green Revolution (which started in 1965) derived from using their labor advantage in labor-intensive land improvement programs. By the time of his study, Green Revolution technology had been amply diffused. Large farmers, who have an advantage in accessing capital-intensive fertilizers and other chemicals, had compensated through greater use of Green Revolution technology for the labor advantage of small farms and equalized efficiency levels.

If there are enough degrees of freedom (i.e., observations over enough years), technical efficiency effects can be specified for each farm, instead of only for large versus small or some other a priori differentiating criterion. Dawson, Lingard, and Woodford (1991) thus analyze a sample of 22 rice farms in central Luzon in the Philippines observed over five discontinuous years. The estimated production function relates the observed output to factors (area, labor, fertilizer, and irrigation), to four year effects, and to 21 farm effects. Using the most efficient farm as the base for the farm effect, the estimated coefficients of the farm dummies measure farm-specific technical efficiency relative to this best farm. They find that there is a wide range of efficiency levels across farms, ranging from 36% to 100% with a median of 58%, suggesting large potential gains in production with improvement in management quality.

9.1.2.3. *Econometric Estimation of Frontier Production Functions**

An earlier approach to the estimation of the production frontier was based on linear programming. It consisted in estimating the parameters of a linear production function subject to the constraints that all observed points be inside the frontier, except for a prespecified percentage of the observations. This discounted the most egregious outliers. See Timmer (1971) for an application of this method to the U.S. states. Since then, econometric techniques for the estimation of a stochastic production frontier have been developed by Aigner, Lovell, and Schmidt (1977) and Meeusen and van den Broeck (1977). This has been applied to the simultaneous estimation of a production frontier and the first-order conditions for profit maximization by Kumbhakar (1987) using a Cobb-Douglas, and by Kalijaran (1990) using a translog. This approach yields consistent and efficient estimates of economic efficiency and its two components, firm-specific technical and input-specific allocative efficiencies.

Let the production frontier be:

$$q^* = f(x), \quad \cdot$$

where q^* is the maximum output a firm could reach by using the inputs x in a technically efficient manner. If the firm is less than maximally technically efficient, the predicted level of output with the observed levels of input is:

$$q = f(x)e^u, \ u \leq 0,$$

where e^u is the firm-specific technical efficiency parameter. If the firm is maximally efficient, $u = 0$. If it is technically inefficient, $u < 0$ and $q < q^*$. Due to random measurement errors, the observed output level q is determined by:

$$q = f(x)e^{u+v}, \ Ev = 0.$$

Assuming profit maximization, both output and input levels are endogenous, with the implication that the production function and the first-order conditions must be estimated simultaneously. The first-order conditions for profit maximization are:

$$pf_i' = p_i, \ i = 1, ..., m,$$

where p is product price, f_i' the marginal physical product of x_i, and p_i the ith factor price. If there are allocative inefficiencies in the use of factors, or mistakes in profit maximization (e.g., divergence between expected and actual real prices), the levels of factor use are determined by:

$$f_i' = p_i / p + u_i^*, \ i = 1, ..., m,$$

where u_i^* is zero if the firm is allocatively efficient. Otherwise, u_i^* can be positive or negative according to the direction of the error in resource allocation. Since there are also measurement errors, the observed levels of factor use are given by:

$$f_i' = p_i / p + w_i, \ w_i = u_i^* + v_i^*, \ E(v_i^*) = 0.$$

If the production frontier is a translog, the system of equations to be estimated is:

$$\ln q = \alpha + \sum_{i=1}^{m} \beta_i \ln x_i + \frac{1}{2} \sum_{i=1}^{m} \sum_{j=1}^{m} \gamma_{ij} \ln x_i \ln x_j + u + v,$$

$$c_i = \beta_i + \sum_{j=1}^{m} \gamma_{ij} \ln x_j + w_i, \ i = 1, ..., m,$$

where c_i is the share of factor i in total revenue, calculated as $p_i x_i / pq$ (see Kalijaran, 1990).

Given a half-normal distribution for u, that is, u is distributed as the negative values of $N(0, \sigma_u)$, a normal distribution $N(0, \sigma_v)$ for v, and a multivariate normal distribution $N(\zeta, \Sigma)$ for the vector w, the model can be estimated using the maximum likelihood approach. This gives estimates of the parameters α, β, γ, σ_u, σ_v, ζ, and Σ.

The actual firm-specific technical efficiency u_k for firm k cannot be measured independently of v_k. However, because these two random variables follow different distributions, one can compute the conditional expected value of u_k, given $(u_k + v_k)$:

$$\hat{\bar{u}}_k = E\left(u_k \middle| u_k + v_k\right) = -\frac{\sigma_u \sigma_v}{\sigma}\left[\frac{\phi(\cdot)}{1-\Phi(\cdot)} - \frac{u_k + v_k}{\sigma}\sqrt{\frac{\gamma}{1-\gamma}}\right],$$

where $\sigma = \sqrt{\sigma_u^2 + \sigma_v^2}$, $\gamma = \sigma_u^2 / \sigma^2$, and $\phi(\cdot)$ and $\Phi(\cdot)$ are the standard normal density and cumulative distributions, respectively, evaluated at $\left((u_k + v_k)/\sigma\right)\left(\sqrt{\gamma/(1-\gamma)}\right)$. This expected value $\hat{\bar{u}}_k$ is used as an indicator of firm-specific technical efficiency.

Allocative efficiency of each firm k with respect to each input i is measured by the estimated residuals w_{ik} and the mean values over the sample firms by the estimates of ζ.

Applying this technique to Filipino rice farmers in Laguna Province, Kalijaran (1990) finds that the average value of $\hat{\bar{u}}_k / \hat{q}_k^*$ over the sample was equal to 0.79. This implies that, on average, production is 21% below the efficiency frontier. Individual farmers' levels of technical efficiency can be explained by regressing $\hat{\bar{u}}_k$ against variables representing the farmers' level of technical knowledge (a number of agronomic practices in crop establishment) and socioeconomic status (education, tenure, and nonfarm income). These variables are all statistically significant, suggesting priorities for the extension services as well as policy interventions to enhance the socioeconomic status of farmers that will result in increased agricultural production. A similar technique has been used by Hussain, Nelson, and Nelson (1991) to analyze the determinants of technical efficiency in wheat production in northern Pakistan.

9.2. Technical Change and Productivity Growth*

Technical efficiency gives a measure of the total factor productivity gap for an individual firm relative to the production frontier which describes the best available technique. The production frontier can itself shift with technical change, thus creating aggregate productivity growth. Indeed, productivity growth has been shown to be a major source of growth of aggregate output (Solow, 1957) and of agricultural output (Lave, 1962; Hayami and Ruttan, 1985). In this section, we first analyze disembodied technical change, which represents a pure shift in the production function. This concept is closely related to total factor productivity growth. We then analyze embodied technological change, where technical change is associated with productivity change in a particular input.

9.2.1. Disembodied Technical Change

Consider a situation where technical change implies a shift in the production function over time. In this case, the production function is:

(1) $q = f(x,t)$,

where t is time. The rate of technical change is then defined as:

$$T(x,t) = \frac{\partial \ln f(x,t)}{\partial t} = \frac{\partial f}{\partial t}\frac{1}{f}.$$

Because this type of technical change does not increase the productivity of a particular input, but rather that of all inputs jointly, it is said to be "disembodied." Specification of technical change as "disembodied" is usually unrealistic. However, it is a convenient specification. For this reason, it has been employed in most studies of technical change.

Total differentiation of the production function (1) gives a decomposition of the sources of growth between technical change and increase in the use of individual factors:

$$(2) \quad \dot{q} = T + \sum_j E_j \dot{x}_j,$$

where $\dot{q}$ and $\dot{x}_j$ are rates of change (that is, $\dot{q} = d \ln q / dt$) and E_j is the output elasticity of factor x_j. From this, we obtain $T = \dot{q} - \sum E_j \dot{x}_j$.

Measurement of technological change therefore requires knowledge of the elasticities E_j. If we assume that there are competitive markets and that firms are profit maximizers, the output elasticities are equal to the input shares in total revenue, $E_j = p_j x_j / pq$, and technological change can be measured by:

$$(3) \quad T = \dot{q} - \sum_j \frac{p_j x_j}{pq} \dot{x}_j.$$

Alternatively, if we assume that producers are cost minimizers, then output elasticities are equal to $E_j = E_{cq}^{-1} p_j x_j / c$, where $c = \sum p_j x_j$ is total cost and E_{cq} is the elasticity of cost with respect to output. Technological change is then measured by:

$$(4) \quad T = \dot{q} - E_{cq}^{-1} \sum_j \frac{p_j x_j}{c} \dot{x}_j.$$

From expression (3), technical change can be identified solely on the basis of observed data, while expression (4) requires the estimation of the cost function before computing technical change.

Technical change need not be specified solely in terms of the production function. By duality, we know that the production process can be completely specified by either the profit or the cost function. Correspondingly, technical change can be defined from the cost function $c(p_x, q, t)$ as:

$$T^* = -\partial \ln c(p_x, q, t) / \partial t,$$

which is the proportional shift in the cost function. Addition of the assumption of cost minimizing behavior for firms gives the following expression:

$$(5) \quad T^* = E_{cq} \dot{q} - \sum_j \frac{p_j x_j}{c} \dot{x}_j,$$

which shows a direct relationship with technological change defined on production in (4), that is, $T^* = E_{cq} T$. Generalization of this approach to a multioutput cost function $c(p_x, q_1, ..., q_n, t)$ yields the following convenient measure of technical change (Capalbo, 1988):

$$(6) \quad T^* = \sum_i E_{cq_i} \dot{q}_i - \sum_j \frac{p_j x_j}{c} \dot{x}_j.$$

9.2.2. *Total Factor Productivity*

Total factor productivity (*TFP*) is a simpler concept than that of technological change and is, therefore, the most common measurement of technical progress. It is defined as the ratio q/X of output q to an index X of all inputs. Differentiating this expression with respect to time gives:

$$\dot{TFP} = \dot{q} - \dot{X}.$$

Alternative specifications of the aggregate input index are used. One of the more common specifications is the Divisia input index, which is based either on cost shares or on input shares in total revenue:

$$\dot{X} = \sum_j \frac{p_j x_j}{c} \dot{x}_j, \text{ or } \dot{X} = \sum_j \frac{p_j x_j}{pq} \dot{x}_j.$$

With the first of these definitions, $X = \sum p_j x_j$ and *TFP* is the inverse of the average cost. If, in addition, there are several products in the output index, this index should be constructed as a Divisia output index,

$$\sum_i \frac{p_i q_i}{\sum_k p_k q_k} \dot{q}_i = \dot{Q}.$$

The resulting $\dot{TFP}$ is the Divisia index of total factor productivity:

(7) $\quad \dot{TFP} = \dot{Q} - \dot{X} = \sum_i \frac{p_i q_i}{\sum_k p_k q_k} \dot{q}_i - \dot{X}$, where $\dot{X} = \sum_j \frac{p_j x_j}{c} \dot{x}_j$ or $\sum_j \frac{p_j x_j}{\sum_k p_k q_k} \dot{x}_j$.

These expressions show that the index of *TFP* constructed on revenue shares corresponds to the index of technological change when there are competitive markets and profit maximization [equation (3)]. Similarly, the index of *TFP* constructed on cost shares corresponds to technical change if there is cost minimization and constant return to scale ($E_{cq} = 1$) [equation (4)]. If $E_{cq} \neq 1$, then the relationship between *TFP* and T is the following:

(8) $\quad \dot{TFP} = \dot{q} - \dot{X} = T + E_{cq}^{-1} \dot{X} - \dot{X} = T + \left(E_{cq}^{-1} - 1 \right) \dot{X}.$

In this final expression, the first term on the right-hand side is the rate of technical change while the second captures the scale effect associated with factor deepening. Using the cost-based definition of technological change with generalization to the multiple-output case and assuming that output prices are equal to marginal cost gives:

$$E_{cq_j} = p_j q_j / c, \quad \dot{Q} = \sum_j \frac{E_{cq_j}}{\sum_k E_{cq_k}} \dot{q}_j, \text{ and}$$

$$(9) \quad T\dot{F}P = \dot{Q} - \dot{X} = \left(\sum_j E_{cq_j} \right) \dot{Q} - \dot{X} + \left(1 - \sum_j E_{cq_j} \right) \dot{Q} = T^* + \left(1 - \sum_j E_{cq_j} \right) \dot{Q}.$$

9.2.3. *Discrete Measures of Technical Change and TFP*

Because data are observed as discrete observations rather than as continuous variables, one needs to define indices of technical change and *TFP* based on such discrete measures. A first approach to this problem approximates the concepts defined in continuous terms above with discrete data. A second approach consists in choosing a specific functional form for the production or the cost function that leads to an exact definition of technical change in discrete terms.

9.2.3.1. *The Tornqvist Approximation*

The Tornqvist approximation of the Divisia index of *TFP* defined in expression (7) (Chambers, 1988, p. 233) is:

$$(10) \quad \Delta TFP = \sum_i \frac{1}{2} \left(r_{it} + r_{i,t-1} \right) \left(\ln q_{it} - \ln q_{i,t-1} \right) - \sum_j \frac{1}{2} \left(s_{jt} + s_{j,t-1} \right) \left(\ln x_{jt} - \ln x_{j,t-1} \right),$$

where r_{it} is the revenue share of output q_i in period t and s_{jt} the ratio of the cost of input x_j to total revenue (or total cost) in period t.

This approximation has been widely used to calculate the annual index of *TFP*. Capalbo (1988) finds that the *TFP* index for U.S. agriculture rose from 100 in 1950 to 165 in 1982, registering an annual growth rate of 1.58%. During the same period, the average annual growth rate in output was 1.75%. This difference implies that factor deepening contributed to annual output growth by only 0.17%. Technological change thus accounted for 90% of total observed output growth and factor deepening for only 10%.

9.2.3.2. *Using the Translog Function*

The use of a translog function allows one to specify exactly technical change or *TFP* indices suitable to discrete data, as opposed to approximating for discrete data an index defined for continuous data as above. However, the specification of a translog production or cost function is, in a sense, also an approximation, since it is unlikely that technology exactly follows a translog function over the range of observations (Capalbo, 1988). This approach allows for the decomposition of *TFP* into technological change and scale effects as first shown in equations (8) and (9).

If one uses a translog production function, the discrete measure of total factor productivity is given by the expression (10) above. With a translog cost function, the discrete measure of total factor productivity is given by:

$$\Delta TFP = T^* + \left(1 - \sum_i E_{cq_i} \right) \sum_i \frac{E_{cq_i}}{\sum_k E_{cq_k}} \left(\ln q_{it} - \ln q_{i,t-1} \right).$$

The elasticities E_{cq_i} and $T^* = -\partial \ln c / \partial t$ can be estimated by fitting the translog total cost function. Applying this method to the same U.S. data, Capalbo finds that the annual rate of *TFP* growth is 1.56%, but that the contribution of T^* is 1.74% while that of nonconstant returns to scale is -0.47%. The rate of technical change in U.S. agriculture was thus higher than growth in total factor productivity. This implies that diseconomies of scale neutralized part of the gains from technology.

The policy implication of the sources of growth studies, initiated by Solow in the 1950s, is to emphasize the role which research, labor skills, and information can play as a source of growth complementary to factor deepening. Viewing productivity gains in this simplistic fashion is, however, insufficient. Because new technologies are in fact associated with new investments and with particular factors of production, one needs to look beyond disembodied technological change into the bias of technical change.

9.2.4. Biased Technical Change

Technical change may be biased toward saving either labor or capital. In addition, the origin of the bias may be embodied in differential productivity growth of a particular factor of production. While the rate of technological change has, as we have seen above, important implications for growth, its bias has important implications for income distribution. Because rate and bias can be affected by the choice of priorities in public investment in research and extension, they offer important instruments for policymakers.

Consider the situation where technical change modifies differentially the productivity of each factor, in addition to creating a pure shift effect as before. The production function becomes:

$$q = f\big[\tilde{x}(x,t),t\big],$$

where $\tilde{x}$ is the effective contribution to q of not only input x but also technological change associated with the use of x. The rate of growth in output is given by:

$$\dot{q} = \sum_i E_{q\tilde{x}_i}\dot{\tilde{x}}_i + T.$$

The first term is a scale-expansion effect, given by a weighted average of the rates of change of the various effective inputs. The second is the pure shift effect, as encountered before. If the effective inputs are specified as:

$$\tilde{x}_j = \lambda_j(t)x_j,$$

then the production function is $q = f(\lambda_1 x_1, ..., \lambda_n x_n, t)$ and the scale effect in output growth is:

$$\sum_j E_{q\tilde{x}_j}(\dot{\lambda}_j + \dot{x}_j).$$

Using a Hicksian definition of the bias of technical change, we will say that, for two factors K and L and a given factor price ratio, p_K / p_L:

a. Technical change is neutral if it leaves the optimum factor ratio K/L unchanged. In Figure 9.3, technological change has shifted the isoquant I to I'. The new equilibrium with constant prices is at B, leaving the factor ratio unchanged.

b. Technical change is labor-saving if the optimum factor ratio K/L rises, with the new equilibrium at B'.

c. Technical change is capital-saving if the optimum factor ratio K/L falls, corresponding to point B''.

In agriculture, a convenient representation of the production function is to decompose capital between land-saving capital (biochemical capital goods K_A and, in particular, fertilizers) and labor-saving capital (machinery K_L and, most specifically, tractors). Technological change can

Figure 9.3. Bias of technological change

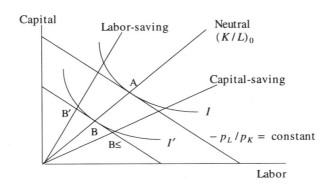

I = unit isoquant before (I) and after (I') neutral technological change

then be aimed at increasing the productivity of land-saving capital (in general, biochemical innovations, and, in particular, the technology of the Green Revolution) with a rate λ_A or at increasing the productivity of labor-saving capital (in general, mechanical innovations) with a rate λ_L. If the primary inputs are land (A) and labor (L), the production function can be written as:

$$q = f\left[f_A(A, \lambda_A K_A), f_L(L, \lambda_L K_L)\right].$$

In this two-tiered production function, the elasticity of substitution between A and $\lambda_A K_A$ within f_A is high. This is also the case between L and $\lambda_L K_L$ within f_L. However, the elasticity of substitution between the aggregate input indices f_A and f_L is low, due to complementarity between these indices of primary factors "land" and "labor." Empirical measurements by Kaneda (1982) confirm these relative magnitudes. Technological change will be biased toward land-saving (the Green Revolution with its yield increasing effect) or toward labor-saving (machines displacing workers) according to the relative magnitudes of the efficiency (or factor-augmenting) parameters λ_A and λ_L.

9.3. Efficiency and Productivity under Transactions Costs

9.3.1. *The Concepts of Transactions Costs and Effective Prices*

Standard Walrasian economics postulates that all markets exist, including those for credit and risk, and that the equilibrium prices these markets determine apply equally to all participants. In practice, especially in the less developed economies, many markets fail either because they do not exist or because there are such high transactions costs associated with their use that it is more advantageous for agents to effect transactions through institutional arrangements other than the market. Transactions costs typically involve the costs of information, search, negotiation, screening, monitoring, coordination, and enforcement (Bardhan, 1989; Hoff and Stiglitz, 1990). In agriculture, transportation costs are also an important type of transactions costs. The result of this pervasive existence of transactions costs is that, even if perfect markets exist in a particular distant location, agents have to incur high costs to access these markets, creating wide bands between sale price and purchase price. We encountered this situation when analyzing household behavior in Chapter 6. We saw that certain transactions will occur at the farm-gate sale or purchase price, while other "transactions" occur within the household when the subjective equilibrium between supply and demand determines a shadow price that falls within the price band.

The consequence of transactions costs is that each decision-making unit faces a unit-specific set of effective prices. Optimum resource allocation will consequently differ for each farm according to the transactions costs-determined effective prices that characterize it. This result has several important implications for policy making.

One implication is that a fundamental result of traditional neoclassical economics, namely that there is separability between efficiency and equity, no longer applies. If markets are perfect, every commodity, whether product or factor, has a single opportunity cost. Specification of ownership does not matter for resource allocation: in the calculus of profit or utility maximization, resources are valued at their opportunity cost, which is the same as the market price. The assignment of property rights is then unrelated to efficiency. Incomes, and consequently equity, are determined ex post relative to resource allocation and do depend on the allocation of property rights. The efficient outcome may not be desirable from an equity standpoint, justifying state intervention. Absence of transactions costs thus implies that achieving efficient resource allocation is separable from equity considerations. In the household model (Chapter 6), for instance, we have seen that, under perfect markets, there is separability between production and consumption decisions.

When transactions costs are present, this fundamental principle breaks down (Bardhan, 1989). Efficiency in resource use depends crucially on the distribution of the assets and property rights. As in the household model, there is no longer separability between efficiency and equity. Redistribution of the assets eventually becomes an important policy tool in achieving a higher level of efficiency. If the poor have lower transactions costs on labor, and production is labor intensive, both efficiency and greater equity may be achieved through a transfer of assets to them. Other policy interventions, such as public investment in infrastructure, education and information, and promotion of service cooperatives, may be effective in reducing transactions costs.

A second important implication is that the combination of rational choice behavior and transactions costs creates incentives for opportunistic behavior, resulting in adverse selection and moral hazard in transactions, both of which have high costs. The first implies ex ante costs of screening out the bad risks among candidates for the transaction while the latter implies ex post costs of monitoring, legal action, and enforcement. This gives rise to the quest for institutions, whether alternative or complementary to the market, that place checks on opportunism and reduce transactions costs. Typical institutions include sharecropping to overcome market failures in supervision and management and to share risk; interlinkage of transactions between credit and labor or credit and sale of product; credit schemes with peer monitoring; mutual insurance networks for risk sharing when there are no contingency markets; and so on. The institution that is most efficient from the standpoint of the principal, given the response expected from other agents, will be chosen, leading to "local" efficiency. This does not mean, however, that the most globally efficient institution will always be chosen. This may be due to existence of transactions costs in institutional change itself, leading to path dependency and permanence of dysfunctional institutions (Akerlof, 1976). Sunken costs, asset specificity, complexity of private bargaining, lack of cooperation, and barriers to entry all serve to block institutional change. Redistributive effects of institutional change may hurt politically dominant agents, with subsequent compensation not credible to them due to lack of commitment mechanisms for the gainers.

9.3.2. *Measurement of Efficiency under Transactions Costs*

While technical efficiency may remain unaltered by transactions costs, this is certainly not the case for allocative efficiency, which needs to be measured relative to firm-specific effective prices. Indeed, if effective prices differ widely, what appear to be allocative inefficiencies relative to market prices may prove to be efficient relative to effective prices.

One convenient approach to measuring efficiency under transactions costs uses the concept of profit efficiency. Profit efficiency is defined as the ability of firm i to achieve the highest level of profit given the specific effective prices p_{ji} and the specific levels of fixed factors z_{ki} of that firm. Figure 9.4 illustrates the principle of the method, with firms differing only along one argument, price p_i or fixed factor z_i. A stochastic profit frontier can be estimated by the same method used to estimate a stochastic production frontier (section 9.1.2.3). Profit inefficiency is defined as profit loss from not operating on the profit frontier. In Figure 9.4, for a firm operating at point F, this is measured by (MF/MP).

Using this methodology, Ali and Flinn (1989) estimated profit efficiency among Basmati rice producers in two villages of Pakistan. Their results, reported in Table 9.1, show that farmers exhibited a wide range of profit inefficiency. The authors pursued their analysis by econometrically identifying factors associated with profit loss. Three groups of factors—institutional, resource base, and socioeconomic—in addition to a village dummy variable, were retained. The results of the regression analysis of profit loss are reported in Table 9.2. Socioeconomic factors account for over half of the explained variability in profit loss. Farm households with more education exhibit significantly less loss of profit than those with less education. Indeed, based on its contribution to R^2, education is the single most important determinant of between-household levels of profit loss. Factors associated with the farmers' resource base have a small impact on loss of profit, and the parameters are not significant. Institutional factors contribute 25% of the explained variability in profit loss between farms, with water shortages a major determinant. Finally, the significant village dummy implies that farmers in the more remote village are less efficient than those in the more accessible village, even when other factors are considered.

Figure 9.4. Frontier and average stochastic profit functions

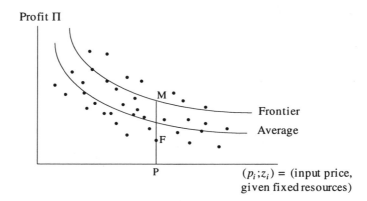

Table 9.1. Frequency distribution of profit loss in Basmati rice production in Pakistan, 1982

Range of profit loss (percentage of maximum profit)	Percentage of sample farmers
0-12	15
12-21	24
21-33	23
33-44	19
44-56	12
56 and above	7

Source: Ali and Flinn, 1989.

9.3.3. Measurement of Total Factor Productivity under Transactions Costs

When there are transactions costs, effective prices differ across farms. Consequently, comparisons of *TFP* across farms need to account for differential optimum factor allocations. If the farms to be compared are multiproduct in nature, *TFP* comparisons must include different product choices. The *TFP* index used will consequently typically be Q/X, where Q is the gross value of output and X is total variable factor cost, both measured at effective prices. In this case, *TFP* is thus the inverse of average effective variable cost. It can differ across farms due to economies of scale, different effective prices, and differences in technical or allocative efficiency.

Table 9.2. Determinant of profit inefficiency (in rupees/ha) among Basmati rice producers in Pakistan, 1982

Variables	Estimated coefficient	t- statistic	Contribution to R^2 (%)
Socioeconomic characteristics			52
Education	−38.0*	8.8	31
Tenancy	−119.8	1.1	5
Off-farm employment	273.5*	2.5	9
Credit nonavailability	204.6*	2.0	7
Resource base			12
Farm size	14.0	0.8	3
Tube-well ownership	−94.8	0.9	4
Tractor use	−110.3	1.1	5
Institutional factors			25
Water constraint	21.0*	3.3	12
Late crop establishment	4.1	1.0	4
Late fertilizer application	14.0*	2.2	9
Village dummy	−258.0*	2.7	11
Intercept	1553.9*	12.6	
R^2	0.5		
F-ratio ($n_1 = 10, n_2 = 181$)	14.8		
Standard error of profit loss	533.6		

Source: Ali and Flinn, 1989.
*Significant at 5%.

Much empirical work has been done to identify the presence of economies of scale in agriculture. While some authors report positive economies of scale (Henry, 1986), most empirical evidence suggests that economies of scale are approximately null (Berry and Cline, 1979). Measurements of technical and allocative efficiency and explanations of their determinants across farms have been analyzed in section 9.3.2 above. Instead, this section focuses on the role of transactions costs in explaining productivity differentials. Not only can the frequent price discrimination against small farms be eliminated by policy reforms, but systematic determinants of differences in effective prices that are due to fundamental structural characteristics of the agrarian economy can be reversed. Most particularly, the role of family labor in farm production and of collateral in accessing credit are important determinants of differences in effective prices, and hence in total factor productivity. Asset redistribution, in the form of land reform, can increase aggregate output by capitalizing on the relative effectiveness of the family farm in mobilizing cheap labor. Promotion of financial institutions such as group lending and credit cooperatives can help reduce credit costs for small farmers (Besley, 1992).

Yield (Q/A) is a specialized productivity indicator which has been extensively used in the debate on land distribution. Although an imperfect indicator of the productivity gains from land reform, yield is easy to measure. As such, there has been an active debate on the determinants of its relation to farm size. In general, an inverse relationship between land productivity and farm size has been observed (Cornia, 1985). This has been attributed to lower effective labor costs on small farms, associated either with captive family labor with no opportunity cost other than leisure, or with lower search, screening, and supervision costs when using family as opposed to hired labor. Many studies have also observed a weakening of this relationship when agriculture becomes more capital-intensive. Adoption of Green Revolution technology is a primary example of capital-intensive changes in farming. Deolalikar (1981) thus observes for India that the small farm sector as a whole enjoys higher yields than the large farm sector, but that this yield advantage diminishes, and in fact reverses, with capital-intensive technical change. Similarly, the inverse relationship which Rao (1975) had observed between land productivity and farm size in the West Godavari District of India before the Green Revolution in 1958–60 had given way to a positive relationship after diffusion of the new technology in 1969–70.

Although greater use of fertilizer and other modern inputs on large farms are usually cited as reversing the standard land productivity/farm size relationship, controversy remains as to why this is true. Subbarao (1982), for instance, convincingly shows that a positive relationship is related to the weak institutional position of small farmers, with associated constraints on access to credit, modern inputs, and irrigation. In the institutionally well-developed regions of India (Punjab, Haryana, western Uttar Pradesh), the inverse relationship has remained despite diffusion of Green Revolution technologies. This suggests that reversal is associated with transactions costs that reflect not inherent structural features of farm size but institutional biases that can be eliminated by policy reform. Redistributive land reform can prove useful only if complemented by the appropriate institutional reforms in support of smallholders. de Janvry and Sadoulet (1989) argue that reversal of the inverse relationship is also associated with greater success by large farmers in using their rent-seeking power to obtain credit subsidies and tax breaks.

This land productivity/farm size debate inevitably questions how household-specific transactions costs affect behavior. It is this behavior that may explain differential productivity levels across farms and, therefore, may ultimately explain social differentiation or the logic for redistributive land reform. Consequently, we turn to examining models of household behavior under transactions costs which explain the relationship between productivity and farm size.

9.4. Household Behavior under Transactions Costs and Productivity Differentials

9.4.1. A Model of Household Behavior

Two of the most common structural features of the agrarian economy are (1) access to credit limited by availability of formal collateral, and (2) moral hazard in hiring labor, implying the need to supervise hired labor, since it has an incentive to shirk. Models of household behavior incorporating these two features have been constructed by Eswaran and Kotwal (1986), Feder (1985), and Carter and Kalfayan (1987). These models set out to predict the nature of the relationship between factor productivity and farm size, and hence to identify policy instruments which affect the direction of this relationship.

In the model constructed by Eswaran and Kotwal (1986), the household problem is defined as follows:

a. The household owns an amount of land $\overline{A}$ and can rent land in or out, resulting in an operational unit of size A that can be greater or smaller than $\overline{A}$. Land transactions are financed at the rental rate r.

b. There is a fixed starting cost $\overline{K}$ to initiate farming, associated with the fixed component of inputs other than land and labor.

c. The household owns a total endowment of labor time $E = 1$, which it can allocate among the following options:

li = work on its own farm,
lo = labor hired out,
$s(h)$ = time spent supervising hired labor, where h is the quantity of labor hired in,
le = leisure.

d. Labor transactions are completed at the wage w. Total labor used on the farm is $L = li + h$.

e. The household has access to a quantity of credit $B(\overline{A})$ proportional to land (assets) owned that serves as collateral.

f. The product price p, the wage w, and the land rental rate r are exogenous, and there are no transactions costs associated with selling or buying these products or factors.

g. The production technology is $q = \varepsilon f(L, A)$, where ε is a stochastic term with $E(\varepsilon) = 1$ representing weather uncertainties and $f(\cdot)$ is homogenous of degree one.

h. Because production is stochastic, the household cannot infer the value of L from knowledge of q. As a consequence, there is an incentive for hired labor to shirk. Family labor does not shirk, since it is the residual claimant on farm profits. Supervision of hired labor consequently needs to be performed by family members in order for supervised labor to become as effective as self-motivated family labor. The supervision function is $s = s(h)$, $s' > 0$, $s'' > 0$, so that supervision costs increase more than proportionately with h. In other words, there are decreasing returns to supervision.

i. The household's utility function u is assumed to be separable in income y and leisure, and to display income risk neutrality:

$$u(y, le) = y + u(le).$$

Given this framework, the household's decision problem is to maximize:

$$\underset{A, li, lo, h, le}{\text{Max}} \; p \, f(L, A) + w(lo - h) - r(A - \overline{A}) - \overline{K} + u(le),$$

subject to the following constraints:

$$li + lo + s(h) + le = 1 \qquad \text{(time constraint)}$$
$$rA + w(h - lo) + \overline{K} \leq r\overline{A} + B(\overline{A}) = B^* \quad \text{(assets constraint)}.$$

Solution of the problem reveals that the household's optimum income strategy depends on its initial asset endowment. As first developed by Roemer (1982), this result thus explains how social classes emerge endogenously as a consequence of rational choice behavior in the context of unequal initial asset distribution. Optimal household strategies are as follows:

Initial assets position B^*	Hire out lo	Own-farm work li	Supervision $s(h)$	Endogenous social class
$B^* < \overline{K}$	+	0	0	Landless worker
$\overline{K} \le B^* < B_1^*$	+	+	0	Worker-peasant
$B_1^* \le B^* < B_2^*$	0	+	0	Family farmer
$B_2^* \le B^* < B_3^*$	0	+	+	Rich farmer
$B^* \ge B_3^*$	0	0	+	Capitalist farmer

Households whose asset position B^* does not allow them to incur the fixed start-up cost $\overline{K}$ do only wage work. They are landless workers and hire out whatever small amount of land they may own. Once $B^* \ge \overline{K}$, the households allocate their labor to both own-farm work and work hired out. They are thus worker-peasants or semiproletarians. As the assets become sufficient, all family labor is absorbed in the family farm. There is a range of asset positions (B_1^* to B_2^*) that corresponds to the family farms. Because shifting to hired labor implies higher labor costs, the richer family farmers will expand their operation by consuming less leisure. With yet more assets, the households hire labor in, and some of the family labor has to be diverted to supervision. They form a class of rich farmers. Finally, with yet more assets, all family labor is used in supervision, making these households pure capitalist farms.

There are several regularities that derive from the model of interest to us here:

a. The labor-to-land ratio $(li + h) / A$ is constant over the asset range of the worker-peasant class and strictly decreasing as assets increase. This is because, while the price of land is constant, the effective price of labor rises beyond B_1^*. In the family farm, increases in B^* induce the households to consume less leisure, thus resulting in a rising perceived price of own labor. For the rich and capitalist farmers, this is further reinforced by the fact that the effective labor cost rises as hired labor needs to be supervised. This effective labor cost rises at an increasing rate with the number of hired workers.

b. The expected yield q/A is constant over the asset range of the worker-peasant class and strictly decreasing as assets increase beyond B_1^*. This explains the inverse relation between land productivity and farm size, which directly follows from (a.) above and the assumption of homogeneity of degree one of the production function. Note that two distortions are needed to produce this result: a transactions cost on labor, implying an increasing effective price, and a constraint on credit due to collateral requirements. If agents were not credit constrained, large farmers using the land less efficiently should lease their land in excess of a family farm operation to households with fewer assets and higher efficiency. With no supervision cost, all farms would use the same factor ratio. If, in addition, there were no differential constraint on borrowing, all farms would be of equal size at equilibrium.

As Eswaran and Kotwal (1986) observe, the inverse relationship between land productivity and farm size can be reversed through adoption of labor-saving capital. Not only would the adoption of labor-saving capital reduce diseconomies of scale introduced by supervision requirements, but it may also introduce economies of scale due to indivisibilities. This is not included in their model, however. Correct specification of reversal in the relationship between yields and farm size would require introducing an additional transactions cost benefiting large farms, such as preferential access to credit, fixed costs in land transactions, or biased technological change in their favor. In this case, the balance between transactions costs on labor, favoring small farms, and transactions costs on capital and land, favoring large farms, would determine the outcome of the yield and *TFP* relations with farm size.

9.4.2. Determinants of the Relation between TFP and Farm Size

To see how the structure of transactions costs affects *TFP* and the role of land reform, we can again use an Eswaran and Kotwal type of model. We make the simplifying assumption that $A = \overline{A}$, that is, there is no asset rental market, where $\overline{A}$ includes not only land but all other fixed capital inputs. The production function is thus $q = f(L, \overline{A})$. Total labor costs are equal to $w_1 h + w_2 li + w_3 s(h)$, where $w_1 h$ represents the wage costs of hired labor h, $w_2 li$ the opportunity cost of family labor li, and $w_3 s(h)$ the cost of supervision of labor $s(h)$. It can be rewritten as $[w + v(h)]L$, where w is the average cost of hired and family labor and $v(h)$ an average supervision cost per unit of labor. This average cost $v(h)$ increases with the share of hired labor in total labor, and hence average labor cost increases with farm size. Total factor productivity is measured by the inverse of the average cost as:

$$TFP = \frac{q}{[w + v(h)]L + rA} \, ,$$

where rA is the cost of land A.

In the absence of any transactions on land, total factor productivity becomes:

$$TFP = \frac{q}{[w + v(h)]L} = \frac{1/p}{\beta_L} \, ,$$

where β_L represents the share of labor costs in total value of production. If agriculture is labor-intensive and there is little substitutability between labor and the other factors of production (represented by $\overline{A}$), β_L increases rapidly as the cost of labor increases, that is, with farm size, and *TFP* falls. This gives us the expected inverse relationship between *TFP* and farm size, justifying redistributive land reform to achieve both equity and efficiency gains. If, however, agriculture is capital intensive, and there is labor-saving technological change as farm size increases such that $\sigma_{LA} > 1$, then β_L falls with the price of labor, and hence with $\overline{A}$, and *TFP* increases with $\overline{A}$. Berry and Cline (1979) thus observe that β_L does fall with farm size in countries with more advanced agriculture. In this case, redistributive land reform can achieve equity gains, but at the cost of efficiency losses, making land reform an ineffective approach to income redistribution. Before we conclude that land reform is "dead," however, it is important to investigate the reasons for the reversal of *TFP*. If, in particular, the reversal is due to successful rent seeking by large farmers in obtaining subsidies to the adoption of labor-saving technological change, the social rationale for land reform may remain. For this purpose, we need to calculate *TFP* at both private and social (denoted with a *) prices.

At social prices, if there is unemployment in the economy at large but not for skilled supervisory labor, then $w^* = 0$, but $v(h) > 0$ for $h > 0$. Also, $r^* = \overline{r}$, the average implicit land rent in the agricultural sector. Under these conditions,

$$TFP^* = \frac{q}{v(h)L + \overline{r}\overline{A}} \, .$$

On small farms, $h = 0$, and $TFP_S^* = \dfrac{q}{\bar{r}\bar{A}}$, while, on large farms,

$$TFP_L^* = \frac{q/\bar{r}\bar{A}}{1 + v(h)L/\bar{r}\bar{A}} < TFP_S^*.$$ Social *TFP* thus decreases with farm size.

Assume, however, that labor-saving technological change $\alpha(C)$ has been adopted on the large farms at a cost C, and that this cost has been subsidized by a rent $R(\bar{A})$. Technological change increases output and reduces supervision costs to a less steep schedule $v'(h) < v(h)$. Thus in this case, at private prices,

$$TFP_S = \frac{q}{wL} < \frac{\alpha(C)q}{[w + v'(h)]L + C - R(\bar{A})} = TFP_L.$$

TFP increases with farm size due to the combined effects of α, $v'(h) < v(h)$, and the $R(\bar{A})$ subsidy, negating efficiency gains from land reform. However, at social prices, the subsidy is a social cost, and we can still have:

$$TFP_S^* = \frac{q}{\bar{r}\bar{A}} > \frac{\alpha(C)q/\bar{r}\bar{A}}{1 + v'(h)L/\bar{r}\bar{A} + C/\bar{r}\bar{A}} = TFP_L^*.$$

Thus, while land reform no longer appears justified at private prices under rent seeking, it may well remain justified at social prices, where the rent subsidy is a social cost (de Janvry and Sadoulet, 1989).

9.5. Transactions Costs and Institutional Solutions: Sharecropping

As of now, we have explored two solutions to the existence of transactions costs: one where the decision-making unit adjusts its production and consumption in accordance with its specific effective prices; and the other where it refrains from using the market and prefers self-sufficiency (as the subjective equilibrium falls within its price band), and the transaction occurs within the decision-making unit itself. There is a third solution, which consists in contracting with an outside agent and completing the exchange through a face-to-face transaction as opposed to an open-market transaction. Transactions thus achieved through contract typically include land, labor, products, credit, insurance, management, and supervision. Analyzing this subject takes us into the vast and fascinating theory of agrarian institutions (see Bardhan, 1983, 1989; Basu, 1984; Hoff, Braverman, and Stiglitz, 1993; Nabli and Nugent, 1989). We provide here an analysis of the choice of contract between a landlord and a peasant-worker as a representative case of agrarian institutions. This case illuminates the unequal relationship of the principal (the dominant landlord) to the agent (the dominated tenant-worker) in the context of several contract options. In a principal-agent relationship, the principal chooses the contract to offer in full knowledge of the optimizing behavior of the agent, under the constraint that the contract be at least as attractive to the agent as the agent's alternative opportunities for employing his resources (Bell, 1989). In this case, the options are a fixed-rent contract, a wage contract, and a sharecropping contract.

From the Marshallian theory of sharecropping, it is well known that output sharing creates a disincentive for the tenant to work (Otsuka and Hayami, 1988). Choice by the landlord of a sharecropping contract will consequently be justified only if it helps overcome other sources of inefficiency. Sharecropping has thus been explained as a mechanism for risk sharing (Cheung, 1969) and for screening of tenants (Newbery and Stiglitz, 1979). The interpretation given by Eswaran and Kotwal (1985) is that it is used to overcome market imperfections other than that of land. If, for instance, (1) both management and supervision are important in production, (2) the landlord is more efficient at management while the tenant is more efficient at supervision, and (3) neither supervision nor management can be bought on the market for a fee, then share-cropping may be a mechanism to effectively gain access to these two factors.

Say that the production function is:

$q = q(t,\ s,\ L,\ M,\ \overline{A})$, where:

t = is management (technical efficiency),
s = labor supervision,
L = labor, with wage w,
M = other variable inputs, such as fertilizers and machinery, with price p_M,
$\overline{A}$ = fixed land and capital.

Assume that the landlord (index 1) is better at management, the tenant (index 2) is better at supervision, and neither service can be bought on the market. If $0 \le \gamma \le 1$ is an efficiency parameter, the two agents have the following efficiency characteristics in each of the two functions:

	Efficiency at supervision	Efficiency at management
Landlord	γ_1	1
Tenant	1	γ_2

We can now explore the relative merits of the three alternative contracts in overcoming market failures for management and supervision. Assume that v is the landlord's opportunity cost of time, u the worker-tenant's reservation income per unit of time, and each partner has a time endowment $E = 1$.

Fixed-wage contract. Under this contract, the landlord makes all production decisions, performs all supervision and management, and is the residual claimant. The landlord's problem is thus:

$$\underset{t_1, s_1, M, L}{\text{Max}}\ \Pi_1^w = \left[pq(t_1, \gamma_1 s_1, L, M) - p_M M - wL\right] + (1 - t_1 - s_1)v .$$

In this expression, t_1 and s_1 are the quantities of management and supervision time contributed by the landlord. On the right-hand side, the term in square brackets is the landlord's expected income in farming and the last term is income in his alternative activity.
Under this contract, the incomes of the two partners are:

$y_1^w = \tilde{\Pi}_1^w$, where $\tilde{\Pi}$ denotes maximum profits, for the landlord, and

$y_2^w = u$ for the tenant.

Fixed-rent contract. The tenant takes all the production decisions, performs all supervision and management, and is the residual claimant. His problem, which is not affected by payment of a lump-sum rent, is:

$$\underset{t_2,s_2,M,L}{\text{Max}} \;\; \Pi_2^r = \left[pq(\gamma_2 t_2,s_2,L,M) - p_M M - wL\right] + (1 - t_2 - s_2)u,$$

where t_2 and s_2 are the quantities of management and supervision contributed by the tenant. As principal, the landlord can charge a fixed rent R that reduces the tenant to his reservation income: $R = \tilde{\Pi}_2^r - u$. The incomes of the two partners are thus:

$y_1^r = R + v$ for the landlord, and

$y_2^r = u$ for the tenant.

Share contract. The two partners decide jointly on M and L, and each partner decides how much to contribute of the factor in which he is most efficient, that is, management t_1 by the landlord and supervision s_2 by the tenant. They first decide on the choice of M and L by solving the joint problem:

$$\underset{M,L}{\text{Max}} \;\; \Pi^{sc}(t_1,s_2) = pq(t_1,s_2,L,M) - p_M M - wL.$$

The formula for sharing the profit Π^{sc} between them is a nonlinear arrangement with a fixed amount α and a share β for the tenant:

landlord's profit: $\quad -\alpha + (1-\beta)\Pi^{sc}$

tenant's profit: $\quad \alpha + \beta\Pi^{sc}.$

Given this, each partner decides how much to contribute of the nonmarket input in which he is most efficient:

landlord problem: $\quad \underset{t_1}{\text{Max}} \; (1-\beta)\Pi^{sc}(t_1,s_2) + (1-t_1)v$

tenant problem: $\quad \underset{s_2}{\text{Max}} \; \beta\Pi^{sc}(t_1,s_2) + (1-s_2)u.$

The solution of these two problems as a noncooperative Nash game gives the two best-response functions:

for the landlord: $\quad t_1 = f_1(s_2,\beta),$
for the tenant: $\quad s_2 = f_2(t_1,\beta),$

which can be solved as $t_1(\beta)$ and $s_2(\beta)$.

As principal, the landlord has the last word in setting the terms of the contract (α, β), and will set α to reduce the tenant to the reservation utility u, and choose $\beta = \tilde{\beta}$ to maximize expected income, that is, the landlord will solve the problem:

$$\text{Max}_{\alpha,\beta} \ y_1^{sc} \ \text{ s.t. } \ \alpha + \beta\Pi^{sc} + (1 - s_2)u = u.$$

The resulting incomes are:

$$y_1^{sc} = \tilde{\Pi}^{sc}\left(t_1(\tilde{\beta}), s_2(\tilde{\beta})\right) + \left(1 - t_1(\tilde{\beta})\right)v + \left(1 - s_2(\tilde{\beta})\right)u - u,$$

$$y_2^{sc} = u.$$

Finally, the landlord should compare the maximum levels of income achieved under the three alternative contracts, that is, y_1^w, y_1^r, and y_1^{sc}, and choose the most profitable contract.

The comparative statics of the choice of contract can be represented in Figure 9.5. If the activity, as defined by crop and technology, is such that efficiency in supervision is easy to achieve by the landlord (γ_1 high), the landlord should choose a wage contract. This will be the case for crops that are heavily mechanized with much labor-saving effect. By contrast, if the activity is such that efficiency in management is easy to achieve by the tenant (γ_2 high), the landlord should offer him a fixed-rent contract. This is the case for traditional crops such as corn

Figure 9.5. Choice of optimum contract

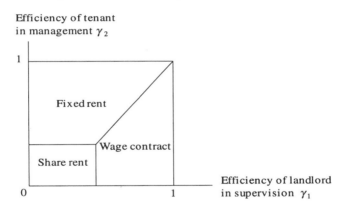

Source: Eswaran and Kotwal (1985)

and rice, in which there is a long peasant tradition and relatively little technological innovation. If the activity is demanding in both management and supervision, then a sharecropping contract will be optimum. The optimum contract will respond to changes in the determinants of γ_1 and γ_2. For instance, if a new technology for traditional crops is introduced that is demanding in technological knowledge and in access to new inputs, thereby making tenant management inefficient, the landlord may switch from a fixed-rent to a sharecropping contract. If there is market integration and the crop becomes a cash crop, greater demands in management will also result in a sharecropping contract being optimal. By contrast, if a labor-intensive crop is introduced, the landlord may switch from wage contracts to share rent. Wells (1983) has shown this to be the case for the strawberry industry in California. Conversely, if a mechanical harvester is adopted, for instance, for harvesting canning tomatoes, shift should be from a share contract, which was previously justified by labor intensity and importance of supervision, to a wage contract.

In conclusion, contracts emerge in response to specific transactions costs. To arrive at a sharecropping solution, two market imperfections are necessary. To reduce the tenant to his reservation wage and maximize his own income, the landlord needs to control two instruments. A fixed fee α achieves the first, and a variable share β achieves the second. The contract that is ultimately chosen by the landlord is "locally superior," that is, superior from the standpoint of the landlord's income. It need not be globally efficient in that both supervision and management are underprovided compared with their marginal costs. Similarly, it need not be equitable in the sense that the worker-tenant always remains at the same level of income u, while all efficiency gains are captured by the landlord. The issue of equity is directly linked to the choice of a principal-agent framework. If a bargaining approach had been chosen instead, the efficiency gains would be shared with a rule that fundamentally depends on the relative power of the two agents (Bell, 1989).

Nonexistence of a market for an input is equivalent to the extreme case of the general problem of moral hazard in market transactions. The idea is that, when it is difficult or costly to observe the input which is actually delivered, the agent will have a tendency to shirk and to underprovide the input for which he is paid. At the extreme, the effective input that is actually delivered is infinitely expensive, which says that, de facto, the market does not perform. In our model, the problem of observability does not apply to the product and to the other variable inputs M, but it applies to the three other inputs: labor, supervision, and management. One solution to shirking is to use supervision, the option which has been chosen in this model for the labor input. Another solution is to let the agent who is the residual claimant on output perform the task, as the agent will receive all the benefits from performing it well. To achieve this, a fixed-rent contract would be offered, here with the individual who performs the tasks of supervision and management. In this particular model, however, this would create inefficiencies due to unequal inabilities among participants in performing these tasks. What the sharecropping contract does is to assign both partners as residual claimants on the output and allow each partner to decide on the amount of supervision or management to provide. Note, however, that because of output sharing, a disincentive problem is created resulting in the Marshallian inefficiency. As a result, the sharecropping option mitigates the efficiency problem but without completely eliminating it. It will be chosen if the efficiency gain from eliminating inefficiencies in the delivery of supervision and management is greater than the inefficiency created by the disincentive effect of sharecropping.

Exercise 9
Relationship between Farm Size and Productivity: The Economics of Land Reform

In this exercise (file 9TFP), we examine the relationship between farm size and productivity. The efficiency criterion used is the overall efficiency in resource utilization, including both technical input-output efficiency, which is usually measured by technological choices and returns to scale, and allocative efficiency, which relates ratios of factor use to their relative costs. For that purpose, we use an index of total factor productivity *TFP*, which is based on the average cost of production. This index of *TFP* is computed with different price systems: market prices, social shadow prices, and effective prices paid by the farmers. The objective of this exercise is

	A	B	C	D	E	F	G	H	I	J	K	L	M
1	Table 9E.1. Relationship between farm size and productivity												
2													
3													
4					Data						Factor ratios		Land
5	Farm	Farm	Number	Average	Average	Avg. gross	Labor	Capital					value
6	group	size	of farms	farm size	land value	receipts	input						
7			N	A	pA.A	pQ	L	pK.K	pQ/L	pQ/pK.K	pQ/A	pQ/pA.A	pA
8													
9			(percent)	(ha)	(U.S.$)	(U.S.$)	(man-years)	(U.S.$)					
10													
11	1	0-10 ha	47.8	3.7	189	318	.951	1495					
12	2	10-50 ha	32.9	25.5	763	782	1.734	3669					
13	3	50-100 ha	7.8	71.9	2452	1165	2.229	4156					
14	4	100-200 ha	4.6	138.9	4247	1223	2.222	6139					
15	5	200-500 ha	3.4	313.2	11112	1565	2.506	9396					
16	6	> 500 ha	3.5	1178.0	17119	2589	3.534	11662					
17													
18	Total factor productivity at constant prices (market or social prices)												
19													
20			Market prices I										
21	Wage		342										
22	Interest rate		0.03										
23					Actual land distribution			Redistribution					
24					Total			Efficiency Welfare					
25				TFP	area	NA.TFP		(percent land)					
26													
27	Group		1	0.846	177	150		50					
28			2	1.077	839	904		50					
29			3	1.213	561	680		100					
30			4	1.141	639	729							
31			5	1.063	1065	1132							
32			6	1.249	4123	5152							
33					7403	8746							
34	Average TFP					1.181		1.213	0.962				
35													
36													
37	Total factor productivity with transactions costs (effective and social prices)												
38													
39			Effective prices IV										
40	Wage wf		0										
41	wnf		342										
42	Supervision s		0.2										
43	Family labor Lf		1.7										
44	Interest rate is		0.25										
45	il		0.03										
46								Actual land distribution			Redistribution		
47				Labor	Interest	Capital	TFP	Total			Efficiency Welfare		
48				costs	rate	costs		area	NA.TFP		(percent land)		
49													
50			1	0	.25	417	.763						
51			2										
52			3										
53			4										
54			5										
55			6										
56													
57	Average TFP												
58													

	A	B	C	D	E	F	G	H	I	J	K	L	M
59	Table 9E.1. Relationship between farm size and productivity (continued)												
60													
61								Effective					
62	Prices			Market	Social	Social	Effective	social					
63				prices	prices	prices	prices	prices					
64				I	II	III	IV	V					
65		Wages		342	0	171	0	171					
66							342	171					
67		Supervision					0.2	0.2					
68		Family Labor					1.7	1.7					
69		Interest		.03	.15	.15	.25	.18					
70							.03	.15					
71													
72	TFP	1		.846									
73		2		1.077									
74		3		1.213									
75		4		1.141									
76		5		1.063									
77		6		1.249									
78													
79	Average TFP												
80		Actual distribution		1.181									
81		Efficiency land reform		1.213									
82		Welfare land reform		.962									

to illustrate the thesis that while large farms may be more efficient under a system of distorted market prices, the allocation of resources as performed on medium-size farms corresponds better to the optimal choice when proper account is taken of social shadow cost and transaction costs in the access to the different factors. The economic and welfare rationales for land reform, and the eventual trade-offs between these two goals, are examined on that basis.

The data reported in the first part of Table 9E.1 draw heavily on a study of northeastern Brazil in Berry and Cline (1979). For each farm-size category, information is given on the output level, measured by average receipts pQ, and on the resources used: labor input L, capital measured by its value $p_k K$, and land. To take into account variability in quality, the land input is measured not by the area but by its estimated value $p_A A$, under the assumption that the value of land incorporates the relevant locational and physical aspects of the land into a single measure of land quality.

1. Analyze the variations in factor use according to farm size by computing the ratios pQ/L, $pQ/p_K K$, pQ/A, and $pQ/p_A A$.

2. The costs of the two assets, land and capital, are calculated by applying the cost of capital (interest rate) i to the asset value reported for each of these two inputs. If w is the cost of labor, the total cost of production is:

$$wL + i(p_K K + p_A A).$$

Then define the index of total factor productivity, *TFP*, by the inverse of the average cost of production:

$$TFP = \frac{pQ}{wL + i(p_K K + p_A A)}.$$

Compute *TFP* for each farm size for a set of "market" prices (case I) in which the wage is the minimum wage, $w = \$/man\text{-}year\ 342$, and the interest rate is heavily subsidized at 3%.

Determination of the correct "social price," or opportunity cost, for labor and capital requires calculation of the equilibrium values for the whole economy, which is practically impossible. Short of that, a range of values can be used for labor from 0 (case II) up to 171 (case III), which is equal to one-half of the minimum wage. For the social price of land and capital, an opportunity cost of 15% per annum is applied. With these values (cases II and III), compute *TFP* at social prices.

Compare the performance of the different farm sizes under these two sets of prices.

3. The previous analysis assumes that all farms face the same prices, with no differential access or transactions costs. We will now introduce two transactions costs, on labor and on capital, to more realistically reflect the prices effectively paid by each class of farm.

For labor, assume that each household has $Lf = 1.7$ man-year units of family labor, the price of which is w_f. Hired labor, with employment equal to $Lnf = L - 1.7$ (when positive), is paid w_{nf}. Assume also that there is a unit supervision cost for this hired labor that increases with the size of the pool of employed: $s(L) = s\,(L - 1.7)$. The total labor cost is thus:

$w_f L$ for the farms not hiring external labor, and

$w_f Lf + w_{nf}\left[1 + s(L - 1.7)\right](L - 1.7)$ for the larger farms.

These two expressions can be combined into a single formula as follows:

$$w_f \min(L, Lf) + w_{nf}\left[1 + s\max(0, L - 1.7)\right]\max(0, L - 1.7).$$

With a distorted labor market encompassing labor surplus in the economy, for family labor in particular, and rigid wages on the market, we can estimate that the opportunity cost is $w_f = 0$ for family labor, and $w_{nf} = 342$, the minimum wage, for hired labor. Assume that the supervision factor s is 0.2. With these values (case IV), compute the effective labor cost for each farm size.

Distortions on the capital market greatly favor large farms. Assume that the interest rate varies linearly with the land value, which serves as the collateral for loans, in such a way that the large farms get credit at the subsidized rate $i_l = 3\%$ while the small farms pay $i_s = 25\%$. The exact formula to use is:

$$i = i_s + \left(i_l - i_s\right)p_A A / 17500.$$

Compute for each farm size the cost of land and capital and *TFP* at these effective prices (case IV).

The determination of social prices includes removing the market distortions but not the transactions costs, which are structural characteristics of variability of access to factors of production by class of farm. For the effective social price of labor, we keep the above formula that includes supervision costs. However, both family labor and hired labor are valued at the social wage, so $w_f = w_{nf} = 171$. As for the interest rates, only a small difference between small and large farms, reflecting the differential risk of default, prevails, with $i_s = 18\%$ and $i_l = 15\%$.

Compute the labor cost, capital cost, and *TFP* at these effective social prices (case V). Compare the performance of the different farm sizes under these different sets of prices.

4. We now consider alternative land reform programs and compute the potential efficiency and welfare gains of each. The average *TFP* in the sector is a weighted average of the TFP_k by farm groups, with weights equal to the land area in each group. With the distribution of number of farms, N_k, and the average farm size, A_k, compute the land distribution by group $N_k A_k$ and the average total factor productivity:

$$TFP = \sum_k N_k A_k TFP_k / \sum_k N_k A_k$$

for the different sets of prices (cases I–V).

Repeat this with two alternative land redistribution schemes: in the first, an "efficiency" oriented land distribution, all the land is attributed in farms of the most socially efficient size, that is, to the 50–100 ha size. In a welfare-oriented distribution, all the land is distributed equally to all farms. This would mean a single farm size of 11.3 ha. As our size groups do not correspond to this specific size, we simulate this "welfare" scheme by giving 50% of the land to each of the two small size groups 1 and 2.

Compare the potential efficiency gains of each of these land reform programs. What are the efficiency costs of a welfare oriented land reform?

5. Assume now that a drastic readjustment of the exchange rate has taken place, which has revalued the prices of the tradables relative to the prices of the nontradables. Consider labor as the only nontradable and agricultural product and capital as tradables. Increase the value of output by 20% in the original data. Increase also the interest rates by 20% in the relevant places. Compute *TFP* at effective prices and at effective social prices. Compare the efficiency gains of land reform now to results obtained in question 4.

References

Aigner, Dennis, C. Knox Lovell, and Peter Schmidt. 1977. "Formulation and Estimation of Stochastic Frontier Production Function Models." *Journal of Econometrics* 6:21–38.

Akerlof, George. 1976. "The Economics of Caste and the Rat Race and Other Woeful Tales." *Quarterly Journal of Economics* 90:599–617.

Ali, Mubarik, and John Flinn. 1989. "Profit Efficiency among Basmati Rice Producers in Pakistan Punjab." *American Journal of Agricultural Economics* 71:303–10.

Bardhan, Pranab. 1983. *Land, Labor, and Rural Poverty.* Oxford: Oxford University Press.

Bardhan, Pranab. 1989. "Alternative Approaches to the Theory of Institutions in Economic Development." In *The Economic Theory of Agrarian Institutions,* edited by P. Bardhan. Oxford: Clarendon Press.

Basu, Kaushik. 1984. *The Less Developed Economy: A Critique of Contemporary Theory.* Oxford: Basil Blackwell.

Bell, Clive. 1989. "A Comparison of Principal–Agent and Bargaining Solutions: The Case of Tenancy Contracts." In *The Economic Theory of Agrarian Institutions,* edited by P. Bardhan. Oxford: Clarendon Press.

Besley, Timothy. 1992. "Savings, Credit, and Insurance," in *Handbook of Development Economics,* J. Behrman and T.N. Srinivasan, eds., draft.

Berry, Albert, and William Cline. 1979. *Agrarian Structure and Productivity in Developing Countries.* Baltimore: Johns Hopkins University Press.

Capalbo, Nancy. 1988. "Measuring the Components of Aggregate Productivity Growth in U.S. Agriculture." *Western Journal of Agricultural Economics* 13:53–62.

Carter, Michael, and John Kalfayan. 1987. "An Economic Model of Agrarian Structure in Latin America." Unpublished paper. University of Wisconsin at Madison, Department of Agricultural Economics.

Chambers, Robert. 1988. *Applied Production Analysis: A Dual Approach*. Cambridge: Cambridge University Press.

Cheung, Steven. 1969. *The Theory of Share Tenancy*. Chicago: University of Chicago Press.

Cornia, Andrea. 1985. "Farm Size, Land Yields, and the Agricultural Production Function: An Analysis for Fifteen Developing Countries." *World Development* 13:513–34.

Dawson, Philip, John Lingard, and Christopher Woodford. 1991. "A Generalized Measure of Farm–Specific Technical Efficiency." *American Journal of Agricultural Economics* 73:1098–1104.

de Janvry, Alain, and Elisabeth Sadoulet. 1989. "A Study in Resistance to Institutional Change: The Lost Game of Latin American Land Reform." *World Development* 17:1397–1407.

Deolalikar, Anil. 1981. "The Inverse Relationship between Productivity and Farm Size: A Test Using Regional Data from India." *American Journal of Agricultural Economics* 63:275–79.

Eswaran, Mukesh, and Ashok Kotwal. 1985. "A Theory of Contractual Structure in Agriculture." *American Economic Review* 75:352–67.

Eswaran, Mukesh, and Ashok Kotwal. 1986. "Access to Capital and Agrarian Production Organization." *Economic Journal* 96:482–98.

Farrell, Michael. 1957. "The Measurement of Production Efficiency." *Journal of the Royal Statistical Society*, ser. A, general, 120:253–81.

Feder, Gershon. 1985. "The Relation between Farm Size and Farm Productivity." *Journal of Development Economics* 18:297–313.

Hayami, Yujiro, and Vernon Ruttan. 1985. *Agricultural Development: An International Perspective*. Baltimore: Johns Hopkins University Press.

Henry, Michael. 1986. "Economies of Scale and Agrarian Structure." *Oxford Agrarian Studies* 15:72–99.

Herdt, R. W., and A. M. Mandac. 1981. "Modern Technology and Economic Efficiency of Philippine Rice Farmers." *Economic Development and Cultural Change* 29:375–98.

Hoff, Karla, Avishai Braverman, and Joseph Stiglitz. 1993. *The Economics of Rural Organization: Theory, Practice, and Policy*. Oxford: Oxford University Press.

Hoff, Karla, and Joseph Stiglitz. 1990. "Introduction: Imperfect Information and Rural Credit Markets— Puzzles and Policy Perspectives." *World Bank Economic Review* 4:235–50.

Hussain, Syed, Charles Nelson, and Gerald Nelson. 1991. "Analysis of Technical Inefficiency in Northern Pakistan: Estimation, Causes, and Policy Implications." Unpublished paper. Texcoco, Mexico: International Center for Wheat and Corn (CIMMYT).

Kalijaran, K. P. 1990. "On Measuring Economic Efficiency." *Journal of Applied Econometrics* 5:75–85.

Kaneda, Hiromitsu. 1982. "Specification of Production Functions for Analyzing Technical Change and Factor Inputs in Agricultural Development." *Journal of Development Economics* 11:97–108.

Kumbhakar, S. C. 1987. "The Specification of Technical and Allocative Inefficiency in Stochastic Production and Profit Frontiers." *Journal of Econometrics* 34:335–48.

Lave, Lester. 1962. "Empirical Estimates of Technological Change in United States Agriculture, 1850–1958." *Journal of Farm Economics* 44:941–52.

Leibenstein, Harvey. 1989. "Organizational or Frictional Equilibria, X–Efficiency, and the Rate of Innovation." *Quarterly Journal of Economics* 83:600–623.

Meeusen, Wim, and Julien van den Broeck. 1977. "Efficiency Estimation from Cobb–Douglas Production Function with Composed Error." *International Economic Review* 18:435–44.

Nabli, Mustapha K., and Jeffrey B. Nugent (eds.). 1989. *The New Institutional Economics and Development: Theory and Applications to Tunisia*. Amsterdam: North-Holland.

Newbery, David, and Joseph Stiglitz. 1979. "Sharecropping, Risk Sharing, and the Importance of Imperfect Competition." In *Risk, Uncertainty, and Agricultural Development*, edited by J. Roumasset et al. Laguna, Philippines: Agricultural Development Council.

Otsuka, Keijiro, and Yujiro Hayami. 1988. "Theories of Share Tenancy: A Critical Survey." *Economic Development and Cultural Change* 57:31–68.

Rao, C. H. H. 1975. *Technological Change and Distribution of Gains in Indian Agriculture*. New Delhi: Macmillan.

Roemer, John. 1982. *A General Theory of Exploitation and Class*. Cambridge: Harvard University Press.

Sidhu, Surjit. 1974. "Relative Efficiency in Wheat Production in the Indian Punjab." *American Economic Review* 64:742–51.

Solow, Robert. 1957. "Technical Change and the Aggregate Production Function." *Review of Economics and Statistics* 39:312–20.

Subbarao, K. 1982. "Technology Gap and the Emerging Size–Productivity Relationships Following the Adoption of New Technology: An Analysis of Evidence from Northwest and Eastern India." Unpublished paper. University of California at Berkeley, Department of Agricultural and Resource Economics.

Timmer, Peter. 1971. "Using a Probabilistic Frontier Production Function to Measure Technical Efficiency." *Journal of Political Economy* 79:776–94.

Wells, Miriam. 1983. "The Resurgence of Sharecropping: Historical Anomaly or Political Strategy?" Unpublished paper. University of California at Davis, Department of Applied Behavioral Sciences.

Yotopoulos, Pan, and Lawrence Lau. 1973. "A Test for Relative Economic Efficiency: Some Further Results." *American Economic Review* 63:214–23.

CHAPTER TEN

Input-Output Tables, Social Accounting Matrices, and Multipliers

Because agriculture is a major sector of most developing countries' economies, agricultural policies affect all other sectors. This results from changes in agriculture's output supply, input demand, employment, and income generation in the rural areas. Conversely, changes in other sectors may affect production, employment, and income distribution in agriculture. The analysis of this type of interactions among sectors and institutions requires economywide frameworks which we will study in this and the following chapters.

The basis of any such multisectoral analysis must be a consistent and complete data set on all transactions among sectors and institutions: consistent in the sense that for every income there should be a corresponding outlay or expenditure; and complete in that both the receiver and the sender of every transaction must be identified. The social accounting matrix (SAM) is a simple and efficient framework to organize economic data in such a way. SAMs have also been used, like their homologue input-output tables, to assess the economywide effects of an increase in demand for one sector or in external transfer to an institution, in what is known as "multiplier analysis."

Analysis of the interactions among sectors is a key element in the debate over the proper role of agriculture and other sectors in the development process. In the 1950s, the prevailing view was that industry was an active sector capable of pulling the whole economy while agriculture was passive, and hence that development should be based on industrialization. The debate then focused on selection of an industrial investment strategy. It opposed the balanced growth-path advocated by Nurske, according to which investment should be pursued simultaneously in several industries, to Hirschman's proposed strategy of judiciously unbalanced growth (Hirschman, 1958). Choice of the strategic sectors in which to invest is based on their capacity to generate forward linkages (which may encourage investment in sectors that require their production as input) or backward linkages (which may encourage investment in sectors producing the inputs that they demand). The measure of these linkages is done from the matrix of interindustry flows, the "input-output" matrix. Agriculture, especially peasant agriculture, is short on linkage effects. Like all primary production, it has few backward linkages, and as producer of final commodities, it has low forward linkages. Hence, this development strategy based on the quest for linkage effects led to the neglect of agriculture. Exhaustion of this industrialization strategy led, in the 1970s and 1980s, to an almost complete reversal in the conception of the role of agriculture in development. This was, in particular, due to extension of the concept of linkage to include income and final consumption linkages. The agricultural sector was recognized as an important source of household incomes, the expenditure of which can induce industrialization under the pull of effective demand (see Chapter 1). Technically, extension of the concept of linkage to include income and final consumption effects was based on extension of the input-output matrix to the SAM which we examine in this chapter. It led to the aggregate measure of farm-nonfarm linkages proposed by Haggblade, Hazell, and Brown (1989).

10.1. Social Accounting Matrices

The general structure of a SAM is represented in Table 10.1. A SAM is a square matrix in which each transactor or account has its own row and column. The payments (expenditures) are listed in columns and the receipts in rows. As each account must balance, the corresponding row and column totals are equal. There are six types of accounts in the SAM: the activities, commodities, and factors (labor and capital) accounts; the current accounts of the domestic institutions, divided into households, firms, and the government; the capital account; and the rest of the world account.

Activity or production accounts are used to buy raw materials and intermediate goods and hire factor services to produce commodities. Their expenditures (column 1) hence include the purchase of intermediate commodities. The remainder is, by definition, value-added, of which a part may be payable to the government as a tax on the activity (e.g., a value-added tax). Value added is then distributed to factors of production in the form of wage payments and of rent to fixed factors. The receipts (row 1) of the activities derive from sales on the domestic market, exports, and export subsidies received from the government. Export taxes to the government are noted as negative export subsidies.

Commodity accounts can best be seen as representing domestic product markets. Note that because commodity accounts are defined separately from activities, they need not have the same sectoral definitions. Commodity accounts (column 2) purchase imports and domestically produced commodities, including services from the trade sector, and pay indirect taxes, including tariffs levied on imports net of subsidies, on commodities. Their receipts (row 2) proceed from sales on the domestic market of intermediate products to activities, of final goods to households and government for consumption, and of investment goods to the capital account.

Factor accounts include labor and capital accounts. They receive payments (row 3) from the sale of their services to activities in the form of wages and rent and income from abroad as remittances and capital income. These revenues are distributed (column 3) to households as labor incomes and distributed corporate and unincorporated profits, and to firms as non-distributed profits after the corresponding taxes have been paid to government.

Institutions include households, firms, and government, with households usually disaggregated in different socioeconomic groups. Distinction is made between current and capital accounts, accounts 4 and 5, respectively. Households' incomes include the factor incomes described above and various transfers coming from other households, from government, from firms (mostly from insurance), or from abroad. Remittances are sometimes introduced here rather than in the labor accounts if information is available at this level. Households' expenditures consist of consumption and income taxes, with residual savings transferred to their capital account. Firms receive profits and transfers and spend on taxes and transfers. Their residual savings go into their capital account. The government account is distinct from administrative activities included in the activity accounts, which buy intermediate goods, pay wages, and deliver "administrative services." This government account spends its current expenditures on directly buying the services provided by the activity account. The other items in the current budget are transfers to households and firms, and the remaining savings are transferred to the capital account. On the income side, the government receives tax revenues and current transfers from abroad.

In principle, a separate *capital account* could be identified for each of the institutions described above. In practice, however, adequate data are seldom available, and only the govern-

Table 10.1. Structure of a social accounting matrix

			Expenditures							
	1	2	3 Factors		4 Institutions			5	6	7
Incomes	Activities	Commodities	Labor	Capital	Households	Firms	Government	Capital account	Rest of world	Total
1 Activities		Domestic sales					Export subsidies		Exports	Production
2 Commodities	Intermediate demand				Households consumption		Government consumption	Investment		Domestic demand
3 Factors										
Labor	Wages								Factor incomes from abroad	Gross national product at factor cost
Capital	Rent									
4 Institutions										
Households			Labor income	Distributed profits	Intrahousehold transfers	Transfers	Transfers		Transfers	Households income
Firms				Nondistributed profits			Transfers		Transfers from abroad	Firms income
Government	Value-added taxes	Tariffs Ind. taxes	Taxes Social sec.	Taxes on profits	Direct taxes	Taxes				Government income
5 Capital account					Households savings	Firms savings	Government savings		Capital transfers	Total savings
6 Rest of world		Imports	Factor payments			Current transfers abroad				Imports
7 Total	Production	Domestic supply	Factor outlay		Households expenditures	Firms expenditures	Government expenditures	Total investment	Foreign exchange earnings	

275

ment capital account is separated from a consolidated capital account of the domestic private institutions. These capital accounts collect savings together with net foreign capital transfers (also called foreign savings) from the rest of the world. This provides the necessary finance for domestic fixed capital formation and changes in stocks.

Transactions between the domestic economy and the *rest of the world* are recorded in the last account. The economy receives income from the rest of the world as payment for exports and pays for imports to the rest of the world. Similarly, some factor payments are received from abroad, offsetting factor payments to the rest of the world, and current transfers to and from abroad are made by the current institutions' account. The current accounts deficit is covered by net foreign capital transfers, which appear as foreign savings. SAMs do not usually contain assets accounts. Thus, if the foreign exchange used by the economy results in a decrease in reserves, the latter should be aggregated to the net foreign capital transfers. The fact that the foreign account deficit exactly matches the deficit in the savings-investment account is a standard result of national accounting. In the SAM framework, it is a mathematical necessity that if all other accounts are balanced, then the last one will also be in equilibrium.

There is no unique way of disaggregating and organizing the data in a SAM. The number of accounts in each category depends on the objectives of the study. We have already mentioned the possibility of disaggregating the household account to show separate socioeconomic classes. Similarly, the government account could be disaggregated into several entities. A SAM which emphasizes agriculture may have several agricultural subsectors rather than only one or two, as is typical in most general-purpose SAMs. SAMs also vary in the way transactions are recorded. We have mentioned the case of remittances, which are received either by the labor factor or by the household. Imports are sometimes also split between intermediate and final goods imports directly bought by the activities and institutions accounts. Also, returns to family labor may be aggregated with the return to fixed factors rather than with labor income. SAMs can also be built for different economic entities. The most common use of SAMs is at the national level, as presented here. However, SAMs have also been built for regional economies and for villages, with an example of the latter presented later in this chapter. The disaggregation scheme and the density of transactions among domestic accounts will clearly differ in these cases. Finally, accounts could be arranged in any order, a feature which is largely a matter of taste and tradition. However, all SAMs must respect the same logic of complete and consistent accounting.

10.2. Example: A Social Accounting Matrix for Ecuador, 1980

SAMs provide a great deal of information about the structure of an economy. An example is given in Table 10.2 with a SAM for Ecuador in 1980. Recall that, by convention, the cell *ij* is a payment from account *j* to account *i*. The reading of this SAM shows the following features of the Ecuadorian economy:

a. *Sectoral structure of domestic production and value added.* Agriculture represents 9% of domestic production $[(t1 + t2)/ta]$, and 12.6% of GDP $[(t1 - c1 + t2 - c2)/(ta - ca)]$. The oil sector is of about the same size, with figures at 8.8% and 12.7%, respectively. Manufacturing production, noted as activities 4 and 5, is larger but nevertheless shows a low level of industrialization accounting for only 18.4% of GDP.

b. *Sectoral contrasts in the generation of income.* Sharp contrasts are seen between sectors whose production mostly generates value added and sectors with high intermediate demand.

Table 10.2. Social accounting matrix, Ecuador, 1980

	Activities: Ag. exports 1	Other ag. 2	Oil 3	Ind. consom. 4	Prod. goods 5	Util. tmsp. 6	Trade-services 7	Govt. services 8	Total activ. a	Commodities: Ag. exports 9	Other ag. 10	Oil 11	Ind. consom. 12	Prod. goods 13	Util. tmsp. 14	Trade-services 15	Govt. services 16	Total commod. c	Factors: Skilled 17	Unskilled 18
Current accounts																				
1 Ag. exports										7,719								7,719		
2 Other ag.											27,489							27,489		
3 Oil												779						779		
4 Ind. cons. goods													67,213					67,213		
5 Prod. goods														45,727				45,727		
6 Util. cnstr. trnsp															77,023			77,023		
7 Trade-services										5,545	7,612	1,682	12,624	30,719		67,369		125,551		
8 Govt. services																	43,081	43,081		
a Total activities										13,264	35,101	2,461	79,837	76,446	77,023	67,369	43,081	394,582		
9 Ag. exports	18	758	26	8,174	2,292	80	148	46	10,784											
10 Other ag.	177	52	176	18,246	139		1,278	416	20,837											
11 Oil			48	307	1,322	3,410	149	322	5,915											
12 Ind. cons. goods	128	1,336	2,825	15,207	636	55	3,082	933	21,425											
13 Prod. goods	1,392	1,846	1,725	4,552	23,022	21,245	8,860	9,519	73,261											
14 Util. cnstr. trnsp	152	245	626	1,355	1,443	2,943	12,125	3,315	23,303											
15 Trade-services	359	240		782	653	7,078	19,859	1,940	31,537											
16 Govt. services																				
c Total commodities	2,226	4,477	5,426	48,623	29,507	34,811	45,501	16,491	187,062											
17 Skilled	95	259	1,295	1,934	2,067	6,448	18,600	21,343	52,041											
18 Unskilled	124	197	443	7,429	5,829	23,711	32,872	5,149	75,754											
19 Ag. labor	2,559	12,670	6	214	146	27	300	98	16,020											
l Total labor	2,778	13,126	1,744	9,577	8,042	30,186	51,772	26,590	143,815											
20 Corporate capital	453	1,316	2,112	7,086	5,384	4,382	4,421		25,154										6,275	31,578
21 Urb. low educ.	1,478	423		7,204	1,070	5,585	8,491		24,251										16,537	18,188
22 Urb. med. educ.	148	269		2,493	1,076	2,224	6,044		12,254										25,249	1,802
23 Urb. high educ.	214	101		157	165	657	3,624		4,918										1,870	7,641
24 Rural non ag.	1,719	40		1,405	275	1,319	3,460		8,218										1,294	13,522
25 Small farms	1,674	1,495		1,980	437	1,287	2,737		9,610										297	1,848
26 Medium farms	1,337	2,508		363	73	289	900		5,470										519	1,175
27 Large farms	2,166	3,884		241	56	554	1,213		8,114											
h Total households	8,736	8,720		13,843	3,152	11,915	26,469		72,835											
28 Firms																				
29 Income tax																				
30 Value-added tax	263	179	31,830	3,215	1,501	845	1,680		39,513											
31 Import tariff										3	-606	88	1,477	11,062				12,024		
32 Government																				
33 Rest of world										10	2,485	5,805	3,794	51,418	3,128	7,887		74,527		
Capital accounts																				
34 Government																				
35 Total private																				
t Total	14,456	27,818	41,112	82,344	47,586	82,139	129,843	43,081	468,379	13,277	36,980	8,355	85,108	138,926	80,151	75,256	43,081	481,133	52,041	75,754

277

Table 10.2. Social accounting matrix, Ecuador, 1980 (cont.)

	Factors			Institutions																Total
	19 Ag. labor	l Total labor	20 Capital	21 Urban low ed.	22 Urban med. ed.	23 Urban high ed.	24 Rural nonag.	25 Small farms	26 Medium farms	27 Large farms	h Total hholds	28 Firms	29 Income tax	30 Indir. tax	31 Import tariff	32 Govt.	33 Rest of world	34 Govt. invest.	35 Private invest.	t
Current accounts																				
1 Ag. exports																	6,737			14,456
2 Other ag.																	329			27,818
3 Oil																	40,333			41,112
4 Ind. cons. goods																	15,131			82,344
5 Prod. goods																	1,859			47,586
6 Util. cnstr. trnsp																	5,116			82,139
7 Trade-services																	4,292			129,843
8 Govt. services																				43,081
a Total activities																	73,797			468,379
9 Ag. exports				812	433	203	159	307	110	119	2,143								350	13,277
10 Other ag.				4,570	2,404	1,153	1,007	3,736	1,153	1,075	15,098								1,045	36,980
11 Oil				529	295	165	123	195	51	49	1,407								1,033	8,355
12 Ind. cons. goods				20,413	12,282	6,323	4,895	11,584	3,639	3,253	62,389								1,294	85,108
13 Prod. goods				8,957	6,943	4,490	3,074	4,780	1,487	1,678	31,409							2,778	31,478	138,926
14 Util. cnstr. trnsp				5,358	4,190	3,019	1,708	2,405	591	925	18,196							15,868	22,784	80,151
15 Trade-services				13,101	10,692	7,006	3,770	5,947	1,555	1,647	43,718									75,256
16 Govt. services				141	129	101	37	62	19	30	519					42,562				43,081
c Total commodities				53,881	37,368	22,460	14,773	29,016	8,605	8,776	174,879					42,562		18,646	57,984	481,133
17 Skilled																				52,041
18 Unskilled																				75,754
19 Ag. labor																				16,020
l Total labor																				143,815
20 Corporate capital			25,154																	25,154
21 Urb. low educ.	968	38,821		1,041	1,151	918	6	12	4	9	3,141	2,000				2,666	33			70,912
22 Urb. med. educ.	291	35,016		986	1,099	920	5	8	3	5	3,026	2,263				2,920	22			55,501
23 Urb. high educ.	130	27,181		774	921	736	1	1		1	2,434	2,213				1,875	10			38,631
24 Rural non ag.	612	10,123					148	246	79	156	629	156				125				19,251
25 Small farms	7,652	22,468					333	554	182	349	1,418	35				437				33,968
26 Medium farms	3,417	5,562					60	102	32	63	257	18				18				11,325
27 Large farms	2,950	4,644					39	64	21	40	164	114				58				13,094
h Total households	16,020	143,815		2,801	3,171	2,574	592	987	321	623	11,069	6,799				8,099	65			242,682
28 Firms			25,154	1,561	1,788	1,819	422	560	327	497	6,974	6,373				26	2,088			40,615
29 Income tax				2,389	4,041	4,213	444	372	42	29	11,530	5,329								16,859
30 Value-added tax																				39,513
31 Import tariff																				12,024
32 Government													16,859	39,513	12,024		931			69,327
33 Rest of world						776					776	7,975				8,026				91,304
Capital accounts																				
34 Government																10,614	14,423			25,037
35 Total private				10,280	9,133	6,789	3,020	3,033	2,030	3,169	37,454	14,139						6,391		57,984
t Total	16,020	143,815	25,154	70,912	55,501	38,631	19,251	33,968	11,325	13,094	242,682	40,615	16,859	39,513	12,024	69,327	91,304	25,037	57,984	

Source: de Janvry, Sadoulet, and Fargeix, 1991.

Agriculture and trade services count 84% and 65% of their production as value added, respectively, computed as $(ti - ci)/ti$ for activity i. This is in contrast to the production goods sector, with high intermediate demand and only 38% of its production distributed in value added. Within value added, further contrast can be made between labor income and profit. In this particular SAM, profits from informal sector firms have been directly attributed to the households that operate them. This is an efficient way of keeping track of the social distribution of asset ownership and of dealing with the lack of separation between the return to labor and the return to the fixed factors that often occurs in these firms. However, this allocation blurs the concepts of factors of production. Labor income accounts for less than 5% of value added in the oil sector and more than 60% in the utilities-construction-transportation sector. Finally, tax rates, which are net of subsidies in this SAM, are significant only for the manufacturing sectors, constituting 8.3% and 9.5% of value added, and for the oil sector. In the latter case, taxes, direct government participation in oil extraction, and subsidies to the refineries are all lumped together, and government captures 89% of value added. This aggregation is acceptable only if the structure of government revenues is not the focus of the analysis.

c. *Import dependency and import tariff rates,* as measured in the columns of the commodity accounts. Imported industrial production goods represent 37% of domestic supply and are taxed at an average rate of 21%.

d. *The structure of external trade.* Imports (row 33, columns 9–16) are dominated by industrial production goods (69% of all imports) and exports (column 33, rows 1–8) by oil (55% of the value of exports). The balance of trade is roughly in equilibrium, as noted by comparing total imports in 33c to total exports in a33. The traditional agricultural exports sector only generates 9% of total exports even though 47% of its production is exported.

e. *The sources of household incomes,* in rows 21 to 27. Interestingly, the households which receive the highest share of their income from wages are the urban households with high education and the small farmers: 70% of urban household income is wage income, with almost all income received by skilled labor. Similarly, 66% of small farmer income is wage income, albeit from unskilled labor. Savings rates average 15% of income, varying from 8.9% in small farms to 15.4% in large farms.

f. *Important macroeconomic features of the economy.* The investment rate in the economy is 27%, with public investment representing 24% of all investment. The balance-of-payments deficit (row 34, column 33) amounts to 5% of GDP. Since the balance of trade is almost in equilibrium, this current deficit is mostly due to transfers abroad, as debt service and capital flight, by urban households, firms, and government. The foreign capital transfer that covers this deficit is shown as a transfer to the government account, corresponding to the institutional arrangement in Ecuador at that time. Total government expenditures (current expenditures, in t32, less savings [row 34, column 33], plus capital expenditures in c34) account for 27% of GDP. Of the government budget, 55% is spent on consumption (administration), 24% on investment, and 10% on transfers abroad (interest payment on debt). The government deficit amounts to 12% of its revenues (in 32t).

A weakness of this SAM, also common to most SAMs, is in the definition of the activities and the confusion that exists with the commodity disaggregation. Activities are intended to each stand for a representative productive agent. Firms that are aggregated under each heading should thus have the same production function, with a unique technology and a similar distribution of factor income. In agriculture, therefore, activities should correspond not to commodity aggregates, but rather to alternative production systems, which each produce a variety of commodities with a given technology. In that sense, for example, in the village SAM from which Table 10.8 described later is derived, the agricultural sector is disaggregated into rainfed and irrigated agriculture, with further disaggregation of rainfed agriculture by farm size. Similarly, within nonagricultural activities, the informal sector should probably be separated from the formal sector.

10.3. Construction of a SAM: Data Requirements

Given the degree of country specificity and the variety of objectives which construction of a SAM may have, it is impossible to define a general set of data needs with which to compile a SAM. The more disaggregated a SAM is intended to be, the more extensive are the data requirements. In all cases, the starting point should be the building of a highly aggregated SAM based on the country's national accounts statistics. Then, disaggregation of the different accounts is based on three sets of data:

a. *Activity and commodity balances,* which are usually easily derived from input-output tables.

b. *Disaggregation of value added* into income by labor categories and profits, which is usually based on employment surveys and sectoral censuses. It is, however, often difficult to properly account for informal sector activities, which are seldom represented in industrial surveys.

c. *Determining incomes and outlays of the private institutions,* and of households in particular, is the most difficult part in the construction of a SAM. On the expenditure side, consumption surveys are often available, and taxes are found in the government budget. On the income side, a multipurpose household survey is needed. If this is not available, some compromises are necessary, using data from family expenditure surveys, or from rural and urban income distribution surveys, or from labor force surveys. If the household survey contains labor force characteristics of household members, then this greatly improves the mapping of factor incomes to households. Incomes and outlays of all firms aggregated together are sometimes available in the national accounts documents. Transfers between government and private institutions are usually available from government statistics. Transfers among private institutions are rarely directly available at the level of disaggregation required and thus need to be estimated on the basis of indirect indicators. A complete balance of payments is necessary to provide information on property income flows and transfers between the domestic economy and the rest of the world. When direct information is not available, household savings may be derived as residuals.

In conclusion, the construction of a disaggregated SAM is very demanding in terms of data. And, even when the statistical material is available, the reconciliation of information from various sources and surveys requires considerable effort. Nevertheless, this cannot be avoided, as a consistent characterization of the interdependencies of the economic and social system is necessary to analyze the implications of policies.

10.4. The Measure of Agricultural Surplus

The concept of agricultural surplus has been central to the history of economic thought on development. It has been used to characterize a variety of different transfers from agriculture to the rest of the economy. Kuznets summarizes the contributions of agriculture to the economy as: (1) supplying food and raw materials, (2) providing an investible surplus of savings, (3) generating income for the rural population that will raise demand for products of other expanding sectors, and (4) relaxing the foreign exchange constraints (Kuznets, 1965). Morrisson and Thorbecke (1990) have proposed using the complete and consistent framework of the SAM to rigorously define agricultural surplus. This is done by constructing a SAM which distinguishes between agriculture and nonagriculture in all the accounts, as shown in Table 10.3. The convention for the notation of the transactions is the standard one, with the first subscript representing the sector receiving the money flow and the second subscript indicating the sector sending the money flow. Hence X_{an} is the purchase of agricultural intermediate goods by the nonagricultural sector. The subscripts a, n, g, and r refer to agriculture, nonagriculture, government, and rest of the world, respectively. An example of such an aggregation for the Ecuadorian matrix is provided as Table 10.4. Complementary information on investment by sectors has been used in order to split the investment account.

The equilibrium between total income and total expenditures of each account lead to 13 identities, which can be written:

$$X_{aa} + X_{an} + C_{aa} + C_{an} + C_{ag} + I_{aa} + E_{ar} = X_{aa} + X_{na} + VL_{aa} + VL_{na} + VK_{aa} + VK_{na} + TI_{ga} + X_{ra}$$

for the first account, and similarly for the other accounts. By adding the identities corresponding to the accounts 1, 3, 5, 7, 9, 10, and 12 and rearranging the terms, one obtains the following expression:

$$\underbrace{[(C_{an} + C_{ag} + X_{an} + VL_{an} + VK_{an}) - (C_{na} + X_{na} + VL_{na} + VK_{na})]}_{A_d} + \underbrace{[(L_{an} + K_{an}) - (L_{na} + K_{na})]}_{B_d}$$

$$-I_{na} = \underbrace{\frac{(TR_{na} - TR_{an})}{C_d}} + \underbrace{\frac{(S_{na} - S_{an})}{D_d}} + \underbrace{\frac{[(TD_{ga} + TI_{ga}) - (TR_{ag} + S_{ag})]}{E_d}},$$

or, $A_d + B_d - I_{na} = C_d + D_d + E_d$.

A_d represents the net outflow of commodities and primary factors from agriculture to the rest of the economy. The final consumption element $(C_{an} + C_{ag} - C_{na})$ is normally expected to be negative, since the rural households consume more nonagricultural goods than the urban households consume agricultural goods. The net flow of intermediate goods is usually positive. The flows of primary factors are generally small. Usually however, the final goods flow dominates the other elements, thus A_d is negative. In the Ecuadorian case, $A_d = -32,052$ million sucres.

B_d represents the net outflow of labor and capital services. Labor services and investment of rural households into nonagricultural activities are usually large compared with urban involvement into agriculture. Hence, the net outflow of services is usually positive, and in the Ecuadorian case it is equal to 40,733 million sucres.

Table 10.3. Social accounting matrix distinguishing between agriculture and nonagriculture

	Expenditures													
	Activities/ commodities		Factors				Institutions			Capital account		Rest of world		
			Labor		Capital		Households/ firms		Govern- ment					
Incomes	A	N	A	N	A	N	A	N		A	N	A	N	Total
Activities/commodities														
A	X_{aa}	X_{an}					C_{aa}	C_{an}	C_{ag}	I_{aa}		X_{ar}		Y_1
N	X_{na}	X_{nn}					C_{na}	C_{nn}	C_{ng}	I_{na}	I_{nn}		X_{nr}	Y_2
Factors														
Labor														
A	VL_{aa}	VL_{an}												Y_3
N	VL_{na}	VL_{nn}												Y_4
Capital														
A	VK_{aa}	VK_{an}												Y_5
N	VK_{na}	VK_{nn}												Y_6
Institutions														
Households/firms														
A			L_{aa}	L_{an}	K_{aa}	K_{an}	TR_{aa}	TR_{an}	TR_{ag}			TR_{ar}		Y_7
N			L_{na}	L_{nn}	K_{na}	K_{nn}	TR_{na}	TR_{nn}	TR_{ng}				TR_{nr}	Y_8
Government	TI_{ga}	TI_{gn}				K_{gn}	TD_{ga}	TD_{gn}	TR_{gg}					Y_9
Capital account														
A							S_{aa}	S_{an}	S_{ag}			S_{ar}		Y_{10}
N							S_{na}	S_{nn}	S_{ng}				S_{rn}	Y_{11}
Rest of world														
A	X_{ra}						TR_{ra}		TR_{rg}	I_{ra}				Y_{12}
N		X_{rn}				K_{rn}		TR_{rn}			I_{rn}			Y_{13}
Total	Y_1	Y_2	Y_3	Y_4	Y_5	Y_6	Y_7	Y_8	Y_9	Y_{10}	Y_{11}	Y_{12}	Y_{13}	

Source: Morrisson and Thorbecke, 1990.

Table 10.4. Social accounting matrix distinguishing between agriculture and nonagriculture, Ecuador, 1980

	Activities		Commodities		Labor		Capital		Households		Firms		Govt	Capital account		Rest of world		Total
	Ag.	Nonag.	Ag.	Nonag.	Ag.	Nonag.	Ag.	Nonag.	Rural	Urban	Ag.	Nonag.		Ag.	Nonag.	Ag.	Nonag.	
Activities																		
Agriculture			35,208													7,066		42,274
Nonagriculture			13,157	346,217													66,731	426,105
Commodities																		
Agriculture	776	30,845							7,666	9,575				1,395				50,257
Nonagriculture	5,927	149,514							53,504	104,134			42,562	6,038	69,197			430,876
Labor																		
Agriculture	15,229	791																16,020
Nonagriculture	675	127,120																127,795
Capital																		
Agriculture	19,225																	19,225
Nonagriculture		78,764																78,764
Households																		
Rural					14,631	28,166	15,146	16,589	2,468				638					77,638
Urban					1,389	99,629	2,633	38,790	55	8,546		6,476	7,461				65	165,044
Firms																		
Agriculture							1,446											1,446
Nonagriculture								23,385	1,806	5,168			26				2,088	32,473
Government	442	39,071	−603	12,627					887	10,643		5,329	68,396				931	137,723
Capital account																		
Agriculture									8,168		1,446	1,329	1,061					12,004
Nonagriculture									3,084	26,202		11,364	9,553				18,994	69,197
Rest of world																		
Agriculture			2,495											4,571				7,066
Nonagriculture				72,032						776		7,975	8,026					88,809
Total	42,274	426,105	50,257	430,876	16,020	127,795	19,225	78,764	77,638	165,044	1,446	32,473	137,723	12,004	69,197	7,066	88,809	

Source: Calculated on the basis of data in Table 10.2.
Note: Figures are in million sucres.

I_{na} is the purchase of nonagricultural commodities for investment in agriculture. It is equal to 6,038 million sucres in the Ecuadorian SAM.

C_d represents the net transfers among households and firms. Its sign depends on whether there are more remittances from rural to urban areas or vice versa. These numbers are usually small. A relatively important component in the Ecuadorian SAM seems to be the payment by rural households of fees and contributions to insurance and other nonagricultural firms, which gives C_d equal to −1,861 million sucres.

D_d represents net savings from agriculture to nonagriculture and is equal to 1,755 million sucres in the Ecuadorian SAM.

E_d is the net monetary transfer of agriculture to the government. It includes taxes paid by agriculture, transfer of the government to rural households, and savings of the government for investment in agriculture. The net of the first two elements is usually negative, representing a tax on agriculture. The last element, government savings for investment in agriculture, gives the distribution of the use of tax revenues in public goods. However, the information is not often readily available, and it was missing in the Ecuadorian SAM. Rather than completely ignoring government's investment in rural areas, we have attributed 10% of capital expenditure to it. On the basis of this assumption, $E_d = -973$ million sucres. This indicates a net transfer from the rest of the economy to agriculture through the government. This result can be justified in the case of Ecuador, where oil is a large source of government revenue.

Together, A_d, B_d, and $-I_{na}$ represent net physical outflows of real commodities and services from agriculture to nonagriculture. It is equal to 2,643 million sucres in Ecuador. The relationship established above shows that it is exactly compensated by a net financial inflow into agriculture, in the form of transfers and savings from nonagriculture to agriculture. One last element of transfer to the agricultural sector is the goods which are provided freely by the government to the rural households (F_d). However, these are not included in the SAM. The domestic agricultural surplus can be defined as:

$$SU_d = A_d + B_d - I_{na} - F_d.$$

Similarly, one can define a foreign agricultural surplus by:

$$SU_f = A_f + B_f - I_{ra},$$

derived from rewriting the account 12 equilibrium as follows:

$$\underbrace{[X_{ar} - (TR_{ra} + X_{ra})]}_{A_f} - \underbrace{K_{ra}}_{B_f} - I_{ra} = \underbrace{-TR_{ar}}_{C_f} - \underbrace{S_{ar}}_{D_f}.$$

In the Ecuadorian case, foreign agricultural surplus is equal to 4,571 million sucres.

A merit of this approach is that it provides a consistent and complete accounting of transactions between agriculture and nonagriculture. What is still missing, however, is an accounting of transfers through price distortions. This cannot be obtained by accounting alone, since it requires the notion of equilibrium prices. This could be developed as an application of the general equilibrium models that we will present in Chapter 12.

10.5. The Input-Output Model

10.5.1 Equations

The input-output table is the subset of a SAM made of the activity and commodity accounts only. To simplify the exposition of the model, commodities and activities have been aggregated. The general structure of such accounts can be seen in Table 10.5. For example, X_{21} is the quantity and $p_2 X_{21}$ is the value of sector 2's output sold to sector 1 to be used as an intermediate input. The excess of each sector's total output over total intermediate sales is marked as final goods, which include net exports, investment, and private and public consumption. The accounts also show the amounts that sectors pay for primary factors of production and various taxes.

Table 10.5. The input-output model

		Sectors (j)			Final demand	Total demand
		1	$\cdots$	n		
Sectors (i)	1	$p_1 X_{11}$	$\cdots$	$p_1 X_{1n}$	$p_1 F_1$	$p_1 X_1$
	$\vdots$	$\vdots$		$\vdots$	$\vdots$	$\vdots$
	n	$p_n X_{n1}$	$\cdots$	$p_n X_{nn}$	$p_n F_n$	$p_n X_n$
Value added						
Labor (k)	1	$w_1 L_{11}$		$w_1 L_{1n}$		
	$\vdots$	$\vdots$		$\vdots$		
	s	$w_s L_{s1}$		$w_s L_{sn}$		
Other		Π_1		Π_n		
Taxes		T_1		T_n		
Total supply		$p_1 X_1$		$p_n X_n$		

p_i Unit price of sector i's output, $i = 1, \ldots n$.
X_{ij} Output of sector i sold to sector j as intermediate input, $i, j = 1, \ldots n$.
F_i Final demand for sector i's output, $i = 1, \ldots n$.
X_i Total supply of sector i, $i = 1, \ldots n$.
w_k Unit price of labor $k, k = 1, \ldots s$.
L_{kj} Amount of labor k used in sector $j, k = 1, \ldots s; j = 1, \ldots n$.
Π_j Profit in sector $j, j = 1, \ldots n$.
T_j Indirect taxes, including tariffs, paid by sector $j, j = 1, \ldots n$.

Input-output tables are often used for assessing the impact of a change in the final demand of a given sector on all sectors of the economy. The technique used for this purpose is attributed to Vassily Leontief and is known as the Leontief model. The basic idea of the model is quite simple. The amount of sector i's output required for the production of sector j's output X_{ij} is assumed to be proportional to sector j's output X_j. Therefore, if a_{ij} is such an input-output coefficient, then:

(1) $X_{ij} = a_{ij}X_j, \quad i, j = 1, \ldots, n.$

The equilibrium between total supply and total demand for each sector is written:

(2) $X_i = \sum_{j=1}^{n} X_{ij} + F_i, \quad i = 1, \ldots, n$, where X_{ij} is intermediate and F_i final demand.

Substituting equation (1) into equation (2) yields:

(3) $X_i = \sum_{j=1}^{n} a_{ij}X_j + F_i, \quad i = 1, \ldots, n.$

This relationship between final demand and production also holds in changes:

(4) $\Delta X_i = \sum_{j=1}^{n} a_{ij}\Delta X_j + \Delta F_i, \quad i = 1, \ldots, n,$

where ΔF_i and ΔX_i represent changes in final demand and output of sector i, respectively. Since (3) and (4) are formally identical, we pursue the discussion using the symbols F and X for level or change indifferently.

Note that if the final demand in a given sector i increases by, say, F_i, initially production increases by the same amount, $X_i^1 = F_i$. However, this increase in production raises the intermediate demand for all sectors, including i itself, by $X_j^2 = \sum a_{ij}X_i^1$. To produce these intermediate inputs, however, more intermediate inputs are needed, and there is a third round of effects $X_j^3 = \sum a_{ji}X_i^2$. This obviously leads to more and more rounds of effects. Thus, sectoral outputs keep rising as a result of the higher intermediate-goods demand each round of effects generates. But, in each round output increases become smaller and smaller such that their total always has a limit. To calculate this limit, it is easier to write equation (3) in matrix form (where $\Rightarrow$ reads "which gives"),

(5) $X = AX + F \Rightarrow (I - A)X = F \Rightarrow X = (I - A)^{-1}F.$

In this equation, X is the vector of outputs, X_i, $i = 1, \ldots, n$; F is the vector of final demands, F_i, $i = 1, \ldots, n$; A is the matrix of a_{ij}'s, i, $j = 1, \ldots, n$; and I is the unit matrix, which has ones on its diagonal and zeros everywhere else. $(I - A)^{-1}$ is a multiplier which can be used to calculate overall changes in sectoral outputs which result from changes in final demand.

Once the change in X is known, changes in primary-input requirements can be similarly calculated. Assume that the amount of labor category k needed for the production of one unit of product j, b_{kj}, is a constant. Therefore, the total amount of labor k required is:

(6) $L_k = \sum_{j=1}^{n} b_{kj}X_j, \quad k = 1, \ldots, s,$

or, in matrix form,

(7) $L = BX,$

where L is the vector of labor requirements, L_k, $k = 1, ..., s$; and B is the matrix of b_{kj}'s, $k = 1, ..., s; j = 1, ..., n$.

Any input-output model has a dual price system, which can be viewed as a set of cost prices in a linear framework. These output prices are calculated by taking the prices of factors and the tax rates as given. Assume that the returns to the fixed factors are also proportional to supply X, that is, $\Pi_j = r_j X_j$, and that indirect taxes are proportional to the market value of the supply, that is, $T_j = t_j p_j X_j$. The cost-price equations are derived by first noting that equality of receipts and payments in each sector implies:

$$(8) \quad p_j X_j = \sum_{i=1}^{n} p_i X_{ij} + \sum_{k=1}^{s} w_k L_{kj} + \Pi_j + T_j, \quad j = 1, ..., n.$$

Dividing both sides of equation (8) by X_j, we have

$$(9) \quad p_j = \sum_{i=1}^{n} p_i a_{ij} + \sum_{k=1}^{s} w_k b_{kj} + r_j + p_j t_j, \quad j = 1, ..., n.$$

Equation (9) can be written in matrix form as:

$$(10) \quad p = A'p + B'w + r + \check{t}p \implies p = (I - \check{t} - A')^{-1}(B'w + r),$$

where p, w, and r represent vectors of output, labor, and fixed-factor prices, respectively, and $\check{t}$ is a matrix with elements t_j, $j = 1, ..., n$, on its diagonal. The prime ($'$) after A and B represents the transpose of these matrices.

Note that these prices are independent of the level of production in the economy. For this reason, Leontief models belong to a genre of general equilibrium models known as fixed-price. In these models, supply is infinitely elastic at the cost price and output is demand-determined.

To calculate the coefficients of a Leontief model by means of financial flows among sectors, the unit of each output or input is chosen such that its price is equal to one. In that case, quantities can be replaced by financial values when calculating a_{ij}'s and b_{ik}'s.

10.5.2 Interpretation and Extension

The crucial assumption in input-output analysis is that sectoral production is completely demand-driven. This assumes that there is excess production capacity in all sectors, and that increasing demand can always be met by higher output with no price increase. Since this assumption is likely to be unrealistic, input-output models are more useful as guidelines to potential induced linkage effects, and as indicators of likely supply bottlenecks that may occur in a growing economy, than as predictive models.

The underlying production function assumes constant return to scale and no substitution among the different inputs. To the extent that prices remain constant, this is acceptable, as substitution among factors is expected to be induced by relative price movements. But, when prices are not constant, this constitutes a severe limitation of fixed (that is, predetermined) price models.

Variants of the basic framework are easily introduced in input-output models:

a. Intermediate inputs can be disaggregated into domestic and imported goods. The multipliers can thus represent more closely the multiplier effect on the domestic economy.

b. When the input-output model is used to look at the effect of small changes in the final-demand vector, a matrix of marginal rather than average coefficients can be used.

c. Input-output multipliers have been used to measure Hirschman's (1977) concept of linkages. Backward linkages are measured by the multipliers described above. Forward linkages are computed in a similar fashion, using a matrix of supply coefficients obtained by dividing the row of intermediate inputs supply by the total supply of a sector. But total linkages cannot be defined as the sum of the two, since they rely on inconsistent theories. Alternatively, the total contribution of a sector to the economy has been measured with the extraction method (Cella, 1984). This method compares the observed total output with the output that would be obtained with the same vector of final demand but a truncated input-output matrix in which, except for the diagonal element, the row and the column of the sector to be isolated would be filled with zeros. The difference between these two output levels measures the total linkage effect of each sector.

d. Alternative models of price formation can be used, provided that they do not depend on the level of supply and demand. For example, enterprises in some industries, especially oligopolistic ones, are believed to use a procedure called markup pricing for determining output prices. The procedure is as follows. First, the variable cost of production, consisting of labor and material expenses, is calculated and a markup then is added to provide for a return to fixed capital and, perhaps, some monopoly profits. Thus, the return to capital depends on all other variable costs rather than being a fixed rate per unit of output, as assumed in the derivation of equation (10). Under markup pricing, we have:

$$(11) \quad p = (I + \breve{r})(A'p + B'w) + \breve{t}p \ \Rightarrow \ p = [I - \breve{t} - (I + \breve{r})A']^{-1}(I + \breve{r})B'w,$$

where r_i is the markup rate in sector i. This methodology was used by Augusztinovics (1989) to represent the Hungarian price system.

10.6. SAM Multipliers

Extension of the input-output model to a SAM framework is performed by partitioning the accounts into endogenous and exogenous accounts and assuming that the column coefficients of the endogenous accounts are all constant. An important issue then is to determine which accounts can be set exogenous and which can be set endogenous. Endogenous accounts are those for which changes in the level of expenditure directly follow any change in income, while exogenous accounts are those for which we assume that the expenditures are set independently of income. Standard practice is to pick, for the exogenous accounts, one or more among the government, capital, and rest of the world accounts, justifying the choice on the basis of macroeconomic theory and the objectives of the study.

Consider the following partitioning of the SAM matrix:

	Endogenous accounts (*n*)	Sum of exogenous accounts (1)	Total
Endogenous accounts (*n*)	*MX*	*F*	*X*
Exogenous accounts (*m*)	*BX*	*L*	
Total	*X*		

X is the vector of total income or expenditure of the endogenous accounts, *F* the vector sum of the expenditures of the exogenous accounts, *L* the column vector of the income of the exogenous accounts, *M* the square matrix (*n* × *n*) of coefficients of the endogenous accounts, and *B* the rectangular matrix (*m* × *n*) of the coefficients with exogenous accounts as rows and endogenous accounts as columns. If Δ represents the operator "change," one may define:

The matrix of multipliers	$(I - M)^{-1}$
The vector of shocks	ΔF
The vector of impacts	$\Delta X = (I - M)^{-1} \Delta F$
The leakages	$\Delta L = B\, \Delta X.$

A shock, or "injection", is given by a change in elements of the exogenous accounts. The model solves for the equilibrium level of all the endogenous accounts. Multipliers, like their input-output analogues, are completely demand-driven. The coefficients in the rows of the exogenous accounts provide the "leakages." These leakages are, for example, the induced demand for imports, the induced government revenues, and the induced savings.

If a single account is taken as exogenous, the fact that the endogenous accounts must all balance at a new equilibrium guarantees that the exogenous account will also balance, since the SAM as a whole must balance. If two or more accounts are set exogenously, then only their sum must balance, given a solution for the endogenous accounts. Each choice of which accounts are endogenous defines a different macro "closure" to the SAM model. Of course, the computed multipliers will be sensitive to the choice of partition, and the resulting choice of model must be justified in terms of both theory and empirical realism for the particular problem under study.

The range of shocks that can be studied with a SAM model is directly derived from the choice of the exogenous accounts. With an exogenous rest of the world account, simulations of changes in exports, or in transfers to different households, to the government (if endogenous), or to the savings account (if endogenous) can be performed. With an exogenous capital account, shocks are mainly changes in investment. With an exogenous government account, changes in demand for administrative services, and in transfers to value added or households can be simulated. In all cases, the multiplier model gives the impact on the structure of production, labor income, incomes of the various socioeconomic households, government revenues, savings, and imports.

Table 10.6 lists some columns of the matrix of multipliers computed from the SAM described above, defining government, capital, and rest of the world accounts as exogenous. Interpretation of the first column indicates that an increase in agricultural exports of one unit induces an increase of production of 1.05 units in this sector, 0.78 units in the trade service sector, and 2.98 units in the whole economy. It also generates 1.89 units of household income, almost equally shared by rural and urban households. By contrast, an increase of one unit in oil exports only generates 1.37 units in domestic production and 0.25 in household incomes. Column 16 shows that an increase in the government demand for administrative services induces large production linkages in the other sectors, totaling 2.94 units in the whole economy, and creating revenues mostly for the urban households. The last two columns show the impact of injections

Table 10.6. Input-output and social accounting matrix multipliers, Ecuador, 1980
(selected columns)

	SAM multipliers					Input-output multipliers			
	Ag. exports	Oil	Production goods	Govt services	Urban high ed.	Small farms	Ag. exports	Oil	Production goods	Govt. services
	1	3	5	16	23	25	1	3	5	16
1 Ag. exports	1.05	.01	.06	.04	.04	.06	1.00	.00	.04	.01
2 Other ag.	.20	.02	.11	.16	.14	.27	.00	.00	.01	.01
3 Oil	.00	1.00	.00	.00	.00	.00	.00	1.00	.00	.00
4 Cons. goods	.52	.07	.30	.43	.41	.67	.01	.00	.02	.03
5 Prod. goods	.20	.05	1.29	.24	.15	.20	.04	.03	1.20	.10
6 Util. cnstr. transp.	.24	.08	.19	.29	.23	.27	.02	.05	.06	.09
7 Trade, services	.78	.14	.64	.77	.69	.90	.07	.05	.23	.15
8 Govt. services	.00	.00	.00	1.00	.00	.00	.00	.00	.00	1.00
9 Ag. exports	.08	.01	.10	.07	.06	.10	.00	.00	.06	.01
10 Other ag.	.27	.03	.15	.22	.19	.36	.00	.00	.01	.02
11 Oil	.04	.01	.05	.04	.03	.03	.01	.01	.04	.01
12 Cons. goods	.65	.08	.38	.55	.52	.85	.01	.00	.03	.03
13 Prod. goods	.61	.16	.89	.72	.46	.60	.13	.10	.62	.31
14 Util. cnstr. transp	.25	.08	.20	.30	.24	.28	.02	.05	.06	.10
15 Trade, services	.50	.09	.34	.50	.49	.58	.04	.03	.06	.08
16 Govt. services	.00	.00	.00	1.00	.00	.00	.00	.00	.00	1.00
17 Skilled	.16	.06	.17	.65	.14	.18				
18 Unskilled	.35	.08	.40	.47	.30	.39				
19 Ag. labor	.28	.01	.07	.09	.07	.14				
20 Corporate capital	.15	.07	.21	.11	.10	.14				
21 Urb. low educ.	.43	.07	.34	.43	.30	.37				
22 Urb. med. educ.	.24	.06	.26	.42	.22	.26				
23 Urb. high educ.	.15	.05	.15	.39	1.14	.15				
24 Rural non ag.	.22	.02	.09	.12	.08	.11				
25 Small farms	.39	.03	.16	.20	.14	1.23				
26 Medium farms	.20	.01	.05	.06	.05	.08				
27 Large farms	.26	.01	.06	.07	.06	.10				
28 Firms	.24	.10	.29	.20	.20	.23				
Total activities	2.98	1.37	2.61	2.94	1.66	2.37	1.15	1.14	1.56	1.39
Total commodities	2.40	.47	2.12	3.40	1.99	2.81	.22	.19	.87	1.56
Total labor	.79	.16	.65	1.21	.51	.71	.24	.09	.33	.74
Total household income	1.89	.25	1.11	1.69	1.97	2.30	.63	.02	16	.06

Source: Calculated on the basis of data in Table 10.2.

to households, where transfers could come either from the government or from the rest of the world.

Comparison of these multipliers with the input-output or production multipliers derived from the Leontief model (Table 10.6) illustrates an important contribution of the SAM approach. First, SAM multipliers are much larger than their corresponding input-output multipliers. Because value added is a leakage, only intermediate demand serves as multiplier in the input-output analysis. In contrast, value added and incomes generate demand linkages in the SAM approach. Second, agriculture usually has very low production multipliers. This has served as a fundamental argument against basing a development strategy on agriculture. It was thought that, with scarce resources, investment should be concentrated on selected industrial sectors with high multipliers (Hirschman, 1977). However, when one considers the linkage effects created by agricultural incomes, as included in the SAM multipliers, the agricultural sectors do not fare any worse than the industrial sectors and, furthermore, induce a relatively more equitable distribution of growth.

Table 10.7 reports simulations of shocks with injection performed in more than one account. In the first experiment, exports are increased by 10,000 million sucres, with a sectoral allocation of this increase proportional to original exports. In the second experiment, a support scheme to the agricultural export sector is implemented as a subsidy to profit, with distribution to the different recipients of this profit in proportion to original profits received. Compared with the impact of an increase in the exports of that sector (column 1 of the multipliers matrix), this support scheme induces less production growth but more income to households, in particular to rural households. The choice of an export promotion policy or a financial support thus depends on whether the principal objective is growth or income. The last experiment shows that a redistribution scheme among households induces growth, particularly of the agricultural sectors. It, however, reduces savings and government revenue, due to tax income, and increases imports. This demonstrates the existence of potential trade-offs from redistribution.

10.7. Applications and Extensions of the SAM Multiplier Analysis

A major use of multiplier models in the SAM framework has been for the analysis of income distribution policy (see surveys by Thorbecke, 1985, Hayden and Round, 1982, and Khan and Thorbecke, 1988, on technology choice and Thorbecke and Berrian, 1992, on budget policy). Most of these studies are applied to national economies. Regional SAMs, however, can illustrate some interesting relationships among entities in an heterogenous economy. Using a regional SAM for the south of Italy, with two "rest of the world" accounts representing the rest of Italy and foreign countries, respectively, D'Antonio, Colaizzo, and Leonello (1988) have shown that the leakages out of the south to the north are so high that any transfer from the north to the south, in fact, benefits the north as it comes back amplified into its economy under the form of demand for its production. Hazell, Ramasamy, and Rajagopalan (1991) used a regional SAM for North Arcot in India to measure the impact of agricultural growth on the local nonfarm economy. SAMs have recently been applied to village economies. Adelman, Taylor, and Vogel (1988) have used a SAM to study the role of remittance incomes in sustaining a Mexican village economy and shaping its income distribution. Subramanian and Sadoulet (1990) have examined the transmission of production fluctuations and technical change in an Indian village economy.

Table 10.7. Policy simulations with SAM multipliers, Ecuador, 1980

	1980 value	Experiment 1 10,000 increase of exports			Experiment 2 10,000 transfer to ag. exports value-added			Experiment 3 10,000 redistribution from rich to poor		
		Shock	Change (value)	(%)	Shock	Change (value)	(%)	Shock	Change (value)	(%)
1 Ag. exports	14,456	913	1,283	8.9		484	3.4		113	0.8
2 Other ag.	27,818	45	1,334	4.8		2,130	7.7		589	2.1
3 Oil	41,112	5,465	5,489	13.4		28	0.1		5	0.0
4 Cons. goods	82,344	2,050	4,771	5.8		5,527	6.7		1,358	1.6
5 Prod. goods	47,586	252	1,445	3.0		1,731	3.6		238	0.5
6 Util. cnstr. trnsp.	82,139	693	2,215	2.7		2,407	2.9		241	0.3
7 Trade, services	129,843	582	5,002	3.9		7,724	5.9		1,109	0.9
8 Govt. services	43,081		19	0.0		43	0.1		−2	0.0
9 Ag. exports	13,277		636	4.8		833	6.3		195	1.5
10 Other ag.	36,980		1,734	4.7		2,865	7.7		793	2.1
11 Oil	8,355		249	3.0		305	3.6		54	0.6
12 Cons. goods	85,108		3,446	4.0		6,998	8.2		1,720	2.0
13 Product. goods	138,926		3,626	2.6		5,258	3.8		723	0.5
14 Util. cnstr. trnsp.	80,151		1,583	2.0		2,505	3.1		251	0.3
15 Trade, services	75,255		2,720	3.6		5,053	6.7		490	0.7
16 Govt. services	43,081		19	0.0		43	0.1		−2	0.0
17 Skilled	52,041		1,268	2.4		1,545	3.0		225	0.4
18 Unskilled	75,754		2,595	3.4		3,385	4.5		507	0.7
19 Ag. labor	16,020		865	5.4		1,094	6.8		295	1.8
20 Corpor. capital	25,154		1,248	5.0	493	1,673	6.7		226	0.9
21 Urb. low educ.	70,912		2,553	3.6	1,608	4,841	6.8	5,235	5,628	7.9
22 Urb. med. educ.	55,501		1,732	3.1	161	2,447	4.4	−5,176	−4,962	−8.9
23 Urb. high educ.	38,631		1,053	2.7	233	1,608	4.2	−3,603	−3,520	−9.1
24 Rural non ag.	19,251		789	4.1	1,871	2,830	14.7	1,421	1,592	8.3
25 Small farms	33,968		1,462	4.3	1,822	3,737	11.0	2,508	2,915	8.6
26 Medium farms	11,325		572	5.1	1,455	2,148	19.0	836	1,003	8.9
27 Large farms	13,094		680	5.2	2,357	3,137	24.0	−1,221	−1,033	−7.9
28 Firms	40,615		1,771	4.4		2,656	6.5		115	0.3
Ag. production	42,274	957	2,616	6.2		2,615	6.2		703	1.7
Nonag. production	426,105	9,043	18,940	4.4		17,459	4.1		2,949	0.7
Urban income	165,044		5,338	3.2	2,002	8,896	5.4	−3,544	−2,855	−1.7
Rural income	77,638		3,504	4.5	7,505	11,853	15.3	3,544	4,477	5.8
Govt. revenues	68,396	4,351	5,521	8.1	165	1,922	2.8	−533	−308	−0.5
Savings	51,593		1,978	3.8	1,588	4,234	8.2	−425	−140	−0.3
Imports	83,279		2,501	3.0	5	3,844	4.6	−72	448	0.5

Source: Calculated on the basis of data in Table 10.2.
Note: Figures are in million sucres, unless otherwise indicated.

Most of the variants and developments of the Leontief model have been or could be applied to the SAM-based linear model. In particular, complete fix-price models can be developed within a SAM. Demand models can be improved by using marginal propensities to consume, or even full demand systems, like the Linear Expenditure System or the Almost Ideal Demand System, both seen in Chapter 2.

Analysis of the process underlying the multiplier effects captured in the SAM multiplier matrix has led to several contributions. Based on the partition of the endogenous section of the SAM into three categories of accounts—activities/commodities, factors, and institutions (mainly households)—the matrix of multipliers can be decomposed into four components: initial injection, transfer effects, open-loop effects, and closed-loop effects. Transfer effects capture the direct effects resulting from interactions within each category of accounts, for example, the intersectoral input-output elements or the transfers among institutions. Open-loop effects capture the interactions among and between the three endogenous categories of accounts, for example, from production activities on factor income, from factor income on household revenues, or from household revenues on production. Closed-loop effects show the full circular effects of an income injection traveling through the system back to its point of origin, for example, from production activities, to factors, to institutions, and then back to activities in the form of consumption demand. Two versions of this decomposition have been used: the original multiplicative decomposition by Pyatt and Round (1989), and an additive rearrangement by Defourny and Thorbecke (1984).

In the structural path analysis of Defourny and Thorbecke, it is each element of the SAM multiplier which is decomposed into direct, total, and global influences. This method shows how influence is diffused from a given pole, through which specific paths it is transmitted, and the extent to which it is amplified by circuits adjacent to these paths. In breaking the multiplier into the different paths, this decomposition can help identify critical links in the transmission of influence. Accordingly, policymakers may want to concentrate their actions in order to enhance the positive effects of interdependence.

Recall that all traditional SAM models are based on the key assumption that production activities are endogenous and demand-driven, reflecting the assumed existence of excess capacity throughout the economy. This is clearly unrealistic for some sectors, agriculture in particular, at least in the short or medium run. Conceding that agriculture is supply-constrained instead requires a modification of the multipliers (Subramanian and Sadoulet, 1990). The agricultural sector cannot indeed be simply shifted to the group of exogenous accounts since, despite being exogenous, it needs to balance. Thus endogenously determined demand for the agricultural sectors must be met by a change in imports or exports. Under these conditions, the village economy analyzed by Subramanian and Sadoulet exhibits much smaller internal multiplier effects arising from any income transfer from outside the village. This can be seen by comparing columns 1 and 2 in Table 10.8. This model can also be used to analyze the impact of any exogenous change in the agricultural sector. Comparison of columns 3 and 4 shows that an irrigation program has a higher multiplier effect on the economy than an annual transfer of comparable value. Simulation of the effects on the village economy of a fall in agricultural output of 10%, shown in columns 4 and 5, reveals that changes in income levels and distribution depend strongly on how factor and intermediate use in agriculture respond to fluctuations in output. Weather fluctuations that affect the crops early in the production cycle will, in fact, result in similar relative declines in incomes for the landless and the farm operators. In contrast, the impact of weather fluctuations that come late in the cropping season, after most of the labor for intermediate work has been used and paid for, falls disproportionately on farmers' profits.

Haggblade and Hazell have developed a family of two-sector, fix-price models and endogenous-price models to measure the farm-nonfarm linkages, usually in the context of regional economies (Haggblade and Hazell, 1989; Haggblade, Hazell, and Brown, 1989; and Haggblade, Hammer, and Hazell, 1991). Fix-price models classify economic activities as tradable or

Table 10.8. Transmission of influence in a village: SAM approach with supply-constrained agriculture

	Experiments				
	1 (Rs)	2 (Rs)	3 (Rs)	4 (%)	5 (%)
Activity outputs					
Rainfed agriculture	1,744	0	−15,248	−10.0	−10.0
Irrigated agriculture	877	0	31,706	−10.0	−10.0
Livestock	1,088	690	1,210	−6.7	−3.5
Agricultural services	93	46	319	−7.8	−5.7
Village production	300	244	283	−6.2	−7.5
Trade	1,953	1,599	1,767	−5.0	−6.5
Factor incomes					
Hired male	271	153	914	−3.0	−2.0
Hired female	158	0	1,199	−7.9	−3.6
Farm servants	121	45	671	−4.1	−1.4
Household income					
Landless	461	240	1,213	−5.2	−3.9
Small farmers	333	120	562	−6.7	−6.6
Medium farmers	576	231	855	−5.6	−6.8
Large farmers	12,156	10,781	8,896	−7.6	−11.7

Source: Subramanian and Sadoulet, 1990.
Note: Column 1: transfer of Rs 10,000 to large farmers, agriculture endogenous.
        Column 2: transfer of Rs 10,000 to large farmers, agriculture exogenous.
        Column 3: irrigation, with benefits only to large farmers.
        Column 4: 10% shock on agriculture with preharvest costs declining proportionately.
        Column 5: 10% shock on agriculture with full preharvest costs committed.

nontradable. In rural regions of developing countries, grains and industrial crops are usually considered tradables, while perishable agricultural commodities and services are nontradables. Both tradable and nontradable outputs have constant prices. This is based on the assumption of an infinitely elastic supply of nontradables. The level of production of tradable products is either demand-constrained (the usual input-output or SAM multiplier model) or supply-constrained (the semi-input-output model). Their empirical results show that:

a. The SAM multiplier model produces unrealistically large multipliers, between 3 and 6.

b. Semi-input-output multipliers differ substantially across regions, from values of 1.3–1.5 in African rural regions, to 1.7–1.8 in Asian cases, and 2.2 in an analysis of Oklahoma. This is related to the increasing input intensity and consumption diversification as income increases.

c. Consumption linkages account for 75% to 90% of the total multiplier in Africa, and 50% to 60% in Asia.

d. Allowing for increasing costs of production in nontradables and for a not perfectly elastic labor supply, price-endogenous models give much lower multipliers. The magnitude of the dampening of the regional multipliers obviously depends on the rigidities of the labor market and of the nontradable supply. In the cases they study, the price-endogenous multipliers are in the range of 75% to 90% of the semi-input-output multipliers.

In these different studies, SAM models have been stretched to accommodate some of the more limiting assumptions made in the standard model. However, this framework remains fundamentally applicable in situations characteristic of the Keynesian environment of a fix-price model, with excess production capacity in most sectors and absence of substitution. This framework cannot reflect the workings of a market economy in which price adjustments play an important role and where there are important substitution possibilities in both production and demand. It thus cannot be used at all to study shocks that encompass important structural changes based on major relative price readjustments, like real exchange rate movements, wage repression, or terms-of-trade effects, all of which are characteristic of the recent major adjustments occurring in developing countries. To capture such features, a nonlinear model with joint determination of prices and quantities must be used. This type of model will be developed in Chapter 12.

Exercise 10
Input-Output and Social Accounting Matrix Multipliers in Morocco

We use, in this exercise (file 10SAM), a social accounting matrix (SAM) for Morocco in 1980 given in Table 10E.1. It includes 26 accounts: 11 productive sectors, 5 factors of production (3 labor categories and 2 capital accounts), 6 households, an account for all firms, and accounts for the government, the rest of the world, and capital, which includes savings and investment. For the following multiplier analysis, the first 23 accounts (production sectors, factors, households, and firms) are considered endogenous, while government, rest of the world, and capital accounts are held exogenous. Note that, to reduce the size of the matrix, activities and commodities have been combined; hence, the sum total is total supply, which includes domestic production and imports, while livestock has been aggregated with other agricultural production and trade with services.

1. Structure of the Economy

Give a rapid description of the main characteristics of the economy based on the analysis of the information contained in the SAM. Include the following: structure of domestic value added (agriculture, industry, and service shares, importance of mining), external trade (dependency ratios, trade deficit, and structure of exports and imports), factor use among the different

	A	B	C	D	E	F	G	H	I	J	K	L	M	N
1		Table 10E.1. Input-output and social accounting matrix multipliers in Morocco, 1980: Data												
2														
3		(in million 1980 dirhams)												
4					Other		Refined	Mills,	Textiles,	Cons.	Prod.	Constr.,		Ag.
5			Cereals	Ag. exp.	ag.	Phosph.	oil	bakery	leather	goods	goods	services	Admin.	workers
6			1	2	3	4	5	6	7	8	9	10	11	12
7														
8		1 Cereals	808		898			2600		613		81	24	
9		2 Ag. exp.		77				65		310		7	2	
10		3 Other ag.	15		568	34		190	2	3822	33	76	23	
11		4 Phosphates				24					627	72		
12		5 Refined oil	120	173	164	226	571	151	5	211	1034	1643	488	
13		6 Mills, bakery			144			1217		101	1	333	26	
14		7 Textiles, leather	1	0	2	9	1	1	486	6	2	19	76	
15		8 Cons. goods	26	14	477	37	13	128	1526	4594	262	1924	311	
16		9 Prod. goods	412	390	103	415	256	146	164	1465	6558	6694	2591	
17		10 Const., services	1258	1863	1153	493	803	362	1606	3629	4739	8263	1671	
18		11 Administration										355		
19		12 Ag. workers	592	494	413									
20		13 Nonag. skilled				176	33	95	53	383	783	1417	3194	
21		14 Nonag. unskilled				273	91	271	319	942	1024	6330	5576	
22		15 Informal capital						859	913	1443	945	10294		
23		16 Formal capital				1786	148	253	89	1270	2265	6282	-50	
24		17 Rural low income	1006	292	3334									1083
25		18 Rural medium inc.	1791	644	1394									417
26		19 Rural high income	1198	1838	589									
27		20 Urban low income												
28		21 Urban medium inc.												
29		22 Urban high income												
30		23 Firms	20	16	14	248	43	77	34	244	402	1275	366	
31		24 Government	880	43	347	664	1291	-1096	84	2447	3960	1991	-298	
32		25 Rest of world	1352	54	503	26	3916	638	32	2694	9243	1418		
33		26 Capital account												
34		Total	9476	5897	10103	4411	7166	5955	5313	24176	31876	48472	13998	1499
35														
36														
37		**Matrix of coefficient**												
38														
39														
40					Other		Refined	Mills,	Textiles,	Cons.	Prod.	Constr.,		Ag.
41			Cereals	Ag. exp.	ag.	Phosph.	oil	bakery	leather	goods	goods	services	Admin.	workers
42			1	2	3	4	5	6	7	8	9	10	11	12
43														
44		1 Cereals												
70														
71														
72		**Matrix of coefficient (I-A)**												
73														
74														
75					Other		Refined	Mills,	Textiles,	Cons.	Prod.	Constr.,		Ag.
76			Cereals	Ag. exp.	ag.	Phosph.	oil	bakery	leather	goods	goods	services	Admin.	workers
77			1	2	3	4	5	6	7	8	9	10	11	12
78														
79		1 Cereals												
102														
103														
104		**Production multipliers: Leontief inverse matrix**												
105														
106														
107					Other		Refined	Mills,	Textiles,	Cons.	Prod.	Constr.,		
108			Cereals	Ag. exp.	ag.	Phosph.	oil	bakery	leather	goods	goods	services	Admin.	
109			1	2	3	4	5	6	7	8	9	10	11	
110														
111		1 Cereals												
126														
127		**SAM multipliers M**												

	O	P	Q	R	S	T	U	V	W	X	Y	Z	AA	AB	AC
	Nonag.	Nonag.	Informal	Formal	Rural	Rural	Rural	Urban	Urban	Urban			Rest of	Capital	
	skilled	unskilled	capital	capital	low inc.	med. inc.	high inc.	low inc.	med. inc.	high inc.	Firms	Govt.	world	account	Total
	13	14	15	16	17	18	19	20	21	22	23	24	25	26	
1															
2															
3															
7															
8					1316	721	300	1680	345	33			114	-57	9476
9					720	395	192	1858	581	84			1606		5897
10					551	302	117	1615	663	105			193	1794	10103
11													3613	74	4411
12					22	72	72	941	810	220			474	-230	7166
13					519	566	376	1784	677	84			59	69	5955
14					458	422	237	1562	666	171			1176	19	5313
15					1399	1213	747	5838	2559	656			2217	236	24176
16					441	433	305	2439	1151	289			1448	6175	31876
17					892	813	584	4914	2585	710			2283	9853	48472
18								33	17	3		13589			13998
19															1499
20															6134
21															14825
22															14455
23															12043
24		50									1085	231	420		7501
25											601	66	1260		6172
26											97	33	420		4174
27		14775	5292								2552	371	1896		24886
28	4698		8897								699	82	474		14849
29	1437		266	1000							714	41			3457
30				11043					900		0	50	544		15275
31					75	62	220	249	1263	277	2408		76		14941
32										286	1115	2481			23757
33					1107	1173	1024	1973	2631	540	6005	-2003	5484		17933
34	6134	14825	14455	12043	7501	6172	4174	24886	14850	3457	15275	14941	23757	17933	
35															
36															
37															
38															
39															
40	Nonag.	Nonag.	Informal	Formal	Rural	Rural	Rural	Urban	Urban	Urban			Rest of	Capital	
41	skilled	unskilled	capital	capital	low inc.	med. inc.	high inc.	low inc.	med. inc.	high inc.	Firms	Govt.	world	account	
42	13	14	15	16	17	18	19	20	21	22	23	24	25	26	
43															
44															
70															
71															
72															
73															
74															
75	Nonag.	Nonag.	Informal	Formal	Rural	Rural	Rural	Urban	Urban	Urban					
76	skilled	unskilled	capital	capital	low inc.	med. inc.	high inc.	low inc.	med. inc.	high inc.	Firms				
77	13	14	15	16	17	18	19	20	21	22	23				
78															
79															
102															
103															
104															
105															
106															
107															
108															
109															
110															
111															
126															
127															

Table 10E.2. Input-output and social accounting matrix multipliers in Morocco: Policy simulations

	Base values X (million DH)	Simulation A			Simulation B			Simulation C			Simulation D			Simulation E		
		Shock ΔF	Impact ΔX (million DH)	Change ΔX/X (%)	Shock ΔF	Impact ΔX (million DH)	Change ΔX/X (%)	Shock ΔF	Impact ΔX (million DH)	Change ΔX/X (%)	Shock ΔF	Impact ΔX (million DH)	Change ΔX/X (%)	Shock ΔF	Impact ΔX (million DH)	Change ΔX/X (%)
1 Cereals																
2 Ag. exp.																
3 Other ag.																
4 Phosphates																
5 Refined oil																
6 Mills, bakery																
7 Textiles, leather																
8 Cons. goods																
9 Prod. goods																
10 Const., services																
11 Administration																
12 Ag. workers																
13 Nonag. skilled																
14 Nonag. unskilled																
15 Informal capital																
16 Formal capital																
17 Rural low income																
18 Rural medium inc.																
19 Rural high income																
20 Urban low income																
21 Urban medium inc.																
22 Urban high income																
23 Firms																
Total production																
Household income																
Government income ΔG																
Imports ΔI																
Savings ΔS																

Policy definitions:

A- Cereal price support of 100 million DH

B- Exports increase by 100 million DH

C- Income transfer of 100 million DH to urban poor households

D- Income transfer of 100 million DH to urban rich households

E- Income redistribution of 100 million DH

sectors (labor and profit shares, and skilled versus unskilled labor). Note that the labor share in agriculture is very small because it includes only the wage labor. Return to family labor is aggregated with return to the fixed factors, land, and capital. To maintain the distributional characteristics of agricultural production, rural households are assimilated with farm size, and returns to the fixed factors in these agricultural sectors are directly attributable to the households. Contrast the structure of production of the different farm sizes. Analysis of the government should include an evaluation of its size (size of the administration sector, government budget as share of GDP), its deficit, and its structure of income and expenditures.

2. Input-Output Multipliers

You must first compute the matrix A of technical coefficients and the matrix $(I - A)$. Each coefficient a_{ij} of the matrix A is computed as the ratio of the corresponding cell of the SAM matrix to the column total. These coefficients represent the direct impacts on production and income of an increase in exogenous demand. To compute the matrix $(I - A)$, consider only the 23 endogenous accounts. Fill in the space with the matrix $-A$. Then go into each diagonal element and, with the editing key F2, add +1.

The input-output multipliers are obtained by inverting the block of $(I - A)$ containing productive sectors only. This is done by using /Data Matrix Inverse, highlighting the area of the matrix you want to invert, and indicating the output range. The diagonal elements are the multipliers on the sector itself. The off-diagonal elements are induced production. The totals are the total production multipliers.

Interpretation

Suppose that the exports of citrus and vegetable (Ag.exp.) increase by 1 million DH. By how much does the sector's production increase? Which other sector will increase its production? By how much will total production increase in the economy?

Which sector has the highest multiplier on itself? The highest total multiplier? Comparing these two series of impacts, which has the highest linkage with the rest of the economy?

3. SAM Multipliers

Invert the block of $(I - A)$, which contains all sectors, factors, households, and firms in the same manner. The result is a matrix M of multipliers containing production effects in the rows corresponding to sectors and income effects in the rows corresponding to factors, households, and firms.

What is now the effect of an increase in the exports of citrus and vegetable by 1 million DH on its sectoral production, on the production of other sectors, on the income of the different households? Why do urban households benefit from this? Compare the total production multipliers (the sums of the production impacts only) with the input-output multipliers.

Which sectors have the highest total production multipliers? Which sectors have the highest impact on income (sum of all household incomes)? Compare the linkages with the rest of the economy (multiplier outside the production sector itself) with those obtained through the input-output analysis.

The columns corresponding to the households give the impact of an income transfer of 1 million DH on the economy. To which groups should this transfer be made to generate the highest production response? Compare also the income multipliers. If you originally gave 1 million DH to the rural poor households, by how much would their income increase? By how much would the other groups' incomes increase? Compare income effects across groups.

Explain these results by the socioeconomic relations that are embedded in the SAM.

4. Simulation of Policies

The simulation of the impact of a more general exogenous change, an increase in export or a transfer in more than one account, for example, is obtained by premultiplying the vector of the initial transfer by the matrix M of multipliers. Each policy to be studied is therefore characterized by a vector of initial shock ΔF. Its impact is measured by the resulting vector ΔX:

$$\Delta X = M \, \Delta F.$$

To perform this operation, enter the initial policy in a column vector ΔF. Zeros need to be explicitly entered, as the operation will not work with blank spaces in place of zeros. Compute the product with the sequence /Data Matrix Multiply.

Induced imports ΔI resulting from the change in the production level can also be computed. They are obtained by premultiplying the vector of resulting change in the endogenous accounts ΔX (production and income) by the vector i' of import coefficients computed in A above:

$$\Delta I = i' \Delta X.$$

This can be done with the same sequence, /Data Matrix Multiply. Induced savings $\Delta S = s' \Delta X$ and government revenues $\Delta G = g' \Delta X$ can similarly be computed.

Perform the following policy experiments in Table 10E.2 and comment on the results.

Policy experiment A. Consider a policy of cereal price support. This can be represented as an income transfer to agricultural profits. Consider a transfer of 100 million DH distributed among the three rural households proportionately to the profit they receive from cereal production. What is the impact on production and income?

Policy experiment B. Consider an increase of Moroccan exports by 100 million DH. This increase in external demand is assumed to be distributed among all sectors in proportion to their initial exports. What is the impact on production and income? Given the induced import change, what is the net change in the balance of trade?

Policy experiments C and D. Simulate income transfers of 100 million DH to urban poor households and to urban rich households. Compare the differential impacts on growth and savings.

Policy experiment E. Analyze an income redistribution of 100 million DH from the three richest groups (urban high- and medium-income and rural high-income) to the three poorer groups (urban low- and rural medium- and low-income households). What is the impact of such a redistribution policy on growth and savings? Comment on the implied short-run/long-run trade-off.

References

Adelman, Irma, Edward Taylor, and Steve Vogel. 1988. "Life in a Mexican Village: A SAM Perspective." *Journal of Development Studies* 25:5–24.

Augusztinovics, Maria. 1989. "Primary Incomes and Intersectoral Pricing." *Journal of Policy Modeling* 11:31–44.

Cella, Guido. 1984. "The Input-Output Measurement of Interindustry Linkages." *Oxford Bulletin of Economics and Statistics* 46:73–84.

D'Antonio, Mariano, Raffaela Colaizzo, and Guiseppe Leonello. 1988. "Mezzogiorno/Centre-North: A Two-Region Model of the Italian Economy." *Journal of Policy Modeling* 10:437–51.

Defourny, Jacques, and Erik Thorbecke. 1984. "Structural Path Analysis and Multiplier Decomposition within a Social Accounting Matrix Framework." *Economic Journal* 89:111–36.

de Janvry, Alain, Elisabeth Sadoulet, and André Fargeix. 1991. *Adjustment and Equity in Ecuador.* Paris: Development Centre, Organization for Economic Co-operation and Development.

Haggblade, Steven, Jeffrey Hammer, and Peter Hazell. 1991. "Modeling Agricultural Growth Multipliers." *American Journal of Agricultural Economics* 73:361–74.

Haggblade, Steven, and Peter Hazell. 1989. "Agricultural Technology and Farm-Nonfarm Growth Linkages." *Agricultural Economist* 3:345–64.

Haggblade, Steven, Peter Hazell, and J. Brown. 1989. "Farm-Nonfarm Linkages in Rural Sub-Saharan Africa." *World Development* 17:1173–1201.

Hayden, Carol, and Jeffrey Round. 1982. "Developments in Social Accounting Methods as Applied to the Analysis of Income Distribution and Employment Issues." *World Development* 10:451–65.

Hazell, Peter, C. Ramasamy, and V. Rajagopalan. 1991. "An Analysis of the Indirect Effects of Agricultural Growth on the Regional Economy." In *The Green Revolution Reconsidered*, edited by P. Hazell and C. Ramasamy. Baltimore: Johns Hopkins University Press.

Hirschman, Albert. 1958. *The Strategy of Economic Development.* New Haven: Yale University Press.

Hirschman, Albert. 1977. "A Generalized Linkage Approach to Development with Special Reference to Staples." *Economic Development and Cultural Change*, suppl., 25:67–98.

Khan, Haider, and Erik Thorbecke. 1989. "Macroeconomic Effects of Technology Choice: Multiplier and Structural Path Analysis within a SAM Framework." *Journal of Policy Modeling* 11:131–56.

Kuznets, Simon. 1965. *Economic Growth and Structure.* New York: Norton.

Morrisson, Christian, and Erik Thorbecke. 1990. "The Concept of Agricultural Surplus." *World Development* 18:1081–95.

Pyatt, Graham, and Jeffrey Round. 1989. "Accounting and Fixed Price Multipliers in a Social Accounting Framework." *Economic Journal* 89:850–73.

Subramanian, Shankar, and Elisabeth Sadoulet. 1990. "The Transmission of Production Fluctuations and Technical Change in a Village Economy." *Economic Development and Cultural Change* 39:131–73.

Thorbecke, Erik. 1985. "The Social Accounting Matrix and Consistency-Type Models." In *Social Accounting Matrices: A Basis for Planning*, edited by G. Pyatt and J. Round. Washington, D.C.: World Bank.

Thorbecke, Erik, and David Berrian. 1992. "Budgetary Rules to Minimize Societal Poverty in a General Equilibrium Context." *Journal of Development Economics* 39:189–205.

CHAPTER ELEVEN

Multimarket Models

11.1. The Multimarket Approach

The multimarket approach extends the analysis of price and nonprice policy instruments from the analysis of their impact in commodity– or factor–specific partial equilibrium models to the interactions among markets on both the product and factor sides. It details the nature of one (for the country as a whole or a region) or more (for several regions, farm sizes, or farming systems) agricultural production systems, each of which is represented by a profit function from which are derived product supplies and factor demands. This producer core is complemented with systems of final demands, factor supplies, income equations, and market equilibrium conditions. The model allows one to follow the impact of particular price and nonprice policies and reforms on production, factor use, the prices (for nontradables) and net exports (for tradables) of products and factors, household incomes, household consumption, government revenues and expenditures, and the balance of trade. The multimarket remains, however, a sectoral as opposed to a general equilibrium model in that it usually does not equilibrate a number of balances which are, as we shall see in Chapter 12, fundamental to general equilibrium analysis, such as savings and investment, the supply and demand of foreign exchange, and fiscal revenues and expenditures. It also treats commodities as pure tradables or nontradables, instead of allowing for imperfect substitution between domestic and traded goods, a flexibility which the CGE models of Chapter 12 allow.

There are two traditions in the use of multimarkets for policy analysis. The first, of a more academic nature, associated with Quizon and Binswanger (1986), consists in proceeding first with rigorous estimation of both the complete producer core and a complete system of final demands. As such, it starts from the methodologies developed in Chapter 2 for the analysis of demand and in Chapter 3 for the analysis of the profit function. The other approach, of a more pragmatic policy-making nature, associated with Braverman and Hammer (1986), consists in specifying only the equations and exogenous variables of a subset of interest in the producer core and of using "best guesses" to quantify the necessary elasticities. While the first approach has the merit of rigor and econometric validation, the second has the advantage of serving as a quick consistency check on complex policy reasonings that involve quantitative trade-offs that are far from intuitively obvious. As we shall argue, the two approaches are not exclusive and should be viewed as mutually reinforcing.

Other approaches have also been used to perform quantitative policy analysis at the sectoral level (Thorbecke and Hall, 1982).

11.1.1. Consistency Frameworks

The objective of this approach, which has been extensively used by the FAO (Computerized System for Agricultural and Population Planning, Assistance, and Training or CAPPA model, FAO, 1991), is to reconcile macroeconomic and population projections with projections of agricultural production and to derive from this the resulting agricultural trade surplus or deficit. It is meant to identify gaps between consumption and production and thus to serve as the basis for policy-oriented dialogue directed at modifying the magnitude of these gaps. The approach consists of the following steps: (1) project population from fertility data; (2) project overall economic growth and income levels; (3) project demand for agricultural products derived from the population and income growth scenarios; and (4) project production based on land and water resources, stocks of fixed factors, expected productivity gains in yields, and market constraints for exportables. Trade gaps and employment effects are then derived. This consistency framework could equivalently be used to derive the production required to achieve desired levels of trade self-sufficiency given the levels of demand implied by population and income projections. Optimistic and pessimistic scenarios for the projections are usually formulated to arrive at a range of results. Policy options are principally directed at relaxing the constraints on domestic production. Inconvenients of the approach are lack of behavioral response by economic agents, rigidity in specifying the determinants of production which are usually of the fixed coefficient type and without allowing for substitutions across products, and lack of attention to the role of prices.

11.1.2. Mathematical Programming Approaches

The programming approach has the advantage of being able to derive optimum policy to satisfy a multiplicity of objectives, of taking into account the role of prices, and of specifying in considerable detail the constraints under which production, income generation, and policy making are taking place. Regional and sector policy analysis models can combine a policymaker model with models representing the behavior of an array of representative farms. We first look at the specification of the policymaker model, then of producers, and finally combine the two into one where policy-making accounts for the responses of producers to changes in the policy instruments. This is then extended to the specification of sectoral models.

a. The policymaker model and the multi-objective programming approach.

The policymaker's objective is to maximize a utility function $U(Y)$ defined on a set of objectives Y, with respect to policy instruments (taxes and subsidies T, and regulations R), under a set of resource constraints K and structural equations F_2:

$$\underset{T,\,R}{\text{Max }} U(Y) \quad \text{s.t.} \quad F_1(T, R) \leq K, \text{ resource constraints,}$$

$$Y = F_2(T, R), \text{ structural equations,}$$

$$T, R \geq 0.$$

Multiple objectives can include such goals as aggregate income, food security, employment, externalities, etc. To accommodate multiple objectives, the programming problem is usually specified as the minimization of deviations from specified levels of each goal, weighted by the relative "costs" of deviations from these target levels for the decision maker. The problem can then be written as:

$$\underset{T,R}{\text{Max}} \sum_i \left(w_i^+ d_i^+ + w_i^- d_i^- \right) \quad \text{s.t.} \quad F_1(T, R) \le K,$$

$$\overline{Y} = F_{2i}(T, R) - d_i^+ + d_i^-, \text{ for all } i,$$

$$d_i^+, d_i^-, T, R \ge 0, \text{ either } d_i^+ \text{ or } d_i^- = 0,$$

where $\overline{Y}_i$ is the target level for objective i, d_i^+ the level of surplus in objective i, d_i^- the shortage in objective i, and w_i^+ the weight attached to a surplus in objective i and w_i^-, the weight attached to a deficit in objective i. A variety of methods has been used to determine these weights. They include: (1) calibrating the weights so that the model reproduces observed decision makers' behavior, for instance the weighing of risk against return (Brink and McCarl, 1978), (2) interactions between the modeler and a decision makers' committee to agree on the choice of weights (Candler and Boehlje, 1971), and (3) direct elicitation of preferences through a survey (Barnett, Blake, and McCarl, 1982). Alternatively, the weights can be systematically varied to describe trade-offs among objectives. For instance, a profit maximization can be weighted against a soil erosion objective, establishing a frontier of efficient trade-offs between the two goals.

b. Producer response model.

Representative farm models are constructed based on a typology of farm types. This typology can focus on regions, farm sizes, tenure types, and/or technological levels according to the purpose of the study. Each farm model can also be a multi-objective program (or a linear programming model if there is only one linear objective such as the maximization of farm restricted profits). The representative farm model is:

$$\underset{x}{\text{Max}} \, u(y) \quad \text{s.t.} \quad f_1(T, R, x) \le k(R), \text{ resource constraints,}$$

$$y = f_2(T, R, x), \text{ structural equations,}$$

$$x \ge 0.$$

In this model, y is the vector of farm objectives (e.g., profit, risk avoidance, diet adequacy, meeting social obligations, etc.), x production decisions, and k resource endowments which are function of the exogenous regulatory environment R.

c. Unified policymaker-producer response: multi-level programming and sectoral models.

These models combine consistently different levels of decision making. For instance, policymakers allocate public resources given predictions of how farmers will react to each possible allocation and subject to resource constraints, while farmers decide on the use of resources under their control given policy decisions (Hazell and Norton, 1986). With one farm, the programming model thus becomes:

$$\underset{T,\,R}{\text{Max}}\ U(Y) \quad \text{s.t.} \quad F_1(T,\,R,\,x) \le K,$$

$$Y = F_2(T,\,R,\,x), \text{ and to}$$

$$\underset{x}{\text{Max}}\ u(y) \quad \text{s.t.} \quad f_1(T,\,R,\,x) \le k(R),$$

$$y = f_2(T,\,R,\,x),$$

$$T,\,R,\,x \ge 0.$$

This model becomes more difficult to solve when there is more than one farm. The solution is found by iterating between farm and overall optima until a stable solution is found.

The sectoral specification of these models requires adding demand schedules for outputs and supply schedules for purchased factors and closing markets for prices and quantities. The constraint K captures regional factor limits, for instance on hired labor, water, draft animals, and machinery shared among farms. Endogenous variables are prices and quantities of products, quantities of factors used, prices of purchased inputs, and shadow prices of owned factors. If the objective of the model is not to derive optimum policy but to simulate reconciliation of behavior of the representative farms in a perfectly competitive market, the policymaker's objective function is replaced by a quadratic objective function equal to the sum of the producer and consumer surplus for each commodity after government taxes and subsidies. Maximization of this objective function, under certain restrictive assumptions, is equivalent to equilibrating supply and demand in all markets (Takayama and Judge, 1971).

As an example, the CHAC model for Mexico is subdivided into 20 district submodels with 33 crops and several alternative technologies for each (Goreux and Manne, 1973). Districts contribute to national supply with differential transport costs. The national objective is set as maximizing the sum of producers and consumers surplus, so that the model solves for product prices that equilibrate national supply and demand. The main policy instruments are investment programs, factor and product price fixing, and trade policies. The impacts of these policy initiatives are followed at the district, sectoral, regional, and national levels. Other models with a regional or sectoral focus include Kutcher and Scandizzo (1981) for Northeast Brazil and McCarl (1992) for Egyptian agriculture with a focus on the allocation of irrigation water.

While advantageous as a tool for specifying technological features, resource constraints, and complex objective functions, the programming approach suffers from the following difficulties:

a. The condition for the maximization of the sum of producer and consumer surplus to correspond to a perfectly competitive equilibrium is that each market is dealt with as a partial equilibrium solution. This implies that the model solution does not take into account the income generated by the sector as a shifter of the model's product demand functions (McCarl and Spreen, 1980).

b. The algorithm to solve a multilevel programming remains cumbersome and not necessarily consistent, and oscillations between local and global optima do not necessarily converge.

c. Specification of the objective function used to derive the optimum policy remains largely arbitrary. An option to avoid specifying the weights attached to different policy objectives is to derive frontiers between policy objectives by maximizing in turn each objective given the level of the others, or vary systematically the weights attached to the different objectives.

d. Finally, the data requirements are extensive, implying costly and time-demanding research and cumbersome policy analysis.

11.1.3. *Multilevel Planning Models*

Quantitative policy analysis at the industry and sectoral levels has also been pursued by building econometric models. These models typically consist in a large number of equations that are estimated from time series data and solved numerically. They reflect the aggregate supply and demand decisions of the agents involved, the complex technological features of each activity and their interrelations with other activities, the role of government interventions, and the determination of market equilibria. They have the advantage of detailing the specific features of each industry and of stressing the role of lagged variables, giving them the possibility for serving as forecasting tools.

Industry models typically focus on vertical market structures. Early examples include the 137 equations model by Raulerson and Laugham (1970) for the Florida concentrated orange juice industry and the 38 equations model by Vernon, Rives, and Naylor (1969) for the tobacco leaf industry. Recent contributions include the 171 equations FAPRI model for 11 crops in the United States and main regions of the world, which is used annually to run ten year projections (Westhoff, Baur, Stephens, and Meyers, 1990), as well as the CARD linked sectoral models for beef, poultry, pork, and feedgrains (Grundmeier, Skold, Jensen, and Johnson, 1989). These models are usually recursive to capture the flow of information through the industry, which helps trace out causality in policy instruments. Sectoral econometric models are typically composed of interlinked commodity submodels, for instance the Ray and Heady (1972) model for the United States which includes six subsectors for livestock, feedgrains, wheat, soybeans, cotton, and tobacco. Typical policy questions are the roles of government price support, acreage allotment, and technological change on production, prices, trade, and farm incomes.

The multimarket approach that we develop in the rest of this chapter goes beyond a consistency approach in that it attributes fundamental importance to market equilibria and to the role of prices. It differs from the programming approaches in that it seeks to conduct policy analysis by simulation of alternative scenarios, as opposed to deriving an optimum policy from a stated objective function. It also differs from the industry or sectoral econometric models in simplifying the technological and linkage specifications of activities and often minimizing estimation requirements, particularly if only local deviations from an initial equilibrium point are analyzed. The cost of this is that it greatly simplifies the technological, linkage, and constraint specifications to what can be captured by a profit function with fixed factors. It also falls short of the general equilibrium models analyzed in Chapter 12 in that it takes the other sectors of the economy as given and does not consider the feedback effects that macroequilbrium constraints may impose on the sector.

We first describe the logic of the multimarket model using a flowchart approach. We then detail the equations of the model, the variables for which it solves, and the policy instruments it permits us to study. Finally, we develop two examples, one in each of the two traditions mentioned above, a model by Quizon and Binswanger (1986) for India and a model by Braverman and Hammer (1986) for Senegal.

11.2. Structural Logic of the Model

The multimarket model incorporates four classes of agents: producers, consumers, suppliers of factors, and government. As opposed to the household model, production, consumption, and labor supply decisions are not integrated, as the country or region mainly contains agents which are specialized in only one of these decisions. As we have seen in Chapter 3, the profit function for a production system represents a state of technology, the contributions to production of a set of private and public fixed factors that are common to the activities of that system (as opposed to being allocated to each activity as in a production function approach), and profit maximization behavior by the agents in that system. In Figure 11.1, the profit function yields a system of supply [equations (1) in section 11.3] and factor demand [equations (2)], the parameters of which satisfy the set of symmetry and homogeneity restrictions established in Chapter 3. Both products and factors can be either traded or nontraded.

On the factor side, each household class (h, containing N_h identical households) supplies factors k as a function of product and factor prices and a set of household characteristics [equations (3)]. Total factor supply is obtained by summing over households both within and across classes. Other factors, particularly those which are imported, are supplied on the factor markets independently of household decisions.

Household income by class is given in equations (4) as the sum of the incomes to the factors supplied by the households in that class and the share of these households' class in sectoral profits Π [equations (5)]. Incomes are also received from earnings in other sectors of the economy and from transfers and remittances. While exogenous in nominal terms, the real value of these other incomes depends on the household-specific cost of living index (CPI). For the nonagricultural households, whose incomes are fixed in nominal terms, real income effects thus come entirely through the impacts of policy on their CPIs. Per capita income in class h can then be calculated in equation (6) by dividing class income by the number N_h of households in that class.

Once per capita incomes are known, the demand system can be specified for each class of households as a function of per capita incomes and consumer prices. Total demand for each commodity is obtained in equation (7) by summing over households within each class and across classes.

Equilibrium conditions on product [equations (8)] and factor markets [equations (9)] depend upon the tradability of each factor and product. For a nontradable, the equilibrium condition is the equality between supply and demand. Any trade in "nontradables" in taken as an exogenous difference between domestic supply and demand. This equilibrium condition determines both equilibrium price and quantity after trade. For tradables, by contrast, prices are the exogenous border prices, with the nominal exchange rate as exogenous, corrected by relevant trade distortions (export taxes, import tariffs, and subsidies to exports or imports). Market equilibrium is achieved through quantity adjustments, where endogenous net exports equilibrate supply and demand at the exogenous domestic price.

The balance-of-trade [equation (10)] and the balance of government revenues [equation (11)] and expenditures are residuals. They are used to indicate the magnitude of the deficits or surpluses of a particular multimarket equilibrium, with no feedback on the exchange rate or the domestic price system.

While the logic of a multimarket can be represented as a flow chart in Figure 11.1, this does not imply causality in the determination of the endogenous variables of the model. In general,

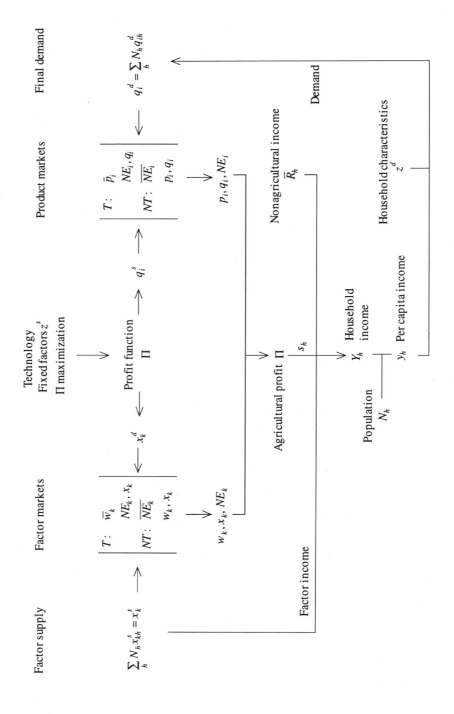

Figure 11.1. Generic structure of a multimarket

all equations are simultaneous and the model must consequently be solved jointly for all the endogenous variables. We now proceed to write this model as a set of equations that can be quantified and solved numerically.

11.3. Equations of a Multimarket Model

Profit function: the producer core

(1) Output supply: $\quad q_i^s = q_i^s(p, w, z^s).$

(2) Factor demand: $\quad x_k^d = x_k^d(p, w, z^s).$

Factor supply

For factors supplied by the agricultural households h:

(3) $\quad x_k^s = \sum_h N_h x_{kh}^s\left(p, w, z_h^x\right).$

For the other inputs:

(3') $\quad x_k^s = x_k^s(p, w, z^x).$

Household income and final demand

(4) Income per class: $\quad Y_h = \sum_k w_k N_h x_{kh} + s_h \Pi + \overline{R}_h,$

(5) where: $\quad \Pi = \sum_i p_i q_i - \sum_k w_k x_k .$

(6) Income per capita: $\quad y_h = \dfrac{Y_h}{N_h}.$

(7) Demand: $\quad q_i^d = \sum_h N_h q_{ih}^d(y_h, p, t, z_h^d).$

Equilibrium conditions

(8) Product markets: $\quad q_i^s = q_i^d + NE_i,$

    if nontradable, $\quad NE_i = \overline{NE}_i,\ (p_i, q_i$ endogenous$),$

    if tradable, $\quad p_i = \overline{p}_i,\ (NE_i, q_i$ endogenous$).$

(9) Factor markets: $\quad x_k^s = x_k^d + NE_k,$

    if nontradable, $\quad NE_k = \overline{NE}_k,\ (w_k, x_k$ endogenous$),$

    if tradable, $\quad w_k = \overline{w}_k,\ (NE_k, x_k$ endogenous$).$

(10) Balance of trade: $\quad BOT = \sum_i NE_i .$

Government revenue:

(11) $G = \sum_i t_i p_i q_i^d + \sum_i \left(\dfrac{t_{Ei}}{1 - t_{Ei}} - \dfrac{t_{Mi}}{1 + t_{Mi}} \right) p_i NE_i + \overline{G},$ where

$$t_M = \frac{p - p^b}{p^b} \text{ (for imports)}, \quad t_E = \frac{p^b - p}{p^b} \text{ (for exports)}.$$

Endogenous variables

$q_i^s,\ q_i^d$	Agricultural product supply and demand.
$x_k^d,\ x_k^s$	Factor demand and supply.
x_{kh}^s	Supply of factor k per capita in household class h.
$Y_h,\ y_h$	Household class h income and per capita income.
Π	Agricultural profit.
w_k or NE_k	Factor price (nontradables) or net exports (tradables).
p_i or NE_i	Product price (nontradables) or net exports (tradables).
BOT	Balance of trade.
G	Government revenue.

Exogenous variables

z^s, z^x, z^d	Shifters of product supplies, factor supply, and final demand functions.
p_i or NE_i	Product price (tradables) or net exports (nontradables).
w_k or NE_k	Factor price (tradables) or net exports (nontradables).
N_h	Population in household class h.
s_h	Share of household class h in agricultural profit Π.
t_i	Consumer tax rates.
t_{Mi}, t_{Ei}	Nominal rates of protection on net imports and exports.
$\overline{G}$	Exogenous government revenue.
$\overline{R}_h$	Nonagricultural income.

Counting the number of equations and endogenous variables gives the following:

Equations	Number of equations	Endogenous variables	Number of new endogenous variables
(1)	N	q_i^s	N
(2)	K	x_k^d	K
(3)	K	x_k^s	K
(4)	H	Y_h	H
(5)	1	Π	1
(6)	H	y_h	H
(7)	N	q_i^d	N
(8)	N	p_i or net exports	N
(9)	K	w_k or net exports	K
(10)	1	Balance of trade	1
(11)	1	G	1

The exogenous variables which serve as policy instruments are trade distortions under the form of taxes and subsidies, fixed factors and exogenous shifters in production (z^s and z^x), household characteristics in demand (z^d), household class sizes (N_h), farm households shares in agricultural profit, and transfers to households ($\overline{R}_h$). The model can thus be used to simulate not only the effects of price policies but also those of a host of structural factors, provided these have been introduced in the equations of the model.

11.4. Writing and Solving a Multimarket

A multimarket is thus a system of $3N + 3K + 2H + 3$ nonlinear equations in the same number of unknowns. However, the last two equations are not simultaneous with the others and may thus be solved separately. If the functional form of all these functions is fully specified, as in the Quizon-Binswanger approach, the model can be solved using a computer algorithm such as the General Algebraic Modeling System (GAMS; see Meeraus, 1983). Even though the model is one of comparative statics and there is no clear concept of historical time, knowledge of the functional forms of the equations in the model permits its use beyond calculating marginal changes around an equilibrium point. This is particularly important when simulating the impact of changes in the fixed factors, as the time lapse involved may be medium run at the least. This is, however, not the approach which has been most commonly followed. Instead, the equations are log-linearized, with the result that all the equations become linear in the rates of change in the endogenous and exogenous variables, and the coefficients are transformed into shares or elasticities (see below). Under this form, the model is the tangent hyperplane approximation to all functions at the base equilibrium point. The model can consequently be used only to study small deviations from this equilibrium point. It cannot, in particular, reproduce a fully consistent new equilibrium point to be used as a new departure for another simulation. Solving the model becomes very easy, since it only requires matrix inversion and multiplication, as we will see below. This is how Binswanger and Quizon (1984) solved their India multimarket. When the full functions have been estimated, instead of simply local elasticities, this type of solution implies a significant loss of information and makes analyzing changes in fixed factors problematic.

More important than ease of calculation, a reason why the multimarket has been solved in log-linear form is that it generally can be written only in that form due to lack of empirical knowledge of the full functional forms. This is the justification for log-linearization given by Braverman and Hammer (1986). Empirical information is usually available only in the form of observed shares and collected or partially estimated elasticities. The model is then specified in a very incomplete form, with only the most relevant equations and exogenous variables included for the specific policy problem at hand. In this case, most of the restrictions on elasticities implied by the profit function or the demand system cannot be imposed due to incompleteness of variables. Among exogenous variables, only those that will be changed in policy experiments need be introduced, greatly simplifying the task of the policy analyst. Clearly, the model can only be used for local simulations around the initial equilibrium point. This reduces the range of experiments that can be conducted. This is particularly the case for policy experiments concerning changes in fixed factors, since these changes have a long gestation period during which population and a number of other exogenous variables may have changed by large amounts, making local analysis inappropriate.

With all the equations linearized, the model can be written in matrix form as:

$A\dot{q} + B\dot{z} = 0$, where:

A is the matrix of coefficients associated with the endogenous variables,
B is the matrix of coefficients associated with the exogenous variables,
$\dot{q}$ is the vector of rates of change in the endogenous variables,
$\dot{z}$ is the vector of rates of change in the exogenous variables.
Solution of the model is obtained simply as:

$$\dot{q} = -A^{-1}B\dot{z} \; .$$

Calculation thus only requires a matrix inversion and multiplication which can be done with a spreadsheet. In log-linearizing the model, it is useful to note that the profit equation (5) becomes:

$$\dot{\Pi} = \sum_i \frac{p_i q_i}{\Pi}\dot{p}_i + \sum_k \frac{w_k x_k}{\Pi}\dot{w}_k,$$

where the profit maximization condition makes the terms in $\dot{q}_i$ and $\dot{x}_k$ disappear.

   Constructing a multimarket in log-linear form is thus particularly simple and relatively undemanding in empirical information. Shares are easy to measure and much prior information is available in the literature on elasticities. In the exercise for this chapter, we will construct a simple multimarket in log-linear form.

11.5. Examples of Multimarket Analyses of Agricultural Policy

11.5.1. Incidence of the Green Revolution and Public Investments in India

   This multimarket model was constructed to analyze a variety of policy scenarios including technical change, subsidies to fertilizers, investment in fixed factors such as irrigation and infrastructure, schemes of taxation and transfers, and consumer food subsidies (Quizon and Binswanger, 1986). The model includes four agricultural product markets (rice, wheat, coarse cereals, and other crops), three factors (labor, draft power, and fertilizer), and eight household classes (four income quartiles each in the rural and urban sectors). The producer core is fully estimated using a translog profit function. The product supply and factor demand system includes a large number of shifters, such as land, rainfall, irrigation, high-yielding varieties, roads, farm capital (animals and implements), regulated prices, and technological change, all of which can be subsequently used as policy instruments. Factor supply functions are also estimated with the following exogenous variables: labor is a function of the real wage and of migration, itself a function of wage; animal draft is a function of the real rental rate; and fertilizer is a function of the price of fertilizer relative to that of nonagricultural goods. Land is in fixed supply and is the claimant to residual farm profits. Final demand is estimated using a LES, and elasticities are predicted for each of the eight income groups. A consumer price index is calculated for each income group. The output, nominal incomes, and nominal prices of nonagricultural activities are fixed. Consequently, changes in agricultural incomes do not affect the nonagricultural economy. Yet the income-group-specific CPIs allow one to calculate real income effects for the urban groups.

11.5.1.1. Technological Change under Alternative Trade Regimes

The first policy question analyzed is how alternative price regimes affect the social incidence of gains from the Green Revolution in different commodities. Technological change scenarios are specified as separate 20% yield increases in specific crops such as rice and coarse cereals. Alternative price formation regimes are either a closed economy or a state-trading economy where the full exogenous 20% production increase is exported. This contrast in trade regimes is an important policy issue in India, which has traditionally been a closed economy in foodgrains. Grains remain a nontradable even when a quantum of grains is exported, since these exports are exogenous. The results are reported in Table 11.1.

The main contrast between closed and export economies is in the effect on domestic prices. With a closed economy, a 20% yield increase in rice induces a 30.9% fall in its price (column 1). Because wheat is a close substitute in consumption, its price falls by 21.1%. A falling price and competition in production with rice result in a decline in production of wheat of 5.9%. These large declines in the prices of key commodities result in a fall of 12% in the GNP deflator. The total increase in agricultural output (5.4%) requires only a moderately higher agricultural employment, which raises the real agricultural wage only slightly (1.5%). Higher wages together with falling farm prices reduce agricultural profits by 7.5%.

The per capita real income effects for the rural and urban groups are determined by the effects on prices, the wage bill, and farm profits. The rural poor are net buyers of foodgrains and consequently benefit from falling prices as well as from higher employment and wages. The large farmers, by contrast, are hurt by technological change: they have a marketed surplus of grains, and the prices of all crops fall, in all cases by more than the increase in output. In the urban sector, all groups are net buyers and greatly benefit from falling food prices. The urban poor, who spend most of their income on food, benefit most. The real income effects are thus progressive on the distribution of income within both the rural and the urban areas.

The consequences of technological change are dramatically different when the additional production is exported (column 2). National income now increases by 5.7%, mainly through an increase of agricultural profits by 36.1%. Government exports combined with higher rural incomes cause an increase in domestic demand, resulting in a 10.1% increase in domestic prices. The price of rice increases by 9.1%. The prices of other crops, which experience no technological change, rise by 14.5% to 19.6%. The rural sector responds to these higher prices by raising agricultural output by 6.2%, with land reallocated from coarse cereals and other crops to rice and wheat. As a result, rice increases by an additional 7.9% over the 20% output effect due to technological change.

Rising prices hurt all urban income groups. The urban poor lose the most, with the poorest showing a decline in cereals consumption of 5%. Although incomes in the rural sector increase, it is the large farmers rather than the rural poor who capture most of the gain from technological change (14.9% for the former versus 1.3% for the latter). Real income effects are thus regressive in both the urban and rural sectors.

Which commodity is chosen for a technological effort leads to sharply different price and income effects. When technical change is in coarse cereals (columns 3 and 4), the aggregate impact is less than in rice because it is a smaller sector: while rice represents 26.7% of total agricultural output, coarse cereals represent only 10.7%. However, coarse cereals have a much lower income elasticity. The income effects of technical change are consequently less effective in increasing demand, and prices fall more sharply, by 35.5% as opposed to 30.9% for rice. Income distribution effects are also different. The rural and urban poor gain disproportionately

Table 11.1. Simulated effects of technical change and increased exports, India
(percentage change)

	20% increase in yield of rice		20% increase in yield of coarse cereal	
	Closed economy (1)	Exports increase (2)	Closed economy (3)	Exports increase (4)
National income per capita	4.1	5.7	1.0	2.1
Output				
Total	5.4	6.2	2.3	2.5
Rice	20.1	27.9	2.8	0.5
Wheat	−5.9	1.8	1.5	1.8
Coarse cereals	4.9	−5.4	12.8	22.2
Other crops	0.2	−1.6	−0.2	−0.7
GNP deflator	−12.0	10.1	−4.9	5.6
Prices				
Rice	−30.9	9.1	−1.8	10.9
Wheat	−21.1	19.6	−4.1	13.6
Coarse cereals	−6.7	13.9	−35.5	−6.2
Other crops	−8.1	14.5	−3.7	6.9
Real wage rate	1.5	2.4	−2.1	2.1
Employment	1.1	0.8	−0.4	0.8
Wage bill	2.7	3.2	−2.5	2.9
Profits	−7.5	36.1	−1.1	15.0
Real income per capita (by quartile)				
Rural				
Poorest	7.5	1.3	4.0	1.5
Second	5.1	6.1	1.8	2.7
Third	3.6	9.2	0.8	3.5
Richest	−1.4	14.9	−0.1	6.2
Urban				
Poorest	12.0	−6.9	3.3	−3.9
Second	13.6	−7.7	1.8	−5.2
Third	11.1	−7.1	1.2	−4.5
Richest	5.7	−4.8	0.1	−2.6
Per capita cereal consumption				
Rural				
Poorest quartile	11.2	2.0	7.8	2.1
Richest quartile	4.3	6.5	−0.7	1.2
Urban				
Poorest quartile	13.1	−5.0	5.6	−2.8
Richest quartile	6.8	3.5	−1.4	−0.4
Aggregate	10.1	3.7	4.2	1.0

Source: Quizon and Binswanger, 1986.

from cheaper coarse cereals because they are the only heavy consumers of these cereals. In addition, gains for rural poor consumers exceed those of urban consumers because the rural poor are heavier consumers. Technical change targeted at coarse grains is thus effective in focusing welfare gains on the poorest of the poor.

Overall, the choice of trade regime under which the Green Revolution occurs is crucial in determining the distribution of its benefits and costs, and much more so than the targeting of technological change on particular crops. While, in all cases, technological change creates net social gains, as measured by increases in national income per capita, it is noteworthy that the technological changes in rice and coarse grains are not Pareto optimal: in a closed economy, the large farmers lose; in an export economy it is the urban households that lose. Because there are net social gains, compensations could be paid, however, thus permitting Pareto optimality after compensation.

11.5.1.2. Fertilizer Subsidies or Public Investment in Irrigation?

Governments that want to stimulate agriculture can choose to either subsidize factor prices or increase public investment. The second policy question consequently compares the income distribution effects of investment in publicly delivered fixed factors (irrigation and infrastructure) with a price subsidy to fertilizers, both in a closed economy. In Table 11.2, irrigated area is increased by 10% (column 1). This leads to a 2.7% increase in total agricultural output and a 5.8% decline in the overall price level due to falling agricultural prices. Agricultural employment and real wages rise with the increased labor requirements in the irrigated areas. These higher wages combine with lower prices, which in all cases fall by more than quantities increase, to reduce farm profits by 4.8%. Gains from investment in irrigation are captured by the urban households through falling prices and by the rural poor and medium income households through the combination of higher wage bills and lower food prices. In a closed economy, large farmers lose from infrastructure investment, as they did from the Green Revolution. Because net social gains are created, the gainers could compensate these farmers to prevent them from opposing these investments.

Column 2 gives the results of a 20% fertilizer subsidy. Note that the results are not quantitatively comparable to those of the irrigation program, since the size of the fertilizer subsidy should have been calculated to have the same budgetary cost as the irrigation program. Qualitative results can, however, be compared. The consequence of increased fertilizer use is a 1.3% increase in agricultural output and a decrease in the aggregate price level of 1.1%. To understand the impact on labor and the distribution of income, it is important to notice that fertilizers have been observed to be labor saving in the estimated labor demand equations. As a result, the agricultural wage declines by 1.9% and agricultural profits increase by 5.6%, due to both lower wages and lower fertilizer costs. Through the negative-employment effect, the net effect is negative on the real income of the rural poor. It is the rural rich who gain most from a fertilizer subsidy. These subsidies are consequently highly regressive on the distribution of income in agriculture. We should note in passing that the budgetary costs of investments in irrigation and fertilizer subsidies are not made explicit in this model. Unless this cost is zero, for example, if they are funded by foreign aid, the national per capita income effect of these policy scenarios is overstated.

Table 11.2. Simulated effects of increased agricultural investment and input subsidies
(percentage change)

	10% increase in irrigated area (1)	20% fertilizer subsidy (2)
National income per capita	1.7	1.3
Output		
Total	2.7	1.3
Rice	0.6	0.3
Wheat	5.1	1.3
Coarse cereals	1.9	-2.1
Other crops	3.5	2.5
GNP deflator	-5.8	-1.1
Price		
Rice	-6.9	-1.8
Wheat	-12.8	-1.8
Coarse cereals	-9.4	1.6
Other crops	-6.4	-1.9
Real wage rate	0.7	-1.9
Employment	0.4	-0.8
Wage bill	1.1	-2.7
Profits	-4.8	5.6
Real income per capita (by quartile)		
Rural		
Poorest	2.9	-0.4
Second	1.7	0.8
Third	0.9	1.5
Richest	-0.7	2.5
Urban		
Poorest	6.0	0.6
Second	5.7	0.7
Third	5.2	0.6
Richest	3.5	0.4
Per capita cereal consumption		
Rural		
Poorest quartile	2.6	-0.7
Richest quartile	-0.1	0.6
Urban		
Poorest quartile	5.6	0.1
Richest quartile	-0.6	-0.3
Aggregate	1.8	0.1

Source: Quizon and Binswanger, 1986.

11.5.1.3. Alternative Approaches to Food Subsidies

Even though we know that cash income transfers are the most effective way of improving the nutritional status of their poor, most governments are using food subsidies to achieve this purpose, and this has been done through a variety of alternative approaches. They include generalized food subsidies such as subsidies to the price of bread in Egypt and unrestricted access to cheap food in government stores in Mexico in the 1970s, and targeted subsidies through the food stamps program in the United States and ration shops in Egypt, Sri Lanka, India, and Bangladesh (Pinstrup-Andersen, 1993). Food subsidies have proved to be both potentially effective in reducing malnutrition and difficult to manage because of the complex indirect effects they unleash. Difficult issues include the risks of serious backlash effects on the excluded poor through rising prices on residual free markets, disincentive effects on producers, runaway costs that unleash inflation or compete with other government expenditures (productive investment and job creation in particular), high costs of effective targeting, and leakages of benefits to the nonpoor (Taylor, Horton, and Raff, 1980). A multimarket offers a convenient tool to capture some of these complex effects. In the multimarket for India, Binswanger and Quizon (1984) analyze three fundamental features in the design of a food subsidies program with the following options:

Targeting of the subsidies: no targeting, urban ration shops open to all urban groups, or food stamps for all poor regardless of residence.

Source of subsidized food: additional imports or domestic production.

Financing of subsidies: foreign aid, excise tax on nonagricultural consumer goods, or forced procurement of foodgrains on the two largest farm-size groups.

Selected results are given in Table 11.3. Following the discussion of Chapter 1, we can assess the alternative policy scenarios simulated following four criteria:

Efficiency: change in real national income.

Welfare: change in real income level of the poorest rural and urban groups.

Equity: income distribution effects within the rural sector and within the urban sector, and between rural and urban (where rural households are poorer than the urban).

Political feasibility: real income effect on the urban rich or the rural rich, or a coalition of both. In India, the political feasibility of food policy is very much dominated by the political power of the rural rich (de Janvry and Subbarao, 1986).

We start by assessing the system that prevailed until recently consisting of urban ration shops, domestic supply, and forced procurement (column 1). By redistributing income, the policy creates a small efficiency gain through the Keynesian demand multiplier it induces. Since there are no imports, the extra demand of the urban groups puts upward pressure on prices. This creates a backlash effect on the rural poor, who must buy food on the residual free market at inflated prices. The urban poor gain, since the subsidies are targeted to the urban sector. Because the urban poor spend a higher share of their income on the subsidized foods, they gain more than the urban rich, and the policy is progressive on the urban distribution of income. The rural rich lose because of forced procurement. As a consequence, the income distribution effect is not clear in agriculture since the rural poor lose. Clearly, the policy is regressive between rural and urban, with the richer urban capturing most of the gains. Finally, political feasibility of the approach would require political dominance of the urban rich over the rural rich. Since this has not been the case in the last two decades, political feasibility of the approach is doubtful, potentially explaining why it could not be sustained and inviting analysis of alternative policy scenarios.

Table 11.3. Untargeted food subsidies and urban ration shops
(percentage change)

Targeting	Urban ration shops	Urban ration shops	Urban ration shops	All poor
Trade	Domestic supply	Domestic supply	Foreign supply	Foreign supply
Financing	Forced procurement	Excise tax	Foreign aid	Foreign aid
National per capita income	0.4	0.5	1.7	4.0
Output				
Total	0.1	0.2	−0.2	−0.4
Rice	0.0	0.3	−0.4	−0.3
Wheat	0.4	0.8	−4.1	−11.6
Coarse cereals	−0.1	−0.6	1.5	4.1
Other crops	0.1	0.3	1.0	2.3
GNP deflator	2.3	6.6	−2.7	−9.2
Price				
Rice	3.0	7.4	−4.9	−14.5
Wheat	3.6	8.0	−11.9	−35.0
Coarse cereals	3.1	7.2	−2.9	−10.1
Other crops	2.9	6.6	−0.7	−4.8
Real wage rate	0.1	−0.4	−0.5	−1.2
Employment	0.0	−0.2	−0.1	−0.2
Wage bill	0.1	−0.6	−0.6	−1.4
Profits	4.7	8.7	−3.0	−12.4
Real income per capita (by quartile)				
Rural				
Poorest	−0.5	−1.8	0.9	17.6
Second	0.2	−0.4	0.3	10.7
Third	−0.9	0.5	−0.1	−0.9
Richest	−1.5	2.2	−0.9	−3.8
Urban				
Poorest	8.1	4.5	12.7	20.1
Second	6.0	1.9	10.4	16.9
Third	3.7	−0.5	7.4	6.6
Richest	2.0	−2.4	3.8	2.8
Per capita cereal consumption				
Rural				
Poorest quartile	−0.5	−1.2	1.7	13.7
Richest quartile	−0.3	1.8	1.5	2.9
Urban				
Poorest quartile	5.7	3.1	11.3	20.0
Richest quartile	1.1	1.2	1.8	1.8

Source: Binswanger and Quizon, 1984.

An alternative possibility is to shift the cost of financing the same food subsidy scheme to the urban rich, by eliminating forced procurement and replacing it by an excise tax which is principally paid by the urban rich, since they are the main consumers of nonagricultural consumer goods (column 2). The implications for efficiency and welfare are qualitatively the same, but domestic prices rise sharply because the food consumption of the rural rich is no longer curtailed by the procurement tax. As producers they gain sharply, and the impact is now regressive on the distribution of income in agriculture, with the rich gaining absolutely and the poor losing absolutely. The urban rich lose because the cost of the tax is far greater than the benefits derived from access to the ration shops. If the rural rich control the policy-making process, political feasibility is now ensured. Indeed, as the political power of the larger farmers has been gradually reinforced by the income gains derived from the Green Revolution, the financing of food subsidies has been gradually shifted from forced procurement to an excise tax.

An alternative is, of course, to import food to meet the increase in demand induced by the subsidies, in order to avoid rising domestic prices and the backlash effect on the nontargeted rural poor (column 3). In this case the transfer of resources from abroad creates a larger efficiency gain. Food imports, principally cheap wheat, create a sharp fall in the price of all agricultural products, either by direct competition in consumption with domestic production in the case of wheat and rice, or by substitution in production in the case of other cereals. Falling agricultural production implies employment and real wage losses for the rural poor. Yet, they gain from falling food prices because most of them are food deficit small farmers. The welfare of the urban poor rise sharply as they cumulate the gains from ration shops and falling prices for the rest of their food purchases. Since the rural rich lose from falling prices, the income distribution effect is sharply progressive in the rural sector. It is also progressive in the urban sector because the poor have higher food budget shares. The scheme is, however, regressive between rural and urban because the latter gain more. As to political feasibility, it will not be achieved if the rural rich dominate the policy agenda. Nevertheless, their losses are smaller than under a forced procurement scheme.

Targeting food subsidies on all poor, both rural and urban, is, of course, the way of achieving high welfare gains in both sectors and high equity gains in both sectors as well (column 4). Here again, there are high efficiency gains. The scheme is thus attractive because it satisfies the efficiency, welfare, and intrasectoral equity criteria. Yet, if the rural rich dominate politically, it will be opposed by them, since imports make prices and hence their real incomes fall. Achieving political feasibility thus requires active political management. Since there are positive net social gains, part of the gains in real national income could be taxed for redistribution toward the rural rich, still leaving a net gain for the poor. Since the urban rich gain, an excise tax on nonagricultural consumer goods could be levied to achieve this income transfer. This transfer could be implemented through a fertilizer subsidy as analyzed in Table 11.2.

Analyzing policy interventions according to the four criteria of political feasibility (as a precondition to be necessarily satisfied, after engaging in political management if necessary), efficiency, welfare, and equity shows that achieving the optimum policy is far from easy, especially if we properly take into account the secondary effects these policies unleash. In addition, it is important to analyze policies as a joint package of interventions. We saw here, for instance, that a key point is to link issues of trade and taxation to the design of food subsidy interventions. The multimarket approach gives an effective tool to evaluate policy packages according to the multiple criteria used above and to search by simulation for feasible and desirable alternatives.

11.5.2. Stabilization Policies and Agriculture in Senegal

Government intervention in Senegalese agriculture has historically been extensive, with agricultural price subsidies absorbing as much as 23% of government expenditures in the early 1980s. With rising inflation and foreign exchange deficits, Senegal had to introduce a set of stabilization policies to reduce the government deficit. One such policy proposed lowering the farm price for peanuts, which had traditionally been maintained above the export price. To

Table 11.4. Structure of the multimarket for Senegal

						Government intervention	Government budget[b]
Producer goods							
	\multicolumn{4}{l}{Regions where produced}			Trade[a]		
	Basin	South	Fleuve	Dakar			
Peanuts	x	x	x		*T* exported	Export subsidy $\bar{p}^p > ep^{\$}$	$-B_2$
Cotton		x	x		*T* exported	Export subsidy $\bar{p}^p > ep^{\$}$	$-B$
Rice		x			*T* imported	Producer subsidy $\bar{p}^p > ep^{\$}$	$-B^p$
Millet	x	x	x		*NT*		
Maize		x			*NT*		

Factors	Market clearing conditions		
Land	Fixed by region, endogenous residual profit Π_{region}		
Labor	Fixed by region, endogenous wage w_{region}		
Fertilizer		Subsidized $\bar{p}_k <$ cost for peanuts and cotton	$-B_1$

Consumer goods			
Peanut oil		Subsidized $\bar{p}^c < ep^{\$}$	$-B$
Rice		Taxed $ep^{\$} < \bar{p}^c < \bar{p}^p$	$+B^c$
Millet			
Maize			

Regional income	$\Pi_{region} + w_{region}L +$ exogenous nonagricultural income

[a]*T* = tradable, *NT* = nontradable.
[b]$+B$ ($-B$) indicates a positive (negative) effect of the intervention on government net revenue.

analyze the implications of this and other components of a policy package, a multimarket was constructed by Braverman and Hammer (1986).

The model focuses on the production system for five crops (peanuts, cotton, rice, millet, and maize) in four regions (the Peanut Basin, South, Fleuve, and Dakar) using three factors (land, labor, and fertilizer). The features of the model are summarized in Table 11.4. As a rule, before conducting a multimarket analysis of price distortions, it is important to clearly understand the functioning of each market on a partial equilibrium basis. We do this by first analyzing price formation on each market.

Peanuts and cotton are tradable cash crops and are entirely bought by a parastatal marketing board at a fixed support price. They are sold at a lower price for both export and processing into peanut oil. These two commodities are the object of the following subsidies: farm price support (export subsidy), fertilizer subsidy, and subsidy to processing into oil. The fertilizer subsidy, by stimulating the production of peanuts, increases the cost of the export subsidy. In Figure 11.2a, the fertilizer subsidy shifts the supply of peanuts and increases the cost of the subsidy to exports.

Figure 11.2. Partial equilibrium analysis of price distortions in the Senegal multimarket

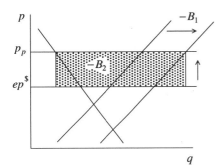

11.2a. Peanut and cotton markets:
Fertilizer ($-B_1$) and exports ($-B_2$)
subsidies

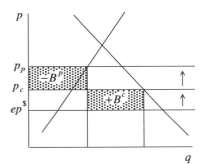

11.2b. Rice market:
Producer subsidy ($-B^p$) and
consumer tax ($+B^c$)

The farm price of rice is supported, with government buying the entire crop, which is relatively small. Senegal has a deficit in rice, and low-price imports from Thailand are subject to an import tariff. The producer price is thus above the consumer price, which is itself above the world market price. As shown in Figure 11.2b, the government's cost is the net between the cost of the subsidy to domestic producers, calculated as the difference between farm and consumer prices, and the tariff revenue on imports. The other two crops, millet and corn, are nontradables with no government intervention.

On the factor side, land and labor are nontradables within each region. For each region, income is thus equal to:

$$\Pi_{region} + w_{region} L + \text{exogenous nonagricultural incomes.}$$

Fertilizer is a tradable with a price below import cost.

Finally, on the consumption side, the consumer price of peanut oil is subsidized with a below-border price. Rice, by contrast, is taxed, with a price above the border price and below the farm price. Millet and maize are bought at equilibrium market prices.

Table 11.5 reports the results of several policy experiments designed at reducing the budget deficit. We only interpret here the results from the first experiment: a 15% decline in the peanut price. The mechanisms involved show the importance of taking into account substitution effects in production and consumption in order to fully assess the results of such a price policy. For example, the direct effect of a falling farm price of peanut is a decline in production of 6.9%. This direct effect reduces the cost of government export subsidies by 22% (not reported in Table 11.5). However, indirect effects reduce this beneficial effect on government subsidies. By substitution in production, the output of cotton increases by 13.1%. This increases the cost of export subsidies to that commodity. Similarly, the production of rice increases by 10.8%. The

Table 11.5. Results of agriculture pricing analysis, Senegal
(percentage change)

	Peanut price lowered 15%	Rice producer price raised 10%	Fertilizer price raised 100%	10% devaluation	Rice consumer price raised 25%
Supply					
Peanut	−6.9	−0.8	−2.3	2.5	−8.4
Rice	10.8	10.2	−2.3	1.8	−5.6
Cotton	13.1	−3.3	−16.3	2.2	−6.9
Millet	4.9	−0.2	−0.6	−3.3	11.3
Maize	4.1	−1.2	0.6	−4.1	0.9
Real income					
Peanut basin	−5.7	0.03	−1.1	3.7	−1.6
South	−4.7	1.5	−1.1	5.3	−5.1
Fleuve	1.2	0.7	−0.4	−0.1	−7.8
Dakar	0.6	−0.03	−0.1	−0.4	−5.1
Demand					
Rice	−9.1	0.6	0.3	6.9	−6.7
Maize	2.6	−0.7	0.4	−2.6	0.6
Peanut	−3.9	0.3	−0.3	3.0	−1.5
Millet	5.3	−0.2	−0.7	−3.6	12.3
Agricultural export earnings	−1.9	−0.7	−5.2	13.3	−8.8
Government deficit in agriculture	−18.1	−0.02	−10.4	24.8	−24.6
Rice imports	−13.9	−1.7	1.0	8.1	−7.0

Source: Braverman and Hammer, 1986.

cost to government of supporting farm prices is thus increased. To make things worse for government, increased domestic production reduces the need for rice imports. Falling real incomes in the areas where peanuts are produced (5.7% in the Peanut Basin and 4.7% in the South) lead to an aggregate decline in the demand for rice of 9.1%. With domestic supply increasing and domestic demand falling, imports are sharply reduced (−13.9%), leading to a fall in government tariff revenues. The net effect is to reduce the direct effect on government deficit in agriculture from 22% to 18.1%.

On the side of nontradables, the quantities produced of millet (4.9%) and maize (4.1%) increase by substitution with peanuts. Millet and maize prices consequently fall, and their demands increase, by 5.3% and 2.6%, respectively. Finally, the domestic demand for peanuts falls, even though peanut prices have remained unchanged, due to income effects in the regions hurt by falling peanut producer prices.

We see through this example that a price intervention in one market creates complex second-round effects in other markets that justify the need to use a multimarket analysis. Other examples of multimarket applications can be found in Braverman, Hammer, and Ahn (1986) for Korea; Braverman, Hammer, and Morduch (1985) for Cyprus; and Aloui, Dethier, and Houmy (1989) for Morocco.

11.6. Conclusion

While consistent econometric estimation of the full producer core and of a complete demand system is desirable, it is evident that this is a large task, highly demanding in data and typically requiring two to three years of econometric analysis. Pressed with the need to produce results, policy analysts will typically engage instead in guesstimation of elasticities and calibration of a log-linearized version of the model.

We find that there is much merit in initiating the development of a multimarket model in this latter fashion. The exercise should start with a solid description of the functioning of each market, of the institutions involved, and of the nature of the policy interventions in each market. These interventions should be characterized market by market in a partial equilibrium framework. The multimarket should then be constructed on the basis of observed shares and best-guess elasticities. This helps policy analysts understand what the model can do, what aspects need to be extended or dropped, and what parameters are the key to answering the policy questions raised. Once the model has thus been used for policy simulations, the analyst has a better feel for which are key parameters in the determination of the results and should be estimated econometrically. This suggests partial estimation of these key parameters. With the results obtained, new rounds of policy simulations should be performed, suggesting again the eventual need for further econometric efforts.

Exercise 11.1
A Multimarket for the Grain-Livestock Sector in North Africa

We develop here a simplified multimarket model for a North African grain-livestock sector (file 111MRKT) based on the study by Dethier (1989). We consider only three products: wheat, barley, and livestock. Although this model is very simple, it embodies two important characteristics of an agricultural sector: the existence of strong substitutability in production between some commodities (wheat and barley) and the use of one product (barley) as an input for another production (livestock). We assume that barley is used only for animal feed and wheat only for human consumption (bread). The base year data for supply, demand, imports, prices, and the total country income are reported in cells A5–J12 of Table 11E.1.

The output supply and derived-demand system therefore includes four equations: output supplies for wheat, barley, and livestock, and the derived demand for barley. The complete specification should express these as functions of the prices p of all competitive outputs and all inputs and of the fixed factors z:

	A	B	C	D	E	F	G	H	I	J	K	L
1	Table 11E.1. A multimarket for the grain-livestock sector in North Africa											
2												
3	Data on the agricultural sector											
4												
5				Quantities (1000 tons)				Prices (DA/ton)				
6				Derived	Final							
7	Commodities		Supply	demand	demand	Imports	Producer	User	Consumer	Border		
8	Wheat (bread)		3000		6000	3000	4800		3000	3500		
9	Barley		1000	1400		400	3900	3500		3000		
10	Livestock		200		200	0	35000		65700	0		
11												
12	Income = 295000000 (thousand DA)											
13												
14	Elasticities			Producer and user price elasticities				Consumer price and income elasticities				
15				Barley		Barley	Consump-					
16	Production		Wheat	producer	Livestock	user	tion	Wheat	Livestock	Income		
17	Wheat		.40	-.08	0	0	Wheat	-.50	.06	0.2		
18	Barley supply		-.30	.50	0	0	Livestock	.05	-.10	0.7		
19	Livestock		0	0	.10	-.05						
20	Barley demand		0	0	.07	-.10						
21												
22	Multimarket model											
23												
24	A matrix	Equation	ΔSw	ΔSb	ΔSl	ΔDb	ΔDw	ΔPl	ΔMw	ΔMb	ΔDl	Δy
25		(1ʻ)	1.00	0	0	0	0	0	0	0	0	0
26		(2ʻ)	0	1.00	0	0	0	0	0	0	0	0
27		(3ʻ)	0	0	1.00	0	0	-0.10	0	0	0	0
28		(4ʻ)										
29		(5ʻ)										
30		(6ʻ)										
31		(7ʻ)										
32		(8ʻ)										
33		(9ʻ)										
34		(10ʻ)										
35												
36	B matrix		ΔPwp	ΔPbp	ΔPbu	ΔPwc						
37		(1ʻ)	.40	-.08	0	0						
38		(2ʻ)	-.30	.50	0	0						
39		(3ʻ)	0	0	-.05	0						
40		(4ʻ)										
41		(5ʻ)										
42		(6ʻ)										
43		(7ʻ)										
44		(8ʻ)										
45		(9ʻ)										
46		(10ʻ)										
47												
48	A inverse		ΔSw	ΔSb	ΔSl	ΔDb	ΔDw	ΔPl	ΔMw	ΔMb	ΔDl	Δy
49		ΔSw										
50		ΔSb										
51		ΔSl										
52		ΔDb										
53		ΔDw										
54		ΔPl										
55		ΔMw										
56		ΔMb										
57		ΔDl										
58		Δy										

	A	B	C	D	E	F	G	H	I	J	K	L
59	Table 11E.1 (continued)											
60	A inverse*B		ΔPwp	ΔPbp	ΔPbu	ΔPwc						
61		ΔSw										
62		ΔSb										
63		ΔSl										
64		ΔDb										
65		ΔDw										
66		ΔPl										
67		ΔMw										
68		ΔMb										
69		ΔDl										
70		Δy										
71												
72	Policy instruments		Initial	New	% change							
73			value	value	Δp							
74		ΔPwp	4800	4320	-10							
75		ΔPbp	3900	3900	0							
76		ΔPbu	3500	3500	0							
77		ΔPwc	3000	3000	0							
78												
79	Results of price policy experiments: A inverse * B * Δp											
80												
81			Initial value	Policy		Copy of policy results						
82		ΔPwp	4800	-10	-10	0	0	0				
83		ΔPbp	3900	0	0	-10	0	0				
84		ΔPbu	3500	0	0	0	10	0				
85		ΔPwc	3000	0	0	0	0	10				
86	Endogenous variables			(% change	(% change over initial values)							
87		Sw	3000		-4.00							
88		Sb	1000		2.95							
89		Sl	200		-.19							
90		Db	1400		-.13							
91		Dw	6000		-.22							
92		Pl	35000		-1.86							
93		Mw	3000		3.56							
94		Mb	400		-7.85							
95		Dl	200		-.19							
96		y	2.95E+08		-.53							
97	Real income		(thousand DA)									
98		CPI	1		-.08							
99		Real y	2.95E+08		-.45							
100	Government budget costs											
101	Producer subsidies											
102		Wheat	3900		-39.45							
103		Barley	900		2.95							
104	Consumer tax (barley) and subsidy (wheat)											
105		Barley	700		-.13							
106		Wheat	3000		-.22							
107	Total government budget cost											
108			7100		-21.37							
109	Balance of trade: import bills											
110		Wheat	10500		3.56							
111		Barley	1200		-7.85							
112		Total	11700		2.39							

$q = q\,(p, z)$.

However, as we will only consider small changes in the solution around the initial observation, we use this system in log-linearized form, and keep only those exogenous variables for which changes will be considered. In this particular case, the system is simplified to include only the prices of wheat, barley, and livestock. This simplification assumes that the prices of the other agricultural commodities and of the other inputs will not change and that there will be no change in the use of fixed factors.

The output supply and derived-demand system is then written:

$$
(1)\text{–}(4)\quad
\begin{bmatrix}
\Delta S_w \\
\Delta S_b \\
\Delta S_l \\
\Delta D_b
\end{bmatrix}
=
\begin{bmatrix}
E_w^{p_w} & E_w^{p_b} & 0 & 0 \\
E_b^{p_w} & E_b^{p_b} & 0 & 0 \\
0 & 0 & E_l^{p_l} & E_l^{p_b^u} \\
0 & 0 & E_b^{p_l} & E_b^{p_b^u}
\end{bmatrix}
\begin{bmatrix}
\Delta \bar{p}_w \\
\Delta \bar{p}_b \\
\Delta p_l \\
\Delta \bar{p}_b^u
\end{bmatrix},
$$

where S_i represents the supply of commodity i, D_b the derived demand for barley input, p_j the producer price of j, and p_b^u the price of barley as an input for the livestock producers. All prices with a bar above are exogenous. The sign Δ is the log differentiation operator, that is, $\Delta x = dx/x$ is the rate of change in x. The $E_i^{p_j}$ are thus the elasticities of supply or derived-demand of i with respect to p_j. These elasticities are provided in cells A14–F20. Note that, from the profit function theory in Chapter 3, the cross-price elasticities between barley and wheat follow the symmetry constraint:

$$
E_b^{p_w} = E_w^{p_b}\, p_w q_w\,/\,p_b q_b.
$$

This also applies to the cross-price elasticities between livestock and barley. Since this is an incomplete system, the additivity constraint cannot be imposed.

The consumer demand system is also log-linearized and simplified to:

$$
(5)\text{–}(6)\quad
\begin{bmatrix}
\Delta D_w \\
\Delta D_l
\end{bmatrix}
=
\begin{bmatrix}
\mathcal{E}_w^{p_w^c} & \mathcal{E}_w^{p_l} & \mathcal{E}_w^y \\
\mathcal{E}_l^{p_w^c} & \mathcal{E}_l^{p_l} & \mathcal{E}_l^y
\end{bmatrix}
\begin{bmatrix}
\Delta \bar{p}_w^c \\
\Delta p_l \\
\Delta y
\end{bmatrix},
$$

where D_i is the consumer demand for commodity i, y is income, and $\mathcal{E}_i^{p_j}$, $\mathcal{E}_i^y$ are the elasticities of demand for i with respect to the consumer price p_j and income, respectively (notice the difference in notations between E for the producer elasticities of output supply and derived demand, and $\mathcal{E}$ for the consumer elasticities of demand). These elasticities are given in cells G14–J20. Note that, because of symmetry in substitution effects (Slutsky equations in Chapter 2), the cross-price elasticities between wheat and livestock are related by:

$$
\mathcal{E}_w^{p_l} = \frac{w_l}{w_w}\,\mathcal{E}_l^{p_w^c} + w_l(\mathcal{E}_l^y - \mathcal{E}_w^y).
$$

The two cereal markets have price controls, with both producer prices ($\bar{p}_w$ and $\bar{p}_b$) and consumer/user prices ($\bar{p}_w^c$ and $\bar{p}_b^u$) fixed by government. These cereals are tradables, and market equilibria are obtained by residual imports, computed as the difference between demand and supply. For wheat, both consumers and producers are subsidized, as the consumer price is below the border price p^b while the producer price is above the border price:

$$\bar{p}_w^c < p_w^b < \bar{p}_w.$$

For barley, users are taxed at a user price above the border price while producers are subsidized at a producer price even higher above the border price:

$$p_b^b < \bar{p}_b^u < \bar{p}_b.$$

By contrast, because livestock is a nontradable, an endogenous market price equilibrates the livestock market. Producer and consumer prices differ by a large multiplicative marketing margin: $p_l^c = kp_l$, where $k = 1.9$. However, because the margin is multiplicative, $\Delta p_l^c = \Delta p_l$, and we do not need to differentiate between the two prices in terms of rates of change. Therefore, the market equilibrium equations are:

Tradables: $S_w(\bar{p}_w, \bar{p}_b, p_l, \bar{p}_b^u) + M_w = D_w(\bar{p}_w^c, p_l^c, y)$, for wheat;

$\qquad\qquad S_b(\bar{p}_w, \bar{p}_b, p_l, \bar{p}_b^u) + M_b = D_b(\bar{p}_w, \bar{p}_b, p_l^c, \bar{p}_b^u)$, for barley;

Nontradable: $S_l(\bar{p}_w, \bar{p}_b, p_l, \bar{p}_b^u) = D_l(\bar{p}_w^c, p_l^c, y)$, for livestock.

In rates of change, these equilibrium equations are:

$$(7), (8) \quad \Delta M_i + \frac{S_i}{M_i}\Delta S_i - \frac{D_i}{M_i}\Delta D_i = 0, \quad i = w, b,$$

$$(9) \qquad \Delta D_l - \Delta S_l = 0.$$

National disposable income y is composed of maximum profits in the whole agricultural sector and of all other incomes $\bar{R}$, which are considered exogenous because they are not affected by agricultural policy:

$$y = \Pi(p, z) + \bar{R} = \sum_i p_i S_i - \bar{p}_b^u D_b + \bar{R}, \quad i = w, b, l,$$

which, in log-linearized form, gives:

$$(10) \quad \Delta y = \sum_i \frac{p_i S_i}{y}\Delta p_i - \frac{p_b^u D_b}{y}\Delta p_b^u.$$

The model thus consists of 10 equations, 10 endogenous variables (S_w, S_b, S_l, D_b, D_w, D_l, p_l, M_w, M_b, and y), and four exogenous variables ($\bar{p}_w$, $\bar{p}_w^c$, $\bar{p}_b$, $\bar{p}_b^u$). By log-linearizing all the equations and grouping the endogenous variables Δu on the left of the equality sign and the exogenous variables Δx on the right, the complete system can be written as:

$$A\Delta u = B\Delta x,$$

where A is the 10×10 matrix of endogenous variable coefficients and B the 10×4 matrix of exogenous variable coefficients. This system can be solved for the rates of change Δu in the endogenous variables as a function of the rates of change Δx in the exogenous variables as:

$$\Delta u \doteq A^{-1} B \Delta x.$$

1. Solving for the Endogenous Variables

In your spreadsheet, construct the A and B matrices by entering in matrix form the model's system of equations with endogenous variables on the left and exogenous variables on the right. The equations of the multimarket to be entered are thus the following:

(1') $\quad \Delta S_w = E_w^{p_w} \Delta \bar{p}_w + E_w^{p_b} \Delta \bar{p}_b$

(2') $\quad \Delta S_b = E_b^{p_w} \Delta \bar{p}_w + E_b^{p_b} \Delta \bar{p}_b$

(3') $\quad \Delta S_l - E_l^{p_l} \Delta p_l = E_l^{p_b^u} \Delta \bar{p}_b^u$

(4') $\quad \Delta D_b - E_b^{p_l} \Delta p_l = E_b^{p_b^u} \Delta \bar{p}_b^u$

(5') $\quad \Delta D_w - \mathcal{E}_w^{p_l} \Delta p_l - \mathcal{E}_w^y \Delta y = \mathcal{E}_w^{p_w^c} \Delta \bar{p}_w^c$

(6') $\quad -\mathcal{E}_l^{p_l} \Delta p_l + \Delta D_l - \mathcal{E}_l^y \Delta y = \mathcal{E}_l^{p_w^c} \Delta \bar{p}_w^c$

(7') $\quad \Delta M_w + \dfrac{S_w}{M_w} \Delta S_w - \dfrac{D_w}{M_w} \Delta D_w = 0$

(8') $\quad \Delta M_b + \dfrac{S_b}{M_b} \Delta S_b - \dfrac{D_b}{M_b} \Delta D_b = 0$

(9') $\quad \Delta D_l - \Delta S_l = 0$

(10') $\quad \Delta y - \dfrac{p_l S_l}{y} \Delta p_l = \dfrac{p_w S_w}{y} \Delta \bar{p}_w + \dfrac{p_b S_b}{y} \Delta \bar{p}_b - \dfrac{p_b^u D_b}{y} \Delta \bar{p}_b^u.$

In your spreadsheet, carefully construct the A matrix in cells C25–L34 and the B matrix in cells C37–F46. Compute the inverse of matrix A by calling the sequence /Data Matrix Inverse, highlight C25–L34, and place the result in C49. Compute the product $A^{-1}B$ by calling the sequence /Data Matrix Multiply, highlight C49–L58, Return, highlight C37–F46, and place the result in C61.

Cells C74–E77 contain a policy matrix with values for each of the four policy variables, corresponding to the initial value, the new value we want to simulate, and the corresponding percentage change between initial and new value that serves as the Δx vector for the policy simulations. Note that, since all the relations are linear (except in section 2, step c below), we use them with Δx and Δu multiplied by 100, in order to be expressed as a percentage change.

To solve the multimarket model and perform a policy experiment, complete the following steps:

a. Go to the area D74–D77 where the policy experiment is defined. Enter the new value for the controlled prices, reducing, for example, the producer price of wheat $\bar{p}_w^p$ to 4320, that is, by

10%, while keeping the other prices constant. The percentage changes are indicated in E74–E77.

b. Multiply $A^{-1}B$ by the vector of exogenous variables by the sequence /Data Matrix Multiply, highlight C61–F70, Return, highlight E74–E77, and place the result in D87.

2. Computing Supply, Demand, Prices, Imports, Government Subsidy Costs, and Balance-of-Trade Effects

You now have, in your policy results vector, the percentage changes induced in the 10 endogenous variables of your model by the change you gave to one of the exogenous variables. This first experiment models a 10% decline in the producer price of wheat. You want to complement this vector of induced changes by a number of useful policy indicators derived from these changes. They include:

a. Change in the consumer price index: $\Delta CPI = \dfrac{p_w^c D_w}{y} \Delta \bar{p}_w^c + \dfrac{p_l^c D_l}{y} \Delta p_l$.

b. Change in real income: $\Delta \text{real } y = \Delta y - \Delta CPI$.

c. Changes in government budget costs (in percentage in change):

Change in producer subsidy for i: $100\left[\dfrac{(\bar{p}_i^1 - p_i^b)(1 + \Delta S_i)}{(\bar{p}_i^0 - p_i^b)} - 1\right]$, $i = w, b$.

Change in consumer subsidy (wheat) or user tax (barley) for i:

$$100\left[\frac{(p_i^b - \bar{p}_i^{c,u1})(1 + \Delta D_i)}{(p_i^b - \bar{p}_i^{c,u0})} - 1\right], \quad i = w, b,$$

where $\bar{p}_i^0$ is the initial price, $\bar{p}_i^1$ the new price, and p_i^b the border price of commodity i. Remember that D86 to D95 must be divided by 100 in order to obtain ΔS_i and ΔD_i. Compute the growth rate of the total budgetary costs.

d. Balance-of-trade effects:

Import bill for i: ΔM_i, $i = w, b$.

Total import bill: $\Delta M = \sum_i M_i \Delta M_i / \sum_i M_i$, $i = w, b$.

Save your vector of policy results D87–D112 by copying their values in E87–E112. Simulate changes in some of the other exogenous variables (producer price of barley, consumer price of bread, and user price of barley paid by livestock producers), which are able to reduce budgetary costs and observe their effects on the endogenous variables you have calculated. Note that the matrix manipulations you have done in steps a and b of section 1 above need to be redone for each experiment.

3. Interpretation of the Results

It is now time to evaluate the policy results.

In the first experiment where the producer price of wheat was lowered by 10%:

a. How does a change in the producer price of wheat affect the supply of barley and why?

b. Why does the demand for wheat fall even though the consumer price of bread has not changed?

c. How do the supply and the price of livestock change and why?

d. Contrast the observed changes in nominal as opposed to real income. How do you explain the difference?

e. The idea of reducing the producer price of wheat was to lower the cost of farm programs on the government budget. Carefully observe the structure of government subsidies and taxes. Note the indirect effects on the subsidies budget to barley at the producer and livestock user levels.

f. Finally, what is the impact on the balance of trade and why?

Analyze similarly the results obtained with the other simulations of price policies.

4. Computing of Income Distribution Effects

By assuming for simplicity that all rural households have the same production patterns and that all households have the same consumption patterns, we have neglected the role of distribution effects in the computation of income effects. However, if sources of income and consumption shares differ across households, changes in prices will affect the real incomes of the different classes of households differently. This is what is analyzed now. The information on income distribution and consumption by class is reported in the area A113–L133 (Table 11E.2).

Six income classes are considered, three urban and three rural. Nominal incomes of the urban classes are unaffected by the agricultural policy. Nominal incomes of the rural classes are related to the previously determined variables as follows:

$$y_k = \alpha_{kw}\Pi_w + \alpha_{kb}\Pi_b + \alpha_{kl}\Pi_l + \bar{R}_k,$$

where the α_{kw}, α_{kb}, and α_{kl} are the shares of income of class k in the maximum profit obtained in wheat Π_w, barley Π_b, and livestock Π_l and $\bar{R}_k$ is the exogenous other income of that class. Differentiation of this equation gives the relative change in class income:

$$\Delta y_k = \alpha_{kw}\frac{p_w S_w}{y_k}\Delta\bar{p}_w + \alpha_{kb}\frac{p_b S_b}{y_k}\Delta\bar{p}_b + \alpha_{kl}\left(\frac{p_l^p S_l}{y_k}\Delta p_l - \frac{p_b^u D_b}{y_k}\Delta\bar{p}_b^u\right).$$

This is the formula used in cells D144–D146, with class income y_k equal to the product of income per capita and population in class k.

The change in cost of living CPI_k is a weighted average of the change in consumer prices, where the weights β_{ki} are the consumption shares:

$$\Delta CPI_k = \beta_{kw}\Delta\bar{p}_w^c + \beta_{kl}\Delta p_l^c$$

and, finally, the change in real income is the difference between the changes in nominal income and in cost of living.

	A	B	C	D	E	F	G	H	I	J	K	L
113	Table 11E.2. A multimarket for the grain-livestock sector in North Africa: Income distribution											
114												
115	Data for Income distribution											
116	Shares of profits by income group (rural households)						Rural incomes structure					
117		Wheat	Barley	Livestock				Wheat	Barley	Livestock	Other	
118	Poor	.4	.4	.80			Poor	.103	.028	.100	.769	
119	Middle	.1	.3	.15			Middle	.030	.024	.022	.924	
120	Rich	.5	.3	.05			Rich	.240	.039	.012	.709	
121												
122	Budget shares in consumption by income group (percentage)											
123	Rural and											
124	urban	Wheat	Livestock									
125	Poor	8	2									
126	Middle	6	4									
127	Rich	4	10									
128												
129	Base incomes per capita (DA/head)				Population (millions)							
130		Rural	Urban				Rural	Urban				
131	Poor	8000	12000		Poor		7	6				
132	Middle	16000	18000		Middle		3	3				
133	Rich	30000	35000		Rich		1	1				
134												
135	Results of policy experiments on income distribution											
136												
137	Policies		Initial value	Policy			Copy of policy results					
138		ΔPwp	4800	-10	-10	0	0	0				
139		ΔPbp	3900	0	0	-10	0	0				
140		ΔPbu	3500	0	0	0	10	0				
141		ΔPwc	3000	0	0	0	0	10				
142	Nominal income											
143		Rural	(DA/head)	(% change)		(% change over initial values)						
144		Poor	8000		-1.21							
145		Middle	16000		-.34							
146		Rich	30000		-2.42							
147	CPI											
148		Rural/urban	(Index)									
149		Poor	1		-.04							
150		Middle	1		-.07							
151		Rich	1		-.19							
152	Real income											
153		Rural	(DA/head)									
154		Poor	8000		-1.18							
155		Middle	16000		-.27							
156		Rich	30000		-2.24							
157		Urban										
158		Poor	12000		.04							
159		Middle	18000		.07							
160		Rich	35000		.19							

Analyze the income distribution effects of changes in the exogenous prices. Explain, in particular, why the nominal income effects and the *CPI* differ across rural classes. Note each time how a particular policy affects the incidence of poverty and the distribution of income. Save your results in the "copy of policy results" area. Repeat the policy experiments you conducted above.

Exercise 11.2
Policy Simulation with a Multimarket for Brazil

This exercise is not programmed in a Lotus spreadsheet. Instead, it comes as a self-contained interactive package that does not give access to the programming itself. It is only usable on IBM-compatible computers. Although the programming follows the same structure as the one described in the Lotus Exercise 11.1, you need not complete Exercise 11.1 to perform

Table 11E.3. Policy simulation with a multimarket for Brazil: Structure of the model

		Regions			Price formation
	North	South	Interior		
Products					
Wheat (h)		x		T	$\bar{p}_h^c < p_h^b < \bar{p}_h^p$
Soybeans (s)		x	x	NT	$\bar{E}_s \begin{cases} \text{oil } (so) \text{ for consumption, } \bar{E}_{so} \\ \text{meal } (sm) \text{ for } m \text{ crops, } \bar{E}_{sm} \end{cases}$
Export crops (e)	x	x		T	$p_e^p = p_e^b / (1 + t + t_E)$
					$p_e^c = p_e^p (1 + t)$
Minimum price crops (m)	x	x	x	NT	$p_m^c = p_m^p (1 + t)$ or $\bar{p}_m$
Inputs					
Credit (r)					$\bar{r}$
Labor (w)	$\bar{w}$	$\bar{w}$	w	NT	interior, $L^I = L_s^I + L_m^I$
Soy meal (sm)				NT	$\bar{E}_{sm}$
Consumption					
Wheat (h)					$\bar{p}_h^c$
Soy oil (so)					
Export crops (e)					$p_e^c = p_e^p (1 + t)$
Minimum price crops (m)					$p_m^c = p_m^p (1 + t)$, $\bar{G}_m$, $\bar{p}_m$

Policy instruments: $\bar{p}_h^c, \bar{p}_h^p, \bar{E}_{so}, \bar{E}_{sm}, \bar{G}_m, \bar{r}, t, t_E$.
T = tradable, NT = nontradable.

the simulation exercise that follows. We will use this multimarket built for Brazil by Braverman, Hammer, and Brandão (1986) at the World Bank to analyze the results of policy simulation.
To gain access to the program, use the following DOS commands:
>b: (if your diskette is in the disk drive b),
>cd 112MRKT (to move to the directory 112MRKT on your exercise diskette).
Type BRAZIL to start the program.

The underlying model and the list of potential policy changes are described in section 1. In section 2, an analysis of some of the main characteristics of the structure of the economy is conducted, based on the database on production, consumption, and prices. Simulations of price and export policies are then performed in section 3. The main structural features of the model are summarized in Table 11E.3.

1. Summary of the Multimarket Model

There are four producer goods: wheat (h); soybeans (s); export crops (e)—coffee, cocoa, and oranges; and the others, named "minimum-price crops" (m).

They are produced in three regions: North (N), South (S), and Interior (I). The South produces all four goods; the North, only e and m; and the interior, only s and m. Each region should be characterized by a system of supply equations which are themselves functions of all competitive crops prices, all factor prices, and all fixed inputs. However, the model is set in deviation around the observed equilibrium point, and only those variables which will be allowed to change in the simulations need to be explicitly written. No fixed factors are thus considered, and only three variable input prices explicitly enter the model: the price of credit r, the price of soybean meal sm in all regions, and the price of labor w in the Interior. The system of output supply S and derived demand for factor L and intermediate inputs D for the Interior is, for example, written as follows:

$$
\begin{aligned}
\dot{S}_s^I &= 0.85\dot{p}_s^p - 0.05\dot{p}_m^p + E_s^{\bar{p}_m}\dot{\bar{p}}_m && +E_s^r\dot{r} + E_s^w\dot{w}^I \\
\dot{S}_m^I &= -0.02\dot{p}_s^p + 0.10\dot{p}_m^p + E_m^{\bar{p}_m}\dot{\bar{p}}_m && +E_m^r\dot{r} + E_m^w\dot{w}^I \\
\dot{L}_s^I &= E_{L_s}^{p_s}\dot{p}_s^p + E_{L_s}^{p_m}\dot{p}_m^p + E_{L_s}^{\bar{p}_m}\dot{\bar{p}}_m && +0.11\dot{r} - 0.36\dot{w}^I \\
\dot{L}_m^I &= E_{L_m}^{p_s}\dot{p}_s^p + E_{L_m}^{p_m}\dot{p}_m^p + E_{L_m}^{\bar{p}_m}\dot{\bar{p}}_m && +E_{L_m}^{p_{sm}}\dot{p}_{sm} && +0.05\dot{r} - 0.36\dot{w}^I \\
\dot{D}_{sm}^I &= E_{D_{sm}}^{p_s}\dot{p}_s^p + E_{D_{sm}}^{p_m}\dot{p}_m^p + E_{D_{sm}}^{\bar{p}_m}\dot{\bar{p}}_m && -1.5\dot{p}_{sm}, && +E_{D_{sm}}^r\dot{r} + E_{D_{sm}}^w\dot{w}^I
\end{aligned}
$$

where

$\dot{x}$ represents the growth rate of variable x,

S_s^I and S_m^I represent the supply of s and m by the Interior region,

L_s^I and L_m^I represent the demand for labor separately for soybeans and minimum-price crop production, respectively,

D_{sm} represents the demand for soybean meals,

p_s^p, p_m^p represent the producer price for soybeans and minimum-price crop,

p_{sm} represents the market price for soybean meal,

$\bar{p}_m$ represents the government guaranteed price for minimum-price crop,

r and w^I represent the interest rate and the wage in the region,

and E_y^x represents the elasticity of y with respect to x, for those elasticities whose values are not given in the different information tables. The other coefficients represent elasticities too.

The maximum profit is:

$$\Pi^I = p_s^p S_s^I + p_m^p S_m^I - r\bar{K}^I - p_{sm}D_{sm}^I - w^I L^I.$$

After differentiation and simplification, this can be written as:

$$\dot{\Pi}^I = \frac{p_s^P S_s^I}{\Pi^I}\,\dot{p}_s^P + \frac{p_m^P S_m^I}{\Pi^I}\,\dot{p}_m^P - \frac{r\overline{K}^I}{\Pi^I}\,\dot{r} - \frac{p_{sm}D_{sm}^I}{\Pi^I}\,\dot{p}_{sm} - \frac{w^I L^I}{\Pi^I}\,\dot{w}^I.$$

The regions each have a consumption system. They consume wheat, soybean oil (*so*), export crops, and minimum-price crops. Their demand is a function of their income and all consumer prices p_j^c. These are written as:

$$\dot{D}_j^i = E_{jy}^i\dot{Y}^i + \sum_{j'}E_{jj'}^i\,\dot{p}_{j'}^c\,,\quad i = N, S, I,\ \text{and}\ j, j' = h, so, e, m,$$

where E_{jy}^i is the income elasticity for commodity j in region i, and $E_{jj'}^i$ is the price elasticity of demand for j with respect to the price of commodity j' in region i.

The regional income is the sum of the agricultural profit, wage income, and a constant nonagricultural income $\overline{R}$:

$$Y = \Pi + wL + \overline{R}.$$

Differentiating this expression yields:

$$\dot{Y}^i = \frac{\Pi^i}{Y^i}\dot{\Pi}^i + \frac{w^i L^i}{Y^i}(\dot{w}^i + \dot{L}^i),\quad i = N, S, I.$$

The multimarket is a system of market equations for all four goods and for labor in the interior region. Different equilibrium mechanisms apply to the different markets.

Wheat Market (Figure 11E.1a)

Supply from the South only; demand from all three regions; producer and consumer prices fixed by the government; residual imports M_h to balance the market:

$$S_h^S + M_h = \sum_i D_h^i,\quad i = N, S, I,\ \text{with}\ M_h\ \text{endogenous}$$

p_h^p and p_h^c exogenously set by the government, with $\overline{p}_h^c < p_h^b < \overline{p}_h^p$.
Thus, the government incurs the cost of both a subsidy to farmers $(-B_p)$ and to consumers $(-B_c)$.

Export Crops Market (Figure 11E.1b)

Supply from the North and the South; demand from all three regions; border price p_e^b as exogenous; producer and consumer prices derived by taking into account export taxes t_E and indirect taxes t; and residual exports E_e to balance the market:

$$S_e^N + S_e^S = \sum_i D_e^i + E_e,\quad i = N, S, I,\ \text{with}\ E_e\ \text{endogenous},$$

$$p_e^p = \frac{p_e^b}{(1 + t + t_E)},\ \text{producer price, and}$$

$p_e^c = p_e^p(1+t)$, consumer price.

With $p_e^b > \bar{p}_e^c > \bar{p}_e^p$, the government captures a revenue from both consumers ($+ B_c$) and exports ($+ B_E$).

Figure 11E.1. Partial equilibrium analysis of price distortions in the Brazilian multimarket

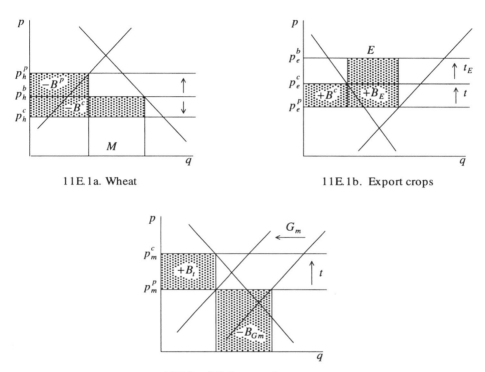

11E.1a. Wheat

11E.1b. Export crops

11E.1c. Minimum-price crops

Minimum Price Crops Market (Figure 11E.1c)

Supply and demand from all three regions. There is an announced support price $\bar{p}_m$ set by the government. Production depends on both the free-market price and the support price. However, the case examined here is for a year in which the free-market price is higher than the announced support price. Therefore, the price is left flexible and equilibrates supply and demand, given an exogenous amount of government purchase $\bar{G}_m$. Using the support price in the supply model is an attempt to capture the risk reduction effect of this support price even when it actually does not apply. Producer and consumer prices differ by the indirect taxes t:

$$\sum_i S_m^i = \sum_i D_m^i + \bar{G}_m, \quad i = N, S, I,$$

$$p_m^c = p_m^p(1+t),$$

$\overline{G}_m$, $\overline{p}_m$, and t exogenously set by the government, and p_m^p endogenous.
The government thus incurs a cost $(-B_{Gm})$ in procurement and a revenue from indirect taxes $(+B_t)$.

Figure 11E.2. Multimarket for Brazil: Soybeans

$$\sum_i S_s^i - \overline{E}_s \quad \to C \begin{cases} \text{oil}: aC - \overline{E}_{so} & \to S_{sm} = D_{sm} & \to p_{sm} \\ \text{meal}: bC - \overline{E}_{sm} & \to S_{so} = D_{so} & \to p_{so} \end{cases} \Bigg\} p_s$$

Soybean Market (Figure 11E.2)

Supply of soybeans from the South and the Interior. These soybeans (s) give two products in fixed proportions: soybean oil (so) for consumption and soybean meal (sm) for feed. The demand for soybean meal is a demand for an input by the producers of cattle. This appears as part of the minimum crops composite. Thus, this is part of a producer output supply and input demand system as specified above. The price p_s is an average of the prices of its components, soybean oil and soybean meal, less fixed-transformation costs d. There are exogenous exports of all three products, and the prices of soybean meal and soybean oil are determined so as to equilibrate the markets:

$\sum_i S_s^i = C + \overline{E}_s$, $i = S, I$, equilibrium condition for soybeans,

$S_{so} = aC - \overline{E}_{so}$, domestic supply for soybean oil,

$S_{sm} = bC - \overline{E}_{sm}$, domestic supply for soybean meal,

$S_{so} = \sum_i D_{so}^i$, equilibrium condition for soybean oil,

$S_{sm} = \sum_i D_{sm}^i$, equilibrium condition for soybean meal,

$p_s = ap_{so} + bp_{sm} - d$, price of soybeans,

where C is domestic availability of soybeans.

Labor Market

In the North and the South, there is an exogenous wage due to labor surplus in the North and integration in a very large labor market in the South. Consequently, these wages will not be allowed to vary in any policy experiments. For this reason, these labor markets are not explicit. By contrast, in the Interior there is an explicit demand for labor which is part of the producer output supply and input demand system and a supply which is a function of the wage. The equilibrium wage balances the market:

$\dot{L} = 0.05\dot{w}$, labor supply,

$L = L_s + L_m$, equilibrium condition,

w, endogenous.

Credit

Subsidized exogenous interest rate $\bar{r}$.

Model Solution

This gives a system of 24 equations that is linearized around the base values and solved for the 24 endogenous variables:

$$S_j^i \text{ (8 nonzero)}, D_k, p_e^p, p_e^c, p_s^p, p_{so}^c, p_{sm}, p_m^p, p_m^c, M_h, L_s, L_m, w,$$

where $j = h, e, s, m;\ k = h, e, so, sm, m;\ i = N, S, I.$

The exogenous variables that can be modified in policy simulations are:

The producer price of wheat, $\bar{p}_h^p$,

The consumer price of wheat (bread), $\bar{p}_h^c$,

The export quota on soybean oil, $\bar{E}_{so}$,

The export quota on soybean meal, $\bar{E}_{sm}$,

The export quota on soybeans, $\bar{E}_s$,

Government purchases of minimum-price crops, $\bar{G}_m$,

The floor price of minimum-price crops, $\bar{p}_m$,

The interest rate for agricultural credit, $\bar{r}$,

The indirect tax rate, t, on export crops and minimum-price crops,

The tax rate on export crops, t_E.

Further results can be derived from the model solution on income distribution, government revenues, and foreign exchange.

In each of the three producing regions, agricultural profits are attributed to three different income groups according to initial shares. The nonagricultural income accruing to the rural groups and the urban nominal income are assumed constant. Group-specific consumption shares are used to compute group-specific consumer price indices. This allows computation of the changes in nominal income and real income by region and class.

Changes in government revenues are computed as the sum of changes in export tax revenues and indirect tax revenues less producers' and consumers' subsidy costs for wheat.

Changes in foreign exchange earnings are the sum of changes in export earnings from the soy products and the export crops less the changes in import costs of wheat.

2. Analysis of the Basic Economic Structure

a. Analyze production in the North. What is produced? What share of the *value* of agricultural production do the export products represent? Is subsistence agriculture (the minimum-price crops) in surplus or deficit? By how much?

b. What share of the production of the export crops is consumed in the country? What are the levels of indirect taxation and of export taxes on these products? You should recall that:

$$p_e^p = p_e^b /(1+t+t_E),$$
$$p_e^c = p_e^p (1+t),$$

where p_e^p, p_e^c, and p_e^b are the producer, consumer, and border prices, respectively, t is the rate of indirect taxation, and t_E is the tax rate on exports.

c. For wheat, Brazil implements a double policy of import substitution and consumer subsidies. What is the rate of protection on domestic production? What is the subsidy rate for consumers? What is the share of imports in total consumption?

d. For the minimum-price crops, what is the level of protection? What is the indirect tax on consumers?

e. In the Northern and Southern regions, the nominal wage for labor is set by the rest of the economy. Only the Interior region has an agricultural labor market that clears by wage determination. What are the elasticities of labor supply and demand on this market?

f. Using budget shares and income and price elasticities in consumption, characterize which goods are relatively more necessary and luxury in nature. Also characterize the substitution possibilities in consumption.

g. Give an example of a product with an elastic supply and one with a low supply elasticity. Are there complementarities in production? What can you say about the substitution effects among products?

3. Policy Simulations

In discussing each result, make sure to clearly identify the causal chains involved.

a. Reduction of the bread subsidy. Simulate the effects of a 10% increase in the consumer price of wheat. What is the impact of this policy on:
   Bread consumption.
   Consumption of other foods. Why? (note the substitutions).
   The other prices (link this to the supply elasticities).
   The government budget.
   The income distribution. Who gains and who loses? Explain why.

b. Reduction of the subsidy to wheat production by decreasing the producer price by 10%. What is the impact of this policy on:
   Wheat production and imports.
   Production of the competitive crop, soybeans.
   The price of soybeans and the impact that this change has on the nominal levels of income in the different regions. To understand this, carefully review the regional structure of production.

c. Discuss another policy of your choice among the list proposed on the diskette.

References

Aloui, Omar, Jean-Jacques Dethier, and Abderrahm Houmy. 1989. "L'impact de la politique d'ajustement sur les secteurs des céréales et de l'élevage au Maroc." Rabat: Ministry of Agriculture and Agrarian Reform, Department of Planning and Economic Affairs.

Barnett, Douglas, Brian Blake, and Bruce McCarl. 1982. "Goal Programming via Multidimensional Scaling Applied to Senegalese Subsistence Farms." *American Journal of Agricultural Economics* 64:720-27.

Binswanger, Hans, and Jaime Quizon. 1984. *Distributional Consequences of Alternative Food Policies in India*. Washington, D.C.: World Bank, Agriculture and Rural Development Department.

Braverman, Avishay, and Jeffrey Hammer. 1986. "Multimarket Analysis of Agricultural Pricing Policies in Senegal." In *Agricultural Household Models: Extensions, Applications, and Policy*, edited by I. Singh et al. Baltimore: Johns Hopkins University Press.

Braverman, Avishay, Jeffrey Hammer, and Antonio Salazar Brandão. 1986. *Economic Analysis of Agricultural Pricing Policies in Brazil: The Wheat and Soybean Case*. Discussion paper. Washington, D.C.: World Bank, Agricultural and Rural Development Department.

Braverman, Avishay, Jeffrey Hammer, and Choong Yong Ahn. 1986. "Multimarket Analysis of Agricultural Pricing Policies in Korea." In *The Theory of Taxation for Developing Countries*, edited by D. Newbery and N. Stern. New York: Oxford University Press for the World Bank.

Braverman, Avishay, Jeffrey Hammer, and Jonathan Morduch. 1985. *An Economic Analysis of Reducing Input Subsidies to the Livestock Sector in Cyprus*. Staff Working Paper no. 782. Washington, D.C.: World Bank.

Brink, Lars, and Bruce McCarl. 1978. "The Tradeoff Between Expected Return and Risk Among Cornbelt Farmers." *American Journal of Agricultural Economics* 60:259-63.

Candler, Wilfred, and Michael Boehlje. 1971. "Use of Linear Programming in Capital Budgeting with Multiple Goals." *American Journal of Agricultural Economics* 53:325-30.

de Janvry, Alain, and Kalandihi Subbarao. 1986. *Agriculture Price Policy and Income Distribution in India*. Delhi: Oxford University Press.

Dethier, Jean Jacques. 1989. "Note on the Analysis of the Impact of Agricultural Policy Reforms in Algeria." Agriculture and Rural Development Department, World Bank.

FAO. 1991. *Working with CAPPA Series*. Rome: Food and Agriculture Organization of the United Nations.

Goreux, Louis, and Alan Manne, eds. 1973. *Multi-level Planning: Case Studies in Mexico*. Amsterdam: North-Holland.

Grundmeier, Eric, Karl Skold, H. H. Jensen, and Stanley Johnson. 1989. *CARD Livestock Model Documentation: Beef*. Iowa State University, Center for Agricultural and Rural Development, Technical Report 88-TR2.

Hazell, Peter, and Roger Norton. 1986. *Mathematical Programming for Economic Analysis in Agriculture*. New York: Macmillan.

Kutcher, Gary, and Pasquale Scandizzo. 1981. *The Agricultural Economy of Northeast Brazil*. Baltimore: Johns Hopkins University Press.

McCarl, Bruce, and Thomas Spreen. 1980. "Price Endogenous Mathematical Programming as a Tool for Sector Analysis." *American Journal of Agricultural Economics* 62:87-102.

McCarl, Bruce. 1992. *Mathematical Programming for Resource Policy Appraisal Under Multiple Objectives*. Madison: University of Wisconsin, The Environmental and Natural Resources Policy and Training Project.

Meeraus, Alexander. 1983. "An Algebraic Approach to Modelling." *Journal of Economic Dynamics and Control* 5:81–108.

Pinstrup-Andersen, Per (ed.) 1993. *The Political Economy of Food and Nutrition Policies*. Baltimore: Johns Hopkins University Press.

Quizon, Jaime, and Hans Binswanger. 1986. "Modeling the Impact of Agricultural Growth and Government Policy on Income Distribution in India." *World Bank Economic Review* 1:101–48.

Raulerson, Richard, and Max Laugham. 1970. "Evaluating Supply Control Policies for Frozen Concentrated Orange Juice with an Industrial Dynamics Model." *American Journal of Agricultural Economics* 52:197-208.

Ray, Daryll, and Earl Heady. 1972. "Government Farm Programs and Commodity Interaction: A Simulation Analysis." *American Journal of Agricultural Economics* 54:578-90.

Robinson, Sherman. 1989. "Multisectoral Models." In *Handbook of Development Economics,* vol. 2, edited by H. Chenery and T. N. Srinivasan. Amsterdam: Elsevier Science Publishers.

Takayama, T., and George Judge. 1971. *Spatial and Temporal Price and Allocation Models.* Amsterdam: North Holland.

Taylor, Lance, Susan Horton, and Daniel Raff. 1980. *Food Subsidy Programs: A Survey.* Cambridge: Massachusetts Institute of Technology, Economics Department.

Thorbecke, Erik, and Lana Hall. 1982. "Nature and Scope of Agricultural Sector Analysis: An Overview." In *Agricultural Sector Analysis and Models in Developing Countries*, edited by E. Thorbecke and L. Hall. Rome: Food and Agriculture Organization of the United Nations, Policy Analysis Division.

Vernon, John, Norfleet Rives, and Thomas Naylor. 1969. "An Econometric Model of the Tobacco Industry." *Review of Economics and Statistics* 51:149-158.

Westhoff, Patrick, Robert Baur, Deborah Stephens, and Williams Meyers. 1990. *FAPRI U.S. Crops Model Documentation.* Iowa State University, Center for Agricultural and Rural Development, Technical Report 90-TR17.

CHAPTER TWELVE

Computable General Equilibrium Models

Computable general equilibrium models (CGE) combine features from the different types of models that we have seen in the previous chapters. They are based on the socioeconomic structure of a SAM, with its multisectoral, multiclass disaggregation. They are, in spirit, close to multimarket models, in which agents' decisions are price responsive and markets reconcile supply and demand decisions. They additionally encompass a certain number of macroeconomic components, such as investment and savings, balance of payments, and government budget. Thus they are best chosen for policy analysis when the socioeconomic structure, prices, and macroeconomic phenomena all prove important.

CGEs have been built to simulate the economic and social impacts of a wide range of scenarios such as the following:

a. Foreign shocks, such as adverse changes in the terms of trade (e.g., an increase in the price of imported oil or a decline in the price of the country's main exports) and forced reduction of foreign borrowing. Because foreign exchange is a particularly scarce resource in many developing countries, the subject of foreign shocks, the tracing out of their impact throughout the economy, and the design of compensating stabilization measures have played a central role in the empirical work with CGEs.

b. Changes in economic policies. Taxes and subsidies are the most commonly analyzed policy instruments, particularly in the trade sector. These models are also used to look at changes in the size and composition of government's current expenditures and investment.

c. Changes in the domestic economic and social structure, such as technological change in agriculture, asset redistribution, and human capital formation.

Several surveys on CGEs have recently appeared in the literature: see Robinson (1989) for a general survey, Decaluwé and Martens (1988) for empirical applications, de Melo (1988) for models with a special focus on trade policy, de Janvry and Sadoulet (1987) for an empirical analysis of agricultural price policies, and Gunning and Keyser (1993) for recent developments. Principles of construction of general equilibrium models are discussed in Dervis, de Melo, and Robinson (1982) and in Shoven and Walley (1992).

CGEs are fundamentally equilibrium models. Thus the proper time frame in which to apply them is the time span that it takes for all markets to reach a new equilibrium after being hit by a shock. In that sense they are often thought of as medium-term models, which solve beyond the period of adjustment disequilibrium, but before major dynamic effects can take place.

CGEs, which solve for a single-period equilibrium, are fundamentally static models. A limited dynamic dimension can be added by considering a sequence of equilibria whereby, in each period, some exogenous variables are updated and some current behavior depends on the solutions from previous periods.

CGEs are almost all set up in "real" terms. There are no assets markets, money is neutral, and all agents make decisions as a function of relative prices. Formally, it implies that the models are homogenous in all prices, and that one price, usually an aggregate domestic price, is chosen as numéraire. Structuralist models, however, differ on this point in the sense that, without necessarily incorporating assets markets, they choose either a wage or the exchange rate to be constant. However, structuralists do not consider this constant price as numéraire, since they argue that decisions on these variables are taken in money terms relative to the preshock price system. We will return to this point later.

12.1. The Structure of CGE Models

A CGE can be described by specifying the agents and their behavior, the rules that bring the different markets in equilibrium, and the macroeconomic characteristics.

12.1.1. Agents and Their Behavior

The agents of the economy are those which have been identified in the SAM, but their rules of behavior are different. Main behavioral differences concern the producers (activity accounts), the traders (commodity accounts), and the households. In a SAM-multiplier model, producers produce whatever is demanded and use factors in fixed proportions, resulting in fixed coefficients in columns. In a CGE, producers are profit maximizers and thus choose their levels of production and their purchases of inputs on the basis of prices. On the supply side (activity rows in the SAM), they also decide whether to sell on the domestic market or to export on the basis of relative prices. In a SAM-multiplier model, imports and domestic production are fixed shares of domestic supply (commodity columns). In a CGE, domestic products and imports are imperfect substitutes, and the composition of domestic supply depends on their relative prices. In a SAM-multiplier model, households' expenditures are determined by constant shares. In contrast, CGE households maximize utility and thus choose their levels of consumption based on income and prices. Other behavioral assumptions of the CGE are not price responsive. Some expenditures, such as those of government, are set constant in nominal or in real terms. Others, such as tax payments, savings, and distribution of factor incomes to the institutions, are given by constant coefficients. The different transfers, such as interhousehold transfers or payments from firms to households, can be of either kind.

12.1.2. Market Equilibrium

In a CGE, all the accounts are endogenous and thus must be in equilibrium. Some actors directly balance their own budgets. Producers sell their total production, factors distribute their income, firms and households spend their income, and investment is determined by available savings. The government budget is usually "balanced" by letting its savings, or deficit if negative, be residually computed. But, for the other accounts, there needs to be a reconciliation between the independent supply and demand decisions. This occurs through the markets: supply and demand of commodities on the product markets, supply and demand of factors on the factor markets, and supply and demand of foreign exchange on the foreign exchange market. The standard rule in these markets is one of price flexibility and endogenous determination of the equilibrium prices, specified as commodity prices, factor prices, and exchange rate, respectively. As we will see later, other rules can be implemented with fixed price and quantity adjustment either on the demand side, like a rationing scheme, or on the supply side, as in a SAM multiplier.

12.1.3. Macroconstraints

There are four main macroeconomic components in a CGE. The first three, the balance of payments, the savings-investment equilibrium, and the government budget, correspond to the three last accounts of the SAM. The fourth component is the aggregate supply of primary factors of production. The overall behavior of the model hinges on the rules which govern these macroconstraints.

In most cases, the balance of payments is constrained to an externally defined level of deficit. Any change in this level of borrowing, or in the conditions of exports or imports, will affect the whole economy through the change of the real exchange rate. In this respect, despite their multisectoral character, CGEs fundamentally behave like the aggregate model described in Chapter 8.

The savings-investment balance plays a small role in most CGEs. Except in the structuralist models (Taylor, 1990) and in the recently developed models with financial sectors, there is no investment behavior per se, and total investment is simply equal to available savings. Furthermore, in a static model, variations of the investment level subsequent to changes in savings have few consequences, as they only affect the level of demand. This does not capture the fact that, from a long-term perspective, investment is a main determinant of growth, and thus any important change in the generation of savings, whether by government or by foreign savings, has important consequences for the economy.

The third macroconstraint derives from a balanced government budget. Unlike sectoral models such as multimarkets, the budgetary consequences of all policies are fully accounted for in a CGE. Thus, for example, liberalization of foreign trade cannot be implemented without either raising other taxes, decreasing government expenditures, or crowding out private investment through government borrowing. Similarly, any sectoral policy of the government will have an impact on other sectors. As a result, which rule is chosen to balance the budget matters very much.

The last important macroeconomic feature is related to the supply of primary factors of production. In most models, capital is considered fixed and fully utilized in every sector. However, labor, or at least certain categories of labor, is mobile across sectors and may or may not be fully employed. Whether or not there is full employment of all these productive resources in the economy is a critical characteristic that strongly determines the response of the model to external shocks and policies. Indeed, while the price system serves to allocate the resources among sectors, the overall level of production is fundamentally determined by the total level of resources productively employed in the economy. If one postulates full employment of resources, reallocation from less productive sectors to more productive sectors, in response to changes in relative prices, can only marginally induce growth. A substantial improvement of incentives would only put pressure on the labor markets and induce wage increases without increasing the overall supply. Less intuitive, but just as true, is the opposite result that a serious recession could not occur in a full-employment economy.

12.1.4. Homogeneity and Numéraire

The behavioral assumptions of a CGE model are usually that agents respond to relative prices rather than to the absolute level of any price. Formally stated, all demand and supply functions of the model are homogenous of degree zero in all prices. The system will then only solve for relative prices. It is standard procedure to set one price or a price index as constant.

This price is called the numéraire. Common practice is to use an aggregate producer price, an aggregate consumer price, or, sometimes, the exchange rate. The numéraire defines a unit of account for all the nominal values. If no other price or nominal values are explicitly set exogenously, then the real values of the system are independent of the choice of numéraire and of the value given to the numéraire. However, care must be given when introducing rigidities, like fixed prices or nominal expenditures, in the model. A fixed wage, for example, has to be interpreted as being fixed in terms of the numéraire. Results will differ according to whether the numéraire is the consumer price index, which then gives a fixed wage in terms of its purchasing power, or rather is an aggregate producer price, which gives a fixed wage in terms of production cost.

While the multisectoral, multiclass design of CGEs is an important characteristic that elicits the distributional impact of shocks and policies, some fundamental macroeconomic mechanisms at work in the model can be better understood in small, aggregate CGEs. Two such mechanisms, the roles of international trade and of the labor market, will be analyzed in the next section, before we continue with a more detailed presentation of the multisectoral models.

Figure 12.1. Foreign trade in a CGE

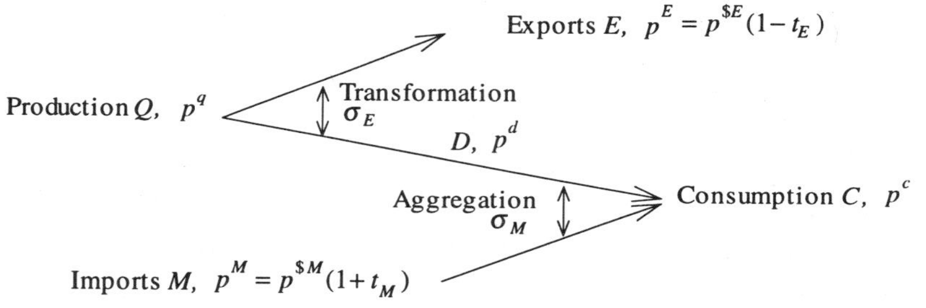

12.2. The Macroeconomics of CGE Models

12.2.1. *Foreign Trade and the Real Exchange Rate*

In SAM-multiplier models, foreign trade was modeled very crudely, with exogenous determination of exports and a fixed proportion of domestic supply imported. In CGEs, by contrast, foreign and domestic commodities are treated as imperfect substitutes. The determination of exports and imports depends on relative prices, as illustrated in Figure 12.1. Domestic production Q is composed of exports E and domestic goods D, with prices p^q, p^E, and p^d. The function for transforming domestic production into E and D is usually a constant elasticity of transformation (CET) function:

(1) $Q = CET(E, D).$

Its elasticity of substitution σ_E reflects the ease with which it is possible to shift the composition of sectoral production between domestic and foreign markets. The optimum ratio of domestic goods to exports (D/E) is then a function of relative prices,

$$(2) \quad \frac{D}{E} = k_E \left(\frac{p^d}{p^E} \right)^{\sigma_E} ,$$

with the producer price p^q as the average sale price.

Symmetrically, consumers consume a composite good C made up of domestic goods D and imports M with price p^M. We assume that the composite commodity is given by a constant elasticity of substitution (CES) aggregation function of M and D, with substitution elasticity σ_M:

$$(3) \quad C = CES(M, D).$$

For consumers maximizing utility, the desired ratio of domestic goods to imports (D/M) is a function of relative prices:

$$(4) \quad \frac{D}{M} = k_M \left(\frac{p^d}{p^M} \right)^{-\sigma_M} ,$$

and the consumer price p^c is the average purchase price.

The prices of foreign goods are determined by international prices, $p^{\$E}$ and $p^{\$M}$, exchange rates, and trade policies:

$$(5) \quad p^E = p^{\$E} \, e \, (1 - t_E)$$

$$(6) \quad p^M = p^{\$M} \, e \, (1 + t_M).$$

Now consider an aggregate, one-sector CGE with this foreign trade specification. For the economy as a whole, a supplementary constraint comes from the necessity of a balance-of-trade equilibrium:

$$(7) \quad p^{\$E} E - p^{\$M} M = 0.$$

This system of seven equations can be solved analytically. Combining equations (2), (4), and (7) yields:

$$k_M \left(\frac{p^d}{p^M} \right)^{-\sigma_M} p^{\$E} = k_E \left(\frac{p^d}{p^E} \right)^{\sigma_E} p^{\$M} ,$$

or $\quad p^d = e \left(\dfrac{k_M}{k_E} \right)^{\frac{1}{\sigma_E + \sigma_M}} \left(p^{\$E} \right)^{\frac{-\sigma_M}{\sigma_E + \sigma_M}} \left(p^{\$M} \right)^{\frac{-\sigma_E}{\sigma_E + \sigma_M}} \left(1 - t_E \right)^{\frac{1}{\sigma_E + \sigma_M}} \left(1 + t_M \right)^{\frac{1}{\sigma_E + \sigma_M}} .$

It reveals that the ratio of domestic price to exchange rate, p^d/e, is influenced by prices of foreign commodities, and thus international prices, and trade taxes, with the extent of influence of foreign prices on domestic price a function of the elasticities of substitution σ_M and σ_E defined above. Note that, although the presentation is a little different, this model is similar to the three-sector model of Chapter 8. We choose here to use the equilibrium of the balance-of-trade condition rather than the equilibrium of the domestic market, but, as is shown there, these two conditions are equivalent. The outcome is thus an equilibrium real exchange rate e/p^d which is a function of external deficit (here for simplicity set equal to zero), international prices, and substitutability between foreign products and domestic goods.

A graphic presentation of this model, adapted from Devarajan, Lewis, and Robinson (1990), is presented in Figure 12.2. It illustrates the mechanisms that reequilibrate the markets after an external shock on the foreign capital flow or on the terms of trade. Assuming that all factors of production are fully employed, production takes place on the production possibility frontier represented in quadrant IV, which depicts the transformation possibility between exports E and domestic commodities D. Corresponding to this production possibility frontier, a consumption

Figure 12.2. Macroeconomic balance in a CGE

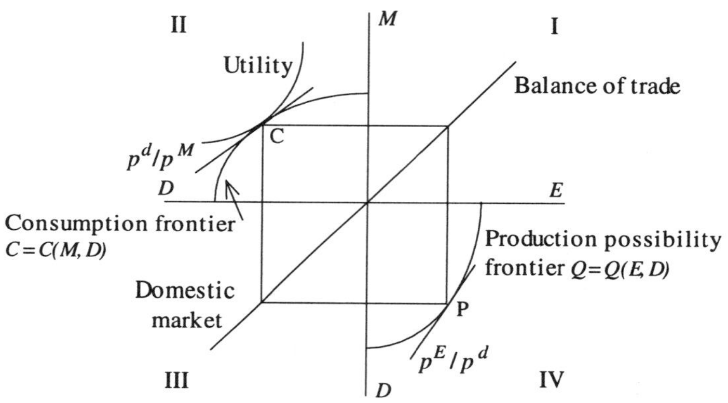

frontier is built in quadrant II as follows: starting from point P, exports E are exchanged in quadrant I, which represents the foreign exchange market, for imports M, and domestic production is delivered by the domestic market, as represented in quadrant III, to the consumer. In quadrant I we have assumed that there is no foreign capital inflow and that the prices of imports and exports are equal. This gives a balance-of-trade line that goes through the origin with a slope equal to one. The consumption of M and D combine in quadrant II at C. Repeating the same transformation from each point of the production frontier, one traces the consumption frontier of quadrant II. The equilibrium solution is then determined in quadrant II by consumer demand behavior. The tangency of the utility curve, which is the import aggregation function, and the consumption possibility frontier determines point C and the equilibrium relative price, p^d/p^M. Working back to the production quadrant, the corresponding production point is P, and the relative price of exports and domestic commodity is given by the tangent to the production possibility frontier at P. The economy produces at point P and consumes at point C.

Consider what would happen if foreign capital inflow increased to some value $B > 0$. This is represented in Figure 12.3. The balance-of-trade line and the consumption possibility frontier shift vertically by this amount B. The new equilibrium consumption is C^*, with more consumption of both D and M and an increase in the price ratio p^d/p^M. On the production side, the relative price has shifted in favor of the domestic good and against the export. This represents an appreciation of the real exchange rate defined as the Dutch disease, as was described in Chapter 8. Production for the domestic market rises and production for exports declines.

Consider now an adverse terms-of-trade shock represented by an increase in the world price of the imported good. This is depicted in Figure 12.4 by a rotation of the balance-of-trade line. The consumption possibility frontier is correspondingly transformed. The characteristics of the new equilibrium depend crucially on the value of the elasticity of substitution σ_M. Figures 12.4a and 12.4b depict the extreme cases of complementarity, $\sigma_M = 0$, and perfect substitutability, $\sigma_M = \infty$. In the first case, consumption of the two commodities will remain in the same proportion, and there will be less consumption of both imports and domestic goods. On the production side, the new equilibrium is P^*. Exports have increased in order to generate foreign exchange to

Figure 12.3. Increase in foreign capital inflow

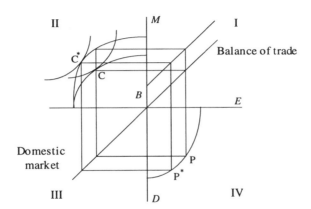

Real exchange rate appreciates: $p^E/p^d \downarrow$.
Exports E decrease and domestic sales D increase.

pay for the more expensive imports, and the price ratio p^E/p^d has also increased to attract resources away from D to E. There has been a real depreciation of the exchange rate and an opening of the economy to foreign trade. In contrast, when domestic goods and imports are perfect substitutes, as represented in Figure 12.4b, the new tangent to the curve C^* is to the left of the old consumption point C. Consumption shifts drastically away from the more expensive imports and toward domestic goods. At the new equilibrium, production of D rises and the real exchange rate appreciates. The economy is now closing to foreign trade. When $\sigma_M = 1$, there is no change in either the real exchange rate or the production structure of the economy.

The real exchange rate will thus depreciate in response to an adverse terms-of-trade shock only when $\sigma < 1$, which is frequently the case for the imports of developing countries. Section 12.4 will use full CGEs of Asian and African countries to show the same contrasted results due to an increase of the cereal import price.

Figure 12.4. Change in world price

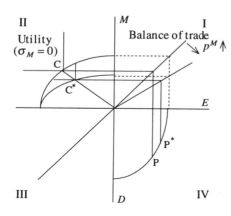
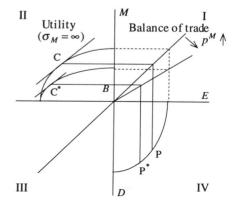

12.4a. Imports and domestic product
complements in consumption.
Real exchange rate depreciates: $p^E / p^d \uparrow$.
E increases and D decreases.

12.4b. Imports and domestic product
perfect substitutes in consumption.
Real exchange rate appreciates: $p^E / p^d \downarrow$.
E decreases and D increases.

12.2.2. The Labor Market Closure

The aggregate level of production, considered fixed in the previous section, is essentially determined by the functioning of the factor markets. To see this, complete the previous model with the following equations determining aggregate output:

Production: $Q = Q(\overline{K}, L)$

Labor demand: $L^d = L(p^q / w)$

Labor supply: L^s

Labor market closures: Full employment: $L^s = L^d$

                         Labor surplus: $w = w(P)$ and $L^s > L^d$.

The first equation states that aggregate output is a function of two factors of production, capital and labor. Capital is assumed to be fixed in the short run, and labor is thus the only variable factor. The profit-maximizing behavior of the productive sector implies that labor demand is a function of the ratio of output price to wage. Consider labor supply to be exogenous. If the labor market is assumed to always be in equilibrium, then a flexible wage adjusts until labor demand is equal to labor supply. Alternatively, if there is some rigidity in the wage forma-tion, with wage above its equilibrium value, then labor is in surplus in the economy. The wage equation sets the wage indexed to a given price index P. Without disaggregating the economy into social groups, we can characterize the workers' welfare by the purchasing power of the wage w/p^c, where p^c is the consumption price.

Consider what will happen in response to the different shocks analyzed above. If there is full employment, aggregate output is always constant and equal to its maximum level. The wage adjusts proportionally to the output price p^q, to maintain constant what is called the *product wage*, w/p^q. How does the real wage, in terms of the aggregate consumer price, vary? The output price is an average of export and domestic prices with weights equal to the sale values of exports and domestic production. Consumer price is, similarly, an average price of import and domestic prices with weights equal to the values of imports and domestic production. The real wage is written:

$$\frac{w}{p^c} = k\frac{p^q}{p^c} = k\frac{(D/Q)\,p^d + (E/Q)\,p^E}{(D/C)\,p^d + (M/C)\,p^M},$$

where k is a factor of proportionality. The real wage will thus decrease whenever the foreign import price increases or there is a real devaluation and capital flow is positive (p^d/e decreases and $p^M M > p^E E$).

The macroeconomic results are quite different when there is a labor surplus and the labor market is in disequilibrium. There will be output growth or decline depending on whether the product wage decreases or increases. This clearly depends on the price to which the wage is indexed. Assume, for example, that the wage is indexed to the domestic price, $P = p^d$, indicating that wages are really determined by the truly domestic or nontradable part of the economy. The product wage is then:

$$\frac{w}{p^q} = k\frac{p^d}{p^q} = \frac{k}{(D/Q) + (E/Q)\,p^E/p^d},$$

and a real devaluation induces growth. If wages were indexed to the consumer price, $P = p^c$, then a real devaluation, induced by a decline in foreign capital flow or by an import price increase in the context of positive capital flow, would induce a recession.

This aggregate model underscores that aggregate output and welfare are two quite distinct concepts that may vary in opposite directions in response to external shocks, and that output response crucially depends on the functioning of the labor markets. In particular, with full employment of all factors, variation in output will only come from reallocation of resources among sectors and will usually only be small.

12.3. Construction of CGE Models

12.3.1. Flow Chart and Functional Specifications

A full presentation of the equations of a CGE is given in Table 12.1. However, the approximate graphical presentation of Figure 12.5 illustrates the functioning of a multisectoral CGE. The model is a system of simultaneous equations expressing the decisions of the agents, which, for the sake of this presentation, we will decompose into a succession of decisions and adjustment processes. Start, for example, with given prices, p^d, p^E, and p^M. The producer price is calculated using the elasticity of transformation between exports and domestic sales. The activities, shown in the upper left corner, use fixed factors of production: capital and land. Given prices and wages, profit maximization behavior determines the activities' demand for labor. If labor markets are perfect, wages, labor supply, and labor demand will adjust until full

Table 12.1   Equations of the computable general equilibrium model

1. Equations of the model

Production

(1) $Q_i^s = CES(\overline{K}_i, L_{ki})$ Production technology

Labor markets

(2) $L_{ki} = CES**(p_i^q, w)$ Labor demand

(3) $L_k^s = L_k^s(w_k, p^c)$ Labor supply

(4) $\sum_i L_{ki} - L_k^s = 0$ Labor market equilibrium

Factor remuneration

(5) $F_k = F_k(w_k L_k^s, t_k)$ Wage income

(6) $V_i = V_i(p_i^q Q_i^s - \sum_k w_k L_{ki}, t_i)$ Nonwage income

Institution disposable income

(7) $Y_h = Y_h(\alpha_{hk} F_k, \alpha_{hi} V_i, t_h)$ Household income

(8) $Y_G = Y_G(Q_i^s, F_k, V_i, Y_h, M, E, t)$ Government income

Savings and investment

(9) $S_G = Y_G - \overline{C}_G$ Government savings

(10) $S_h = s_h Y_h$ Household savings

(11) $S = \sum S_h + S_G + RF$ Total savings

(12) $I_i = k_i S / p_i^k$ Investment by sector

(13) $p_i^k = p_i^k(p^c)$ Price index for investment by sector i

Product demand

(14) $Z_i = \sum_j \Gamma_{ij} I_j$ Demand for investment goods

(15) $C_{hi} = C_{hi}\left[(1 - s_h)Y_h, p^c\right]$ Household consumption

(16) $p_i^c = CES^\circ(p_i^d, p_i^M)$ Composite consumer price

(17) $C_{Gi} = c_{Gi} \overline{C}_G$ Government consumption

External market

(18) $D_i / M_i = d_i = CES*(p_i^d, p_i^M)$ Ratio of domestic to import demand

(19) $p_i^M = p_i^{\$M} e (1 + t_{Mi})$ Import price

(20) $M_i = \left[\sum C_{hi} + C_{Gi} + Z_i + (AQ)_i\right] / (1 + d_i)$ Imports

(21) $E_i / D_i = CET*(p_i^E, p_i^d)$ Ratio of exports to domestic sales

(22) $p_i^E = p_i^{\$E} e (1 - t_{Ei})$ Export price

(23) $p_i^q = CET^\circ(p_i^d, p_i^E)$ Composite producer price

(24) $\sum_i p_i^{\$M} M_i - \sum_i p_i^{\$E} E_i - F = 0$ Equilibrium

Equilibrium on the product markets

(25) $Q_i^d = \left[\sum C_{hi} + C_{Gi} + Z_i + (AQ)_i\right] d_i / (1 + d_i) + E_i$ Demand for domestic commodities

(26) $Q_i^d = Q_i^s$ Equilibrium

Numéraire

(27) $P = \sum_i \beta_i p_i^c = 1$ Consumer price index as numéraire

Table 12.1 Equations of the computable general equilibrium model (cont.)

2. Exogenous variables and parameters

$\overline{K}_i$	Capital stock in sector i
F	Foreign capital flow
$p_i^{\$M}, p_i^{\$E}$	Foreign prices of imports and exports
t_k, t_i, t_h	Taxes on labor category k, nonlabor income i, and household h
t_{Ei}, t_{Mi}	Export taxes and import tariffs
a_{hk}, a_{hi}	Share of household h in wage income k and nonwage income i
$\overline{C}_G, c_{Gi}$	Total and shares in government consumption
s_h	Household saving rate
k_i, G_{ji}	Share of savings invested in sector i and capital composition in sector i
$A, (AQ)_i$	Matrix of input-output coefficients and intermediate demand for good i
b_i	Weights in aggregate price index

3. Endogenous variables

Q_i^s	Domestic production in sector i
L_{ki}, L_k^s, w_k	Demand in sector i, supply, and wage of labor of category k
F_k	After-tax wage income of skilled category k
V_i	After-tax nonwage income in sector i
Y_h, Y_G	Income of household h and government revenues
S_h, S_G	Savings of household h and government
I_i	Investment in sector i
C_{hi}, C_{Gi}, Z_i	Private and government consumption and demand for investment
D_i, Q_i^d	Domestic and total demand for domestic good
M_i, E_i	Imports and exports
d_i	Ratio of domestic demand to imports
e	Exchange rate
p_i^d, p_i^q	Producer price of domestic and composite goods
p_i^c, p	Consumer price of composite goods and aggregate price index
p_i^k	Price of capital goods in sector i
p_i^M, p_i^E	Import and export prices in domestic currency

4. Functions

CES	Constant elasticity of substitution function
*CES**	Derived demand relation from cost minimization in a CES
*CES***	Derived demand relation from profit maximization in a CES
CES°	Derived aggregate price from a CES aggregation function
CET	Constant elasticity of transformation function
*CET**	Derived ratio of demand from profit maximization in a CET
CET°	Derived aggregate price from a CET aggregation function

Figure 12.5. CGE flow chart

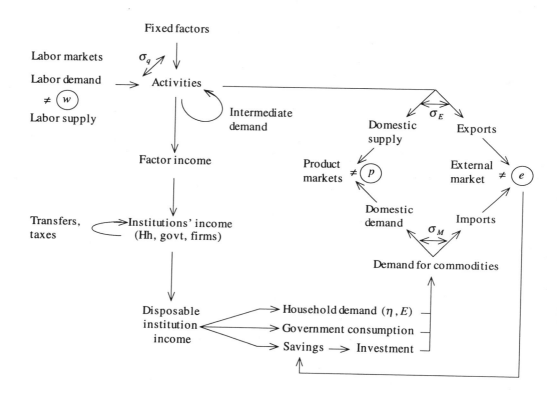

The symbol $\neq \; \boxed{p}$ represents a market mechanism with equilibrium price p
σ_q are elasticities of substitution between factors of production
σ_M are elasticities of substitution between imports and domestic goods
σ_E are elasticities of transformation between exports and domestic goods
η and E are income and price elasticities of household consumption

employment is reached. Factor incomes are then distributed to the institutions, households, firms, and government. Transfers among institutions, such as taxes to government, distribution of profits, and government transfers to households and firms, modify initial incomes and define the disposable income of the institutions.

The savings-consumption behavior of these institutions is analyzed next. For the government, this proceeds from explicit policies. Firms are usually assumed to save all residual income. Households have constant but socially differentiated saving rates and explicit demand systems derived from utility maximization. The consumer prices necessary for these decisions are determined from domestic prices, imported prices, and elasticities of substitution between imports and domestic goods. Savings determine the total level of investment. Allocation between sectors is exogenous, and the commodity composition of investment demand is derived from exogenous coefficients. Adding consumption and investment demand yields total commodity demand. The distribution of this demand between imports and domestic goods, a function of relative prices and the elasticities σ_M, defines domestic demand and import demand by commodity.

On the producer side, allocation of production between domestic and export markets depends on relative prices and elasticities of transformation σ_E. This defines domestic supply and exports by commodity. On the foreign exchange market, imports form total demand of foreign exchange and exports form total supply. Domestic market disequilibria between supply and demand for the different commodities and disequilibrium on the foreign exchange market are simultaneously resolved by adjustment of the domestic prices and the exchange rate. We thus reach the end of the circle with a new set of prices p^d, p^E, and p^M. We can then think of a new round in which producers' decisions are modified to adapt to new prices, incomes adjust, and so on. This continues until the process converges to a set of prices that ensure equilibrium of all markets.

This pictorial description confirms that the only areas in which there are behavioral relationships that go beyond fixed values or fixed shares are in production, consumption, imports, and exports decisions. Production is usually represented by fixed input-output coefficients for intermediate goods and CES functions for labor and capital, with elasticities of substitution σ_q. Labor categories are themselves aggregated with either a Cobb-Douglas or a CES function. The household demand system is either the Linear Expenditure System (LES) or the Almost Ideal Demand System (AIDS), characterized by income elasticities η and the matrix of price elasticities E. As seen above, imports derive from a CES aggregation function of imports and domestic goods, with elasticities σ_M, and exports from the CET transformation possibility function between exports and domestic goods, with elasticities σ_E. Alternative specifications can, evidently, be substituted for any of these functions, especially when empirical work supports them.

12.3.2. Data Requirements

CGE models are not estimated, only "calibrated." This calibration is based first and foremost on exact replication of the base year data compiled in the SAM.

The SAM gives a consistent and complete record of nominal values of transactions in the base year. Measurement units for labor categories are chosen so that all wages are initially equal to one. Similarly, measurement units for quantities of domestic commodities, imports, and exports are chosen so that the consumer prices of domestic goods and imports, the world price of exports, and the exchange rate are all equal to one in the base year. With this normalization rule, all initial quantities and prices can be computed and parameters that are directly computed from shares can be easily derived. Share parameters of the CES and CET are also directly derived from observed values in the SAM.

Only the four sets of elasticities described above are necessary to complete the parameter requirements for the model: the elasticities of substitution σ_q between labor and capital, the income and price elasticities of household consumption η and E, the elasticities of substitution σ_M, and the elasticities of transformation σ_E. These must be collected from independent studies.

Estimated demand systems are often available, although some reconciliation is generally necessary between the aggregation schemes of the available analyses and of the model. As seen in Chapter 2, LES parameters can be recovered from estimated income elasticities by income class and a value for the flexibility of money. Values for the flexibility of money have an order of magnitude relatively well established from international comparisons, ranging from -3 to -1 for per capita incomes ranging from those of Chile and Argentina to that of the United States (Chapter 2), and from -7.5 to -2 as income rises from \$100 to \$3000 1970 U.S. dollars (Lluch, Powell, and Williams, 1977). Import and export functions can be estimated from time series usually available in national accounts. Because econometric estimates of the elasticities of substitution among factors are seldom available, most CGEs are built with approximate values for these parameters. Luckily, experience has shown that the empirical results obtained from simulations with CGEs are quite insensitive to the specific values of all these elasticities, although, as we have seen in the previous section for σ_M, they crucially depend on their order of magnitude. In fact, the possible range of substitutability is relatively well represented by four values: 0.3 for very low substitutability, 0.8 for medium-low, 1.2 for medium-high, and 3.0 for very high. The use of these educated guesses, which should not obscure the need for better specification, serves to obtain preliminary solutions that can be used to initiate a policy dialogue.

Dynamic models are much more demanding. Information must be acquired on the allocation of investment and depreciation rates to update the capital stocks, on population growth and mobility across labor categories to update the supply of labor, and on eventual changes in parameters. The change in productivity coming from technological change, which is potentially linked to the degree of renewal of capital and thus to investment, represents the most important parameter in this estimation process. Dynamic models are validated by comparing a base run with the country's historical path before any counterfactual experiments are performed.

12.3.3. Alternative Closure Rules: Structuralist Models

Low, or even zero, substitutability between products or factors in the core model already represents a certain degree of rigidity in the economy. More fundamental structuralist features are introduced in CGE models by alternative rules of functioning of some of the markets, more commonly referred to as market imperfections.

As seen above, the rules in the labor markets are an important determinant of the results. In some labor markets, an infinitely elastic supply at a given wage rate is more realistic than the neoclassical market-clearing mechanism. The relevant rules of wage formation then need to be specified. One theory assumes fixed nominal wages, thus reflecting short-run institutional constraints on the adjustment of wages to the cost of living. Another wage theory specifies fixed real wages, in accordance with an institutionalized subsistence level or efficiency theory of wage. Note, however, that real CGEs cannot accommodate this distinction, as there is no inflation, and "nominal" is defined relative to the numéraire. Models that follow this theory thus differ in the reference price with respect to which the wage is fixed. Any other empirical model of wage formation and, in particular, a model of partial adjustment to some prices and/or the unemployment level, can be specified. The choice among these alternative specifications of wage formation has both important macroeconomic and distributional implications.

With respect to product markets, price regulation, as is often the case in the agricultural sector, can substitute for the market-clearing mechanism. The adjustment mechanism then needs to be specified. Excess supply and demand of goods can be absorbed by variation of stocks, or by exports or imports. Alternatively, specific rules for quantity rationing can absorb the excess demand. In the industrial sectors, a downward stickiness of prices with a resulting cut in production and excess capacity in terms of installed capital is commonly observed. This situation is modeled through a markup-pricing rule and production levels which adapt exactly to demand.

On the external markets, regulated exchange rates are also a common feature of developing countries. Note, however, that the exchange rate that is used here is a real exchange rate due to the price normalization of the model. As it was discussed in Chapter 8, the mere fixing of the official exchange rate does not entail control of the real exchange rate. The models can, however, be used to simulate the adjustment of the economy under a fixed real exchange rate. Specification of such an exogenous exchange rate generates disequilibrium on the external market, which is eliminated by alternative rationing schemes or by a compensating capital inflow.

Finally, the savings-investment equilibrium can have alternative formulations. In some models an investment-driven closure is justified by an active participation of the state in the investment program. This is a common feature in many developing countries. Because investment is then exogenous, savings must be raised to match this program. A possible closure is to assume that government savings complement private savings, and that another component of the government budget becomes residual. An alternative is to allow foreign borrowing to complement domestic savings at the required level. A more fundamental change of the macroeconomic closure occurs when the price index does not serve as a numéraire and the adjustment of savings to exogenous investment comes through a more general adjustment of the economy. Two cases of this are the classical Keynesian multiplier and the Kalecki closure rule used in Taylor's (1990) Latin American structuralist models. In the first case, all prices are markup prices and relative wages are fixed, with one of the wages serving as the numéraire. The level and the structure of production are completely demand-determined. At equilibrium, savings are necessarily equal to the corresponding demand for investment goods. This is essentially the SAM-multiplier model. In the second case, prices are flexible and nominal wages and the exchange rate are fixed. The price level adjusts to match demand with output. Because wages and the exchange rate are fixed, savings adjust to investment through changes in real wages and the real exchange rate. Empirical models usually encompass a mix of these two cases, with markup prices in some industrial sectors and flexible prices in other sectors.

12.3.4. Exogenous Variables: Definition of Shocks and Policies

The range of simulations and policy experiments that can be done with CGEs includes variation in any of the exogenous variables or parameters that are significant to the overall model:

International contextual variables: prices of major imports or exports, transfers from the rest of the world, and balance-of-payments deficit (examples in Benjamin, Devarajan, and Weiner, 1989; Sanderson and Williamson, 1985; Clarete and Roumasset, 1990).

Domestic structural parameters: productivity parameters, level of fixed factors of production, aggregate level of labor supply (see Narayana, Parikh, and Srinivasan, 1987, for a study of investment in irrigation).

Policy instruments: tax and subsidy rates, government expenditures, government transfers (examples in Moran and Serra, 1993; de Melo, 1988).

Parameters of the model, such as elasticities of substitution or supply elasticities, may also be altered. Such simulations may be performed as sensitivity analyses. Sensitivity analyses are useful in assessing the robustness of the results to parameters which are only approximately known. Alternatively, parameter changes may denote a real structural change due to a change in behavior, in the environment, or in a policy not explicitly represented in the model. It is clear that the link from the assumed change to the parameter needs, in that case, to be established outside the model.

12.4. Examples of CGE Analysis of Policy Scenarios

12.4.1. GATT and Increase in Food Import Price for Low-Income Countries

Table 12.2 gives the effects of rising world prices of cereals and animal products, a potential outcome of the GATT negotiations, simulated with CGEs for archetype economies representative of two contrasted subsets of low-income countries: African countries where cereal imports are not competitive with domestic production, and Asian countries which produce cereals that are competitive with imports (Sadoulet and de Janvry, 1992). The two models have the same macroeconomic closures: the numéraire is the aggregate producer's price, foreign borrowing is exogenous, the exchange rates are flexible, there is a surplus of unskilled labor, all other markets are clearing through prices, and the government budget deficit is maintained constant through a proportional change in expenditures. The long-term effect is given by assuming that total factor productivity is affected by the levels of private and public investment.

There are very sharp contrasts in the results obtained with the two archetypes. In both cases, GDP falls, but for very different reasons. Accordingly, differential policy measures should be implemented in order to restore growth and protect the welfare of the poor. These results show the following:

a. In Africa (column 1), the consumer price of food crops increases by only 3% and the consumption of both imported cereals and domestically produced food falls. Cereal imports are reduced by less than the 20% rise in the import price of cereals, with the result that the cereals import bill increases, forcing the country to *devalue* its currency. Resources are reallocated from less tradable agricultural crops to agroexports. The policy implication for these countries is to capitalize maximally on exchange rate devaluation by specializing further in the production of their comparative advantage crops and trading for the rest.

b. The social cost, measured by the change in real income of the five social classes, is spread among all classes. The losses are, however, regressive in agriculture because larger farmers are already more engaged in the production of agroexports, whose prices rise. In the urban sector, the poor lose little, as the rise in food prices is small. The rich lose from the reduction in economic growth.

c. By contrast, in Asia (column 2), the rising world cereals price is transmitted to the whole food crops sector, where producer prices increase by 8.8%. This leads to both a sharp fall in the

Table 12.2. Impact of a 20% increase in price of cereals and animal products on poor African and Asian countries (percent changes over base values)

	Short run Africa	Short run Asia	Long run Asia	Food subsidies Africa	Food subsidies Asia	Income transfers Africa	Income transfers Asia	Food aid Africa	Food aid Asia
Macroeconomy									
GDP at market prices	−0.3	−0.8	−1.5	−2.6	−2.0	−1.0	−1.5	0.2	0.0
Absorption	−0.8	−1.0	−1.6	−3.0	−2.1	−1.4	−1.6	−0.3	−0.2
International trade									
Exchange rate	0.7	−4.8	−4.9	0.2	−4.2	0.5	−4.7	0.8	−4.9
Agricultural exports	0.6	−3.9	−4.5	−1.2	−3.9	0.2	−4.0	0.8	−3.7
Cereal imports	−10.7	−76.7	−76.9	−5.9	−52.7	−10.0	−71.3	−11.7	−90.6
Producer prices									
Agricultural terms of trade	−0.4	5.3	5.0	4.4	7.9	0.4	6.4	−0.8	3.8
Price of agricultural exports	0.7	−3.5	−3.4	0.2	−2.9	0.4	−3.4	0.7	−3.7
Price of food crops	0.1	8.8	8.6	6.4	12.0	0.9	9.6	−1.1	5.4
Agricultural production									
Export crops	0.6	−2.3	−2.7	−1.2	−2.3	0.2	−2.4	0.7	−2.2
Food crops	0.0	2.9	2.3	1.3	3.7	0.2	3.0	−0.3	1.6
Government budget									
Government deficit	1.0	−6.9	−7.2	0.3	−6.1	0.7	−6.8	1.1	−7.2
Export taxes	1.4	−8.4	−9.2	−1.0	−7.9	0.7	−8.5	1.5	−8.5
Food subsidies		5.7	4.9		11.8		7.1		0.2
Tariff revenues	0.0	−3.6	−4.3	−2.2	−3.8	−0.6	−3.9	0.4	−3.3
Current expenditures	0.2	−5.2	−6.2	−11.4	−16.5	−4.2	−12.7	0.5	−3.9
Investment									
Public investment	0.0	−5.5	−6.6	−11.1	−16.8	−4.2	−13.0	0.4	−4.3
Private investment	−0.2	1.6	1.0	−0.9	1.2	−0.4	1.5	−0.2	1.6
Real incomes									
Landless and small farmers	−2.0	−2.5	−3.0	2.2	−1.6	−0.6	−0.9	−0.2	−0.6
Medium farmers	−1.5	0.1	−0.5	1.5	1.3	−1.4	−0.2	−1.3	0.5
Large farmers	−0.4	5.2	4.3	0.7	7.1	−0.7	4.3	−0.5	2.5
Urban poor	−0.7	−2.6	−3.1	−4.8	−3.1	0.4	0.2	0.2	0.1
Urban rich	−0.7	−2.0	−2.6	−5.9	−4.4	−2.6	−3.9	−0.3	−1.2
Consumption									
Food consumption	−2.3	−3.7	−4.3	1.0	−0.7	−1.9	−3.2	−1.3	−1.6
Consumer price of food	3.0	9.0	8.8			3.6	9.8	1.9	5.6

Source: Sadoulet and de Janvry, 1992.

consumption of cereals and an increase in the domestic production of food crops. The result is that cereal imports fall by much more than the 20% increase in the world cereals price, resulting in a foreign exchange savings and a *revaluation* of the exchange rate. International trade thus shrinks in Asia while expanding in Africa. This contrast in the impacts of the same external price shock on the real exchange rate and on the structure of trade in Africa and Asia illustrates the reasoning done with the aggregate model in section 12.2.1. The policy implication for Asia is to enhance the supply response to rising cereals prices by improving the elasticity of supply and seeking productivity gains in food production for import substitution. This calls for greater public investment in food production and promotion of new technological packages.

d. The social effects of rising world prices are also quite different in the Asian context. The large farmers' real incomes increase sharply in relation to their large marketed surplus of food. The small farmers and landless lose, as they are net buyers of food at the inflated price. The urban rich are negatively affected by the reduction in direct and indirect employment linked to falling government expenditures.

e. There is a sharp contrast in the impact of rising world prices on government across continents. In Africa, increased trade tax revenues allow the government to maintain the level of public investment, while in Asia the government has to sharply reduce its expenditures. Column 3 gives the long-run negative consequences of this budget adjustment. In spite of the modest protection of private investment achieved in the short run, the fall in public and private investment over time leads to a long-run fall in GDP. Thus absorption, defined as domestic consumption and investment, falls correspondingly and the real income of each social class worsens over time. International loans must be sought in order to protect investment in food production or in other nonagricultural sources of growth.

f. Three approaches to compensation are examined in columns 4 to 9. When food subsidies are introduced to maintain the consumer price of food constant at the preliberalization level, the macroeconomic effects are enormously costly. The tremendous loss in growth due to these effects thus affects the urban poor anyway. The alternative of targeted income transfers sharply reduces the macroeconomic and public expenditure costs of protecting the poor. However, this scheme is unlikely to be politically feasible, given its high cost to the nonpoor. Targeted income transfers under the form of international food aid effectively protect the welfare of the poor. As with all food aid programs, producer prices of food crops fall. This indicates that while targeted food aid is important as a short-run instrument to palliate the negative welfare effects of rising food prices, it does not substitute for a long-run strategy of agricultural development.

12.4.2. Stabilization Policies in Response to External Shocks: Efficiency, Welfare, and Political Feasibility

We present here the simulation results of alternative approaches to stabilization and adjustment obtained with a CGE model for Ecuador which has both real and financial sectors (de Janvry, Sadoulet, and Fargeix, 1991). This is the model that was used to generate the GDP and rural income trajectories in Figure 1.1. The objective of presenting these results is to illustrate use of the policy evaluation criteria discussed in Chapter 1. These criteria are:

Economic performance (efficiency) measured by: changes in real GDP, in the real exchange rate, in the rate of inflation, and in employment.

Welfare measured by:

For *equity*: changes in the real income of several classes of households, ranging from small to large farmers in the rural sector, and from low to high education households in the urban sector.

For *poverty*: changes in poverty indices measuring the incidence of poverty in the population, the absolute number of poor, and the Foster-Greer-Thorbecke (FGT) poverty index.

Political feasibility measured by:

Factor incomes: changes in skilled labor income, in agricultural export profits, and in manufacturing profits. These factor incomes capture the response of the dominant corporatist forces in society.

Political feasibility indexes: changes in the indices representing political response under democracy (real income changes weighted by the number of people in each group) and economic power (real income changes weighted by the average per capita income of each group).

The model has several features that are important to know in order to interpret the results: (1) wages only partially adjust to inflation and to the level of unemployment; (2) government current expenditures are principally wages paid to skilled civil servants which create effective demand, while government capital expenditures employ unskilled labor in construction projects and create both short-run effective demand and medium-run productivity gains; (3) poor households have highly diversified sources of income, with the rural poor earning 66% of their income on labor markets and the urban poor 43% of their incomes from profits in informal sector activities.

Variables are at their observed levels in year 1 (Table 12.3). Stabilization policies are introduced in year 2 to counteract a foreign sector shock created by a 40% reduction in the government's foreign borrowing capacity and a 30% fall in the price of oil exports. The three policy responses which government can introduce in year 2 are: (1) exchange rate adjustment with no fiscal measures; (2) fiscal austerity to maintain the government deficit at the preshock level; and (3) a combination of fiscal austerity for stabilization and trade liberalization for adjustment as pursued by the Ecuadorian government.

The results show that, in terms of efficiency, there is a trade-off between the short run, where letting the exchange rate bear the burden of adjustment without stabilization policies is best, versus the long run, where stabilization and liberalization have a high growth payoff. This captures one of the main dilemmas of stabilization and the political temptation to postpone introduction of remedial measures. In terms of welfare, there is a conflict in the short run between rural incomes that would benefit from strong stabilization and adjustment versus the urban interests that will be hurt by falling government expenditures and the loss of employment associated which a sharper recession induced by these policies. They consequently are the ones who prefer minimizing policy adjustment, letting the exchange rate balance foreign accounts. In the long run, however, all incomes benefit from the policy which ensures the strongest growth recovery, that is, stabilization and liberalization. Absolute poverty would similarly increase less in the short run under exchange rate management, while it increases least in the long run with stabilization and adjustment.

Finally, which policy is implemented depends on political support. Policies with negative short-run political feasibility indices are infeasible, even if they are politically feasible in the long run. We see that the dominant corporatist interests are strongly opposed to stabilization and liberalization: skilled labor loses jobs from fiscal austerity and decline of employment in the import substitution industries exposed to international competition; manufacturing profits in what is largely import substitution industries are similarly hurt; and export-oriented agribusiness

Table 12.3. Simulations of stabilization policies in response to terms of trade and debt shock in Ecuador

	Base values[c]	Exchange rate adjustment			Fiscal adjustment			Stabilization and liberalization		
	Year 1	Year 2	Year 3	Year 7	Year 2	Year 3	Year 7	Year 2	Year 3	Year 7
Policies										
Govt. current expend.	42,562	1.5	3.0	9.3	−16.5	−15.2	−10.0	−10.0	−8.7	−3.0
Govt. capital expend.	18,646	1.5	3.0	9.3	−16.5	−15.2	−10.0	−7.5	−6.1	−0.4
Money supply [a]	28.0%	40.0	40.0	40.0	40.0	40.0	40.0	30.0	30.0	30.0
Average tariff rate	16.1%	0.0	0.0	0.0	0.0	0.0	0.0	−38.3	−38.3	−38.3
Economic performance										
Real GDP	293,341	−0.1	−2.2	−1.8	−3.0	−3.6	2.8	−1.8	−2.1	3.0
Exchange rate [a]	25.0%	75.3	42.4	39.8	81.1	38.5	38.0	62.1	29.2	28.6
Inflation [b]	25.8%	46.7	46.1	40.3	48.3	41.7	38.8	34.6	31.2	29.1
Employment (index)	100	2.5	−4.7	−4.7	0.0	−5.5	−1.6	−1.0	−4.9	−2.2
Welfare										
Class incomes										
Rural small farmers	33,968	0.2	−1.6	−2.5	−1.9	−2.0	3.8	0.9	0.9	5.4
Rural large farmers	13,094	2.8	0.8	−3.7	1.8	2.4	6.6	4.6	5.0	7.5
Urban low education	70,912	−1.6	−3.7	−2.0	−4.7	−5.9	0.6	−1.9	−2.7	2.8
Urban high education	37,893	−3.7	−4.0	−2.0	−10.1	−10.1	−4.6	−5.1	−5.1	−0.3
Povert indices										
Poor (% of pop.)	36.3	38.8	42.3	48.3	43.3	45.2	44.8	39.4	41.4	43.6
Number of poor (index)	100	108.8	120.8	148.3	121.5	129.1	137.5	110.5	118.2	133.8
FGT Index	24.5	28.9	38.4	64.5	39.0	45.6	48.5	29.8	35.5	46.0
Political support										
Factor incomes										
Skilled labor income	52,039	−3.4	−2.3	0.1	−12.9	−12.4	−8.2	−6.3	−5.9	−2.0
Agric. exports profits	9,189	18.8	9.0	−1.9	20.6	13.8	12.7	17.5	12.3	10.3
Manufacturing profits	8,535	−14.5	−15.9	−6.0	−14.9	−14.5	−1.1	−14.9	−13.5	−1.5
Indices										
Democratic		−0.7	−2.5	−2.5	−3.4	−3.9	2.0	−0.5	−0.7	4.0
Economic		−1.4	−3.0	−2.4	−4.9	−5.5	0.4	−1.6	−1.9	2.9

Source: Calculations based on the CGE model in de Janvry, Sadoulet, and Fargeix, 1991.
Note: Results for years 2 to 7 (except in rows footnoted [a] and [b]) are in percentage deviation from year 1.
[a]Growth rate. [b]Value. [c]In millions of 1980 sucres, unless otherwise indicated.

interests would prefer the stronger exchange rate devaluation associated with fiscal adjustment. It is, by contrast, the democratic forces which are most strongly in favor of liberalization, but this in the longer run. In the short run, democratic forces lose from liberalization, but less than from the other policy alternatives. Making the liberalization package politically acceptable thus requires two aspects of political management: actively seeking government support in popular forces as opposed to corporatist interests; and engaging in extensive policy dialogue to help democratic forces assess the liberalization program not against the status quo ante (incomes in year 1) but against the counterfactual of the implications of the alternative policy package that could be introduced, namely exchange rate and fiscal adjustments. A policy which is best in the long run from the standpoints of efficiency and welfare, and which is politically feasible in the long run, thus needs an active role of the state in managing its short-run acceptability. Quantitative policy analysis, which reveals the nature of the intertemporal and interclass distribution of gains and losses from these different policy options, is thus a useful basis on which to anchor a policy dialogue that is an integral part of the political management of policy reform.

12.5. Extensions and Recent Developments

Recent developments of CGE modeling have been conducted in the following areas:

a. Oligopolistic behavior in certain industries and the resulting impact on price formation (de Melo and Roland-Holst, 1992; Devarajan and Rodrik, 1991).

b. Scale economies and optimal protection to capture the benefits which they create (Harris, 1984; Devarajan and Rodrik, 1989).

c. Optimal policy choice. In these models, the CGE equations, which express the structural relationship of the economy, perform as the constraint set, and the policy is determined by maximizing a planner's objective function. The objective function might include GNP, aggregate employment, or external balance. The instruments might include exchange rates, taxes, and government expenditures (Adelman, Yeldan, Sarris, and Roland-Holst, 1989).

d. Integration of a multimarket specification for the agricultural sector into a CGE (Sadoulet and de Janvry, 1992). This allows one to better characterize the substitutions and complementarities among activities in agriculture, and their use of common fixed factors, as opposed to the standard CGE formulation of separate production functions for each activity which derives from the industrial origin of these models.

e. Asset markets and the endogenization of interest rates and inflation. This opens the field to studies of the sectoral and social impact of monetary policies and, more generally, stabilization policies (Bourguignon, de Melo, and Morrisson, 1991; de Janvry, Sadoulet, and Fargeix, 1991).

f. Multicountry models to assess multilateral trade reform (Mercenier, 1992; Robinson, Burfisher, Hinojosa-Ojeda, Thierfelder, 1993).

Areas which are still widely unexplored include the following:

The introduction of uncertainty and the corresponding behavior of agents.

The introduction of active income strategies on the part of institutions.

Disequilibrium and adjustment mechanisms.

True dynamic behavior (see Kharas and Shishido, 1986).

Transactions through contracts.

12.6. When to Use a CGE

In a sense, CGE models summarize and aggregate most of the knowledge accumulated in the previous chapters. Therefore, there is great temptation to consider them as the panacea, as models that can answer all questions. However, this is an illusion for at least two reasons. The first is purely technical; it is an issue of the mere size of the model. With a model that encompasses macroeconomic, sectoral, and social effects, it is almost impossible to disaggregate any of these aspects in much detail. Typical models consider from 8 to 12 sectors, 2 to 4 labor types, and 6 to 8 household types, because, with more disaggregation, the number of parameters on which estimates/guesstimates have to be made, and the difficulty of interpretation of the results, blurs the central results. For the same reason, every model will be specialized to the questions of concern, with a focus, for example, on labor markets, on the multiple roles of government, on agriculture, or on macroeconomics. This argument about disaggregation and specialization mirrors what has already been discussed about the SAM, extending it also to the realm of behavioral specifications.

The second reason for not substituting a CGE for any other approach is theoretical. Even with the capacity to increase the size of the model to capture details in all areas, there may be absolutely no need to do so. Phenomena with microeconomic or sectoral implications, but no intersectoral and/or macroeconomic effects, will not gain anything under CGE analysis. Similarly, pure macroeconomic analysis would not gain from detailed specification of factor markets and institutions.

A second subject of debate concerns the use of the more theoretically framed CGEs versus the econometrically estimated models. As we have seen before, the empirical requirements to set up a CGE are small. This is due to the combination of calibration procedure, which forces the model to replicate a base year, and the rigorous theoretical basis of all decisions, which imposes profit or utility maximization for producers and consumers. Hence, few parameters are required beyond the base SAM, and these are either independently estimated or taken from the literature. In contrast, other models (Cavallo and Mundlak, 1982, for example) are based on the econometric estimation of all behavioral functions. In that context, reduced forms for production and employment by sector, consumption by commodity, and investment by sector are independently estimated. An advantage of the econometric approach is that it allows for the introduction of lagged variables and a variety of exogenous variables, without having to formally specify the underlying theory. Its drawback is that the estimation is not done in a system approach and thus does not guarantee any basic conditions of consistency or additivity constraints. There obviously can be no definite verdict on which approach is superior. Note, however, that the introduction of some econometrically estimated functions may improve the actual empirical analysis done with CGEs, especially for the variables which seem not to behave as closely to theory as model builders would like. With that respect, investment decision rules and wage equations are the prime candidates for econometric estimation. In addition, import functions need to be improved, as the actual CES model does not reproduce the major changes in trade volume and structure that occur in the growth process. Recently, several models have used the AIDS system, resulting in marked improvements over the CES specification (Robinson, Burfisher, Hinojosa-Ojeda, and Thierfelder, 1993). Because external trade is at the core of the CGE analysis, it is important that any alternative formulation be based on solid theoretical behavior.

Given the strengths and weaknesses of the CGE models, when are they best used? Certainly not in forecasting, as they lack any proper dynamic features. Neither should CGEs be employed for detailed predictions of the impact of very specific policy packages, as they cannot properly model the particularities of any specific policy. However, CGEs can serve as policy laboratories within the process of broad policy analysis. They underscore the main linkages among the different economic and social sectors of the economy and help one understand the ramifications and trickle-down effects induced by a policy or a shock. They can thus be used to explore alternative policy choices, particularly their intersectoral, inter social groups, and intertemporal effects, and their impacts on a whole range of efficiency, equity, poverty, and political feasibility indicators. Very powerful exercises with CGEs are sensitivity analyses on the value of a parameter or on a functional form. If one can identify, as in the example on the impact of a GATT shock described above, the substitutability between imports and domestic crops as the key parameter that conditions the macroeconomic effects, this justifies undertaking further empirical analysis to estimate its value. By contrast, if one determines that the exact value of a parameter, within the range that we can attribute to it with confidence, does not affect the effects in any significant way, then policy analysis can be pursued without waiting for further investigation.

Exercise 12
The Economics of Food Subsidies in a Computable General Equilibrium Model

In this exercise, a CGE model is used to analyze a food subsidization policy and its alternative financing methods. We will see how consumption subsidies may crowd out investment by increasing the government deficit. Alternative policies that allow for maintaining investment are increases in taxes, cuts in other government expenditures, or appeals to foreign aid. They illustrate the trade-offs that the implementation of a consumer subsidy program must face.

Because the result of any such policy package is dependent on how the economy works, it is essential to properly understand the assumptions that have been chosen in this particular model. This is explained in sections 2 and 3 after presentation of the database.

1. Database

As discussed in the chapter, the database for a CGE consists of a social accounting matrix (SAM) and sets of elasticities for production, imports, exports, and demand. These are reported in rows 1 to 20 of the spreadsheet in Table 12E.1. The SAM is an aggregated version of the Moroccan SAM used in the SAM-multiplier exercise of Chapter 10. Because we want to examine food subsidies, it has been aggregated to emphasize the food sector. There are three sectors: agriculture, the food sector, and the rest of the economy, which includes industry, trade, and services. Production proceeds with two factors of production: capital and labor. The return to capital is attributed partly to firms, corresponding to the formal sector, and partly to households, corresponding to the informal sector. Domestic production pays taxes to the government account. The sectoral accounts combine the activity and commodity accounts of the standard SAM. Note that the value of domestic production is the sum of expenditures on intermediate demand, labor, capital, and taxes, as reported in cells B19 to D19. Subtracting exports from this domestic production yields production sold on the domestic market. This domestic sale combined with imports constitutes total domestic supply, as found in cells B20 to D20. The rest of

Table 12E.1. The economics of food subsidies in a computable general equilibrium model: Data and parameters

Data: SAM and Elasticities

Social accounting matrix, Morocco 1980 (million DH)

	Ag.	Food	Other	Labor	Firms	Rural	Urb. low	Urb. high	Govt	Invt	World	Total
Agriculture	2365	5228	2655			4615	5152	1810		1738	1912	25475
Food	402	2480	3595			3141	4703	2369		186	1167	18043
Other	5897	4528	45728			6430	12809	8231	13589	16009	10103	123324
Labor	4500	1028	19930									25458
Firms		1086	13647									14733
Rural households	9134			4549	1734				330		2100	17847
Urban low households		564	4598	14775	2552			129	371		1896	24885
Urban high households		1016	8276	6134	1513				123		188	17250
Government	1269	127	8915		2358	357	249	1540				14815
Capital account					6005	3304	1972	3171	-2003		5484	17933
Rest of world	1908	1986	15980		571				2405			22850
Total	25475	18043	123324	25458	14733	17847	24885	17250	14815	17933	22850	
Production	23567	16057	107344									
Domestic supply	23563	16876	113221									

Elasticities

Production/trade

	Ag.	Food	Other
Capital-labor	0.8	0.8	0.8
Imports	1.3	1.3	1.3
Exports	-2.0	-2.0	-2.0

Consumption

Income elasticities	Rural	Urb. low	Urb. high
Agriculture	0.80	0.70	0.30
Food	0.94	0.75	0.66
Other	1.17	1.21	1.25
Frisch parameter	-4.0	-3.0	-2.0

Production CES

	Ag.	Food	Other
total capital	9134	2666	26521
L share param.	.3	.2	.4
-rhoc	-.3	-.3	-.3
constant	3.2	7.7	4.6

Domestic supply CES

	Ag.	Food	Other
prod for dom market	21655	14890	97241
M share param.	.13	.18	.09
-rhom	.2	.2	-.3
constant	1.4	1.5	1.4

Derived parameters

IO

	Ag.	Food	Other
Agriculture	.100	.326	.025
Food	.017	.154	.033
Other	.250	.282	.426
Pvao	.579	.230	.433
Labor	.179	.580	.241

Shares in capital income

	Ag.	Food	Other
Firms	.000	.407	.515
Rural households	1.000	.600	.000
Urban low househ.	.000	.212	.173
Urban high househ.	.000	.381	.312

Subs. quant. & marg. budg. sh.

Subsistence quantities:

	Rural	Urb. low	Urb. high
Agriculture	3692	3950	1539
Food	2403	3527	1587
Other	4545	7632	3079

Marginal budget shares:

	Rural	Urb. low	Urb. high
Agriculture	.26	.16	.04
Food	.21	.16	.13
Other	.53	.69	.83

Shares in expend. net of taxes

	Rural	Urb. low	Urb. high
	.140	.206	.122
	.160	.010	.089
	.189	.080	.202

Tax rates on income

Rural households	Urban low househ.	Urban high househ.
.020	.010	.089

Tax rates on production

	Ag.	Food	Other
Government	.054	.008	.083
Capital account	.485	.008	.202
Rest of world	.046	.083	

Real expenditures

	Govt	Invt (Shares)	World (Cst term)
Agriculture		.097	1912
Food		.010	1167
Other	13589	.893	10103
Rural households	330		2100
Urban low househ.	371		1896
Urban high househ.	123		188
	2405		

Table 12E.2. The economics of food subsidies in a computable general equilibrium model: Simulations

Exogenous variables

Wage	1.000
Exchange rate	1.000
Govt. expenditures	13589

	Ag.	Food	Other	Capital	Urban high
Import price $	1.0	1.0	1.0		
Export price $	1.0	1.0	1.0		
Tax rates	.054	.008	.083	.160	.089
Consumer subsidies	.000	.000	.000	[F36]	[136]

Endogenous variables

	Ag.	Food	Other
Nonnormalized p	1.000	1.000	1.000
Domestic price	1.000	1.000	1.000
Consumer price	1.000	1.000	1.000
Pva	.579	.230	.433
Labor	4500	1028	19930
Production	23567	16057	107344
Real imports	1908	1986	15980
Real exports	1912	1167	10103

Social accounting matrix, Morocco 1980 (million DH)

	Ag.	Food	Other	Labor	Firms	Rural	Urb. low	Urb. high	Govt.	Invt.	World	Total	Excess demand
Agriculture	2365	5228	2655			4615	5152	1810		1738	1912	25475	.000
Food	402	2480	3595			3141	4703	2369		186	1167	18043	.000
Other	5897	4528	45728			6430	12809	8231	13589	16009	10103	123324	.000
Labor	4500	1028	19930									25458	
Firms	0	1086	13647									14733	
Rural households	9134	0		4549	1734				330		2100	17847	
Urban low househ.	0	564	4598	14775	2552			129	371		1896	24885	
Urban high househ.	0	1016	8276	6134	1513				123		188	17250	
Cons. subsidies	0	0	0									0	
Government	1269	127	8915		2358	357	249	1540				14815	
Capital account					6005	3304	1972	3171	-2003		5484	17933	
Rest of world	1908	1986	15980		571	0	0	0	2405			22850	
Total	25475	18043	123324	25458	14733	17847	24885	17250	14815	17933	22850		

Matrix (dExc.Dem/dp)^-1

	Ag	Food	Other	New Prices
	-0.012	-0.002		1.000
	-0.004	-0.007		1.000
				1.000

	A	B	C	D	E	F	G	H	I	J	K	L	M
81	Table 12E.3. Food subsidy policy with alternative financing: Simulation with a CGE												
82													
83									Alternative financing				
84						Government deficit			Income tax		Cut in govt. expend.	Foreign debt	
85		Base value	Active column	% change		Value	% change	Value	% change	Value	% change	Value	% change
86													
87	Real GDP	63779	63779	0.0									
88	Absorption	80782	80782	0.0									
89	Trade deficit ($)	6692	6692	0.0									
90	Investment	17933	17933	0.0									
91	Exchange rate	1.00	1.00	0.0									
92	Current deficit ($)	5484	5484	0.0									
93	Sectoral performance												
94	Real supply												
95	Agriculture	23567	23567	0.0									
96	Food	16057	16057	0.0									
97	Other	107344	107344	0.0									
98	Producer prices												
99	Agriculture	1.000	1.000	0.0									
100	Food	1.000	1.000	0.0									
101	Other	1.000	1.000	0.0									
102	Government												
103	Basic tax on food	127	127	0.0									
104	Food subsidies	0	0										
105	Govt. surplus	-2003	-2003	0.0									
106	After-tax real income												
107	Rural hh	17490	17490	0.0									
108	Urban low hh	24636	24636	0.0									
109	Urban high hh	15710	15710	0.0									
110	Food imports	1986	1986	0.0									
111													

the SAM is in standard form. The households are aggregated in three groups: all rural, urban low-income, and urban-high income. All savings are combined into one capital account which invests. The rest of the world receives payments for imports, profit repatriation from firms, and interest payments from the government. It pays for exports and sends remittances to households. The net of these transactions, the deficit of the current account, is added to the domestic savings account in cell L16.

2. Derived Model Parameters

The next step, reported in rows 21 to 40, is to derive the parameters of the model. As the SAM transactions are given as values, we first need to choose a set of prices and corresponding measuring units to compute quantities. Note that the existence of sales taxes and tariffs may create a wedge between the price received by the sector and the price paid by the consumers. In our case, however, with only taxes on production, there is a unique domestic price per product, and the procedure of normalization is easier. We set the initial value of the three domestic product prices, all foreign prices, the exchange rate, the wage rate, and the rental rate of capital to one. Hence, the values given in the SAM for production, imports, exports, and consumption can be read as quantities of commodities, and the values given to labor and capital payments can be read as quantities of labor and capital.

Many parameters are simple shares computed from the SAM data. Input-output coefficients are computed in cells B26 to D28. We assume that the return to capital is distributed in constant shares (B31–D34) between the formal sector and the households. Production tax rates (B36–D36) are computed as the ratio of tax payments to value of domestic production. Other tax rates are computed as shares of total income (F36–I36). Distribution of labor income to households is computed with constant shares (E32–E34). Income to firms after taxes is also distributed in constant shares among distributed profits to households (F32–F34), expatriated profits (F38), and savings (F37). Investment demand is proportional to total investment (K26–K28). Government expenditures and remittances from the rest of the world are assumed to be constant in real terms.

The production function is chosen to be CES in labor and capital. Based on observed capital (sum of rows 10 to 13, reported in cells Q27–S27) and labor (B9–D9), and the elasticity of substitution σ given in Q5–S5, the parameters of the CES function are computed by solving the system of production constraint and first-order condition for profit maximization:

$$Q = A\left(\alpha_L L^{-\rho} + (1 - \alpha_L)K^{-\rho}\right)^{-1/\rho}, \text{ with } \rho = 1/\sigma - 1,$$

$$pva \, dQ/dL = w,$$

where $pva = [p(1 - tax) - \text{intermediate costs}]$ is the unit return to K and L, called the value-added price. Assuming $p = w = 1$, this gives:

$$\alpha_L = L^{1-\rho}/\left(L^{1-\rho} + K^{1-\rho}\right) \text{ and } A = Q/\left[\alpha_L L^{-\rho} + (1 - \alpha_L)K^{-\rho}\right]^{-1/\rho}.$$

These values are computed in Q28–S30. Two derived expressions of a CES are currently used in this model:

$$(1) \quad L = K\left[\left(\frac{w}{pva}\frac{1}{A\lambda}\right)^{\sigma-1}\frac{1}{1-\lambda}-\frac{\lambda}{1-\lambda}\right]^{\sigma/(1-\sigma)} \quad \text{, and}$$

$$(2) \quad L = K\left(\frac{w}{r}\frac{1-\lambda}{\lambda}\right)^{-\sigma}.$$

Imports and domestic products are assumed to be imperfect substitutes, and domestic supply to be a CES aggregate of imports and domestic sales (production minus exports). The parameters of CES aggregates are similarly computed in Q34–S37.

Exports are assumed to derive from a demand function from the rest of the world. External demand is a function of the ratio of the Moroccan prices in dollars (p/e) to the world price $p^{\$}$ with an elasticity ε given in Q7–S7:

$$E = E_0(p/ep^{\$})^{\varepsilon}.$$

E_0 is simply the initial value reported in L26–L28.

The private consumption system is specified as the Linear Expenditure System, discussed in Chapter 2. For each household group, the consumption c_i of commodity i is a function of total expenditure y and prices p_j:

$$c_i = a_i + b_i(y - \sum_j p_j a_j)/p_i.$$

The parameters a_i, called the subsistence quantities, and b_i, the marginal budget shares, are derived from the observed value of consumption, the income elasticity η_i, and the flexibility of money (Frisch parameter) ω as follows:

$$b_i = \eta_i p_i c_i / y \quad \text{and} \quad a_i = c_i(1 + \eta_i / \omega).$$

These are computed in cells G26 to I31.

3. Closure Rules

As discussed in the chapter, the behavior of a model strongly depends on what has been assumed in the representation of the functioning of the different markets. Hence, it is important to specify that:

The stock of capital in each sector is assumed to be fixed, labor is assumed to be mobile across sectors, and total labor is available in surplus, at a fixed wage. Hence, employment will simply be equal to labor demand. In the product markets, variable prices allow for clearing of the markets. In the foreign exchange market, the exchange rate is exogenous, and the deficit of current account is endogenous.

The model is homogenous in all prices. Hence, a numéraire is chosen by fixing an aggregate price equal to one. Accordingly, wage and exchange rates can be interpreted as real wage and real exchange rates. The weights for this aggregate price are the initial values of domestic production.

4. Simulation Procedure

The simulation is organized in rows 41 to 80. First, a number of exogenous variables are entered. These include the world prices, the exchange rate, the wage rate, government expenditures, and some tax rates. Tax rates and government expenditures are repeated here to allow for their modification without disturbing the original block of data in rows 1 to 40. This keeps the original data set intact to allow for an easy return to the base run. A row has also been provided for the introduction of consumer subsidies for policy simulations.

The calculation proceeds iteratively as follows:

a. A set of domestic prices in cells B53–D53 (disregard their formulae for now) are normalized to add up to one in B54–D54. From these, we strip away the tax rate and the intermediate costs to get the value-added price (B56–D56).

b. The first-order condition of profit maximization [equation (1) above] gives employment as a function of value-added price and the wage (B57–D57). Production is computed as the CES aggregate of fixed capital and labor (B58–D58). Exports are computed as a function of world prices and domestic prices (B60–D60). Imports (B59–D59) are computed as a function of domestic sales, and the ratio of domestic to import prices [from the equivalent of equation (2) above]. Knowing the quantity of imports and domestic products sold on the market, and taking out consumer subsidies, we are able to compute an average price for the consumer (B55–D55).

c. With these base values computed, the values of a new SAM are calculated in A65–M78. You should scan through the different cells of the matrix to see how the model incorporates the parameters and exogenous variables computed in rows 21 to 40, as well as those that we have repeated to modify in rows 44 to 51. Until the model has converged to equilibrium values, some of the SAM accounts will not be balanced. The labor, firms, households, government, and capital accounts will be eventually balanced by construction, but the products and rest of the world accounts will not. This is because the labor, firms, household, and capital accounts take total incomes from the total row (M69 to M76) and distribute them as expenditures. Government equilibrium is achieved by setting the savings (J76) equal to the difference between revenue (M75) and expenditures (J65 to J73 and J77). Similarly, for the external accounts, foreign savings (L76) are set equal to the balance of current accounts. The only accounts that need to be explicitly balanced are the product accounts. In fact, we only need to balance two of these accounts, as the third will be automatically balanced by Walras's law. This is the purpose of the adjustment procedure explained in the next step.

d. Excess demands for domestic products are computed in cells O65–O67. For example, real demand for agricultural products is equal to the value of domestic demand (B65–K65) divided by consumer price (B55) plus exports (B60) minus imports (B59). Excess demand is computed as the difference between real demand and production (B58) as a percentage of production. For calculating price adjustments in response to excess demands, we use the Newton-Raphson method. It adjusts the price vector by a quantity Δp proportional to the vector of excess demand ΔED, $\Delta p = \alpha M \Delta ED$, where M is the inverse of the derivatives of excess demands with respect to prices, and α is a step length.[1] By trial and error, we choose $\alpha = 0.3$. The matrix M for the first two sectors has been calculated at the base values and written in cells P65–Q66 (recall that we only need to balance two of these accounts); the adjusted prices are computed in S65–S66. The price of the third sector is only transferred.

e. These adjusted prices also appear in B53–D53, and serve for the next iteration. Recalculations toward a new equilibrium are done by pressing F9 several times. You should see the excess demand values decrease; stop the iteration procedure when you reach values that are smaller than 0.001. [The spreadsheet has been organized to correspond to a recalculation scheme that follows a columnwise approach. Hence, if you encounter a problem of convergence, reset the setting with the command /Worksheet Global Recalculation, select Columnwise, and press Enter.]

5. Policy Simulation and Display of Results

Now carry out the following policy experiments and prepare a report evaluating alternative policies. Some important results are summarized in table form in rows 81 to 112. The results from the simulation above are reported in an "active" column, C87 to C110. Comparison with base values is computed in the block of cells D87–D110. After each simulation you should copy the numerical values of your results (C87 to D110) to the space provided in columns F to M.

a. First, to see the impact of food subsidies on this economy, suppose that the government provides a 10% subsidy. This policy change can be implemented in the model by simply entering 0.10 in cell C51. Recalculate the equilibrium. Explain what happens to sectoral real outputs, government surplus, investment, trade deficit in foreign currency, aggregate GDP and absorption, and the real income indices of households. Compare your results with the original presubsidy equilibrium.

b. The above experiment demonstrates that food subsidies cause a major decrease in investment, which has been crowded out by government deficit. How can the country pursue a food subsidization policy while maintaining the original level of investment? One way is to reduce the government deficit by increased taxation. Because the ultimate goal of subsidizing food is redistribution of income in favor of the poor, it makes sense to concentrate increased taxation on the rich. To see how this policy can be modeled, enter 0.15 as the new exogenous value of the tax rate on urban high-income households in cell F50, and find the new equilibrium. What is the new level of investment? You may have to raise the tax rate somewhat to increase the investment to the original value of 17930 million DH. Try various numbers and find a tax rate that yields an investment of 17930 ± 20 million DH. Once you have found the appropriate tax rate, save the results. Compare the sectoral real outputs, government surplus, aggregate GDP and absorption, and the household real income indices you have just found with those of the pre- and postsubsidy equilibria.

---

1. It is based on the following relationship between prices and excess demand: $\Delta ED = [dED/dp] \, \Delta p$, where $[dED/dp]$ is the matrix of first derivatives of excess demand with respect to domestic prices. It should be pointed out that the matrix of first derivatives can be numerically calculated by fixing all output prices (in cells B52–D52) to one, changing them one by one to 1.001, and then recalculating the worksheet twice to find the change in the excess demands. Multiplying these changes by 1,000 yields the first derivatives of excess demand functions. For each price change, one finds a vertical vector of excess demand derivatives. These vectors can be put together as a matrix which is inverted through the Data/Matrix/Inverse function. The reported inverse matrix of first derivatives is evaluated at the original equilibrium for which the model is calibrated. In principle, this matrix should be updated at each iteration. However, the present model converges quickly without updating the price adjustment coefficients; adding a program for updating would only slow down recalculations. This is why we have ignored the changes in $[dED/dp]^{-1}$ as the price vector changes.

c. A second way to reduce the deficit is through reduction of government expenditures. This can be modeled by resetting the tax rate on urban rich households at its original level (= I36 in cell F50) and multiplying government expenditures in cell B46 by a fixed number, say 0.90. Reestablish the equilibrium. Notice what happens to investment. You may need to adjust the scaling factor a bit to get the investment in the 17930 ± 20 million DH range. Once you have found such a scaling factor, save the results and compare them with those of previous equilibria. As you will discover, after subsidization and government expenditure reduction, the distribution of benefits to households is more egalitarian. Can you tell who is really paying for the subsidies in this case?

d. Finally, to maintain investment while subsidizing food, the government may call upon a foreign source. In the closure of our model, foreign capital inflow is endogenous, while the exchange rate is exogenous. Hence, the causality runs from exchange rate to capital inflow. For example, you will read the first simulation results as: given the subsidy program and a fixed exchange rate, the foreign deficit will increase to $5575. Alternatively, one can read the results in the other direction and say: if the availability of foreign exchange is $5575, the equilibrium exchange rate is equal to one. With this symmetry of interpretation in mind, you will search for the real exchange rate and corresponding foreign capital inflow that will allow maintenance of the investment level in the 17930 ± 20 range. To perform this experiment, reset the government expenditure level to its original value, and change the exchange rate in cell B45. Reestablish the equilibrium. Note that you need an *appreciation* of the exchange rate to induce an *increase* of the foreign capital inflow. Compare the results with those of the previous policy experiments. Again, the variables of interest are sectoral real outputs, aggregate GDP and absorption, government surplus, and household real income indices.

References

Adelman, Irma, Erinc Yeldan, Alexander Sarris, and David Roland-Holst. 1989. "Optimal Adjustment to Trade Shocks under Alternative Development Strategies." *Journal of Policy Modeling* 11:451–505.

Benjamin, Nancy, Shantayanan Devarajan, and Robert Weiner. 1989. "The 'Dutch' Disease in a Developing Country." *Journal of Development Economics* 30:71–92.

Bourguignon, François, Jaime de Melo, and Christian Morrisson. 1991. "Poverty and Income Distribution During Adjustment: Issues and Evidence from the OECD Project." *World Development* 19:1485–1508.

Cavallo, Domingo, and Yair Mundlak. 1982. *Agriculture and Economic Growth in an Open Economy: The Case of Argentina.* Research Report no. 36. Washington, D.C.: International Food Policy Research Institute.

Clarete, R. L., and James Roumasset. 1990. "The Relative Welfare Cost of Industrial and Agricultural Policy Distortions: A Philippine Illustration." *Oxford Economic Papers* 42:462–472.

Decaluwé, Bernard, and André Martens. 1988. "CGE Modeling and Developing Economies: A Concise Empirical Survey of 73 Applications to 26 Countries." *Journal of Policy Modeling* 10:529–68.

de Janvry, Alain, and Elisabeth Sadoulet. 1987. "Agricultural Price Policy in General Equilibrium Models: Results and Comparisons." *American Journal of Agricultural Economics* 69:230–46.

de Janvry, Alain, Elisabeth Sadoulet, and André Fargeix. 1991. "Politically Feasible and Equitable Adjustment: Some Alternatives for Ecuador." *World Development* 19:1577–95.

de Melo, Jaime. 1988. "Computable General Equilibrium Models for Trade Policy Analysis in Developing Countries: A Survey." *Journal of Policy Modeling* 10:469–503.

de Melo, Jaime, and David Roland-Holst. 1992. "Tariffs and Export Subsidies When Domestic Markets Are Oligopolistic." In *Applied General Equilibrium and Economic Development*, edited by Jean Mercenier and T. N. Srinivasan. Ann Arbor: University of Michigan Press.

Dervis, Kamal, Jaime de Melo, and Sherman Robinson. 1982. *General Equilibrium Models for Development Policy.* Cambridge: Cambridge University Press.

Devarajan, Shantayanan, Jeffrey Lewis, and Sherman Robinson. 1990. "Policy Lessons from Trade-Focused, Two-Sector Models." *Journal of Policy Modeling* 12:625–57.

Devarajan, Shantayanan, and Dani Rodrik. 1989. "Trade Liberalization in Developing Countries: Do Imperfect Competition and Scale Economics Matter?" *American Economic Review* 79:283–87.

Devarajan, Shantayanan, and Dani Rodrik. 1991. "Pro-Competitive Effects of Trade Reform: Results from a CGE Model of Cameroon." *European Economic Review* 35:1157–84.

Gunning, Jan Willem, and Michiel Keyser. 1993. "Applied General Equilibrium Models for Policy Analysis." In *Handbook of Development Economics,* vol. 3, edited by T. N. Srinivasan and J. Behrman. Amsterdam: Elsevier Science Publishers.

Harris, Richard. 1984. "Applied General Equilibrium Analysis of Small Open Economies with Scale Economies and Imperfect Competition." *American Economic Review* 74:1016–32.

Kharas, Homi, and Hisanobu Shishido. 1986. "A Dynamic-Optimizing Model of Foreign Borrowing: A Case Study of Thailand." *Journal of Policy Modeling* 8:1–26.

Lluch, Constantino, Alan Powell, and Ross Williams. 1977. *Patterns in Household Demand and Saving.* London: Oxford University Press.

Mercenier, Jean. 1992. "Can '1992' Reduce Unemployment in Europe?" Unpublished paper. University of Montreal, Centre de Recherche et Développement en Economie.

Moran, Cristián, and Pablo Serra. 1993. "Trade Reform under Regional Integration: Policy Simulations Using a CGE model for Guatemala." *Journal of Development Economics* 40:103–32.

Narayana, N. S. S., K. S. Parikh, and T. N. Srinivasan. 1987. "Indian Agricultural Policy: An Applied General Equilibrium Model." *Journal of Policy Modeling* 9:527–58.

Robinson, Sherman. 1989. "Multisectoral Models." In *Handbook of Development Economics,* vol. 2, edited by H. Chenery and T. N. Srinivasan. Amsterdam: Elsevier Science Publishers.

Robinson, Sherman, Mary Burfisher, R. Hinojosa-Ojeda, Karen Thierfelder. 1993. "Agricultural Policies and Migration in a United States-Mexico Free Trade Area—A Computable General Equilibrium Analysis." *Journal of Policy Modeling* 15:673–701.

Sadoulet, Elisabeth, and Alain de Janvry. 1992. "Agricultural Trade Liberalization and the Low Income Countries: A General Equilibrium-Multimarket Approach." *American Journal of Agricultural Economics* 74:268–80.

Sanderson, Warren, and Jeffrey Williamson. 1985. *How Should Developing Countries Adjust to External Shocks in the 1980s? An Examination of Some World Bank Macroeconomic Models.* Staff Working Paper no. 708. Washington, D.C.: World Bank.

Shoven, John, and J. Walley. 1992. *Applied General Equilibrium.* New York: Cambridge University Press.

Taylor, Lance. 1990. "Structuralist CGE Models." In *Socially Relevant Policy Analysis,* edited by L. Taylor. Cambridge: MIT Press.

APPENDIX

Some Mathematical Tools

A.1. Elasticity

Suppose that $q = f(x)$ is a demand (or supply) curve, where x is an exogenous variable such as income, price, fixed factor, etc., and q the quantity demanded (supplied). Marginal changes such as dq/dx are in the measurement units of q and x and hence difficult to compare with other marginal changes. By contrast, the elasticity is easier to use, as it is unit free. The elasticity is defined as the percentage change in the dependent variable due to a percentage change in the independent variable:

$$\text{Elasticity of } q \text{ with respect to } x = E_q^x = \frac{\% \text{ change in } q}{\% \text{ change in } x} = \frac{dq/q}{dx/x} = \frac{dq}{dx}\frac{x}{q}.$$

If the absolute value of the elasticity, $\left| E_q^x \right|$, is greater than one, the curve is called elastic; if $0 < \left| E_q^x \right| < 1$, the curve is called inelastic.

Using logarithmic functions, the elasticity can also be written: $E_q^x = \dfrac{d \ln q}{d \ln x}$.

A.1.1. Income Elasticity of Demand

Consider the relationship between demand and income y, at given prices p, called the Engel function (Figure A.1). The elasticity of demand with respect to income is written:

$$\eta = \frac{dq/q}{dy/y} = \frac{dq/dy}{q/y} = \frac{\text{marginal propensity to consume}}{\text{average propensity to consume}}.$$

If $\eta > 1$, demand increases more than proportionally to income, and hence the expenditure share of this good increases as income increases. If $\eta < 1$, the expenditure share declines as income increases. This is usually the case for food consumption.

A.1.2. Price Elasticity of Demand

Price elasticities are usually negative, since demand decreases when price increases. Consider how the expenditure pq changes as the price p increases:

$$\frac{d(pq)}{dp} = q + p\frac{dq}{dp} = q(1 + E_q^p).$$

Hence, if $E_q^p > -1$ (inelastic demand), $d(pq)/dp > 0$, an increase in price induces an increase in expenditure despite a decrease in demand, because the change in quantity is smaller than the

---

For further complements, see James Henderson and Richard Quandt, *Microeconomic Theory: A Mathematical Approach* (New York: McGraw-Hill, 1971); and C. E. Ferguson, *The Neoclassical Theory of Production and Distribution* (Cambridge, England: Cambridge University Press, 1969).

change in price. If $E_q^p < -1$ (elastic demand), $d(pq)/dp < 0$, expenditure pq decreases with a price increase. This is because the decline in demand is larger than the price increase.

The same reasoning applies to factor demand in production. The cost of any single factor will increase or decrease in response to its own price increase depending on whether the demand elasticity is greater or lower than -1.

Figure A.1. Engel functions

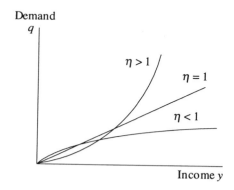

A.1.3. *Cross-Price Elasticity of Demand*

The elasticity of demand for good i as a function of a change in the price of good j is:

$$E_{q_i}^{p_j} = \frac{\partial q_i}{\partial p_j} \frac{p_j}{q_i} = \frac{\text{\% change in quantity of } i}{\text{\% change in price of } j}.$$

If $E_{q_i}^{p_j} > 0$, i and j are gross substitutes,

If $E_{q_i}^{p_j} < 0$, i and j are gross complements.

Note that the symbol ∂ is commonly used instead of d for partial derivatives of a function of several variables.

A.1.4. *Special Functional Forms*

The demand function $q = ap^E y^\eta$ exhibits constant elasticities. It is called the log-linear function since:

$$\ln q = \ln a + E \ln p + \eta \ln y,$$

where the price and income elasticities are equal to E and η, respectively.

In the analysis of production, this functional form is the Cobb-Douglas production function:

$$q = ak^\alpha l^\beta, \quad \text{or}$$

$$\ln q = \ln a + \alpha \ln k + \beta \ln l,$$

where k and l represent capital and labor and α and β their elasticities of production.

By contrast, the linear demand curve, $q = a - bp$, has a variable elasticity. The demand curve is defined for price varying between 0 and a/b. The elasticity at any point is:

$$E = \frac{p}{a - bp}(-b) = \frac{-p}{a/b - p},$$

which varies from 0 to $-\infty$ when the price increases from 0 to a/b. Demand is inelastic for low prices and elastic for high prices. It is unit elastic, $E = -1$, when $p = a/2b$, the mid-point of the demand curve (Figure A.2).

Figure A.2. Price elasticity of demand

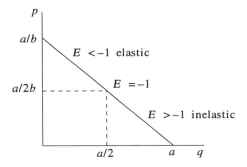

A.2. Taylor Expansion and Log-Linearization of a Function

A.2.1. *Taylor Expansion, Cobb-Douglas, and Translog Functions*

The Taylor expansion gives an approximation of a function $f(x)$ at some arbitrary point x_0. It is written:

$$f(x) = f(x_0) + f'(x_0)(x - x_0) + \frac{f''(x_0)}{2!}(x - x_0)^2 + \ldots.$$

The first-order approximation takes the first two terms and is a linear function: $f(x) \approx a + bx$. The second-order approximation, which takes the first three terms, is a second degree polynomial: $f(x) \approx a + bx + cx^2$. This allows one to consider the choice of a linear or quadratic function as an approximation to any more complex function.

A useful form of the Taylor expansion uses the logarithmic transformation to arrive at elasticities rather than marginal changes. Consider the function $q = f(x)$. Using the identity $x = e^{\ln x}$, this function can be written:

$$\ln q = \ln f(e^{\ln x}), \text{ or } \ln q = g(\ln x).$$

The first- and second-order Taylor expansions of this last expression are:

$\ln q \approx a + b \ln x$, and

$\ln q \approx a + b \ln x + c(\ln x)^2$.

If q is a function of several variables x_i, these expressions are written:

(1) $\ln q \approx a + \sum_i b_i \ln x_i$, and

(2) $\ln q \approx a + \sum_i b_i \ln x_i + \sum_{ij} c_{ij} \ln x_i \ln x_j$.

Equation (1) is the Cobb-Douglas function, while equation (2) is the translog function. These two functions are commonly used for production and profit analysis. And, as was noted above, they can always be considered first- and second-order approximations of any more complex production or profit function.

A.2.2. Log-Linearization of a Model

The approximation above can justifiably be used when one considers small changes in variables around a given point. Total differentiation of the first-order Taylor expansion in logarithmic form [equation (1)] can then be written:

(3) $d \ln q = \sum_i E_i \, d \ln x_i$,

where the parameters $E_i \, (= b_i)$ are elasticities.

Note that $d \ln q$ is the growth rate $\dot{q}$ of q, $d \ln q = \dfrac{dq}{q} = \dot{q}$. Hence expression (3) can also be written as:

(4) $\dot{q} = \sum_i E_i \, \dot{x}_i$.

In the particular case of a linear function such as $q = \sum_i b_i x_i$, this transformation gives:

(5) $\dot{q} = \sum_i \dfrac{b_i x_i}{q} \, \dot{x}_i$,

where the coefficients $b_i x_i / q$ represent the share of the variable x_i in q.

The transformation of a general function $q = f(x_i)$ into $\dot{q} = \sum E_i \dot{x}_i$ is called its log-linearization. The log-linearization of all the equations of a model greatly simplifies its solution, as it transforms the model in a system of linear equations in rates of change of all the variables. Typically, models are composed of a number of nonlinear functions that are approximated by equations like (4), and of identities or linear functions that are approximated by equation (5). Hence all the parameters of the log-linearized model are shares or elasticities.

Note, however, that it is only an approximation. Hence, once log-linearized, the model can only be used to simulate the impact of small changes in the exogenous variables around the initial equilibrium point where the shares and elasticities are measured.

As an example of log-linearization, consider a model of production and consumption of food with endogenous price and income. This can represent either a farm household with market failure and determination of a shadow price internal to the household (Chapter 6), or a closed economy with a nontradable equilibrium price (Chapter 11). Supply q^s of food is a function of the price p and fixed factors of production z^s. Consumption q^c of food is a function of income, price, and household characteristics z^c. The income y of the household consists of farm income pq^s and an exogenous off-farm income R. The system is written as:

$$q^s = q^s(p, z^s)$$
$$q^c = q^c(p, y, z^c)$$
$$y = pq^s + R$$
$$q^s = q^c.$$

The log-linearization of the system is written as:

$$\dot{q}^s = E_s^p \dot{p} + E_s^{z^s} \dot{z}^s$$
$$\dot{q}^c = E_c^p \dot{p} + \eta \dot{y} + E_c^{z^c} \dot{z}^c$$
$$\dot{y} = \alpha_q(\dot{p} + \dot{q}^s) + \alpha_R \dot{R}$$
$$\dot{q}^s = \dot{q}^c,$$

where $\alpha_q = pq^s / y$ and $\alpha_R = R / y$ are the shares of farm and off-farm income in total income. This linear system in rates of change solves for the rates of change in price, quantity, and income as a function of the rates of change in the exogenous variables $\dot{z}^s$, $\dot{z}^c$, and $\dot{R}$.

A.3. Optimization Problems

A.3.1. Unconstrained Maxima and Minima

Consider the case of a function of one variable, $y = f(x)$. This function has a (relative) maximum at the point $x = a$ if $f(a) \geq f(x)$ for all values of x in a small neighborhood around a and a (relative) minimum at $x = b$ if $f(b) \leq f(x)$ for all values of x in a small neighborhood around b.

At an extremum (maximum or minimum), the slope is zero:

$$\frac{dy}{dx} = 0 \text{ (first-order condition)},$$

and the extremum is:

$$\left. \begin{array}{l} \text{a maximum if } \dfrac{d^2y}{dx^2} < 0 \text{ at this point} \\ \text{a minimum if } \dfrac{d^2y}{dx^2} > 0 \text{ at this point} \end{array} \right\} \text{ (second-order condition)}.$$

Together, these conditions constitute a necessary and sufficient condition for an extremum.

For a function of several variables, $y = f(x_1, ..., x_n)$, a necessary condition for an extremum is that the first-order conditions

$$\frac{\partial y}{\partial x_1} = \frac{\partial y}{\partial x_2} = \cdots = \frac{\partial y}{\partial x_n} = 0 \quad \text{or} \quad f_1 = f_2 = \cdots = f_n = 0$$

be satisfied. The second-order sufficient conditions are a generalization of the sign condition written for the one variable case. They involve sign constraints on the elements of the matrix of second-order derivatives. However, they are often found to be difficult to check rigorously and are often neglected.

A.3.2. Constrained Optimization

In most of the maximization problems encountered in economics, a certain number of constraints limit the space of the possible solution. For example, consumers are maximizing utility u subject to a budgetary constraint, and firms are maximizing profits π subject to technological relationships and resource constraints. The behavior of agents is represented as a problem of optimization under constraint. For example, the consumer's problem is written as:

$$\text{Max}_{q} \; u(q) \quad \text{s.t.} \quad \sum_i p_i q_i = y.$$

Similarly, using q to denote the vector of outputs and x the vector of inputs, the producer's problem is written as:

$$\text{Max}_{q,x} \; \pi(q, x) \quad \text{s.t.} \quad g(q, x) = 0,$$

or, for the case of a single output q:

$$\text{Max}_{q,x} \; \pi(q, x) \quad \text{s.t.} \quad q = g(x).$$

In some cases, one can solve the constraint for one of the variables and substitute the expression in the objective function. The constrained problem in n variables becomes an unconstrained optimization problem in $(n-1)$ variables. In the consumer case, for example, one can write:

$$q_1 = (y - \sum_{i \geq 2} p_i q_i) / p_1,$$

and rewrite the optimization problem as:

$$\text{Max}_{q_2, ..., q_n} \; u\left((y - \sum_{i \geq 2} p_i q_i) / p_1, q_2, \cdots, q_n\right).$$

This can also be done for the producer case, if the technology constraint gives explicit relations of the type $q = g(x)$.

However, this substitution is not possible when constraints are implicit functions, like $g(q, x) = 0$, or when there are inequality constraints, like $h(q) \geq 0$. For these cases, we have to directly address the problem of optimization under constraint. A mathematical technique to find such constrained optimum is that of Lagrange multipliers.

Consider the general case: maximize $u(q_1, ..., q_n)$ with respect to $q_1, ..., q_n$ subject to the condition that $q_1, ..., q_n$ satisfy the equation, $g(q_1, ..., q_n) = y$. The Lagrange multiplier technique proceeds as follows: form the function

$$V = u(q_1, ..., q_n) + \lambda[y - g(q_1, ..., q_n)],$$

where λ is a variable, the Lagrange multiplier, and maximize V with respect to $q_1, ..., q_n$, and λ. Since $g(q_1, ..., q_n) = y$, the value of V is not changed by introduction of a Lagrange multiplier. But the optimizing values now have to satisfy an additional equation, namely the side condition $g(\cdot) = y$, since the first-order conditions for an extremum become:

$$\frac{\partial V}{\partial q_1} = u_1 - \lambda g_1 = 0$$
$$\vdots$$
$$\frac{\partial V}{\partial q_n} = u_n - \lambda g_n = 0$$
$$\frac{\partial V}{\partial \lambda} = y - g(q_1, ..., q_n) = 0.$$

These conditions constitute a system of $n + 1$ equations in $n + 1$ unknowns, which is the *structural form* of the model. They can be solved for $q_1, ..., q_n$, and λ, which give the coordinates of the extremum, or the *reduced form* or solution of the model. In particular, the n equations:

$$q_i = q_i(p_1, ..., p_n, y), \ i = 1, ..., n$$

are the ordinary or Marshallian demand equations, with own-price slopes $\partial q_i / \partial p_i$. These price slopes can be decomposed into a price effect where the utility level is kept constant (the Slutsky substitution effect or Hicksian price effect) and an income effect which is the response to the income transfer needed to keep utility constant in spite of the change in purchasing power associated with the price change. Price slopes can thus always be decomposed into two effects:

$$\frac{\partial q_i}{\partial p_i} = \left. \frac{\partial q_i}{\partial p_i} \right|_{\text{utility=constant}} - q_i \frac{\partial q_i}{\partial y} \ \text{ or, in elasticity terms,}$$

$$E_{ii} = \left. E_{ii} \right|_{\text{utility=constant}} - w_i \eta_i,$$

where E_{ii} is the Marshallian or ordinary price elasticity, $\left. E_{ii} \right|_{\text{utility=constant}}$ the Hicksian or compensated price elasticity, w_i the budget share $p_i q_i / y$, and η_i the income elasticity.

Besides being a convenient mathematical tool, the Lagrange multiplier often has an interesting interpretation of its own. Solving the system above, we obtain $q_1(y), ..., q_n(y), \lambda(y)$.

Substituting in the objective function yields $u[q_1(y),\dots,q_n(y)]$. Consider now the effect of a marginal change in the constraint on the objective function:

$$\frac{du}{dy} = \sum_i u_i \frac{dq_i}{dy}.$$

From the first-order conditions above, $u_i = \lambda g_i$. Differentiation of the constraint $g(q) = y$ with respect to y gives:

$$\sum_i g_i \frac{dq_i}{dy} = 1.$$

Hence, we find that:

$$\frac{du}{dy} = \sum_i u_i \frac{dq_i}{dy} = \sum_i \lambda g_i \frac{dq_i}{dy} = \lambda.$$

The Lagrange multiplier λ equals the incremental change of the objective function obtained from an incremental change in the constraint. In other words, λ is the marginal value of relaxing the constraint. For example, in the consumer case where the constraint is income, λ represents the marginal utility of income.

If k represents the available supply of some inputs, λ represents the marginal value of this input in terms of the objective function; hence it is often called the "shadow price" of this input. In the case of a producer that operates under a limited availability of one input x_1, the problem is:

$$\underset{q,x}{\text{Max}} \ \pi(q,x) \ \text{s.t.} \ g(q,x) = 0 \ \text{and} \ x_1 \leq k.$$

The Lagrange method presented above, generalized to the case of an inequality constraint, is:

$$\underset{q,x}{\text{Max}} \ \pi(q,x) + \lambda_g g(q,x) + \lambda_1(k - x_1).$$

In this case, λ_1 represents the marginal profitability of the resource k.

Example 1: Derivation of demand functions in the consumer behavior model. Consider an individual who spends disposable income y on n commodities $q_1,\dots,q_n$ during a certain time period. We assume this individual to have a Stone-Geary utility function (see Chapter 2):

$$u = u(q_1,\dots,q_n) = \prod_{i=1}^{n}(q_i - c_i)^{b_i},$$

or $\quad \ln u = \sum_{i=1}^{n} b_i \ln(q_i - c_i),$

where b_i and c_i are parameters and $\sum b_i = 1$. Utility functions must be stable during the time period, continuous with respect to the quantities consumed $q_1,\dots,q_n$ of the n goods, and have finite first- and second-order derivatives for all possible values of $q_1,\dots,q_n$. These conditions are satisfied for $q_i > c_i$. Prices of the n goods consumed are $p_1,\dots,p_n$.

The individual's budget constraint is:

$$\sum_{i=1}^{n} p_i \, q_i = y.$$

To determine the utility maximizing levels of quantities, we maximize:

$$V = u(q_1, \dots, q_n) + \lambda \left(y - \sum_{i=1}^{n} p_i \, q_i \right) \quad \text{with respect to } q_1, \dots, q_n, \lambda.$$

The first-order conditions are the *structural form* of the model:

$$\frac{\partial V}{\partial q_1} = u_1 - \lambda p_1 = b_1 \frac{u}{q_1 - c_1} - \lambda p_1 = 0$$

$$\vdots$$

$$\frac{\partial V}{\partial q_n} = u_n - \lambda p_n = b_n \frac{u}{q_n - c_n} - \lambda p_n = 0$$

$$\frac{\partial V}{\partial \lambda} = y - \sum_{i=1}^{n} p_i q_i = 0,$$

or, equivalently,

$$\frac{u_1}{p_1} = \dots = \frac{u_n}{p_n} = \lambda \ \text{ or } \ \frac{u_i}{u_j} \equiv \frac{MU_i}{MU_j} \equiv MRS_{i,j} = \frac{p_i}{p_j}, \ \text{for all } i \text{ and } j.$$

Hence, the first-order conditions for a maximum require equality of the ratio of marginal utilities (*MU*) or, equivalently, of the marginal rate of substitution (*MRS*) between goods to the price ratio for all pairs of commodities consumed.

The first-order conditions constitute a set of $n + 1$ equations in $n + 1$ unknowns that can be solved for $q_1, \dots, q_n, \lambda$ in terms of $p_1, \dots, p_n, y$. For the Stone-Geary, the first-order conditions can be rewritten as:

$$\frac{u}{\lambda} = p_i \frac{q_i - c_i}{b_i} = \frac{\sum_i p_i (q_i - c_i)}{\sum_i b_i} = y - \sum_i p_i c_i.$$

The solution gives the *reduced form* of the model, which is the system of demand equations. This is the Linear Expenditure System:

$$q_1 = q_1(p_1, \dots, p_n, y) = c_1 + \frac{b_1}{p_1}\left(y - \sum_i p_i c_i\right)$$

$$\vdots$$

$$q_n = q_n(p_1, \dots, p_n, y) = c_n + \frac{b_n}{p_n}\left(y - \sum_i p_i c_i\right).$$

Example 2: Derivation of supply and factor demand functions in the producer behavior model. Consider a production function, $q = f(x_1, x_2, z)$, p the product price, p_1 and p_2 the prices of variable factors x_1 and x_2, and c the cost of fixed factor z. The objective function is to:

Maximize profits, $\pi = pq - p_1 x_1 - p_2 x_2 - c$, with respect to x_1 and x_2.

The first-order conditions are:

$\dfrac{\partial \pi}{\partial x_1} = pf_1 - p_1 = 0$, where $f_1 = \dfrac{\partial q}{\partial x_1}$ is the marginal productivity of x_1,

$\dfrac{\partial \pi}{\partial x_1} = pf_2 - p_2 = 0$, where $f_2 = \dfrac{\partial q}{\partial x_2}$ is the marginal productivity of x_2, or

$VMP_1 = p_1$,

$VMP_2 = p_2$, where $VMP_i = pf_i$ is value marginal productivity of factor i.

The *structural form* of the model is thus composed of the three equations:

$q = f(x_1, x_2, z)$, production function,

$VMP_1 = p_1$,

$VMP_2 = p_2$, first-order conditions for profit maximization.

The structural form can be solved for the *reduced form* of the model that gives the endogenous variables as a function of the exogenous variables:

$q = q(p, p_1, p_2, z)$, supply function,

$x_1 = x_1(p, p_1, p_2, z)$,

$x_2 = x_2(p, p_1, p_2, z)$, factor demand functions.

The maximum profit obtained is:

$$\pi(p, p_1, p_2, z) = pq(p, p_1, p_2, z) - \sum_i p_i x_i(p, p_1, p_2, z).$$

As an example, consider the case where the production function is a Cobb-Douglas, $q = A x_1^{\alpha_1} x_2^{\alpha_2} z^{\alpha_3}$, with $\alpha_1 + \alpha_2 + \alpha_3 = 1$. This expression can be substituted in the objective function, leading to a nonconstrained maximization problem:

Objective function: $\displaystyle \operatorname*{Max}_{x_1, x_2} \pi = pA x_1^{\alpha_1} x_2^{\alpha_2} z^{\alpha_3} - p_1 x_1 - p_2 x_2 - c$.

First-order conditions:

$$\frac{\partial \pi}{\partial x_1} = pA\alpha_1 x_1^{\alpha_1 - 1} x_2^{\alpha_2} z^{\alpha_3} - p_1 = 0 \quad \text{or} \quad p\alpha_1 \frac{q}{x_1} = p_1,$$

$$\frac{\partial \pi}{\partial x_2} = pA\alpha_2 x_1^{\alpha_1} x_2^{\alpha_2 - 1} z^{\alpha_3} - p_2 = 0 \quad \text{or} \quad p\alpha_2 \frac{q}{x_2} = p_2,$$

$$q = A x_1^{\alpha_1} x_2^{\alpha_2} z^{\alpha_3}.$$

This shows that the elasticities of production α_i are the shares of each factor's return in total revenue:

$$\alpha_i = \frac{p_i x_i}{pq}.$$

The reduced form of the model gives the system of output supply and factor demand:

$$q = A^{1/\alpha_3} \left(\frac{\alpha_1}{p_1} \right)^{\alpha_1/\alpha_3} \left(\frac{\alpha_2}{p_2} \right)^{\alpha_2/\alpha_3} p^{(\alpha_1 + \alpha_2)/\alpha_3} z,$$

$$x_1 = \frac{\alpha_1}{p_1} pq, \quad \text{and} \quad x_2 = \frac{\alpha_2}{p_2} pq.$$

A.4. Functional Forms of Production Functions

A.4.1. *Cobb-Douglas (CD)*

$q = A\, x_1^{\alpha_1}\, x_2^{\alpha_2}$, where A is the parameter of total factor productivity.

Elasticity of production for factor $x_i = \dfrac{\partial q}{\partial x_i} \dfrac{x_i}{q} = \alpha_i.$

Returns to scale are characterized by the proportional change in output due to a joint proportionate change of all inputs: $(dq/dx)(x/q)$ for $dx_1 = dx_2 = dx$. Returns to scale are said to be increasing, (constant, or decreasing) when $(dq/dx)(x/q) > 1$ $(= 1,\text{ or} < 1)$. For the Cobb-Douglas production function:

$$\frac{dq}{dx}\frac{x}{q} = \alpha_1 + \alpha_2 \geq \text{ or } \leq 1.$$

Marginal productivity of each factor: $q_i' = \partial q / \partial x_i = \alpha_i\, q / x_i$.

Marginal rate of substitution, defined as the necessary change in x_2 to maintain q constant after x_1 has changed:

$$\tau = -\frac{dx_2}{dx_1}\bigg|_{q\,cst} = \frac{\partial q/\partial x_1}{\partial q/\partial x_2} = \frac{\alpha_1}{\alpha_2}\frac{x_2}{x_1}.$$

The elasticity of substitution measures the ease of substitution among factors. It is defined as the proportionate change in the input ratio relative to the proportionate change in the ratio of marginal productivities:

$$\sigma = \frac{d\ln(x_2/x_1)}{d\ln(q_1'/q_2')} = 1.$$

If the objective is to *minimize variable costs*, $p_1 x_1 + p_2 x_2$, for a given output q, the derived factor demands are:

$$x_1 = \left[\frac{1}{A}\left(\frac{\alpha_2}{\alpha_1}\frac{p_1}{p_2}\right)^{-\alpha_2} q\right]^{\frac{1}{\alpha_1+\alpha_2}}, \text{ and } x_2 = \left[\frac{1}{A}\left(\frac{\alpha_1}{\alpha_2}\frac{p_2}{p_1}\right)^{-\alpha_1} q\right]^{\frac{1}{\alpha_1+\alpha_2}}.$$

Properties of the CD factor demand system:

a. Homogenity of degree zero in prices.

b. Symmetry: $\dfrac{\partial x_1}{\partial p_2} = \dfrac{\partial x_2}{\partial p_1}.$

c. Elasticity of factor demand with respect to output: $\dfrac{dx_1}{dq}\dfrac{q}{x_1} = \dfrac{dx_2}{dq}\dfrac{q}{x_2} = \dfrac{1}{\alpha_1+\alpha_2}.$

d. Elasticity of factor demand with respect to relative factor prices:

$$\frac{dx_1}{dp_1/p_2}\frac{p_1/p_2}{x_1} = \frac{-\alpha_2}{\alpha_1+\alpha_2} \quad , \quad \frac{dx_2}{dp_2/p_1}\frac{p_2/p_1}{x_2} = \frac{-\alpha_1}{\alpha_1+\alpha_2}.$$

If the objective is *profit maximization*, the supply and factor demands are obtained by solving for the following first-order conditions:

$$\begin{cases} x_i = \alpha_i \dfrac{p}{p_i} q, \text{ hence } \alpha_i = \dfrac{p_i x_i}{pq} \text{ is the factor share} \\ q = A x_1^{\alpha_1} x_2^{\alpha_2}. \end{cases}$$

If there is decreasing return to scale, $s = \alpha_1 + \alpha_2 < 1$. The supply function is then:

$$q = A^{\frac{1}{1-s}}\left(\frac{\alpha_1}{p_1}\right)^{\frac{\alpha_1}{1-s}}\left(\frac{\alpha_2}{p_2}\right)^{\frac{\alpha_2}{1-s}} p^{\frac{s}{1-s}}.$$

If there is constant return to scale, q can only be determined if there is one fixed factor, $x_1 = \bar{x}_1$. The supply function then becomes:

$$q = A^{1/\alpha_1} \left(\alpha_2 \frac{p}{p_2} \right)^{\alpha_2/\alpha_1} \bar{x}_1.$$

Replacing q in the first-order conditions for each factor by the supply function gives the factor demands in terms of prices only.

A.4.2. Constant Elasticity of Substitution (CES)

$$q = A\left(\alpha_1 x_1^{-\rho} + \alpha_2 x_2^{-\rho}\right)^{-\frac{1}{\rho}}, \text{ with } A > 0, \ 0 < \alpha_i < 1, \text{ and } \alpha_1 + \alpha_2 = 1.$$

The CES production function reduces to CD for $\rho = 0$.

Returns to scale: $\dfrac{dq}{dx}\dfrac{x}{q} = 1$, that is, it is homogenous of degree one.

Marginal productivity of each factor: $\dfrac{\partial q}{\partial x_i} = \alpha_i \, A^{-\rho} \left(\dfrac{q}{x_i} \right)^{1+\rho}.$

Marginal rate of substitution: $\tau = -\dfrac{dx_2}{dx_1}\bigg|_{q\,cst} = \dfrac{\alpha_1}{\alpha_2}\left(\dfrac{x_2}{x_1}\right)^{1+\rho}.$

Elasticity of substitution: $\sigma = \dfrac{1}{1+\rho}.$

Input demand derived from *cost minimization*:

$$x_1 = \frac{1}{A}\, \alpha_1^\sigma \, p_1^{-\sigma} \left[\alpha_1^\sigma \, p_1^{1-\sigma} + \alpha_2^\sigma \, p_2^{1-\sigma} \right]^{\frac{\sigma}{1-\sigma}} q,$$

$$x_2 = \frac{1}{A}\, \alpha_2^\sigma \, p_2^{-\sigma} \left[\alpha_1^\sigma \, p_1^{1-\sigma} + \alpha_2^\sigma \, p_2^{1-\sigma} \right]^{\frac{\sigma}{1-\sigma}} q.$$

Properties of the CES factor demand system:
a. Homogenity of degree zero in prices.
b. Symmetry: $\dfrac{\partial x_1}{\partial p_2} = \dfrac{\partial x_2}{\partial p_1}.$

Input demand and output supply derived from *profit maximization*: since there is constant return to scale, q can be determined only if there is one fixed factor $x_1 = \bar{x}_1$. Then:

Demand: $\quad x_2 = \bar{x}_1 \left(\dfrac{\alpha_2}{\alpha_1} \right)^{\frac{\sigma}{1-\sigma}} \left[\left(A\dfrac{p}{p_2} \right)^{1-\sigma} \alpha_2^{-\sigma} - 1 \right]^{\frac{\sigma}{1-\sigma}},$

Supply: $\quad q = A^{1-\sigma}\left(\dfrac{p_2}{\alpha_2 p}\right)^{\sigma} x_2.$

A.4.3. Translog Production Function

$$\ln q = \ln \gamma_0 + \alpha_1 \ln x_1 + \alpha_2 \ln x_2 + \beta_1 (\ln x_1)^2 + \beta_2 (\ln x_2)^2 + \gamma_1 \ln x_1 \ln x_2.$$

Returns to scale: $\alpha_1 + \alpha_2 + 2\beta_1 \ln x_1 + 2\beta_2 \ln x_2 + \gamma_1 (\ln x_1 + \ln x_2)$, variable.

Constant returns to scale version (which is identical to a Taylor expansion of a CES):

$$\ln \frac{q}{x_1} = \ln \gamma_0 + \alpha_2 \ln \frac{x_2}{x_1} + \beta_2 \left(\ln \frac{x_2}{x_1}\right)^2.$$

Marginal productivity: $\quad \dfrac{\partial q}{\partial x_i} = \dfrac{q}{x_i}\left(\alpha_i + 2\beta_i \ln x_i + \gamma_1 \ln x_j\right), \quad j \neq i.$

Elasticity of substitution: $\quad \sigma = -\dfrac{A+B}{q}\left(A + B - 2\alpha_2 \dfrac{A}{B} - 2\beta_2 \dfrac{B}{A} - 2\gamma_1\right)^{-1}, \quad$ variable,

where: $\quad A = \beta_1 + 2\beta_2 \ln x_2 + \gamma_1 \ln x_1$
$$B = \alpha_1 + 2\alpha_2 \ln x_1 + \gamma_1 \ln x_2.$$

A.5. Functional Forms of Demand Systems: Derivation of Elasticities

A.5.1. Linear Expenditure System (LES)

$$p_i q_i = c_i p_i + b_i \left(y - \sum_j c_j p_j \right),$$

where:

$c_i p_i$ = committed level of expenditures (subsistence),

$y - \sum c_i p_i$ = "supernumerary" or uncommitted income.

Income elasticity: $\quad \dfrac{\partial q_i}{\partial y} = \dfrac{b_i}{p_i}, \quad$ and $\quad \eta_i = b_i \dfrac{y}{p_i q_i} = \dfrac{b_i}{w_i}.$

Cross-price elasticity: $\quad \dfrac{\partial q_i}{\partial p_j} = -\dfrac{b_i}{p_i} c_j, \quad$ and $\quad E_{ij} = -\dfrac{b_i c_j p_j}{p_i q_i}, \quad i \neq j.$

Own-price elasticity: $\quad \dfrac{\partial q_i}{\partial p_i} = -\dfrac{b_i}{p_i^2}\left(y - \sum_{j \neq i} c_j p_j\right) = \dfrac{c_i}{p_i}(1 - b_i) - \dfrac{q_i}{p_i},$

$$\text{and} \quad E_{ii} = -1 + (1 - b_i)\frac{c_i}{q_i}.$$

Flexibility of money: $\quad \omega = \dfrac{\partial \lambda}{\partial y}\dfrac{y}{\lambda} = \dfrac{\eta_i(1 - w_i\eta_i)}{E_{ii} + w_i\eta_i} = -\dfrac{y}{y - \sum\limits_j c_j p_j}\ .$

A.5.2. Almost Ideal Demand System (AIDS)

$$\frac{p_i q_i}{y} = a_i + \sum_j b_{ij} \ln p_j + c_i \ln \frac{y}{P},$$

$$\ln P = a_0 + \sum_k a_k \ln p_k + \frac{1}{2}\sum_k \sum_j b_{jk} \ln p_k \ln p_j\,.$$

If P is approximated by the Stone geometric price index P^*,

$$\ln P^* = \sum_k w_k \ln p_k \quad \text{and} \quad \frac{\partial \ln P}{\partial \ln p_i} \approx \frac{\partial \ln P^*}{\partial \ln p_i} = \frac{w_i}{p_i}\,.$$

Income elasticity:

$$\frac{\partial q_i}{\partial y} = \frac{1}{p_i}\left(a_i + \sum_j b_{ij} \ln p_j + c_i \ln \frac{y}{P}\right) + \frac{c_i}{p_i} = \frac{1}{p_i}\left(\frac{p_i q_i}{y}\right) + \frac{c_i}{p_i}, \quad \text{and} \quad \eta_i = 1 + \frac{c_i}{w_i}\,.$$

Own-price elasticity:

$$\frac{\partial q_i}{\partial p_i} = -\frac{y}{p_i^2}\left(a_i + \sum_j b_{ij} \ln p_j + c_i \ln \frac{y}{P}\right) + b_{ii}\frac{y}{p_i^2} - c_i\frac{y w_j}{p_i^2}, \quad \text{and} \quad E_{ii} = -1 + \frac{b_{ii}}{w_i} - c_i\,.$$

Cross-price elasticity:

$$\frac{\partial q_i}{\partial p_j} = b_{ij}\frac{y}{p_i}\frac{1}{p_j} - c_i\frac{y}{p_i}\left(\frac{w_j}{p_j}\right), \quad \text{and} \quad E_{ij} = \frac{b_{ij}}{w_i} - \frac{c_i}{w_i}w_j\,.$$

Flexibility of money: $\quad \omega = \dfrac{\partial \lambda}{\partial y}\dfrac{y}{\lambda} = -1\,.$

Author Index

Adams 22
Adelman 1, 2, 291, 361
Ahn 160, 323
Aigner 246
Akerlof 255
Akino 200
Alderman 129, 166, 167
Alexander 129
Ali 255
Aloui 323
Anderson, J. 99
Anderson, K. 206
Antle 125
Antonovitz 96, 98, 99
Asikoglu 227
Askari 90
Augusztinovics 288
Ayer 200
Azam 156

Baanante 67
Balassa 181
Ball 68
Bapna 67, 68, 73
Bardhan, K. 148
Bardhan, P. 1, 254, 262
Barnett 304
Barnum 141
Barten 41, 45, 46
Basu 128, 262
Bates 206
Baur 306
Becker 24, 141
Behrman 32, 51, 52, 90, 92
Bell 128, 262, 266
Benjamin, D. 160
Benjamin, N. 355
Benson 129
Berrian 291
Berry 257, 261, 268
Berthélemy 156
Besley 156, 164, 257
Bieri 37
Binswanger 67, 68, 73, 76, 120, 168, 302, 306, 311, 312, 317
Blake 304
Blanciforti 44, 47
Blyn 128
Boehlje 304
Bollino 41, 44

Bourguignon 144, 361
Bowers 76
Brandt 49
Braverman 102, 132, 262, 302, 306, 311, 320, 323, 332
Brink 304
Brown, A. 36, 38
Brown, J. 273, 294
Bruce 48, 91
Burfisher 361, 362
Buschena 116

Candler 304
Capalbo 249, 251
Cardoso 1
Carter, C. 201
Carter, M. 258
Cavallo 232, 362
Cella 288
Chalfant 46, 125
Chambers 162, 251
Chavas 98
Chayanov 141
Chen 21
Cheung 263
Chiappori 144
Chou 168
Christensen 41
Clarete 355
Cline 257, 261, 268
Colaizzo 291
Corden 181
Cornia 9, 258
Cuddihy 92, 95
Cummings 90
Currie 189

D'Antonio 291
Davis 201
Dawson 246
de Janvry 24, 37, 120, 125, 134, 148, 154, 156, 162, 258, 262, 317, 341, 356, 358, 361
de Londoño 33, 49
de Melo 7, 24, 341, 356, 361
Deaton 32, 36, 38, 40, 41, 43, 49, 51, 53, 164, 167
Debertin 84
Decaluwé 341
Defourny 293
Delgado 128, 140

Deolalikar 32, 51, 52, 258
Dervis 7, 24, 341
Dethier 323
Devarajan 346, 355, 361
Dillon 99
Domenech 232
Dornbusch 215
Dorosh 233

Eckstein 100
Edwards 232
Ellis 140, 144
Esfahani 67
Eswaran 258, 259, 260, 263
Evenson 73, 78
Ezekiel 97

Fafchamps 126, 154, 156
Falcon 32
Faletto 1
Faminow 129
Fargeix 24, 358, 361
Farrell 243
Feder 161, 258
Fei 2, 21
Ferguson 373
Finkelshtain 125
Fisher, B. 100
Fisher, I. 15
Flinn 255
Folbre 52
Foster 19
Fox 7
Frisch 36
Fulginiti 67, 70, 85, 206

Garcia 52, 167
García García 220, 233
Gardner 2, 98, 176, 206
Gerschenkron 1
Geweke 45
Goetz 162
Goodwin 49
Goreux 305, 306
Gorman 47
Goungetas 46
Gray 46
Green 44, 47, 96, 98
Greenfield 96
Greer 19
Griliches 200
Grundmeier 306
Gunning 341

Haggblade 273, 294
Hall 201, 302
Hammer 102, 132, 294, 302, 306, 311, 320, 323, 332

Harberger 223
Hardaker 99
Harris 361
Harrison 141
Hartley 96
Hayami 200, 206, 248, 263
Hayden 291
Hays 128
Hazell 2, 273, 291, 294, 304, 306
Heady 306
Heathfield 84
Hein 45
Helmers 215
Henderson 97, 373
Henry 257
Herdt 244
Hill 225
Hinckley 99
Hinojosa-Ojeda 361, 362
Hirschman 1, 2, 273, 288, 291
Hoff 254, 262
Hoover 33, 49
Horton 317
Houmy 323
Houthakker 38
Hueth 14
Hussain 248

Jacinto 52
Jardine 217
Jarvis 96
Jensen 306
Johansson 11
Johnson, H. 1
Johnson, S. 46, 306
Jorgenson 41
Judge 98, 128, 305
Just 14, 90

Kalfayan 258
Kalijaran 246, 247, 248
Kanbur 132
Kaneda 253
Kao 98
Keyser 341
Khan, H. 291
Khan, M. 220
Kharas 361
King 44, 47
Knudsen 51, 127
Konandreas 112, 130, 131
Kotwal 258, 259, 260, 263
Kreps 5
Krueger 1, 184, 191
Krugman 4
Kumar 148
Kumbhakar 246
Kutcher 305

Kuznets 2, 281

Lambert 161
Laraki 52, 53
Lau 41, 64, 160, 161, 168, 245, 246
Laugham 306
Lave 248
Leibenstein 242
Leonello 291
Leontief 285
Levy 18
Lewis 346
Lin 160, 161, 168
Lingard 246
Lipton 199
Lloyd 17
Lluch 354
Lopez, M. 184
Lopez, R. 68, 160
Lovell, C. K. 246
Lovell, M. 102
Lucas 99
Luo 161

Maddala 45, 162
Magnac 161
Mandac 244
Manne 305, 306
Martens 341
Matlon 140
McCalla 201
McCarl 304, 305
McCoy 128
McElroy 52, 144
Meeraus 311
Meeusen 246
Mellor 2
Mercenier 361
Meyers 306
Michel 182
Monke 6
Montes Llamas 220, 233
Moran 356
Morduch 167, 168, 323
Morrisson 156, 281, 361
Moscardi 120, 125
Mount 120
Muellbauer 41, 43
Mundlak 75, 76, 84, 90, 232, 362
Murphy 189
Muth 99

Nabli 262
Narayana 356
Nash 127
Naylor 306
Nelson, C. 248
Nelson, Gerald 248

Nelson, Glenn 96
Nerlove 86, 96
Newbery 112, 113, 120, 263
Norton, G. 201
Norton, R. 304, 306
Nugent 262
Nurske 273

Ohkawa 2
Olson 206
Ostry 220
Otsuka 263
Owen 200

Paarsch 96
Pandya-Lorch 140
Parikh 356
Parks 43
Paxson 166, 167
Pearson 6, 32
Penn 184
Perrin 67, 70, 85
Persson 6
Peters 96
Peterson 200
Pinckney 131
Pinstrup-Andersen 33, 49, 52, 317
Pollak 46, 47
Pope 98
Posada 200
Powell 354
Prais 38
Pyatt 21, 293
Pyle 116

Quandt 97, 373
Quizon 67, 68, 73, 302, 306, 311, 312, 317

Raff 317
Rajagopalan 291
Raki 156
Ramasamy 2, 291
Ranis 2
Rao, C. 258
Rao, M. 90
Raulerson 306
Rausser 206
Ravallion 128, 129
Ray 306
Reardon 140
Reutlinger 130
Rezende Lopes 132
Rives 306
Robinson 7, 24, 341, 346, 361, 362
Rodrik 361
Roe 99
Roemer 259
Roland-Holst 361

Roningen 48
Rose 46
Rosenzweig 51, 168
Rosovsky 2
Roumasset 120, 355
Round 291, 293
Roy 116
Ruttan 201, 248

Sadoulet 24, 134, 154, 156, 162, 258, 262, 291,
    293, 341, 356, 358, 361
Sah 176
Salazar Brandão 132, 332
Sanderson 355
Sarris 361
Scandizzo 48, 51, 91, 305
Schiff 184, 185
Schluter 120
Schmidt 246
Schmitz 14, 189, 200, 201
Schuh 200
Schultz, T. P. 51
Schultz, T. W. 176
Schweinberger 17
Scobie 200, 217
Seckler 200
Sen 2, 51
Senauer 52
Sengupta, J. 7
Sengupta, S. 51
Serra 356
Shideed 99
Shishido 361
Shogren 206
Shonkwiler 99
Shoven 341
Sidhu 67, 246
Singh 141, 148, 160
Skold 306
Solow 248, 252
Spreen 96, 305
Squire 141, 148, 160
Srinivasan 356
Stephens 306
Stiglitz 1, 3, 4, 112, 113, 120, 176, 254, 262, 263
Stone 41, 42
Strauss 32, 51, 141, 148
Streeten 1
Subbarao 258, 317
Subramanian 32, 51, 291, 293
Sullivan 48
Swinnen 206

Tabellini 6
Takayama 128, 305
Tan 132
Taylor, E. 291
Taylor, L. 317, 343, 355

Telser 116
Theil 21, 41
Thierfelder 361, 362
Thomas 32, 51, 52
Thorbecke 7, 19, 281, 291, 293, 302
Timmer 32, 129, 191, 246
Tinbergen 6
Tobin 45
Townsend 167
Tsakok 177, 181
Turnovsky 116
Tweeten 198

Uctum 227
Udry 167, 168

Valdés 112, 130, 131, 184, 185, 231, 232, 233
van den Broeck 246
van der Zee 206
Vasavada 203
Vernon 306
Vogel 291
von Braun 140

Wainio 48
Wales 46, 47
Walley 341
Wallis 100
Waugh 97
Webb 184
Weiner 355
Weiss 4
Wells 265
Wessells 45
Westhoff 306
White, F. 99
White, K. 46
Wibe 84
Wickens 96
Wignaraja 232
Williams, J. 98
Williams, R. 354
Williamson 355
Wolpin 168
Woodford 246
Wright 97, 98
Wyeth 129

Yeldan 361
Yotopoulos 64, 160, 168, 245, 246

Zellner 45
Zilberman 116
Zusman 4

Subject Index

adaptive expectations 87
adverse selection 4, 254
Africa
    archetype economy CGE 356
    household model 154
    NPC and RPC 179
    supply response for groundnuts 102
agrarian institutions 241
agricultural development-led industrialization 2
agricultural policy 2
    European Community 194
    United States 194
agricultural research 51
agricultural structural adjustment program 156
agricultural surplus 281
agriculture
    role in economic development 1
    sources of growth 241
almost ideal demand system (AIDS). *See* demand
    system
Argentina.
    price policy 70
Asia
    archetype economy CGE 356

base run 7, 9, 10
border price 176
Brazil
    multimarket 332
    price stabilization program 132

calibration 7, 10, 353
calorie intake 32, 50, 51, 53, 56
    effect of food subsidies 57
captive labor 140
cereal imports, CGE analysis 356
certainty equivalent
    action certainty equivalent price 121
    income 116
    welfare certainty equivalent price 122
CHAC model 305
cheap food policy 197
closure rules
    in CGE 354
    in SAM 289
Cobb-Douglas 376
    labor aggregation 353
    normalized profit function 64, 169

production function 62, 374, 382, 383
profit function 63, 245
supply function 63, 75
cobweb model 97
Colombia
    calorie intake 49
    equilibrium exchange rate 220
    real exchange rate 227
comparative advantage. *See* domestic resource cost
compensating variation 13
computable general equilibrium models (CGE) 341
    archetype economies 356
    closure rules 354
    Ecuador 358
    financial sector 358, 361
    model structure 342
    Morocco 363
    multimarket CGE integration 361
    numéraire 344
    parameter requirements 354
    policy experiments 355
    when to use 362
consistency frameworks 303
constant elasticity of substitution (CES). *See also*
    production function
    import aggregation 345
    labor aggregation 353
constant elasticity of transformation (CET). *See also*
    production function
    exports 353
constrained optimization 378
consumer behavior 34
consumer subsidy equivalent (CSE) 184
consumer surplus 11, 189
consumption smoothing 164, 167
contracts
    fixed-rent 264
    fixed-wage 263
    sharecropping. *See* sharecropping
cost function 61, 66, 249
    translog 251
Côte d'Ivoire
    DRC 188
    NPC, EPC, and REPC 182
credit constraint 150, 151, 153, 156. *See also*
    liquidity constraint

decision prices 152

demand analysis 32
    constant elasticity demand equation 33
    decision to consume 45
    estimation from cross-section data 38
    estimation under restrictions 45
    in household model 146
demand system
    almost ideal demand system 43, 353, 362, 387
    estimation 41
    generalized almost ideal demand system 44
    linear expenditure system 42, 47, 353, 381, 386
    linear logarithmic expenditure system 168
demographic differentiation 141
development economics 1
discount rate 165
domestic resource cost (DRC) 185
    Côte d'Ivoire 188
    Morocco 188
dual price system 287
duality 63, 249
Dutch disease 206, 223

economies of scale 3, 257
    analysis in CGE 361
Ecuador
    CGE model 358
    social accounting matrix 276
    stabilization policies 9, 358
effective exchange rate 214, 217
efficiency 358
    allocative 243
    economic 243
    effect of price distortions 191
    measurements 244
    of sharecropping 263
    profit 255
    technical 242
Egypt
    inequality 22
    supply response for crops 92
elasticities
    demand
        calorie elasticities 51
        compensated 379
        estimation 38
        in household model 146
        income elasticities 34
        Marshallian/Hicksian 379
        of substitution 345
        price elasticities 35, 53, 373
        quality elasticities 49
        substitutes/complements 35, 374
    supply 69, 70, 80
        aggregate supply 75, 76
        fixed factors 80
        homogeneity and symmetry properties 64
        in household model 155
        long-run supply 73, 81

    of substitution 345, 354, 384, 385, 386
elasticity 373
elasticity approach to exchange rate 219, 228
Engel curve 37, 53, 373
environmental protection through taxes 203
equity 359
equivalent variation 13
European Community
    agricultural policy 194
exchange rate
    Colombia 220
    depreciation/appreciation 214, 225, 347, 371
    devaluation/revaluation 80, 214, 349, 356
    effective 214
    equilibrium 177, 218, 219, 232, 346
    Japan 223
    nominal 214
    overvaluation 185, 198
    Pakistan 215, 233
    real. *See* real exchange rate
exchange rate adjustment 359
expectations formation
    adaptive 87
    autoregressive schemes 98
    conditional price expectations 99
    futures prices 98
    naive 94
    price support programs 98
    rational. *See* rational expectations
expected prices 69
expected utility 116, 122
export function
    constant elasticity of transformation 353
    export demand 368
exportables 229
externalities 3

factor demand 63, 78, 307, 309
    estimation 67
factor subsidies 182
    fertilizer in India 315
    fertilizer in Senegal 321
farm-gate prices 177
fiscal policy 225, 359
fix-price models 287, 294
fixed factors. *See also* public goods
    in production 62, 67, 70, 72, 78, 356
flexibility of money 37, 42, 44, 47, 56, 354,
    368, 387
food security 5, 129
    India 134
food self-sufficiency 125, 134
food subsidies 32, 56
    CGE analysis 358, 363
    India 317
    Morocco 52
    multimarket analysis 317
foreign capital flow 225, 346, 371

Frisch parameter. *See* flexibility of money
frontier production function 246
full income constraint 142, 143, 145

generalized almost ideal demand system (GAIDS). *See* demand system
generalized Leontief. *See* profit function

Hicksian demand curve 13
home time 143, 147
homogeneity of output supply system 63
household model 140
    Africa 154
    calibration 163
    dynamics 164
    estimation 160
    Morocco 156
    nonseparable. *See* nonseparable household model
    separable. *See* separable household model
    Taiwan 168
    when to use 159
household unit 144
households
    behavior 258
    characteristics in demand 46
    response to price risk 124

imperfect substitutes 204, 344
import function
    constant elasticity of substitution (CES) 345
importables 229
incidence parameter or ω factor 230
income distribution 4
income risk 120
income stabilization 113
index
    Divisia 250
    index of variability 126, 131
    poverty index
        Foster-Greer-Thorbecke 359
        Sen 19
    price index
        Fisher's ideal 15
        geometric 43, 387
        in AIDS 43
        Laspeyres 15, 56
        Paasche 15
    Theil inequality index 21, 23
India
    fertilizer subsidies 315
    food security 134
    food subsidies 317
    multimarket 312
    public goods 68, 315
    technological change 313
    village SAM 293
inequality measures

decomposition by source 21
    Gini coefficient 20, 22, 23
    Lorenz curve 20
    Mexico 22
    Theil index 21, 23
input-output
    model 285
    table for Morocco 295
    tables 273
intrahousehold decision 51, 144
inverse relationship between farm size and
    land productivity 258, 260
    total factor productivity 261

Japan
    exchange rate 223
    real exchange rate 227

Kalecki closure rule 355
Keynesian multiplier 355

labor market closure 348
labor supply 142, 147
labor surplus 348
Lagrange multiplier 34, 165, 379
land reform 241, 258, 261, 262, 266
Leontief model. *See* input-output model
life-cycle model 164
linear expenditure system (LES). *See* demand system
linkages
    agriculture 2
    agriculture/industry 273
    backward/forward 288
    farm-nonfarm 294
liquidity constraint 166, 167, 168. *See also* credit constraint
log-linearization 311, 375, 376
Lucas critique 99

macroconstraints in CGE 343
marginal productivity 383, 385
marginal rate of substitution 383, 385
market dynamics
    cobweb model 97
    storage 98
market failures 149, 151, 154
market integration 126, 128
marketed surplus 147, 162
markup price 288, 355
Marshallian inefficiency. *See* sharecropping
mathematical programming 303
Mexico
    CHAC model 305
    inequality 22
    poverty 18
moral hazard 4, 255
Morocco

CGE model 363
  DRC 188
  food subsidies 52
  household model 156
  input-output table 295
  social accounting matrix 295
multi-objective programming 303
multilevel planning models 306
multimarket CGE integration 361
multimarket models 302, 341
  Brazil 332
  India 312
  North-Africa 323
  Senegal 320
multiplier analysis 273
  input-output 286
  social accounting matrix 288, 291

Nerlovian model
  elasticities 90
  general 86
  restricted 88
  simplified 88
net present value 165
new home economics 141
nominal exchange rate 214
nonseparable household model 149
  results 154
nontradables 150, 151, 177, 229, 294, 309
normalized Cobb-Douglas. *See* profit function
normalized quadratic. *See* profit function
North Africa
  multimarket 323
numéraire 342, 344

opportunistic behavior 254
optimization problems 377
output supply 63, 78, 307, 309
  estimation 67

Pakistan
  exchange rate 215, 233
  profit efficiency 255
Pareto optimal policy 14
partial equilibrium analysis 176, 189
partial-adjustment 87
peasant household. *See* household model
permanent income model 165, 167
policy analysis
  counterfactual 9
  evaluation 10
  simulation 6
policy analysis matrix 6
policy laboratory 363
political economy of price distortions 206
political feasibility 23, 317, 359
poverty measures

Foster, Greer, and Thorbecke index 359
  headcount ratio 17
  income gap 17
  Mexico 18
  Sen poverty index 19
price bands 149, 162
price distortions 176, 177, 179, 185, 189, 204
  multiple price interventions 201
  political economy of 206
price policy. *See also* price distortions
  Argentina 70
  Senegal 320
price risk
  households' response 124, 150
price stabilization 113, 122, 126, 127, 135
  price band 132
price transmission 129
price variability 121
  measure 126
primary factors
  supply of 309, 343
principal-agent 262, 266
producer subsidy 194
producer subsidy equivalent (PSE) 184
producer surplus 189
production function
  Cobb-Douglas 62, 374, 382, 383
  constant elasticity of substitution 367, 385
  constant elasticity of transformation 344
  translog 247, 386
profit efficiency 255
  Pakistan 255
profit function 61, 62, 63, 78
  estimation 67
  generalized Leontief 65, 163
  normalized Cobb-Douglas 64, 169
  normalized quadratic 65, 69, 78
  translog 66, 70
propensity to consume 373
protection, effective 179
  effective protection coefficient (EPC) 179
  effective subsidy coefficient (ESC) 184
  real effective 179
protection, nominal
  Côte d'Ivoire 182
  nominal effective rate of protection (NERP) 181
  nominal protection coefficient (NPC) 178
  nominal rate of protection (NRP) 178
    direct, indirect, total 184
protection, real
  Africa 179
  Côte d'Ivoire 182
  real effective 179
  real protection coefficient (RPC) 179
  real rate of protection (RRP) 179
  real rate of relative protection (RRRP) 184
public goods 3, 72, 76, 81
  India 68, 315

purchasing power parity (PPP)
    equilibrium exchange rate 218
    exchange rate 179
    real exchange rate 217

quantity restrictions in trade 197

Ramsey rule 194, 198
rational expectations
    criticisms 102
    estimation 100
    model 99
real exchange rate 214, 215, 218
    CGE analysis 355
    Colombia 227
    commodity boom 223
    elasticity approach 228
    equilibrium 346
    Japan 227
    productivity change 223
    trade policies 226
    ω-approach 229
real income 14
reference prices 176
restricted profit 62, 189
returns to scale 383, 385, 386
risk
    cost of risk 116, 119
    income risk 113
    price risk 113
    production risk 112
risk aversion 116, 118, 150, 168
    absolute 118, 119
    empirical measures 120, 125
    relative 118, 119
    welfare and supply 123
risk coping 167
risk management 166, 167, 168
risk neutrality 116
    welfare and supply 121
risk premium 116, 118, 125
risk sharing 119, 167, 263
role of the state 1

safety-first 116
sectoral models 304
semi-input-output multipliers 295
Senegal
    multimarket 320
    price policy 320
separability between efficiency and equity 254
separability in demand 36, 56
    pointwise separability 36
separability in household model 150, 167. *See also*
    household model
    tests of separability 160
separable household model 145

comparative statics 146
food consumption 146
labor supply 147
marketed surplus 147
results 148
shadow price 150, 151, 380
    estimation 161
sharecropping 262, 264
    Marshallian inefficiency 263, 266
Shephard duality 63, 67
Slutsky equations 35, 147
social accounting matrix 273, 341, 342
    Ecuador 276
    Indian village economy 293
    Morocco 295
    open- and closed-loop effects 293
    regional analysis 291
    village economy 291
social classes 259
social differentiation 140
social price 269
sources of growth 241, 249, 252
stabilization policies
    Ecuador 9, 358
Stone-Geary utility function 42, 380
structural path analysis 293
substitutes/complements 35, 374
supernumerary income 42, 386
supervision costs 259
supply
    ex ante vs. ex post 113
supply response. *See also* output supply
    aggregate 73
    elasticity 84
        short run 87
    for beef 95
    for crops in Egypt 92
    for groundnuts in Africa 102
    for maize in Thailand 92
    for tree crops 96
    in nonseparable household model 155
    reduced form approaches 85
    short run vs. long run 72
    structural form approaches 84
    with price bands 162
sustainability 5
symmetry of output supply system 63

Taiwan
    household model 168
tax policy
    CGE analysis 356
    export tax 191
    import tariffs 196
    on a nontradable 197
Taylor expansion 375
technological change 25, 26, 199, 248
    bias 252

disembodied 248
India 313
labor- and land-saving 253
rate 248
treadmill 200
terms-of-trade shock 347
Thailand
supply response of maize 92
Tornqvist approximation 251
total factor productivity 248, 250, 256, 261
Tornqvist approximation 251
tradables 176, 294, 309
trade liberalization 359
trade policies 230. *See also* price policy
transactions costs 4, 149, 241, 254
transitory income 166
translog 376
cost function 251
indirect utility function 163
production function 247, 386

welfare
aggregate 17
effects of price distortions 190
measures of 11

ω-approach
equilibrium exchange rate 232
real exchange rate 229